Crime
Prevention

International Perspectives,
Issues, and Trends

Crime
Prevention

International Perspectives, Issues, and Trends

Edited by
John A. Winterdyk

CRC Press
Taylor & Francis Group
Boca Raton London New York

CRC Press is an imprint of the
Taylor & Francis Group, an **informa** business

CRC Press
Taylor & Francis Group
6000 Broken Sound Parkway NW, Suite 300
Boca Raton, FL 33487-2742

First issued in paperback 2020

ISBN-13: 978-1-4987-3367-0 (hbk)
ISBN-13: 978-0-367-59550-0 (pbk)

Library of Congress Cataloging-in-Publication Data

Names: Winterdyk, John, author.
Title: Crime prevention : international perspectives, issues, and trends /
John A. Winterdyk.
Description: 1 Edition. | Boca Raton, FL : CRC Press, 2017.
Identifiers: LCCN 2016029691| ISBN 9781498733670 (hardback) | ISBN 1498733670
(hardback) | ISBN 9781315314211 (eISBN) | ISBN 131514215 (eISBN) | ISBN
9781315314204 (web pdf) | ISBN 1315314207 (web pdf)
Subjects: LCSH: Crime prevention.
Classification: LCC HV7431 .W548 2017 | DDC 364.4--dc23
LC record available at https://lccn.loc.gov/2016029691

Visit the Taylor & Francis Web site at
http://www.taylorandfrancis.com

and the CRC Press Web site at
http://www.crcpress.com

This book is dedicated to those willing to consider exploring and using crime prevention as a primary response model to addressing the complexities of crime and justice. This includes especially my former mentors who introduced me to the principles of crime prevention, my students, and those colleagues who have made the journey a little easier by their interest and intellectual challenges in my learning process.

Contents

Foreword

Prevention is perhaps one of the most difficult goals to achieve regardless of what field it is being attempted in, be it a physical field like engineering or a social one like health. However, for some fields, the idea of prevention is more familiar and its importance is more generally accepted than others.

For example, within engineering, it goes without question that a basic goal for the design and building of a bridge must be that it will be constructed in such a way as to prevent it collapsing under heavy use or in adverse weather conditions such as a flood. To achieve this preventive goal, engineers will study, estimate, and apply optimal strength and usage parameters in order to prevent the risk of an adverse outcome. As users of that bridge, we understand this and, for the most part, accept and trust this advice. More importantly, we expect that these calculations are done carefully and that appropriate preventive/safety measures are in place. In fact, we would be astonished and incensed if the safety of the public was compromised by these preventive measures not being undertaken.

Similarly, we are all familiar with the preventive messages coming from health experts about how to prevent and minimize our exposure to various forms of illness such as infectious diseases like hepatitis or polio, or lifestyle-related disease such as cancer or diabetes arising from obesity, now so common in the developed world. While some types of preventive health messages may often be more contentious or difficult to sell than others (e.g., an effective tobacco smoking cessation message may be more difficult to deliver than a message to promote the breast feeding of newborn children), there is usually a general acceptance of the legitimacy of the basis of the message (i.e., it is based on a scientific evidence) and its objectives are seen as desirable and beneficial from either a personal (e.g., the avoidance of an illness) or a public health/utilitarian perspective (e.g., reduced rates of illness in the community and associated costs), or both.

However, there are several other fields in which the prevention goal remains less well understood or generally accepted. As a result, these still struggle for the sort of political and community legitimacy and traction that some other fields enjoy.

Two quite closely related fields that typically experience this challenge are the prevention of alcohol and other drug-related harm and crime prevention. It has perhaps been my misfortune to have spent my professional career working in both of these fields. I have seen and worked with these challenges in different and diverse roles as a senior government executive, as an academic and researcher, and as a member of different civil society organizations. This has led me to appreciate that there are dimensions to the achievement of prevention that extend beyond the accumulation of a viable and well-documented scientific evidence base about effective policies, strategies, programs, and practices, as vitally important as these are. Some of these factors include perceptions about the legitimacy of the relevant prevention goal from the perspective of those affected by the problem that is trying to be prevented as well as opportunities for participation and engagement in the development and implementation of any proposed solutions. This is because, to a large extent, the most effective strategies for prevention in both alcohol and other drug and crime prevention fields involve action that will involve some form of redistribution of power among stakeholders and communities affected by the identified problems, once the nature of these problems have been finally agreed upon, of course. Furthermore, the scale and nature of the causes of the observed problems will frequently extend beyond the immediate community or region and across fields ranging from social physical planning processes, to access to and the delivery of human services, and into questions of social and economic equity and the wider physical environment. Inevitably, criminal justice processes end up being identified as just one part of a suite of measures needed to achieve a comprehensive prevention or crime control strategy. Indeed, in many settings, the criminal justice sector may even be part of the problem.

This is where the value of this collection extends well beyond its deceptively modest title of *Crime Prevention: International Perspectives, Issues, and Trends*. Most reviews of current knowledge about crime prevention tend to limit themselves to specific areas or topics of crime prevention research, policy, and practice without providing an adequate understanding of the extremely broad range of inputs, processes, and associated outcomes that are really a part of the modern approach to crime prevention safety. Furthermore, other reviews frequently overlook the fact that what we understand as current good practice in crime prevention has developed from the way that we have incorporated effective processes for learning from the successes, and failures, of earlier crime prevention efforts. Too often this very important task of reflecting, learning, and building on past experience is referred to merely as "building the evidence base" when in fact it is the much more complex task of building and applying a proper understanding how what was done to achieve a particular result was, at least in part, a product of the context and time within which the crime prevention effort was undertaken.

Effective crime prevention is not just the successful implementation of a set of projects to address a series of current problems. Rather, it is a continuous process that needs to be dynamically planned, implemented, and appropriately supported over time with an understanding that the issues to be addressed tomorrow and into the future will not be the same as today's problems, assuming of course that the current prevention effort has been effective. It is one of the great strengths of this current volume that its essays provide us with the insight and skills to be better able to achieve this goal. They show us that our current successes in preventing crime and assisting to improve overall community safety did not come out of nowhere.

Furthermore, as we have learned more about how to undertake effective crime prevention, we have also come to learn about what can go wrong and where future threats can be found. For example, while one chapter clearly explains how we need to think about future threats in terms of vectors that are not currently factored into our planning and development processes, such as the potential impact of global climate change on both the immediate and underlying causes of crime including access to basic resources like housing and employment as well as its effect on migration and social dislocation, another chapter demonstrates how we have frequently failed to give adequate consideration to the governance and administrative requirements for sustaining crime prevention effort. Each of these themes addresses issues that frequently lie outside the normal planning parameters for prevention of crime policy makers. They also highlight the importance of engaging with those who may be seen as unconventional stakeholders in the crime prevention enterprise, as well as potentially influential partners and collaborators. This is well illustrated by the essays that seek to refocus our process for engagement with the business sector, as well as rethinking the role of civil society and the place of "victims" within the matrix of action that produces effective crime prevention.

Finally, what this volume does so well is to help us to understand, develop, and work with an agenda for the prevention of crime that is sophisticated yet accessible at the same time; evidence based but also responsive and engaging for stakeholders; as well as being transparent and legitimate in a way that builds appropriate governance structures for sustainable implementation. It also demonstrates the breadth and range of issues that need to be considered to be parts of the crime prevention agenda while at the same time making it clear that the science of crime prevention is a well-developed and comprehensive set of tools that can be legitimately applied to problems as diverse as the effects of climate change on global populations, violence against women and children, as well as specific socially marginalized groups in communities, transnational organized crime, local corruption, and the resurgence of forms of fraud newly enabled through social media and personal technology.

In other words, this book shows that contemporary crime prevention really is as sophisticated as any form of rocket science. But at the same time, contemporary crime prevention is highly participatory and accessible and is capable of being responsive to a rapidly changing crime environment and community needs and expectations. The lessons from this book go a long way to equipping us with the tools for achieving the political and community traction and legitimacy necessary for crime prevention to be effective and sustainable over time.

Professor Peter Homel, PSM
Griffith Criminology Institute
Griffith University, Australia

Peter Homel, PSM, is a widely published internationally recognized expert on crime prevention policy and program design, implementation, management, and evaluation. He has particular experience in the translation of evidence and research into sustainable practice.

He is currently a professor at the Griffith Criminology Institute at Griffith University in Australia. Previously, he was principal criminologist (Crime Prevention) at the Australian Institute of Criminology. Before that, he was the first director of the Crime Prevention Division within the New South Wales (NSW) Attorney General's Department and the deputy director of the Drug Alcohol Directorate at NSW Health.

He has worked extensively with government and nongovernment agencies for almost 40 years and continues to work closely with international bodies including the United Nations Office on Drugs and Crime and the UN-Habitat program. He is currently an executive board member of the Australian Crime Prevention Council and the International Centre for the Prevention of Crime.

Over the past two decades, he has evaluated major national crime prevention programs in Australia, the United Kingdom, and Canada, and has been assisting with the development of new programs in SE Asia and the Middle East.

In 2000, he was awarded the Public Service Medal (PSM) for outstanding public service and innovation in the field of crime prevention. In 1997, he undertook a Fulbright Professional Award at the RAND Corporation in California.

Some Relevant Publications

A'mer, F., Friedrich, R., Homel, P., Itawi, F., Jaradat, J., Kaufmann, R., Luethold, A., Masson, N., Rahhal, O., Al-Sharif, H., and Zeidani, M. 2012. Developing a community safety plan for Hebron. Geneva Centre for the Democratic Control of the Armed Forces (DCAF). http://www.dcaf.ch/Publications/Developing -a-Community-Safety-Plan-for-Hebron.

Harris, R., Edwards, D., and Homel, P. 2014. Meeting the challenge of drug and alcohol management at events and venues: The Australian case. *Event Management* 18(4): 457–470.

Harris, R., Edwards, D., Homel, P., and Fuller, G. 2015. An empirical basis for the ratio of crowd controllers to patrons. NDLERF Monograph Series No. 54. Canberra: National Drug Law Enforcement Research Fund. http://www .ndlerf.gov.au/publications/monographs/monograph-54.

Homel, P. 2006. Joining up the pieces: What central agencies need to do to support effective local crime prevention. In Knutsson, J. and Clarke, R. (eds.), *Implementation of Local Crime Prevention Measures*. Crime Prevention Studies Vol. 20. New Jersey: Prentice Hall, 111–139.

Homel, P. 2009. Improving crime prevention knowledge and practice. Trends and Issues in Criminal Justice. No. 385, Canberra: Australian Institute of Criminology. http://www.aic.gov.au/en/publications/current%20series/tandi /381-400/tandi385.aspx.

Homel, P. 2009. Lessons for Canadian crime prevention from recent international experience. *Institute for the Prevention of Crime (IPC) Review* 3: 13–39.

Homel, P. 2010. Delivering effective local crime prevention: Why understanding variations in municipal governance arrangements matters. In Idriss, M. et al. (eds.), *2010 International Report on Crime Prevention and Community Safety: Trends and Prospects*. Montréal: International Centre for the Prevention of Crime, 118–119.

Homel, P., and Carroll, T. 2009. Moving knowledge into action: Applying social marketing principles to crime prevention. Trends and Issues in Criminal Justice. No. 381, Canberra: Australian Institute of Criminology. http://www .aic.gov.au/publications/current%20series/tandi/381-400/tandi381.aspx.

Homel, P., and Fuller, G. 2015. Understanding the local government role in crime prevention. Trends and Issues in Crime and Criminal Justice No. 505. Canberra: Australian Institute of Criminology. http://aic.gov.au/media_library /publications/tandi_pdf/tandi505.pdf.

Homel, R., and Homel, P. 2012. Implementing crime prevention: Good governance and a science of implementation. In Welsh, B. and Farrington, D. (eds.), *The Oxford Handbook on Crime Prevention*. Oxford: Oxford University Press, 423–445.

Homel, P., and Kirvan, M.A. 2012. Crime prevention: Celebrating its inroads, accelerating its progress. In Redo, S. (ed.), *Blue Criminology: The Power of United Nations Ideas to Counter Crime Globally*. Helsinki: European Institute for Crime Prevention and Control (HEUNI), 98–100.

Homel, P., Morgan, A., Behm, A., and Makkai, T. 2007. The review of the National Community Crime Prevention Programme: Establishing a new strategic direction. Report to the Attorney-General's Department. Canberra: Australian Institute of Criminology (unpublished report).

Homel, P., Nutley, S., Tilley, N., and Webb, B. 2004. *Investing to Deliver. Reviewing the Implementation of the UK Crime Reduction Programme*. London: Home Office Research Study 281.

Hulme, S., and Homel, P. 2015. Evaluation of the Victorian Community Crime Prevention Program: Final Report. Special Report. Canberra: Australian Institute of Criminology. http://aic.gov.au/media_library/publications/special /008/Evaluation-Victorian-CCPP.pdf.

Morgan, A., and Homel, P. 2011. A model performance measurement framework for community based crime prevention. Technical and Background Paper. No. 40. Canberra: Australian Institute of Criminology. http://www.aic.gov.au /documents/B/D/9/{BD9D5686-84DE-4914-ADFC-E9F4D6C3CE36}tbp040 .pdf.

Morgan, A., and Homel, P. 2013. Evaluating crime prevention: Lessons from large-scale community crime prevention programs. Trends and Issues in Crime and Criminal Justice No. 458. Canberra: Australian Institute of Criminology. http://www.aic.gov.au/publications/current%20series/tandi/441-460/tandi458 .html.

Nutley, S., and Homel, P. 2006. Delivering evidence-based policy and practice: Lessons from the implementation of the UK Crime Reduction Programme. *Evidence and Policy* 2(1): 5–26.

Willis, K., Anderson, J., and Homel, P. 2011. Measuring the effectiveness of drug law enforcement. Trends and Issues in Crime and Criminal Justice. No. 406, Canberra: Australian Institute of Criminology. http://www.aic.gov au/documents/7/C/3/{7C3C0834-EE1D-4013-88D1-938A0D934782}tandi406 .pdf.

Willis, K., and Homel, P. 2008. Measuring the performance of drug law enforcement. *Policing: A Journal of Policy and Practice* 2(3): 311–321.

Acknowledgment

Most of us are well familiar with the ancient African proverb: "It takes a village to raise a child." Well, a parallel analogy can be said about the preparation of this book. Although I will shamelessly lay claim to the concept of this book, its genesis lies in the teaching and inspirations of some of my undergraduate and graduate mentors who planted the seeds and encouraged me (and my fellow classmates) to challenge the status quo of crime control, treatment, suppression, and punitive intervention that seemed to dominate criminal justice policy during my formative education in criminology during the 1980s. Furthermore, the actualization of this book would not have come to fruition were it not for the collective contribution of all those who not only contributed to this book but a number of whom also shared their thoughts about the framework and content for the book. Without this community of dedicated and scholarly feedback, I would still be on a "Walkabout" trying to figure out what and how to bring the book to life.

In addition to the "global village" of contributors, I am/was particularly blessed to have the unwavering support from former CRC Senior Acquisition Editor Carolyn Spence. Not only did she embrace the initial proposal for the book, she provided her professional support and insight into some key elements of the book as well. To the "community village" of other CRC staff who helped chaperone such initiatives to completion, I am also dearly indebted. You are a brilliant team to work with.

Finally, there are the more intimate members in the "global village"—my family. Again, as John Donne wrote in 1624: "no man is an island, entire of itself; every man is part of a continent." I have admittedly spent a disproportionate amount of my adult life pursuing my passion for learning and academia. However, without the unwavering support of my partner in life and happiness—Rose—I would never have been able to accomplish a fraction of what I've done. Yet, she also ensured with measured patience that I make time for that which is more important—family. I have been blessed during the preparation of this book to see my small intimate village of four (which includes our two sons) grow—we became first-time grandparents and are thrilled that our intimate village will grow and thrive to contribute to the global village.

Since I started this Acknowledgment with a quote, I would like to end it with yet another equally eloquent quote (paraphrased) that indirectly speaks to the power and underlying message throughout this book: "We can start building a good community when once we decide that we can and must all be a good neighbors."

As much as this book is the ensemble of many people helping directly and indirectly to seeing this anthology come to life, I remain the sole bearer of any limitations that one might find in these pages and collectively share any of its accolades with those who were instrumental in informing both the content and creation of this book.

About the Editor

Dr. John A. Winterdyk has published extensively in the areas of criminology theory, youth at risk, corrections, and criminal justice–related issues, including articles in the *Canadian Journal of Criminal Justice* and *Criminal Justice Review*, among others. He gained his PhD from Simon Fraser University and has recently returned to Mount Royal University (MRU) after time spent in Germany as a Visiting Scholar at the Max Planck Institute in Freiburg. He has published a number of books, including a recently edited book entitled *Border Security in the Al-Qaeda Era*, co-edited with Kelly Sundberg (MRU), as well as editing a book on human trafficking with Philip Reichel (University of Northern Colorado) and Benjamin Perrin (University of British Columbia). He is also working on a fourth edition of a textbook on youth justice. He recently completed a book entitled *Inequality, Diversity and Canadian Justice* (Nelson) with Doug King. Dr. Winterdyk's current research interests include Canadian border security, in particular looking at the effect the establishment of the Canada Border Services Agency has on the Canadian public's perception of border security. Dr. Winterdyk recently completed a cross-national research project looking at combating human trafficking with scholars from Canada, the United States, and Austria, funded through the National Institute of Justice, and taken part in studies on identity theft (the first of its kind in Canada) and on mass marketing fraud. Dr. Winterdyk recently served as guest editor for a special issue on genocide for the *International Criminal Review* as well as a co-guest editor (with Philip Reichel) of the *European Journal of Criminology*, which looks at human trafficking. His research projects include human trafficking, fear of crime, border security, and prison gangs. In January 2010, Dr. Winterdyk became the director of the Centre for Criminology and Justice Research Project's pilot study, *Human Trafficking: Formalizing a Localized Response*.

Since graduating from Simon Fraser University (PhD in criminology, 1988). John has taught in the Department of Economics, Justice, and Policy Studies at Mount Royal University (MRU, Calgary, Alberta). In additional to his position at MRU, John has held adjunct positions at St. Thomas University (Fredericton, New Brunswick), the Polytechnic of Namibia (Windhoek, Namibia), and the University of Regina (Canada). John is the former and founding director for the Centre of Criminology and Justice Research at MRU and 2009 recipient of the Distinguished Scholarship award. He has published extensively in the areas of youth justice, human trafficking, international criminal justice, and criminological theory.

To date, he has authored/edited nearly 30 textbooks and is currently working on a number of projects including an international handbook on human trafficking, an introductory Canadian criminology textbook, and a monograph that will profile the "pioneers" of Canadian criminology and criminal justice. In addition to his numerous peer-reviewed articles, John was served as special guest editor for five different peer-reviewed journals (themes: genocide, human trafficking, human rights, terrorism, and crime prevention). Current areas of research include comparative criminology/criminal justice, restorative justice, corrections, crime prevention, and trafficking in persons. John also serves on a number of provincial, national, and international boards. In his free time, John is an avid cyclist.

About the Contributors

Matjaž Ambrož, PhD, is an associate professor of criminal law (Faculty of Law, University of Ljubljana) and a researcher at the Ljubljana Institute of Criminology, where he currently leads a research project on criminal offenses of school workers. He has been a visiting research fellow at Max Planck Institute for Foreign and International Criminal Law (Freiburg, Germany) in 2003, 2007, and 2015. He has recently published a monograph, *Perpetration and Participation in Criminal Law* (2014), and coauthored a monograph, *Brain in the Dock: Neuroscience, Criminal Law and Criminology* (2015). His current research interests include substantive criminal law, sociology of criminal law, theories on justifying legal punishment, implementation of penal sanctions, and crime prevention. E-mail: matjaz.ambroz@pf.uni-lj.si

Mike B. Beke is a consultant working for the firm Blomeyer & Sanz. His principal research area relates to justice and home affairs in the EU in which he specialized in anti-corruption and good governance studies. Mike conducted impact assessments and policy evaluations for the EU institutions, in particular for the European Parliament Committees on Budgetary Control and on Organised Crime, Corruption and Money Laundering, on topics ranging from tax fraud, corruption in public procurement, to administrative law. Currently, he is a member of the European Commission's network of local correspondents on corruption, established to periodically analyze the Spanish state of play in anti-corruption activities. In 2012, before working at Blomeyer & Sanz, Mike worked on corruption research for Transparency International Spain and EU governance for the Centre for European Policy Studies in Brussels.

Dr. Gisela Bichler is a professor of Criminal Justice at California State University, San Bernardino, and director of the Center for Criminal Justice Research. Dr. Bichler regularly works with a range of criminal justice agencies, community groups, and city governments to develop solutions to local crime and public safety issues that remove the opportunity for crime by invoking stronger place management and adopting a range of crime-control strategies based on the situational crime prevention framework. Her current research examines the structure of illicit networks associated with criminal enterprise groups, transnational illicit markets, terrorism, and gang violence. Recent publications have appeared in the *Journal of Research in Crime* *and Delinquency, Policing: An International Journal of Police Strategies and Management, Global Crime, Crime and Delinquency, Security Journal, Crime Patterns and Analysis,* and *Psychological Reports.*

Melanie Burton is currently a PhD candidate in the Faculty of Law at the University of New South Wales in Sydney Australia. She also works as a research assistant on various projects for the Gendered Violence Research Network and the Faculty of Arts and Social Sciences at the University of New South Wales. Melanie has a background of study and practice in clinical psychology, completing her Master of Psychology and Postgraduate Diploma in Clinical Psychology at the University of Otago in Dunedin, New Zealand, in 2010. Her current research interests are on sexual and gendered violence with a specific focus on child sexual offenders and offenses.

Jesse Cale is a senior lecturer in Criminology in the School of Social Sciences at the University of New South Wales (UNSW) in Sydney Australia. He received his PhD in Criminology from Simon Fraser University in 2010 and has also worked as a research and policy analyst for the provincial government of British Columbia, Canada. Before commencing at UNSW, he was a research fellow in the Key Centre for Ethics, Law, Justice, and Governance at Griffith University (Brisbane, Australia). His main areas of research are sexual offenders and offenses, developmental and life-course criminology, victimization and victimology, and crime prevention and social policy. His studies have been published in various journals including *Aggression and Violent Behavior, Criminal Behaviour and Mental Health, Criminal Justice and Behavior, Homicide Studies, Journal of Criminal Justice, Psychology Crime and Law,* and *Sexual Abuse: A Journal of Research and Treatment.*

Dr. Irwin M. Cohen has been a faculty member of criminology and criminal justice in the School of Criminology and Criminal Justice at the University of the Fraser Valley in Abbotsford, British Columbia, since 2003; was the director of the School from 2010 to 2013; and is currently the RCMP Research Chair for Crime Reduction and the director of the Centre for Public Safety and Criminal Justice Research. Dr. Cohen has taught a wide range of undergraduate and graduate courses. Dr. Cohen has also published many scholarly articles and book chapters, delivered many lectures, conference papers, and workshops, and written policy reports on a wide range of topics including terrorism, youth justice issues, policing, public policy, and aboriginal issues.

Dr. Raymond R. Corrado is a professor in the School of Criminology at Simon Fraser University and was an associate faculty member in the Psychology Department and the Faculty of Health Sciences. He is a visiting fellow at Clare Hall College and the Institute of Criminology, University of Cambridge, and recently had a three-year appointment as a visiting professor in the Faculty of Law at the University of Bergen. He is a founding member of the Mental Health, Law, and Policy Institute at Simon Fraser University. Dr. Corrado was also a former co-director of the BC Centre for Social Responsibility and former director of the Centre for Addictions Research British Columbia, SFU Site. He is on the editorial boards of six major criminology and forensic mental health journals. He has co-authored nine edited books including *Multi-Problem Violent Youth, Issues in Juvenile Justice, Evaluation and Criminal Justice Policy*, and *Juvenile Justice in Canada*, and has published more than 200 articles, book chapters, and reports on a wide variety of theory and policy issues, including youth/juvenile justice, violent young offenders, mental health, adolescent psychopathy, aboriginal victimization, child/adolescent case management strategies, and terrorism. Currently, Dr. Corrado is a principal investigator and co-principal investigator of several research projects including three large-scale studies on incarcerated serious and violent young offenders, comprehensive risk management instrument for violent children and youth, and early childhood aggression. He received his PhD from Northwestern in Chicago.

Yvon Dandurand is a criminologist; a member of the School of Criminology and Criminal Justice, University of the Fraser Valley; and a fellow and senior associate of the International Centre for Criminal Law Reform and Criminal Justice Policy, a United Nations–affiliated institute. He specializes in comparative criminal law and criminal justice research and has been extensively involved in numerous children's rights and youth justice reform and policy development projects in Canada and abroad. He has developed and implemented assessment tools and performance indicators and other monitoring mechanisms in the areas of child protection and juvenile justice. He developed the *Criteria for the design and evaluation of juvenile justice reform programs* for the Interagency Panel on Juvenile Justice. He also participated in the development of the *Mapping and Assessment Toolkit* for child protection systems published by UNICEF. He recently worked as the UNODC lead consultant for the development of the United Nations *Model Strategies and Practical Measures on the Elimination of Violence against Children in the Field of Crime Prevention and Criminal Justice* and created a checklist to facilitate the implementation of that new child rights–based instrument.

Dr. Garth Davies is an associate professor of Criminology at Simon Fraser University. His most recently completed work involves the social psychology of radicalization. He has also been involved in the development of the Terrorism and Extremism Network Extractor, a web crawler designed to investigate extremist activities on the Internet. The crawler is presently being adapted to examine violent extremism on the dark net. Dr. Davies is also the co-director of the Terrorism, Risk, and Security Studies professional online Masters program at Simon Fraser University.

Jaap de Waard is a senior policy advisor at the Netherlands Ministry of Security and Justice. He is the former secretary of the European Crime Prevention Network (EUCPN). He has published widely on crime prevention models, international trends in the private security industry, and international benchmark studies in the field of crime control. He is a regular presenter at national and international conferences and expert meetings in the field of law enforcement and crime prevention. He is a research fellow at the International Victimology Institute (INTERVICT), Tilburg University, the Netherlands.

Jaap studied Information Science with special emphasis on the application and usage of knowledge in organizations, along with the interaction between people, organizations, and any existing information and knowledge systems.

Benjamin Flander, PhD, is an assistant professor at the Faculty of Criminal Justice and Security, University of Maribor, Slovenia. His areas of specialization are constitutional law and human rights in criminal justice systems. He is the coauthor of recently published chapters in *Trust and Legitimacy in Criminal Justice* (2015, edited by Gorazd Meško and Justice Tankebe) and *International Developments and Practices in Investigative Interviewing and Interrogation* (edited by David Walsh et al.). He is the author of two books. Lately, his research interests include Nietzsche, postmodernism, advanced critical legal studies, and critical criminology. Since 2012, he has been active as an evaluator at the Group of States against Corruption (GRECO). E-mail: benjamin.flander@fvv.uni-mb.si

Richard Grimes qualified as a solicitor in 1977 and worked initially in a law center and later as a full-equity partner for a provincial law firm, handling a wide range of, principally, publicly funded cases. He has retained an interest in law teaching and research as well as legal practice in the belief that the one informs the other and has worked at several universities in England and Ireland. In 1990, he joined Sheffield Hallam University where he established an in-house solicitor's practice in which undergraduate law students handled real cases under professional supervision. He was seconded to the University of the South Pacific from 1995 to 1997 where he became the director of the Institute for Justice and Applied Legal Studies. In 1998, he was appointed head of Law and professor of Legal Education at the University of Derby, and in 2000, he joined the College of Law as professor and director of Pro Bono Services and Clinical Legal Education. From 2006 to 2010, Richard acted as an independent consultant on a variety of projects in the United Kingdom and further afield including in Afghanistan, Georgia, Iran, and Nigeria, working with national governments, donor agencies, law schools, the legal profession, and NGOs. He was director of Clinical Programmes at the York Law School, University of York, from 2010 to 2016 and helped pioneer a fully integrated clinical approach to study using problem-based learning. He has now returned to a consultancy role. He has published widely on clinical legal education issues, in the legal skills field, and on various substantive law matters. He remains committed to learning by doing and to improving access to justice more generally.

Rita Haverkamp was appointed, in 2013, to the position of professorship in the Department of Crime Prevention and Risk Management at Eberhard Karls University in Tübingen, Germany. She is currently a member of the Scientific Advisory Committee on the Dialogue on Societal Aspects of Security Research that is funded by the German Federal Ministry of Education and Research. In addition, Haverkamp serves on the Research Advisory Board of the Federal Criminal Police Office.

Professor Haverkamp completed her doctoral thesis on "Electronic Monitoring of Criminal Offenders" at the Max Planck Institute for Foreign and International Criminal Law in Freiburg, Germany. Her habilitation thesis on "Women in Prison against the Background of the European Prison Rules" was completed at the Ludwig-Maximilians-University in Munich in 2008. Before achieving her professorship, Rita worked as a senior researcher (2008–2013) at the Department of Criminology of the Max Planck Institute for Foreign and International Criminal Law where she focused mainly on terrorism and security-related research.

Jackie Jones is a professor of Feminist Legal Studies at the University of the West of England and a human rights activist. She specializes in women's human rights but has written articles and chapters on the rights of transsexuals, gender, asylum, sexuality, and same-sex marriage. She is president of the European Women Lawyers Association, chair of the Wales Assembly of Women, and trustee of two women's rights organizations in the United Kingdom. She, along with others, has written a draft UN Convention/Optional Protocol to Eliminate Violence against Women and Girls, working closely with Professor Rashida Manjoo, the former UN Special Rapporteur on Violence against Women, Its Causes and Consequences. Jackie has written several pieces on human trafficking and helped progress the agenda on human trafficking in Wales from 2007 to 2010 working with Parliamentarians on awareness raising and a specific Wales report. She has given evidence to the Westminster Parliament and the National Assembly for Wales on State obligations to enact gender-specific laws to combat violence against women and regularly attends governmental meetings to discuss equality and women's rights issues in the United Kingdom and in Europe, as well as the United

Nations Commission on the Status of Women. She was national coordinator of the EU Progress–funded project, European Women Shareholders Demand Gender Equality (www.ewsdge.org).

Michael Kilchling, Dr. jur., is a senior researcher at the Department of Criminology of the Max Planck Institute for Foreign and International Criminal Law in Freiburg/Germany (MPI) and lecturer at the University of Freiburg where he teaches criminology, penology, prison law, and juvenile justice law. His main research interests include penal sanctions and sanctioning systems, juvenile justice, victim/offender mediation and other forms of restorative justice, victimology, organized crime, money laundering and the financing of terrorism, confiscation, and asset recovery. He liaises with the Max Planck Partner Group for Balkan Criminology, a joint venture of the MPI and the Faculty of Law of the University of Zagreb/Croatia, and is one of the course directors of the International Spring Course "Crime Prevention through Criminal Law and Security Studies" of the Zagreb Faculty of Law and of the annual "Balkan Criminology" course, both held at the Inter University Centre in Dubrovnik/Croatia. He was a member of several international expert groups at the Council of Europe and the EU Commission; at the Council of Europe, he was a member of the Group of Specialists on Assistance to Victims and Prevention of Victimization that prepared the Recommendation R(2006)8 on Assistance to Crime Victims. He is a co-editor of *Balkan Criminology News*, the newsletter of the Max Planck Partner Group for Balkan Criminology, and a member of the international advisory board of *Restorative Justice—An International Journal*. Besides his academic activities, he volunteers as a member of the board of the European Forum for Restorative Justice, currently as its chair, and as a member of the scientific council of the German association of victim support groups (ado).

Dr. J. Bryan Kinney is an associate professor in the School of Criminology at Simon Fraser University, where he has completed his MA and PhD in Criminology. He is also the assistant director for the Institute for Canadian Urban Research Studies. His research interests include environmental criminology, geography of crime, police studies, crime prevention and crime reduction, quantitative research methods, court sentencing patterns, and historical criminology.

Helmut Kury, Prof. Dr. habil. Dipl. Psych., Prof. h.c. mult., studied psychology and economy at the University of Freiburg/Germany. Throughout his academic career, he served as an assistant teacher at the University of Freiburg, Department Psychology (1970–1973); he was a senior researcher at Max Planck Institute for Foreign and International Penal Law—Department of Criminology; and he served as a professor at the University of Freiburg/

Germany (1973–1980 and 1988–2006, pensioner). From 1980 to 1988, he was first director of the Criminological Research Institute (KFN) of Lower Saxony in Hannover/Germany.

His main research interests include the resocialization of offenders, evaluation of different treatment programs, juvenile delinquency, psychological diagnostic of prisoners and sex offenders, expert testimonies in court, fear of crime, and community crime prevention, among other areas. Kury has published some 700 articles in national and international journals and has edited a score of books covering such topics as crime, criminology, forensic psychology, family, and criminal behavior. His most recent publications include the following: *Punitivity—International Developments.* 3 Vols. (2011), Bochum: Brockmeyer, edited with E. Shea; *Forensic Psychology* (2012), Stuttgart: Kohlhammer; edited with H. Obergfell-Fuchs; and *Women and Children as Victims and Offenders. Background, Prevention, Reintegration*, 2 Vols. (2016), Heidelberg, New York: Springer; edited with S. Redo and E. Shea.

Benoit Leclerc is an associate professor of Criminology and Criminal Justice at Griffith University in Brisbane, Australia. He was involved in research and clinical work with adolescent and adult sex offenders at the Philippe-Pinel Institute of Montréal for seven years and received his PhD from the Université of Montréal, Canada. His research interests include script analysis, offender decision-making, situational crime prevention, and sexual offending. His most recent funded project involves the study of the effectiveness of situational crime prevention to prevent sexual offenses. His research has been published in various journals including *British Journal of Criminology, Criminal Justice and Behavior, Criminology, Journal of Interpersonal Violence, Child Abuse & Neglect, Journal of Research in Crime and Delinquency*, and *Sexual Abuse: A Journal of Research and Treatment.*

Elliott Mann, BA, studies at the School of Criminology at Simon Fraser University, where he is currently completing a master's degree in Criminology. He completed his undergraduate degree in Criminal Justice at Mount Royal University and was placed on the President's Honor Roll. His research interests include environmental criminology, crime prevention and CPTED, and geography of crime.

Dr. Nerea Marteache is an assistant professor of Criminal Justice and the assistant director of the Center for Criminal Justice Research at California State University, San Bernardino. Her scholarship involves two complementary subject areas—crime prevention through opportunity reduction and the analysis and evaluation of criminal justice policy. From 2005 to 2008 she worked as a researcher at the Department of Justice of the Government of Catalonia (Spain), mainly in the areas of juvenile justice, corrections, and court performance evaluation. Dr. Marteache's current research examines the opportunity structure of theft by employees, wildlife crime, and crime in transportation systems. Her recent scholarly work includes book chapters and publications in *European Journal on Criminal Justice and Research*, *European Journal of Criminology*, *Journal of Public Transportation*, *Journal of American College Health*, and *Crime Science*.

Dr. Veronica Martinez Solares played a key role in developing the materials for the politicians who successfully legislated Mexico's model national law on crime prevention. She was the lead expert in developing the model framework for national crime prevention for 10 Latin American countries in partnership with the EFUS and other partners for EUROsociAL. She has a growing list of publications and has worked on numerous projects to develop effective crime prevention, victim assistance, police reform, and modern justice in Latin America, including on grants from the British Council, the Canadian International Development Research Centre, the Legal Defence Institute from Peru, the Citizen Security Studies Centre from Chile, and the Organization of American States. She is invited increasingly to speak in both English and Spanish in North and Latin America on these issues.

Gorazd Meško, PhD, is a professor of criminology and the head of the Institute of Criminal Justice and Security at the Faculty of Criminal Justice and Security, University of Maribor, Slovenia. He is a member of the Max Planck Partner Group for Balkan Criminology and an International Ambassador of the British Society of Criminology. He received the "Zois Award" for his outstanding achievements in scientific, research and development activities in social sciences in 2014. He has recently edited *Handbook on Policing in Central and Eastern Europe* (2013, with Charles B. Fields, Branko Lobnikar, and Andrej Sotlar) and *Trust and Legitimacy in Criminal Justice: European Perspectives* (2015, with Justice Tankebe). His current research interests include crime prevention, provision of safety/security, and legitimacy. E-mail: gorazd.mesko@fvv.uni-mb.si

Anne Miller holds a masters' in public policy and public administration, Anne is a credentialed evaluator through the Canadian Evaluation Society, an accredited SROI practitioner, and licensed SROI trainer through the Social Value Network International. Working as the director of SROI and Evaluation at a consulting firm in Canada, Anne supported the Government of Alberta in reviewing the SROI analyses of 88 crime prevention projects funded under Alberta's Safe Communities Secretariat (2011–2014). She has conducted significant research in crime-related financial proxies and has contributed to providing training in SROI and cost analysis for many government departments and crime prevention programs.

Monica Pauls, MA, has been working as a researcher in the social science field for more than a decade. Upon completing her masters' degree, she worked as the coordinator for Alberta-based Research Projects at the Canadian Research Institute for Law and the Family. Monica went on to teach at Mount Royal University, but continued to conduct research as both an independent consultant and as a member of the academic community. Her scholarly interests include at-risk children and youth, interpersonal violence, youth empowerment, social movements and community change, and evaluation. She is well versed in both quantitative and qualitative methodologies and has experience with various analytical software programs. Monica is currently appointed as assistant professor in the Department of Child Studies and Social Work at Mount Royal University.

Michael Platzer served for 34 years in the United Nations Secretariat in various capacities, in the Office of the Secretary-General, human rights, technical cooperation, HABITAT, UNDP, peacebuilding/reconstruction, and the UNODC. He has taught at Australian, Austrian, American, and Caribbean universities. Dr. Platzer was liaison officer for the Academic Council on the United Nations System to the Vienna-based UN organizations and chair of the Vienna NGO Alliance for Crime Prevention and Criminal Justice. For the past three years, he has led a campaign to stop Femicide: A Global Issue That Demands Action, which has resulted in two General Assembly resolutions, many symposia, and five publications. His primary interests are the education of the "succeeding generations," innovative teaching techniques, social media advocacy, environmental protection, juvenile justice reform, prisoners' rights, guidelines for chaplains witnessing torture, victim rights, rights of migrants, social integration, and assistance to refugees. In addition to teaching, he is also busy organizing workshops and conferences, conducting surveys, and publishing research. His last UN assignment was Regional Representative to the Caribbean, on behalf of UNODC. Practical projects, which assisted youth, the poor, vulnerable people, and women, have always been his priorities.

Sławomir Redo (Dr. hab., Law/Criminology) is an independent academic, and senior adviser at the Academic Council on the United Nations System (Liaison Office at Vienna, Austria). He teaches a graduate interdisciplinary course on "The United Nations and Crime Prevention" at several international universities.

Redo was a UN Senior Crime Prevention and Criminal Justice Expert and staff of the United Nations Office on Drugs and Crime who, for 30 years, had worked on technical assistance projects implementing the UN law against organized crime and many other UN crime prevention and criminal justice standards and norms.

He has published some 70 articles mainly on the United Nations law and practice of crime prevention and criminal justice. He co-edited three criminological books, including For the Rule of Law: Criminal Justice Teaching and Training across the World. In 2012, he published Blue Criminology. The Power of United Nations Ideas to Counter Crime Globally. He also co-edited Women and Children as Offenders and Victims of Crime. Suggestions for Succeeding Generations (Springer, 2016).

Dr. John Rook is a passionate servant leader who champions the belief that poverty can be solved. With a doctorate from Oxford University, he has spent years both at the front lines and in academia to gain both a theoretical and practical understanding of the issues facing people in poverty. He has published a Greek workbook and numerous journal articles, and has a children's book on homelessness in progress.

For six years, he chaired the National Council of Welfare, a federal body reporting to the Minister of Human Resources and Skills Canada proposing recommendations for improving Canadian lives to the Canadian Parliament. From 2000 to 2010, he worked for the Salvation Army, and for six years, he was CEO of their Community Services, which included the Booth Centre and Centre of Hope homeless projects and Child & Family Services.

He has received numerous recognitions for his work from the City of Burlington, Ontario's Celebration of Service Award (1996), to the Queen Elizabeth II Diamond Jubilee Medal (2013). He sat on the Provincial Interagency Council on Homelessness and chaired the research committee. He is a board member of the Basic Income Canada Network and Vibrant Communities Calgary. He is the founding director of the Canadian Poverty Institute at Ambrose University in Calgary. Currently he is director of Programs and Strategic Initiatives at The Mustard Seed in Calgary, Alberta, Canada.

Samantha Sexsmith is a recent recipient of a master's degree in Public Policy from the School of Public Policy in Calgary, Alberta. Before moving to Calgary, Samantha received an honour's bachelor degree in Criminal Justice and Public Policy from the University of Guelph. Samantha has previously worked on the front lines with incarcerated youth, which ultimately sparked her academic interests, but she now remains focused on research and policy analysis. Samantha's research focuses heavily on alternative methods to incarceration for youth crime, but she is currently working with Dr. John Rook on research related to poverty and homelessness.

Margaret Shaw, PhD, is a sociologist and criminologist, and was director of analysis and exchange at the International Centre for the Prevention of Crime (ICPC) from 1999 to 2011. She now works as an independent consultant, including with ICPC. Before joining ICPC, she worked for more than 20 years as a research and policy advisor in the Home Office, England. Between 1986 and 1999, she was a lecturer and associate professor in the Department of Sociology and Anthropology at Concordia University, Montréal, and undertook research for federal, provincial, and municipal governments and police organizations in Canada. She has undertaken extensive research internationally including for UN HABITAT, UNODC, UN WOMEN, and WHO and published widely on crime prevention, youth violence, justice and rehabilitation, gender, women's imprisonment and safety, human trafficking, and evaluation. In 2013, she was awarded the *Saltzman Prize for Contributions to Practice* by the Division of Women and Crime, American Society of Criminology, and in 2014, she received the *G.O.W. Mueller Award for Distinguished Contributions to International Criminal Justice*, from the International Division of the Academy of Criminal Justice Sciences.

Jan van Dijk has a degree in law from Leiden University (1970) and a PhD in criminology from the University of Nijmegen (1977). He is a former director of the Research Centre and Directorate of Crime Prevention of the Dutch Ministry of Justice and a former professor of criminology at the Universities of Leiden and Tilburg. He served as officer in charge of the United Nations Centre for International Crime Prevention in Vienna between 1998 and 2006. He is currently a visiting professor at Lausanne University, Switzerland. He is vice-president of the Group of Experts on Action against Trafficking in Human Beings (GRETA) of the Council of Europe and vice-president of the Dutch State Compensation Fund for Victims of Violent Crime. He is a member of the Research Council of the Dutch National Police (Politie en Wetenschap).

van Dijk published extensively on victims' rights, crime prevention, and human trafficking. His latest monograph in English is *The World of Crime: Breaking the Silence on Problems of Security, Justice and Development* (Sage, 2008). In 2011, he published with Rianne Letschert the edited book *The New Faces of Victimhood: Globalization, Transnational Crimes and Victim Rights* (Springer). In 2012, he published with A. Tseloni and Graham Farrell *The International Drops in Crime* (Palgrave/Macmillan). In 2009, he received the Sellin-Glueck Award of the American Society of Criminology, and in 2012, he received the Stockholm Prize in Criminology.

Paul van Soomeren is one of the founders of DSP-groep (http://www .dsp-groep.eu/home/) and works as a management consultant and policy researcher for national and local authorities, the EU, and international organizations and institutions. DSP-groep is a leading institute for policy research and social innovation, established in 1984 and based in Europe (Amsterdam-NL). Areas of expertise include crime prevention, safety and (social) security, youth, welfare and health care, leisure/sports, and culture.

He is the director of the board of the International CPTED Association (crime prevention through environmental design) and the European Designing Out Crime Association (http://www.e-doca.eu/). In that capacity, he travels all over the world to lecture on these subjects.

Areas of expertise include urban planning and design, crime prevention, safety/security, education, and social management. Paul is a member of the international COST action Management Committee and is a visiting professor of the Adelphi Research Institute of the University of Salford (UK).

Paul studied Social Geography, and Urban and Regional Planning at the University of Amsterdam. He worked for the Ministries of Justice and Interior Affairs (National Crime Prevention Institute) for three years before he founded DSP-groep in 1984.

Irvin Waller is an influential author and speaker, professor of Criminology, and president of the International Organization for Victim Assistance. He won awards in the United States and internationally for his contributions to the UN General Assembly resolution that adopted the Declaration on Principles of Justice for Victims in 1985. His work to stop victimization—the ultimate victim right—has won recognition across the world, particularly for his role as the founding executive director of the International Centre for Prevention of Crime, affiliated with the UN. He has advised the governments of more than 50 countries in both the affluent and developing world, including that of Mandela. His recent trilogy of books provide policymakers with effective actions based on the accumulated evidence and international best practices to stop violent crime and assist victims. They are translated into Spanish, Chinese, and other languages. They include *Less Law, More Order—The Truth about Reducing Crime* (2006), *Rights for Victims of Crime: Rebalancing Justice* (2011), and *Smarter Crime Control: A Guide to a Safer Future for Citizens, Communities and Politicians* (2014).

Scott Walsh was born and brought up in Lancashire, North West England. After leaving school with limited qualifications, he moved from job to job working, among other things, as an apprentice baker and in local cotton mills. After a troubled few years that included various encounters with the law and several custodial sentences, Scott started to improve his position, first attending college and then volunteering to help with a variety of youth projects. He has worked with young offenders for the past eight years specializing in RJ. He received a major Ministry of Justice award for crime prevention in 2010 and now regularly lectures on RJ and is involved in the development and delivery of RJ programs and in the training of RJ facilitators. In 2015, he decided to study law at degree level (which he is enjoying immensely) and he hopes to eventually qualify and practice as a solicitor.

D. Gaye Warthe, PhD, MSW, RSW, is an associate professor and chair of the Department of Child Studies and Social Work at Mount Royal University, Calgary. Dr. Warthe has extensive practice experience including working with child protection, pregnant and parenting adolescents, and education, and as a medical social worker at a children's hospital. As a private consultant, she contributed to the development and implementation of domestic violence screening protocols, was involved in establishing the domestic violence court in Calgary, and was the lead consultant on a Family and Sexual Violence Sector Review. Dr. Warthe is the principal investigator on a relationship violence prevention project at Mount Royal called Stepping Up; she developed the Dating Relationship Scales to measure dating violence in young adults and is the principal investigator in a multiyear dating violence prevalence study. Dr. Warthe was on the Advisory Committee of Shift: The Project to End Domestic Violence and currently serves on the Steering Committee for RESOLVE Alberta; she is a member of the board with Discovery House Family Violence Prevention Society and the Alberta Council of Women Shelters.

Introduction

> One insight that Friedrich Nietzsche shares with Emile Durkheim...is that strong political regimes have no need to rely upon intensely punitive sanctions. Punitiveness may pose as a symbol of strength, but it should be interpreted as a symptom of weak authority and inadequate controls.
>
> **D. Garland**
> *1996, p. 445*

Today, there is no shortage of literature questioning the relative efficiency and effectiveness of any state's criminal justice system (CJS). Why then, despite a plethora of initiatives, do society's most marginalized sectors (e.g., aboriginal/indigenous and other [minority] ethnic groups; physically, emotionally, or mentally challenged people, children, and youth; Roma; minority ethnic groups, etc.) continue to be overrepresented within and not receive basic rights and support from the CJS? Why do these groups seem to be socially dominated, for example, victim to exploitation, harassment, profiling, lack of equal opportunity, and so on? One explanation is that those identifying with one or more such groups tend to be poverty stricken or have low socioeconomic standing relative to their fellow citizens. Haugen and Boutros (2014) provide a compelling overview of how countries whose economies are not well established and where poverty is a major concern* also tend to have various levels of inefficiency and corruption within, and a lack of state funding for their CJS, which essentially contribute to the breakdown of their society and the perpetual crime problems. The point about funding also mirrors one of the conclusions that Farrell and Clark (2004) draw from their analysis, that "criminal justice expenditure levels are significantly tied to levels of available public monies as determined by the strength of a national economy" (p. 22).† Similarly, Dandurand (2014, p. 383) points out that "criminal justice systems around the world are frequently being questioned both in terms of their effectiveness and their efficiency." Drawing

---

* According to World Bank data from 2011, approximately 14.5% of the world's population lives in poverty (at $1.25 a day). The hardest hit areas are the sub-Saharan region at 46.8%, followed by fragile and conflict-affected zones at 42.7%, while Europe and Central Asia have the lowest poverty rate at 0.5% (see http://data.worldbank.org/topic/poverty). Reporting on data collected by World Issues, Shah (2013) reports that 80% of the world's population lives on less than US$10/day.
† For example, countries such as Switzerland, Denmark, United States, and Singapore had the highest per capita spending across the CJS while also having very robust economies.

on a range of international examples, Dandurand tenders a number of recommendations that collectively speak to new and better capacity building initiatives throughout the CJS. While having introspective suggestions, Dandurand intentionally situate(s) these changes within a financial or resource context. In Canada, for example, between 2003 and 2013, the CJS budget increased 66% despite a steadily decreasing crime rate (Story and Yalkin 2013). In their comprehensive review of global expenditures on criminal justice (CJ), Farrell and Clark (2004) observed that approximately 62% of global CJ budget is spent on policing, 3% on prosecution, 18% on courts, and 19% on incarceration. These are all reactive investments in crime control. Interestingly, no mention is made of money being allocated to crime prevention initiatives—a proactive initiative.

Even though politicians and civil servants express the need to formulate policy based on informed evidence, the burgeoning costs, relatively inefficiency, and effectiveness of the CJS have not been affected by many reforms despite clear and compelling evidence of viable alternatives. Furthermore, as Garland (1996) reports in his analysis of the strategies of crime control, the normality of crime rates and the limitations of criminal justice agencies to effectively respond to the changing rates have created a predicament for governments, which, in turn, can be used to explain the contradictory character of recent crime-control policy. For example, it could be claimed that many CJSs are being expanded despite an overall decline in world crime rates (see Chapter 17). Furthermore, when comparing the prison rates for 11 countries for the period from 2005 to 2009, only two countries, the Netherlands and Finland, experienced a drop in their prison population rates (Walmsley n.d.). Prisons are very expensive and reoffending rates, internationally, hover around 40% (UN Minister of Justice 2010). UN data also show that the *per capita* of police officers increased throughout most of the 20th century, with a global per capita in 2006 of around 300 while the UN recommends the minimum strength needs only to around 222 (Twelfth United Nations Congress on Crime Prevention and Criminal Justice 2010, p. 19). What is not taken into account are the increasing associated costs of maintaining law enforcement agencies; these budgets have continued to grow despite a global leveling of police numbers. Speaking to this general point, the British-based National Audit Office (2012, p. 9) reported that "international comparisons have an important role to play in building understanding of how individual criminal justice systems are functioning."

Despite the challenges of making international comparisons (see Dammer and Albanese 2013; Reichel and Albanese 2014; Winterdyk 2015), it is clear that most governments around the world are relying increasingly on neo-conservatism ideas* to reduce their criminal justice expenditures by "tinkering"

---

* For further discussion on the concept of neo-conservativism see, for example, J. Clarke (2004). *America Alone: The Neo-Conservatives and the Global Order.* Cambridge, United Kingdom: Cambridge University Press.

with how they formally administer justice. Bear in mind, however, the cautionary comments of Sherman et al. (1997) that crime prevention, while not a perfect solution, holds considerably more promise than the "dominate" approach of trying to *control* crime. After all, it is unlikely that we can control the crime "opportunities" continually proffered by new technology, social change, and the adaptive and innovative (e.g., rational choice theory) behavior of prospective offenders (see Ekblom 2012). Yet, we should be mindful of the provocative point made by esteemed American political scientist James Q. Wilson (1931–2012) in his 1974 essay: "Crime and the criminologists." Wilson notes how it was only in the aftermath of the political failures of social reforms in the late 1960s (i.e., deinstitutionalization and philosophy of reintegration), which also coincided with a rising crime rate and public concern over law and order, that we began to see the policy analysis and legislation on crime control being influenced by sociological and psychological theories that were simply not robust enough to be used as justification for any social policy (Hope 2000). The (re)emergence of crime prevention as a crime-control strategy was seen initially as a simplified explanation and response to the "failings" of more traditional interpretation of crime and responses to it (Ekblom 2012; Garland 2001). While a substantive body of literature supports *proactive* over *reactive* measures for maintaining social order (see, generally, Sherman et al. 2006), we remain burdened with predominantly punitive and retributive approaches to maintaining law and order.

As reflected in the title of this book, the focus is on crime prevention as opposed to crime control. Before launching into the diverse range of themes, topics, and issues related to crime prevention efforts within an international context, we begin by summarizing the two main ideological perspectives on maintaining law and order. We then offer an overview of what crime prevention is, its approaches, and some of the key theories used to explain crime from a crime prevention standpoint. Then, we conclude with a few comments on initiatives aimed at measuring the relative effectiveness of crime prevention and offer an idea of what the future might hold.

Retributivism versus Utilitarianism

Retribution: "Just Deserts... Making the Punishment Fit the Crime"

We shut our eyes likewise to the fact that the control performance is frightfully expensive and inefficient.

K. Menninger
1969, p. viii

The etymology of crime can trace its origins to the Latin *cerno*, which translates to "I decide, I give judgment." Today, the conventional meaning of a crime denotes an act or behavior that, in accordance with a state's Criminal/Penal Code, is subject to a punitive response—punishment. The history of punishing someone for wrongdoing can also be traced back to pre-literate cultures when police forces didn't exist; serious offenses had to be dealt with quickly and generally deemed fair in the eyes of the church, which had a powerful role in enforcing morality at that time.* Philosophically, punishment can be divided into two schools of thought—*retribution* and *utilitarianism.*

In ancient Greece, retribution was the fundamental and universal principle of justice and formed the foundation upon which morality and Greek science were built. More recently, the Swiss child-psychologist Jean Piaget (1896–1980) was among the first to point out that, when left to their own devices, children will seek retribution when wronged. Only as we age and learn to modulate our sense of justice do we become able to desist from taking justice into our own hands (i.e., theory of cognitive development).†

I suspect that most readers are familiar with the ruthless phrase sometimes used by those who feel they have been unjustly harmed; they want their proverbial "pound of flesh." Those familiar with Shakespeare's *Merchant of Venice* (4:1), 1596, know the origin and meaning behind this phrase, which was used by the moneylender Shylock who was insistent that Antonio pay dearly with his flesh for not having paid Shylock back:

> The pound of flesh, which I demand of him, is deerly bought; 'tis mine, and I will have it.‡

As the story unfolds, the presiding judge, Portio, makes it clear that Shylock deserves compensation for his pound of flesh, money lent but not paid back, but without an ounce of blood because it was not asked for. Upon further reflection, Shylock accepts the ruling, but then later abandons his quest for revenge in favor of mercy.

> While we can credit Shakespeare for the colorful retributive phrase, the notion of exacting "justice," or "just deserts," first coined in 1976 (*Doing Justice*), by the British lawyer/penal theorist Andrew von Hirsch, asserts that punishment should be proportionate to the seriousness of the crime. This approach supersedes the classical principle of "utilitarianism" (see below) and any thought

---

* Some of the earliest written codes intended to maintain order and a just approach to crime control include the Sumerian *Code of Ur-Nammu* (circa 2100 BC), *Hammurabi Code* (circa 100 BC), and the *Mosaic Code* circa 640 BC).

† For more details on the theory of cognitive development see B.J. Wadsworth (1996), *Piaget's Theory of Cognitive and Affective Development: Foundations of Constructivism* (5th ed.). White Plains, NY, England: Longman Publishing.

‡ Old English spelling.

about treating or preventing a/the offender/crime. The just deserts model, while arguably more sophisticated than Immanuel Kant's (1724–1804) doctrine of "an eye for an eye"—law of vengeance (i.e., *Lex Talionis*), or "like for like" as described in Part 2 (Section 7) of Kant's 1785 *Metaphysics of Morals*, is not without its critics. Nevertheless, Kant's doctrine embraced the principles of natural law, humans as free and rational beings (see Corrado and Mattehesuis 2014), and the assumption of the social contract. This latter idea was adapted from the French philosopher and writer J.J. Rousseau (1712–1778), who argued that any sense of retributivism is dependent on the expressed guilt by the offender. Once established, punishment is deemed necessary as a means of obtaining (public) security and would supposedly ensure a fair and impartial sentence.* However, as Hudson (1996) points out, in treating similar crimes alike, such practice fails to take into consideration any of the structural or economic factors such as poverty (also see Crocker and Johnson 2010; Haugen and Boutros 2014). In dealing solely with the crime, the just desert model negates the possibility that any human condition, or element, underlies the motive behind the crime and thus dilutes the notion of the fair and equitable sentence envisioned by "true justice" philosophy.

Although space does not allow for a more protracted discussion of the merits of retribution, we conclude by pointing out that despite the proliferation of federal and international criminal laws (see Einarsen 2014) and expanding CJSs with their skyrocketing budgets, we are being shackled by a system that not only overcriminalizes behavior but also has proven to be not very effective at preventing crime or rehabilitating offenders.

Utilitarianism: "The Greater Good"

The utilitarian theory justifies punishment as a means to discourage, or "deter," future transgressions/transgressors. As first introduced by the Scottish scholar David Hume (1711–1766)† and later refined by Jeremy Bentham (1748–1832), the principle of utilitarianism refers to doing what is in the greatest good for a society—"the greatest happiness principle." According to utilitarian principles, punishment is "consequential" in nature. That is, unless the punishment serves the specific good of ensuring the safety and well-being of a society, it can be construed as "cruel and unusual." For example, if an inmate is suffering from a terminal illness, it may not serve

---

* During the 1970s, the just desserts model gained wide acceptance and many countries revised their sentencing guidelines to reflect the three key types of justice sentencing, for example, fixed sentences, presumptive guidelines with limited flexibility that were subject to specific conditions, and advisory guidelines under which proscribed situations, judges could exercise their discretion.
† Hume was one of the first empiricists and reasoned that *desire* as opposed to *reason* governed human behavior.

society to detain him or her indefinitely if he or she is no longer capable of committing a crime.

Virtually every country has a Criminal/Penal Code and a formalized CJS, whose primary function is to maintain social order, premised on crime control, or as English criminologist Jason Ditton (1979) defined it— "controlology." By nature and by definition, most CJSs are reactive in so much that a formal response cannot be applied unless a formal offense has been committed and the court has made a determination of the behavior or act in question.

Viewed from a psychological perspective, the "fear" (i.e., risk) of punishment—loss of freedom and dignity—assumes not only that humans are capable of making rational decisions regardless of their individual emotional and cognitive development but also that it is possible to proscribe a formal response proportionate to "the harm done" using what Jeremy Bentham* has termed *ethical calculus* (a pseudo-mathematical concept). However, as Ariely (2012) observed, most of us consider ourselves to be good people and therefore doing a "little wrong" won't hurt because on measure we are essentially good/law-abiding people who can rely on our own sense of morality to gauge how far we can transgress the norms and values of society without considering ourselves to be "bad." However, as Ariely points out, we are neither well equipped nor well qualified to judge our own moral performance. For example, how do we "know" when doing good enough is good enough? Would killing Adolf Hitler be considered a "good" act if it put an end to the Holocaust? Did the 2011 assassination of Osama bin Laden and founder of Al-Qaeda put an end to their terrorist activities?† While any attempt to engage in rich discourse over these examples is beyond the scope of the Introduction (and the objective of this book), what many of the early thinkers either directly or indirectly acknowledged is that criminal behavior is dependent on the opportunity to learn the behavior—that is, crime is rooted in social causation or "pleasure pursuit" as described by Geis (1972, p. 57). Therefore, if crime is largely learned and a predictable expression of our pursuit of pleasure/happiness (i.e., a calculable temptation), then we should also be able to design crime prevention approaches that will reduce the likelihood of a crime by neutralizing or eliminating the desire and temptation in the first place.‡

---

* Bentham was referred to as a "radical fool" by the German philosopher Johann W. von Geothe.
† The Al-Qaeda in Yemen claimed responsibility for the January 2015 terrorist massacre in Paris, France.
‡ Denunciation theory is a hybrid of retribution and utilitarianism. However, like retribution, it is grounded in the principle that offenders deserve to be held accountable (i.e., punished) for their wrongdoing. Arguably, the crimes in most Criminal Codes reflect those behaviors that a society disapproves of and which require some form of regulatory response (Zaibert 2006).

Crime Prevention Approaches: "An Ounce of Prevention Is Worth a Pound of Cure"

> As with other social problems, it is perhaps more sensible to think of prevention strategies.
>
> **V. F. Sacco and L. W. Kennedy**
> *2010, p. 315*

Crime prevention, although a simple term like *crime*, is complex in its expressions. In general, crime prevention refers to the array of strategies implemented by business, communities, governments, individuals, and nongovernment agencies/organizations to target the various environmental, cultural, economic, and social factors affecting the risk of crime and victimization (IPC 2008; Jacobs 1962; van Dijk and de Waard 1991). As Wilson (2011) points out, unlike most conventional approaches to crime control, crime prevention focuses on criminogenic situations as opposed to trying to deal with the criminal after the fact. Above all else, crime prevention is a *management* approach to crime control.

We will next summarize several of the main approaches to crime prevention that differ in terms of the intervention focus and types of activities delivered. Most of these approaches will be explored in greater detail in some of the subsequent chapters.

Environmental Crime Prevention

The environmental approach seeks to physically alter specific characteristics of the environment that are thought to contribute (i.e., risk factors) to the occurrence of criminal events (Ekblom 2012; Poyner 1983; Sutton et al. 2008). There are two specific environmental crime prevention approaches.

Urban Design and Planning

One of the more popular and broader planning initiatives includes CPTED (Crime Prevention through Environmental Design) and urban renewal projects. Specifically, these approaches seek to reduce the opportunities for crime through the design and management of the built (e.g., buildings, roadways, lighting, public spaces, etc.) and the existing environment (e.g., high shrubs, "blind spots," etc.). As will be discussed in Chapter 14 by J. Bryan Kinney et al., CPTED is increasingly being incorporated during the redevelopment and regeneration of urban areas experiencing social decay.

Evidence in support of CPTED is growing; although, unlike other approaches to crime prevention, CPTED has not been systematically evaluated (Shaftoe and Read 2005). Research demonstrates a strong correlation between certain characteristics of the built environment and crime levels, although the research into certain relationships (such as between through-movement/connectivity and crime) has been inconsistent (Armitage and Monchuk 2011). While further research into the impact of CPTED is warranted, as described in Chapter 14, there is sufficient evidence to support the application of CPTED principles.

Situational Crime Prevention—Stopping Opportunities

> [C]rime prevention through environmental design (and situational prevention) is an approach that promises to be more effective than any traditional police methods.
>
> **B. Poyner**
> *1983, p. i*

Although the concept has a rich informal history, the formal approach of situational crime prevention was brought to the fore by Ronald Clarke (1983) and represents a radical departure from most crime-control approaches by focusing on the social setting for crime rather than the offender. The principles are simple: (1) reduce the opportunities for offenders to commit crime, (2) modify the environment to cause the potential offender to question whether they can get away with the crime, and (3) modify the environment or setting so that it appears more difficult, riskier, and less rewarding to engage in the crime (see Clarke 1997). The early Neighborhood Watch programs were an excellent and comparatively inexpensive example of situational crime prevention. Yet, as will be touched on in several chapters, situational crime prevention has evolved in a number of significant ways while remaining true to its fundamental approach. Over the years, for example, Clarke, along with some of his colleagues, has developed 25 techniques of situational prevention aims by which to reduce crime (see Clarke and Eck 2003 for further details).

Crime Prevention through Social Development—Strengthening Neighborhoods

As stated earlier, combating crime is an expensive, resource-intense business. However, it is also generally recognized that many crimes are the result of social ills. The Crime Prevention through Social Development (CPSD) strategy thus embraces approaches designed to influence the underlying social and economic causes of crime, as well as offender motivation. It is a longer-term approach that involves mobilizing the dynamic forces within a community (e.g., housing, health and educational achievement, or community cohesion through community development measures) to target and reduce a crime problem in the most effective and most efficient way.

Drawing on many of the conventional theories of crime, and as will be explored in Chapter 8 by Matjaž Ambrož et al., CPSD theory recognizes the complexity of the causes of crime and thus attempts to identify the various risk factors (e.g., poverty, poor parental skills, school dropout, low self-esteem, bad associates/friends, substance abuse, etc.) and develop social programs that can effectively eradicate the problem.

Developmental Crime Prevention—Early Intervention

Developmental crime prevention (DCP) is a variation of a CPSD approach in that it focuses on the way a crime occurs, or the way a victimization happens. During the late 1990s up to the beginning of the new millennium, DCP initiatives were quite popular in Australia (see Homel 2006; Homel et al. 1999; Weatherburn 2004). DCP is premised on the belief that early intervention in a young person's development (e.g., parenting and early childhood support, literacy training and alternative learning programs, anti-bullying initiatives in schools, etc.) can produce significant long-term social and economic benefits. Such initiatives aim to identify, measure, and manipulate *risk* and *protective factors* (e.g., resources or services to individuals, families, schools, or community factors, etc.) that are important in predicting future offending, as confirmed by research (Homel 2006). Chapters 6 and 10 offer topic-specific examples.

Finally, in addition to the social benefits of DCP approaches, these outcomes are also associated with significant financial savings, both for the community and for the participant (see Homel 2006 and generally Chapter 19 by Anne Miller).

Community Development—Collaborating for Community Safety

> convivencia ciudadana… ideal for coexistence of very diverse cultural, social, or political groups… stable and potentially permanent living together….

> **International Report**
> *2010*

Community development is premised on the notion that changing the physical or social organization of communities may constructively affect the behavior and quality of life of people who live there (Tonry and Farrington 1995). As various ecological theories tell us, the risk of becoming involved in crime, or being victimized, is greater in communities that have high levels of social exclusion or a lack of social cohesion. Also underlying the community development approach is the belief that crime in a particular community is not principally the result of the actions of a small number of criminogenically disposed individuals, but the consequence of a series of structural determinants present within particular communities (e.g., differential rates of access to housing, employment, education and health services, among other factors; Welsh and Hoshi 2006). The underlying assumption is that if crime-promoting structural stress factors can be reconfigured or removed (e.g., "the broken window syndrome"), crime will be reduced (Hope 1995). Community development strategies can aim to build social cohesion and address factors leading to community disorganization, empower communities to participate in decision-making processes, and increase resources, services, and economic opportunities in disadvantaged communities or address low-level physical or social disorders considered to be precursors to more serious problems (Lane and Henry 2004; Welsh and Hoshi 2006; also see Chapter 7 by Helmut Kury).

Finally, before we review the three levels of crime prevention, it is perhaps worth bearing in mind that regardless of which approach one might favor or explore, it is important to acknowledge that unlike how conventional CJSs are administered, the various approaches speak to the need for a degree of public responsibility, or what Edmond Cahn called "consumers of justice" (cited in Menninger 1972, p. 78)—we need to educate ourselves* and assume a certain degree of responsibility for public safety as opposed to solely relying on our respective crumbling CJSs. The contributors to this book reflect such a sentiment in their respective chapters.

Levels of Crime Prevention

In 1976, Brantingham and Faust pointed out that the term *prevention* must be widely misunderstood to have been used so inappropriately throughout the CJS in discussions on prime intervention strategies. In the same article, they introduced a now widely accepted conceptual model that defines the three levels of crime prevention. Borrowing from their own work and combining the three elements of crime (i.e., offender, crime, and situation) by Sacco and Kennedy (1995), Hasting (2008, p. 3) created a table incorporating both the levels and elements of crime. Table I.1 is an adaptation of Hasting's conceptualization with examples added in the boxes.

Crime Prevention Theories

...the appropriate application of that theory, the potential pay-offs can only be realized if the environment into which strong analytical capacity is inserted is capable of making good use of it.

N. Tilley
2002, p. 10

---

* Although the rate of increase has slowed, the United Nations Education, Scientific and Cultural Organization estimated that approximately 84% of the world's population and engage in basic reading and writing skills. This is up from around 76% in 1990 (International Literacy Data 2013).

Table I.1   A Crime Prevention Typology

Levels of Intervention

	Offender(s)	Situation	Victim(s)
Primary	Creating employment opportunity for the unemployed	School-based programs	Providing the elderly with an alarm device to reduce risk of victimization
Secondary	Youth programs	Neighborhood dispute centers in high-risk neighborhoods	Retail stores using drop boxes to limit the amount of money available at any one time
Tertiary	Confining offenders to a period of detention	Constructing physical barriers to limit opportunity of prospective offenders	The use of CCTVs in high-risk crime areas

Elements of Crime Event[a]

Source: Adapted from Hasting, R. (2008). Achieving crime prevention: Reducing crime and increasing security in an inclusive Canada, p. 3. Retrieved from canada.metropolis .net/pdfs/hastings_achieving_crime_prevention_e.pdf.

[a]   A criminal event could arguably also include *law* (without a law there is no crime), *target* distribution (opportunity), and *location* (see Brantingham and Jeffery 1991). However, for the purpose of illustrating the levels of crime prevention, the other elements are not considered essential.

Throughout this reader, you'll encounter a number of different theoretical perspectives upon which the various crime prevention initiatives have been premised. However, by way of introduction, in Table I.2, we will briefly summarize several of the major theories that typically underpin crime prevention efforts. However, as Hope and Karstedt (2003, p. 1) observed, the "contemporary approaches to crime prevention are deficient… precisely because they ignore the collective, social and structural dimensions either as necessary components of their theory of practice, or as objects of intervention in their own right." Nevertheless, the basic idea behind all the theories is that crime and victimization is not random but predictable (Hasting 2008).

Cost–Benefit Analysis and Crime Control

As Aos et al. (2004, p. 413) noted in his assessment of prevention programs, "money matters." Depending on one's point of view, the adage "crime doesn't pay" is arguably a misnomer. While it is true that most criminals eventually get caught and crime truly doesn't pay, if you work in the CJS as an officer/ agent of the system, salaries are generally very respectable, job security is high (provided you do your job there is almost guaranteed certainty that your position will not be terminated), and working benefits are quite enviable compared to many other professions. However, when one takes into account the relative efficiency and effectiveness of the different elements of the CJS, there

Table I.2   Summary of the Major Crime Prevention Theories

Theory	Fundamental Premise(s)	Strengths	Critique
Environmental criminology— Brantingham and Brantingham 1991; Park and Burgess 1925	Crime occurs within an environment that is characterized by its space (geography), time, law, offender, and target or victim. CPTED.	By understanding the interaction of time, space, target, and so on, it is possible to "map" geographic profiling criminal behavior.	Risk interpreting environmental correlations as causal relationships. Potential risk of shifting crime control/risk management to an individual or civil responsibility.
Rational choice— Cornish and Clarke 1986	Offending occurs after offenders' weight matters (i.e., decision making) in relation to their personal needs and situational risk factors of committing the crime.	Explains why high-risk youth do not persistently reoffend. Used to establish control policies. Not limited by social class or social variables.	The claim that people maximize manifest payoffs is unfalsifiable and too generalist to be of substantive value.
Routine activity— Cohen and Felson 1979	Crime is a function of the presence of a motivated offender, the availability of a suitable target, and the absence of a capable guardian.	Can explain crime fluctuations. Shows how victim behavior can influence criminal choice of target.	Motivation is not evenly distributed across the population and the key elements of the theory may be simplified assumptions that do not accurately reflect the complexity of human behavior.
Crime pattern— Brantingham and Brantingham 1984	Criminal opportunities are not random and offenders and victims are not pathological in their use of time and space. Behavior and mobility is predictable— referred to as a "crime template."	Takes into account elements of routine activity, social networks, and urban structure. Can explain why crimes are committed in certain areas.	It may be considered "antisocial" because it offers no opportunity to help individuals/settings at risk of being victimized.

is pause to question the relative cost–benefit of conventional crime control, and as Aos et al. (2004, p. 440) observes, it is "possible to take an 'economic approach' to the public policy options facing decision makers" in the CJS.

In recent years, and as will be addressed at various levels throughout this book, evaluations of crime prevention projects have become more sophisticated to reflect the complexity of the theoretical models of crime prevention and perhaps more importantly the complexity of measuring relative effectiveness. For example, since the late 1960s, we have evolved from relying on single measures (e.g., recidivism, fear of crime, victimization, etc.) as indicators of "success," to using multiple indicators and different methods and designs to measure the same thing (Knutsson and Tilley 2010). One of the more recent measures introduced into the evaluation equation has been cost–benefit analysis. For example, Roman et al. (2010) prepared an entire edited book on cost–benefit analysis and crime control. Again, in Chapter 19, Anne Miller will discuss and explore one of the leading cost–benefit strategies.

The Future of Crime Prevention

Just as the whole complexion of crime changes with the various advancements and social, economic, and political fluctuations, so too must, and will, the state of crime prevention. However, as is reflected throughout this book, there is no uniform protocol in how to prevent crime (see Box I.1).

Therefore, although it may be impossible to predict where crime prevention will be in 5 or 10 (or more) years from now, one thing that is reasonably certain is that it will continue to undergo constant and (at times) rapid change. For example, in the 1970s, crime prevention gained public support in response to target hardening programs (e.g., use deadbolts, property identification, the "Club," etc.). While such techniques are still commonly used today, we have evolved to increasingly using such techniques as house alarms and electronic monitoring, biometrics, and so on. Similarly, when I was a young graduate student, I was involved in evaluating the first crime prevention initiative to reduce corner store robberies in Canada. Modeled after the successful "Robbery Prevention Kit" developed by Southlands (7-Eleven) Corporation in the States, the program proved highly successful, and it was instrumental in establishing a permanent Crime Prevention Unit in the Vancouver Police Force. However, even this program has evolved and has become a somewhat standardized practice among a wide range of convenience-oriented services, for example, gas stations, late-night fast-food outlets, and so on (see Roesch and Winterdyk 1986).

As suggested in several of the chapters (see Chapters 17 through 19), the future of crime prevention, while at times appearing subject to the political stability and relative economic sustainability of countries, is essentially

BOX I.1   THE UNITED NATIONS AND CRIME PREVENTION

Established in 2003, the United Nations Office on Drugs and Crime (UNODC) was a merger between the United Nations Drug Control Program and the Centre for International Crime Prevention. Today, the UNODC operates in all regions of the world through its extensive network of field officers. In addition to its various roles, the UNODC provides technical support in developing countries emerging from conflict to address crime problems (i.e., organized crime, trafficking, cybercrime, etc.). In addition to helping countries build professional capacity to prevent crime, the UNODC also offers assistance in establishing proactive legal frameworks to prevent/deter crimes. The UN's focus on crime prevention was further strengthened with the adoption of the 2002 "Guidelines for the Prevention of Crime," which promote a multidisciplinary and cross-sectoral approach to crime prevention. In particular, the approach combines social (see Chapter 8) and situational prevention (see Chapter 13) with community-centered (see Chapter 7) crime prevention. The Guidelines center around five key areas:

1. The strategic planning of crime prevention
2. The structuring of institutional responsibilities for crime prevention
3. Different national crime prevention approaches
4. Implemental issues, including good practices and lessons learned
5. International cooperation, networking, and technical assistance

   Together, the Guidelines capitalize on a knowledge-based approach (see Chapter 17) to crime prevention. For further information, see https://www.unodc.org/unodc/en/commissions/CCPCJ/.

a more promising and necessary approach to crime than the conventional crime-control practices that have historically characterized the international community (see Chapter 17), and where applied and in some cases prioritized as a response mechanism to crime, crime prevention initiatives have demonstrated that they generally represent more cost-effective and cost-efficient strategies (see Chapter 19) in response to burgeoning criminal justice budgets. However, crime prevention initiatives will also need to find ways to contend with the delicate balance between crime control, protecting victims, and how far people will go to ensure and maintain public safety. For example, the extensive use of such situational crime prevention strategies as CCTVs, the proliferation of security screening border crossing or airports, and so on have been widely embraced in a growing number of countries. Yet, as the World Bank reported in 1997, "...crime and violence have emerged in recent years as major obstacles to the realization of development objectives in Latin America and the Caribbean." Furthermore, in poor countries (e.g., Latin America and many African countries), the capacity to support crime prevention initiatives and establish safety nets remains weak, and the fear of crime, corruption, and general insecurity remains high, which contributes to the cycle of violence and perpetuation of the cycle of poverty (see Chapter 12).

As reflected in the range of topics and themes covered in this book, the question is thus not whether crime prevention is here to stay, but how to document its effectiveness and how to promote and sustain credible public and institutional support at all levels. The chapters by Margaret Shaw (Chapter 16), Irvin Waller and Veronica Martinez Solares (Chapter 17), and Jan van Dijk et al. (Chapter 18) present a sound argument and model for building and promoting crime prevention initiatives; however, it remains to be seen if crime prevention will become a universal priority. In order to reach such a lofty status, the future of crime prevention will ultimately depend on community buy-in because crime is a community problem (e.g., social disorganization, poverty, negative peer influences, etc.). Therefore, while crime prevention is not just a fad, its future success is dependent on effective marketing and strict measuring of outcomes to convince both the public and policymakers/ decision makers of the efficiency and cost-effectiveness of prevention programs. As Redo (2012, p. 219) points out in his work, "blue criminology" (referring to the efforts of the UNODC) "is basically focused on peoples (community/individuals)" (also, see Chapter 1).

Finally, the future of crime prevention will also depend on the growth of professionally skilled crime prevention experts. For, as C. Wright Mill (cited in Hope and Karstedt 2003, p. 461) observed, "if ever there was a social problem that required the connection of 'the personal troubles of milieu' with 'the public issues of social structure,' then crime reduction is surely it." Yet, in saying so, I am reminded of what J.Q. Wilson said in 2011 when asked to comment about America's future. After pointing out that a number of years ago he had made a prediction in one of his published essays, he acknowledged that: "It was hopelessly, embarrassingly wrong... Since then I have embraced the view that social scientists should never predict; leave that job to pundits" (Wilson 2011).

Format of the Book

For this reader, the first of its kind, a range of topics and themes were identified, which reflect the diversity in which crime prevention techniques have been actualized and proven (to varying degrees) successful. After identifying a list of topics, they were circulated among a number of international crime prevention specialists for feedback. From the final topic list, an array of international experts was invited to contribute to this project. By trying to ensure a degree of international representation in this book, it will hopefully also ensure that a global lens is shed upon the topic that will also serve to demonstrate that crime prevention is not only an international phenomenon, but one that offers considerable practical appeal to conventional criminal justice responses to crime or social injustices. Each contributor was then provided with a set of common criteria and asked to discuss, examine, and evaluate the (contemporary) approaches to crime prevention in relation to their theme/topic.

The book is divided into three informal parts. The first three chapters provide a broad, global overview of crime prevention and the social, economic, and political challenges involved in making mandates mainstream within the CJS. In Chapter 1, Redo provides a comprehensive overview of some of the novel ideas about the United Nations post-2015 goals toward sustainable goals for crime prevention that address such diverse themes as developing a culture of lawfulness, the implications of climate change on crime and poverty, and the importance of educational crime prevention methods. In Chapter 2, Dandurand draws on the UN model of crime prevention and addresses the issue of preventing violence against children. As Dandurand points out, not only is violence against children pervasive but it cuts across all boundaries of race, gender, geography, religion, and culture, and it targets among the most vulnerable in society. In Chapter 3, Marteache and Bichler cover a comparatively new and novel topic in relation to crime prevention—transportation systems. Using the Pareto principle (i.e., 80% of the effects come from 20% of the cause), they explain how transportation-based crime problems can be addressed through various crime prevention approaches.

Chapter 4 by Cale, Burton, and Leclerc focuses on the prevention of child sexual abuse. As they point out, the problem of child sexual abuse is probably far more extensive than official data indicate, and similar to Dandurand's contribution (Chapter 2), the victims represent the more vulnerable sector of society. Then, in Chapter 5, the topic shifts to another topical subject matter; that of domestic violence. After presenting a contextual understanding of the subject area, Pauls, Warthe, and Winterdyk explore how crime prevention strategies are a more effective approach to addressing the problem. The subject of preventing human trafficking is the theme of Chapter 6. Focusing specifically on sexual exploitation, Jones begins with a rich discussion of some of the fundamental problems confronting societies' efforts to combat human trafficking and then reviews the general prevention obligations of States before discussing one of the key crime prevention initiatives—criminalizing demand.

Chapters 7 and 8 shift to two thematic approaches to crime prevention. In Chapter 7, Kury offers a rich overview and understanding of how and why community crime prevention can be an effective scheme for responding to/preventing crime. In the chapter, Kury also describes why using punishment to deter crime is a less effective approach to crime control. Then, in Chapter 8, Ambrož, Meško, and Flander offer an insightful and critically reflective accounting of the important role social crime prevention approach can play in crime prevention strategies.

Chapter 9, authored by Grimes and Walsh, presents a unique approach on how restorative justice (RJ) can serve as an effective crime prevention alternative to conventional crime control. Drawing on a personal accounting, the chapter serves to illustrate how RJ can be an effective crime prevention option. Then, in Chapter 10, Platzer addresses from a crime prevention perspective the topic of femicide. Although a practice that prevailed since the dawn of time, it is has not received much attention until recently. However, Platzer provides a thorough overview of the nature and extent of femicide and discusses how crime prevention strategies are essential to addressing this "hidden crime."

How we might prevent terrorism is the topic of Chapter 11. In this chapter, Corrado, Cohen, and Davies first place terrorism within a criminological context before identifying and discussing how crime prevention policy can be used to address the risk and threats of terrorism. This is followed by another unique contribution by Rook and Sexsmith who in Chapter 12 tackle the topic of poverty and crime prevention. They begin by articulating the relationship between poverty and crime and then they carefully examine and discuss how crime prevention policy can begin to address the plight of poverty and crime. The topic of preventing corporate crime is the focus of Chapter 13. In this chapter, Beke offers a rich overview of the concepts and causes of corporate crime and presents a summary of the main theories in corporate crime prevention. The chapter concludes by reviewing a range of intervention and prevention strategies before discussing the role of sanctions as a primary prevention strategy.

Meanwhile, Chapter 14 by Kinney, Mann, and Winterdyk addresses one of the "original" crime prevention technique and methods. The chapter focuses on CPTED, and in addition to looking at the differences between first- and second-generation CPTED, the authors explore some of the international projects and findings as well as discuss some of the challenges confronting the relative impact of CPTED.

In Chapter 15, Haverkamp and Kilchling explore and discuss "lessons learnt from victimology" as they pertain to crime prevention and the victim. In this chapter, the authors not only explore the nexus between the victim and offender but carefully point out how, from a crime prevention perspective, this area requires more careful analysis for "more reality-oriented crime prevention programs."

The final four chapters embrace a broader perspective on the role of crime prevention in the crime management discourse. In Chapter 16, Shaw explores and critically examines the politics of crime prevention. Among other issues, she concludes with a discussion of some of the challenges for the development of crime prevention in the future. Then, in Chapter 17, Waller and Martinez Solares address the importance of putting crime prevention into practice. They point out how many of the prevailing barriers to fully embracing crime prevention policies hinder the advancement of the crime prevention philosophy but through an array of examples show that crime prevention is the "smarter" path to crime control. However, as van Dijk, van Soomeren, and de Waard discuss in Chapter 18, one of the biggest challenges form crime prevention to become mainstream in any CJS is the issue of sustainability within a "rocky" social and political climate. Using a case example, they show how even the best of intentions can be sidelined as a result of (political) ideological differences.

The final chapter by Miller, Chapter 19, focuses on the practical and pragmatic issue of "the value of crime prevention." Miller examines whether crime prevention is a cost-effective and cost-efficient alternative to conventional crime control. Although not a straightforward answer is provided, the author presents a compelling argument that the use of crime prevention strategies is economically a more practical approach to managing crime in society.

In the end, while I have made every effort to ensure strong international representation and to cover a diverse range of themes or topics where crime prevention has proven effective, there are a bevy of topics that could not be included for practical and pragmatic reasons. Therefore, as with most sojourns into new territories as enriching as this book will hopefully be, there remains room for additional topics and discourse about crime prevention. For example, although van Dijk and his colleagues comment on the challenges crime prevention presents in some jurisdiction today, using "Google trends" and search for *crime prevention* reveal that, since 2004, there has been a dramatic drop in interest on the Internet. However, places like South Africa, Australia, and the Philippines still show strong interest in the topic, and in terms of topics of interest, the top three queries involved prevention of crime, community crime prevention, and crime prevention programs.*

I have also drawn on colleagues who I felt could lend an international lens to their topic. Nevertheless, as is the case with any written product, it is never the definitive work. However, since this book does represent the first known effort to cover the topic of crime prevention across a wide spectrum of issues, themes, and topics, challenges and limitations are to be expected. Yet, it is also recognized that some topics were not included (e.g., preventing youth crime, preventing smuggling, etc.). This was largely attributed to page constraints. However, it also opens the door for another rendition of this

* For further information, see https://www.google.ca/trends/explore#q=crime%20prevention.

initiative and perhaps one that, while sharing some of the characteristics on the ever-growing popularity of "handbooks," will also continue to offer a more expansive coverage of such critical topics.

References

Aos, S., Lieb, R., Mayfield, J., Miller, M., and Pennucci, A. (July 2004). *Benefits and Costs of Prevention and Early Intervention Programs for Youth.* Olympia, WA: Washington State Institute for Public Policy.

Ariely, D. (2012). *The (Honest) Truth about Dishonesty.* New York: Harper Collins.

Armitage, R., and Monchuk, L. (2011). Sustaining the crime reduction impact of designing out crime: Re-evaluating the Secured by Design scheme 10 years on. Security Journal 24: 320–343.

Brantingham, P.J., and Brantingham, P.L. (1991). Environmental Criminology. Prospect Heights, IL: Waveland Press.

Brantingham, P.J., and Faust, F.L. (1976). A conceptual model of crime prevention. *Crime and Delinquency* 22(3): 284–296.

Brantingham, P.J., and Jeffery, C.R. (1991). Afterword: Crime, space, and criminological theory. In P.J. Brantingham and P.L. Brantingham (Eds.), *Environmental Criminology.* Thousand Oaks, CA: SAGE Pub.

Brantingham, P.L., and Brantingham, P.J. (1984). Patterns in Crime. New York: Macmillan.

Clarke, R.V. (1983). Situational Crime Prevention: Its Theoretical Basis and Practical Scope. *Crime and Justice* 4: 225–256.

Clarke, R.V. (Ed.). (1997). *Situational Crime Prevention: Successful Case Studies* (2nd ed.). Guilderland, NY: Harrow and Heston.

Clarke, R.V., and Eck, J. (2003). *Become a Problem-Solving Crime Analyst.* London: Jill Dando Institute of Crime Science, University College London.

Cohen, L., and Felson, M. (1979). Social change and crime rate trends: A routine activity approach. American Sociological Review 44(4): 588–608.

Cornish, D., and Clarke, R.V. (Eds.). (1986). *The Reasoning Criminal.* New York: Springer-Verlag.

Corrado, R., and Mattehesuis, J. (2014). Development psycho-neurological research trends and their importance for reassessing key decision-making assumptions for children, adolescents, and young adults in juvenile/adult and adult criminal justice systems. *Bergen Journal of Criminal Law and Criminal Justice* 2(2): 141–163.

Crocker, D., and Johnson V.A. (2010). *Poverty, Regulation and Social Justice Readings on the Criminalization of Poverty.* Halifax, NS: Fernwood Pub.

Dammer, H., and Albanese, J. (2013). *Comparative Criminal Justice Systems* (5th ed.). Belmont, CA: Wadsworth.

Ditton, J. (1979). *Contrology: Beyond the New Criminology.* Macmillan Pub.

Dandurand, Y. (2014). Criminal Justice Reform and the System's Efficiency. *Criminal Law Forum* 25: 383–440.

Einarsen, T. (2014). New frontiers in international criminal law: Towards a concept of universal crimes. *Bergen Journal of Criminal Law and Criminal Justice* 2(2): 1–21.

Ekblom, P. (Ed.). (2012). *Design against Crime: Crime Proofing Everyday Products.* London: Lynne Reinner Pub.

Farrell, G., and Clark, K. (2004). What does the world spend on criminal justice? HEUNI Paper No. 20: Helsinki, Finland.

Garland, D. (1996). The limits of the sovereign state. *BJC* 36(4): 445–471.

Garland, D. (2001). *The Culture of Control: Crime and Social Order in Contemporary Society.* Oxford: Oxford University Press.

Geis, G. (1972). Jeremy Bentham. In H. Mannheim (Ed.), *Pioneers in Criminology* (2nd ed.). Montclair, NJ: Patterson Smith.

Hasting, R. (2008). Achieving crime prevention: Reducing crime and increasing security in an inclusive Canada. Retrieved from canada.metropolis.net/pdfs/hastings_achieving_crime_prevention_e.pdf.

Haugen, G.A., and Boutros, C. (2014). *The Locust Effect.* New York: Oxford University Press.

Homel, P. (2006). Joining up the pieces what central agencies need to do to support crime prevention. In J. Knuttson and R.V. Clarke (Eds.), *Putting Theory to Work: Implementing Situational Crime Prevention and Problem Oriented Policing* (Crime prevention studies, Vol. 20), 111–113. Monsey, NY: Criminal Justice Press.

Homel, R. et al. (1999). *Pathways to Prevention: Developmental and Early Intervention Approaches to Crime in Australia.* Canberra: Commonwealth Attorney-General's Department.

Hope, T. (1995). Community Crime Prevention. In *Building a Safer Society: Strategic Approaches to Crime Prevention*, edited by M. Tonry and D.P. Farrington. Vol. 19 of *Crime and Justice: A Review of Research.* Chicago: University of Chicago Press.

Hope, T. (2000). Introduction. In T. Hope (Ed.), *Perspectives on Crime Reduction. The International Library of Criminology, Criminal Justice and Penology.* Aldershot, Hants: Ashgate Pub.

Hope, T., and Karstedt, S. (2003). Towards a new social crime prevention. In H. Kury and J. Obergfell-Fuchs (Eds.), *Crime Prevention: New Approaches*, 459–460. Mainz, Germany: Weisser Ring Pub.

Hudson, B. (1996). *Understanding Justice.* Buckingham, UK: Open University Press.

International Literacy Data 2013. (2013). UNESCO. Retrieved from http://www.uis.unesco.org/literacy/Pages/data-release-map-2013.aspx.

International Report—Crime prevention and community safety: Trends and perspectives. Centre for the Prevention of Crime, Montreal, Canada. Retrieved from: http://www.crime-prevention-intl.org/fileadmin/user_upload/Publications/Crime_Prevention_and_Community_Safety_ANG.pdf.

IPC (Institute for the Prevention of Crime). (2008). *What Is Crime Prevention?* Ottawa, Canada: University of Ottawa.

Jacobs, L. (1962). *The Death and Life of Great American Cities.* London: Johnathan Cape.

Knutsson, J., and Tilley, N. (Eds.). (2010). *Evaluating Crime Reduction Initiatives.* London: Lynne Reiner Pub.

Lane, M., and Henry, K. (2004). Beyond symptoms: Crime prevention and community development. *Australian Journal of Social Issues* 39(2): 201–213.

Menninger, K. (1972). *A Guide to Psychiatric Books.* New York: Grune & Stratton.

Menniger, K. (1969). *The Crime of Punishment.* New York: Penguin Books.

National Audit Office. (2012). *Comparing international criminal justice systems.* London: UK., Ministry of Justice. Retrieved from http://www.nao.org.uk /wp-content/uploads/2012/03/NAO_Briefing_Comparing_International _Criminal_Justice.pdf.

Park, R.E., and Burgess, E.W. (1925). *The City.* Chicago: University of Chicago Press.

Poyner, B. (1983). *Design against Crime: Beyond Defensible Space.* London: Butterworths.

Redo, S.M. (2012). *Blue Criminology: The Power of the United Nations Ideas to Counter Crime Globally.* Helsinki, Finland: European Institute for Crime Prevention and Control, affiliated with the United Nations.

Reichel, P., and Albanese, J. (Eds.). (2014). *Handbook of Transnational Crime and Justice* (2nd ed.). Thousand Oaks, CA: SAGE.

Roesch, R., and Winterdyk, J. (1986). The implementation of a robbery information/ prevention program for convenience stores. *Canadian Journal of Criminology* 28: 279–290.

Roman, J.K., Dunworth, T., and Marsh, K. (Eds.). (2010). *Cost–Benefit Analysis and Crime Control.* Washington, DC: The Urban Institute Press.

Sacco, V.F., and Kennedy, L.W. (1995). *The Criminal Event: An Introduction to Criminology in Canada.* Toronto: Nelson.

Sacco, V.F., and Kennedy, L.W. (2010). *The Criminal Event: An Introduction to Criminology in Canada* (5th ed.). Toronto: Nelson.

Shaftoe, H., and Read, T. (2005). Planning out crime: The appliance of science or an act of faith? In: N. Tilley N. (ed.) *Handbook of Crime Prevention and Community Safety.* Devon, UK: Willan Publishing.

Shah, A. (2013). Poverty, facts and statistics. Retrieved from http://www.globalissues .org/article/26/poverty-facts-and-stats.

Sherman, L.W., Farrington, D.P., Welsh, B.C., and MacKenzie, D.L. (Eds.). (2006). *Evidence-Based Crime Prevention.* Revised ed. New York: Routledge.

Sherman, L.W., Gottfredson, D., MacKenzie, D. et al. (1997). Preventing crime: What works, what doesn't what's promising: A report to the United States Congress. Washington, DC: National Institute of Justice.

Story, R., and Yalkin, T.R. (2013). *Expenditure Analysis of Criminal Justice in Canada.* Ottawa: Office of the Parliamentary Officer. Retrieved from http://www.pbo -dpb.gc.ca/files/files/Crime_Cost_EN.pdf.

Sutton, A., Cherney, A., and White, R. (2008). *Crime Prevention: Principles, Perspectives and Practices.* Melbourne, Australia: Cambridge University Press.

Tilley, N. (Ed.). (2002). *Analysis for Crime Prevention.* Monsey, NY: Criminal Justice Press. Crime Prevention Studies Vol. 13.

Tonry, M., and Farrington, D.P. (Eds.). (1995). *Crime and Justice, Building a Safer Society: Strategic Approaches to Crime Prevention.* Chicago: The University of Chicago Press. Vol. 19.

Twelfth United Nations Congress on Crime Prevention and Criminal Justice. (2010). Vienna, United Nations. Retrieved from http://www.un.org/en/conf/crime congress2010/.

van Dijk, J.J.M., and de Waard J. (1991). Two-Dimensional Typology of Crime Prevention Projects. Washington, DC: NCJRS.

von Hirsch, A. (1976). *Doing Justice: The Choice of Punishments.* New York: Hill and Wang.

Weatherburn, D. (2004). *Law and Order in Australia: Rhetoric and Reality*. Sydney, Australia: The Federation Press.

Welsh, B.C., and Hoshi, A. (2006). Communities and Crime Prevention. In L.W. Sherman, D.P. Farrington, B.C. Welsh, and D.L. MacKenzie (Eds.), *Evidence-Based Crime Prevention*. New York: Routledge.

Wilson, J.Q. (1974). Crime and the criminologists. *Commentary.* Retrieved from https://www.commentarymagazine.com/article/crime-and-the-criminologists/.

Wilson, J.Q. (2011). Optimistic or pessimistic about America: James Q. Wilson. *Commentary.* Retrieved from https://www.commentarymagazine.com/2011/11/06/optimistic-or-pessimistic-about-america-james-q-wilson/.

Winterdyk, J. (Ed.). (2015). *Juvenile Justice: International Perspectives, Models, and Trends*. Boca Raton, FL: CRC Press.

Zaibert, L. (2006). *Punishment and Retribution*. Hants, UK: Ashgate Pub.

The Transformative Power of the United Nations Post-2015 Sustainable Development Goals and Crime Prevention Education for a New Culture of Lawfulness

1

SŁAWOMIR REDO

Contents

Learning Outcomes
After reading this chapter, you should be able to

- Familiarize yourself with some salient issues on the United Nations Sustainable Development Goals (SDGs) agenda 2016–2030 relevant to crime prevention education for a culture of lawfulness

1

- Appreciate the relevance and limits of climatological research to crime and welfare concerns, including some relating to violence and poverty and the ambiguous nexus between them and illegal/irregular migration
- Acknowledge the difference between the pre-SDGs criminological perspectives on South–North differences on governance and reformist motivation for crime prevention
- Appreciate the role of moral education in these terms with a view to balancing out innovation and anticorruption education
- Learn about some educational crime prevention methods to interculturally motivate and rationalize learners' thinking for problemsolving of local and global nature
- Familiarize yourself with some of the key recommendations for educationists to transform the SDGs ideas through into programs with a view to a more humane and effective crime prevention education for sustainable development worldwide.

Introduction

Poverty is the parent of revolution and crime.

Aristotle
384–322 BC

Sustainable development requires human ingenuity. People are the most important resource.

Dan Shechtman
2001

This chapter has two key objectives. First, to familiarize such learners with some salient crime prevention issues in the United Nations (UN) Declaration on Sustainable Development Goals (SDGs Declaration [SDGsD]) 2016–2030 (A/RES/70/1 2015). Second, to engineer a more interculturally effective delivery of the UN crime prevention message, the seminal content of which is in that declaration and for which instrumentalities are at the disposal and the initiative of international organizations and entities with their projects and events.

Legislative Background

Among these organizations and entities, there is the intergovernmental 14th UN Congress on Crime Prevention and Criminal Justice (Japan 2020). The 14th Congress, a quinquennial event since 1955, will assess the implementation of the 2015 Declaration of the 13th Congress (Doha, Qatar), built around the above SDGsD (at that time forthcoming). The Doha Declaration sets before

Member States the goal of integration of crime prevention, criminal justice, and other rule-of-law aspects into their domestic educational systems. At the 13th Congress, Member States pledged to integrate crime prevention and criminal justice strategies into all their relevant social and economic policies and programs, in particular those affecting youth, with a special emphasis on programs focused on increasing educational and employment opportunities for youth (15–24 years of age) and young adults (18–29 years of age). The Doha Declaration emphasized that education for all children and youth, including the eradication of illiteracy, is fundamental to the prevention of crime and corruption and to the promotion of a culture of lawfulness that supports the rule of law and human rights while respecting cultural identities (A/70/174 2015).

The SDGsD sets the goal to

> ensure that all learners acquire the knowledge and skills needed to promote sustainable development, including, among others, through education for sustainable development and sustainable lifestyles, human rights, gender equality, promotion of a culture of peace and non-violence, global citizenship and appreciation of cultural diversity and of culture's contribution to sustainable development.
>
> **SDG 4.7**

Very much concerned with a lack sustainability of development, since 1987, the UN in its sustainable development (SD) agenda has gradually built up the argument that in "The Future We Want" (A/RES/66/288),* the greatest global challenge facing the world today is poverty eradication. Poverty, as defined by the UN, is the effect of all sorts of environmental and socioeconomic abuses that serves to spawn "gnawing deprivation" (absolute poverty/ excessive inequality) (A/69/700, paragraph 67).

At the core of environmental and socioeconomic abuses is the abuse of natural resources (e.g., oil, gas, and coal). Since 1988, the UN Intergovernmental Panel on Climate Change (UNIPCC) started comprehensive investigations on how some forms of the abuse of nonrenewable resources may be related to global climate change and its consequences. In 2014, the Secretary-General (S-G) stated that: "[t]ackling climate change and fostering sustainable development agenda are two mutually reinforcing sides of the same coin" (A/69/700, paragraph 49).

Reportedly, the December 2014 globally averaged temperature across land and ocean surfaces was 0.77°C (1.39°F) above the 20th-century average of 12.2°C (54.0°F), the highest on record for December since records

---

* This is the title of the Outcome Document of the United Nations Conference on Sustainable Development (2012), otherwise called the "Rio+20 resolution." The first United Nations Conference on Environment and Development was held 20 years earlier (Rio de Janeiro, June 3–14, 1992).

began in 1880, surpassing the previous record set in 2006 by 0.02°C (0.04°F) (National Centres for Environmental Information 2015). According to a "best estimate" global average temperature, by 2017, it may increase by 2°C to 2.4°C above preindustrial levels (UNIPCC 2007, pp. 227–228). Whether or not this authoritative prediction indeed materializes, climate change has surely become a new factor believed to contribute to the impoverishment and to certain forms and dynamics of crime.

Accordingly, in the UN Population Fund Activities report, research that suggests that the reduction of total greenhouse gas emissions eventually counters poverty is cited:

> [D]ollar-for-dollar, investments in voluntary family planning and girls' education would also in the long run reduce greenhouse-gas emissions at least as much as the same investments in nuclear or wind energy... Strong family planning programmes are in the interests of all countries for greenhouse-gas concerns as well as for broader welfare concerns.
>
> **UNFPA**
> *2009, pp. 26–27*

Consequently, global inequalities of climate change must also affect justice, human rights, and crime prevention issues (UNDP 2007, p. 185). Indeed, "[t]here are many predictions that global warming could result in hundreds of millions of people suffering from hunger, malnutrition, water shortages, floods, droughts, heat stress, diseases triggered by extreme weather events, loss of livelihoods and permanent displacement" (Kang 2007, p. 1). Dealing with these potential deprivations will require developing and implementing a new environmental ethics of humanity to live in harmony with nature, in the interest of "the priority of the natural order of sociability and common good with respect to contracts" (Hittinger in Rommen 1936/1998, p. xxix).

The SDGsD is one of the legal conduits through which the UN projects its new morality into other areas of human activity: "Transforming our World" (A/RES/70/1 2015) for the "Future We Want for All."* As both slogans suggest, the UN SDGs framers do not accept the irreversibility of the negative effects of climate change. Rather, they chart the avenues for their mitigation. Goal 13.3 states this plainly "Improve education, awareness-raising and human and institutional capacity on climate change mitigation [emphasis added], adaptation, impact reduction and early warning."

The SDGsD envisions a world that is just, equitable, and inclusive. It credits global climate changes for at least a part of the present governance problems in the above regard, including criminal justice administration and crime prevention in the world.

---

* This is the slogan of the UN Secretariat derived from the above footnoted Outcome Document.

This vision interplays with that of the 12th Congress (2010). In its Salvador Declaration, it also placed crime prevention and the criminal justice system for the rule of law in the SD's center. It further recognized that long-term sustainable economic and social development and the establishment of a functioning, efficient, effective, and humane criminal justice system have a positive influence on each other (A/RES/65/230 2010).

All these declarations are political acts and they are predetermined by the UN Charter. Together, the declarations outline new standards and norms for a just conduct, even when neither its framers nor academics are sure if indeed the reasons for and the results of that conduct in terms of the SD's causal nexus are clear enough. In other words, in the UN, confusion prevails on the "root causes" of armed conflicts, for instance, whether these include poverty and climate change or both are not in that root but are threats to peace and security (Spijkers 2011, pp. 200–201).

Notwithstanding that ambiguity, the UN reports that "crime is both cause, consequence of poverty" (GA/SHC/3817 2005). In its legal instruments, it clearly stresses that in poverty's eradication, centrality of governance and the execution of the just conduct by either institutionalizing or enhancing the rule of law in a pluralistic context are important. The Doha Declaration is a case in point. It further emphasizes that, to achieve SD, we need to counter the destabilizing effects of crime, with crime prevention efforts alongside effective criminal justice institutions underpinned by human rights (A/RES/70/174 2015, paragraphs 3–5 and 8).

This policy position cannot be scientifically validated by involving the control-group method, as far as the UN technical assistance is concerned, that is, rendered by the UN Secretariat (Redo 2012, pp. 186–187). Mostly driven by a political mandate, UN criminology therefore cannot have some features of academic criminology, driven by concept and method. Yet, regarding other methods and projects pursued domestically by Member States, the Doha Declaration emphasizes the role of evidence-driven crime prevention and criminal justice (A/RES/70/174 2015, paragraph 5(a)).

Within that field, except rather precise criminal justice and human rights UN terminology, other UN terms and concepts tend to be quite vague (Redo 2013). For example, in the UN policy statements, "development" and "security" are often linked to one another. However, when it comes to evidencing how they are interrelated in terms of cause and effect, the UN points that the links between them are "intrinsic" and "inextricable" (A/59/565 2004, p. viii and paragraph 30). In short, whether within the UN or outside of it, nobody knows for sure what exactly are "development" and "security" and how precisely they affect one another.

Such ambiguities are natural. They persist because UN logonomics has its own legal and linguistic rules for a production of meaning within a larger UN social contract (i.e., Charter) of its 193 Member States.

This aspirational UN contract implies fostering impersonal social justice that involves independent personhood of citizens with their unique combination of characteristics. Each one represents the whole of humankind, whose rights, both inherent and inalienable, should be preserved and respected (Annan 2014, p. 62). One may claim them individually through various legal recourses up to the UN human rights treaty machinery that keenly acknowledges such rights (Spijkers 2011, pp. 303–304).

Implementing the UN contract is not an easy process. For example, if Western expert opinions are reliable, then no more than 20%–30% of the world's current population is individualistic in social nature (Dumont 1986, p. 62; Hofstede 1991, p. 17; Triandis 1996, p. 407), while all people are inborn egoists. Consequently, this essay seeks to clarify some of the latent cross-cultural communication ambiguities caused by the UN "language" that prompts different expectations. This clarification will hopefully help in the education of crime prevention aspects of the SDGsD to be less a "dialogue of the deaf" and more personally responsive.

Historical Background

Regarding the first objective, those concerned with the questions of access to justice and the rule of law may recall the expert contemplations on climate and crime by the French legal and moral philosopher Charles-Luis de Montesquieu (1689–1755). Supported by some 3000 citations in his *The Spirit of Laws* (Montesquieu 1748/1949), claiming to treat "all the peoples of Europe with the same impartiality as … the peoples of the island of Madagascar" (1949/II: 997), he argued that people's different spirit, their moral characteristics, and the way of thinking and acting result from a unique combination of climate, religion, laws, maxims of government, history, mores, and manners.

In Montesquieu's opinion, climate affects countries and the character of its residents because "the empire of the climate is the first, the most powerful, of all empires" (Montesquieu 1772/2001, p. 328). Furthermore, because of climate, people are inclined toward certain sorts of sociopolitical governance. Accordingly, the closer we move toward the tropics, the further we move from principles of morality and the rule of law. Montesquieu dismissed the possibility of attaining freedom and welfare in southern countries. He argued that their people will remain there enslaved, poor and passive, while countries become autocratic. The effect of climate can be seen even for some portions of countries. For example, he remarked that "In the north of China people are more courageous than those in the south; and those in the south of Korea have less bravery than those in the north" (Montesquieu 1772/2001, p. 291).

Regarding the character of people, Montesquieu claimed that the ideal one can develop in France's climate, which is neither too warm nor too cold. However, generally, people in colder climates have fewer vices and express more sincerity and frankness. By contrast, Northerners find pleasure in mental activities, while Southerners are happier by simply relaxing. This is because in excessive heat, human thermodynamics affects the mind, depriving it of curiosity and enterprising spirit, as if that thermodynamics irrevocably dooms people's mind—a true early-Darwinian notion (Stokes 1995, p. 125). To counter their vices, Montesquieu suggested that laws in warmer climates should be more explicit and strict in encouraging industriousness and regulating violence, sexual behaviors, and even the consumption of alcohol, but the greatest punishment for Southerners is to rationalize their mind (Stokes 1995, p. 249).

Current Climatological Research on Governance and Crime Prevention

Currently, three pre-SDGs strands in the focus of this essay address the relationships between climate and crime; however, none of them is directly relevant to a long-term climate change and crime. The first is structural and concentrates on governance. The second is situational and concentrates on temperature and violence, while the third is ethno-climatologist and concentrates on moral judgments. Both the second and third strands corroborate some of Montesquieu's criminological claims. Collectively, they all contribute to the SDGs-chartered crime prevention in the context of teaching it—the second objective of this chapter.

Continuing with the first objective and contrary to Montesquieu's earlier claims, there is no scientific support for *climatological determinism* today. For example, there is no way to explain climatologically why homicide rates in Western Europe dramatically decreased over the past 700 years (Pinker 2011). Furthermore, climatological determinism cannot explain the distinct welfare differences between the two contemporary Koreas (the Democratic Republic of Korea and the Republic of Korea) and in China, nor can it explain the differences between the two Germanys (1949–1990) (the Federal Republic of Germany [FRG] and the German Democratic Republic), Poland (1945–1989–2015) and Japan (from 1868 onward), or Botswana and Ghana (Africa), among many other countries. These welfare differences have nothing to do with warmer or colder climate but with the overpowering role of market economies, which are liberal in some countries (e.g., Botswana, Ghana, Japan, FRG, and Poland) or precariously liberalizing in others (e.g., China).

Regardless of climate, there are considerable differences in the development of an inclusive political system (i.e., democracy) and inclusive market economy with established and secure property and welfare rights that encourage investment, productivity, and innovation. The interplay of these elements may give policymakers a legitimate framework and motivation to break away from the self-sustaining cycle of poverty, to develop themselves and their country in the future by pursuing laws, policies, and practices that assist modernization (Acemoglu and Robinson 2012).

Other analyses point to environmental scarcity of renewable resources (e.g., cropland, freshwater, forests, wildlife, pastures, etc.) as a potential criminogenic factor (see Homer-Dixon 1991, 1994, 1999). Anderson and DeLisi (2011) argue that such shortages can lead to civil unrest and civil war, to migration to adjacent regions and conflict with the people who already live in that region, and even to genocide and war.

Not corroborated statistically, such governance arguments sound less convincing than the following scarcity-focused econometric study. Along such lines of reasoning, Mehlum et al. (2006) documented near-perfect correlations between 1833 and 1865 in Bavaria: positive between property crime and rye prices, and negative between beer prices and violent crime.

Criminologists corroborate this theme but expand its conclusions regarding the pathway of deprivation conflict and changes that occur in routine and other crime, owing to rural–urban migration that may exacerbate the security and other welfare concerns of urban residents (Crank 2003; Crank and Jacoby 2015).

Regarding situational research, since the time of Lombroso's (circa late 1800s and early 1900s), it has been suggested that warm weather prompts violent but not property crime (Anderson 2001, p. 34; Anderson and DeLisi 2011; Lombroso 1899/1911). Moreover, the analysis of archival data of serious civil disorders in the United States (1967–1971) suggests "a curvilinear relationship between ambient temperature and the incidence of collective violence" (Baron and Ransberger 1978, p. 354). The frequency of riots increased with ambient temperature up through approximately 85°F (29.4°C) and then decreased sharply as temperature continued to increase. Regarding victimology, this analysis did not take into account the number of days when the temperature was above 90°F (32.2°C)—regarded as the tipping point that influences people's fear of specific forms of property and violent crime (Cohn 1990). In sum, a meta-analysis of all such studies shows that the higher average temperature there is in any place and the closer this place is to the equator, the more crime there is (Ellis et al. 2009, Chapter 2).

Similarly exceptional is the finding regarding domestic violence and other assaults: Humidity levels have been found to be slightly negatively correlated to the latter, but not the former. That decrease may be credited to air pollution, as humidity levels are higher before and after a rainfall, which removes pollution from the air (Semmens et al. 2002).

Currently, it is not possible to draw any firm conclusions about the possibly more intricate relationships between temperatures and crime, between rain and crime, or between wind and crime. This is not only because of various uncertainties as how to measure the potential local, regional, and interregional influences of such natural factors but also because of the possibly correlated impact of the intermediate psychological or material factors. Regarding psychological factors, Agnew (2012, p. 21) speculates that as the century progresses, "climate change will increase strain, reduce social control, weaken social support, foster beliefs favourable to crime, contribute to traits conducive to crime, increase certain opportunities for crime, and create social conflict."

Regarding material factors, they have been studied more systematically than ever before. One such local study went into assessing the longitudinal 20-year long changes in dynamics of violent crime, credited to anomalous warm temperatures. It found that in neighborhoods with higher levels of social disadvantage, they are more likely to experience higher levels of violence as a result of such warm temperatures (Mares 2013). The criminological insights into countering urban crime and other social unrest are complementary and prospective (see Crank 2003).

Finally, the UN Office of High Commissioner for Human Rights cautioned that there is little empirical evidence to substantiate the projected impacts of environmental factors on armed conflict (A/HRC/10 2009, paragraph 64). The subsequent meta-review of the relationship between one and another found it inconclusive (Theisen et al. 2013), while another review on the relationships between urban violence and global warming dismissed it because of the flaws in statistical sample selection and analytical coherence (Buhaug et al. 2014).

Interestingly, both reviews have neither drawn on the respective criminological meta-reviews (Ellis et al. 2009, Chapter 2) nor drawn on later discipline-proper climatological studies (Ranson 2012). Their findings are more pronounced concerning the criminogenic effects of climate change than the weighted UNIPCC-related findings, with one analysis finding sounding rather dramatic. Based on a 30-year panel of monthly crime and weather data for 2997 U.S. counties, temperature has a strong positive effect on criminal behavior, with little evidence of lagged impacts. "Between 2010 and 2099, climate change will cause an additional 22,000 murders, 180,000 cases of rape, 1.2 million aggravated assaults, 2.3 million simple assaults, 260,000 robberies, 1.3 million burglaries, 2.2 million cases of larceny, and 580,000 cases of vehicle theft in the United States," claims its author (Ranson 2014).

In contrast with the pre-SDGs review of ethno-climatology studies that showed that they were predetermined by concepts and methods to legitimize moral judgments about racial differentiation ("racialization") or ideological forms of political dominance (Livingstone 2002), the latter analysis is not tainted by this argument. However, as any such long-term prognosis, it may be unduly simplified and, surely, very deterministic.

Next, we will concentrate only on such judgements regarding long-term climate changes projection on crime and welfare concerns. Therefore, regardless of the expressions of the SDGs findings, it is generally acknowledged that crime prevention experts are seldom concerned with the effects climate change has on crime. Their perspective is likewise hardly concerned with crime prevention and criminal justice issues, unless addressed within the Environmental Justice (EJ) framework. As a result, the intergovernmental declarations may not immediately capture the attention of respective actors because the UN declarations may not reach or attract them.

In their interest, before the acknowledgment of some of the salient crime prevention SDGsD issues, two UNIPCC long-term views that may set the introductory tone are brought up here. First, the UNIPCC, in its most recent and authoritative climatological assessment of the scientific literature, argues that human security will progressively be threatened as climate changes. However, the UNIPCC upholds the earlier cited conclusion that there is no strong positive relationship between warming and armed conflict (UNIPCC 2014, p. 772).

Second, since future generations are not able to directly influence the welfare of today, the UNIPCC is uncertain about the more precise consequences of climate change for SD (UNIPCC 1995, p. 14). Save for migration, there are no other criminologically relevant concerns registered by the UNIPCC.

Two Strands for the SDGs-Related Crime Prevention Education

This chapter acknowledges the stochastic, non-Eurocentric, moral climatological perspective of the new SDGsD that is charted by the Rio+20 Outcome Document. In two different but related themes, it projects the UNIPCC's welfare concerns into crime prevention education. The first theme involves welfare as a common UN objective in article 55 of the Charter, here narrowed to criminological aspects (UN 2003, paragraphs 73 and 74). The second theme involves welfare as a factor that may (de)motivate learning to pursue a progressive crime prevention reform—an issue to be eventually addressed by the second objective of this essay.

In 2014/2015, the UN Open-Ended Working Group on Sustainable Development Goals elaborated the narrative for and the draft of the SDGsD containing 17 goals to be reached until 2030. Across them, the UN General Assembly eventually listed five interrelated essential SD elements: People, Planet, Prosperity, Peace, and Partnership (A/RES/70/1 2015). Not all of these elements are (in)directly related to climate change or to crime, but all five represent the defining SD elements.

The following ideas may help strategize crime prevention education in terms of three SD elements: People, Prosperity, and Peace.

People: Absolute Poverty, Property, Gender Equality, and Violence

> We are determined to end poverty and hunger, in all their forms and dimensions, and to ensure that all human beings can fulfil their potential in dignity and equality and in a healthy environment.
>
> **A/RES/70/1**
> *2015, p. 2/35*

Eradication of poverty "in all its forms and dimensions" by 2030 is part of the welfare manifesto that may mislead those who interpret it verbatim. What the SDGs framers really mean is eradicating extreme poverty, quantified internationally to be at the level of U.S.$1.25 for all people everywhere (SDG 1.1) or above that value—for half of men, women, and children of all ages living in poverty according to national poverty threshold (SDG 1.2).

The relationships between poverty and crime are manifold. In keeping first with the UNIPCC's and SDGs' focus on migration, the criminogenic impact on poverty-stricken people cannot be underestimated. Transnationally, such migrants not only are the clientele of organized criminal groups who facilitate their smuggling but also are of great concern for the sending and receiving States (see Reuveny 2007, p. 669). In recent years, these areas have also experienced environmental migration to Europe; this underpinning led to the speculation of the resulting frictions between major powers (Reuveny 2007).

As a result of the (mass) migration, the sending (i.e., states of origin) States lose human and social capital capable of producing country's wealth. The receiving States, meanwhile, are obliged to address humanitarian challenges (e.g., shelter, food, etc.), human rights concerns (e.g., access to justice, asylum, deportation), welfare concerns, security concerns, and other crime prevention concerns, including anticorruption or the enculturation in domestic standards and norms (proper parenting and household relationships), so that migrants will eventually become good and productive residents.

To date, there is no body of modern crime prevention research that could comprehensively help in meeting such challenges. Therefore, only as a signpost may one note that there are two fundamental by products of poverty and crime, namely, *hunger* and *indignity*.

Concerning hunger and crime, this relationship has been well documented in the criminological literature since the Second World War. An increase in crime is possible because of food rationing. Additionally, the business made on war by "white collar" criminals enables them to earn colossal profits (Barnes and Teeters 1951, pp. 9–11). However, more recently, Krause (2011) conducted a comparative study of 182 countries covering the period between 1986 and 2009. He found a robust correlation between high rates of intentional homicide and higher levels of extreme poverty and hunger, but not with hunger alone (Krause 2011, p. 155).

Concerning indignity, it originally involved "honor" crimes (i.e., crimes usually involving the use of violence committed by people who want to defend the reputation of their family and community). At the UN, crime prevention is not the only form in which human dignity as a value is violated. Ever since the UN Charter in 1945 (which was followed by the Universal Declaration of Human Rights [UDHR] in 1948), the UN has universalized dignity and preconditioned it by economic, social, and cultural rights that should assure free individual development and worthy existence (articles 22 and 23). The content of that concept has been broad in scope and is not related to any particular philosophy (see Spijkers 2011). Hence, now "dignity" also means "to end poverty and fight inequalities" (A/69/700, p. 16/34).

In economically underdeveloped countries, poverty persists because of the discriminatory property rights. It prevents them and their residents (particularly women) from fully exercising their economic, social, and cultural rights (A/69/700, paragraphs 67 and 68, chapter IV.B and SDGs 1.4, 3b, 5a). Consequently, regarding SDGs 16.1 and 16.2, preventing the various forms of violence and slavery including trafficking in women and children, one of the forms of organized crime, is really about regulating the right to property to/ of a person or his or her freedom.

The fight for freedom by abolishing this kind of property "rights" has been at the core of world's history. For example, Indian criminological studies show that property-less women are much more often abused by their partners than those with property (Agarwal and Panda 2007), and to a lesser extent, this continues to be an issue in developed countries where domestic violence has not been found to be correlated with property-less women (Schröttle and Vogt 2016). Nonetheless, various studies show that impoverished families have a much higher rate of social problems, including domestic violence, other crimes, and delinquency, than do socially stable families.

Based on the study of female homicide victimization rates from 1985 to 2010 across 33 European countries, Stamatel (2014) concluded:

> Better economic conditions reduce female homicide victimization, as they do for violence more generally. Gender dynamics play a contradictory role: less traditional gender roles increase the risk of victimization, whereas improving the collective status of women in society reduces that risk. Most importantly, controlling for these known predictors of female homicide victimization, the historical legacies and socio-historical contexts of nations matter greatly for explaining variation across Europe.

J.P. Stamatel
2014, p. 596

In summary, not only does the criminogenic role of property-related and other economic predictors matter greatly, but so does the individual sense of justice. As both evolve, crime prevention education must follow new horizons.

Prosperity: Relative Deprivation, Innovation and Crime Prevention

> We are determined to ensure that all human beings can enjoy prosperous and fulfilling lives and that economic, social and technological progress occurs in harmony with nature.

A/RES/70/1
2015, p. 2/35

To grow a strong, inclusive, and transformative economy is the essence of prosperity in the UN SDGs terms (A/69/700, p. 16/34). In keeping further with the aforementioned UNIPCC's focus on the human security aspect of migration, welfare for foreign immigrants in comparison with welfare support for local citizens of the host country may give rise to xenophobic feelings by those who financially receive less than what immigrants receive. Moreover, among those who live on welfare, when compared to the lowest wage, it may be demotivating to produce the fruits for economic, social, and technological progress. This may then lead to a socially problematic and impoverished population. Moreover, only "as individuals strive to do better, they partly but never fully succeed since their reference points continue to rise along their earning power" (Becker and Rayo 2010, p. 181).

Nevertheless, they may still take a chance in enriching themselves illegitimately. Enrichment, however, may not necessarily be material (i.e., motivated by greed). For example, Montesquieu's "crimes of passion," including domestic violence, rape, "joyriding," taking crack, and hate crimes, can be expressions of people's frustration (WHO 2002, pp. 31–33). However, regardless of any real motivation, such crimes can be detrimental to one's positive self-development.

Therefore, in terms of crime prevention education for prosperity, the following points are considered important.

In market societies that facilitate the formation of distinct cognitive skills and habits, such people can prosper better than in other less advanced markets. However, the labor market of developed countries is oversupplied with educated people, and short of people with new skills, especially those who may be instruments of development in the new world economy (Hanushek and Wößmann 2007, pp. 10–11).

The case for the compelling interdependence between education and prosperity can be found in the recent statistical publications by the United Nations Industrial Development Organization (UNIDO 2013). The UNIDO argues that the higher a country's industrialization measured by Manufacturing Value Added (MVA) *per capita*, the higher the rate of enrolment in primary school, as well as the life expectancy at birth. The depth of the food deficit (measured by a daily calorie intake below or above the global standard) is significantly lower when MVA *per capita* is high. The same UNIDO paper informs that a 1% annual increase in MVA decreases the "poverty head count" by almost 2% and the number of deaths related to conflict by 4.5%. However, in either case, there may be other variables that may qualify the reliability and validity of this finding.

Moreover, since the MVA does not include information about the competitiveness of countries' industries, UNIDO's *Competitive Industrial Performance Report 2012–2013* (UNIDO 2014), self-proclaimed as "the most comprehensive global comparative analysis of industrial competitiveness, including 135 countries in the world" (UNIDO 2014, p. vi), investigated why some countries are more industrially competitive in terms of export than others. By examining the internal relations within the MVA's internal components, the report found that, indeed, innovative countries (in a high-tech sense) yield a higher total MVA. Hence, eventually, they are more industrially competitive than other countries with a low value of innovations. On aggregate, at the core of UN's "Prosperity," that is, "productive and fulfilling lives … inclusive and sustainable economic growth," is innovation that powers high-tech industries.

In summary, education is deemed to be a necessary precondition for prosperity to prevail. In determining which model (i.e., natural sciences vs. social sciences or engineering vs. law) might best contribute to prosperity, one recent econometric study reported that growth depends positively on the rule of law and the investment ratio. Negatively, however, it depends on the fertility rate, the ratio of government consumption to GDP, and inflation (Barro 2003). Therefore, a culture of lawfulness is the necessary precondition to economic growth through education (see, e.g., Easterly 2001). In conclusion, such a growth is an effect of moral and economic entrepreneurship for SD.

Peace: Security, the Rule of Law and Justice

> We are determined to foster peaceful, just and inclusive societies which are free from fear and violence. There can be no sustainable development without peace and no peace without sustainable development.
>
> **A/RES/70/1**
> *2015, p. 2/35*

In the opinion of the UN, a "tax" is now tantamount to undermining one of the SDGs (No. 16), to "[p]romote peaceful and inclusive societies for SD, provide access to justice for all and build effective, accountable and inclusive institutions at all levels" (A/RES/70/1 2015, p. 26/35). The UN has planned this in SDG 16.5 by aiming to "substantially reduce corruption and bribery in all their forms reduction" (A/RES/70/1 2015). Ironically, both formulations seemingly contradict one another: promoting peace and social tolerance, and increasing the nontolerance to corruption and bribery.

This UN normativity is logonomically very complex (Redo 2013), but there is no contradiction between the two formulations. This was first signaled as such at the UN Security Council by its president who reaffirmed that corruption is a threat to peace and security (S/PRST/2010/4 2010, p. 2). Later reports demonstrate the detrimental effect of corruption on governance and the rule of law in a country (IEP 2016).

The "Peace" element presents only cursory references to both ("strengthen the rule of law"/"ensure equal access to justice"). In both cases, this is a major departure from treating the rule of law and justice as overwhelming objectives of the UN.

The UN Charter mentions "justice" in various places and ways. However, in none of them is there a clear definition. While the Preamble to the Charter only alludes to it (see articles 1(1) and 2(3)), it only speaks about achieving justice. In the opinion of the Charter's commentators, "justice … means something different from international law (…) and (…) refers to natural law" (Simma et al. 2002/II, p. 36).

Within the UN Charter's mandate involving the maintenance of peace and security, the Security Council involves de facto not substantive justice but procedural justice. In this sense, the Security Council resembles a global police precinct as opposed to a court of justice. Although the General Assembly and the Economic and Social Council occasionally do "condemn" Member States for their activities, they are really not involved in making legally valid judgements and strive to uphold "equity" (distributive justice)—one of the purposes of public international law. This is particularly evident when such actions and measures pertain to economically or otherwise underprivileged social groups, especially women and children, and improving education for prevention.

Teaching Crime Prevention and Culture of Lawfulness across the World

In relation to the second objective of this chapter, as put by the UN S-G, a change of "old mind-sets, behaviors and destructive patterns" is needed for global transformation of economy, environment, and society (A/69/700, paragraph 159).

In accordance with the UN logonomic rules, this call involves combining "fire with water," that is, the *attitude*-driven intercultural transmission of the UN crime prevention *values* that contribute to the rationalization of mind-sets, behaviors, and the prevention of destructive patterns. This interplay of both eastern and western perspectives (see Clarke 2006, p. 118) has been quite successful with regard to instilling a greater SD awareness, of which EJ is an evident part. The SDGsD contributes to the UN logonomics, now in the Rio+20 spirit.

In this spirit, we will offer some observations on EJ attitudes and values in the present SDGs call. The SDGs prescribe the conduct, but hardly effect its implementation. Quite rightly, they are the case of nomen omen "declarative knowledge" (Ryle 1949, p. 30).

Because of this, delivering locally in the organization's own terms, a UN crime prevention message ("operational knowledge") has proven to be difficult. For example, regarding welfare concerns, legal culture of Confucianism promotes benevolence not as a part but a form of good governance, a kind of "procedural justice"/attitude that assures mutual satisfaction with the living conditions. "Justice" in Confucianism is neither a part of beneficence nor benevolence. Rather, it is an innate attitude of anybody in whatever capacity (personal/official). A person may lose and recover "justice" in personal, filial, or social interest, so as to restore a reciprocal affective relation with others. Another example: In UN logonomics, "hate crimes" are a form of prejudice of others meant as "inferior" (from the Greek *hustereo*, meaning "the worse" or "the lesser").

In light of such conflicting understandings, taking the SDGsD as a canon for programming a new mind-set is quite a challenge. Making the present culture of lawfulness to conform normatively across the world with the declaration requires not only the continuation of promotion of values but also work on changing the attitudes.

Since there is no ultimate single concept of justice as a value, Montesquieu's views about North–South virtues and vices are Eurocentric. However, such is not the case with his other character-related comparative observations. Indeed, in one cross-cultural psychological experiment involving 2900 college students who were surveyed across 26 countries, researchers found that impact on learning (see Pennebaker et al. 1996). The findings showed that the respondents considered Northerners and Southerners within their own countries to be respectively less or more emotionally expressive and found that within-country North–South stereotypes exist.

The same logic begs the question how crime prevention teaching can assist in rationalizing crime prevention responses according to the various legal cultures within which this North–South stereotyping naturally operates. In full awareness that there neither is a single right answer to this question, the following observations support the importance of developing individual personhood for the social contract civic obligations implied by a progressive welfare reform, stipulated by article 55 of the UN Charter.

From a reformist perspective, it must be recalled that, generally, learning and innovation (a) in manufacturing industries builds technological capabilities and (b) must be combined with anticorruption education. Thus, the obvious way to improving the law-abiding and other educational performances of underprivileged learners is through financing and implementing an equal-opportunity SDGs policy across pupils/students of different socioeconomic background that blends both. However, the ensuing returns on investment in the educational performance of such socioeconomically underprivileged learners are not without their challenges (see Keane and Roemer 2009).

In regard to trying to make higher returns, two complimentary cost-effective ways are proposed. Both involve supporting pro-social– and pro-skill–oriented reformist motivation to equalize individual welfare chances of learners by building up their civic commitments.

The first approach is through motivating learners to break away from the sectarian stereotyping of self and others. The World Bank experiment conducted in India (Hof and Pandey 2004), a country known from its very rigid social stratification, compellingly proved the following:

a. The negative learner's self-perception works like a self-fulfilling prophecy. It locks in the economic disadvantage because of the pre-defined content of own expectations.
b. These expectations are not a consequence of a "culture of poverty" per se but of its enduring legacy that hampers positive personal attitudinal changes.
c. Since the aggregate effect of economic deprivation (injustice) on the expectations associated with the in-group is clearly negative, motivating learners to perform better may alleviate their enduring feeling of personal inferiority. In the long run, it may alleviate prejudice of others and the impoverished future in general cultures (Redo 2014; see also Steele and Aronson 1995; Augostinos and Rosewarne 2001).

The second approach involves understanding the learners' foundational thinking and then rephrasing their different concepts "so as to develop a progressive and logical train of critical thought" (UNESCO 2009, p. 34) through a participatory/interactive and affective thinking group discussion with more questions than a person may answer. This is done by a predetermined and sequentially interrogative, inferential inductive logic of "particular-to-general-to-generic": A case-specific question "A" entails a less minor question "B" (and vice versa); yet, both lead to a generalizable question "C," which implies a self-evident answer. In other words, one does not have to answer a question in order to apply a rule. Thus, only questions play the role of premises and conclusions and carry the message what to think. Without making any use of answers to the first and next question just transformed, a learner ends up with a question of a required final form—a genuine answer in itself (see, e.g., Leszczyńska-Jasion et al. 2013).

Socrates (469–399 BC)—"the first criminal justice educator" (Holland 1980, p. 1)—could have originally asked these questions. This method of inquiry enables learners to make their own logical connections, and it serves to improve an overall sense of justice.

Currently, the Socratic method experiments with universal moral philosophy questions for enhancing global civic education among kids (Lipman 2008) and adolescents (UNESCO 2006), occasionally with a view to problem-solving. It has not yet reached the stage, or form, in crime prevention education, nor did it result in socially progressive reformist action. However, this inductive case method for internal transformation no doubt may help as it serves to facilitate a more precise response to universal questions, such as "What is genocide?", "What is torture?", "What is justice?", "Should children who come to a country as refugees have the same rights as children born in that country?", and "What is sustainable development?" The answers to such questions come in reply to someone's own thinking what something is. They coincide with the prescriptive (peremptory) global legal concepts and definitions or the balance of findings corroborating the etiology and reducibility of some forms of crime or abuse.

The evaluation of such global civic education projects suggests that they are promising (Topping and Trickey 2007a,b), but they are not without some conceptual and operational challenges (Farahani 2014). Nonetheless, one recently evaluated moral philosophy project that in 2012–2014 involved some 3000 pupils aged 8–11 in 48 state primary schools across England yielded an improvement in their maths and literacy progress—the equivalent of 2 months' worth of teaching. The project yielded even faster rates of progress for pupils from impoverished families and from ethnic minority groups (e.g., 3 months for math and 4 months for reading) (EEF 2016).

These kinds of moral philosophy projects are implemented not only in primary- and secondary-level schools of some 60 countries with different legal cultures (EEF 2016) but also at the tertiary level (Ryan et al. 2013). The projects' conceptual and institutional endorsements by UNESCO (2006) and UNICEF (2009) signal the viability of bridging Western and Eastern moral philosophy issues in one civic education through collectively refining affective thinking (Lipman 2003, p. 266) for its eventual rationalization and application in constructive decision-making.

Discussing such universal moral values enlivens our security checks over conscience of humankind. Hence, the S-G's call for changing the old mindsets, behaviors, and destructive patterns certainly may have a useful and progressive SDGs tool. Through the global consensus on the definitions preset through the UN Charter and elaborated in the subsequent legal instruments (including the UDHR), this social science method for problem-solving is applicable to all levels of formal education anywhere. However, there is no doubt that such an education in universal moral issues will yield different answers in sending and receiving countries, because of the level of socioeconomic development and democratic institutions. This is precisely the reason why the UNESCO's and UNICEF's respective involvement may advance them through the primary/tertiary education in developed and developing countries.

Conclusion

The primary focus of this chapter was on some salient crime prevention issues reported in the UN Declaration on Sustainable Development Goals 2016–2030 and on engineering a more interculturally effective delivery of the related crime prevention message.

In order for this to happen, greater attention needs to be paid to including SD as a key element for various crime theories. Nowadays, they deal only narrowly with the SD concept (Redo 2012), and even less with the UNIPCC's concern about the climate-related exacerbation of welfare losses of present and future generations. And yet, in criminological terms, the impoverished future implies that absolute and relative resource deprivation as a result of welfare losses will facilitate various crimes and abuses affecting a culture of lawfulness.

Figure 1.1 incorporates the above UNIPCC and other criminological concerns (Crank and Jacoby 2015; Homer-Dixon 1999) into one strategic UN SDGsD model that includes prevention. This model is paradigmatic but not causal, more visionary than evidentiary. It consists of two perpendicular axes: "Climate stress" and "Governance/Crime prevention/Culture of lawfulness." In between them are (a) sustainable livelihoods that affect (b) migration and mobility, (c) cultural change, (d) conflict, (e) crime and abuse—all interlaced as local, national, and transnational/international governance problems whose solutions include (f) prevention.

The local governance problems are as follows: crime and conflict resulting from (e.g., supply/demand-induced scarcity) national (e.g., crimes associated with inequality and possible punitive reaction by a State), transnational/international, and organized crime; hate and other culture identity–related crime (e.g., honor killings); and corruption, immigrant welfare crime, and terrorism. On the assumption that crime prevention returns to security and culture of lawfulness are the highest at the axes' common starting point (Heckman 2008), the (f) curve accordingly runs in-between them.

Against this background, for the educationists and other readers of this chapter, there are four general UN SDGsD messages involving primary crime prevention.

The first message involves various forms of property and personal "welfare" crime: domestic or transnational (organized or not) must be the focus of educational policies ensuing from the climate change and SD in general. In the UN SDGs, there are numerous references to various forms of crime and other abuses (Zvekic 2015).

The second concerns the importance of centralized governance in any country's success to attain the SDGs by 2030. This assertion is enshrined in the UN resolution on the "Guidelines for the prevention of urban crime" (E/1995/9). It calls authorities to design and implement integrated crime prevention as a

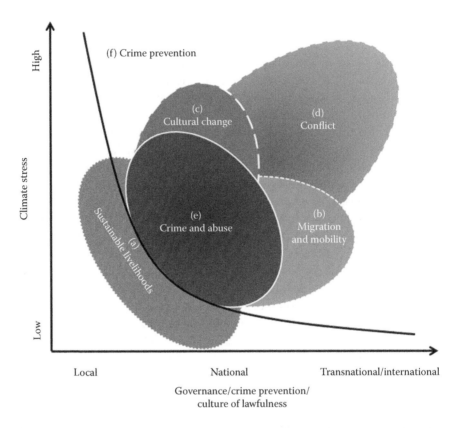

Figure 1.1 Climate change, governance, crime prevention, and culture of lawfulness on the United Nations post-2015 sustainable development agenda. (Adapted from UNIPCC 2014:777, with inputs from Homer-Dixon, T.F. [1999]. *Scarcity and Violence*. Princeton: Princeton University Press; and Crank, J.P., and Jacoby, L.S. [2015]. *Crime, Violence, and Global Warming*. London: Routledge, Taylor & Francis Group.)

pluralistic endeavor including many stakeholders. The guidelines call upon central authorities to (a) provide active support, assistance, and encouragement to local actors; (b) coordinate national policy and strategies with local strategies and needs; and (c) organize consultation and cooperation mechanisms between the various administrations concerned at the central level.

The third one is about the importance of limiting the excessive criminogenic income inequalities by modifying the property rights in various dimensions. In terms of the SDG 10 ("to reduce inequality within and among countries"), this should be done by removing the respective discriminatory laws, policies, and practices. This can take many different forms. Among them are the exclusionary laws, policies, and practices that facilitate violence and discrimination against women, including the denial of their access to and rights over land, inheritance, and property. The UN SDGs framers must be aware of it, but when it comes to legislative action and implementation, not much comes into the picture (A/70/137 2015, paragraph 22). Therefore, if the North–South dialogue is to be actualized, then legislators must acknowledge and address these elements.

Finally, I would like to conclude with a case for the role of temperature in social relations raised by Friedrich Engels (1820–1895) and ask in a Socratic manner whether the following makes sense:

> The contempt for the existing social order is most conspicuous in its extreme form—that of offences against the law. If the influences demoralising to the working-man act more powerfully, more than usual, he becomes an offender as certainly as water abandons the fluid for the vaporous state at 80 degrees, Réaumur.
>
> **F. Engels**
> *1844/1943, p. 130*

From the standpoint of this criminological inquiry into the effects of climate change (and in contrast with the first motto of this chapter), this metaphor seems rather nonsensical. Yet, it serves to alert us to some important long-range messages.

First, plausible as is the explanation of certain criminological claims in terms of temperature, climate, cultural (individualism/collectivism), or psychological (egoism/self-interest) terms, it is really the power of one or the other ideology that overrides them and leads to (de)modernization, (de)humanization, and (de)individualization. Under the sun, there is probably no better explanation for the contrast in welfare and economy between the two Koreas, the two Germany's, and Poland before and after 1989, but the (de)motivating power of ideology on individuals and a good governance, secular or not.

Second, recent historical and laboratory research on the dynamics of the aforementioned U.S. civil serious disorders led to conclude that "[w]hen the number of committed opinion holders is below 10%, there is no visible progress in the spread of ideas… Once that number grows above 10%, the idea spreads like flame" (Szymański in the interview, Minority Rules 2016; Redo 2016). This may be the alternative explanation for a tipping point that prompts the underprivileged people to become violent, as if that 10% were an indicator of a social change in any direction. This may be true, but only if other ideas cannot counter the criminogenic spread of poverty (Waagen et al. 2015), with the spread originally and metaphorically scaled by Engels.

Third, ideas communicated in the UN SDGsD offer another way between command and market economy for building an inclusive, peaceful, prosperous, and sustainable world. Although the latter economy is intuitively bound with self-interest (Wolpert 1992), the Declaration pursues a new way of thinking and acting, by going beyond that interest for a constructive self-realization of countries and individuals, in accordance with the UN spirit and law.

However, all these messages should not undermine the role of interim recommendations regarding preventing the illegal migration, not directly related to the climatic conditions, but to the gnawing poverty. Very relevant to building the leitmotif for the SDGs-driven crime prevention education is therefore the following quote:

> It is a day at the beginning of January 1997. At the center of the shining lump of fish there is something strange, big and dark. Nobody is surprised because all sorts of things are found in the smack: Punic amphora and plastic tanks, tires and equipment discarded by cruise ships, as well as, when all goes well, bigger preys such as swordfish and tuna fish. But that thing does not look like a fish, nor like an amphora, nor like a boat relic. A jet of water liberates "the thing" of mud and seaweed. It is the body of a man. A dark-skinned man.

> **C. Lombardi-Diop**
> *2008, p. 168*

Four Criminological Recommendations Follow from This Dramatic Account

First, countering the smuggling of migrants by organized crime groups requires even more coordinated and effective international law enforcement and other measures to reduce the massive profits made on it by their members.

Second, while organized criminals appear impervious to other forms of preventing their profitable acts, those States must develop a self-sustained capacity to create decent life chances for their own people and be able to eventually finance this on their own. This is a sign of good governance, which 50 years since the start of the de-colonialization should begin yielding measurable results. The UN is full of well-intended declarations by Member States. The excuses of some of them are that colonial legacies (especially in Africa) prevent them from doing better and, hence, prevent from priming justice over loot.

On the way to 2030 and after, the homegrown greed, corruption, and hypocrisy are not good conduits to fight the self-sustaining cycle of poverty and crime. Anywhere, but particularly in developing countries, only a genuine and well-motivated commitment to take local affairs in own hands and create life chances for everybody may stop these self-deprivations. Only then will "the [foreign] polluter pays" principle work both ways. Hence, it is not only Montesquieu who may guide us regarding access to justice; the North–South and South–South UN SDGs that engage the Southern countries in a genuine effort to take their fate in their own hands, on the principle of shared responsibility, may do so as well.

Third, the idea of global citizenship involving shared responsibility should draw more on the environmental ethics calling to live in harmony with nature. While a systemic expansion of this ethics into harmonious coexistence in other walks of life is conceptually difficult, EJ and justice in general are at the root of natural law. Education in justice and crime prevention through an intergenerational learning process (similar to that for EJ) should contribute to a new culture of lawfulness with shared prosperity.

Last, but not least, in this global paradigm, UNICEF, UNESCO, the UN Academic Impact Initiative, the EU's Bologna Process through their UN SDGs, and new initiatives should take the lead in the methods and ways to transform a culture of lawfulness through civic education that modifies old mind-sets, deracializes them, rationalizes behaviors, and prevents destructive patterns.

May the 14th Congress find the UN Member States on this path.

Glossary of Key Terms

Climate change: Warming of the climate system involving increases in global average air and ocean temperatures, widespread melting of snow and ice, and rising global average sea level (IPPC 2007, Sec. 6.1).

Corruption: The misuse of a public or private position for direct or indirect personal gain (United Nations 2004).

Crime prevention: Strategies and measures that seek to reduce the risk of crimes occurring, and their potential harmful effects on individuals and society, including fear of crime, by intervening to influence their multiple causes or risk factors (United Nations 2010).

Culture of lawfulness: Dominant or mainstream culture, ethos, and thought in a society sympathetic to the rule of law. In a society governed by the rule of law, people have the ability to participate in the making and implementation of laws that bind all the people and institutions in society, including the government itself (Godson 2000).

Dignity: A nonphilosophical and secular UN concept purposely undefined by the organization. Dignity arises from globally shared moral intuition, is self-evident in nature and inherent to any person regardless of his or her socioeconomic status, and gives rise to individual human rights of any character (Spijkers 2011, Chapter 6).

Hunger: Not having enough to eat to meet energy requirements for normal growth and development and an active and healthy life, due to food insecurity and malnutrition caused by un sustainable agriculture and food systems (UN n.d.; WFP n.d.).

Inclusiveness: The extent to which individuals are incorporated within a wider moral and political community. Inclusiveness involves and values diversity, by increasing social equality and the participation of diverse and disadvantaged populations (O'Brien and Yar 2008, p. 153; York Institute, n.d.).

Innovation: The socioeconomic process of translating an idea, a good, or service that creates value for sustainable livelihood and development globally and locally, with due account of culture-specific factors. It contributes to improving individual and collective legitimate life chances and facilitates countering poverty and crime.

Justice: For the UN, justice is an ideal of accountability and fairness in the protection and vindication of rights and the prevention and punishment of wrongs. Justice implies regard for the rights of the accused, for the interests of victims, and for the well-being of society at large. It is a concept rooted in all national cultures and traditions and, while its administration usually implies formal judicial mechanisms, traditional dispute resolution mechanisms are equally relevant (S/2004/616, paragraph 7).

Migration: Refers here to the smuggling and other international irregular forms of, more often than not, South–North migration.

Motivation: The process that initiates, guides, and maintains goal-oriented behaviors. Motivation is what causes a person to act (VW n.d.).

Poverty: The nonfulfillment of preferences and the nonsatisfaction with basic needs or denial of choices and opportunities for living a tolerable life, which includes adequate food, water, health care, and education (UNDP 1997, p. 3). The UN SDGs define absolute poverty in terms of individual consumption levels of less than U.S.$1.25 a day.

Reform: Refers here to progressive socioeconomic development with due account of culture-specific factors. It is a conscious international and domestic moral and economic entrepreneurship to promote UN Charter's "higher standards of living, full employment, and conditions of economic and social progress." In the process of the elaboration and implementation of the United Nations crime prevention and criminal justice standards and norms, including treaty law instruments, this development implies progressive humanistic treatment of offenders and victims of crime, juvenile delinquents, and children in conflict with the law. It also includes enhancing of the performance of criminal justice system, the right to defense, the eventual abolition of death penalty, and the respective improvements in countering various forms of crime, whether traditional or modern.

Sustainable development: Sustainable development in its original sense given by the World Commission on Environment and Development

(1987), chaired by Gro Harlem Brundtland, Norway's then Prime Minister, communicates that in the interest of the right to development of future generations, the development of economy and civilization should not be pursued at the cost of exhausting the nonrenewable natural resources and the destruction of environment. Currently, this concept extends to a self-generating, creative, albeit also conflicting, mechanism for renewing socioeconomic and other resources. It is geared toward their multiplication and, generally, the broadening of human intergenerational capital in any creative areas of humankind, including science and education—the necessary doorway to a change in mindset and behavior (Redo 2012, p. 233).

United Nations: The United Nations is an international organization founded in 1945. It is currently made up of 193 Member States. The mission and work of the United Nations are guided by the purposes and principles contained in its founding Charter.

Discussion Questions

1. The involvement of transnational organized crime in the smuggling of migrants requires law enforcement and judicial measures to undercut the financing of this process and the seizure and forfeiture of assets. Search for cases involving countering this crime in this manner, then offer viable and democratic legal solutions that internationally facilitate the improvement in fighting the smuggling of migrants.

2. While climate change and poverty may (dis)jointly drive domestic and international crime and migration, what would be needed in the migrant-sending countries in terms of building their own prosperous development to benefit from their human capital (UN SDGs' "People")?

3. Find examples of crime trends studies focused on the issue of poverty in which chosen for the analysis independent poverty variables lead to strikingly different interpretations of the correlated with them crime data.

4. Identify criminological studies that deal with the question of SD beyond EJ issues.

5. Taking note of the dramatic consequences of illegal migration documented by the case of "a dark-skinned" man quoted in this chapter, consider, on the basis of global treaties dealing with migration and the right to education, whether or not those who survived the ordeal of smuggling into your country could exercise their right to education, and if they are eligible to political asylum, in case they document their political persecution in the sending country.

6. Pro-reformist positive motivation includes rational thinking. In terms of canons of logical thinking, what methods other than the Socratic type of inquiry may be included? For example, how could you prove, in terms of Aristotle's logic, that the motto of this chapter carries a syllogistically compelling and educationally important crime prevention message?

Suggested Reading

Kury, H., Redo, S., and Shea, E. (2016). *Women and Children as Victims and Offenders: Background–Prevention–Reintegration. Suggestions for Succeeding Generations*, ed. H. Kury, S. Redo, and E. Shea. Berlin–Dordrecht–Heidelberg–New York: Springer, particularly Introduction (vol. I: part I, chap. 4, part III, chap. 3; vol. II: part V, chap. 5; final discussion: chaps. 1 and 5; post scriptum).

Sławomir, R. (2012). *Blue Criminology. The Power of the United Nations Ideas to Counter Crime Globally*, Helsinki: European Institute for Crime Prevention and Control, affiliated with the United Nations.

Sławomir, R. (2013). The United Nations rule of law, "common language of justice" and the post-2015 educational agenda: Some academic and policy aspects. *Comparative Law Review* 16: 211–246, http://dx.doi.org/10.12775/CLR.2013.023 (accessed January 16, 2016).

Waagen, A., Gunjan, V., Chan, K., Swami, K., and D'Souza, R. (2015). Effect of zealotry in high-dimensional opinion dynamics models. *Phys. Rev. E 91*, http://dx.doi.org/10.1103/PhysRevE.91.022811 (accessed January 16, 2016).

Recommended Web Links

http://www.unesco.org/new/en/education/themes/leading-the-international-agenda/education-for-sustainable-development/

The United Nations Educational and Scientific and Cultural Organization offers a variety of high-quality expert-group or peer-reviewed analyses; recommendations, reports, handbooks, and manuals on education and sustainable development among which there are intercultural publications on moral philosophy that draws on the Socratic method.

https://sustainabledevelopment.un.org/

This United Nations HQ website is a source of intergovernmental and civil society documentation with the most politically important problematics in which various United Nations organs, other entities, and actors keep stock of the respective resolutions, statements, interventions, reports, and publications regarding the organization's sustainable development goals agenda 2016–2030.

https://academicimpact.un.org/

This global initiative of the United Nations Department of Public Information aligns institutions of higher education with the United Nations in furthering the realization of the purposes and mandate of the organization through activities and research in a shared culture of intellectual social responsibility.

http://acuns.org/category/publications/

This is a website of the Academic Council on the United Nations System (ACUNS), a nongovernmental organization in general consultative status with the Economic and Social Council, and a global professional association of educational and research institutions, individual scholars, and practitioners active in the work and study of the United Nations, multilateral relations, global governance, and international cooperation. ACUNS promotes teaching on these topics, as well as dialogue and mutual understanding across and between academics, practitioners, civil society, and students. Researchers and students can find on the website most relevant UN discussion topics and information on the UN publications.

References

A/70/137. (16 July 2015). Summary report of the 2014 parliamentary hearing. Note by the President of the General Assembly.

A/HRC/10. (15 January 2009). Report of the Office of the United Nations High Commissioner for Human Rights on the relationship between climate change and human rights.

A/RES/59/565. (2004). A more secure world: Our shared responsibility, Report of the High-level Panel on Threats, Challenges and Change, 1 December 2004. United Nations, New York.

A/RES/65/230. (21 December 2010). Salvador Declaration on comprehensive strategies for global challenges: Crime prevention and criminal justice systems and their development in a changing world.

A/RES/70/1. (25 September 2015). Transforming our world: The 2030 Agenda for sustainable development.

A/RES/70/174. (17 December 2015). Doha Declaration on integrating crime prevention and criminal justice into the wider United Nations agenda to address social and economic challenges and to promote the rule of law at the national and international levels, and public participation. Thirteenth United Nations Congress on Crime Prevention and Criminal Justice.

Acemoglu, D., and Robinson, J.A. (2012). *Why Nations Fail: The Origins of Power, Prosperity, and Poverty*. New York: Crown Business.

Agarwal, B., and Panda, P. (2007). Toward freedom from domestic violence: The neglected obvious. *Journal of Human Development* 8(3): 359–388.

Agnew, R. (2012). Dire forecast: A theoretical model of the impact of climate change on crime. *Theoretical Criminology* 16(1): 21–42.

Anderson, C.A. (2001). Heat and violence. *Current Directions in Psychological Science* 10: 33–38.

Anderson, C.A., and DeLisi, M. (2011). Implications of global climate change for violence in developed and developing countries. In *Social Conflict and Aggression*, eds. J.P. Forgas, A.W. Kruglanski, and K.D. Williams, 249–265. London: Psychology Press.

Annan, K. (2014). The very heart of the UN's mission. In *Kofi Annan. We the Peoples. A UN for the 21st Century*, ed. E. Mortimer, 121–128. Boulder and London: Paradigm Publisher.

Augostinos, M., and Rosewarne, D.L. (2001). Stereotype knowledge and prejudice in children. *British Journal of Developmental Psychology* 19(11): 143–156.

Barnes, E.H., and Teeters, N.K. (1951). *New Horizons in Criminology*. New York: Prentice-Hall, Inc.

Baron, R.A., and Ransberger, V.M. (1978). Ambient temperature and the occurrence of collective violence: The "Long, hot summer" revisited. *Journal of Personality and Social Psychology* 36: 351–360.

Barro, R. (2003). Determinants of economic growth in a panel of countries. *Annals of Economics and Finance* 4: 231–274.

Becker, G.S., and Rayo, L. (2010). Why Keynes underestimated consumption and overestimated leisure for the long run. In *Revisiting Keynes. Economic Possibilities for Our Grandchildren*, ed. L. Pecchi and G. Piga, 179–184. Cambridge: The MIT Press.

Buhaug, H., Nordkvelle, J., Bernauer, T., Böhmelt, T., Brzoska, M., Busby, J.W., Ciccone, A., Fjelde, E. et al. (2014). One effect to rule them all? A comment on climate and conflict. *Climatic Change* 127: 391–397.

Clarke, J.J. (2006). *Oriental Enlightenment. The Encounter between Asian and Western Thought*. New York–London: Routledge.

Cohn, E.J. (1990). Weather and crime. *The British Journal of Criminology* 30(1): 51–64.

Crank, J.P. (2003). Crime and justice in the context of resource scarcity. *Crime, Law & Social Change* 39: 39–67.

Crank, J.P., and Jacoby, L.S. (2015). *Crime, Violence, and Global Warming*. London: Routledge, Taylor & Francis Group.

Dumont, L. (1986). *Essays on Individualism. Modern Ideology in Anthropological Perspective*. Chicago: University of Chicago Press.

E/1995/9. (24 July 1995). Guidelines for the prevention of urban crime.

Easterly, W. (2001). *The Elusive Quest for Growth: An Economists' Adventures and Misadventures in the Tropics*. Cambridge: The MIT Press.

EEF/Education Endowment Foundation. Philosophy for children, evaluation report and executive summary. (2016). Independent evaluators: S. Gorard, N. Siddiqui, and B.H. See. Durham, UK: Durham University. Retrieved from https://educationendowmentfoundation.org.uk/.../Philosophy_for_Childr...

Ellis, L., Beaver, K., and Wright, J. (2009). *Handbook of Crime Correlates*. Oxford: Elsevier/Academic Press.

Engels, F. (1844/1943). *The Condition of the Working-Class in England in 1844*, ed. D. Price. London: George Allen & Unwin.

Farahani, M.F. (2014). The study on challenges of teaching philosophy for children. *Procedia—Social and Behavioral Sciences* 116: 2141–2145.

GA/SHC/3817. (7 October 2005). Crime is both cause, consequence of poverty, Third Committee told as it begins discussion of crime prevention, international drug control.

Godson, R. (2000). *A Guide to Developing a Culture of Lawfulness*. Symposium on the Role of Civil Society in Countering Organized Crime: Global Implications of the Palermo, Sicily, December 14, 2000, Palermo, Italy. Retrieved from http://www.cicad.oas.org/apps/Document.aspx?Id=309.

Hanushek, E.A., and Wößmann, L. (2007). The role of school improvement in economic development, NBER Working Paper No. 12832, Cambridge: National Bureau of Economic Research. Retrieved from http://www.nber.org/papers/w12832.

Heckman, J.J. (2008). The case of investing in disadvantaged young children. Big ideas for children: Investing in our nation's future. Washington, DC: First Focus.

Hoff, K., and Pandey, P. (2004). An experimental investigation of an Indian caste. World Bank Policy Research Working Paper 3351, Washington, DC: World Bank. Retrieved from http://elibrary.worldbank.org/. doi/pdf/10.1596/1813-9450-3351.

Hofstede, G. (1991). Empirical models of cultural differences. In *Contemporary Issues in Cross-Cultural Psychology*, ed. N. Bleichrodt, and P.J.D. Drenth, 4–20. Amsterdam: Swets & Zeitlinger, Inc.

Holland, K.M. (1980). Socrates—The first criminal justice educator. *Criminal Justice Review* 5(2): 1–4.

Homer-Dixon, T.F. (1991). On the threshold: Environmental changes as causes of acute conflict. *International Security* 16(2): 76–116.

Homer-Dixon, T.F. (1994). Environmental scarcities and violent conflict: Evidence from cases. *International Security* 19(1): 5–40.

Homer-Dixon, T.F. (1999). *Scarcity and Violence*. Princeton: Princeton University Press.

IEP/Institute for Economics and Peace. (2016). Peace and Corruption. Sydney. Retrieved from http://economicsandpeace.org/research/.

Kang, K.-W. (2007). Climate Change and Human Rights. Address by Ms. Kyung-wha Kang Deputy High Commissioner for Human Rights, Office of the United Nations High Commissioner for Human Rights. Retrieved from http://www.ohchr.org/en/NewsEvents/Pages/DisplayNews.aspx?NewsID=200&LangID=E#sthash.4M8scgS8.dpuf.

Keane, M.P., and Roemer, J.E. (2009). Assessing policies to equalize opportunity using an equilibrium model of educational and occupational choices. *Journal of Public Economics* 93(7): 879–898.

Krause, K. (ed.). (2011). *Global Burden of Armed Violence 2011: Lethal Encounters*. Geneva Declaration on Armed Violence and Development. Cambridge, UK: Cambridge University Press.

Lipman, M. (2003). *Thinking in Education*. New York: Cambridge University Press.

Lipman, M. (2008). *A Life Teaching Thinking*. Montclair, NJ: Institute for Advancement of Philosophy for Children.

Leszczyńska-Jasion, D., Urbański, M., and Wiśniewski, A. (2013). Socratic trees, *Studia Logica* 101: 959–986.

Livingstone, D.N. (2002). Race, space and moral climatology: Notes toward a genealogy, *Journal of Historical Geography* 28(2): 159–180.

Lombardi-Diop, C. (2008). Ghosts of memories, spirits of ancestors: Slavery, the Mediterranean, and the Atlantic. In *Recharting the Black Atlantic: Modern Cultures, Local Communities, Global Connections*, ed. A. Oboe and A. Scacchi, 162–180. New York–Abingdon: Routledge.

Lombroso, C. (1899/1911). *Crime: Its Causes and Remedies*. Boston: Little, Brown & Company.

Mares, D. (2013). Climate change and levels of violence in socially disadvantaged neighbourhood groups. *Journal of Urban Health: Bulletin of the New York Academy of Medicine* 90(4): 768–783.

Mehlum, H., Miguel, E., and Torvik, R. (2006). Poverty and crime in 19th century Germany. *Journal of Urban Economics* 59: 370–388.

Minority Rules: Why 10 Percent Is All You Need. (2016). Retrieved from http://freak onomics.com/2011/07/28/minority-rules-why-10-percent-is-all-you-need/.

Montesquieu, C. (1748/1949). Essai sur les causes qui peuvent affecter les esprits et les caracteres. In *Oeuvres completes de Montesquieu*, ed. R. Callois, 2 vols. Paris: Gallimard.

Montesquieu, C. (1772/2001). *The Spirit of Laws*, translated by T. Nugent. Kitchener, ON: Batoche Books.

National Centres for Environmental Information (NOAA). (2015). Global Analysis— December 2014. Retrieved from https://www.ncdc.noaa.gov/sotc/global/20141 2+&cd=2&hl=en&ct=clnk&gl=at.

O'Brien, M., and Yar, M. (2008). *Criminology: The Key Concepts*. London–New York: Routledge.

Pennebaker, J.W., Rimé, B., and Blankenship, V.E. (1996). Stereotypes of emotional expressiveness of Northerners and Southerners: A cross-cultural test of Montesquieu's hypotheses. *Journal of Personality and Social Psychology* 70(2): 372–380.

Pinker, S. (2011). *The Better Angels of Our Nature: Why Violence Has Declined*. London: Penguin Books.

Ranson, M. (2012). Crime, weather, and climate change. MRCBG Associate Working Paper Series No. 8. Harvard Kennedy School. Retrieved from http://www.hks .harvard.edu/content/download/67660/1243450/version/1/file/ranson_2012-8 .FINAL.pdf.

Ranson, M. (2014). Crime, weather, and climate change. *Journal of Environmental Economics and Management* 67(3): 274–302.

Redo, S. (2012). *Blue Criminology. The Power of the United Nations Ideas to Counter Crime Globally*. Helsinki: European Institute for Crime Prevention and Control, affiliated with the United Nations.

Redo, S. (2013). The United Nations rule of law, "common language of justice" and the post-2015 educational agenda: Some academic and policy aspects. *Comparative Law Review* 16: 211–246.

Redo, S. (2014). Education for succeeding generations in culture of lawfulness. In *Current Problems of the Penal Law and Criminology*, ed. E.W. Pływaczewski, 698–722, Warszawa: Wydawnictwo C.H. Beck.

Redo, S. (2016). New instruments and approaches for countering social exclusion: A criminological contribution to the United Nations post-2015 educational agenda. In *Current Problems of the Penal Law and Criminology*, Vol. 7, ed. E.W. Pływaczewski and E.M. Guzik-Makaruk.

Reuveny, R. (2007). Climate change-induced migration and violent conflict. *Political Geography* 26(7): 656–673.

Rommen, H. (1936/1998). *The Natural Law: A Study in Legal and Social History and Philosophy*, translated by T.R. Hanley, Introduction and Bibliography by R. Hittinger. Indianapolis: Liberty Books.

Ryan, E., Xin, S., Yuan, Y., You, R., and Li, H. (2013). When Socrates meets Confucius: Teaching, creative and critical thinking across cultures trough multilevel Socratic method. *Nebraska Law Review* 92(2): 290–331.

Ryle, G. (1949). *The Concept of Mind*. New York: Barnes & Noble.

S/2004/616. (23 August 2004). The rule of law and transitional justice in conflict and post-conflict societies. Report of the Secretary-General.

S/PRST/2010/4. (24 February 2010). Threats to peace and security, Statement by the President of the Security Council, United Nations.

Schröttle, M., and Vogt, K. (2016). Women as victims and offenders: The facts and their validity. In *Women and Children as Victims and Offenders: Background–Prevention–Reintegration. Suggestions for Succeeding Generations*, eds. H. Kury, S. Redo, and E. Shea. Berlin–Dordrecht–Heidelberg–New York: Springer.

Semmens, N., Dillane, J., and Ditton, J. (2002). Preliminary findings on seasonality and the fear of crime. *The British Journal of Criminology* 42(4): 798–806.

Simma, B., Mosler, H., Randelzhofer, A., Tomuschat, C., Wolfrum, R., Paulus, A., and Chaitobu, E. (2002). *The Charter of the United Nations: A Commentary*. New York: Oxford University Press.

Spijkers, O. (2011). *The United Nations, the Evolution of Global Values and International Law*. Cambridge: Intersentia.

Stamatel, J.P. (2014). Explaining variations in female homicide victimization rates across Europe. *European Journal of Criminology* 11(5): 578–600.

Steele, C.M., and Aronson, J. (1995). Stereotype threat and the intellectual test-performance of African-Americans. *Journal of Personality and Social Psychology* 69(5): 797–811.

Stokes, K.M. (1995). *Paradigm Lost: A Cultural and Systems Theoretical Critique of Political Economy*. New York–London, England: Armonk.

Theisen, O.M., Gleditsch, N.P., and Buhaug, H. (2013). Is climate change a driver of armed conflict? *Climatic Change* 117(3): 613–625.

Topping, K.J., and Trickey, S. (2007a). Collaborative philosophical enquiry for school children: Cognitive effects at 10–12 years. *British Journal of Educational Psychology* 77(1): 271–288.

Topping, K.J., and Trickey, S. (2007b). Collaborative philosophical inquiry for school-children: Cognitive gains at 2-year follow up. *British Journal of Educational Psychology* 77(4): 787–796.

Triandis, H.C. (1996). The psychological measurement of cultural syndromes. *American Psychologist* 51(4): 407–415.

UNDP/United Nations Development Programme. (2007). *Human Development Report*. New York: United Nations.

UNESCO. (2006). *Intersectoral Strategy on Philosophy*. Paris: UNESCO.

UNESCO. (2009). *Philosophy. A School of Freedom.* Paris: UNESCO.

UNFPA. (2009). *State of World Population 2009. Facing a Changing World: Women, Population and Climate.* New York: United Nations.

UNICEF. (2009). *School Resource Pack for Ages 11–16.* London: UNICEF.

UNIDO. (2013). *The Industrial Competitiveness of Nations. Looking Back, Forging Ahead.* Vienna: UNIDO.

UNIDO. (2014). How industrial development matters to the well-being of the population. Some statistical evidence, Working Paper 04/2014. Vienna: UNIDO.

UN/United Nations. (n.d.). Retrieved from http://www.un.org/en/zerohunger/#&panel1-1.

United Nations. (2003). *Repertory of Practice of United Nations Organs.* Codification Division, Office of Legal Affairs United Nations. Retrieved from http://legal.un.org/cod/.

United Nations Handbook on Practical Anti-Corruption Measures for Prosecutors and Investigators. (2004). Vienna: UNODC.

United Nations. (2010). *Handbook on the United Nations Crime Prevention Guidelines: Making Them Work.* Vienna: UNODC.

United Nations Intergovernmental Panel on Climate Change. (1995). *Climate Change 1995, Second Assessment Report.* Cambridge: Cambridge University Press.

United Nations Intergovernmental Panel on Climate Change. (2007). *Climate Change 2007, Fourth Assessment Report.* Cambridge: Cambridge University Press.

United Nations Intergovernmental Panel on Climate Change. (2014). *Climate Change 2014, Fifth Assessment Report.* Cambridge: Cambridge University Press.

United Nations Office of the High Commissioner for Human Rights. (2000). *ABC of Teaching Human Rights. Human Rights Topics for Upper Primary and Lower and Senior Secondary School.* Geneva: United Nations.

VW/VeryWell. (n.d.). Retrieved from http://psychology.about.com/od/mindex/g/motivation-definition.htm.

Waagen, A., Gunjan, V., Chan, K., Swami, A., and D'Souza, R. (18 February 2015). Effect of zealotry in high-dimensional opinion dynamics models. *Phys. Rev. E 91.* Retrieved from http://dx.doi.org/10.1103/PhysRevE.91.022811.

WFP/World Food Programme. (n.d.). Retrieved from https://www.wfp.org/hunger/glossary.

Wolpert, L. (1992). *The Unnatural Nature of Science.* Cambridge: Harvard University Press.

World Commission on Environment and Development. (1987). Our Common Future. Retrieved from http://www.un-documents.net/our-common-future.pdf.

World Health Organization (WHO). (2002). World report on violence and health. Geneva: World Health Organization.

York Institute/York Institute of Health Research. (n.d.). Retrieved from http://yihr.abel.yorku.ca/peu/?page_id=5.

Zvekic, U. (2015). Organised crime and corruption in the context of development. In *Vienna Vision: Peaceful, Inclusive, Prosperous and Sustainable World*, ed. M. Dimitrijević, 44–49. Vienna: Academic Council on the United Nations System.

Preventing Violence against Children
The UN Model Strategies

2

YVON DANDURAND

Contents

Learning Outcomes
After reading this chapter, you should understand

- The many ways in which children can be victims of violence and why the prevention of **violence against children** must be a priority for action
- The important roles of the **criminal justice system** and the **child protection system** in preventing violence against children
- That children are also victims of violence as a result of their involvement in the criminal justice system
- That proactive, comprehensive, context-specific, and sustainable prevention measures are required to address the complex and multidimensional risk factors that increase the vulnerability of children to different forms of neglect, exploitation, and violence

Introduction

> Every society, no matter its cultural, economic or social background, can and must stop violence against children.
>
> **United Nations**
> *2006, p. 5*

Violence against children takes many different forms: neglect, physical and emotional abuse, infanticide, sexual abuse, rape, trafficking, torture, inhuman and degrading treatment or punishment, forced and child marriage, killings in the name of honor, forced labor, and many others (United Nations 2006). It takes place in every setting, including those where children ought to be safe—at home, in schools, or in care institutions.

Violence against children has serious and damaging consequences in childhood, adolescence, and throughout adulthood. These consequences have far-reaching social, emotional, and economic costs to individuals, families, and communities (Teten Tharp et al. 2012; United Nations 2006). For children who survive violence, the experience can have lifelong adverse health, social, and economic consequences, including disability from physical injury, a deterioration of physical and mental health, and an increase in risk behavior and exposure to further violence. The Adverse Childhood Experiences study, a large-scale investigation of the associations between childhood maltreatment and later-life health and well-being in the United States, provides clear evidence of the impact of child abuse and mistreatment, or **adverse childhood experience**, on the future health and quality of life of the children (Edwards et al. 2005).

Most countries lack the necessary data gathering mechanisms to properly document the prevalence of violence against children (World Health Organization [WHO] 2006). Offenses against children are often unreported to the authorities or are only reported after substantial delays. Surveys of children are complicated by methodological and ethical challenges (UNICEF 2014b, 2015b). Yet, when the data exist, they usually reveal how incredibly widespread the problem is (UNICEF 2014b). In India, for example, a national government survey involving 17,000 children and adults found that 50% of children reported emotional abuse, 66% reported physical abuse, and 53% of them reported sexual abuse (Kacker et al. 2007).

The 2006 World Report on Violence against Children provided an alarming global picture of violence against children (Pinheiro 2006). The study confirmed, if that was necessary, the magnitude and impact of violence against children. Its main message, however, was that violence against children is preventable (Pinheiro 2006, p. 6).* Preventing the victimization of children through all available means must be recognized as a priority. The multidimensional nature of violence against children calls for a multifaceted response and complementary strategies to respond to the diverse manifestations of violence in the many settings in which it occurs—in private and in public life; in the home, the workplace, educational and training institutions, and the community; within the criminal justice system (CJS); or in situations of armed conflict or natural disaster. For example, according to a recent national victimization study conducted in Canada, just under one-third of Canadians reported experiencing some form of abuse at the hands of an adult before the age of 15. These abused individuals reported violent victimization rates that were more than double those of people who did not experience child maltreatment (Perreault 2015).

As was reported to the Human Rights Council by the Special Representative of the Secretary General on Violence against Children (SRSGVAC):

> Countless girls and boys of all ages continue to be exposed to the cumulative impact of different forms of violence as a result of reactive, ill-coordinated and ill-resourced national strategies; dispersed and poorly enforced

---

* The report also contains several general recommendations concerning the prevention of violence against children.

legislation; and low levels of investment in family support and gender- and child-sensitive approaches and mechanisms to support child victims and fight impunity.

SRSGVAC
2014, p. 6

Many countries have adopted laws that define and condemn various forms of violence against children as serious crimes, but not all of them have insured that the police and other criminal justice institutions actually take these crimes seriously and accept their respective responsibilities with respect to child protection and the prevention of violence against children. Reducing violent crimes against children is not always identified as a crime prevention or policing priority (Dandurand 2014). Law enforcement and criminal justice institutions, however, have yet to strengthen their efforts to prevent violence against children and to increase their diligence in investigating, convicting, and rehabilitating perpetrators of violent crimes against children.

This chapter reviews some of the key prevention strategies identified during the consultation process that led to the recent adoption of the *United Nations Model Strategies and Practical measure on the Elimination of Violence against Children in the Field of Crime Prevention and Criminal Justice* (hereinafter the Model Strategies) (United Nations 2014b). This may convince the readers of the importance of implementing evidence-based, comprehensive, and multisectoral prevention strategies and policies to address the factors that give rise to violence against children and expose them to the risk of violence.

Proactive Prevention of All Forms of Violence against Children: A State Obligation

States have the duty to take appropriate measures to effectively protect children from all forms of violence. Article 19 of the 1989 *Convention on the Rights of the Child* (CRC) requires State parties to "take all appropriate legislative, administrative, social and educational measures to protect the child from all forms of physical or mental violence, injury or abuse, neglect or negligent treatment, maltreatment or exploitation, including sexual abuse, while in the care of parent(s), legal guardian(s) or any other person who has the care of the child." The Convention establishes the State's obligation to protect children against all kinds of violence and to prevent such violence. It implies a duty on the part of the CJS, among others, to prevent violence against children.

One may argue that when the CRC was adopted, there still prevailed a deep-rooted scepticism about the willingness, capacity, and ability of the police and other criminal justice institutions to intervene competently, sensitively, and effectively in the often delicate situations involving violence against children (Dandurand 2014). Since a lot of the violence occurs in private settings, such as the family, these institutions often resisted the idea of getting involved in these situations. The same was true then of the perception of the CJS's role in responding more generally to domestic violence (see Chapter 5). However, societal expectations are changing and many countries now recognize the unique and crucial role the CJS must play in preventing and responding to violence against children.

In fact, since the adoption of the CRC, other international conventions and protocols were also adopted that called for the criminalization of various forms of violence against children and concurrently created an obligation for law enforcement and criminal justice institutions to prevent, investigate, punish, and otherwise control these crimes. This was the case, for example, of *Optional Protocol to the Convention on the Rights of the Child on the sale of children, child prostitution and child pornography** and the *Protocol to Prevent, Suppress and Punish Trafficking in Persons, Especially Women and Children.*†

The United Nations Committee on the Rights of the Child summarized the States' obligations to prevent violence against children as follows:

> (...) child protection must begin with proactive prevention of all forms of violence as well as explicitly prohibit all forms of violence. States have the obligation to adopt all measures necessary to ensure that adults responsible for the care, guidance and upbringing of children will respect and protect children's rights. Prevention includes public health and other measures to positively promote respectful child-rearing, free from violence, for all children, and to target the root causes of violence at the levels of the child, family, perpetrator, community, institution and society.

Committee on the Rights of the Child
2011, paragraph 46

Every component of the CJS needs to review and revise its policies and practices with respect to its response to violence against children. In particular, the police need to reevaluate their own response to the problem. A very small proportion of child abuse cases come to the attention of the police, but the number of cases will continue to increase over time (HMIC 2015b). Police forces are just beginning to tackle child protection cases while trying at the same time to respond to the increasing numbers of nonrecent cases of abuses that are increasingly being reported (HMIC 2015a). An inspection

---

* Optional Protocol to the Convention on the Rights of the Child on the sale of children, child prostitution and child pornography, General Assembly resolution 54/263, Annex II.
† Protocol to Prevent, Suppress and Punish Trafficking in Persons, Especially Women and Children, supplementing the United Nations Convention against Transnational Organized Crime, General Assembly resolution 55/25, Annex II.

into how police forces deal with the online sexual exploitation of children conducted in England and Wales by the Inspector of Constabulary (HMIC) highlighted how the prevention of child sexual exploitation in a virtual world requires a different style of policing from the conventional methods of the past (HMIC 2015b). As the HMIC report warns: "(the) dangers in the virtual world are now part of the everyday risk to children. There is a lack of recognition that dealing with these risks is already part of everyday policing" (HMIC 2015b, p. 40). Police services everywhere need to reconsider how they can protect and safeguard children who are being bullied, harassed, and exploited through online activities.

The United Nations Model Strategies

In December 2014, the United Nations General Assembly adopted the *United Nations Model Strategies and Practical Measures on the Elimination of Violence against Children in the Field of Crime Prevention and Criminal Justice* (United Nations 2014b) (also see Chapter 1 for more detail). As stated in the instrument itself, the Model Strategies were formulated in order to help States address the need for integrated violence prevention and child protection strategies and offer children the protection to which they have an unqualified right. The Model Strategies affirm the complementary roles of the justice system, on the one hand, and the child protection, social welfare, health and education sectors, on the other, in creating a **protective environment** and in preventing and responding to violence against children (Dandurand 2015a).

The Model Strategies use the same broad definition of violence against children as that found in article 19 of the CRC mentioned above. The main purpose of this new international instrument is to offer a comprehensive and practical framework to assist governments in the review of national laws, procedures, and practices to ensure that they effectively prevent and respond to violence against children and fully respect the rights of child victims of violence in accordance with the CRC and other relevant human rights standards.

Taking into account the high risk faced by children in conflict with the law, especially those who are deprived of their liberty, the Model Strategies also identify measures to prevent the victimization of children in contact with the CJS, as accused, offenders, victims, or witnesses. In that respect, the Model Strategies are meant to guide the review of laws, policies, and procedures, as necessary, to ensure compliance with international standards and ensure that the process of juvenile justice and criminal justice reform is framed by a child- and gender-sensitive approach. With respect to perpetrators of violence against children, the Model Strategies involve ensuring that decisions on the arrest, detention, and terms of any form of release of an alleged perpetrator of violence against a child take into account the need for the safety of the child.

As discussed at greater length in Chapter 2, the new instrument proposes a total of 17 strategies organized into three distinct groups: general prevention strategies to address violence against children as part of broader child protection and crime prevention initiatives, strategies and measures to improve the ability of the CJS to respond to crimes of violence against children and to protect child victims effectively, and strategies and measures to prevent and respond to violence against children in contact with the justice system.

The Model Strategies can be used to assess the present situation in a country or the progress made in improving the criminal justice response to violence against children. In fact, a checklist based on the Model Strategies has been developed and is now available from the United Nations Office on Drugs and Crime (UNODC) (Dandurand 2015b). The Model Strategies are expected to encourage practitioners and researchers to explore and test different ways of implementing the proposed measures, evaluate their impact, and share information and best practices.

Prohibiting Violence against Children

A first essential strategy (*Model Strategy I*) consists of prohibiting all forms of violence against children. The establishment of a sound legal framework that prohibits violence against children and empowers authorities to respond appropriately to incidents of violence is obviously important. The strategy involves formally prohibiting cruel, inhumane, or degrading treatment or punishment of children in all settings, something that is already an obligation for State parties to the CRC, but not necessarily criminalizing all forms of violence.

At the same time, the strategy also involves revising all laws (including criminal procedure law) to remove any provision that justifies, allows for, or condones violence against children or may increase the risk of violence against children.* For example, a recent UNICEF study analyzing domestic laws relating to violence against children in ASEAN countries documented the numerous legal exceptions that apply to violence against children in the context of relationships (e.g., parent–child, teacher–pupil, and husband–wife) that effectively deny children legal protection from violence (UNICEF 2015a). It revealed age-based and gender-based legal provisions that are incompatible with the rights of the child and deprive children of the legal protection they would be entitled to if they were adults.

---

* These are areas where Parliamentarians can play a very important role (see Inter-Parliamentary Union and UNICEF 2007).

BOX 2.1   PREVALENCE OF FEMALE GENITAL MUTILATION/CUTTING

UNICEF estimated that more than 125 million women in 29 countries have been victims of genital mutilation or cutting. It identified eight countries in which more than 80% of girls and women of reproductive age have been cut: Somalia (98%), Guinea (96%), Djibouti (93%), Egypt (91%), Eritrea (89%), Mali (89%), Sierra Leone (88%), and Sudan (88%). It identified a further five countries in which FGM/C prevalence are between 51% and 80%: Gambia (76%), Burkina Faso (76%), Ethiopia (74%), Mauritania (69%), and Liberia (66%) (UNICEF 2013b).

Criminalizing Specific Forms of Violence against Children

Specific forms of violence against children must be criminalized, including the following: engaging in sexual activities with a child; sexual abuse; sexual exploitation and sexual harassment; abuses facilitated by the use of new information technologies; the sale of or trafficking in children; forced labor; offering, obtaining, procuring, or providing a child for prostitution; forced marriage; or genital mutilation (see Box 2.1).

The criminalization of some of these conducts is already required by the CRC or another convention or protocol to which States may be a party. For example, article 35 of the CRC states that: "States Parties shall take all appropriate national, bilateral and multilateral measures to prevent the abduction of, the sale of or traffic in children for any purpose or in any form," and similar criminalization requirements are found in the following: article 1 of the Optional Protocol to the Convention on the Rights of the Child on the sale of children, child prostitution and child pornography; the Protocol to Prevent, Suppress and Punish Trafficking in Persons, Especially Women and Children, supplementing the United Nations Convention against Transnational Organized Crime; article 18 of the Council of Europe 2007 Convention on the Protection of Children against Sexual Exploitation and Sexual Abuse; and article 3 of the Convention Concerning the Prohibition and Immediate Action for the Elimination of the Worst Forms of Child Labour.*

Prohibition of Harmful Practices

Countless number of girls and boys fall victim to harmful practices undertaken under different pretexts or grounds, including female genital mutilation

---

* *Convention Concerning the Prohibition and Immediate Action for the Elimination of the Worst forms of Child Labour,* 1999 (No. 182), International Labour Organization.

or cutting, forced marriage, breast ironing, and witchcraft rituals. A comprehensive prohibition of all forms of violence against children must specifically target all harmful practices against children. This must be supported by detailed provisions in relevant legislation to secure the effective protection of girls and boys from those practices, to provide means of redress, and to fight impunity. This particular aspect of the strategy is controversial in many parts of the world because it essentially affirms the supremacy of international human rights law over cultural, traditional, and sometimes religious practices (Dandurand 2014).

What is particularly important is the removal from national legislation of any legal provisions that justify or allow for consent to harmful practices against children. It is also necessary to ensure that resorting to informal justice systems does not jeopardize children's rights or preclude child victims from accessing the formal justice system (SRSGVAC and Plan International 2012, p. 40). What are also necessary are legislative and other measures to ensure the effective and sometimes proactive investigation of incidents and to establish the responsibility of perpetrators of harmful practices against children.

Improper disciplinary practices in the home and the use of corporal punishment at home and in schools are other examples of problematic practices. UNICEF's recent statistical analysis of violence against children revealed that the use of violent discipline in the home was widespread in most of the 42 countries it surveyed (UNICEF 2014b). In six of the seven countries surveyed in the East Asia-Pacific region, more than two-thirds of children had experienced violent discipline in the home (Kilbanem 2013; UNICEF 2014c). In the schools of many countries, corporal punishment is a persistent problem, even when the practice has been banned completely. This indicates that when dealing with well-established cultural practices, a legal prohibition in itself is often not sufficient to abolish the practice completely. Other means are also necessary in order to actively enforce the ban and ensure compliance with the law (Veriava 2014).

Corporal punishment at home and in the school is viewed very differently across cultures (UNICEF 2014b). Rules or expectations of behavior within a cultural or social group can encourage violence. Effective prevention requires an understanding of the norms that govern a society or a community. It also requires interventions that challenge cultural and social norms supportive of violence (WHO 2010). As Fairholm and Singh (2010) observed, "culture has been used throughout history as an excuse to hurt children" (p. 11). Efforts to denounce these cultural excuses and justifications continue to face barriers of disbelief, denial, and outright opposition (see Box 2.2).

The United Kingdom and other countries have adopted legal measures to prohibit and prevent such practices.* In Canada, for example, a new law came

---

* For example, in the United Kingdom: the *Anti-social Behaviour, Crime and Policing Act 2014*, 2014 Chapter 12, sections 120–121.

BOX 2.2   CHILD AND FORCED MARRIAGES

Some estimates of child marriage globally suggest that, each year, as many as 14.2 million girls are married before the age of 18, and that as much as one-third of these marriages are entered into before the age of 15 (UNICEF 2014a; United Nations Population Fund 2012). Child marriage overwhelmingly affects young women and girls, and victims of child marriage are often subjected to significant harms, including early sexualization, maternal health problems, a lack of sexual and reproductive freedom, increased risk of intimate partner violence, and other significant health and social consequences (Fonteneau and Huyse 2014; Godha et al. 2013; Raj and Boehmer 2013; Sabbe et al. 2015).

The issue of child marriages is particularly sensitive in migrant-receiving Western nations, where policymakers struggle to balance the need to address the problem of forced and child marriage internally—which is increasingly portrayed as a "cultural" problem, imported by immigrants—and their national values of multiculturalism and inclusion (Anis et al. 2013; Fonteneau and Huyse 2014; Gill and Van Engeland 2014). On the one hand, child marriage is widely identified as an expression of deeply embedded social norms and gender-based discrimination, patriarchy, male domination, and stereotypical gender roles (Anis et al. 2013; Fonteneau and Huyse 2014; Gangoli et al. 2006; Greene 2014; Jain and Kurz 2007; UNFPA 2012; UNICEF 2014a). On the other hand, whenever one refers to cultural values and practices, one may expect some defensive posturing on the part of various individuals, groups, and communities and may understandably fear ostracism and other repercussions when such cultural practices are denounced (Bokhary and Kelly 2010).

into force in 2015 that amended the *Immigration and Refugee Protection Act*, the *Civil Marriage Act*, and the *Criminal Code of Canada*.* The law established a new national minimum age for marriage of 16, below which no marriage is lawful. It created a new offense prohibiting the active and knowing participation in a forced marriage ceremony by any person. However, such legal measures must be reinforced by other education and advocacy measures that can successfully challenge the values, attitudes, and beliefs that condone and justify this form of violence against children (Phillips 2012; UNFPA 2012; UNICEF 2013b).

---

* An Act to Amend the Immigration and Refugee Protection Act, the Civil Marriage Act and the Criminal Code and to Make Consequential Amendments To other Acts, S.C. 2015, c. 29.

Comprehensive and Context-Specific Prevention Programs

A second broad strategy (*Model Strategy II*) consists of developing and implementing comprehensive prevention programs and action plans. States are called upon to play a leadership role in developing effective crime prevention strategies and in creating and maintaining institutional frameworks for their implementation and review. This emphasizes the important role of criminal justice agencies, working together with child protection, social welfare, health and education agencies, and civil society organizations to develop comprehensive and effective violence prevention programs. In that regard, the Committee on the Rights of the Child (2011) explained that prevention includes public health and other measures to positively promote respectful child-rearing, free from violence, for all children, and to target the root causes of violence at the levels of the child, family, perpetrator, community, institution, and society.

The participation of children in the development of prevention strategies is crucial. In that regard, the Committee on the Rights of the Child (2009b) also stressed the importance of consulting children in the formulation of legislation and policy related to these and other problem areas and involved in the drafting, development, and implementation of related plans and programs.

Proactive, comprehensive, context-specific, and sustainable prevention measures are required to address the complex and multidimensional risk factors that increase the vulnerability of children to different forms of neglect, exploitation, and violence.* The Model Strategies identify a number of priorities for action that should be addressed in a prevention plan.

Preventing Violence against Children in Vulnerable Situations

The same model strategy also addresses the need to adopt special protection measures for groups of children that may be especially vulnerable. The Committee on the Rights of the Child (2003, 2006a,b, 2007, 2014) has often drawn attention to the need for special vigilance with respect to the risks of violence faced by various marginalized vulnerable groups of children (see Box 2.3). It also provided a long list of children in potentially vulnerable positions. In a given context, such a list may include, among others, children working or living on the streets, suffering from mental illness or a substance abuse disorder, seeking refuge from war or natural disasters, living with HIV/AIDS, or exposed to violence and harassment because of their sexual identity (Dandurand 2014).

---

* See also Committee on the Rights of the Child (2011, paragraph 72); UNICEF, UNHCR, Save the Children and World Vision (2013); WHO (2006).

> ### BOX 2.3   INFORMATION TECHNOLOGY
> ### AND VIOLENCE AGAINST CHILDREN
>
> A recent study on the effects of new information technologies revealed the extent to which the expansion of availability and accessibility of information and communication technologies created distinct threats to children's safety (UNODC 2014). These technologies have become instrumental in the commercial sexual exploitation of children, and they have created new threats in the forms of cyber-enticement and solicitation, cyber-bullying, cyber-harassment, and cyber-stalking. These new threats dictate the adoption of specific prevention measures and point at the important role that the private sector must play in such initiatives.

The Risk of Violence against Children Committed by Children

Keeping in mind that children and youth are themselves the most frequent victims of youth violence, it stands to reason that a comprehensive strategy must also focus on preventing youth violence by addressing known risk factors and implementing evidence-based prevention programs (WHO 2015).

The problem of child sexual exploitation in gangs and in groups, for example, deserves special attention. For instance, in the United Kingdom, the Office of the Children's Commissioner conducted a two-year inquiry that identified several factors that can increase a child's vulnerability to being sexually exploited in gangs or in groups (Berelowitz et al. 2012). These include living in a chaotic or dysfunctional household; a history of abuse; physical and emotional abuse and neglect; experiencing a recent bereavement or loss; and in cases of sexual exploitation in a street gang, gang association either through relatives, peers, or intimate relationships, or living in a gang neighborhood.

There are certain features of gang-associated sexual violence and exploitation that are unique to, or exacerbated by, the gang environment, including the following: sex used as a means of initiating young people into a gang; sexual activity in return for (perceived) status or protection; young women "setting up" people in other gangs; establishing a relationship with, or feigning sexual interest in, a rival gang member as a means of entrapment; rape; and so on (Beckett et al. 2012). Incidents of gang-associated sexual violence and exploitation are rarely reported.

The Recruitment in Gangs and Extremist Groups

Measures to prevent the recruitment of children and youth into violent youth gangs or extremist groups are also necessary (Howell 2010). A review of 14 impact evaluation studies of gang projects conducted across Canada identified three models in particular that should be considered for replication in communities that experience youth gang issues. They involved comprehensive social integration interventions through targeted outreach (National Crime Prevention Centre 2007; Smith-Moncrieffe 2013). In the United States, the 2007 report of the Office of Juvenile Justice and Delinquency Prevention introduced a gang prevention model based on a balanced approach encompassing prevention, intervention, and suppression activities (Office of Juvenile Justice and Delinquency Prevention 2007). Some of the prevention programs, particularly the early prevention measures targeting youth at risk, could also be adapted and included in initiatives to prevent the radicalization of youth and their recruitment by extremist networks and groups (Dandurand 2015c).

Violence in Schools

In schools, it is often necessary to adopt measures to protect children from the violent and exploitative behavior of other children and from various forms of bullying. Educators and school psychologists have also reflected on rights-based frameworks to protect children within schools (Fiorvanti and Brassard 2014). Training programs are developed to equip teachers with the necessary ability and competence to detect and respond to abuse and neglected children (Baginsky and MacPherson 2005; Kenny 2004; Fayez et al. 2015). A fair amount of research has also been conducted on how to prevent bullying in schools; the lessons learned through this research were synthesized by the National Crime Prevention Centre (2008), which concluded that a "whole-school" approach is an effective and lasting approach to prevent bullying in schools (see Box 2.4).

A project of the Indian Red Cross Society in partnership with the Canadian Red Cross in Tamil Nadu, India, offers an example of children and youth involvement in a violence prevention strategy developed for school settings (Indian Red Cross Society and Canadian Red Cross 2015). It includes child protection committees made of teachers, police, parents, and youth; school codes of conduct; education of parents; and youth peer education.

**BOX 2.4   FREQUENCY OF BULLYING
IN THE UNITED STATES**

The U.S. Department of Health and Human Services (2014) reported that, nationwide, during the 12 months preceding the survey, 9.6% of students had been bullied on school property and 14.8% of students had been electronically bullied, including being bullied through e-mail, chat rooms, instant messaging, websites, or texting.

Preventing Child Trafficking and Commercial Sexual Exploitation

Specific prevention measures are also required to prevent the violence associated with trafficking in children, and various forms of exploitation of children by criminal groups should be addressed by specific prevention measures, including measures to prevent the following:

- The recruitment, use, and victimization of children by criminal groups, terrorist entities, or violent extremist groups
- The sale of children, trafficking in children, child prostitution, and child pornography
- The production, possession, and dissemination of images and all other materials that depict, glorify, or incite violence against children, including when perpetrated by children, particularly through information technologies, such as the Internet, in particular social networking environments

Prevention Planning

Model Strategy II also involves developing and implementing at every level of government comprehensive plans for the prevention of violence against children in its various forms based on in-depth analysis of the problem and incorporating best crime prevention practices. Considering the fact that a comprehensive approach is bound to require coordinated action at various levels (legislative, policymaking, training, monitoring, research, public education, etc.), effective engagement of relevant actors at all these levels is necessary.

A comprehensive plan of action should build on

- Well-defined responsibilities for the relevant institutions, agencies, and personnel involved in implementing preventive measures
- Appropriate coordination of preventive measures among government agencies and between governmental and nongovernmental agencies
- Reliance on evidence-based methods for effectively identifying, mitigating, and reducing the risk of violence against children
- Close interdisciplinary cooperation, with the involvement of all relevant agencies, civil society groups, local and religious leaders, and, where relevant, other stakeholders
- The participation of children and families in policies and programs for the prevention of criminal activities and victimization (United Nations 2014b)

In some instances, governments are incorporating measures to prevent violence against children in a plan to prevent gender-based violence (United Nations 2014a). In the United Kingdom, for example, preventive measures are taken on the basis of the 2010 strategy "Call to End Violence against Women and Girls" and related annual action plans.* In other countries and regions, specific plans have been adopted to counter violence against children (see SRSGVAC 2013b; also see League of Arab States 2014).

Public Education and Awareness Raising

The WHO (2010) systematically reviewed various violence prevention interventions with some evidence of effectiveness by types of violence prevented. A comprehensive prevention program invariably requires a broad public education and awareness raising campaign. Crime prevention and law enforcement organizations, in cooperation with educational institutions, nongovernmental organizations, relevant professional associations, and the media, can implement and support effective public awareness and public education initiatives that prevent violence against children by promoting respect for their rights and by educating their families and communities about the harmful impact of violence. Together, they can raise awareness of how to prevent and respond to violence against children among persons who have regular contact with children in the justice, child protection, social welfare, and health and education sectors and in areas relating to sport, culture, and leisure activities.

Mobilizing the Media

The media can contribute to community efforts to prevent and respond to violence against children and to promote changes in social norms that tolerate such violence. Media-led ethical guidelines can be formulated to ensure the child-friendly coverage of cases involving child victims, taking into consideration the child's right to privacy.

Challenging Harmful Practices

World Vision and Ipsos Reid conducted research around the world to better understand public attitudes and perceptions about violence against children and how to protect them. One of the main findings of this research was that there is often a discrepancy between what danger people think children are vulnerable to and what they are actually exposed to (World Vision and Ipsos

---

* See http://www.gov.uk/government/publications/ending-violence-against-women-and-girls -action-plan-2013.

Reid 2014). The survey illustrated the importance of changing perceptions, attitudes, and beliefs that have long allowed the problem to persist, and highlighted the imperative to invest in families as the most effective and powerful agents to prevent violence.

The 2006 United Nations study also referred to the need to challenge the societal acceptance of violence, which explains that, in too many instances, both children and perpetrators may accept physical, sexual, and psychological violence as inevitable and normal (United Nations 2006). Interventions that effectively challenge that societal acceptance have been widely used (WHO 2010). It is possible to involve children, their families, communities, relevant professionals, religious leaders, and criminal justice in discussing the impact and detrimental effects of violence against children and ways to prevent violence and eliminate harmful practices. In doing so, it is of course absolutely necessary to challenge attitudes that condone or normalize violence against children, including the tolerance and acceptance of corporal punishment and harmful practices, and the acceptance of violence.

Promoting Research and Data Collection, Analysis, and Dissemination

A third strategy (*Model Strategy III*) addresses the need to promote research and collect data on violence against children, including on violence against children in contact with the justice system. In most countries, the current situation is such that data of this kind are not only rare but also rarely reliable. The strategy identifies specific types of data and research that should be encouraged as a practical basis for developing evidence-based policies and interventions and for monitoring the success of existing programs (United Nations 2014b, paragraph 18). In the United States, for example, the National Center for Injury Prevention and Control has clearly demonstrated the value of surveillance systems that identify the prevalence and magnitude of various forms of violence against children (Teten Tharp et al. 2012).

Greater attention is needed to improving data collection on violence against children. For example, a UNICEF review of available data on violence against children in East Asia and the Pacific region confirmed that many countries of the region still have little to no data on violence against children and that this hinders policy and program development for the protection of children (UNICEF 2014b, p. 41).

The culture of silence that surrounds most forms of violence against children results in high levels of underreporting, exacerbating difficulties in collecting data. The 2012 Joint report of the SRSGVAC and the

Special Rapporteur on the Sale of Children, Child Prostitution and Child Pornography (SRSCCPCP) on "Safe and Child-sensitive Counselling, Complaint and Reporting Mechanisms to Address Violence against Children" recommended that "(d)ata and research should be strengthened to overcome the invisibility of violence and the persistent lack of information on the outcome of violence-related cases and to evaluate the impact of relevant initiatives on the children concerned. Children's views and experience should inform this process; (...)" (SRSGVAC and SRSCCPCP 2012, p. 23).

Establishing Effective Detection and Reporting Mechanisms

A fourth strategy (*Model Strategy IV*) involves the establishment of effective detection and reporting mechanisms as a core element of the child protection system. It is absolutely crucial to ensure that safe child- and gender-sensitive approaches, procedures, and complaint reporting and counseling mechanisms are established by law and are easily accessible to all children and their representative or a third party without fear of reprisal or discrimination (United Nations 2014b, paragraph 19d). The model strategy includes measures to ensure that criminal justice professionals are aware of risk factors and can recognize signs that a child is at risk, as well as measures to legally require professionals who routinely come into contact with children in the course of their work to notify appropriate authorities if they suspect that a child is or is likely to become a victim of violence.

A joint report of the SRSGVAC and the SRSCCPCP explained that "more often than not, children lack trust in available services, fearing they will not be believed and judged rather than listened to. They also frequently fear public exposure, stigmatization, harassment and reprisals if they make incidents of violence known. In most cases, children are unaware of the existence and role of counselling, reporting or complaint mechanisms" (SRSGVAC and SRSCCPCP 2012, p. 21).

Another measure included in this strategy consists of adopting legislation, if necessary, and working with Internet service providers, mobile phone companies, search engines, public Internet facilities, and others to facilitate the detection and the investigation of child pornography. The Internet is also significantly misused as a tool for the dissemination of acts of child abuse or exploitation.* Furthermore, law enforcement agencies need the human resources, technical capacity, and appropriate tools to thoroughly and effectively investigate such crimes.

---

* See Report of the SRSCCPCP (United Nations 2013).

Offering Effective Protection to Child Victims of Violence

Model Strategy V includes two groups of measures to ensure that the CJS does as much as it can, in collaboration with child protection agencies, to protect child victims of violence against further violence and do so while using **child-sensitive approaches**. In particular, it refers to the need to ensure that national standards, procedures, and protocols are developed and implemented in order to respond with sensitivity to child victims of violence who must be removed from a dangerous context and need temporary protection and care in a safe place pending a full determination of the best interests of the child. It also refers, among many other things, to the need to ensure that relevant authorities have the legal authority to issue and enforce protection measures such as restraining or barring orders in cases of violence against children, including removal of the perpetrator from the domicile, and prohibiting further contact with the victim, as well as to impose penalties for breaches of those orders.

Ensuring Effective Investigation and Prosecution of Incidents of Violence against Children

Model Strategy VI is about the effective investigation and prosecution of incidents of violence against children. In countries such as Canada where there is a broad social awareness of the problem and a fairly high level of confidence in the police, a large number of cases are typically reported to the police each year. For example, there were 14,000 children who were victims of a police-reported sexual offense in Canada in 2012 (Cotter and Beaupré 2014). In many cases, the victims delayed reporting the incident. In many other instances, the identification of the perpetrator is a relatively simple matter, but the gathering of sufficient evidence to proceed with charges is often an arduous and time-consuming task. The police must engage in proactive investigations regardless of whether an official complaint has been lodged by the child or someone else. The new instrument invites countries to adopt and implement policies and programs aimed at guiding all decisions concerning the investigation and prosecution of offenses of violence against children and ensuring the fairness, integrity, and effectiveness of such decisions.

Enhancing Cooperation among Various Sectors

Model Strategy VII acknowledges the complementary roles of the CJS and the child protection, health, education, and social service sectors and, in some cases, informal justice systems in creating a protective environment and preventing and responding to incidents of violence against children. The strategy consists of ensuring effective coordination and cooperation among these various systems and agencies and establishing stronger operational links, particularly in emergency situations, between these agencies while protecting the privacy of child victims of violence. However, it can often be challenging to ensure effective interagency and intersectorial cooperation. In many jurisdictions, that challenge is being addressed systematically, often through legislation and a formal clarification of the concerned agencies respective mandates.

In New Zealand, for example, the *Vulnerable Children Act 2014** and the Children's Action Plan both emphasize the importance of interagency cooperation and provide a framework for professionals from different sectors to work more closely together to protect children against violence. To support such effective collaboration, governments often have to provide statutory or other guidance such as that adopted in England and Wales (United Kingdom 2013).

Improving Criminal Proceedings in Matters Involving Child Victims of Violence

Because criminal proceedings can have a detrimental or even traumatic impact on child victims and witnesses, the United Nations adopted in 2005 the *Guidelines on Justice in Matters Involving Child Victims and Witnesses of Crime*.† It later produced a *Model Law on Justice in Matters Involving Child Victims and Witnesses of Crime* (UNODC 2009). In 2010, the Council of Europe adopted guidelines on child-friendly justice to help governments ensure that children are treated properly by and in the justice system (Kilkelly 2010).

Model Strategy VIII is largely inspired by these various instruments and suggests several measures that States should consider in developing legislation, procedures, policies, and practices for children who are victims of crime or witnesses in criminal proceedings.

Ensuring That Sentencing Reflects the Serious Nature of Violence against Children

Model Strategy IX is meant to ensure that the serious nature of violence against children is reflected in sentencing practices and that, in doing so,

---

* New Zealand, *Vulnerable Children Act 2014*, Public Act 2014, no. 40.
† Guidelines on Justice in Matters involving Child Victims and Witnesses of Crime, Economic and Social Council resolution 2005/20, annex.

courts have access to a full range of sentencing alternatives. The strategy, however, acknowledges the fact that many of the perpetrators of violence against children are themselves children and that the principle of the best interests of the child apply whether the child is a victim or perpetrator of violence. Some of the criminal justice practices applied to child perpetrators of violence against children can have a very detrimental impact on their social and psychological development. This is the case, for example, of the practice of placing children on a sex offender registry (Human Rights Watch 2013).

Strengthening Capacity and Training of Criminal Justice Professionals

Model Strategy X refers to a host of measures to build the capacity of the CJS and CJS professionals to respond more effectively to violence against children. Very importantly, however, it refers also to the need to develop specialized expertise among these professionals and to establish specialized teams and functions within the system. Specialized training is of course recommended (Penal Reform International 2013b). The strategy also includes measures that can be taken by professional associations.

Preventing and Responding to Violence against Children within the Justice System

A whole section of the Model Strategies relates to measures to prevent children from being victimized during their contacts with the justice system (including the juvenile justice system). This is because of the heightened risk of violence faced by children in conflict with the law. Considering that one important objective of the CJS is the protection of children's rights, violence against children within that system thwarts its achievement and is counterproductive to any efforts of rehabilitation and reintegration of the child (Dandurand 2014; OHCHR/UNODC/SRSG-VAC 2012). It is also very sad to observe that many children in conflict with the law were themselves victims of abuse or neglect (Representative for Children and Youth and Office of the Provincial Health Officer 2009).

In that regard, the Model Strategies emphasize the need to prevent children from becoming involved in the CJS, and it introduces a number of measures for preventing the risk of violence against children at various stages of their contacts with that system. Measures are proposed to limit the involvement of children in the justice system, prevent violence associated with law enforcement and prosecution activities, ensure that deprivation of liberty is only used as a measure of last resort, and prohibit violent, arbitrary, or inhumane punishment of children. Finally, the Model Strategies identifies oversight and accountability measures that are crucial to the prevention of violence against children within the justice system.

Model Strategy XI involves implementing measures to reduce the number of children in contact with the justice system (see Article 40(3)(b) of the CRC). In particular, **diversion** and restorative justice programs* are recommended. A report of the International NGO Council on Violence against Children adds that diversion should not be limited to minor or first-time offenses, but considered also wherever it would serve the best interest of the child (International NGO Council on Violence against Children 2013). With respect to indigenous children, the Committee on the Rights of the Child encourages States to "take all appropriate measures to support indigenous peoples to design and implement traditional restorative justice systems as long as those programmes are in accordance with the rights set out in the Convention, notably with the best interests of the child" (Committee on the Rights of the Child 2009a, paragraph 75).

Model Strategy XII is about the prevention of violence and mistreatment associated with law enforcement and prosecution activities. The UN Study on Violence against Children (United Nations 2006, p. 197) found that police and other security forces are often responsible for violence against children and that arrest is one of the situations in which this occurs. The "Five years on" follow-up study found that children are at high risk of violence from their first point of contact with the law (NGO Advisory Council 2011, p. 21). The strategy involves, among others things, ensuring that all arrests are conducted in conformity with the law, to limit the apprehension, arrest, and detention of children to situations in which these measures are necessary as a last resort, and to promote and implement, where possible, alternatives to arrest and detention. As part of this strategy, it is most important to ensure that children are informed of their rights and have prompt access to legal aid during police interrogation and while in police detention, and that they may consult their legal representative freely and fully confidentially. Article 37(d) of the CRC states that every child deprived of his or her liberty has a right to prompt access to legal and other appropriate assistance. The *United Nations Principles and Guidelines on Access to Legal Aid in Criminal Justice Systems* calls upon States to ensure that effective legal aid is provided promptly at all stages of the criminal justice process.[†]

---

* See, in that regard, the *Basic Principles on the Use of Restorative Justice Programmes in Criminal Matters*, Economic and Social Council resolution 2002/12, Annex. Also see UNODC 2006 and SRSG on Violence against Children 2013a.

[†] United Nations Principles and Guidelines on Access to Legal Aid in Criminal Justice Systems, Economic and Social Council resolution 2005/20, annex, Principle 7.

A very important strategy, reflecting a principle enshrined in the CRC, is *Model Strategy XIII*, which includes a number of measures to ensure that deprivation of liberty is used only as a measure of last resort and for the shortest appropriate period of time. Article 37(b) of the CRC stipulates that "the arrest, detention or imprisonment of a child shall be in conformity with the law and shall be used only as a measure of last resort and for the shortest appropriate period of time." Article 40(4) of the Convention stipulates that "a variety of dispositions, such as care, guidance and supervision orders; counselling; probation; foster care; education and vocational training programs and other alternatives to institutional care shall be available to ensure that children are dealt with in a manner appropriate to their well-being and proportionate both to their circumstances and the offence." The Committee on the Rights of the Child mentioned the need to prevent violence in care and justice settings by "inter alia, developing and implementing community-based services in order to make use of institutionalization and detention only as a last resort and only if in the best interest of the child" (Committee on the Rights of the Child 2011, paragraph 47). The Bangkok Rules also recommend avoiding the institutionalization of children in conflict with the law to the maximum extent possible and adds that, when making such decisions, the "gender-based vulnerability of juvenile female offenders shall be taken into account in decision-making."*

Alternatives to incarceration are particularly important in the case of aboriginal children who, as a group, are often overrepresented in detention facilities (Committee on the Rights of the Child 2009a, paragraph 74). In British Columbia, Canada, aboriginal children were found five times more likely to be incarcerated than youth in the general study population (Representative for Children and Youth and Office of the Provincial Health Officer 2009). A survey of youth in custody in that province in 2013 revealed that a little more than half of these youth were aboriginal (McCreary Centre 2013).

Model Strategy XIV reaffirms the prohibition against torture and other cruel, inhuman, or degrading treatment or punishment, while *Model Strategy XV* addresses the need to prevent and respond to violence against children in places of detention. Places of detention can be defined very broadly, and during the preparation of the new instrument, there were many references to the conditions of detention of irregular migrant or asylum-seeking children (Thomas and Devaney 2011) and, in other circumstances, the detention of children in military prisons (UNICEF 2013a). The strategy includes a large number of measures (e.g., reducing delays in criminal proceedings, shortening the length of pretrial detention, avoiding pretrial

---

* *United Nations Rules for the Treatment of Women Prisoners and Non-custodial Measures for Women Offenders* (Bangkok Rules), General Assembly resolution 65/229, annex, Rule 65.

detention, improving conditions of detention) that can be taken to prevent violence against children in places of detention, including measures to prevent overcrowding, to separate children from adults, and to ensure that all detention facilities adopt and implement child-sensitive policies, procedures, and practices, and to monitor compliance with them. It is also necessary to prohibit and effectively prevent the use of corporal punishment as a disciplinary measure, to adopt clear and transparent disciplinary policies and procedures that encourage the use of positive and educational forms of discipline, and to establish in law the duty of managers and personnel of detention facilities to record, review, and monitor every instance in which disciplinary measures or punishment are used (International NGO Council on Violence against Children 2013; Penal Reform International 2012a,b,c, 2013a,b).

Very importantly, the strategy refers to the strict measures needed to ensure that all alleged incidents of violence, including sexual abuse of children in a place of detention, are immediately reported and independently, promptly, and effectively investigated by appropriate authorities and, when well founded, effectively prosecuted. Finally, in view of the crucial importance of independent monitoring and inspection mechanisms, measures are recommended to ensure effective monitoring of, regular access to, and inspection of places of detention by independent bodies, human rights institutions, ombudspersons, or members of the judiciary, who are empowered to conduct unannounced visits, conduct interviews with children and staff in private, and investigate allegations of violence.

Model Strategy XVI addresses the need to detect, assist, and protect children victimized as a result of their involvement with the justice system as alleged or sentenced offenders. It refers, among other things, to the crucial importance of establishing complaint mechanisms for child victims of violence within the justice system that are safe, confidential, effective, and easily accessible. In accordance with the *Declaration of Basic Principles of Justice for Victims of Crime and Abuse of Power,* States must ensure that child victims and witnesses are provided with appropriate access to justice and fair treatment, restitution, compensation, and social assistance.* The International NGO Council on Violence against Children noted that "(t)he absence of meaningful complaint mechanism leaves children involved in the juvenile justice system with little recourse when violence is perpetrated against them. Children all too often have no avenue to draw attention to police or institutional violence other than through the police or institutions themselves"

---

* *Declaration of Basic Principles of Justice for Victims of Crime and Abuse of Power,* General Assembly resolution 40/34.

(International NGO Council on Violence against Children 2013, p. 24; see also Penal Reform International 2013c).

The last strategy in this group (*Model Strategy XVII*) concerns the strengthening of accountability and oversight mechanisms within the CJS. It includes a number of measures to take all appropriate measures to promote transparency and combat impunity and the tolerance of violence against children within the justice system, including awareness-raising programs, education, and effective prosecution of violent offenses committed against children within the justice system.

Conclusion

Although we have provided an overview of generally recognized violence prevention strategies, it must be acknowledged that hard evidence on the relative effectiveness of these strategies is often still lacking. The adoption of the Model Strategies created an opportunity for researchers and practitioners to begin to correct this situation. The new instrument is expected to encourage practitioners and researchers to explore and test different ways of implementing the proposed measures, evaluate their impact, and share information and best practices.

In September 2015, world leaders adopted the *2030 Agenda for Sustainable Development* (United Nations 2015). The agenda and its 17 sustainable development goals will inform national and international policy priorities at the highest level for the next 15 years. One of the specific targets identified in the agenda, under Goal 16, is to "end abuse, exploitation, trafficking and all forms of violence and torture against children" (target 16.2) and efforts will be made internationally to measure whether progress is being achieved toward that target. This, too, is a great opportunity to address the issue more systematically and to ensure that CJSs everywhere attack the task of preventing violence against children in a much more effective and coherent manner.

Glossary of Key Terms

Adverse childhood experience: An adverse childhood experience is a traumatic experience in a person's life occurring before the age of 18 that the person remembers as an adult.

Child protection system: The national legal framework, formal and informal structures, functions, and capacities to prevent and respond to violence against and abuse, exploitation, and neglect of children.

Child-sensitive approach: An approach that takes into consideration the child's right to protection and individual needs and views in accordance with the child's age and level of development.

Criminal justice system: The laws, procedures, professionals, authorities, and institutions that apply to victims, witnesses, and persons alleged as, accused of, or recognized as having infringed criminal law.

Diversion: A process for dealing with children alleged as, accused of, or recognized as having infringed criminal law as an alternative to judicial proceedings, with the consent of the child and the child's parents or legal guardian.

Protective environment: An environment conducive to ensuring to the maximum extent possible the survival and development of the child, including physical, mental, spiritual, moral, psychological, and social development, in a manner compatible with human dignity.

Violence against children: All forms of physical or mental violence, injury or abuse, neglect or negligent treatment, maltreatment, or exploitation against children, including sexual abuse.

Discussion Questions

1. What are the most common forms of violence against children? Can they all be prevented?
2. How could we improve the CJS efforts to prevent violence against children?
3. Why is it so important to challenge cultural values and beliefs that condone, tolerate, or promote violence against children? How can this be achieved?
4. In your own community, how would you recognize the children who are in the most vulnerable situations?
5. Why is it absolutely crucial to ensure that safe procedures and complaint, reporting, and counseling mechanisms are easily accessible to all children? Do such mechanisms exist in your community? Are they used?

Suggested Reading

UNICEF. (2014). *Hidden in Plain Sight—A Statistical Analysis of Violence against Children.* New York: UNICEF. http://files.unicef.org/publications/files/Hidden_in_plain_sight_statistical_analysis_EN_3_Sept_2014.pdf

UNODC. (2009). *Handbook for Professionals and Policymakers on Justice in Matters Involving Child Victims and Witnesses of Crime.* http://www.unodc.org/documents/justice-and-prison-reform/hb_justice_in_matters_professionals.pdf

UNODC. (2015). *Checklist to the United Nations Model Strategies and Practical Measures on the Elimination of Violence against Children in the Field of Crime Prevention and Criminal Justice.* http://www.unodc.org/documents/justice-and-prison-reform/14-08452_Ebook.pdf

Recommended Web Links

Special Representative of the Secretary General on Violence against Children. https://srsg.violenceagainstchildren.org/.

WHO. (2009). *Violence Prevention: The Evidence*. This report presents seven briefings on violence prevention and the available evidence on their impact. http://apps.who.int/iris/bitstream/10665/77936/1/9789241500845_eng.pdf?ua=1.

Acknowledgments

The author gratefully acknowledges the contribution of two research assistants: Sean Plecas and Ruben Timmerman.

References

Anis, M., Kananur, S., and Mattoo, D. (2013). *Who, If, When to Marry: The Incidence of Forced Marriage in Ontario*. Toronto: South Asian Legal Clinic of Ontario.

Baginsky, M., and MacPherson, P. (2005). Training teachers to safeguard children: Developing a consistent approach. *Child Abuse Review* 14: 317–330.

Beckett, H., Brodie, I., Factor, F., Melrose, M., Pearce, J., Pitts, J., Shuker, L., and Warrington, C. (2012). *Research into Gang-Associated Sexual Exploitation and Sexual Violence*. London: Office of the Children's Commissioner and University of Bedfordshire.

Berelowitz, S., Firmin, C., Edwards, G., and Gulyurtlu, S. (2012). "*I Thought I Was the Only One. The Only One in the World.*" *Interim Report. The Office of the Children's Commissioner's Inquiry into Child Sexual Exploitation in Gangs and Groups*. London: Office of the Children's Commissioner.

Bokhary, F., and Kelly, E. (2010). Child rights, culture and exploitation: UK experiences of child trafficking. In *Child Slavery Now*, ed. G. Craig, 145–159. London: The Policy Press.

Committee on the Rights of the Child. (2003). *General Comment No. 3—HIV/AIDS and the rights of the child*.

Committee on the Rights of the Child. (2006a). *General Comment No. 8—The right of the child to protection from corporal punishment and other cruel or degrading forms of punishment*.

Committee on the Rights of the Child. (2006b). *General Comment No. 9—The rights of children with disabilities*.

Committee on the Rights of the Child. (2007). *General Comment No. 10—Children's rights in juvenile justice*.

Committee on the Rights of the Child. (2009a). *General Comment No. 11—Indigenous children and their rights under the convention*.

Committee on the Rights of the Child. (2009b). *General Comment No. 12—The rights of the child to be heard*.

Committee on the Rights of the Child. (2011). *General Comment No. 13—The right of the child to freedom from all forms of violence*.

Committee on the Rights of the Child. (2014). *General Comment No. 18. Joint General Recommendation/General Comment No. 31 of the Committee on the Elimination of Discrimination against Women and No. 18 of the Committee on the Rights of the Child on Harmful Practices.*

Cotter, A., and Beaupré, P. (2014). Police-reported sexual offences against children and youth in Canada, 2012. *Juristat.* Ottawa: Canadian Centre for Justice Statistics.

Dandurand, Y. (2014). Article 19 of the CRC and the criminal justice system's duty to protect children against violence. *Canadian Journal of Children's Rights* 1(1): 44–84.

Dandurand, Y. (2015a). *Introducing the United Nations Model Strategies and Practical Measures on the Elimination of Violence against Children in the Field of Crime Prevention and Criminal Justice—A New Tool for Policymakers, Criminal Justice Officials and Practitioners.* UNODC and Thailand Institute of Justice. New York: United Nations.

Dandurand, Y. (2015b). *Planning the Implementation of the United Nations Model Strategies and Practical Measures on the Elimination of Violence against Children in the Field of Crime Prevention and Criminal Justice—A Checklist.* UNODC. New York: United Nations.

Dandurand, Y. (2015c). Social inclusion programmes for youth and the prevention of violent extremism. In *Countering Radicalisation and Violent Extremism among Youth to Prevent Terrorism*, eds. M. Lombardi et al., 23–26. Amsterdam: IOS Press.

Edwards, V.J., Anda, R.F., Dube, S.R., Dong, M., Chapman, D.F., and Felitti, V.J. (2005). The wide-ranging health consequences of adverse childhood experiences. In *Victimization of Children and Youth: Patterns of Abuse, Response Strategies*, eds. K. Kendall-Tackett and S. Giacomoni. 8.1–8.12. Kingston, NJ: Civic Research Institute.

Fairholm, J., and Singh, G. (2010). *Handbook on Preventing Violence against Children.* Ottawa: Canadian Red Cross.

Fayez, M., Takash, H.M., and Al-Zboon, E.K. (2015). Combating violence against children: Jordanian pre-service early childhood teachers' perceptions towards child abuse and neglect. *Early Childhood and Care* 184(9–10): 1485–1498.

Fiorvanti, C.M., and Brassard, M.R. (2014). Advancing child protection through respecting children's rights: A shifting emphasis for school psychology. *School Psychology Review* 43(4): 349–366.

Fonteneau, B., and Huyse, H. (2014). *Child and Forced Marriage: A Blind Sport in the Belgian Development Co-Operation?* Brussels, Belgium: Research Institute for Work and Society.

Gangoli, G., Razak, A., and McCarry, M. (2006). *Forced Marriage and Domestic Violence among South Asian Communities in North East England.* Bristol: University of Bristol and North Rock Foundation.

Gill, A.K., and Van Engeland, A. (2014). Criminalization or 'multiculturalism without culture'? Comparing British and French approaches to tackling forced marriage. *Journal of Social Welfare and Family Law* 36(3): 241–259.

Godha, D., Hotchkiss, D.R., and Gage, A.J. (2013). Association between child marriage and reproductive health outcomes and service utilization: A multi-country study from South Asia. *Journal of Adolescent Health* 52(5): 552–558.

Greene, M.E. (2014). *Ending Child Marriage in a Generation: What Research Is Needed?* New York: Ford Foundation.

HMIC. (2015a). *In Harm's Way: The Role of the Police in Keeping Children Safe.* London: Her Majesty's Inspector of Constabulary.

HMIC. (2015b). *Online and on the Edge: Real Risks in a Virtual World—An Inspection into How Forces Deal with the Online Sexual Exploitation of Children.* London: Her Majesty's Inspector of Constabulary.

Howell, J.C. (2010). Gang prevention: An overview of research and programs. *Juvenile Justice Bulletin.* Washington (DC): U.S. Department of Justice, OJJDP.

Human Rights Watch. (2013). *Raised on the Registry—The Irreparable Harm of Placing Children on Sex Offender Registries in the U.S.* Washington, DC: HRW.

Indian Red Cross Society and Canadian Red Cross. (2015). *Preventing Violence against Children and Youth as Part of Disaster Risk Reduction and Health Programs.* New Delhi and Ottawa: IRCS and CRC.

International NGO Council on Violence against Children. 2013. *Creating a non-violent juvenile justice system,* October 2013.

Inter-Parliamentary Union and UNICEF. (2007). *Eliminating Violence against Children.* Handbook for Parliamentarian No. 13. Geneva: IPU and UNICEF.

Jain, S., and Kurz, K. (2007). *New Insights on Preventing Child Marriage: A Global Analysis of Factors and Programs.* Washington, DC: International Center for Research on Women.

Kacker, L., Varadan, S., and Kumar, P. (2007). *Study on Child Abuse: India 2007.* New Delhi: Ministry of Women & Child Development, Government of India.

Kenny, M.C. (2004). Teachers' attitudes toward and knowledge of child maltreatment. *Child Abuse and Neglect* 28(12): 1311–1319.

Kilbanem, T. (2013). *Addressing Violence and Abuse—Global Data Collection on Child Discipline.* Bangkok: UNICEF EAPRO.

Kilkelly, U. (2010). *Guidelines on Child-Friendly Justice: A Summary.* Document prepared by the Directorate General of Human Rights and Legal Affairs, Council of Europe, Strasbourg, December 15, 2010.

League of Arab States. (2014). *The Comparative Arab Report on Implementing the Recommendations of the UN Secretary-General Study on Violence against Children.* Cairo: Secretariat General of the League of Arab States (LAS), Department of Family and Childhood–Social Affairs Sector.

McCreary Centre. (2013). *Time Out III—A Profile of BC Youth in Custody.* Vancouver: McCreary Centre Society, August 2013.

National Crime Prevention Centre (NCPC). (2007). *Addressing Youth Gang Problems: An Overview of Programs and Practices.* Ottawa: Public Safety Canada.

National Crime Prevention Centre (NCPC). (2008). *Bullying Prevention: Nature and Extent of Bullying in Canada.* Ottawa: Public Safety Canada.

NGO Advisory Council. (2011). *Five years on: A global update on violence against children.* A report from the NGO Advisory Council for follow-up to the UN Secretary-General's study on violence against children, October 2011.

Office of Juvenile Justice and Delinquency Prevention. (2007). *Best Practices to Address Community Gang Problems; The OJJDP's Comprehensive Gang Model.* Washington (DC): U.S. Department of Justice, Office of Justice Programs.

OHCHR/UNODC/SRSG-VAC. (2012). *Prevention of and responses to violence against children within the juvenile justice system* (Joint Report of the Office of the High Commissioner for Human Rights, the United Nations Office on Drugs and Crime and the Special Representative of the Secretary General on Violence against Children on prevention of and response to violence against children within the juvenile justice system, June 2012, A/HRC/21/25).

Penal Reform International. (2012a). *A Review of Law and Policy to Prevent and Remedy Violence against Children in Police and Pre-Trial Detention in Georgia.* London: Penal Reform International.

Penal Reform International. (2012b). *A Review of Law and Policy to Prevent and Remedy Violence against Children in Police and Pre-Trial Detention in Jordan.* London: Penal Reform International.

Penal Reform International. (2012c). *A Review of Law and Policy to Prevent and Remedy Violence against Children in Police and Pre-Trial Detention in Pakistan.* London: Penal Reform International.

Penal Reform International. (2013a). *A review of Laws and Policies to Prevent and Remedy Violence against Children in Police and Pre-Trial Detention in Bangladesh.* Dhaka: Penal Reform International and Bangladesh Legal Aid and Services Trust.

Penal Reform International. (2013b). *Protecting Children's Rights in Criminal Justice Systems: A Training Manual and Reference Point for Professionals and Policymakers.* London: PRI.

Penal Reform International. (2013c). *The Right of Children Deprived of Their Liberty to Make Complaints.* London: PRI.

Perreault, S. (2015). Criminal victimization in Canada, 2014. *Juristat.* Ottawa: Statistics Canada.

Phillips, R. (2012). Interventions against forced marriage: Contesting hegemonic narrative and minority practices in Europe. *Gender, Place and Culture* 19(1): 21–41.

Pinheiro, P.S. (2006). *World Report on Violence against Children* (by the Independent Expert for the United Nations Secretary-General's Study on Violence against Children). Geneva: United Nations.

Raj, A., and Boehmer, U. (2013). Girl child marriage and its association with national rates of HIV, maternal health, and infant mortality across 97 countries. *Violence against Women* 19(4): 536–551.

Representative for Children and Youth and Office of the Provincial Health Officer. (2009). *Kids, Crime and Care—Health and Well-being of Children in Care: Youth Justice Experiences and Outcomes.* Victoria, February 23, 2009.

Sabbe, A., Oulami, H., Hamzali, S., Oulami, N., Le Hjir, F.Z., Abdallaoui, M., and Leye, E. (2015). Women's perspectives on marriage and rights in Morocco: Risk factors for forced marriage in the Marrakech region. *Culture, Health & Sexuality* 17(2): 135–149.

Smith-Moncrieffe, D. (2013). *Youth gang prevention fund projects—What did we learn about what works in preventing gang involvement?—Research Report 2007–2012.* Ottawa: Public Safety Canada, National Crime Prevention Centre.

SRSGVAC (Special Representative of the Secretary General on Violence against Children). (2013a). *Promoting Restorative Justice for Children.* New York: United Nations.

SRSGVAC (Special Representative of the Secretary General on Violence against Children). (2013b). *Toward a World Free from Violence; Global Survey on Violence against Children*. New York: United Nations.

SRSGVAC. (2014). *Annual Report of the Special Representative of the Secretary-General on Violence against Children*, Human Rights Council, A/HRC/25/47, January 3, 2014.

SRSGVAC and Plan International. (2012). *Protecting Children from Harmful Practices in Plural Legal Systems with a Special Emphasis on Africa*. New York: Office of the Special Representative of the Secretary on Violence against Children.

SRSGVAC and SRSCCPCP. (2012). *Safe and Child-Sensitive Counselling, Complaint and Reporting Mechanisms to Address Violence against Children*. Geneva: UNOHCHR.

Teten Tharp, A., Simon, T.R., and Saul, J. (2012). Preventing violence against children and youth. *Journal of Safety Research* 43: 291–298.

Thomas, N., and Devaney, J. (2011). Safeguarding refugee and asylum-seeking children. *Child Abuse Review* 20: 307–310.

UNICEF. (2013a). *Children in Israeli Military Detention—Observations and Recommendation*. Jerusalem, February 2013.

UNICEF. (2013b). *Female Genital Mutilation/Cutting: A Statistical Overview and Exploration of the Dynamics of Change*. New York: United Nations Children's Fund.

UNICEF. (2014a). *Ending Child Marriage: Progress and Prospects*. New York: United Nations Children's Fund, Division of Data, Research and Policy.

UNICEF. (2014b). *Hidden in Plain Sight—A Statistical Analysis of Violence against Children*. New York: UNICEF.

UNICEF. (2014c). *Violence against Children in East Asia and the Pacific—A Regional Review and Synthesis of Findings*. Bangkok: UNICEF EAPRO.

UNICEF. (2015a). *Legal Protection from Violence: Analysis of Domestic Laws Relating to Violence against Children in ASEAN Countries*. Bangkok: UNICEF EAPRO.

UNICEF. (2015b). *Manual for the Measurement of Indicators of Violence against Children*. New York: UNICEF.

UNICEF, UNHCR, Save the Children, and World Vision. (2013). *A better way to protect ALL children: The theory and practice of child protection systems*, Conference Report, New York: UNICEF.

United Kingdom. (2013). *Working Together to Safeguard Children: A Guide to Interagency Working to Safeguard and Promote the Welfare of Children*. London: HM Government, March 2013.

United Nations. (2006). *Report of the Independent Expert for the United Nations Study on Violence against Children*. A/61/299, August 29, 2006.

United Nations. (2013). *Report of the Special Rapporteur on the Sale of Children, Child Prostitution and Child Pornography*, Najat Maalla M'jid, A/HRC/25/48, December 23, 2013.

United Nations. (2014a). *National Measures Taken to Prevent, Investigate, Prosecute and Punish Gender-Related Killings of Women and Girls*. E/CN.15/2014/CRP.4

United Nations. (2014b). *United Nations Model Strategies and Practical Measures on the Elimination of Violence against Children in the Field of Crime Prevention and Criminal Justice*. General Assembly resolution 69/194.

United Nations. (2015). *Transforming Our World: The 2030 Agenda for Sustainable Development*. General Assembly resolution 70/1. A/RES/70/1.

United Nations Population Fund (UNFPA). (2012). *Marrying Too Young—End Child Marriage*. New York: United Nations.

UNODC. (2006). *Handbook on Restorative Justice Programmes*. New York: United Nations.

UNODC. (2009). *Justice in Matters Involving Child Victims and Witnesses of Crime— Model Law and Commentary*. New York: United Nations.

UNODC. (2014). *Study Facilitating the Identification, Description and Evaluation of the Effects of New Information Technologies on the Abuse and Exploitation of Children*, E/CN.15/2014/CRP.

U.S. Department of Health and Human Services. (2014). *Youth Risk Behavior Surveillance—United States, 2013*, Surveillance Summaries/Vol. 63/No. 4.

Veriava, F. (2014). *Promoting Effective Enforcement of the Prohibition against Corporal Punishment in South African Schools*. Pretoria: Pretoria University Law Press.

World Health Organization (WHO). (2006). *Preventing Child Maltreatment: A Guide to Taking Action and Generating Evidence*. Geneva: World Health Organization.

World Health Organization (WHO). (2010). *Violence Prevention—The Evidence*. Geneva: World Health Organization.

World Health Organization (WHO). (2015). *Preventing Youth Violence: An Overview of the Evidence*. Geneva: World Health Organization.

World Vision and Ipsos Reid. (2014). *Fearing Wrong. Why What Doesn't Scare Us Should*. Uxbridge (UK): World Vision.

Crime Prevention and Transportation Systems

3

NEREA MARTEACHE
GISELA BICHLER

Contents

Learning Outcomes
After reading this chapter, you should be able to

- Discuss how the Pareto principle helps us understand crime concentration
- Estimate the likelihood that crime incidents occur on any segment of a transportation system
- Describe how international crime problems can be resolved with collaborative multijurisdictional efforts
- Be able to determine the scope of a transportation related crime and to identify its unique set of challenges

Introduction

> Transportation is the center of the world! It is the glue of our daily lives. When it goes well, we don't see it. When it goes wrong, it negatively colors our day, makes us feel angry and impotent, curtails our possibilities.
>
> **Robin Chase**
> *Founder and CEO of Buzzcar, co-founder and former CEO of Zipcar, Forbes*
> *June 22, 2012*

> I would like, if I may, to take you on a strange journey.
>
> **The Criminologist:** *The Rocky Horror Picture Show*
> *1975*

Think about the places you went to last week, and how you got there. You may have walked down the street to get a cup of coffee; maybe you drove your car to work or commuted via train or subway; perhaps, you flew across country for a family reunion. In order to get where you needed to be, you used a transportation system. Some systems are completely public, such as the subway; others involve a mix of public and privately controlled vehicles and channels (i.e., driving your car [privately owned] on a public street). Sometimes, our journeys require us to use multiple transportation modalities. For example, you may walk to a bus stop, take the bus to the subway, and then, from a subway station, you catch a taxi to the airport. In this example, the trip also involves different systems (i.e., public transit system composed of buses and a subway, and commercial systems such as air travel).

Transportation systems are also critical to the movement of objects and, as such, are pivotal to all of our economic systems. Look around your home or office. Did you create all of the objects within reach? It is more likely that many of the items were produced somewhere else, perhaps, on the other side of the world. Unless you live and work on a farm, or an island, which is completely self-sufficient, at some point you will need to obtain supplies, whether directly from a store or indirectly by placing an order online. To reach you, objects need to move. This is an essential feature of modern economies. Industry needs to bring products to market. If a supply chain breaks down, the economy collapses. Simply stated, to exist in this modern age, we need functional transportation systems: they glue social systems together and enable us to exist in our modern consumer-based economy.

Disruptions in Transportation Systems Erode Public Trust

Despite our best efforts to design, implement, and maintain transportation systems, the flow of goods and people can be disrupted in different ways:

- Delays: materials and people often have to transfer to other lines or systems while on route and delays may create domino effects, causing backlogs along several legs of the system
- Damage: materials may arrive broken, requiring repair or replacement
- Loss/casualties: people may be injured or killed and materials may be destroyed
- Diversion: materials and people do not reach their intended destination

Crime is one of the factors that can disrupt the flow of people/goods. Copper wire theft, having reached almost "epidemic" proportions in some parts of the world (Koba 2013), is an excellent example. When thieves steal the copper wire from train switches and signal gear, freight and commuter rail stop, leading to delays. Some other examples of crime that can lead to service disruptions and affect public perception of safety in the transportation system are fare evasion, vandalism, pickpocketing, luggage theft, and passenger-on-passenger assaults. In some cases, the system itself can enable crime. For example, a pickpocket may ride the train during busy commuting times, taking wallets with impunity, and moving with the flow of people to avoid detection, or ducking into the crowd to evade arrest. When crime happens on the system, while the system is in operation, it can lead to disruptions in service.

Disruptions have consequences that extend far beyond immediate effects, such as being late to an appointment or not being able to purchase the latest cell phone. In most countries, transportation systems are regulated to some extent by public authorities. Thus, when a transportation system functions poorly, the authority's governance ability is called into question, which, in turn, erodes public trust. This may prompt individuals and businesses to withdraw, leading to a reduction in operating budgets and also, more often than not, reductions in scheduled services.

Managing Crime in the System

As illustrated by John Eck's crime triangle (Figure 3.1), routine activities theory (RAT) (Cohen and Felson 1979; Felson 1995, 2006) provides a useful framework for thinking about crime events. RAT is a general theory of crime events that helps us identify which factors coalesce to generate the crime patterns we see. According to RAT, in order for a crime to happen, it is necessary that a motivated offender coincides in the same place with a suitable target (triangle) and that there are no controllers present who can prevent the crime from happening (arrows). Handlers are the people who can influence an offender and divert them from their original intention of committing a crime. Guardians are in charge of protecting the targets, which can be people (in personal crimes such as homicides or sexual assaults) or

Figure 3.1 Eck's crime triangle.

objects (in crimes such as theft or vandalism). Managers are the people who are responsible for what happens in the location they are in charge of. Only when target and offender coincide in space and time, and those controllers are absent, weak, or corrupt, can crime happen.

When we think about strengthening the crime prevention apparatus of transportation systems, we often look for ways to enhance the capacity of place managers. Why? Because transportation systems, such as buses, subways, trains, ships, and planes, operate under a company or transport authority (and sometimes more). There is always some agency responsible for making sure that things are running smoothly in the system. For this reason, improving place management is one of the most effective techniques to prevent crime in transportation systems and will be the focus of the strategies suggested in this chapter. As will be discussed below, preventing crime happening in transportation systems has its unique sets of challenges. They need to be taken into account if we want our preventative efforts to be successful.

Chapter Organization

Crime affecting transportation systems can be (1) "static," that is, they happen in or around public transit facilities such as bus or subway stops, airports, train stations, or truck stops, or (2) "in transit," that is, on a moving train, plane, subway, bus, truck, and so on. At the same time, when asked to think about how objects and people move about, most people envision traveling through the air and over land and sea. Because of the central importance of transportations in our modern society, and the fact that crime can occur on the system, or be enabled by it, this chapter examines issues of transportation-related crime with examples of "static" and "in transit" crimes for all three major transportation channels—air, land, and sea.

We organized this chapter around three challenges associated with understanding and preventing crime on transportation systems: (1) identifying where crime concentrates; (2) protecting targets that are on the move; and (3) managing crime risks when multiple jurisdictions are involved. Although multiple studies will be cited, we have chosen three examples that illustrate these issues in each of the main transportation channels.

1. Air: Theft from Baggage at Airports
2. Land: Perceptions of Safety in a Commuter Rail System
3. Sea: Maritime Piracy

Every inquiry into diagnosing a crime problem begins with figuring out where crime concentrates. Contrary to popular perceptions, crime is not randomly distributed across space and time or among targets. Using a study about baggage theft at airports, the reader will learn about the 80/20 rule, which suggests that if we were to compare facilities within a system, for example, airports in the United States, not all facilities suffer equally from crime problems. Generally, approximately 80% of crime problems occur at 20% of facilities. By identifying these crime-prone locations, we can maximize the effect of crime prevention initiatives.

The second issue confronting us is that in many instances, the targets we are trying to protect are on the move. Yet, there is limited information about where objects or people are within the system at any one point in time. Thus, to resolve transit crime problems, it is necessary to develop estimation techniques and new data collection methods (i.e., geocoded reports of crime using smartphones). Using a commuter rail example, the reader will learn about an innovative way of estimating where passenger-on-passenger aggression occurs.

Finally, transportation systems often cover broad distances, or link up with systems in different territories. This means that the management and oversight of objects and people involves cooperation among different authorities, and sometimes, jurisdictions overlap. This generates problems with surveillance and place management. To illustrate how this complex issue can be dealt with, our discussion turns to the issue of piracy on the high seas.

Each section will include a textbox containing the description of the case study that will be used to exemplify the concepts explained. Therefore, please make sure to read the textbox carefully. At the end of the chapter, you will find discussion questions that will guide you in thinking more critically about the key ideas raised in the chapter. As with other chapters in this book, key terms in bold text also appear in a glossary of terms found at the end of the chapter.

Hot Routes, Risky Transportation Hubs

When confronted with any crime problem, the first thing we need to do is to thoroughly understand the characteristics and trends of the problem at hand. How is it committed? Where does it tend to happen? Does it occur during the day, or at night? Are there seasonal trends? What targets are mostly affected? As you will learn in this section, crime does not occur randomly. It concentrates in certain areas, times, and establishments, and it disproportionally affects certain products or victims. This is true for crime in transportation systems as well.

To illustrate this issue, we have chosen an example of crime in air transportation: "Thefts from Baggage at Airports in the United States." In Box 3.1, we describe the problem and display some of its concentration patterns.

Studying Concentration

One way of exploring patterns of concentration is to apply the **Pareto principle**, also known as the **80–20 rule**, which states that, for many events, roughly 80% of the effects come from 20% of the causes. When applied to crime, we can reconceptualize this principle as suggesting that the majority of the offenses occur in a few locations, that a small group of very active offenders commit most of the crime, or that a handful of products are disproportionally targeted by thieves, just to cite a few examples. We can graphically display this pattern by using a bar graph, listing all locations (or offenders, or products) from the one with the most crime to the one with the least. If crime concentrates in a few of them, the graph will have a reclining J shape, just like in Figure 3.1. This type of graph is called a **J curve**.

Studying patterns of concentration is very important for crime prevention, because

1. *It leads our analysis.* Studying in depth the most problematic places, offenders, or products immediately suggests reasons why that might be so. We can also compare the ones with the highest amounts of crime to the ones with the lowest, in order to determine what differences between them may be facilitating crime.
2. *It allows us to focus our crime prevention efforts and resources where they are most needed, so we have the greatest impact.* Focusing law enforcement efforts on a small number of problems supports several modern policing practices (i.e., intelligence-led policing, problem-oriented policing, and focused deterrence).

BOX 3.1   THEFT FROM BAGGAGE AT U.S. AIRPORTS

Before a trip, we pack our bags with everything we will need at our destination. If we travel by car or by train, our luggage stays with us the whole time. When traveling by air, we surrender our baggage to the airline at the airport of origin, and we recover it at the baggage claim area of the destination airport.

Literally, millions of bags are checked in every year in the United States and, in most cases, the passenger simply goes on with his or her life after picking up the luggage at the conveyor belt, but sometimes, upon opening the suitcase at the destination, the passenger finds out that some of the things that were inside the bag when it was checked in are no longer there. The passenger/traveler has been the victim of a theft.

Some of the questions that arise are as follows: Who did it? How did this happen? Where did it happen? Is this a very common crime? What items are most at risk of being stolen? In her research, Marteache (2013) arrived at the conclusion that theft from checked luggage must be committed mostly by baggage handlers and security employees such as Transportation Security Administration officers, as they are the ones who have access to the luggage while it is in transit. Regarding the question of where theft is most likely to happen, determining the exact location where crime occurs in transportation systems is challenging, as targets are on the move. We will talk more about this in the next section. In this example, we know that something went missing at some point between checking a bag at the start of the trip and retrieving the bag upon arrival. Bags are thought to be at greater risk at the start of the journey because they tend to spend more time at the origin airport while waiting to be loaded onto the plane than at the destination, where everybody is in a hurry to get their bags and leave the airport.

Different patterns of concentration were observed when studying this problem. There were a total of 494 commercial airports in the United States in 2009. Of those, 263 experienced at least one theft. Only 97 airports had 10 or more thefts. Figure 3.2 shows how thefts concentrated in a few airports, while most airports experienced little or no theft at all.

Table 3.1 lists the airports reporting the highest volume of theft from luggage in 2009. You will notice that many of these international airports are either located in destination cities that attract many

Figure 3.2 U.S. airports ranked from the one with the highest to the one with the lowest number of thefts from checked luggage in 2009 (*N* = 263). (Adapted from Marteache, N. (2013). *Employee Theft from Passengers at U.S. Airports: An Environmental Criminology Perspective* (PhD), Rutgers University, Newark, NJ.)

Table 3.1   Top 10 U.S. Airports with the Highest Volume of Theft from Checked Luggage in 2009

Rank	Airports	No. of Thefts
1	JFK—John F. Kennedy International Airport	455
2	MCO—Orlando International Airport	327
3	LAX—Los Angeles International Airport	312
4	ATL—Hartsfield-Jackson Atlanta International Airport	270
5	MIA—Miami International Airport	257
6	SEA—Seattle-Tacoma International Airport	229
7	LAS—McCarran International Airport	226
8	PHL—Philadelphia International Airport	220
9	EWR—Newark International Airport	218
10	BOS—Boston (Logan) International Airport	200

Source: Adapted from Marteache, N. (2013). *Employee Theft from Passengers at U.S. Airports: An Environmental Criminology Perspective* (PhD), Rutgers University, Newark, NJ.

tourists, or they are important hubs supporting international travel to and from the United States.

Not every item packed had the same chances of being stolen. For example, in the United States, in one of every four thefts, the item missing was a camera, a GPS device, a DVD player, or some other electronic device. Clothing and jewelry were also among the most stolen items (see Figure 3.3).

Finally, thefts peaked during the winter months, even though the number of bags checked was higher in the summer. Winter clothing provides the opportunity to hide stolen items more than summer clothing does (see Table 3.2).

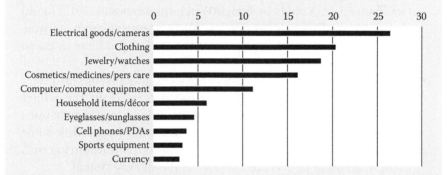

Figure 3.3 Items most commonly stolen from checked baggage in 2009 (in percentage). (Adapted from Marteache, N. (2013). *Employee Theft from Passengers at U.S. Airports: An Environmental Criminology Perspective* (PhD), Rutgers University, Newark, NJ.)

Table 3.2   Seasonal Variation of Theft from Luggage, 2009

	% of Theft from Checked Luggage	% of Checked-In Bags
January	9.7	7.5
February	7.5	7.0
March	8.4	8.6
April	8.0	8.4
May	8.9	8.4
June	8.7	9.0
July	8.8	9.7
August	7.5	9.4
September	7.8	7.8
October	8.4	8.3
November	7.0	7.7
December	9.2	8.2
Total in 2009	100.0	100.0

Source: Adapted from Marteache, N. (2013). *Employee Theft from Passengers at U.S. Airports: An Environmental Criminology Perspective* (PhD), Rutgers University, Newark, NJ.

Concentration of Crime in Transportation Systems

Crime occurring in transportation systems also concentrates

- On certain *targets*

    As evidenced in the research presented in Box 3.1 on theft from baggage at airports, not all items packed in suitcases had the same risk of being stolen. Electronics were stolen at a much higher rate (see Figure 3.3). A study by FreightWatch International (2013) found that, in some European countries, pharmaceutical products were being targeted at much higher rates than other products in cargo theft incidents.

- On certain *times* of the day, days of the week, months, or seasons

    Table 3.2 shows that theft from baggage peaks in the winter months. Some crimes such as vandalism of bus stops may happen mostly at night while nobody is around to see it happen, while some others like pickpocketing in the subway will concentrate during rush hour, when more targets are available in the subway system.

- On certain geographic *areas*, *segments*, or *lines*

    The examples provided in the next two sections of this chapter show different patterns of concentration. The section "Targets Are on the Move" explains how passenger complaints clustered in some lines of a commuter rail system (Metrolink). Within each line, some segments (line portions between two train stations) are riskier than others. In the section "Multiple Jurisdictions at Play," we will discuss how transportation channels also exist on the high seas leading to hotspots for piracy and armed robbery at sea.

- On certain *facilities*

    Facilities are homogeneous sets of establishments with specific public or private functions (Clarke and Eck 2007), such as train stations, bus stops, parking lots, marine ports, and so on. The analysis of theft from baggage at U.S. airports described at the beginning of this section is a clear example of a risky facilities analysis. Some airports experienced a lot of theft, while others had very little or none. Even within airports of similar size, we can find big differences. For instance, JFK International Airport in New York and Denver International Airport had around 23 million passengers each in 2009. However, the number of thefts at JFK (455 thefts) was twice as much as the number of thefts at Denver (188 thefts) that year (Marteache 2013).

Why does crime concentrate? When referring to theft targets, some products are more attractive to offenders than others because they are higher in value and are easier to steal, and the risk of detection is low. If we talk about certain areas, lines, or facilities, it is important to know whether they are located in high-crime areas, they contain many appealing targets, or they attract a large number of offenders, among others.

Another factor that is always important to take into consideration is how well the place where crime occurs is managed. Places that are well regulated, where rules are enforced and place managers make sure that things run smoothly by taking care of any issues that arise, are much less likely to experience crime. The probability of successfully committing a crime is much lower when everybody cares about what is going on. Some policies and practices that make crime more difficult are also ways to deter offenders, such as cashless buses in which you need to have purchased a ticket before boarding (it prevents robbery from bus drivers) or fully automated systems of luggage screening, which prevent theft from baggage by airport personnel.

Studying concentration in transportation systems can sometimes be complicated, because targets, victims, and offenders are not static, they move within the system. We will address this issue in the following section.

Targets Are on the Move

By definition, transportation systems are dynamic environments. Passengers and objects travel from one location to another, sometimes directly, sometimes stopping at one or more intermediate points. For instance, when going on vacation, you may take the bus from your home to the airport, where you will take a direct flight—or two or more connected flights—to the destination city. Upon arrival, you may rent a car, hop on the subway, or take a taxi to your hotel. If, during that trip, you would lose your sunglasses, it would probably be difficult to pinpoint exactly when and where you left them, because you have been on the move. That is exactly what happens with most crime affecting transportation systems: targets and victims are in transit. While for some types of offenses determining the location where a crime happened is not an issue (i.e., vandalism of bus stops), often it is very difficult to do so, because of difficulties in figuring out exactly where and when something occurred, as the victim only finds out about the crime at some point after the event (i.e., theft from checked-in luggage). Crime data tend to include only the origin and destination of the trip and the time frame between departure and arrival, which constitutes a challenge when we want to study how crime concentrates in the system (see Box 3.2).

Determining Where and When In-Transit Crimes Happen

When studying crimes that have occurred in transit, there are two options. First, we can *assume* that the crime occurred at origin/departure, at destination/

arrival, or at some middle point of the trip. This is what happened in the research on theft from passengers' luggage at airports presented in the section "Hot Routes, Risky Transportation Hubs." Given the lack of information on where and when the theft had occurred, and the fact that the origin airport presented broader opportunities for employees to steal from checked baggage than the destination airport (owing to accessibility and time constraints), all thefts were assigned to the origin airports. However, if we are interested in deploying law enforcement personnel or place managers to resolve crime and public safety issues, we need a way of quantifying which trip segment poses the greatest likelihood of generating problems.

As described in the case study presented in Box 3.2, we can *estimate* the likelihood that the crime occurred at a certain time or location, provided that we have the origin and destination, and the departure and arrival times of the person or object in transit. To do so, we can use the following estimation processes:

a. **The Interstitial Analysis Method** (Newton et al. 2014)

We use this method when we know that something happened in transit (while a target or victim was going from point A to point B), but we do not know exactly *where* it happened. An example could be a male tourist who takes the subway to go to another location that is three subway stops away. He has his wallet with him when he boards the subway car, but upon exiting the subway, he realizes that he no longer has it. Somewhere along the way, he was pickpocketed. We can estimate the probability that the incident happened in a certain place by dividing the trip in segments (in this case, if the tourist went through three stations before exiting, each segment would be the portion of the trip between stations). Figure 3.4 illustrates how this calculation is done (Trip 3 in the figure). We divide the incident by the number of segments (1/3 = 0.33) and we find out that each segment has a 33% probability that the incident happened in it. We do that for all pickpocketing incidents reported in the subway and then aggregate the risk of each segment. That will tell us what the most problematic locations in the transit system are.

b. **The Aoristic Analysis Technique** (Ratcliffe 2002)

This technique is quite similar to the Interstitial Crime Analysis method described above, but it is applied to time, instead of space. It is used when we know that something happened in a location, but we are not sure exactly *when* it happened. For instance, a subway car is tagged while it is stored overnight. We know what happened, and where, but not exactly when, since the car could have been tagged at any point between midnight and 5 a.m. The risk of the one incident happening is divided by the five hours during which the subway car

BOX 3.2   PERCEPTIONS OF SAFETY
ON A COMMUTER RAIL SYSTEM

Southern California (United States) is known for its car culture and its terrible traffic. A recent study by TomTom, the GPS manufacturer, found that Los Angeles is the most congested city in the United States.* Public transportation systems such as buses, subways, or trains can help alleviate this situation, but only if they are considered to be safe, affordable, and reliable.

Marteache et al. (2015) studied perceptions of safety among passengers of Metrolink, a regional commuter rail service that operates in Southern California and serves 55 stations located in different cities in the Greater Los Angeles area. They looked at riders' complaints on passenger-on-passenger aggression, misbehavior by conductors or sheriffs (supervision), and on-time performance and crowding of trains (both are indicators of situations that can increase rider tension) between 2009 and 2012. Details about the data used in this research can be found in Table 3.3. One of the goals of the project was to determine whether reported problems spread evenly throughout the system and, if they do not, in what line segments (portions of the train line between stations) do incidents concentrate. As observed in the section "Hot Routes, Risky Transportation Hubs," analyzing concentration is key to preventing crime!

In order to study the pattern of concentration of incidents that led to complaints, it was essential to know where in the system the problem had happened. Unfortunately, the complaint system was not designed to include the exact location where passengers experienced something that concerned them; instead, only the origin and destination of the trip were listed. This situation is common to most public transportation systems and constitutes an important obstacle in the study of crime (Newton 2004).

An estimation method (see Figure 3.4) was used to determine where problems were likely to have occurred. Each incident was divided among the number of segments included in the complainant's trip, to establish the likelihood that the incident happened at each line segment. After that, all probabilities for each segment were added up to arrive at the total estimated probability of problems occurring in each segment. This estimation process is called "interstitial analysis," and it was developed by Andrew Newton in a study of London's subway system, the Underground (Newton et al. 2014).

* http://www.tomtom.com/en_us/trafficindex/#/city/LOS

Table 3.3   Description of Customer Complaints about Incidents Occurring while Onboard or during Boarding/Alighting

Category	Description	Number of Complaints
Passenger-on-passenger aggression	Victimization or witnessing aggressive behavior by a passenger on another rider, including assaults, verbal threats, as well as defiance and disorderly conduct	163
Supervision	Statements about a conductor or sheriff not enforcing rules, behaving inappropriately, aggressiveness, or failing to respond to a request	455
Rider tension		
On-time performance (OTP)	Concerns about delays and disruptions to regular service (excluding planned maintenance)	1423
Crowding	Statements about inability to find seating, and congestion in vestibules and stairs (e.g., too many bicycles or luggage blocking movement)	82

Source: Adapted from Marteache, N., Bichler, G., and Enriquez, J. (2015). Mind the gap: Perceptions of passenger aggression and train car supervision in a commuter rail system. *Journal of Public Transportation* 18(2): 61–73.

Note: Only formal complaints (e-mail, letters, or phone) are included; tweets and Facebook posts are not. Cases were lost because of missing information about the origin or destination of the trip.

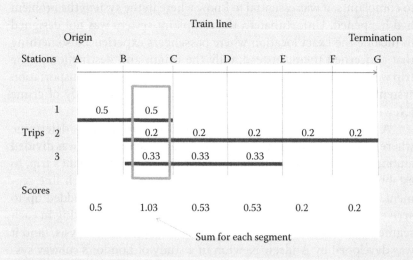

Figure 3.4 Interstitial estimation process. (Adapted from Marteache, N., Bichler, G., and Enriquez, J. (2015). Mind the gap: Perceptions of passenger aggression and train car supervision in a commuter rail system. *Journal of Public Transportation* 18(2): 61–73.)

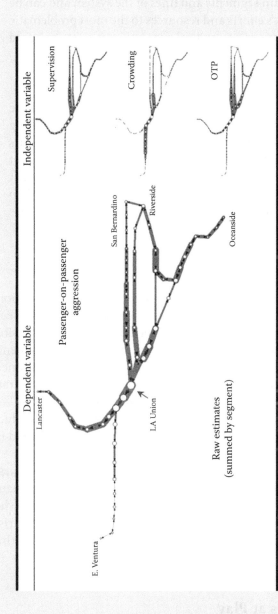

Figure 3.5 Visualization of Metrolink commuter rail network reflecting customer complaints by trip segment 2009–2012. Note: OTP refers to on-time performance. The thickness of the lines between stations (represented by circles) indicates the probability that complaints are associated with incidents occurring on that trip segment. Stations vary in size based on their central positioning in the system based on the system's connectivity. (Adapted from Marteache, N., Bichler, G., and Enriquez, J. (2015). Mind the gap: Perceptions of passenger aggression and train car supervision in a commuter rail system. *Journal of Public Transportation* 18(2): 61–73.)

Note: Station symbols vary in size to reflect a statistic called betweenness centrality. Bigger symbols identify stations that are more central to the flow of passengers throughout the entire system (across different lines).

The estimation was used to display concentration of risk of all four variables in the system (Figure 3.5). These networks show where complaints clustered in certain segments and lines of the system and can be used to direct Metrolink's efforts and resources to the most problematic segments in order to improve passengers' perception of safety onboard the trains.

was in that location (1/5 = 0.2), and that gives us that each of those five hours had a probability of 20% that the incident occurred during that time frame. If another car was tagged as well, but spent 10 hours in that location, each hour had a 10% probability that the incident occurred during that hour. If we do that for all tagging incidents that happened in the same subway yard in the last month, and we add up the accumulated risk for each hour, we will find out what hours are riskier for graffiti on subway cars.

Crime Prevention on the Move

Moving targets not only represent a challenge for studying concentration, they also make the design of prevention strategies difficult. As can be seen in Figure 3.5, riders' complaints about passenger-on-passenger aggression originate on certain trip segments; they build up in contiguous segments and then progressively decrease. Risk tends to concentrate in certain lines; it is not evenly distributed across the system. A good crime prevention strategy would take into account those rhythms and could include "moving" or "dynamic" place managers. Some examples could include multiple conductors on the train, or reinforced supervision at the beginning and the end of the parts of the lines considered riskier.

Another problem inherent to preventing crime in transportation systems is the fact that, very often, several jurisdictions are involved in the management or supervision of safety in the system. How do we determine who is responsible for doing what? What are the consequences of the multijurisdictional problem? The section "Multiple Jurisdictions at Play" addresses this issue.

Multiple Jurisdictions at Play

Transportation systems can be large, covering vast territories and, in doing so, crossing different jurisdictions. Consequently, a web of cooperative relationships is required to operate the system. For example, the Metrolink commuter rail system described above is operated by the Southern California Regional Rail Authority. It is the third largest commuter rail agency in the United States based on its 512-mile directional route network. Metrolink operates seven lines across six counties and serves 55 stations, most of which are located in different cities. While Metrolink operates the trains under the oversight of a politically appointed board of supervisors with representation from each county served, conductor services are subcontracted to Amtrak (a medium- and long-distance intercity train system), the Los Angeles Sheriff's Department provides policing services onboard trains, and stations are operated by city governments with security at stations being privately contracted by each city. At various locations, the system connects with Amtrak, light rail, and local bus services. This means that daily operations require extensive coordination among many different public agencies, private corporations, and other transportation system providers. The operational context of Metrolink is not particularly unusual in that multijurisdictional cooperation is often an important consideration when we think about preventing crime in any transportation system.

The case study used in this section to illustrate the challenges inherent to preventing crime in multijurisdictional transportation systems is Maritime Piracy (see Box 3.3). While most people are familiar with how air and land transportation operate (e.g., planes, trains, trucks, buses, etc.), most of us are unaware of how maritime transportation systems work. For this reason, we have included a section with background information on this topic before addressing the issue of piracy.

Background Information on Maritime Transportation

Law enforcement and crime prevention on the world's waterways poses considerable challenges to all coast guard fleets. As discussed in the section "Targets Are on the Move," objects and people are constantly in transit. The challenge of dealing with crime problems is compounded by the inherent complexity of maritime transportation. If an incident occurs on a ship, owned by a British firm, registered in Panama, and operated by a Philippine crew, while it is sailing around the Horn of Africa, which coast guard do you call? Who responds to the crime?

Since few people have experience with maritime systems, it is important to describe the geography that we are dealing with and the legal constraints imposed on coast guard fleets. Obviously, the size of each jurisdiction is vast: a nation's maritime jurisdiction generally extends from the low water mark of the shoreline up to 200 nautical miles seaward. To demonstrate how immense a maritime jurisdiction can be, consider the territory falling under the scope of the United States Coast Guard (USCG). The USCG polices a 3.4 million–square mile zone and regulates maritime activity along a 9500-mile coastline. One might think that this jurisdiction is large enough, but there is more. Extending beyond this perimeter is the continental shelf, and the *high seas*. The high seas are considered public waters and given that vessels are constantly on the move in this vast area, it could take several days to reach a ship in trouble.

The legal constraints on coast guard services can also be considered a crime prevention challenge. Establishing legal jurisdiction over incidents occurring onboard a vessel involves two considerations: (1) the nationality of the vessel and (2) the location of the vessel.

1. Vessel Nationality

   For a ship to sail on the high seas and then dock at a foreign port, they must have a nationality. In nautical language, this is a "flag." Ships acquire a nationality by registering with a country, referred to as the *flag state*. All nations, including those with no coastline, have the right to navigate the high seas and to maintain a registry of ships. What is material to this chapter is that if a crime incident occurs on the high seas, the flag state has full jurisdiction over the vessel. However, it might be the case that the vessel in question is thousands of miles away from the home state. This raises an important logistical issue: How can each nation respond to events occurring so far from home?

2. Vessel Location

   The second factor that is considered when figuring out the jurisdiction over a maritime crime is the location of the vessel at the time of the incident. If a vessel experiences an incident while underway within the territorial seas of another country, that country's coast guard service shoulders the primary responsibility for dealing with the issue. However, not all coast guard fleets have the same capacity. Some nations do not have the resources to handle all of the crimes occurring within its jurisdiction. This raises another logistic issue: How can a nation protect its fleet when crimes occur out of its jurisdiction, in areas with minimal law enforcement presence?

From this discussion, we can see that if an incident occurs on the open seas, out of reach of the flag nation, or in an area without adequate local coast guard support, the ship master and crew are pretty much on their own to deal with the problem. In Box 3.3, we discuss how the challenges associated with geography and jurisdictional constraints contributed to the development of high-risk regions for maritime piracy. We will also introduce the mechanisms used to overcome these impediments.

BOX 3.3   MARITIME PIRACY

Piracy is an international crime involving acts of violence, vessel deten-tion, or depredation by the crew or passengers of a private ship against another ship, persons, or property aboard, while in international waters. If the same act of violence occurs while a vessel is within its home territorial waters, it is considered an act of armed robbery. Thus, by its very definition, piracy is a complex crime, requiring international cooperation to detect and neutralize threats.

While piracy is an age-old crime problem, it is only in the last couple of decades that we have been able to analyze how this problem affects the global maritime system. The International Maritime Bureau Piracy Reporting Center (IMB PRC), a division of the International Chamber of Commerce, is instrumental in this regard. IMB PRC records and publishes reported acts of piracy and armed violence (https://www.icc-ccs.org/piracy-reporting-centre). By operating a 24-hour free report-ing service, this independent nongovernmental organization fulfills a critical role in maritime security: they provide the information needed to analyze pirate behavior (modus operandi), location and time of attack, and the success of the evasive maneuvers taken by the crew.

Reviewing the IMB PRC data, we see that between 2005 and 2012, the seas off Somalia, the Gulf of Aden, the Gulf of Guinea, and the wider Western Indian Ocean were especially hard hit by piracy. Figure 3.6 illustrates the geographic concentration of piracy off the Somali coast between 2005 and 2010.

Many of these high crime areas are on the high seas or nearby nations dealing with serious internal conflict or fiscal crisis, and thus, these nations are unable to maintain a strong coast guard fleet. These areas are devoid of effective place managers, suggesting that the lack of supervision of critical sea lanes leaves vessels at higher risk of attack.

Between 1984 and 2013, the International Maritime Organization documented 6752 reported incidents of piracy and armed robbery against ships. The dramatic rise in the number of reported incidents is concentrated in two periods: 1999–2004 and 2008–2011. Some argue that these periods correspond with sociopolitical issues occurring in the regions described above, thereby providing more evidence that crime prevention efforts need to focus on establishing multijurisdic-tional, cooperative initiatives, particularly in high crime areas.

Using nine years of information about Somali-based pirate activ-ity (1325 incidents), Townsley et al. (2015) provide some answers about how to resolve this crime problem. Townsley and colleagues found that

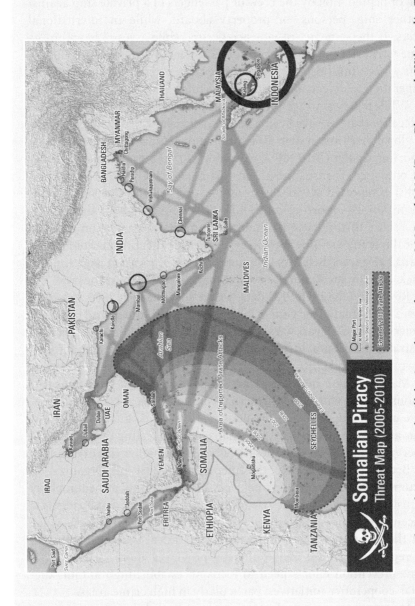

Figure 3.6 Pirate attacks on shipping vessels off the Somali coast between 2005 and 2010. (From Planemad, Wikimedia Commons. https://commons.wikimedia.org/wiki/File:Somalian_Piracy_Threat_Map_2010.png.)

between 2006 and 2014, increasing joint naval patrols in the high-risk region of the Indian Ocean (increasing place management at sea) had a significant but short-lived effect on reducing piracy. Tactical displacement occurred as pirates developed new strategies, such as launching attacks from mother ships, which enabled pirates to continue executing successful attacks and spreading piracy across the Indian Ocean. A more important finding was that increasing guardianship (e.g., adding armed guards to the crew and armed escort vessels) generated a significant and sustained reduction in piracy across the entire region. Increased guardianship was enabled by two critical changes: (1) insurance firms amended their policies, which encouraged companies to modify their operational policies, and (2) interagency cooperation led the response to the problem and multinational collaboration significantly extended the law enforcement capacity of local authorities.

Super Controllers

A critical factor to resolving piracy problems in high-risk regions is the influence of **super controllers**. Super controllers create incentives for others that have the ability to directly intervene and prevent crime in high-risk situations. As described in Box 3.3, Townsley et al. (2015) found that the Somali-based piracy problem was addressed in part because private insurance firms changed the terms of their policies, which encourages shipping conglomerates to adjust operational protocols (e.g., adding professional armed security to the crew). Offering insurance discounts associated with implementing crime prevention strategies encourages private industry to adopt target-hardening measures that they may otherwise deem too expensive to implement. However, super controllers can only be effective if it is possible to generate cooperation among different actors, often among a set of public and private agencies. Below, we highlight three types of mechanisms that enable multijurisdictional cooperation, aimed at dealing with specific problems in transportation systems.

1. Development of Brokers to Network among Security Organizations
    When multiple jurisdictions overlap, private industry and public agencies must overcome organizational silos to share information, coordinate crime control functions, and deploy resources. Investigating the Port of Melbourne, one of the busiest ports in Australia, Brewer (2015) discovered that no less than 16 different types of actors interacted to provide security services at the port. Mapping out the relationships used to share information and coordinate crime control

activities led to the discovery that a small number of actors bridged organizational silos. A set of actors had strategically positioned themselves to coordinate the network of security organizations. From the private realm were the Port of Melbourne Corporation and the Tenanted Facility Operator, who worked closely with three public agencies—the Australian Customs and Border Protection Services, the Victoria Police, and the Australian Federal Police. Many of these relationships were informal, generated by entrepreneurial actors seeking out their counterpart in other organizations.

The effect of these informal brokers within the security networks is that of a super controller in that they incentivize other organizations to adopt specific actions/policies to prevent crime. Maintaining these relationships requires continued interaction and information sharing. Given their relatively close proximity in that these brokers operated out of the same facility, this is not an exceptionally difficult objective to accomplish. Next, we discuss how multiorganizational coordination among agencies, often from different countries, requires more formal arrangements.

2. Interagency Cooperation to Extend Enforcement Capacity

Many nations do not have the capacity to thoroughly inspect and respond to issues occurring onboard vessels sailing within its maritime jurisdiction or docking at its ports. To compensate, nations commit to bilateral and multilateral agreements that, in effect, pool resources. The mechanism used is, in the context of maritime transportation, a multinational memorandum of understanding (MoU). Originating in 1982, the Paris MoU is the longest-standing harmonized inspection program targeting seagoing vessels. Inspection information, including notifications of deficiencies and detentions, is publicly available (https://www.parismou.org/). The 27 nations* that are party to this agreement follow an inspection protocol that targets high-risk foreign flagged vessels for detailed inspection. Risk is calculated based on company performance and registry (flag nation) performance over a rolling three-year window. Through this coordinated inspection program, more than 18,000 vessels are examined each year. Since the vessels that ply the high seas stop at many ports of call, this coordinated system of inspection and data sharing ensures that most vessels are investigated regularly as they travel along their shipping routes.

---

* In 2016, the Member States of the Paris MoU included Belgium, Bulgaria, Canada, Croatia, Cyprus, Denmark, Estonia, Finland, France, Germany, Greece, Iceland, Ireland, Italy, Latvia, Lithuania, Malta, the Netherlands, Norway, Poland, Portugal, Romania, the Russian Federation, Slovenia, Spain, Sweden, and United Kingdom.

The legal framework set by national governments and supported by conventions established by international organizations is critical to extending the enforcement capacity of agencies in charge of the safety and security of transportation systems that extend across several jurisdictions.

3. Information Sharing

The Paris MoU of harmonized inspection is effective in policing foreign vessels owing to the ability to share information. Maintaining centralized data systems is critical to identifying problematic vessels, irresponsible registries (flag nations failing to police their fleet), and problematic companies that sail substandard ships. In addition to naming vessels, operators, and flag states, the detentions and specific inadequacies of shipping operations are exposed. Making this information public provides additional information that underwriters can use to assess the risks involved with maritime transport undertaken by specific vessels. In turn, this supports the development of insurance policies aimed at reducing loss.

Sharing relevant information between agencies (and with the public in general) is essential to extend the surveillance capabilities of all agencies and stakeholders involved in or affected by crime in transportation systems. It also makes the detailed examination of trends and patterns of the crimes possible, which, as is explained in the "Approaching Crime Prevention in Transportation Systems" section, is the first step toward a successful crime prevention strategy.

Approaching Crime Prevention in Transportation Systems

Crimes in transportation systems vary in their degree of complexity, depending on how many of the challenges discussed in this chapter are present in the problem. Any good crime prevention strategy starts with a very thorough analysis of the problem at hand, a study of the characteristics of the crime, its patterns of concentration, the agencies and stakeholders involved, and all the factors that seem to be related to the commission of the crime.

Some of the questions that one needs to ask before choosing and implementing a set of strategies to prevent crimes happening in transportation systems are the following:

1. What exactly is happening? (you need to define your problem)
2. Who are the victims? And the offenders?
3. How is the crime being committed?

4. What are the patterns of concentration? How do you explain such trends?
5. Is the problem static (i.e., graffiti at subway stations) or dynamic/ en route (i.e., pickpocketing happening in the subway cars)?
6. Is the problem local (i.e., vandalism of bus stops in the city center), regional (i.e., passenger aggression in a commuter rail system), national (i.e., theft from cargo being transported from one part of the country to another), or international (i.e., piracy in the high seas)?
7. What jurisdiction is responsible for addressing the problem? If there are several agencies involved, is their action coordinated? How?

Only once we have learned "everything" (or as much as reasonably possible) there is to know about the problem will we be ready to design and implement measures that make the crime more difficult to commit, and therefore less attractive. In doing so we increase the likelihood that the prospective offender will be discouraged from committing the crime. Being aware of the special characteristics of crime in transportation systems is key for its successful prevention. In addition, we must consider the scope of the system itself, because sometimes multijurisdictional efforts are required to resolve crime problems that affect complex systems.

Glossary of Key Terms

Aoristic analysis technique: A technique used when the exact time of the crime is unknown. This method estimates the probability that the crime happened in each temporal unit of the time frame in which the crime occurred.

Crime triangle: The crime triangle is a model developed by John Eck that is used to explain some of the key tenets of routine activities theory. It links each element of a crime (suitable targets, motivated offenders, and the place the incident occurs at) with the crime control entity that could intervene to prevent the crime from occurring (capable guardians, intimate handlers, and place managers).

Interstitial analysis method: A technique used when the exact location of the crime is unknown because it happened in transit. This method estimates the probability that the crime happened in each of the segments of the trip.

J curve: A bar graph that has the shape of a reclining "J," as it displays the concentration of crime in a few locations (or offenders, or products), when we list the one with the most crime to the one with the least.

Pareto principle or the 80–20 rule: A principle that states that 80% of all effects come from 20% of the causes, or that a small percentage of some things are responsible for a large percentage of the outcomes.

Piracy: Piracy is an international crime involving acts of violence, vessel detention, or depredation by the crew or passengers of a private ship against another ship, persons, or property aboard, while in international waters.

Routine activities theory: Routine activities theory is a general theory of crime events that states that, in order for a crime to happen, it is necessary that three elements converge in time and space: a motivated offender, a suitable target, and the lack of a capable guardian.

Super controllers: Institutions, organizations, and people that can provide incentives for others that have the ability to directly intervene and prevent crime in high-risk situations to act.

Important Names

Ronald V. Clarke
John Eck
Andrew Newton
Jerry Ratcliffe
Michael Townsley

Discussion Questions

1. Why is it important to study how crime concentrates?
2. In what different ways does crime concentrate in transportation systems?
3. If a crime event has happened en route, how can we determine where or when the crime likely happened?
4. What possible crime prevention strategies can be used for crimes that happen in transit?
5. What types of mechanisms can be used when we have a crime problem that crosses different jurisdictions?

Recommended Web Links

The 2009 National Household Travel Survey (NHTS) provides information to assist transportation planners and policymakers who need comprehensive data on travel and transportation patterns in the United States: http://nhts.ornl.gov/tools.shtml.

The International Maritime's Bureau Piracy Reporting Centre live map shows all piracy and armed robbery incidents reported during the current year: https://icc-ccs.org/piracy-reporting-centre/live-piracy -map. Details on each incident can be found in the live piracy report here: https://icc-ccs.org/piracy-reporting-centre/live-piracy-report.

References

Brewer, R. (2015). The malleable character of brokerage and crime control: A study of policing, security, and network entrepreneurialism on Melbourne's waterfront. *Policing and Society: An International Journal of Research and Policy*, doi: 10.1080/10439463.2015.1051047.

Clarke, R.V., and Eck, J.E. (2007). *Understanding Risky Facilities*. Problem-Oriented Guides for Police, Problem-Solving Tools Series. Washington, DC: Office of Community Oriented Policing Services, U.S. Department of Justice.

Cohen, L.E., and Felson, M. (1979). Social change and crime rate trends: A routine activity approach. *American Sociological Review* 4:588–608.

Felson, M. (1995). Those who discourage crime. In *Crime and Place*, eds. J.E. Eck and D. Weisburd, Crime Prevention Studies, Vol. 4, pp. 53–66. Monsey, NY: Criminal Justice Press.

Felson, M. (2006). *Crime and Nature*. Thousand Oaks, CA: Sage Publications.

FreightWatch International. (2013). 2013 Global Cargo Theft Threat Assessment. Accessed https://www.naed.org/NAEDDocs/Research/Legal%20Issues/Freight Watch%202013%20Global%20Cargo%20Theft%20Threat%20Assesment%20 Full_0.pdf (December 7, 2015).

Koba, M. (2013). Copper theft "like an epidemic" sweeping U.S. CNBC, July 30, 2013. Accessed http://www.cnbc.com/id/100917758 (December 29, 2015).

Marteache, N. (2013). *Employee Theft from Passengers at U.S. Airports: An Environmental Criminology Perspective* (PhD), Rutgers University, Newark, NJ.

Marteache, N., Bichler, G., and Enriquez, J. (2015). Mind the gap: Perceptions of passenger aggression and train car supervision in a commuter rail system. *Journal of Public Transportation* 18(2): 61–73.

Newton, A.D. (2004). Crime on public transport: "static" and "non-static" (moving) crime events. *Western Criminology Review* 5(3): 25–42.

Newton, A.D., Partridge, H., and Gill, A. (2014). Above and below: Measuring crime risk in and around underground mass transit systems. *Crime Science* 3(1): 1–14.

Ratcliffe, J.H. (2002). Aoristic signatures and the spatio-temporal analysis of high volume crime patterns. *Journal of Quantitative Criminology* 18(1): 23–43.

Townsley, M., Leclerc, B., and Tatham, P.H. (2015). How super controllers prevent crimes: Learning from modern maritime piracy. *British Journal of Criminology* 54(4): 741–764.

Primary Prevention of Child Sexual Abuse

4

Applications, Effectiveness, and International Innovations

JESSE CALE
MELANIE BURTON
BENOIT LECLERC

Contents

Learning Outcomes
After reading this chapter, you should be able to

- Identify some of the key risk factors for child sexual abuse
- Identify some of the key protective factors against child sexual abuse
- Give examples of primary prevention strategies for child sexual abuse

- Discuss strengths and limitations of different primary prevention strategies for child sexual abuse
- Identify avenues for future research in evaluating primary prevention strategies for child sexual abuse

Introduction

Prevention works! Sexual violence is a major public health issue that affects everyone, directly or indirectly, and results in long-term social and economic costs.

Minnesota Department of Public Health
2002

One of the key debates in the sex offending literature involves the notion that incarcerated sex offenders/those in treatment for sexual offenses possibly represent only a minority of actual sex offenders. The basis for this argument is the fact that the vast majority of sex crimes go undetected for various reasons. The **dark figure** for sex crimes is possibly quite more substantial than for certain other types of violent crimes. For example, it is fairly well established that many sex offenders commit a single sex offense in their criminal career and never reoffend sexually. Others, however, commit offenses against different victims over the course of their criminal career, some of which may not come to the attention of authorities. Similarly, some sex offenders may abuse the same victim repeatedly, over the course of months or years without the crimes ever being reported and the offender being caught (e.g., see Lussier and Cale 2013, for a review of the criminal careers of sex offenders).

Critically, there are many reasons that victims may not disclose sexual abuse experiences, particularly child victims. For example, research evidence suggests that in a vast majority of child sexual abuse (CSA) cases, the perpetrator and victim are known to one another (Finkelhor et al. 2005). Therefore, children may find it difficult to report abuse experiences perpetrated by someone known to them, particularly a relative, for fear of not being believed, or even out of a sense of not wanting the perpetrator to get into trouble, for example. At the same time, perpetrators often use a variety of tactics to maintain a victim's silence ranging from buying the victim gifts to using threats to ensure their silence. These dynamics in addition to the severe consequences of CSA on victims, families, and even the broader community make it all the more important to try and prevent these types of offenses from ever occurring in the first place. Therefore, in this chapter, we discuss some of the main primary prevention strategies for CSA, review the evidence of their application and effectiveness, and discuss new international innovations in the primary prevention of CSA.

Types of Sexual Violence Prevention

Once a sex offender has been charged and convicted with an offense, there are several forms of institutional-based treatment programs (e.g., in prisons, hospitals, and residential treatment facilities) and similar community-based programs available that are designed to prevent them from committing further offenses. These types of programs can be understood as tertiary prevention/ intervention strategies because they represent long-term responses consisting of specialized sex offender treatment and management that are designed to prevent further offending after it has already occurred (**Association for the Treatment of Sexual Abusers [ATSA]** 2015). Arguably, this is where the bulk of resources are devoted when it comes to preventing (subsequent) sex crimes. Secondary prevention programs also occur after sexual violence has been perpetrated and often involve attempting to reduce harm to victims immediately following sexual violence, for example, providing immediate counselling for victims. Secondary prevention strategies can also be directed toward specific audiences, such as individuals who have perpetrated sexual violence or those who have been victimized (ATSA 2015).

As we pointed out in the Introduction to this chapter, sex offenders who end up in custody are really only the tip of the iceberg when it comes to the actual prevalence of sex offenders in the wider community. In addition, there is evidence to suggest that repeat sex offenders have numerous victims over the course of their criminal career. Therefore, secondary and tertiary prevention strategies for sexual violence are targeted toward a very limited segment of the population of perpetrators of this particular kind of offending (see Box 4.1). In light of this, we now focus our discussion on primary prevention of sex offending and, specifically, sexual offenses against children.* Primary prevention strategies are those that are employed before any sexual violence has occurred to prevent sex offenses altogether in the first place. However, in order to understand prevention of any kind, it is first necessary to understand the causes of the phenomenon we are trying to prevent, in this case, CSA.

Understanding the Basis for CSA

To date, the majority of theories about sex offenders have emerged from the field of psychology and have been just that: theories about the (typically individual-level) characteristics of sex offenders. For example, numerous psychological theories of sex offenders have been developed to inform

---

* For a review of interventions for violence against women, see Wathen and MacMillan (2003).

BOX 4.1   WHEN DO WE INTERVENE?

The following is an excerpt from the Association for the Treatment for Sexual Abusers Sexual Violence Prevention Fact Sheet that can be found at: https://www.atsa.com/sexual-violence-prevention-fact-sheet.

"The field of public health prevention defines three levels of intervention in a social and/or health problem. Based on when the intervention is used in targeting prevention of problem, they are:

Primary Prevention: Approaches that are employed before any sexual violence has occurred to prevent initial perpetration and victimization. Primary prevention includes building an environment that encourages well-being and healthy choices. This could include approaches such as public dissemination of information and resources. Primary Prevention can be directed toward either at 'Universal' or 'Selected' audiences. Universal reflects strategies aimed at everyone in the population of interest, independent of risk. Selected denotes strategies directed toward those in the population at increased risk for sexual violence perpetration or victimization.

Secondary Prevention: An immediate response after sexual violence has been perpetrated. Secondary prevention deals with the short-term consequences of violence; it attempts to reduce the harm to the victims in the immediate aftermath of the violence (e.g., separating the victim and the perpetrator; providing immediate crisis for counselling for the victim), and to locate, contain, and address the perpetrators. Secondary and Tertiary prevention can be directed towards 'indicated' audiences, reflecting strategies aimed at individuals who have perpetrated sexual violence or those who have been victimized.

Tertiary Prevention: A long-term response after sexual violence perpetration. Tertiary prevention addresses the lasting consequences of victimization (e.g., by providing ongoing counselling for victims) and the provision of specialized sex offender treatment and management to the perpetrators of sexual violence to minimize the possibility of re-offense. Tertiary prevention also includes intervention in family violence to prevent reoccurrence of the situations and behaviors that cause harm."

treatment with these individuals (i.e., tertiary prevention/intervention). While these theories are critical to inform treatment to prevent reoffending, in order to prevent sex crimes from occurring in the first place, we need to understand the multilevel causes of sex offending, and these extend beyond the scope of characteristics of individual offenders. CSA stems from a variety of individual-level influences, as well as interpersonal and relationship-level influences, community-level influences, and societal level influences. Therefore, several theorists in the field have turned their attention toward integrated and ecological theoretical models to explain sex offending.

Integrated theoretical models of CSA place perpetrators within a broader framework of multilevel systems that impact one another over time (e.g., Belsky 1980; Coulton et al. 2007; Smallbone and Cale 2015). Thus, integrated and ecological explanatory models of sex offending are central to primary prevention research because they are capable of identifying multilevel **risk factors** and **protective factors** (e.g., family, peer, organizational, neighborhood, and sociocultural) to inform both the timing and context of prevention (Mendelson et al. 2012). While it is beyond the scope of this chapter to elaborate on the various integrated theories that are out there (for a recent theory, see Smallbone and Cale 2015), Box 4.2 highlights examples of multilevel risk factors that increase the likelihood of CSA.

Taking into consideration the multilevel risk factors for CSA, we now turn to examples of primary prevention strategies that have been implemented to prevent/reduce the likelihood of CSA in the first place. CSA primary prevention approaches involve two distinct points of focus: (1) the prevention of children becoming victims of CSA and (2) the prevention of potential offenders from engaging in CSA, targeting different ecological levels within each focus (Smallbone et al. 2008).

Child-Focused Primary Prevention of CSA

The key focus of CSA primary prevention strategies has been on education directed primarily toward children as well as toward parents/families and childcare professionals (Finkelhor 2009). The proliferation of education prevention programs for CSA began in the late 1970s and they were widely circulated throughout the 1980s (especially in the United States). The aim of these programs is to provide group-based education on personal safety to children to enhance their awareness of danger and increase competencies and coping skills to deal with potential perpetrators. Primary and secondary school-based settings have provided the main platform for such efforts, a major advantage being their ability to reach large numbers of demographically diverse children. Part of the rationale behind large-scale/widespread

BOX 4.2   MULTILEVEL RISK FACTORS FOR CSA

The points below represent *examples* of risk factors that increase the likelihood for CSA to occur. It is important to note that none of these are direct causes of CSA; they are neither necessary nor sufficient conditions for the occurrence of CSA. Rather, their occurrence and particularly their co-occurrence increase the likelihood for CSA to occur. CSA occurs within the context of multilevel risk factors, which means that CSA prevention, and particularly primary prevention, is a process of reducing risk factors and building protective factors with victims and their families, potential perpetrators, and the social environments in which they coexist.

1. Situational risk factors
   a. Lack of child supervision
   b. Alcohol/drug intoxication (i.e., perpetrator)
   c. Environmental factors (e.g., secluded locations)
2. Individual-level risk factors
   a. Perpetrator characteristics
      i. Sexual preferences toward children/attitudes and beliefs supportive of sexual activity with children
      ii. Poor adult attachment patterns (e.g., problems forming and maintaining age-appropriate intimate relationships)
      iii. Emotional congruence with children
      iv. Childhood sexual abuse experiences
      v. Alcohol/drug use and abuse
      vi. Impulsivity/antisociality
   b. Victim characteristics
      i. Female gender
      ii. Preadolescence (i.e., age)
      iii. Low self-esteem
3. Interpersonal/relationship-level risk factors
   a. Family dysfunction
   b. Parental absence/unavailability
   c. Poor relationships with parents
4. Community-level risk factors
   a. Social disorganization
5. Societal-level risk factors
   a. Closed sub-cultures (e.g., that promote secrecy)

education initiatives is also to avoid any potential stigma of identifying specific children at risk of sexual abuse, as well as delivering a cost-effective and less intrusive intervention (Collin-Vézina et al. 2013). These education-based programs tend to focus on teaching children definitions of sexual abuse, recognizing what constitutes inappropriate sexual behavior, teaching strategies to children for avoiding risky situations and how to resist the advances of perpetrators, and conveying the message that children should tell a trusted adult if they have experienced any inappropriate sexual behavior (e.g., MacIntyre and Carr 2000; Rispens et al. 1997). In addition, these type of programs often also aim to encourage reporting of ongoing abuse and to alleviate the negative consequences for children who may have experienced CSA by reducing feelings of guilt and self-blame (Finkelhor 2009). Box 4.3 highlights an

---

BOX 4.3   THE CANADIAN CENTRE
FOR CHILD PROTECTION

The Canadian Centre for Child Protection is a charitable organization that began in 1985 in the province of Manitoba following the disappearance and murder of 13-year-old Candace Derksen. The mission statement of the Canadian Centre for Child Protection delineates four broad goals of the Centre:

1. Reducing the incidence of missing and sexually exploited children
2. Educating the public on child personal safety and sexual exploitation
3. Assisting in the location of missing children
4. Advocating for, and increasing awareness of, issues related to missing and sexually exploited children

To achieve these goals, the Centre hosts a multitude of prevention initiatives involving: training and programs related to the personal safety of children, education programs for children, families, schools, youth-oriented institutions, and communities more broadly; tracking recording and reporting child pornography, online luring, child sex tourism, child prostitution, and child trafficking; recording data on trends in child victimization; collecting tips on missing children; advocacy around issues related to missing and sexually exploited children; and coordinating other nonprofit, government, industry, and community individuals, groups, and organizations in the area of child protection.

innovative initiative from the Canadian Centre for Child Protection addressing some of these key issues.

Evaluations of child-focused education programs have reported improvements in knowledge relating to CSA and preventive skills (e.g., Barron and
Topping 2010; Berrick and Barth 1992; Boyle and Lutzker 2005; Briggs and
Hawkins 1994; Davis and Gidycz 2000; Finkelhor et al. 1995; Rispens et al.
1997; Wurtele et al. 1992); however, both advocates and critics alike acknowledge that the extent to which these programs in fact *prevent* CSA is not
entirely clear (see, e.g., Rheingold et al. 2015; Smallbone et al. 2008; Wurtele
2009). A recent study has also provided evidence on the need to understand
circumstances under which victim disclosure is more or less likely in order to
shape the content of these programs accordingly (Leclerc and Wortley 2015).
The key criticisms of child-focused education programs center on (a) the relevance of the content and (b) the conceptual foundations (Collin-Vézina et
al. 2013).

In terms of content, concerns have been raised that such CSA education
programs may have potentially negative consequences including increased
anxiety in children (i.e., fear of victimization), false reports of CSA, and
increased risk of physical harm by a perpetrator in cases where children
resist (e.g., Binder and McNeil 1987; Finkelhor and Dziuba-Leatherman
1995; Nibert et al. 1989; Wurtele 2009; Wurtele and Miller-Perrin 1992;
Wurtele et al. 1989). For example, teaching preadolescent children that
they should resist the advances of potential perpetrators is particularly
contentious because there is typically little to no guidance in programs
around how children should resist physically or verbally to abusive adults
(Smallbone et al. 2008). Critically, children most vulnerable to experiencing CSA are also those who lack confidence and who have low self-esteem
(e.g., Elliott et al. 1995). Therefore, these are also children who benefit least
from the content of education programs as they are unlikely to implement
self-protection strategies or resist the advances of an adult (see Bagley et al.
1996; Fryer et al. 1987).

In terms of the conceptual foundations, one of the key criticisms is the
fact that children are most likely to be sexually abused by someone known to
them such as a relative or an acquaintance compared to a stranger. Examining
1037 cases of CSA from police files in Canada, Fischer and McDonald (1998)
found that 44% of the offenses were perpetrated by a family member. The
other 56% were often perpetrated by someone relatively well known to the
child victim such as a babysitter, day care worker, family friend, and so on. In
addition, the average age at first abuse victimization in childhood is approximately nine years old for both boys and girls (Finkelhor and Araji 1986).
This in turn makes it particularly challenging for children to be able to resist
advances and take control of the interactions because the perpetrators in
these cases often hold a position of authority, to some extent or another, over

the child. In effect, these large-scale and widespread education-based prevention programs are heavily focused on informing children about a victimization context that is among the least likely to occur (Smallbone et al. 2008). While this is by no means to suggest these programs are not worthwhile, it is necessary to consider the possibility that they do not inform prevention of perhaps the most common CSA contexts.

In one of our studies of adult sex offenders who committed offenses against school-aged children in youth-oriented institutions, we asked offenders what some of the key individual characteristics were that they targeted when selecting a child victim in these settings (see Leclerc and Cale 2015). Interestingly, 75% of the offenders in the sample indicated that they still targeted a child whom they perceived knew they should not talk to strangers or accept car rides from strangers. More than half of these offenders still committed an offense against a child who knew what constituted inappropriate sexual behaviors, and approximately one-third even indicated they committed an offense against a child who was capable of defending themselves or who verbally resisted advances. On the other hand, these particular offenders were least likely to target children whom they perceived they could not trust; these offenders were less likely to target children whom they perceived to be assertive. A characteristic such as being assertive, but more generally, a child's capacity to effectively/successfully navigate psychological, social, and cultural aspects of development, has been referred to as "resilience" (Ungar 2008). As such, resilience building has been incorporated into many child-focused education programs by focusing on developing the protective factors that reduce vulnerability to CSA, such as self-confidence and self-esteem (Barron et al. 2015; MacIntyre and Carr 2000; Smallbone et al. 2008). This practice is supported in a recent study by Leclerc et al. (2011) who found that the most effective self-protective strategies for children were to say that they did not want to have sexual contact and saying "no" to the offender.

Family-Focused Primary Prevention of CSA

Moving beyond the child, the family is the next most proximal level of a child's ecological system, and the influence of parents/guardians on the sexual and nonsexual behavior and development of children has been well documented (e.g., Aspy et al. 2007; Bancroft 2003; Lussier et al. 2011b). While parent-focused and family-focused interventions (e.g., parenthood education, family support, and home visitation services) have demonstrated promise in reducing child maltreatment (e.g., Chaffin et al. 2004; Kolko et al. 2011; Lutzker et al. 1984; Runyon et al. 2009), such efforts have focused primarily on physical and emotional abuse, largely neglecting CSA.

Unlike other forms of child maltreatment (e.g., neglect, physical, and emotional abuse), parents are less likely to be perpetrators of CSA (Smallbone et al. 2008). This means that CSA prevention strategies should educate parents to increase their awareness of the potential for CSA posed by other family members, family friends, neighbors, partners, and other visitors. The goal of such strategies is to assist parents in taking protective measures to increase the safety of their children (Mendelson and Letourneau 2015; Smallbone et al. 2008). In addition, in contrast to other forms of child maltreatment (e.g., neglect, physical abuse), males make up the vast majority of sex offenders against children. Therefore, in comparison to general maltreatment programs that tend to be oriented toward engaging mothers, parent- and family-oriented CSA prevention strategies need to ensure that they target and engage men/fathers within their programs too and focus on enhancing attachment bonds between both male and female parents, and their children (e.g., Finkelhor and Daro 1997; Smallbone et al. 2008).

Where parent-oriented CSA prevention programs have been implemented so far, they have centered on education and have been found to increase parental knowledge about CSA and to increase parental discussions with their children about CSA (e.g., Burgess and Wurtele 1998; Hebert et al. 2002; Wurtele et al. 1992, 2008). However, further evaluation studies are needed to implement and assess the positive and negative outcomes for CSA of parent- and family-oriented prevention programs (Mendelson and Letourneau 2015; Smallbone et al. 2008).

Primary Prevention of CSA in Youth-Oriented Organizations

Childcare professionals (e.g., teachers, day care workers, coaches, leaders, and clergy) within youth-oriented organizations/institutions have been proposed as a further target for primary prevention initiatives (Rheingold et al. 2015). Beyond their central role in identifying instances of CSA and intervening with victims, childcare professionals have frequent contact with large numbers of children, and therefore can potentially be provided with approaches to prevent victimization and perpetration (Rheingold et al. 2012, 2015). Importantly, however, not only do childcare professionals need training to identify and intervene in CSA; in some cases, professionals are the perpetrators of CSA.

Currently, there are few studies examining prevention strategies that target childcare professionals; however, recommendations have been made and many youth-oriented institutions have put primary prevention strategies for CSA in place (Mendelson and Letourneau 2015; Rheingold et al. 2015; Saul and Audage 2007; Terry and Ackerman 2008; Wurtele 2012). For example, since the late 1980s, Boy Scouts of America have implemented youth protection policies to provide extra barriers to child abuse, such as the requirement that at least two adults supervise all scouting activities ("two-deep leadership") to restrict, or minimize, opportunities for staff to be unsupervised with children. A further example is the Catholic Church, which has installed a code of conduct ("The Charter" established in 2003) and CSA training for Clergy (Terry and Ackerman 2008; Wurtele 2012). To some extent, these types of primary prevention strategies in institutions also fall under the auspices of **situational crime prevention**—a criminological perspective increasingly being applied to CSA (e.g., Kaufman et al. 2010; Leclerc et al. 2014). For example, youth-oriented organizations often implement policies to limit contact between childcare professionals and children outside of the organization (e.g., rules that coaches are not permitted to go on trips alone with children or that teachers are not permitted allowed to be alone with a student in a classroom with a closed door after school hours) (Wurtele 2012). In effect, these prevention measures are designed to eliminate the opportunities for CSA to take place, by increasing the risk or effort necessary to commit them (e.g., Leclerc and Cale 2015; Leclerc et al. 2005).

Before hiring childcare professionals, organizations are strongly encouraged to utilize screening and recruitment practices (e.g., criminal checks, in-depth interviews, and background Internet searches), which have the potential to identify individuals who are unsuitable for working with children and who may have the potential to sexually abuse children (Rheingold et al. 2015; Wurtele 2009, 2012). However, there are some practical issues associated with this. First, any job involving prolonged contact with children necessitates some degree of emotional congruence with children; high-quality prospective employees need to be able to relate well with children in order to deal with them effectively. Thus, while this may be a risk factor for CSA, it is also a desired quality for an adult employee in such contexts. Furthermore, there are likely ethical and human rights issues associated with screening individuals who have been sexually abused themselves. There is related privacy issues associated with accessing prior Internet activity as well. Finally, screening criminal backgrounds will likely not identify many child sex offenders, as the majority of child sex offenders, particularly intrafamilial offenders (i.e., those who offend against child victims in their own family) are never caught and do not have prior criminal convictions (e.g., Lussier et al. 2011a). In a study by Wortley and Smallbone (2013), 90% of offenders incarcerated for CSA had no prior history of sex offenses. Therefore, relying on screening alone to prevent CSA within youth-oriented institutions is unreliable and may create a false sense of security (Leclerc and Cale 2015).

There is research evidence to support some of these claims. For example, in our study of offenders in youth-oriented institutions discussed earlier (Leclerc and Cale 2015), we also asked offenders the most common locations in which they committed sexual offenses against children. Half of the offenders indicated they committed the offenses in their own home. In other words, several of these offenders did not commit acts of sexual abuse in the organization/institution itself (see also Erooga et al. 2012; Sullivan and Beech 2004). This was followed by committing offenses against their child victims in cars, or in isolated or out-of-the-way places (i.e., secluded public locations). Only approximately one-fifth of the offenders committed their offenses in the actual organization (e.g., school, youth center, sporting club, etc.). In terms of screening for criminal backgrounds, only approximately one-fifth of these offenders had ever been arrested for a prior offense. Critically, more than three-quarters of these offenders reported that they themselves had been sexually abused as a child (see also Sullivan and Beech 2004), and on average, they spent two years in a youth-oriented institution before the first time they abused a child and spent approximately 16 years working in these organizations before they were caught for CSA (see also Erooga et al. 2012).

Perpetrator-Focused Primary Prevention of CSA

General Deterrence Strategies

Another essential element for the prevention of CSA is preventing potential perpetrators from sexually abusing children in the first place. Typically, this has involved the prevention of perpetration via **general deterrence** strategies. However, like for any crime, general deterrence relies on the assumption or belief on the part of potential offenders that if they commit an offense, there is a high likelihood they will be caught and successfully prosecuted for the offense. In principle, they would be deterred from committing an initial offense based on awareness of prosecution outcomes for known offenders (i.e., the legal threat of punishment, such as imprisonment, sex offender registration, and community notification). In addition, the social consequences (e.g., the social stigma of being labeled a pedophile or a sex offender) that may follow prosecution for offending may match or overshadow the fear of legal consequences, thereby increasing deterrence effects even further.

There is some research evidence that general deterrence does have a positive impact on primary prevention of CSA. Letourneau et al. (2010) found that there was a significant general deterrent effect following the implementation of a **sex offender registration and notification** program that was implemented in South Carolina, in the United States. More specifically, following the implementation of this program, there was a reduction in first-time sex crime arrests in the following decade. Clearly, however, CSA is still a serious problem in society. In addition, when general deterrence fails (i.e., when an offense is committed), the response tends to be to increase in the severity of legal consequences (Smallbone et al. 2008). This response assumes that potential offenders are rational and will desist from engaging in criminal behavior if the consequences are perceived to be sufficiently punitive. Without the public dissemination of laws and penalties prohibiting sexual activities with children, instances of CSA would likely increase considerably. However, it is unclear whether such increases in the severity of consequences contribute anything further to primary prevention. Studies have demonstrated that potential offenders pay far more attention to the perceived positive outcomes of an offense rather than to the potential consequences. For perpetrators of CSA, the rewards produced by offending behavior (i.e., instant outcome of self-gratification) may be far more influential than the potential longer-term outcome of persecution (e.g., Smallbone et al. 2008).

Developmental Prevention

A more positive proactive alternative to general deterrence strategies, which are based on punitive consequences, is to strengthen the natural prosocial resilience within the general population, via **developmental prevention**. The presence of strong prosocial internal and external controls (e.g., perspective taking, self-regulation, and positive attachments) may prevent CSA motivations from developing in the first place (Smallbone et al. 2008). In light of this, developmental prevention is aimed at generally improving life-course outcomes for children. For example, programs that would fall into this category of primary prevention are aimed at improving early attachment relationships between parents and children and providing support and assistance to children at various stages of development such as the transition to school, adolescence, young adulthood, and parenthood (see David Farrington and Brandon Welsh's 2006 book entitled *Saving Children from a Life of Crime: Early Risk Factors and Effective Interventions*). Therefore, while such programs are not necessarily aimed at specifically preventing CSA, this is an approach to preventing the development of antisocial tendencies that in many cases includes vulnerabilities associated with the onset of CSA perpetration. In effect, this type of primary prevention aims to reduce developmental risk factors for antisocial behavior (such as early attachment failures in childhood, poor school adjustment, and noninvolvement in early parenting as an adult) and strengthen protective factors against antisocial behavior. Generally, research studies have demonstrated that when implemented effectively, developmental prevention programs have wide-ranging positive effects, such as better long-term health outcomes and even reducing the likelihood of offending (Farrington and Welsh 2006). However, at the time of finalizing this chapter, there were no studies we were aware of that have examined the specific impact of general developmental prevention programs on CSA later on in life. This represents a significant gap in the prevention literature.

Innovations in Primary Prevention of CSA

Critically, not all perpetrators of CSA report an ongoing sexual interest in children. Unfortunately, the prevalence of sexual interest in children among offenders arrested for or convicted of CSA is still not entirely clear from studies. Nonetheless, sexual interest in children has been indicated as a major risk factor for CSA and is also a predictor of sexual recidivism (Hanson and Busssiere 1998; Hanson and Morton-Bourgon 2005). Some researchers have questioned whether it is possible that sexual attraction toward children may represent a sexual orientation. This view has substantial scientific, clinical, legal, and societal implications (for a discussion, see an article by Seto (2012) titled "Is pedophilia a sexual orientation?" in the *Archives of Sexual Behavior*). Given the focus of this chapter on primary prevention, below we discuss the clinical implications of conceptualizing **pedophilia** (i.e., a specific sexual preference toward children) as a sexual orientation.

While the focus of this chapter has been on CSA, there is evidence that there are some (typically) male adults in society that have age-inappropriate sexual interests in children, but have never acted on them or committed an act of CSA. Some scientists have estimated that anywhere between 1% and 5% of adult males in the population may have a sexual preference toward children (see Seto's (2008) book entitled *Pedophilia and Sexual Offending against Children: Theory, Assessment, and Intervention*). Furthermore, there are increasing clinical accounts of individuals seeking treatment because of their attraction toward children and, at the same time, have never acted on these impulses. Several recent news stories have also shed some light on this phenomenon and documented such accounts:

- *How many men are paedophiles?* http://www.bbc.com/news/magazine-28526106
- *Many researchers taking a different view of pedophilia.* http://articles.latimes.com/2013/jan/14/local/la-me-pedophiles-20130115
- *Is pedophilia a sexual orientation?* http://www.thestar.com/news/insight/2013/12/22/is_pedophilia_a_sexual_orientation.html

This raises interesting questions from a primary prevention perspective. For example, what, if any, services exist for adults who have sexual interests toward children, but have never offended against a child? It would seem prudent that strategies geared toward the primary prevention of CSA perpetration should focus on such individuals. However, there currently are few avenues available for nonoffenders who are seeking help for their sexual interest in children. One initiative that has been developed to intervene with potential child sex offenders is the Berlin *Prevention Project Dunkelfeld*,

BOX 4.4 PREVENTION PROJECT DUNKELFELD

Prevention Project Dunkelfeld (PPD) was launched in 2005 and aimed toward providing treatment for individuals who self-identified as having a sexual interest in children. This project was accompanied by a large-scale media campaign to encourage potential participants who were experiencing distress because of their sexual interests to seek treatment, while ensuring their anonymity and confidentiality to avoid labeling or societal stigma. While the program focuses on preventing the onset of CSA, and therefore includes many individuals who have never committed an act of CSA, some participants may have in the past committed an act of CSA. The project provides treatment broadly based on **cognitive–behavioral therapy** to prevent these individuals from acting on their impulses and committing acts of CSA. The program provides therapy and teaches skills and techniques including, but not limited to, self-efficacy, self-monitoring of sexual fantasies and interests, positive coping strategies, and self-regulation techniques.

In 2015, a study by Professor Klaus M. Beier and colleagues from the Department of Health and Human Sciences, and Institute of Sexology and Sexual Medicine at Berlin University Hospital "Charité" that was published in the *Journal of Sexual Medicine* provided an initial evaluation study of PPD. The findings from their research demonstrated evidence of decreases in emotional deficits and cognitions supportive of CSA in a treatment group, as well as increases in sexual self-regulation. They concluded that the PPD had an effect on reducing certain risk factors associated with CSA and that future research examining factors associated with problematic sexual behaviors is needed.

"Dunkelfeld" means "Dark Field," or in other words refers to the "dark figure" of undetected sex offenses in this context.

More information on the program can be found at: https://www .dont-offend.org/.

which was launched in 2005 to prevent the onset of CSA through therapy with individuals who are sexually attracted to children (Box 4.4).

Conclusions and Future Issues Concerning Primary Prevention of CSA

In this chapter, we covered some of the key primary prevention strategies for CSA and their focus. These programs show promise and are but one group of strategies aimed toward addressing the important issue of CSA in society. It is important to reiterate there are no "silver bullet" solutions to preventing CSA, but rather multiple avenues to address the problem. Primary prevention strategies for CSA have primarily been targeted toward educating children and parents on risks and reporting, and more recently toward reducing opportunities for CSA to occur, and targeting motivations for CSA in potential offenders. It is also vitally important that prevention strategies take into consideration ever-changing technological landscapes that facilitate CSA. Researchers and law enforcement are increasingly investigating online child sex offenders and how they use the Internet to facilitate different types of CSA, such as the production and distribution of child pornography (see Cohen-Almagor 2013). Anthony Beech and colleagues also identified other ways that child sex offenders use the Internet such as to communicate with other individuals with a sexual interest in children and developing and maintaining offending networks (Beech et al. 2008). They concluded that there is a vast amount of child pornography available on the Internet and that there is a trend toward increasingly extreme child pornography involving younger and younger children. The unregulated nature of the Internet has made it difficult for any sort of primary prevention along these lines; however, Beech and colleagues noted that criminal justice agencies have been quick to react/respond to the growing threat of online CSA. Moving forward, a monumental challenge will be developing innovative strategies toward preventing CSA in this context.

Glossary of Key Terms

Association for the Treatment of Sexual Abusers (ATSA): An international multidisciplinary professional association for the prevention of sexual violence and abuse. ATSA plays an important role in promoting evidence-based research and practice, public policy and community strategies around the prevention, assessment, treatment, and management of sex offenders or those at risk of committing sex offenses.

Child sexual abuse (CSA): It broadly refers to the involvement of any child in sexual activity with another person who may be another child, adolescent, or adult, that they do not fully comprehend, and are unable to give informed consent to, and that violates specific laws of a given society.

Cognitive–behavioral therapy: A type of therapy that helps people change problematic thinking habits and is often applied in therapy with sex offenders.

Dark figure: A term used by criminologists to describe the amount of undiscovered crime.

Developmental prevention: It involves the organized provision of resources to individuals, families, schools, and communities to prevent the development of crime and other social problems.

General deterrence: Defined as the impact of the threat of legal punishment on the public at large.

Pedophilia: It refers to sexual desire or sexual interest toward children in adults.

Protective factors (against criminal behavior): These refer to personal characteristics or environmental conditions that reduce the likelihood of crime or other negative outcomes.

Risk factors (for criminal behavior): These refer to personal characteristics or environmental conditions that reduce the likelihood of crime or other negative outcomes.

Sex offender registration and notification: A system that is employed in various countries that allows governments to track the activities of known sex offenders in the community once they have been released from prison.

Situational crime prevention: A term used by criminologists that refers to crime prevention strategies that are aimed at reducing the criminal opportunities that arise from the routines of everyday life.

Discussion Questions

1. On the basis of the review of primary prevention strategies for CSA covered in this chapter, which do you think have the most promise? How can we improve the effectiveness of different primary prevention programs aimed at CSA?

2. In the chapter, we discussed some of the clinical implications of conceptualizing pedophilia as a sexual orientation, but what are the concomitant scientific, societal, and legal implications of taking this view?

3. What kind of primary prevention strategies for CSA can be implemented in cyberspace? Looking forward, what might be some of the best ways to deal with the role of technology in this type of offending?

Suggested Reading

Kaufman, K.L., Hayes, A., and Knox, L.A. (2010). The Situational Prevention Model: Creating safer environments for children and adolescents. In *The Prevention of Sexual Violence: A Practitioner's Sourcebook*, ed. K.L. Kaufman. Holyoke, MA: NEARI Press.

Seto, M.C. (2008). *Pedophilia and Sexual Offending against Children: Theory, Assessment, and Intervention*. Washington, DC: American Psychological Association.

Smallbone, S., and Cale, J. (2015). An integrated life-course developmental theory of sexual offending. In *Sex Offenders: A Criminal Career Approach*, ed. A. Blokland and P. Lussier, 43. New York: John Wiley & Sons Inc.

Smallbone, S., Marshall, W.L., and Wortley, R. (2008). *Preventing Child Sexual Abuse: Evidence, Policy and Practice*. Cullompton, Devon, UK: Willan Publishing.

Recommended Web Links

https://www.atsa.com/
> Website for the professional Association for the Treatment of Sexual Abusers.

https://www.dont-offend.org/
> Official website for Prevention Project Dunkelfeld network.

http://www.stopitnow.org/
> Stop It Now! is a worldwide nonprofit organization working to prevent the perpetration of child sexual abuse through a public health approach with an emphasis on adult and community responsibility.

https://www.protectchildren.ca/app/en/media_release_teatree_tells
_kit
> The Canadian Centre for Child Protection launched Teatree Tells: A Child Sexual Abuse Prevention kit, to help parents and educators with children four to six years of age deal with issues related to child sexual abuse.

References

Aspy, C.B., Vesley, S.K., Oman, R.F., Rodine, S., Marshall, L., and McLeroy, K. (2007). Parental communication and youth sexual behaviour. *Journal of Adolescence* 30(3): 449–466. doi:10.1016/j.adolescence.2006.04.007.

Association for the Treatment of Sexual Abusers (ATSA). (2015). Sexual Violence Prevention Fact Sheet. Association for the Treatment of Sexual Abusers. https://www.atsa.com/sexual-violence-prevention-fact-sheet.

Bagley, C., Thurston, W.E., and Tutty, L.M. (1996). *Understanding and Preventing Child Sexual Abuse: Critical Summaries of 500 Key Studies*. Aldershot, UK: Arena.

Bancroft, J. (2003). *Sexual Development in Childhood*. Vol. 7. Bloomington, IN: Indiana University Press.

Barron, I.G., Miller, D.J., and Kelly, T.B. (2015). School-based child sexual abuse prevention programs: Moving toward resiliency-informed evaluation. *Journal of Child Sexual Abuse* 24(1): 77–96. doi: 10.1080/10538712.2015.990175.

Barron, I.G., and Topping, K.J. (2010). School-based abuse prevention: Effect on disclosures. *Journal of Family Violence* 25(7): 651–659. doi: 10.1007/s10896-010-9324-6.

Beech, A.R., Elliott, I.A., Birgden, A., and Findlater, D. (2008). The Internet and child sexual offending: A criminological review. *Aggression and Violent Behavior* 13(3): 216–228. doi: http://dx.doi.org/10.1016/j.avb.2008.03.007.

Belsky, J. (1980). Child maltreatment: An ecological integration. *American Psychologist* 35(4): 320–335. doi: 10.1037/0003-066X.35.4.320.

Berrick, J.D., and Barth, R.P. (1992). Child sexual abuse prevention: Research review and recommendations. *Social Work Research and Abstracts* 28(4): 6–15. doi: 10.1093/swra/28.4.6.

Binder, R.L., and McNeil, D.E. (1987). Evaluation of a school-based sexual abuse prevention program: Cognitive and emotional effects. *Child Abuse & Neglect* 11(4): 497–506. doi: http://dx.doi.org/10.1016/0145-2134(87)90075-5.

Boyle, C.L., and Lutzker, J.R. (2005). Teaching young children to discriminate abusive from nonabusive situations using multiple exemplars in a modified discrete trial teaching format. *Journal of Family Violence* 20(2): 55–69. doi: 10.1007/s10896-005-3169-4.

Briggs, F., and Hawkins, R.M. (1994). Follow-up data on the effectiveness of New Zealand's national school based child protection program. *Child Abuse & Neglect* 18(8): 635–643. doi: http://dx.doi.org/10.1016/0145-2134(94)90013-2.

Burgess, E.S., and Wurtele, S.K. (1998). Enhancing parent-child communication about sexual abuse: A pilot study. *Child Abuse and Neglect* 22: 1167–1175.

Chaffin, M., Silovsky, J.F., Funderburk B. et al. (2004). Parent–child interaction therapy with physically abusive parents: Efficacy for reducing future abuse reports. *Journal of Consulting and Clinical Psychology* 72(3): 500–510. doi: 10.1037/0022-006X.72.3.500.

Cohen-Almagor, R. (2013). Online child sex offenders: Challenges and countermeasures. *The Howard Journal of Criminal Justice* 52(2):190–215. doi: 10.1111/hojo.12006.

Collin-Vézina, D., Daigneault, I., and Hébert, M. (2013). Lessons learned from child sexual abuse research: Prevalence, outcomes, and preventive strategies. *Child and Adolescent Psychiatry and Mental Health* 7: 22. doi: 10.1186/1753-2000-7-22.

Coulton, C.J., Crampton, D.S., Irwin, M., Spilsbury, J.C., and Korbin, J.E. (2007). How neighborhoods influence child maltreatment: A review of the literature and alternative pathways. *Child Abuse & Neglect* 31(11–12): 1117–1142. doi: 10.1016/j.chiabu.2007.03.023.

Davis, M.K., and Gidycz, C.A. (2000). Child sexual abuse prevention programs: A meta-analysis. *Journal of Clinical Child Psychology* 29(2): 257–265. doi: 10.1207/S15374424jccp2902_11.

Elliott, M., Browne, K., and Kilcoyne, J. (1995). Child sexual abuse prevention: What offenders tell us. *Child Abuse & Neglect* 19(5): 579–594. doi: http://dx.doi.org/10.1016/0145-2134(95)00017-3.

Erooga, M., Allnock, D., and Telford, P. (2012). Sexual abuse of children by people in organisations: What offenders can teach us about protection. In *Creating Safer Organisations: Practical Steps to Prevent the Abuse of Children by Those Working With Them*, ed. M. Erooga, 63–84. London: John Wiley & Sons, Ltd.

Farrington, D.P., and Welsh, B.C. (2006). *Saving Children from a Life of Crime: Early Risk Factors and Effective Interventions*. New York: Oxford University Press.

Finkelhor, D. (2009). The prevention of childhood sexual abuse. *The Future of Children* 19(2): 169–194.

Finkelhor, D., and Araji, S. (1986). *A Sourcebook on Child Sexual Abuse*. Newbury Park, CA: Sage Publications.

Finkelhor, D., Asdigian, N., and Dziuba-Leatherman, J. (1995). Victimization prevention programs for children: A follow-up. *American Journal of Public Health* 85(12): 1684–1689.

Finkelhor, D., and Daro, D.A. (1997). Prevention of child sexual abuse. In *The Battered Child (5th ed., rev. and exp.)*, eds. R.E. Helfer and R.S. Kempe, xxiii, 470. Chicago: University of Chicago Press.

Finkelhor, D., and Dziuba-Leatherman, J. (1995). Victimization prevention programs: A national survey of children's exposure and reactions. *Child Abuse & Neglect* 19(2):129–139. doi: http://dx.doi.org/10.1016/0145-2134(94)00111-7.

Finkelhor, D., Ormrod, R., Turner, H., and Hamby, S.L. (2005). The victimization of children and youth: A comprehensive, national survey. *Child Maltreatment* 10(1): 5–25. doi: 10.1177/1077559504271287.

Fischer, D.G., and McDonald, W.L. (1998). Characteristics of intrafamilial and extrafamilial child sexual abuse. *Child Abuse & Neglect* 22(9): 915–929. doi:10.1016/S0145-2134(98)00063-5.

Fryer Jr, G.E., Kraizer, S.K., and Mlyoshi, T. (1987). Measuring actual reduction of risk to child abuse: A new approach. *Child Abuse & Neglect* 11(2): 173–179. doi: http://dx.doi.org/10.1016/0145-2134(87)90055-X.

Hanson, R.K., and Bussière, M.T. (1998). Predicting relapse: A meta-analysis of sexual offender recidivism studies. *Journal of Consulting and Clinical Psychology* 66(2): 348–362. doi: 10.1037/0022-006X.66.2.348.

Hanson, R.K., and Morton-Bourgon, K.E. (2005). The characteristics of persistent sexual offenders: A meta-analysis of recidivism studies. *Journal of Consulting and Clinical Psychology* 73(6): 1154–1163. doi: 10.1037/0022-006X.73.6.1154.

Hebert, M., Lavoie, F., and Parent, N. (2002). An assessment of outcomes following parents' participation in a child abuse prevention program. *Violence and Victims* 17(3): 355–372.

Kaufman, K.L., Hayes, A., and Knox, L.A. (2010). The Situational Prevention Model: Creating safer environments for children and adolescents. In *The Prevention of Sexual Violence: A Practitioner's Sourcebook*, ed. K.L. Kaufman. Holyoke, MA: NEARI Press.

Kolko, D.J., Iselin, A.R., and Gully, K.J. (2011). Evaluation of the sustainability and clinical outcome of alternatives for families: A cognitive-behavioral therapy (AF-CBT) in a child protection center. *Child Abuse & Neglect* 35(2): 105–116. doi: http://dx.doi.org/10.1016/j.chiabu.2010.09.004.

Leclerc, B., and Cale, J. (2015). Adult sex offenders in youth-oriented institutions: Evidence on sexual victimisation experiences of offenders and their offending patterns. *Trends and Issues in Crime and Criminal Justice* 497: 1–8.

Leclerc, B., Chiu, Y., and Cale, J. (2014). Sexual violence and abuse against children: A first review through the lens of environmental criminology. *International Journal of Offender Therapy and Comparative Criminology*. doi: 10.1177/0306624x14564319.

Leclerc, B., Proulx, J., and McKibben, A. (2005). Modus operandi of sexual offenders working or doing voluntary work with children and adolescents. *Journal of Sexual Aggression* 11(2): 187–195. doi: 10.1080/13552600412331321314.

Leclerc, B., and Wortley, R. (2015). Predictors of victim disclosure in child sexual abuse: Additional evidence from a sample of incarcerated adult sex offenders. *Child Abuse & Neglect* 43: 104–111. doi: http://dx.doi.org/10.1016/j.chiabu.2015.03.003.

Leclerc, B., Wortley, R., and Smallbone, S. (2011). Victim resistance in child sexual abuse: A look into the efficacy of self-protection strategies based on the offender's experience. *Journal of Interpersonal Violence* 26(9): 1868–1883. doi: 10.1177/0886260510372941.

Letourneau, E.J., Levenson, J.S., Bandyopadhyay, D., Sinha, D., and Armstrong, K.S. (2010). Effects of South Carolina's sex offender registration and notification policy on adult recidivism. *Criminal Justice Policy Review* 21(4): 435–458. doi: 10.1177/0887403409353148.

Lussier, P., Bouchard, M., and Beauregard, E. (2011a). Patterns of criminal achievement in sexual offending: Unravelling the "successful" sex offender. *Journal of Criminal Justice* 39(5): 433–444. doi: http://dx.doi.org/10.1016/j.jcrimjus.2011.08.001.

Lussier, P., and Cale, J. (2013). Beyond sexual recidivism: A review of the sexual criminal career parameters of adult sex offenders. *Aggression and Violent Behavior* 18(5): 445–457. doi: http://dx.doi.org/10.1016/j.avb.2013.06.005.

Lussier, P., Corrado, R., Healey, Tzoumakis, J.S., and Deslauriers-Varin, N. (2011b). The Cracow instrument for multi-problem violent youth: Examining the postdictive validity with a sample of preschoolers. *International Journal of Child, Youth and Family Studies* 2(2.1): 294–329.

Lutzker, J.R., Wesch, D., and Rice, J.M. (1984). Research and treatment in child abuse and neglect: A review of project '12-ways': An ecobehavioral approach to the treatment and prevention of child abuse and neglect. *Advances in Behaviour Research and Therapy* 6(1): 63–73. doi: http://dx.doi.org/10.1016/0146-6402(84) 90013-4.

MacIntyre, D., and Carr, A. (2000). Prevention of child sexual abuse: Implications of programme evaluation research. *Child Abuse Review* 9(3): 183–199. doi: 10.1002/1099-0852(200005/06)9:3<183: AID-CAR595>3.0.CO;2-I.

Mendelson, T., and Letourneau, E.J. (2015). Parent-focused prevention of child sexual abuse. *Prevention Science* 16(6): 844–852. doi: 10.1007/s11121-015 -0553-z.

Mendelson, T., Pas, E.T., Leis, J.A., Bradshaw, C.P., Rebok, G.W., and Mandell, W. (2012). The logic and practice of the prevention of mental disorders. In *Public Mental Health*, ed. W.W. Eaton, 459–509. New York: Oxford University Press.

Minnesota Department of Public Health. (2002). Retrieved from http://www.health .state.mn.us/injury/topic/svp/about.cfm.

Nibert, D., Cooper, S., and Ford, J. (1989). Parents' observations of the effect of a sexual-abuse prevention program on preschool children. *Child Welfare* 68(5): 539–546.

Rheingold, A.A., Zajac, K., Chapman, J.E. et al. (2015). Child sexual abuse prevention training for childcare professionals: An independent multi-site randomized controlled trial of stewards of children. *Prevention Science* 16(3): 374–385. doi: 10.1007/s11121-014-0499-6.

Rheingold, A.A., Zajac, K., and Patton, M. (2012). Feasibility and acceptability of a child sexual abuse prevention program for childcare professionals: Comparison of a web-based and in-person training. *Journal of Child Sexual Abuse* 21(4): 422–436. doi: 10.1080/10538712.2012.675422.

Rispens, J., Aleman, A., and Goudena, P.P. (1997). Prevention of child sexual abuse victimization: A meta-analysis of school programs. *Child Abuse & Neglect* 21(10): 975–987. doi: http://dx.doi.org/10.1016/S0145-2134(97)00058-6.

Runyon, M.K., Deblinger, E., and Schroeder, C.M. (2009). Pilot evaluation of outcomes of combined parent–child cognitive–behavioral group therapy for families at risk for child physical abuse. *Cognitive and Behavioral Practice* 16(1): 101–118. doi: http://dx.doi.org/10.1016/j.cbpra.2008.09.006.

Saul, J., and Audage, N.C. (2007). *Preventing Child Sexual Abuse within Youth-Serving Organizations: Getting Started on Policies and Procedures.* Atlanta, GA: Centers for Disease Control and Prevention, National Center for Injury Prevention and Control.

Seto, M.C. (2008). *Pedophilia and Sexual Offending against Children: Theory, Assessment, and Intervention.* Washington, DC: American Psychological Association.

Seto, M.C. (2012). Is pedophilia a sexual orientation? *Archives of Sexual Behavior* 41(1): 231–236. doi: 10.1007/s10508-011-9882-6.

Smallbone, S., and Cale, J. (2015). An integrated life-course developmental theory of sexual offending. In *Sex Offenders: A Criminal Career Approach,* ed. A. Blokland and P. Lussier, 43. New York: John Wiley & Sons Inc.

Smallbone, S., Marshall, W.L., and Wortley, R. (2008). *Preventing Child Sexual Abuse: Evidence, Policy and Practice.* Cullompton, Devon, UK: Willan Publishing.

Sullivan, J., and Beech, A. (2004). A comparative study of demographic data relating to intra- and extra-familial child sexual abusers and professional perpetrators. *Journal of Sexual Aggression* 10(1): 39–50. doi: 10.1080/13552600410001667788.

Terry, K.J., and Ackerman, A. (2008). Child sexual abuse in the Catholic Church: How situational crime prevention strategies can help create safe environments. *Criminal Justice and Behavior* 35(5): 643–657. doi: 10.1177/0093854808314469.

Ungar, M. (2008). Resilience across cultures. *British Journal of Social Work* 38(2): 218–235. doi: 10.1093/bjsw/bcl343.

Wathen, C.N., and MacMillan, H.L. (2003). Interventions for violence against women. *Journal of the American Medical Association* 289(5): 589–600. doi:10.1001/jama.289.5.589.

Wortley, R., and Smallbone, S. (2013). A criminal careers typology of child sexual abusers. *Sexual Abuse: A Journal of Research and Treatment* 26(6): 569–585. doi: 10.1177/1079063213503689.

Wurtele, S.K. (2009). Preventing sexual abuse of children in the twenty-first century: Preparing for challenges and opportunities. *Journal of Child Sexual Abuse* 18(1): 1–18. doi: 10.1080/10538710802584650.

Wurtele, S.K. (2012). Preventing the sexual exploitation of minors in youth-serving organizations. *Children and Youth Services Review* 34(12): 2442–2453. doi: http://dx.doi.org/10.1016/j.childyouth.2012.09.009.

Wurtele, S.K., Kast, L.C., and Melzer, A.M. (1992). Sexual abuse prevention education for young children: A comparison of teachers and parents as instructors. *Child Abuse & Neglect* 16(6): 865–876. doi: http://dx.doi.org /10.1016/0145-2134(92)90088-9.

Wurtele, S.K., Kast, L.C., Miller-Perrin, C.L., and Kondrick, P.A. (1989). Comparison of programs for teaching personal safety skills to preschoolers. *Journal of Consulting and Clinical Psychology* 57(4): 505–511. doi: 10.1037/0022-006X.57.4.505.

Wurtele, S.K., and Miller-Perrin, C.L. (1992). *Preventing Child Sexual Abuse: Sharing the Responsibility.* Lincoln, NE: University of Nebraska Press.

Wurtele, S.K., Moreno, T., and Kenny, M.C. (2008). Evaluation of a sexual abuse prevention workshop for parents of young children. *Journal of Child & Adolescent Trauma* 1(4): 331–340. doi: 10.1080/19361520802505768.

Preventing Domestic Violence

An International Overview

5

MONICA PAULS
D. GAYE WARTHE
JOHN A. WINTERDYK

Contents

Learning Outcomes
After reading this chapter, you should be able to

- Recognize how our understanding of domestic violence is based on our experiences, on our interactions with others, and on the social context within which we live
- Make connections between such understanding and the range of strategies that are implemented in an effort to prevent domestic violence
- Realize the challenges in defining, measuring, and explaining domestic violence at a global level
- Understand the continuum of prevention strategies that exist and how they are influenced by a variety of factors.

Introduction

> ...our failure to conceive of another way may be due to a want of imagination
> or experience, rather than to the inherent impossibility of alternative ways.
>
> **M.C. Nussbaum**
> *2000, p. 254*

Domestic violence is a widespread social problem, cutting across boundaries of class, age, ethnicity, and sexual orientation (McCue 2008). Seen in both developed and developing countries, it is considered one of the most frequent forms of interpersonal violence (Flury et al. 2010; McCue 2008). Domestic violence has devastating and far-reaching implications, ranging from physical and mental health impacts to significant economic consequences, and while the need to address this issue has been repeatedly acknowledged, the problem is not going away (World Health Organization [WHO] 2014). Responses to domestic violence range from justice sanctions, treatment, intervention, to prevention; in this chapter, we focus on how prevention efforts are related to our understandings of domestic violence. As we'll see, responses vary according to context, are often developed in absence of data to inform the focus and direction of programs, and do not reflect the scale and severity of this universal issue (WHO 2014).

Understanding Domestic Violence

> ...rather than simply reflecting an objective "truth" of domestic violence
> and, therefore, what is best to be done about it, there are competing sets of
> understandings or discourses of violence that policies draw on and that,
> therefore, influence different policy approaches.
>
> **S. Murray and A. Powell**
> *2009, p. 534*

It is important to reflect on how we conceptualize domestic violence, in order to challenge the underlying assumptions that shape our ideas. **Social constructionism** looks at how we arrive at knowledge and how we understand things in relation to the social structures within which we live. As the social context changes over time, so do our perceptions and understandings (Hahn Rafter 1990). Certain behaviors may have been acceptable at one point in time, but are redefined as social institutions change and challenges to the status quo arise (Chevigny 2001; Hahn Rafter 1990). Through a social constructionist lens, we see that our understandings of the world are produced by culture, social structures, and the values of the people in power (Hahn Rafter 1990). In a criminological context, the Canadian criminologist Ezzat Fattah (1997) used the concepts of "evolutive" (i.e., changing) and "relative" (i.e., different meaning in different social, cultural, economic, and political context). By applying this approach to our understanding of domestic violence, we realize the roots of our knowledge; this allows us to challenge assumptions and think about the issue in a different way (Burr 2015; Murray and Powell 2009).

Societal understandings of gender provide a useful example. Traditional gender roles in the past served a particular social function, which also allowed for certain behaviors to be considered acceptable (Hahn Rafter 1990). This was rooted in the construction and maintenance of male power, which promoted women's subordination (Hahn Rafter 1990). As people began to question these definitions and as the institution of the family changed, gender roles were redefined (Hahn Rafter 1990). This type of change has had extensive implications in regard to domestic violence, including changes to rape law and the reconceptualization of what is acceptable within a marital relationship* (Hahn Rafter 1990; Murray and Powell 2009). According to Easteal (1994), "[t]he definition of domestic violence changes over time as society slowly shifts its values about what is and is not permissible behavior within a marriage or other intimate relationship" (as cited in Murray and Powell 2009, pp. 86–87).

Interpretation

Evolutive and relative understandings lead to a variety of interpretations of domestic violence. These competing interpretations result in different outcomes; what we do about something is based on how we understand it (Bacchi 1999). The prevailing view is that domestic violence is a gender-based crime. A long history of a patriarchal society has created a social context where women are considered an oppressed group (McCue 2008). Violence against women is possible because of this context and has resulted in a dominant view that all women are vulnerable because they are women (i.e., Universal Risk Theory) (Evans 2005). The definition, understanding, and response to domestic violence have been built historically on a gender analysis, with a link to female inequality and oppression (Murray and Powell 2009).

---

* For example, in Canada, before 1983, rape was considered a sexually motivated crime that involved vaginal or anal penetration and did not apply to a marital relationship. The Criminal Code of Canada was changed in 1983, replacing rape with the crime of sexual assault; a broader definition that includes a range of unwanted coercive behaviors, which also applies to a marital relationship. Other examples include Sweden, where the definition of rape was broadened to include a larger number of sexual crimes in 2005, and the criminalization of marital rape in Spain in 1992.

There is no denying that the majority of victims of domestic violence are women (Wells et al. 2012b). Findings from several population-based studies, such as the WHO's (2006) multicountry study on women's health and domestic violence, estimate that between 15% and 71% of women are physically or sexually assaulted by an intimate partner at some point in their lives (Abramsky et al. 2011; Heise and Garcia-Moreno 2002). Studies in the United States show that in 85% of domestic violence cases reported to police, the victims are women (Heise and Garcia-Moreno 2002; McCue 2008), and the European Commission of Justice (2010) reports that one in five women in Europe experience an incident of domestic violence in their lifetime.

However, defining domestic violence solely from a **gender perspective** is limiting in that it legitimizes only women as victims (Bacchi 1999). A gender analysis assumes that domestic violence occurs in heterosexual relationships, but there is a growing awareness of domestic violence that occurs in lesbian, gay, bisexual, and transsexual relationships (McCue 2008). Definitions based on inequality between the sexes and social contexts where women are more disadvantaged than men result in identification processes that fail to acknowledge other types of victims (Flury et al. 2010; Murray and Powell 2009). These definitions also do not include factors such as ethnicity, race, and class, but rather position *all* women as vulnerable (Murray and Powell 2009); this strengthens the assumption that male power underlies all forms of victimization (Evans 2005).

Nevertheless, since domestic violence has been more widely recognized as a crime, it has become clear that victims of domestic violence can also include children, men, people of transgender, the elderly, and other vulnerable groups (see Box 5.1). Bacchi (1999) suggests that we consider what assumptions underlie the interpretation, the effects of the interpretation, who is constituted with the interpretation, who benefits, who doesn't, and what is problematic about the interpretation as we strive to understand social problems.

Gender responses to domestic violence are focused on supporting female victims and may not consider other approaches to the problem (McCue 2008; Murray and Powell 2009). Many policies around domestic violence privilege gender inequality, maintaining assumptions of homogeneity among women and men (Evans 2005). Increasingly, there is a call for gender sensitivity in violence prevention. Gender-sensitive approaches not only acknowledge the inequality between genders but also recognize that violence is experienced differently by different gender groups. In addition, we need to recognize that one is never "just gender," but there are multiple components to a person's identity. It is important to consider all forms of social marginalization and how these are linked to violence (Evans 2005). This requires a differential response both with intervention and prevention strategies (United Nations 2010). Policies and programs would require adjustment if we consider domestic violence as more than a gender/power issue. For example, including

BOX 5.1   ELDER ABUSE

Elder abuse/neglect/maltreatment is a subject that, despite its long history, was only brought to the public attention in the 1980s (Jackson and Hafemeister 2011, 2013). While elder abuse is still largely overlooked in comparison to other forms of domestic violence, evidence provided by a United Nations report indicate that more attention is needed in order to prepare for the future as the population continues to age (World population aging: 1950–2050 2001). Yet, alarmingly, society as a whole does not appear to be prepared to deal with this segment of the population, nor is it interested to meet their needs (Malks and Cartan 2010). Confluent to the rise in the aging population and subsequent burden placed on their children, caretakers, and guardians is the rise in the number of reports of abuse (i.e., physical, sexual, psychological, financial, and medical) and neglect of elders. In 2015, the WHO estimated that around 1 in 10 older people experience abuse every month.* And although reports of elder abuse have been increasing, it is estimated that nearly 80% of all such incidents go unreported (Friese and Collopy 2010). Hence, the "dark figure" of elder abuse speaks to a growing concern and issue of this form of domestic violence/intimate partner violence (IPV). Launched by the United Nations in 2006, June 15th is now "World Elder Abuse Day" and October 1 is now "International Day of Older Persons." These secondary forms of prevention along with an expanding number of other prevention-oriented programs such as those promoted by the International Network for the Prevention of Elder Abuse, as well as the efforts of a growing number of countries, are at least serving to shed light on this form of domestic violence.

* For a more detailed accounting of the scope of the problem, see http://www.who .int/mediacentre/factsheets/fs357/en/.

poverty (see Chapter 12) as an underlying cause would mean thinking about responses that fall outside of the criminal justice system (Evans 2005).

Various research studies suggest that before the issue of domestic violence (on a global scale) can be understood, there is a need to explore the very real issue of violence against women (Garcia-Moreno 2001). To accomplish this goal, vested parties must understand and recognize that domestic violence and violence against women are not necessarily one and the same. Table 5.1 shows that in addition to supporting the theory that violence against women *is* gender-based violence, there are the many factors that perpetuate violence against women and not necessarily domestic violence.

Table 5.1   Factors That Perpetuate Domestic Violence

Factors	May Include
Cultural	• Gender-specific socialization • Cultural definitions of appropriate sex roles • Expectations of roles within relationships • Belief in the inherent superiority of males • Values that give men proprietary rights over women and girls • Notion of the family as the private sphere and under male control • Customs of marriage (bride price/dowry) • Acceptability of violence as a means to resolve conflict
Economic	• Women's economic dependence on men • Limited access to cash and credit • Discriminatory laws regarding inheritance, property rights, use of communal lands and maintenance after divorce or widowhood • Limited access to employment in formal and informal sectors • Limited access to education and training for women
Legal	• Lesser legal status of women either by written law or practice • Laws regarding divorce, child custody, maintenance, and inheritance • Legal definitions of rape and domestic abuse • Low levels of legal literacy among women • Insensitive treatment of women and girls by police and judiciary
Political	• Underrepresentation of women in power, politics, the media, and legal and medical professions • Domestic violence not taken seriously • Notions of family being private and beyond control of the state • Risk of challenge to status quo/religious laws • Limited organization of women as political force • Limited participation of women in organized political system

Source: Adapted from Heise, L.L., Pitanguy, J., and Germaine, A. (1994). Violence against Women. The Hidden Health Burden. Discussion paper no. 225, p. 46. Washington DC: The World Bank. https://www.unicef-irc.org/publications/pdf/digest6e.pdf.

Definition

Given the general lack of consensus concerning the definition, and the fact that it remains one of the "least recognized human rights violations in the world" (Heise et al. 2002, p. 55), domestic violence is difficult to reliably measure. Domestic violence needs to be seen as a pattern of behavior and not an isolated incident. From a human rights perspective, it is a form of oppression, centered on the operation of fear, terror, and control, made possible by the current social context (McCue 2008; Pain 2014). Domestic violence has been referred to as a form of terrorism, which occurs in the home (i.e., place of residence) as opposed to the public realm, and although it receives less attention than other forms of violence, the serious physical and mental health consequences are starting to be realized (Pain 2014).

It is worthwhile to consider the terms commonly used to reference violence that occurs in the context of an intimate relationship: domestic violence, violence against women, IPV, dating violence, and partner violence. While these are often used interchangeably, IPV seems to have overtaken the use of domestic violence; this term is more neutral and includes unmarried couples, as well as both heterosexual and homosexual relationships (Wells et al. 2012b). The definition of domestic violence has also been broadened in some contexts. For example, in Alberta, Canada, a recently passed private members bill defines domestic violence as "physical, sexual, psychological, and emotional abused forced confinement, stalking, and threats that create a reasonable fear of property damage or personal injury" (Koshan and Watson Hamilton 2015). A range of relationships is identified in this definition, including "spousal, cohabitating, dating, parental, family and caregiving relationships" (Koshan and Watson Hamilton 2015). In the United Kingdom, the government definition of domestic violence was changed in 2012 to include 16- to 17-year-olds and to reflect coercive control as core to domestic violence. This was done to recognize that domestic violence is not an isolated incident of abuse, but rather a complex pattern of repeated abuse or threats of abuse that occurs in a context of power and control. In addition, the term *domestic violence* was changed to domestic violence and abuse (Gov.uk 2013).

The challenges in defining domestic violence, violence against women, or IPV can be further illustrated in the following examples. The Maputo Protocol or the Protocol to the African Charter on Human Rights and Peoples' Rights on the Rights of Women in Africa (drafted in 1995 and ratified in 2005) uses a broader definition of violence against women. The Protocol defines violence against women as "all acts perpetrated against women which cause or could cause them physical, sexual, psychological, and economic harm…" By contrast, the Inter-American Convention of the Prevention, Punishment, and Eradication of Violence against Women (adopted in 1994)* defines violence against women as "any act or conduct, based on gender, which causes death or physical, sexual or psychological harm or suffering to women, whether in the public or the private sphere." Finally, as evidence of the evolving definition of domestic violence/IPV, and violence against women, the **European Istanbul Convention**† defines violence against women as a violation of human rights and a form of *discrimination* against women (Article 3—Definitions) (Council of Europe Convention 2011).

---

* Although most inter-American countries ratified the convention between 1995 and 1998, Jamaica was among the last to ratify the Convention in 2005, and the Bahamas includes an exception in that they have no obligation to provide any form of compensation from public funds to any woman who has been a victim of violence.
† Formally known as the Council of Europe Convention on preventing and combating violence against women and domestic violence. The Protocol came into force in 2014. As of late 2015, the Protocol had been signed by 40 countries. Among those who had not signed the Protocol were Ireland, Switzerland, Bulgaria, Latvia, and several other former Soviet states.

Regardless of the terminology used, a common definitional component is that the violence occurs in the context of an intimate hetero or same-sex relationship at any stage, from dating, common-law marriage, to relationships that have been terminated. People identifying as women, men, and transgender can be victims or perpetrators of violence, although terminology such as "violence against women" acknowledges the gendered nature of violence in intimate relationships. Excluded from this definition is sexual violence perpetrated by a stranger or an individual not known to the victim.

Definitions must address the relationships, types of violence, purpose, and consequences of abuse. Types of violence that can occur in intimate relationships include emotional abuse, stalking, physical abuse, sexual assault, and homicide (Breiding et al. 2015; Heise and Garcia-Moreno 2002). This intentionally broad description of types of violence is potentially problematic because virtually any act could be deemed violent or abusive. Therein lies the question of what is meant by "violence."

What distinguishes violent from nonviolent behavior are the purpose and consequence. The purpose of violent behavior is to control or exploit through neglect, intimidation, inducement of fear, or by inflicting pain (Calgary Domestic Violence Committee 1996). Ganley (2002) describes domestic violence as "purposeful instrumental behavior ... directed at achieving compliance from or control over the victim" (p. 62). The key to differentiating abuse and violence from unhealthy behaviors that can occur in relationships is the pattern of behavior that results in physical, mental, or financial consequences for victims, families, communities, and society (Sinha 2013). While violence is conceptualized and measured as discrete events, Smith et al. (1995) argue that what we are referring to is actually a chronic pattern of behavior with cumulative and multiple effects.

Measurement

Challenges associated with defining domestic violence extend to measurement and data collection. Measuring domestic violence first requires that definitions be operationalized to establish what data will be included and excluded. For example, the initial step in measurement might be to determine the criteria for who will be asked, the types of abuse to be measured, whether standardized scales will be used and, if so, which scales. Sampling and ethical issues associated with asking questions about violence, as well as access to resources and information for respondents requiring support, are all issues that influence the quality of the data collected. Whether the data can be useful to describe the problem internationally requires some agreement between countries as to the type of data collected and from whom. In practical terms, the international community can likely report what countries are measuring domestic violence, but it is highly unlikely that what is measured will be comparable. At the most basic level, countries defining the problem as violence against women are unlikely to ask men about their experiences of violence (Measuring Intimate Partner [Domestic] Violence 2010).

In the absence of a universal definition, studies of domestic violence across the globe are looking at the various risk and protective factors that increase or decrease the likelihood of violence in interpersonal relationships (see Table 5.2).

Table 5.2   Intimate Partner Violence Risk Factors

Risk Factors	May Include
Individual risk factors	• Low self-esteem • Low income • Low academic achievement • Young age • Aggressive or delinquent behavior as a youth • Depression • Anger and hostility • Antisocial personality traits • Borderline personality traits • Prior history of being physically abusive • Unemployment • Emotional dependence and insecurity • Belief in strict gender roles (e.g., male dominance and aggression in relationships) • Desire for power and control in relationships • Perpetrating psychological aggression • Being a victim of physical or psychological abuse (consistently one of the strongest predictors of perpetration) • History of experiencing poor parenting as a child • History of experiencing physical discipline as a child
Relationship factors	• Marital conflict—fights, tension, and other struggles • Marital instability—divorces or separations • Dominance and control of the relationship by one partner over the other • Economic stress • Unhealthy family relationships and interactions
Community factors	• Poverty and associated factors (e.g., overcrowding) • Low social capital—lack of institutions, relationships, and norms that shape a community's social interactions • Weak community sanctions against IPV (e.g., unwillingness of neighbors to intervene in situations where they witness violence)
Societal factors	• Traditional gender norms (e.g., women should stay at home, not enter workforce, and be submissive; men support the family and make the decisions)

Source: Adapted from Centers for Disease Control and Prevention, The Social–Ecological Model: A Framework for Prevention (March 25, 2015), accessed April 20, 2015, http://www.cdc.gov/violenceprevention/overview/social-ecologicalmodel.html.

Risk factors differ in different parts of the world (Abramsky et al. 2011; Flury et al. 2010); "[w]hat constitutes empowerment in one setting may represent an unacceptable transgression of gender norms elsewhere" (Abramsky et al. 2011, p. 15). Some of the factors presented are not as common in nations where women and men are both provided with equal socioeconomic and educational opportunities (Fulu and Miedema 2015), and while there has been a greater focus on individual risk factors, community and societal factors may be more influential in certain contexts (Heise and Garcia-Moreno 2002).

The most consistent individual **risk factors** are young age, lower education, marital status (being separated or divorced), alcohol/drug use by either the partner or the victim (however, we generally understand use or abuse of substances as a consequence rather than a cause), and experiencing violence in childhood or adolescence. Societies where men have greater financial and decision-making power in the home and where it is more difficult to access divorce put women at greater risk (Abramsky et al. 2011; Heise and Garcia-Moreno 2002).

Generally, a higher socioeconomic status is considered a **protective factor**; although domestic violence is seen across all socioeconomic groups, women living in poverty are at greater risk. However, it is difficult to know whether it is poverty itself or the other factors that accompany it (e.g., financial stress, lack of access to resources) that increase the risk of domestic violence. Other protective factors include completion of postsecondary education (for both a woman and her partner), the presence of female working groups, societies that have community sanctions for perpetrators, and societies that have services for victims (Abramsky et al. 2011; Heise and Garcia-Moreno 2002).

Prevalence

Although consideration of risk factors is helpful in understanding the issue and designing appropriate responses, it does not help in determining prevalence. Prevalence depends on victims who come forward to report (McCue 2008). This brings us back to the issue of definition, since how we define domestic violence determines who we legitimize as being victims (Murray and Powell 2009).

Cross-sectional population-based surveys provide the best estimates of the prevalence of the issue, although it is recommended that such numbers be thought of as minimum levels of violence (Watts and Zimmerman 2002). More than 50 population-based surveys on IPV have been conducted in various parts of the world over the past two decades. Even though findings vary greatly, studies indicate that between 10% and 50% of women who have ever had an intimate partner have been physically assaulted by their partner at some point in their lives (Watts and Zimmerman 2002).

The WHO (2014) reported that 57% of countries have national surveys to collect data on issues related to IPV. WHO estimates that between 24.6%

Table 5.3   Global Prevalence of Intimate Partner Violence

Prevalence of Intimate Partner Violence by WHO Region (2010) (WHO 2014)		Prevalence of Physical or Sexual Intimate Partner Violence by Region (Devries et al. 2013)	
WHO Region	Prevalence (%)	Region	Prevalence (%)
Region of the Americas	29.8	North America and Latin America	21.32–40.63
African region	36.6	Sub-Saharan Africa	29.67–65.64
Eastern Mediterranean region	37.0	–	–
European region	25.4	Europe	19.3–27.85
Southeast Asia region	37.7	Asia	16.3–41.73
Western Pacific region	24.6	–	–

Source: Adapted from World Health Organization (2014). Global status report on violence prevention 2014. Jointly published by WHO, the United Nations Development Programme, and the United Nations Office on Drugs and Crime, Geneva, Switzerland. http://www.who.int/violence_injury_prevention/violence/status_report/2014/en/; and from Devries, K.M. et al. *Science* 340, 6140, 1527–12528, 2013. Reprinted with permission from AAAS.

and 37.7% of women experience IPV globally (WHO 2014) (see Table 5.3). However, differences in definition, data collection methods, sampling, and culture affect prevalence rates and our ability to make comparison between countries (Watts and Zimmerman 2002). Table 5.3 demonstrates the range in prevalence rates by considering two studies, the *Global Status Report on Violence Prevention 2014* by the WHO (2014) and *The Global Prevalence of Intimate Partner Violence against Women* by Devries et al. (2013). Comparisons of the data are essentially not possible, considering the variation in definition, measurement, and populations sampled (see Table 5.3).

If we hope to address the issue of domestic violence effectively, we need to question our understanding, for "how violence is conceptualized and defined will determine what is visible, seen and known…" (Itzin 2000, as cited in Murray and Powell 2009, p. 357).

Explaining Domestic Violence

The importance of understanding the causes of domestic violence is not simply an academic exercise. Our understanding of factors that contribute to violence influences the choice of strategies to intervene and prevent violence. The Centre for Disease Control and Prevention (CDC) uses the **social–ecological framework** developed by Dahlberg and Krug (2002) to account for multiple theories used to explain domestic violence at the individual, relationship, community, and societal levels (see Table 5.3).

The social–ecological model increases our understanding of what factors contribute to domestic violence by incorporating aspects of multiple theories and perspectives, such as feminist perspectives and social learning theory. The model also suggests points of prevention and intervention, contributing to its utility (Dahlberg and Krug 2002; Heise 1998). For example, if, at the societal level, attitudes that support violence contribute to the risk of domestic violence, a public education campaign may be a promising direction for prevention activities. Using a number of models, theories, and perspectives to understand domestic violence helps highlight the complexity of factors that contribute to risk and resiliency. This model was first described by Bronfenbrenner (1977) as the ecological model and the multiple levels included the individual or micro-system and broadened to the societal influences or macro-system. An identified strength of the model is the ability to investigate interrelationships between multiple levels, which allows for the incorporation of more than one explanatory theory (Bondurant 2001).

Patriarchy, power and control, structural inequality, and oppression are central themes in a feminist analysis of domestic violence (Jackson 1999). Feminist theory provides a gendered analysis of domestic violence: women experience abuse because the existing social structures support one group having power over another. Abuse and violence reinforce social structures and the entitlement experienced by the group that holds power (Jackson 1999; Johnson and Ferraro 2000; Loseke and Kurz 2005; McPhail et al. 2007, p. 818). Power and inequality are concepts that help explain other risk factors associated with domestic violence, specifically that groups with less power are at increased risk of violence. Risk factors include age, gender, race, and ability. The United Nations and the WHO (2002) support a gendered analysis of domestic violence. The WHO acknowledges that women can be violent in relationships with men and that violence can occur in same-sex relationships; however, "the overwhelming health burden of partner violence is borne by women at the hands of men" (WHO 2002, p. 1).

Alternately, **social learning theory** conceptualizes violence as a learned behavior. Violent acts result from a limited repertoire of skills or knowledge specific to problem solving, anger management, conflict resolution, or coping with stress. Therefore, individuals who use violence in relationships do so because they have not learned any other way to behave, not because they are attempting to control another person. Learning new skills and behavior related to problem solving or conflict resolution would therefore result in a reduction of violence. The overall simplicity of social learning theory holds broad appeal; however, while there is general agreement that there is an impact on children and adolescents who witness or are victimized in their families and learn that violent behavior is a primary tactic for resolving conflict in relationships, the nature of that impact varies (Barnes et al. 1991; Brownridge 2004; Cunningham et al. 1998; Forbes and Adams-Curtis 2001;

Foshee et al. 1999; Kaura and Allen 2004; Skuja and Halford 2004; Straus and Savage 2005). Johnson and Ferraro (2000), in reviewing research from the 1990s, suggested that the intergenerational transmission of violence explains only a small proportion of partner violence and, thus, renamed the phenomena "intergenerational non-transmission of violence" (p. 957).

International Research and Responses to Domestic Violence

Until recently, domestic violence has received limited international attention. Patterns and responses vary across the globe, and we have been unable to get a comprehensive picture of this issue worldwide. The WHO (2014) report, noted above, states that 87% of the 133 countries surveyed have enacted laws relevant to domestic/family violence prevention, but only 44% reported that those laws are fully enforced (see Box 5.2). Categorically, for rape, 64% of countries reported that related prevention laws are fully enforced, 38% of countries reported fully enforced laws for removal of violent spouse from home, and 43% of countries reported fully enforced laws against rape in

---

BOX 5.2   COUNTRIES THAT HAVE NO LAW AGAINST DOMESTIC VIOLENCE AND COUNTRIES THAT HAVE RECENTLY INTRODUCED NEW LEGISLATION AGAINST DOMESTIC VIOLENCE

Armenia	Burkina Faso	Cameroon
Congo	Ivory Coast	Egypt
Haiti	Iran	Latvia
Lebanon	Nigeria	Pakistan
Russian Federation	Syria	

Since 2000, many countries have either introduced new legislation on domestic violence or amended their existing legislation to align their laws with growing international standards. Several examples include the following:

Albania 2003	Bosnia and Herzegovina 2005	Lithuania 2008
Norway 2009	Saudi Arabia 2013 (considered a landmark bill that outlaws domestic abuse)	

marriage. Furthermore, of the 133 countries, some 68% had established a prevention action plan for IPV. The report reveals that while the international
community is developing a growing awareness of domestic violence/IPV,
there still remains much work to be done and it would appear that there is
considerable room for capacity building (see Chapter 1 for further discussion).

Notwithstanding the above issues, there are a number of international
conventions and accords that reflect not only the growing awareness but also
the concerted effort by the international community to respond proactively to
these types of offences. Below is a summary of what are arguably some of the
key international conventions and agreements to prevent domestic violence:

- **Declaration on the Elimination of Discrimination against Women
  (1967)**: The declaration stated that "discrimination against women,
  denying or limiting as it does their equality of rights with men, is fundamentally unjust and constitutes an offence against human dignity."
- **Convention on the Elimination of All Forms of Discrimination
  against Women (1979)**: The Convention's origin lies in the 1948
  International Bill of Human Rights. The document incorporates The
  Universal Declaration of Human Rights, The International Covenant
  on Civil and Political Rights (ICCPR), and The International
  Covenant on Economic, Social, and Cultural Rights. Together, they
  proclaim: "the right to equality, liberty and security and the rights to
  be free from discrimination, torture and degrading and inhumane
  treatment."

  This Convention defines discrimination as "...any distinction,
  exclusion or restriction made on the basis of sex which has the effect
  or purpose of impairing or nullifying the recognition, enjoyment or
  exercise by women, irrespective of their marital status, on a basis
  of equality of men and women, of human rights and fundamental
  freedoms in the political, economic, social, cultural, civil or any
  other field." Furthermore, the signatory states commit themselves
  to ending all forms of discrimination against women: by persons,
  by organisations or by enterprises. In addition, "sufficient legal protection must include the abolishment of discriminatory laws, along
  with the establishment of tribunals and public laws institutions."

  Finally, as of late 2015, only five countries have not signed the
  Convention (e.g., Iran, Niue, Sudan, Somalia, and Tonga), and two
  (one being the United States) are only signatory members. Every state
  party must release regular reports, which since 2008 is scrutinized by
  the Office of the High Commissioner for Human Rights in Geneva
  on the Elimination of Discrimination against Women (CEDAW).
- **General Recommendation 19 on Violence against Women, adopted
  by the Committee on the Elimination of Discrimination against**

Women (CEDAW) (1992): The Committee adopted General Recommendation 19, which includes violence in the prohibition of gender-based discrimination: "violence that is directed at a woman because she is a woman or that affects women disproportionately [is discrimination]." It includes acts that inflict physical, mental or sexual harm or suffering, threats of such acts, coercion and other deprivations of liberty. Violence against women is an internationally recognized human rights violation when either a public official or a private person commits the violence. State participating to the CEDAW must take all the necessary measures to eliminate violence, including legal sanctions, civil remedies, preventative measures (such as public information and education campaigns), and protective measures (such as support services for victims).

- **UN World Conference on Human Rights in Vienna (1993)**: The conference generated a platform for women via the Global Campaign for Human Rights, which resulted in the Vienna Declaration and Programme of Action, which state that women's rights are human rights.

- **Declaration on the Elimination of Violence against Women (1993) (DEVAW)**: The declaration states that "violence against women constitutes a violation of the rights and fundamental freedoms of women and impairs or nullifies their enjoyment of those rights and freedoms..."

  The DEVAW, although it is not binding, is the first significant legal instrument that highlights sex discrimination, and advocates for "all measures" to be taken to "abolish existing laws, custom regulations and practices that are discriminatory against women, and to establish adequate legal protection for equal rights of men and women" (Article 2). The Declaration classifies violence against women into three primary categories: (1) that occurring in the family (domestic violence), (2) that occurring within the general community, and (3) that perpetrated or condoned by the State.

- **Beijing Declaration and Platform of Action (1995)**: The Fourth World Conference on Women in 1995 resulted in the Beijing Declaration. The declaration strengthens the fundamental principle that the rights of women and girls are not separate from universal human rights. It calls upon governments to take measures that include the National Plans of Action, and to follow up on local implementation efforts.

  The definition of violence, contained in the Platform for Action, is extended to "any act of gender-based violence that results in, or is likely to result in, physical, sexual or psychological harm or suffering to women, including threats of such acts, coercion or arbitrary deprivation of liberty, whether occurring in public or private life."

BOX 5.3   PURPLE RIBBON CAMPAIGN

The Purple Ribbon Campaign was started by Mary Durant from Berlin, New Hampshire, in the United States in 1994. The project represented the collective effort of a number of adult rape and abuse survivors who "wanted a better and safer world for children and adult victims of violence." Since its modest beginnings, the campaign is now an international project whose long-term goal is to bring to an end all interpersonal violence. The campaign's information has been translated into some 40 languages. The campaign relies on information dissemination, and while domestic violence plays an important role in their campaign, their crusade is against all types of interpersonal abuse that results in harm to the victim. Their motto reads: "Break the silence and break the cycle! Speak out! Do not protect perpetrators with your silence!!!"

Another indication of the growing international movement to fight domestic violence has been symbolized by the **Purple Ribbon Campaign**, which is designed to promote awareness of domestic violence (see Box 5.3). Also, a growing number of dedicated journals (e.g., *Trauma, Violence, & Abuse*; *Journal of Family Violence*; and *Domestic Violence and Children*), as well as numerous national and international conferences on domestic violence and sexual abuse, have contributed greatly to awareness efforts.

Prevention

As described in the Introduction to this book, prevention strategies are influenced by a number of factors. As previously discussed in this chapter, the definition of domestic violence, theories used to understand and explain violence, and the degree to which domestic violence is identified as problematic all play a role in prevention efforts. Countries and communities that define domestic violence narrowly are unlikely to collect data on the experience of victimization among all members of the community or to invest in broad-based prevention strategies. While a narrow definition can increase the focus on a particular group or component, it can also minimize less common experiences of violence. Alternately, a broad focus can highlight the impact of violence for whole communities or can diffuse efforts and resources, potentially minimizing the impact of prevention initiatives.

The collection of data on the incidence and prevalence of domestic violence supports the need for resources. However, if data are not collected on the experience of *all* domestic violence victims, it is unlikely that resources will be allocated for *all* populations (e.g., victims in same-sex relationships). The understanding of the cause of violence is equally important in designing prevention efforts. If domestic violence is explained with theories that focus on the lack of social and legal sanctions, then prevention efforts will likely target changing cultural and social norms. If the belief exists that domestic violence is the result of a lack of knowledge or skill, educational programs would be a logical choice to prevent domestic violence (Dahlberg and Krug 2002, p. 12).

The social–ecological model discussed earlier supports the use of multiple theories to explain violence and can be used to conceptualize prevention on a continuum, from efforts aimed at the micro level targeting individuals to macro-level interventions aimed at societal change. Ideally, prevention will encompass activities at the primary, secondary, and tertiary level. Primary prevention focuses on reducing the incidence, secondary prevention focuses on early case finding to prevent reoccurrence, while tertiary prevention seeks to minimize the effects of the problem (Wolfe and Jaffe 1999, pp. 135–136).

Table 5.4 describes examples of primary, secondary, and tertiary prevention for individuals, community, and society. Primary prevention activities include providing information on domestic violence in public areas, media campaigns, and mandatory education in schools and in the workplace. Targeting groups at increased risk for violence is an example of secondary prevention (Barnes et al. 1991). Asking about relationship violence in health or counseling programs or collaborating with the community to provide groups for women and men who have witnessed parental violence or have been the victim of violence in a previous relationship are examples of targeted prevention. Tertiary prevention at the micro level includes referrals to specialized resources for individual disclosing victimization, and tertiary prevention at the macro level includes the development of policies or legislation that increases safety for victims.

Prevention activities that are part of a continuum provide for the information to be repeated using diverse formats, in different contexts, and at multiple levels, reducing the likelihood of "erosion of knowledge" (Legge et al. 2004, p. 75). O'Leary et al. (2006) recommend violence prevention activities at the individual or community level target those at risk, be interactive, use cognitive–behavioral techniques, and be sensitive to culture. Universal prevention has been used to target changing norms for inappropriate behavior. A combination of targeted and universal programs from micro to macro levels enhances opportunities to prevent violence from occurring and prevent a reoccurrence when violence has been identified (see Box 5.4).

Recommendations for primary prevention of domestic violence from national and international agencies concerned with domestic violence commonly identify the following elements (Warthe 2014):

Table 5.4 Continuum of Violence Prevention Strategies

	Primary (Universal)	Secondary (Targeted)	Tertiary
Individual	• Universal screening for domestic violence in counseling and health centers to increase awareness • Education and awareness promoting healthy relationships	• Universal screening for domestic violence in counseling and health centers to support early intervention • Access to specialized programs and services for victims/survivors • Programs for groups at risk of victimization/perpetration • Bystander intervention programs • Parenting or peer mentoring programs designed to promote healthy relationships	• Assistance with safety planning for individuals disclosing victimization (counseling/health center or by phone with a community agency) • Referral to programs and services providing specialized support/counseling • Services are comprehensive, available, integrated with other services (e.g., health, mental health), and informed by evidence (WHO 2014)
Community	• Provide information on domestic violence using multiple forms of media • Establish a committee populated by key stakeholders and interested community members to establish an agenda for violence prevention	• Provide 24-hour resource information in key areas where people gather and where there is some degree of privacy, for example, in bathrooms, in public buildings in bathrooms, human resource and counseling offices, and health centers	• Develop policies for managing disclosures of violence • Key systems including health and education develop partnerships with agencies providing specialized services and support

(Continued)

Table 5.4 (Continued) Continuum of Violence Prevention Strategies

	Primary (Universal)	Secondary (Targeted)	Tertiary
Society	• Strengthen data collection to better describe scope of problem, inform action plans (UN Population Fund 2013; WHO 2014) • Address social and cultural norms that support domestic violence and maintain inequalities between groups (e.g., gender, people with disabilities, race, economic class) (CDC 2015) • Address the social and physical environment to reduce risk and increase resilience; this includes policies that promote a prevention agenda within schools and the workplace (CDC 2015)	• Identify groups at risk and ensure policies exist to support primary prevention and early intervention	

Source: Adapted from Warthe, D.G. (2007). *Fields of Service: Dating Violence.* Unpublished manuscript, Faculty of Social Work, University of Calgary, Calgary, Alberta, p. 21.

BOX 5.4   THE COST SAVINGS OF PREVENTION

The need for evidence-based practices and policies has encouraged economic measures of social problems. Estimating the economic cost of
domestic violence justifies investment in prevention efforts (Rossiter
2011). Several studies in Canada have estimated the cost of violence
against women. The definition of violence and the measures of cost vary
in these studies, as any economic estimate of a social problem relies on
a variety of counts, prevalence, morbidity, and mortality of the issue.
However, it is abundantly clear that the prevention of first-time victimization or perpetration of domestic violence will result in economic
cost savings (Wells et al. 2012a).

An analysis of the economic cost of domestic violence in Alberta,
Canada, by Wells et al. (2012a) was conducted based on data from two
national surveys (the Uniform Crime Report and the General Social
Survey) that were used to calculate an annual domestic violence incidence rate for the province, and a per-woman cost of domestic violence
identified in a previous study by Varcoe et al. (2011). The researchers
estimated that the province of Alberta has spent more than 600 million
in the past five years, even after a woman had left the abusive relationship. This estimate was based on the costs of basic health and non–health
care supports and services, and did not include other public sector costs
(e.g., police, lost time at work, effects on children, etc.). Varcoe and colleagues found that each domestic violence case that is prevented saves
$11,370 spent on intervention; this suggests a possible cost savings for
Alberta of approximately $9.6 million, further emphasizing the need to
identify cost-effective prevention strategies (Wells et al. 2012a).

- Increased awareness
- Changing cultural and social norms that contribute to violence
- Initiatives that are grounded in the community
- A range of programs targeted at groups at risk of victimization or
  perpetration (see Box 5.5)
- A network of policies that support prevention
- Data collection system that includes monitoring the incidence of
  violence.

A common approach to prevention is raising awareness of the causes,
scope, and consequences of domestic violence through public information
campaigns (Family Violence Prevention Fund 2002; Harvey et al. 2007; Wells
2011). Public awareness campaigns have been used to provide information,

**BOX 5.5   USING RESTORATIVE JUSTICE
IN RESPONSE TO DOMESTIC VIOLENCE**

In 2015, a European consortium led by the Verwey–Jonker Institute in Utrecht, the Netherlands, released a paper on the use of restorative justice (RJ) in cases of IPV (Lunnemann and Wolthuis 2015). The project involved six European countries, and the research team examined the relative effectiveness of the application of RJ principles when used in cases involving IPV. The project included interviews with 32 victims and 19 offenders in five of the countries. The study found that the most common RJ practice for such cases was victim–offender mediation (VOM).

It was noted that RJ practice and regulations between and even within countries varied in how VOM was practiced. For example, in some countries, it is mandatory to end a VOM with a written agreement, while in others, it is not. The study also found that selection criteria (e.g., gender, age, cultural background, education and employment status, family situation, etc.) varied between the countries. Regardless, all six participating countries used some iteration of VOM when dealing with IPV cases. The findings of the research showed that using VOM in IVP cases resulted in satisfaction rates among most, but not all, of the participants.

It was further noted that while most of the participants in the United Kingdom felt that VOM was a useful tool, "the feminist movement is strongly against restorative justice..." (p. 18). A feminist analysis recognizes the dynamics of IPV as motivated by a desire for power and control; this negates the use of mediation, which assumes an equal distribution of power, as a response. The researchers in this study point out that while offenders might avoid prison time, by participating in the VOM program, offenders take responsibility for their actions and for the outcome for the victim. It was also observed that as promising as VOM proved to be in IPV cases, the practices differ between countries and "there are still many aspects that need improvement..." (p. 22).

dispel myths, and engage specific groups in action to end violence. Public awareness campaigns can contribute to public discourse and minimize isolation for individuals and families.

Related to raising awareness, efforts to change the cultural and social norms that contribute to violence are the most common approach to domestic and sexual violence prevention with approximately half of 133 countries reporting implementing such strategies in 2014 (WHO 2014, p. 28). This is particularly true for countries that use the social–ecological model of violence prevention, as norms that support the use of violence in intimate relationships are identified as a root cause of violence (Victoria Health 2011; Wells et al. 2012b, p. 10). The WHO (2014) includes the need for changing gender norms to support "gender equitable" relationships (p. 75).

In order to be effective, violence prevention needs to be grounded in the community, reflect the needs and "vulnerabilities" specific to community, and be accountable to community (McInturff 2013, p. 30). This is especially relevant in an international context as an approach that might be effective or relevant in one community may not have the same outcomes elsewhere. Community responses involve the leadership and include opportunities for broad participation of members (Family Violence Prevention Fund 2002; Harvey et al. 2007). The United States Agency International Development Plan, for example, identifies the importance supporting of gender equity at the community level by "elevating" leadership roles of women and girls as one strategy to prevent domestic violence (US AIDS 2012, p. 40). Although participatory approaches can take significant amounts of time, they contribute to the capacity to build and sustain programs and services (McInturff 2013, p. 30).

Targeted prevention programs focus efforts on populations or groups that have been identified to be at risk for experiencing domestic violence or where primary prevention is most likely to make a difference. The WHO in their *Global Status Report on Violence Prevention* (2014) indicates that 22% of the 133 countries surveyed have school-based dating violence prevention programs, with the majority of these occurring in the region of the Americas. Other examples of targeted prevention include family-based approaches recognizing the correlation between child maltreatment and domestic violence (Harvey et al. 2007; Wessels et al. 2013) and initiatives to reduce alcohol and substance misuse (Jewkes 2002; Victoria Health 2011; Wells et al. 2012b). Groups that experience higher rates of domestic violence include younger women, pregnant women, indigenous women, and people with disabilities (DisAbled Women's Network 2010; Sinha 2013; Victoria Health 2011; Wells et al. 2012b). The WHO report (2014) identifies that 42% of countries globally target the economic empowerment of women and use gender equity training as a strategy to prevent domestic violence (p. 75). Key to the success of implementing targeted programs is ensuring that evidence exists to support effectiveness and ongoing evaluation (Harvey et al. 2007). Targeted programs should exist as part of continuum prevention efforts in a community (Tutty and Bradshaw 2003).

Policies that support prevention include the development of a national strategy or plan to prevent and respond to domestic violence at the primary, secondary, or tertiary level (McInturff 2013). This represents a long-term commitment rather than short-term solutions and typically requires some type of funding to support the strategy. Policy and protocols can also be implemented locally to support a range of prevention activities in the workplace, schools, and health centers. Police and courts can develop and implement policies for responding that increase safety to contribute to systems that are victim centered.

Ongoing research and measurement of domestic violence is a key element of most prevention strategies (Jewkes 2002; McInturff 2013; US AIDS 2012; Wells et al. 2012b). The WHO (2014) reported that 43% of countries have national surveys to collect data on issues related to domestic violence (p. 74). Measurement provides both benchmarks and data on progress toward the goal of the elimination of violence. Considering domestic violence from different perspectives, such as taking a public health approach or using a broad definition, will result in increased clarity about the data collected and the gaps and contribute to building a strategy for prevention (Flury et al. 2010; Murray and Powell 2009).

Conclusion

As demonstrated in this chapter, domestic violence rarely occurs spontaneously or in isolation from underlying power imbalances that give approval to and legitimate its use in certain circumstances. It is also acknowledged that domestic violence is a universal problem that knows no social, cultural, or economic boundaries. Hence, the authors of this chapter attempted to provide a theoretical context by which to comprehend this issue from a global perspective; the identified challenges with developing a universal understanding only highlights the diversity in our world. We may never get to a place of international agreement around the definition, measurement, and best prevention strategies for domestic violence, because we all construct our understandings of the issue based on different cultural, environmental, and structural foundations. But, perhaps it is more important to acknowledge the connection between understanding, identification, and response, so that prevention is most appropriate for the context of our lives.

Despite the challenges of developing a shared definition and accurate measures of domestic violence, worldwide, there is evidence of the issue being addressed, such as the implementation of national action plans and violence prevention laws. Furthermore, there is evidence of a greater understanding of domestic violence, such as evolving definitions and farther-reaching measurement strategies, and there is evidence of preventative activity, such as an increase of targeted programs along the continuum. We can learn from each other (e.g., public awareness and social marketing campaigns), and we have; recognition of a range of victims, implementation of best practices for prevention, and changes to legislation are evidence of a global effort to fight this growing problem. However, gaps still exist, particularly around the collection of data. This can be addressed by ensuring that definitions are sensitive to not only gender but also other factors, as that is how we will legitimize and best understand the experiences of victims. Definitions, at the very least, should be consistent at a national level; agreement at that level will enable baseline measures and longitudinal comparisons (WHO 2014). From there, prevention strategies will be most successfully executed. The international picture should not be ignored, but we should learn from our differences in understanding and our approaches to ending the cycle of violence (see Box 5.6).

Finally, preventing domestic violence and its various related expression from occurring will require a paradigm shift in attitudes, behavior, and the

BOX 5.6   THE INTERNATIONAL CONTEXT FOR LEGISLATING AGAINST DOMESTIC VIOLENCE

- October 2006: Secretary-General's in-depth study on all forms of violence against women (A/61/122/Add.1 and Corr.1) (available online in all United Nations official languages: http://www.un.org/womenwatch/daw/vaw/v-sg-study.htm)
- December 2006: General Assembly resolution 61/143 on the intensification of efforts to eliminate violence against women
- March 2008: Launch of the Secretary-General's Campaign "UNiTE to End Violence against Women," 2008–2015: One of the five key goals of the campaign, to be achieved in all countries by 2015, is the adoption of legislation on violence against women in accordance with international human rights standards (see http://endviolence.un.org)
- October 2008: General Assembly resolution 63/155 on the intensification of efforts to eliminate violence against women
- March 2009: Launch of the Secretary-General's database on violence against women, which provides the first global "one-stop shop" for information on measures undertaken by Member States of the United Nations to address violence against women, including legislation (United Nations, 2010, http://www.un.org/womenwatch/daw/vaw)
- December 2015: An international conference to end violence against women; 35 stakeholders pledged action to end violence against women (UN Women, 2015, http://www.unwomen.org/en/news/stories/2015/12/global-pledges-ramp-up-campaign-to-end-violence-against-women)

conditions (e.g., social, cultural, economic, and political) that predispose individuals to become victims or perpetrators of violence. We need to continue to enliven our understanding of the factors that place individuals at risk of victimization or perpetration. Fortunately, our knowledge about prevention of domestic violence has grown significantly in the past 20- to 30-odd years, but considerable work still needs to be conducted to sort out the complex interaction of the risk and protective factors in order to identify and develop the most effective ways of changing the prevailing norms and social and structural conditions that can precipitate the crime and the collateral harm for individuals and society at large.

Glossary of Key Terms

Domestic violence: Although there is little agreement on a universal definition of domestic violence, most definitions include the nature of the relationship and the types of violence.

European Istanbul Convention: A Council of Europe convention on preventing and combating violence against women and domestic violence, entered into force on August 1, 2014.

Gender perspective: Considering the impact of gender on people's roles, experiences, and interactions.

Patriarchy: A form of social organization where men hold the power and women are largely excluded from it.

Protective factors: Any characteristic, internal or external to an individual, that decreases the likelihood of something harmful happening to them.

Purple Ribbon Campaign: An international campaign organized to create public awareness and positively change societal attitudes and behaviors about male violence against women, symbolized by a purple ribbon.

Risk factors: Any characteristic, internal or external to an individual, that increases the likelihood of something harmful happening to them.

Social constructionism: A sociological theory that explains that people's understandings of the world are based on their own experiences, their interactions with others, and the social context within which they live.

Social–ecological framework: A model that considers the interplay between various personal and environmental factors in explaining social behavior.

Social learning theory: A sociological theory that explains that people learn by observing others. Based on the work of Albert Bandura (1977).

Discussion Questions

1. What do you consider to be the primary causes of domestic violence? To what extent, if any, do patriarchal values play a role, or what might the primary risk factors be (e.g., socioeconomic vs. psychological, substance abuse, mental health, unemployment, etc.)? How does your perspective impact a crime prevention strategy?
2. What role, if any, should law enforcement play when responding to a domestic violence situation?
3. To what extent, if any, do the feminist perspective and the battered women's movement still play a role in informing domestic violence crime prevention initiatives?
4. The human rights perspective views all forms of violence against women as a form of torture. Do you agree with this perspective and how might it influence any crime prevention strategy?
5. How does your perspective or understanding of domestic violence influence the choice prevention or intervention strategies?
6. Do you believe that domestic violence can be prevented? What would need to happen for this to occur?

Suggested Reading

Annotated bibliography focusing on the scope of the problem/prevalence, health and social consequences, and existing and promising interventions: http://johnjayresearch.org/pri/files/2015/03/IPV-Annotated-Bibliography-PRI.pdf

Centers for Disease Control and Prevention: http://www.cdc.gov/violenceprevention/index.html

Current information on prevalence, research, and promising practices: World Health Organization: http://www.who.int/violence_injury_prevention/violence/activities/intimate/en/

National Resource Center on Domestic Violence: http://www.nrcdv.org/

UN Women: http://www.unwomen.org/en/what-we-do/ending-violence-against-women

Recommended Web Links

https://www.childwelfare.gov/topics/systemwide/domviolence/prevention/
    The Child Welfare Information Gateway website provides information, resources, and tools covering topics on child welfare, child abuse and neglect, out-of-home care, adoption, and so on.
http://www.stopvaw.org/Stop_Violence_Against_Women

Stop Violence Against Women is a project of The Advocates for Human Rights. The website is a forum for information, advocacy, and change in the promotion of women's human rights around the world.

http://www.who.int/mediacentre/factsheets/fs239/en/

The Media Centre of the WHO presents a fact sheet on Violence against women: Intimate partner and sexual violence against women.

http://preventdomesticviolence.ca/

Shift: The Project to End Domestic Violence was created by the Brenda Strafford Chair in the Prevention of Domestic Violence at the University of Calgary in Alberta, Canada. Shift takes a primary prevention approach to stop first-time victimization and perpetration of domestic violence.

References

Abramsky, T., Watts, C.H., Garcia-Moreno, C., Devries, K., Kiss, L., Ellsberg, M., Jansen, H.A., and Heise, L. (2011). What factors are associated with recent intimate partner violence? Findings from the WHO multi-country study on women's health and domestic violence. *BMC Public Health* 11: 109.

Bacchi, C.L. (1999). *Women, Policy and Politics: The Construction of Policy Problems*. London, England: Sage Publications.

Bandura, A. (1977). *Social Learning Theory*. Englewood Cliffs, NJ: Prentice Hall.

Barnes, G.E., Greenwood, L., and Sommer, R. (1991). Courtship violence in a Canadian sample of male college students. *Family Relations* 40(1): 37–44.

Bondurant, B. (2001). University women's acknowledgement of rape: Individual, situational, and social factors. *Violence Against Women* 7(3): 394–313.

Breiding, M.J., Basile, K.C., Smith, S.G., Black, M.C., and Mahendra, R.R. (2015). *Intimate Partner Violence Surveillance: Uniform Definitions and Recommended Data Elements, Version 2.0*. Retrieved from Centers for Disease Control and Prevention website: http://www.cdc.gov/violenceprevention/pdf/intimatepartner violence.pdf.

Bronfenbrenner, U. (1977). Toward and experimental ecology of human development. *American Psychologist* 32: 513–531.

Brownridge, D.A. (2004). Understanding women's heightened risk of violence in common-law unions: Revisiting the selection and relationship hypotheses. *Violence Against Women* 10(6): 626–651.

Burr, V. (2015). *Social Constructionism* (3rd ed.). Florence, KY: Taylor & Francis.

Calgary Domestic Violence Committee. (1996). *Domestic Violence Protocol Project*. Unpublished manuscript.

Centers for Disease Control and Prevention, The Social-Ecological Model: A Framework for Prevention (March 25, 2015), accessed April 20, 2015, http://www.cdc.gov/violenceprevention/overview/social-ecologicalmodel.html.

Chevigny, P.G. (2001). From betrayal to violence: Dante's Inferno and the social construction of crime. *Law and Social Inquiry* 26(4), 787–818.

Council of Europe Convention. (2011). Europe Treaty Series—No. 210 Council of Europe Convention on preventing and combating violence against women and domestic violence. Retrieved August 27, 2016 from: https://rm.coe.int /CoERMPublicCommonSearchServices/DisplayDCTMContent?documentId =090000168008482e.

Cunningham, A., Jaffe, P.G., Baker, L., Dick, T., Malla, S., Mazaheri, N., and Poisson, S. (1998). *Theory-Derived Explanations of Male Violence against Female Partners: Literature Update and Related Implications for Treatment and Evaluation.* London, ON: London Family Court Clinic.

Dahlberg, L.L., and Krug, E.G. (2002). Violence: A global public health problem. In *World Report on Violence and Health*, eds. E.G. Krug, L.L. Dahlberg, J.A. Mercy, A.B. Zwi, and R. Lozano, 1–21. Geneva: World Health Organization.

Devries, K.M., Mak, J.Y.T., Garcia-Moreno, C., Petzold, M., Child, J.C., Falder, G., Lim, S., Bacchus, L.J., Engell, R.E., Rosenfeld, L., Pallitto, C., Vos, T., Abrahams, N., and Watts, C.H. (2013). The global prevalence of intimate partner violence against women. *Science* 340(6140): 1527–1528.

DisAbled Women's Network (DAWN-RAFH) Canada. (2010). Women with disabilities and violence fact sheet. Montreal, QC: DAWN-RAFH Canada. Retrieved August 28, 2016 from http://www.dawncanada.net/pdf/WomenDisabilities Violence.pdf.

Easteal, P. (1994). Violence against women in the home: How far have we come? How far to go? Family Matters, 37, Australian Institute of Family Studies. Retrieved August 28, 2016 from: https://aifs.gov.au/publications/family-matters/issue-37 /violence-against-women-home.

European Commission of Justice. (2010). Domestic violence against women report. Retrieved August 27, 2016 from: http://ec.europa.eu/public_opinion/archives /ebs/ebs_344_en.pdf.

Evans, S. (2005). Beyond gender: Class, poverty and domestic violence. *Australian Social Work* 58(1): 36–43.

Family Violence Prevention Fund. (2002, September). National consensus guidelines on identifying and responding to domestic violence victimization in health care settings. San Francisco. Retrieved August 27, 2016 from: http://www.endabuse .org/programs/healthcare/files/Consensus.pdf.

Fattah, E.A. (1997). *Criminology: Past, Present and Future: A Critical Overview.* New York: St. Martin's Press.

Flury, M., Nyberg, E., and Riecher-Rossler, A. (2010). Domestic violence against women: Definitions, epidemiology, risk factors and consequences. *Swiss Medical Weekly* 140, w13099.

Forbes, G.B., and Adams-Curtis, L.E. (2001). Experiences with sexual coercion in college males and females: Role of family conflict, sexist attitudes, acceptance of rape myths, self-esteem, and the big-five personality factors. *Journal of Interpersonal Violence* 16(9): 865–889.

Foshee, V.A., Bauman, K.E., and Linder, F. (1999). Family violence and the perpetration of adolescent dating violence: Examining social learning and social control processes. *Journal of Marriage and Family* 61: 331–342.

Friese, G., and Collopy, K.T. (2010). *EMS Magazine* 39(7): 59–64.

Fulu, E., and Miedema, S. (2015). Violence against women: Globalizing the integrated ecological model. *Violence Against Women* 21(12): 1431–1455.

Ganley, A. (2002). Understanding Domestic Violence: Preparatory Reading for Participants, Alaska Network on Domestic Violence and Sexual Assault, 71 (Feb. 2002), http://andvsa.org/wp-content/uploads/2009/12/60-ganely-general-dv-article.pdf.

Garcia-Moreno, C. (2001). *Putting Women First: Ethical and Safety Recommendations for Research on Domestic Violence against Women.* Geneva, Switzerland: WHO. Retrieved from http://www.who.int/gender/violence/womenfirtseng.pdf.

Gov.uk. (2013). *Information for Local Areas on the Change to the Definition of Domestic Violence and Abuse.* Retrieved from https://www.gov.uk/government/uploads/system/uploads/attachment_data/file/142701/guide-on-definition-of-dv.pdf.

Hahn Rafter, N. (1990). The social construction of crime and crime control. *Journal of Research in Crime and Delinquency* 27(4): 376–389.

Harvey, A., Garcia-Moreno, C., and Butchart, A. (2007, May 2–3). Primary prevention of intimate-partner violence and sexual violence: Background paper for WHO expert meeting May 2–3, 2007. New York: WHO. Retrieved August 27, 2016 from: http://www.who.int/violence_injury_prevention/publications/violence/IPV-SV.pdf.

Heise, L.L. (1998). Violence against women: An integrated, ecological framework. *Violence Against Women* 4(3): 262–290.

Heise, L., Ellsberg, M., and Gottmoeller, M. (2002). A global overview of gender-based violence. *International Journal of Gynecology and Obstetrics* 78(1): S5–S14.

Heise, L., and Garcia-Moreno, C. (2002). Violence by intimate partners. In *World Report on Violence and Health*, eds. E. Krug, L.L. Dahlberg, J.A. Mercy, A.B. Zwi, and R. Lozano, 87–121. Geneva: World Health Organization.

Heise, L.L., Pitanguy, J., and Germaine, A. (1994). Violence against Women. The Hidden Health Burden. Discussion paper no. 225, p. 46. Washington, DC: The World Bank. https://www.unicef-irc.org/publications/pdf/digest6e.pdf.

Jackson, S.M. (1999). Issues in the dating violence research: A review of the literature. *Aggression and Violent Behavior* 4(2): 233–247.

Jackson, S.L., and Hafemeister, T.L. (2011). Risk factors associated with elder abuse: The importance of differentiating by type of elder maltreatment. *Violence and Victims* 26(6): 738–757.

Jackson, S.L., and Hafemeister, T.L. (2013). *Understanding Elder Abuse.* Washington, DC: National Institute of Justice.

Jewkes, R. (2002). Intimate partner violence: Causes and prevention. *Lancet* 359(9315): 1423–1429.

Johnson, M.P., and Ferraro, K.J. (2000). Research on domestic violence in the 1990s: Making distinctions. *Journal of Marriage and Family Therapy* 62: 948–963.

Kaura, S.A., and Allen, C.M. (2004). Dissatisfaction with relationship power and dating violence perpetration by men and women. *Journal of Interpersonal Violence* 19(5): 576–588.

Koshan, J., and Watson Hamilton, J. (2015, December 4). The Residential Tenancies Act and domestic violence: Facilitating flight? [Blog post]. Retrieved from http://ablawg.ca/2015/12/04/the-residential-tenancies-act-and-domestic-violence-facilitating-flight/comment-page-1/.

Legge, R., Josephson, W.L., Hicks, C., and Kepron, L. (2004). Dating violence: Effects of the Canadian Red Cross prevention program, What's Love Got to Do with It? In *Within Our Reach: Preventing Abuse across the* Lifespan, eds. C.A. Ateah and J. Mirwaldt, 61–75. Winnipeg, MB: Fernwood.

Loseke, D.R., and Kurz, D. (2005). Men's violence toward women is the serious social problem. In *Current Controversies on Family* Violence (2nd ed.), eds. D.R. Loseke, R.J. Gelles, and M.M. Cavanaugh, pp. 79–94. Thousand Oaks, CA: Sage.

Lunnemann, K., and Wolthuis, A. (2015, November). Restorative justice in cases of domestic violence. Verwey–Jonker Institute, Utrecht, the Netherlands, prepared for the Directorate-General Justice, European Commission.

Malks, B.F., and Cartan, H. (2010). Creating large system that work. *Journal of Elder Abuse and Neglect* 22(3–4): 365–374.

McCue, M.L. (2008). *Domestic Violence: A Reference Handbook* (2nd ed.). Santa Barbara, CA: ABC-CLIO, LLC.

McInturff, K. (2013). *The Gap in the Gender Gap: Violence Against Women in Canada*. Ottawa, ON, Canada: Canadian Centre for Policy Alternatives.

McPhail, B.A., Busch, N.B., Kulkarni, S., and Rice, G. (2007). An integrative feminist model: The evolving feminist perspective on intimate partner violence. *Violence Against Women* 13: 817–841. doi:10.1177/1077801207302039.

Measuring Intimate Partner (Domestic) Violence. (2010). Washington, DC: Nation Institute of Justice. Retrieved August 27, 2016 from: http://www.nij.gov/topics /crime/intimate-partner-violence/pages/measuring.aspx.

Murray, S., and Powell, A. (2009). "What's the problem?" Australian public policy constructions of domestic and family violence. *Violence Against Women* 15(5): 532–552.

Nussbaum, M.C. (2000). *Women and Human Development: The Capabilities Approach*. New York: Cambridge University Press.

O'Leary, D.K., Woodin, E.M., Fritz, P.A.T. (2006). Can we prevent hitting? Recommendations for preventing intimate partner violence between young adults. *Journal of Aggression, Maltreatment & Trauma* 13: 121–178.

Pain, R. (2014). Everyday terrorism: Connecting domestic violence and global terrorism. *Progress in Human Geography* 38(4): 531–550.

Rossiter, K.R. (2011). *Domestic Violence Prevention and Reduction in British Columbia (2000–2010)*. New Westminster, BC, Canada: Justice Institute for British Columbia.

Sinha, M. (2013). *Measuring Violence against Women: Statistical Trends*. Retrieved from Statistics Canada website: http://www.statcan.gc.ca/pub/85-002-x/2013001 /article/11766-eng.htm.

Skuja, K., and Halford, W.K. (2004). Repeating the errors of our parents? Parental violence in men's family of origin and conflict management in dating couples. *Journal of Interpersonal Violence* 19(6): 623–638.

Smith, P.H., Earp, J.A., and DeVellis, R. (1995). Measuring battering: Development of the Women's Experience with Battering (WEB) scale. *Women's Health: Research on Gender, Behavior, and Policy* 1(4): 273–288.

Straus, M.A., and Savage, S.A. (2005). Neglectful behavior by parents in the life history of university students in 17 countries and its relation to violence against dating partners. *Child Maltreatment* 10(2): 124–135.

Tutty, L., and Bradshaw, C. (2003). *Violence against Women and Girls: Why Should I Care?* Toronto, ON: Canadian Women's Foundation. Retrieved July 20, 2007 from http://www.cdnwomen.org/eng/1/index.asp.

United Nations. (2010). *Handbook for Legislation on Violence against Women.* Department of Economic and Social Affairs, Division for the Advancement of Women. New York: United Nations. http://www.un.org/womenwatch/daw /vaw/handbook/Handbook%20for%20legislation%20on%20violence%20 against%20women.pdf.

United Nations Population Fund. (2013). The role of data in addressing violence against women and girls. United Nations Population Fund Gender, Human Rights and Culture Branch, Technical Division, New York. http://www.unfpa .org/sites/default/files/resource-pdf/finalUNFPA_CSW_Book_20130221 _Data.pdf.

UN Women (2015, December 11). Global pledges ramp up to end violence against women. Retrieved from http://www.unwomen.org/en/news/stories/2015/12 /global-pledges-ramp-up-campaign-to-end-violence-against-women.

US AIDS. (2012 February). USAID Evaluation Policy: Year One First Annual Report and Plan for 2012 and 2013. Retrieved from: https://usaidlearninglab.org/sites /default/files/resource/files/usaid_evaluation_policy_year_one.pdf.

Varcoe, O., Hankivsky, M., Ford-Gilboe, J., Wuest, P., Wilk, J., Hammerton, J., and Campbell, J. (2011). Attributing selected costs to intimate partner violence in a sample of women who have left abusive partners: A social determinants of health approach. *Canadian Public Policy—Analyse de politiques* 37(3): 1–21.

Victoria Health. (2011). Preventing violence against women in Australia: Research summary. Victoria Health Promotion Foundation, Carlton, Australia. Retrieved from https://www.vichealth.vic.gov.au/Publications.

Warthe, D.G. (2014). *Prevention.* Presentation at the Ending Family Violence: Intervention to Prevention A Family Violence Research Symposium, Edmonton, Alberta. Retrieved from http://www.research4children.com/theme/common /page.cfm?i=10002366.

Warthe, D.G. (2007). *Fields of Service: Dating Violence.* Unpublished manuscript, Faculty of Social Work, University of Calgary, Calgary, Alberta.

Watts, C., and Zimmerman, C. (2002). Violence against women: Global scope and magnitude. *Lancet* 359(9313): 1232–1237.

Wells, L. (2011). Final Report Shift: The Project to End Domestic Violence—Research in the Calgary Aboriginal Community. Calgary, AB, Canada: University of Calgary.

Wells, L., Boodt, C., and Emery, H. (2012a). Preventing domestic violence in Alberta: A cost savings perspective. *The School of Public Policy, University of Calgary,* 5(17): 3–17. Retrieved August 28, 2016 from http://preventdomesticviolence.ca /sites/default/files/research-files/Economic%20Impact%20of%20Domestic%20 Violence%20in%20Alberta.pdf.

Wells, L., Claussen, C., and Cooper, M. (2012b). *Domestic and Sexual Violence: A Background Paper on Primary Prevention Programs and Frameworks.* Calgary, AB: The University of Calgary. Shift: The project to end domestic violence.

Wessels, I., Mikton, C., Ward, C.L., Kibane, T., Alves, R. et al. (2013). Preventing violence: Evaluating outcomes of parenting programmes, Geneva, Switzerland: WHO. Retrieved August 27, 2016 from: http://apps.who.int/iris/bitstream/10665 /85994/1/9789241505956_eng.pdf.

Wolfe, D.A., and Jaffe, P.G. (1999). Emerging strategies in the prevention of domestic violence. *The Future of Children* 9: 133–144.

World Health Organization. (2002). Intimate partner facts. Retrieved from http://www.who.int/violence_injury_prevention/violence/world_report/factsheets/en/ipvfacts.pdf.

World Health Organization. (2006). Intimate partner violence and alcohol fact sheet. Retrieved August 27, 2016 from: http://www.who.int/violence_injury_prevention/violence/world_report/factsheets/ft_intimate.pdf.

World Health Organization. (2014). Global status report on violence prevention 2014. Jointly published by WHO, the United Nations Development Programme, and the United Nations Office on Drugs and Crime, Geneva, Switzerland. http://www.who.int/violence_injury_prevention/violence/status_report/2014/en/.

World population aging: 1950–2050. (2001). Vienna, Austria: United Nations, Department of Economics and Social Affairs—Population Division.

Preventing Human Trafficking for Sexual Exploitation
Ending Demand

6

JACKIE JONES

Contents

Learning Outcomes
After reading this chapter, you should understand

- The global definition of human trafficking
- The problems with getting convictions
- The general prevention obligations of States
- The link between prostitution and trafficking for the purposes of sexual exploitation
- The harm in prostitution
- The rationale for criminalizing demand

Introduction

> The strength of the so-called 'Nordic' model—of shifting criminal responsibility onto those who create demand, rather than those who fulfill it—is most obviously seen in changing attitudes to the acceptability of men to purchase sex.
>
> **APPG on Prostitution and the Global Sex Trade**
> *2014, p. 2*

The scale of human trafficking is difficult to quantify reliably because of its hidden nature (Winterdyk and Reichel 2010; Winterdyk et al. 2012). However, it is generally agreed that it exists, is growing year-on-year, and is one of the top three criminal trades in the world alongside the illegal arms trade and drug smuggling. In 2012, the U.S. Trafficking in Persons Report (**TIP Report**) estimated that around 27 million people around the globe were victims of trafficking (TIP Report 2012, p. 7). UNICEF estimates that as many as 2 million children are prostituted in the global commercial sex trade. There are no global data on age. The European Union has data from the Member States who were able to provide a more detailed breakdown by age across 2010–2012: 45% of registered victims were aged 25 or older, 36% were aged 18–24, 17% were aged 12–17, and 2% were aged 0–11 (EUROSTAT 2015). According to the United Nations Office on Drugs and Crime (UNODC 2014) *Global Report on Trafficking in Persons 2014*, at least 152 different nationalities were trafficked and detected in 124 different countries, with *domestic* trafficking accounting for 27% of all detected cases worldwide. Collectively, women and girls represent around 75% of all victims of trafficking (85% in the EU; EUROSTAT 2015). It is a gross manifestation of gender-based violence and gender inequality. In 2012, the International Labour Organization (**ILO**) revised upward its estimate of the number of people in forced labor globally to 21 million, of which around a quarter are children and around 18.7 million (90%) are exploited by private agents in the "private economy, by individuals or enterprises" (also see Chapter XX) (ILO 2012). In 2015, the ILO estimated that the profits from forced labor in the private economy stood at US$150 billion every year (ILO 2015). One can, therefore, safely say that the myriad forms of human trafficking affect every country, every age group, every ethnicity, all economies, and all genders.

Since the late 1990s to early 2000, human trafficking has also gained increasing worldwide attention, not least because of the apparent contradictions inherent in the trade: millions of people are forced to undertake work for little or no money, yet there are very few convictions in any country on the planet (in 2014, there were just under 4500 convictions, only 216 for forced labor; TIP Report 2015); normative criminal sanctions exist in at least 166 countries (TIP Report 2015), yet the enslavement of people for exploitative purposes appears to be rampant; the trade is seen as a major criminal activity, yet there are hardly any specific, holistic prevention measures in place (Annison 2013; Laczko and Danailova-Trainor 2009). It appears, therefore, that the criminal justice responses to human trafficking have to date not yielded a great number of positive results. Does this mean that the criminal justice system is failing the victims of human trafficking or does it mean that a different approach is required?

This chapter argues that more creative prevention work is required in order to stem the tide of human trafficking. Even though human trafficking can involve a wide range of exploitive activities (e.g., sexual exploitation of children in tourism, organ/tissue trafficking, forced labor, domestic servitude, etc.), this chapter will focus on human trafficking for sexual exploitation, as it is the most prevalent form of human trafficking—followed by forced labor and then debt bondage (Human Rights Commission). Human trafficking is a complex issue (Gallagher 2010) and the response mechanisms have until recently been primarily focused on two facets: (1) raising awareness of what human trafficking is, that it exists in the world and is widespread, and (2) passing normative instruments that criminalize human trafficking in most (and in some jurisdictions all) of its forms but without a significant increase in conviction rates (see below). These two activities are, to some extent of course, the precursor to other prevention measures (bearing in mind that continued awareness raising and educational and training courses are also a key part of prevention work). Yet it is not enough. The United Nations has outlined the four "Ps"—protection, prosecution, prevention, and public education/partnership—as the best way to tackle human trafficking. We are some way away from all four P's being properly utilized in the fight against trafficking.

This chapter focuses on all four Ps but categorizes its main aim as prevention. It will be suggested that prevention work in this field must take the form of ending the demand for sex as a means to undermine and alleviate human trafficking for the purposes of sexual exploitation. Furthermore, it will be contended that there is a clear nexus between the liberalization of the sex industry and the lack of prevention of sex trafficking that requires urgent action. The means used to end the demand is to criminalize it, to seek enforcement of the criminal laws, to educate the public concerning the harm caused to women in prostitution, and to prevent women from entering or remaining in prostitution by providing exit strategies for them. In other words, it is time to introduce the Nordic Model globally. This, it is suggested, is a pragmatic, holistic, and effective way to tackle trafficking for the purposes of sexual exploitation.

Human Trafficking Defined: Regional and Domestic Variations

The first international legal definition of trafficking was agreed in 2000 by way of annex to the United Nations Convention against Transnational Organized

Crime.* It is, therefore, an example of a crime control/management convention (Bruckmueller and Schumann 2012; Milivojevic and Segrave 2012, p. 236) that focuses attention on organized criminal gangs, rather than on the victims of trafficking (for an overview, see Gallagher 2001 and Kaye and Winterdyk 2012, pp. 58–61). The Protocol to Prevent, Suppress and Punish Trafficking in Persons, Especially Women and Children, defines trafficking in section 3:

> "Trafficking in persons" is the recruitment, transportation, transfer, harbouring or receipt of persons, by means of the threat or use of force or other forms of coercion, of abduction, of fraud, of deception, of the abuse of power or of a position of vulnerability or of the giving or receiving of payments or benefits to achieve the consent of a person having control over another person, for the purpose of exploitation...
>
> Exploitation shall include, at a minimum, the exploitation of the prostitution of others or other forms of sexual exploitation, forced labour or services, slavery or practices similar to slavery, servitude or the removal of organs.
>
> The consent of a victim of trafficking to the intended exploitation... shall be irrelevant where any of the means set forth in [above] have been used. The recruitment, transportation, transfer, harbouring or receipt of a child for the purpose of exploitation shall be considered "trafficking in persons" even if this does not involve any of the means set [above]. "Child" shall mean any person under eighteen years of age.

According to this definition, all three elements must be present: an *act* (e.g., recruitment, transport) by a *means* (e.g., threats, coercion, etc.) in order to *exploit* (e.g., in the provisions of sexual services). It is an example of an international definition that is still unclear to policymakers (Roots 2013). The wording of the Protocol suggests only the movement of people. This partly explains the reason many laws are border control measures rather than human rights/prevention measures (Kara 2009, pp. 4–5). In fact, the Protocol does not require movement of the victim across borders, international or otherwise. This is an important aspect of trafficking because many people are trafficked within borders into the sex industry; for example, in the Netherlands (EUROSTAT 2015) and India, whereas countries such as the United Kingdom mostly suffer from international trafficking.

The definition does require "exploitation." This, however, has always been and remains a contested issue (Kara 2009; Rijken 2013). The Protocol provides guidance as to the minima necessary for exploitation to exist, including

---

* There have been other international normative instrument on slavery. One example is the International Convention for the Suppression of the Traffic of Persons and of the Exploitation of the Prostitution of Others 1949. But there are many more.

"the exploitation of the prostitution of others or other forms of sexual exploitation, forced labour or services, (including begging), slavery or practices similar to slavery, servitude or the removal of organs" (see Gallagher 2001 for controversy over definitional issues). However, this is a minimum and is open to interpretation. Domestic laws around the globe vary as to their definition of "exploitation," especially what constitutes "sexual exploitation" (see Box 6.1). It is in this area that the issue of consent, coercion, and exploitation can be seen to be extremely problematic.

The three examples presented in Box 6.1 illustrate that regional and domestic transposition of "exploitation" and, for our purposes, "sexual exploitation" is varied and thus a continuing challenge to a global application of the Protocol. What is included and left out is affected by a State's understanding of sexual exploitation as a gender equality issue and the State's understanding of the nuances of human trafficking. These challenges persist in relation to State parties' adaptation of other parts of the Protocol into their particular domestic legal system(s) as well (Smith and Kangaspunta 2012; Winterdyk et al. 2012, p. 8). For instance, many domestic jurisdictions slice up the offense of trafficking. Until 2015 with the passing of the Modern Slavery Act, the United Kingdom generally used ordinary criminal laws, rather than specific trafficking ones, to prosecute traffickers (this is one of the reasons why conviction rates are low, see below). India amended its Penal Code (Criminal Law [Amendment] Act of 2013) to include a specific offense of slavery (see Box 6.2). It does not, however, explicitly recognize and penalize all forms of labor trafficking (http://www.jgu.edu.in/chlet/pdf/Indias-Human -Trafficking-Laws-Report-Book_Feb-2015.pdf) (see also Bruckmueller and Schumann 2012, p. 102).

Regional anti-trafficking conventions and laws have also influenced these definitions and consequent designated crimes. An example is the European Union, which has taken action in the field of human trafficking for several years in the form of decisions, directives, and action plans, as well as incorporating it into the EU Charter of Fundamental Rights. The most well known is the 2011 Anti-Trafficking Directive,* which makes trafficking a gender issue (as does the Council of Europe Convention on Action against Trafficking in Human Beings 2005; see Elliott 2015).

Laws or policies, therefore, foreground particular parts of the Palermo Protocol according to the culture and ideology prevalent in the society under scrutiny. These variations, therefore, pose challenges for any effective, universal policy or measure to tackle trafficking, let alone prevention work. So too what is tolerated as acceptable exploitation. Examples stem from cultural norms, practices, and traditions, and many of these are harmful,

---

* Directive 2011/36/EU on preventing and combating trafficking in human beings and protecting its victims: OJ L 101, 4.15.2011, p. 1.

BOX 6.1   EXAMPLES OF LAWS ON "SEXUAL EXPLOITATION"

The United Kingdom defines sexual exploitation in the Modern Slavery Act 2015 as follows:

Sexual exploitation
(3) Something is done to or in respect of the person—

    a. which involves the commission of an offence under—
        i. Section 1(1)(a) of the Protection of Children Act 1978 (indecent photographs of children), or
        ii. Part 1 of the Sexual Offences Act 2003 (sexual offences), as it has effect in England and Wales, or
    b. which would involve the commission of such an offence if it were done in England and Wales.
        ii. includes, *inter alia*, rape, assault by penetration, sexual assault, causing a person to engage in sexual activity without consent, prostitution, trafficking into, out of and within the UK for sexual exploitation.

In the United States, "severe forms of trafficking in persons" is defined as "sex trafficking in which a commercial sex act is induced by force, fraud, or coercion, or in which the person induced to perform such act has not attained 18 years of age; or... the recruitment, harboring, transportation, provision, or obtaining of a person for labor or services through the use of force, fraud, or coercion for the purpose of subjection to involuntary servitude, peonage, debt bondage, or slavery" (*Victims of Trafficking and Violence Protection Act of 2000* [TVPA] [P.L. 106–386]). It makes no mention of exploitation (but is implied) and force, fraud, or coercion must be present.

The European Union Statistical Office (EUROSTAT 2015) gathers information according to the Anti-Trafficking Directive* that includes as "sexual exploitation" the following categories:

- Street prostitution
- Window prostitution and brothels
- Strip clubs/bars
- Pornography industry
- Massage parlors
- Others and unknown

---

* Directive 2011/36/EU on preventing and combating trafficking in human beings and protecting its victims: OJ L 101, 4.15.2011, p. 1.

> ### BOX 6.2 INDIA: INDIAN PENAL CODE (IPC)
>
> 370. Buying or disposing of any person as a slave.—Whoever imports, exports, removes, buys, sells or disposes of any person as a slave, or accepts, receives or detains against his will any person as a slave, shall be punished with imprisonment of either description for a term which may extend to seven years, and shall also be liable to fine.

especially for women and girls (Convention on the Elimination of All Forms of Discrimination against Women [**CEDAW**]). This latter point has been acknowledged in the latest **TIP Report** (2015):

> Steadily increasing efforts to combat human trafficking around the globe challenge certain cultural norms. The Palermo Protocol, which has been accepted by 166 States parties and does not allow for any cultural variations, requires the criminalization of all forms of trafficking in persons, as do newly enacted domestic anti-trafficking laws. Likewise, public awareness campaigns and other prevention efforts can also push some traditions to change. In the Middle East, small robots have replaced young boys as jockeys in the sport of camel racing, and in East Asia and the Pacific, some governments have begun to strengthen their responses to child sex tourism by increasing public awareness that it is a crime and denying entry to known foreign sex offenders. African societies are beginning to recognize child domestic servitude as a crime and an injustice to children who instead deserve an education and a supportive environment in which to live. Efforts to prosecute, protect, and prevent human trafficking should continue to hasten the decline of harmful practices that had been defended as culturally justified and thus used to embolden those willing to enslave others.
>
> **TIP Report**
> *2015, p. 18*

Some of these practices, according to the international legal definition, constitute instances of human trafficking. For instance, it may well be acceptable in certain cultures to sell a child, most probably a girl child, into domestic servitude because she is more valuable for her family sending back remittances than taking up space and food at home.* Yet according to the legal definition, this is an example of human trafficking. It is clear from the examples cited in the TIP Report quote that in many parts of the world, measures to combat trafficking are in their infancy (see Box 6.3) partly because of cultural issues despite the fact that the Palermo Protocol does not permit any variation based on culture, suggesting the strength of regional/local cultural norms and how they influence State inaction.

---

* Related to the illegal selling of children is the clandestine practice of intercountry adoption system (see, e.g., Smolin 2006).

BOX 6.3   ORGANIZATION OF AMERICAN STATES

"OAS efforts to combat trafficking in persons began in 1999 when the Inter-American Commission of Women (CIM) co-sponsored a research study on trafficking in persons in nine countries in Latin America that offered broad recommendations for its elimination. In 2003 and 2004, the OAS General Assembly passed two resolutions on the subject, the latter of which created an OAS Coordinator on the Issue of Trafficking in Persons, originally based in the CIM and now part of the Department of Public Security within the Secretariat for Multidimensional Security of the OAS.

Since 2005, OAS has organized, facilitated, and implemented training programs, promoted anti-trafficking policies, and provided opportunities for the exchange of information and best practices to assist member states in their anti-TIP efforts....

By 2012, OAS had trained over 1,000 police, immigration officers, prosecutors, and judges from the English-speaking Caribbean and Central American countries to prevent and combat trafficking in persons. OAS officials helped police academies across the region incorporate the topic of trafficking in persons into their regular training curricula" (Seelke 2015, p. 10).

In Serbia, the government has focused its prevention strategy on, inter alia, awareness-raising campaigns in the media and on television with a special series entitled *Modern Slavery* (Fosson 2011, p. 189).

It is equally true that in many countries, comprehensive prevention work has not yet begun (see Box 6.3). The demand side of the sex industry is an example of a harmful cultural and social practice that requires a criminal sanction (normative instrument) in the fight against trafficking and patriarchy (see below; Jeffreys 2009) and social measures to prevent it from recurring.

This is not to suggest that there are no prevention programs taking place around the world. In fact, there are many. The point is, despite these programs, human trafficking appears to be rampant. One reason is the lack of enforcement of specific criminal laws dealing with human trafficking across the globe where these exist.

Lack of Convictions as a Prevention/Deterrent Strategy

When it comes to human trafficking for the purposes of sexual exploitation, the police often know where the traffickers are and they know where they can find trafficking victims because for prostitution to thrive, as it does, it must be accessible to the buyers—they must be able to find where the women in prostitution are selling sex. It is impossible, therefore, for it to "go underground" (Europol 2014; Swedish Police 2016; UNODC 2009, p. 12). However, many state authorities demonstrate little interest in trying to find the traffickers or to prosecute any offense relating to the sex industry (e.g., brothel keeping in the United Kingdom). It is not a priority crime (see below for possible explanations). That is made obvious when one looks at the statistics of prosecutions around the world, even in countries that pride themselves in the fight against human trafficking. A 2009 Report by the EU Agency for Fundamental Rights entitled *Child Trafficking in the EU* revealed that EU Member States underuse criminal laws for prosecuting child traffickers. Indeed, in "five Member States no final convictions were issued in the period 2000–2007" (EU FRA 2009). This trend is the same where the victims are adults. The low conviction rates are an extremely worrying trend and appear to be replicated in most countries around the world. According to the 2009 UNODC Global Report on Trafficking in Persons, despite the fact that the number of convictions is increasing, they are not doing so proportionately to the growing awareness of the problem. The Report found that "as of 2007/08, two out of every five countries covered by the report had not recorded a single conviction. Either they are blind to the problem, or they are ill equipped to deal with it" (Atak and Simeon 2014; UNODC 2009). It is clearly not being taken seriously by the criminal justice system. By way of comparison, the annual **TIP Report** gathers statistics for global investigations, convictions, and sentences of trafficking for sexual exploitation and from 2007 for forced labor. Prosecutions remain steady at between 5000 and 10,000 in the countries providing statistics (around 167) for trafficking for sexual exploitation. Despite the increase in the number of prosecutions being brought, there is actually a decrease in the number of convictions: from a peak of 5776 in 2013 to 4443 in 2014. For labor exploitation, the numbers are significantly lower—between 500 and 600 annually, with two peak years (2012 and 2013). This correlates with international attention being focused on labor trafficking as a crime. Both figures are very low compared to the millions of people trafficked every year. What is even worse is the number of convictions: only around 4400 in 2014 (the highest number to date) for all forms of trafficking, including for sexual exploitation and only around 220 for forced labor (see Table 6.1). This is appalling.

Clearly, these statistics presented in Table 6.1 indicate a lack of priority in prosecuting and convicting traffickers under domestic criminal laws. Why such low conviction rates? There are several explanations.

First, many local law enforcement agencies and the police still have no, or little, training in how to investigate, how to prosecute, and how to identify victims of trafficking. This has been recognized in many nongovernmental organization (NGO) and government-sponsored reports and requires

Table 6.1   Prosecution Rates Globally

Year	Prosecutions	Convictions	Victims Identified
2004	6885	3026	
2005	6178	4379	
2006	5808	3160	
2007	5682 (490)	3427 (326)	
2008	5212 (312)	2983 (104)	30,961
2009	5606 (432)	4166 (335)	49,105
2010	6017 (607)	3619 (237)	33,113
2011	7909 (456)	3969 (278)	42,291 (15,205)
2012	7705 (1153)	4746 (518)	46,570 (17,368)
2013	9460 (1199)	5776 (470)	44,758 (10,603)
2014	10,051 (418)	4443 (216)	44,462 (11,438)

Source: U.S. Trafficking in Persons Reports. (2012 and 2015). http://www.state.gov/j/tip/rls /tiprpt/2012/192361.htm (accessed November 12, 2015); http://www.state.gov/docu ments/organization/245365.pdf (forced labor figures in brackets).

addressing as part of a comprehensive prevention strategy (Annison 2013; ECPAT; Anti-Trafficking Monitoring Group). There is therefore a lack of understanding (Kara 2009), for instance, comprehending what makes trafficking (a human rights issue) different from smuggling (a border control issue). Much more training needs to take place.

Second, corruption and bribes play a part, as well as the role officials play in the trafficking chain (Atak and Simeon 2014, p. 1029), and there have been calls from the Bench to include anticorruption clauses in a redefinition of international law to assist (or set up) effective monitoring mechanisms for human trafficking (Kendall 2011). In any case, why would officials prosecute those who provide them with a supplementary income?

Third, some regions suffer from political instability and lack of engagement by state officials. For instance, in Latin America and the Caribbean in 2014, there were 944 prosecutions, down from 1182 in 2013. In Europe, 4199 prosecutions were recorded and there were 1585 convictions in 2014, and in East Asia and the Pacific, 1938 prosecutions were recorded and there were 969 convictions (Seelke 2015, p. 13). The development of different layers of laws and policies in Europe and the State and media interest help push up prosecution rates, but still conviction rates should be much higher (demonstrating the need for holistic approaches).

Fourth, a crime-control model is used instead of a human rights–centered approach. The fundamental difference in approach leads to a victim of trafficking being seen as either a criminal (and arrested as such; crime control) or someone in need of protection (with support being offered; human rights). We need both approaches in order to combat human trafficking comprehensively.

Fifth, the definition of human trafficking offered in the Palermo Protocol is complicated and hardly clear (Gallagher 2010, p. 464; Roots 2013). It is, consequently, very difficult to prove all of the elements necessary in order to gain convictions. That is the main reason many domestic laws are written, and then rewritten, or ordinary criminal laws are employed instead of the specific human trafficking ones. It poses a continuing challenge, one that can be addressed for human trafficking for the purposes of sexual exploitation by criminalizing demand.

Sixth, the racist nature of trafficking for any reason, and especially for sexual exploitation with demand requesting certain ethnic and racial features. As a consequence, many indigenous women and girls are trafficked from their reservations or small villages to cater to different tastes. Country examples include Canada, Mexico, and several Asian countries. Most women and girls are from lower social strata or in care; there is a clear lack of interest in providing women and girls in prostitution justice where they have been harmed.*

Seventh, human trafficking is big business, especially trafficking for sexual exploitation. The 2009 UNODC Report explains that "traffickers only sell persons for sexual exploitation when the market conditions make it profitable" (UNODC 2009). A 1998 **ILO** Report estimated that the sex industry in the Philippines, Thailand, Malaysia, and Indonesia alone accounted for 2%–14% of **GDP** in those countries. The report states that:

> Prostitution has changed recently in some SE Asian countries. The scale of prostitution has been enlarged to an extent where we can justifiably speak of a commercial sex sector that is integrated into the economic, social and political life of these countries. The sex business has assumed the dimensions of an industry and has directly or indirectly contributed in no small measure to employment, national income and economic growth.
>
> **L.L. Lim**
> *1998, p. vi*

It is estimated that around 5% of the Netherland's **GDP** comes from the legalization of brothel prostitution in 2001, whereas in China, it is estimated to be worth around 8% of **GDP** (around US$700 billion) (Jeffreys 2009, p. 5). Thus, the trafficking of women and children for the sex industry has become an extremely valuable commodity for governments and recruitment firms around the world. It is in this way that governments cause harm to their own citizens (and "others"), maybe not directly exploiting them, but allowing the exploitation to continue. It is clear that in many countries, government officials (police, etc.) receive kickbacks to turn a blind eye to these situations or do not prosecute even where criminal acts are taking place openly. van Duyne and Spencer (2011) and Jakobsson and Kotsadam (2013) describe human trafficking as an economic crime.

---

* The series of killings of women in prostitution in Toronto in the 1990s.

Finally, and for further discussion below, not acknowledging the link between trafficking for sexual exploitation and the sex industry is another reason for the failure to prosecute. The media endorsed (at best) ambivalence or (at worst) acceptance of prostitution, and the sexual exploitation of humans, especially children, demonstrates a tacit approval.

The Link between Trafficking for Sexual Exploitation and Prostitution

Perhaps surprisingly, the link between trafficking for sexual exploitation and the sex industry, particularly prostitution, has been contested. So too that prostitution can be seen as harmful practice that supports gender inequality (Finkel and Finkel 2015; but see Britton and Dean 2014, p. 322; Jeffreys 2009, 2012, p. 80; Samarasinghe and Burton 2007; Tyler 2012, p. 87). Astonishing is the fact that the definition in the Palermo Protocol clearly mentions it: "the exploitation of the prostitution of others or other forms of sexual exploitation, forced labour." Yet, it is predictable, considering the profits involved within the industry, the people who most use it, and the consequent financial (and other) losses to any move to criminalize it.

The link between trafficking for sexual exploitation and the sex industry has been articulated for a number of years now. In her first report, Sigma Huda (2006), the United Nations Special Rapporteur on Trafficking from 2004 to 2008, found that prostitution is generally a form of trafficking:

> For the most part, prostitution as actually practised in the world usually does satisfy the elements of trafficking. It is rare that one finds a case in which the path to prostitution and/or a person's experiences within prostitution do not involve, at the very least, an abuse of power and/or an abuse of vulnerability. Power and vulnerability in this context must be understood to include power disparities based on gender, race, ethnicity and poverty. Put simply, the road to prostitution and life within "the life" is rarely one marked by empowerment or adequate options.

Since then, there is a growing movement that supports this position and more individuals in power who are willing to speak out. For example, in her 2012 speech, Michelle Bachelet, former and current president of Chile, and former executive director of UN Women, at the United Nations General Assembly Interactive Dialogue on fighting human trafficking as part of a wider violence against women and children agenda, stated that:

> It is difficult to think of a crime more hideous and shocking than human trafficking. Yet it is one of the fastest growing and lucrative crimes. And an

estimated 80 per cent of those trafficked are used and abused as sexual slaves. This human rights violation is driven by the demand for sexual services and the profit they generate; the commodification of human beings as sexual objects, and the poverty, gender inequalities and subordinate position of women and girls that provide fertile ground for human trafficking. We have all heard stories of parents selling their daughters. What we haven't heard so much are the stories of illegal recruiters and traffickers that cash in on *gender-based vulnerabilities.*

M. Bachelet
2012

The **TIP Report** (2015) also clearly reiterates the link between prostitution and sex trafficking.

When an adult engages in a commercial sex act, such as prostitution, as the result of force, threats of force, fraud, coercion or any combination of such means, that person is a victim of trafficking. Under such circumstances, perpetrators involved in recruiting, harboring, enticing, transporting, providing, obtaining, or maintaining a person for that purpose are guilty of the sex trafficking of an adult. Sex trafficking also may occur within debt bondage, as individuals are forced to continue in prostitution through the use of unlawful "debt," purportedly incurred through their transportation, recruitment, or even their crude "sale"—which exploiters insist they must pay off before they can be free. An adult's consent to participate in prostitution is not legally determinative: if one is thereafter held in service through psychological manipulation or physical force, he or she is a trafficking victim and should receive benefits outlined in the Palermo Protocol and applicable domestic laws.

TIP Report
2015, p. 7

Trafficking does not mean prostitution. They are not synonymous but linked. Prostitution becomes an offense and a harm when there is commercial exploitation of a person. If a woman or child is sexually exploited and any person gains out of the same, it amounts to commercial sexual exploitation. Trafficking is the process of recruiting, contracting, procuring, or hiring a person for the sex trade. Therefore, trafficking is a process and prostitution is a result. The "demand" for prostitution (and the sex industry) generates, promotes, and perpetuates trafficking. Demand is created by the (mainly) men who pay for commercial sex. Traffickers, pimps, brothel owners, and other facilitators profit from this demand by supplying the women and girls who are exploited every day in the commercial sex industry. Trafficking is also a means for other types of violations in the sex industry such as developing pornographic material, promoting sex tourism, sexual exploitation under the facade of bar tending, massage parlors, and so on, or even for exploitative labor where sexual abuse may or may not coexist. According to Jakobsson and Kotsadam (2013), trafficking has been found to be more prevalent where prostitution is not illegal. Thus, addressing the demand for commercial sex is a key component of any plan to prevent sex trafficking and sexual exploitation.

Currently, States deal with prostitution in a variety of ways (see Germany, Australia, the Netherlands; see also Bindman and Doezema 1997; Leishman 2007). Generally, many countries' laws distinguish between at least two different types of prostitution: forced and free prostitution. The former is seen to result from coercion, vulnerability, deception, or other pressures. Most define the former as human trafficking, but not the latter. For example, in the United States, sex trafficking is not considered a "severe form of trafficking" under law unless it is associated with commercial sex acts generated by force, fraud, or coercion. This distinction is illusory. How does one prove coercion in these circumstances? Is it assumed a woman, if she is in the sex industry, gives her free will to all forms of sexual practices? Surely not. In any case, Kara points out that "[m]ost men who purchase sex from slaves seek low-price sexual gratification and lack the moral discrimination between 'free' and 'forced'" (Kara 2009, p. 204). These are continuing challenges that should be addressed by criminalizing demand.

The research base supporting the argument that the exploitation and vulnerability, alongside the violence and coercion is widespread in the sex industry passes the legal threshold to amount to human trafficking is growing (see above, Farley et al. 2003; Turner 2012; Tyler 2012). In addition, a considerable body of evidence exists about the multiple harms experienced by women who sell sex: sexual and physical violence; increased likelihood of murder; negative impacts on sexual, mental, and physical health from living with risk, threats, and the actuality of violence, including posttraumatic stress disorder; and problematic substance misuse as a psychological survival tactic. Various authors have cataloged the sexual and physical violence that is the "normal" experience for women in prostitution* (e.g., Commission on the Sex Buyer Law 2016; Jeffreys 2012; Macleod et al. 2008; Turner 2012, p. 38).

This violence can often be traced back to childhood sexual abuse (NHS Scotland 2009), and it leads individuals to being particularly vulnerable to trafficking (Wilson 2015) or entering prostitution as an economic necessity. In South Africa, a study of 349 women involved in street prostitution found that half were under 24 years and 10% were under 18, with a significant

---

* "Including Baldwin (1993, 1999); Barry (1979, 1995); Boyer, Chapman, and Marshall (1993); Dworkin (1981, 1997, 2000); Farley, Baral, Kiremire, and Sezgin (1998); Giobbe (1991, 1993); Hoigard and Finstad (1986); Hughes (1999); Hunter (1994); Hynes and Raymond (2002); Jeffreys (1997); Karim, Karim, Soldan, and Zondi (1995); Leidholdt (1993); MacKinnon (1993, 1997, 2001); McKeganey and Barnard (1996); Miller (1995); Silbert and Pines (1982a, 1982b); Silbert, Pines, and Lynch (1982); Valera, Sawyer, and Schiraldi (2001); Vanwesenbeeck (1994); and Weisberg (1985)" see Farley (2004) for references cited.

BOX 6.4   EVERYDAY SEXUAL VIOLENCE

A five-country study found that 62% ($n = 475$) had been raped since entering prostitution, and nearly half (46%) had been raped more than five times (Farley et al. 2003). The BBC blog running during the period of the murders of five women in Ipswich (England) in December 2006 was replete with postings from women across the globe about the everyday violence they encountered when selling sex (Kelly et al. 2009, p. 40; see also Commission on the Sex Buyer Law 2016, p. 6).

relationship between the numbers of years spent in the sex industry and hard drug use (Kelly et al. 2009, p. 41) (see Box 6.4).

It is also costly to states, societies, and individuals. In the United Kingdom, a 2008 report estimated that the cost to the "state of the violence perpetrated against women in prostitution likely exceeds £1 billion every year. When trafficking of women into the prostitution trade was taken into account, the estimated human and economic cost of the UK's prostitution trade rose to £2.11 billion" (Commission on the Sex Buyer Law 2016, p. 20).

The **EVAW** Coalition,[*] trafficking-specific organizations such as the Coalition Against Trafficking in Women (**CATW**), other feminist organizations, and individuals therefore argue that prostitution meets the definition of violence against women in the 1993 Vienna Declaration, as "gender-based violence that results in, or is likely to result in, physical, sexual or psychological harm or suffering to women" (**DEVAW**, Article 1; see also Ross 2014, p. 332). In the **CEDAW**'s formulation, such gender-based violence is a form of discrimination that "impairs or nullifies the enjoyment by women of human rights and fundamental freedoms under general international law or under human rights conventions" (General Recommendation 19, paragraph 7). It also fuels the underlying causes of human trafficking that governments have signed up to prevent.[†]

---

[*] EVAW Coalition is a coalition of organizations and individuals campaigning to end all forms of violence against women set up in 2005 in the United Kingdom. See http://www.endviolenceagainstwomen.org.uk.

[†] Only Palau and the United States have not ratified the agreement while a number of other countries have ratified the agreement but with various reservations. Such responses reflect the continuing power of patriarchy and privilege that keeps women from being empowered to leave oppressive situations.

International Law State Prevention Obligations

As part of its international law obligations, a State party to the Palermo Protocol or other international or regional human rights instruments* that contain articles on anti–human trafficking and violence against women must prevent trafficking occurring, to focus on "factors that make people vulnerable to traffickers in the first place" (Ross 2014, p. 325; Turner 2012) and that create, or sustain, a culture where traffickers can operate with impunity (Ertürk 2006; Gallagher 2010; Samarasinghe and Burton 2007). These obligations are active, rather than passive, ones, with States obliged to pass normative instruments to criminalize trafficking and to ensure compliance with these laws. The obligations are contained in several instruments, dependent on ratification. General international obligations will be mentioned here plus the Council of Europe Convention by way of example of what more could be achieved.

Article 9(1) of the Palermo Protocol obligates states to establish comprehensive policies to prevent and combat trafficking and to protect victims of trafficking from revictimization. This is part of a multifaceted approach as outlined above (Ross 2014; Samarasinghe and Burton 2007). Article 9(4) demands that States "take or strengthen measures ... to alleviate the factors that make persons, especially women and children, vulnerable to trafficking, including poverty, underdevelopment and lack of equal opportunities." Article 9(5) obligates states to "adopt or strengthen legislative or other measures ... to discourage the demand that fosters all forms of exploitation of persons, especially women and children that leads to trafficking." Jeffreys (1997) (quoted in Jeffreys 2009, p. 170) points out that "this approach is based upon the understanding that men's prostitution behaviour is socially constructed. It is learned behaviour and in societies where it is socially discouraged or penalized it is possible to decrease this behaviour." Article 31 of the Transnational Crime Convention details how states' obligations are ongoing, active ones; for instance, States should undertake awareness-raising campaigns, rehabilitation of offenders, and reexamination of legislative programmes to ensure they are fit for purpose (see Annex I to the Convention for a list of prevention measures; Ross 2014, p. 325) (see Box 6.5).

---

* Examples include the International Covenant on Economic, Social and Cultural Rights; Convention on the Rights of the Child; Convention on the Elimination of all Forms of Discrimination against Women; European Convention of Human Rights; the Maputo Protocol; the Inter-American Convention on International Traffic in Minors; the SAARC Convention on Preventing and Combating Trafficking in Women and Children for Prostitution; European Parliament resolution of February 26, 2014 (2013/2103(INI)) and February 2, 2004 (2004/2220(INI)).

> **BOX 6.5   AN EXAMPLE OF A PREVENTION MEASURE**
>
> In San Francisco, California, a First Offender Prostitution Program (FOPP), also known as "john school," exists as a court diversion program for apprehended clients of the sex industry. It is a "demand reduction strategy" (SAGE; FOPP).

Article 8 of **CEDAW** and Article 6 of **DEVAW*** both oblige states to combat and suppress "all forms of traffic in women and exploitation of the prostitution of others." "Exploitation of prostitution" is not "prostitution." However, in 1999, the Swedish government describe their model as evidence of compliance with Article 6 obligations, where the purchase of sexual services is criminalized on the basis that prostitution is incompatible with gender equality and the integrity of the person. This model tackles the root causes of trafficking (women in prostitution are overwhelmingly from lower socioeconomic classes and abused in childhood) with its exit strategies. Strategic objective d.3 of the Beijing Platform for Action obligates states to "take appropriate measures to address the root factors, including external factors, that encourage trafficking in women and girls for prostitution and other forms of commercialized sex."

Principle 2 of the UNHCR Guidelines describes the responsibilities of states:

> States have a responsibility under international law to act with due diligence to prevent trafficking, to investigate and prosecute traffickers and to assist and protect trafficked persons.

A State can be held responsible for acts perpetrated by a criminal or groups of criminals that harm a person who has been trafficked (Gallagher 2010, Chapter 4; Obokata 2006). Thus, if a State does not criminalize prostitution where this is a harm of and by itself, then the State can be held liable for the harm caused in two ways.

The first is where the assessment of state liability revolves around two questions:

1. Is the situation, action, or omission attributable to the State?
2. If yes: is the situation, act, or omission a breach of an international obligation of that State?

---

* See also the UN Committee on the Elimination of all Forms of Discrimination against Women Concluding Observations for Finland (UN Doc CEDAW/C/FIN/CO/7 (2014), paragraph 21), Republic of Korea (U.N. Doc. CEDAW/C/KOR/CO/7 (2011), paragraph 23(f)), and Botswana (U.N. Doc. CEDAW/C/BOT/CO/3 (2010), paragraph 28).

Article 27 of the Vienna Convention on the Law of Treaties makes clear that where a State has an obligation under international law (e.g., having ratified the Palermo Protocol), it is irrelevant whether or not a State has designated the act as lawful under national law. Thus, even where a State has not criminalized prostitution, it will be held liable where, for example, State officials are found to be complicit in breaching international law obligations, for instance, where a State official takes a bribe in order not to report a person being held against their will in prostitution. On the other hand, a State that criminalizes prostitution (or indeed the sex industry) and that has passed effective laws to criminalize human trafficking and enforces them would not be held liable for a breach of its international law obligations on trafficking for sexual exploitation where third parties are involved.

The second way a State can be held liable under international law is the "due diligence" standard (Clapham 2006; Gallagher 2010, Chapter 4, pp. 382–388; Ross 2014, pp. 333–335). This is where the State is not held liable for acts by others; rather, it is held liable for its own failure to protect, investigate, compensate, and prevent the act of the third party. In the *Velásquez Rodríguez* Case, the Court held that a State will be liable when "a violation of … rights … has occurred with the support or the acquiescence of the Government, [or when] the State has allowed the act to take place without taking measures to prevent it or to punish those responsible" (at paragraph 173; see also *Godinez Cruz v. Honduras*). In *Osman v. UK*, the **ECtHR** (European Court of Human Rights) held that the State could be held liable for failure of its police forces to respond to harassment that led to death. In *Akkoç v. Turkey*, putting in place effective criminal laws to protect the right to life was the State's primary duty as well as having effective "law-enforcement mechanisms for the prevention, suppression and punishment of breaches" (at paragraph 77). This has been echoed by the African Commission on Human and Peoples' Rights in *SERAC and CESR v. Nigeria* (at paragraph 46), the Inter-American Commission on Human Rights in *Fernandes v. Brazil*, and the **CEDAW** Committee in its Ciudad Juarez Inquiry Report in relation to violence against women (including trafficking). In 2006, the UN Special Rapporteur on Violence against Women dedicated an entire report on the use of the due diligence standard to prevent violence against women (Ertürk 2006, https://documents-dds-ny .un.org/doc/UNDOC/GEN/G06/103/50/PDF/G0610350.pdf?OpenElement). As Gallagher points out, while States may try to absolve themselves of responsibility for acts of organized criminals by designating them "private acts," the State will nevertheless be liable where it can be shown that "the State did not reasonably use whatever means it has available to prevent the breach in question…. While determination on this point will depend heavily on the facts of a particular case and the nature of the obligations in question, the increasingly accepted standard of 'due diligence' renders it unlikely that States will be able to avoid responsibility for acts of private persons or entities when their ability to influence an alternative outcome can be established" (Gallagher 2010, p. 249).

It is the argument of this chapter that the body of evidence of the widespread harm in terms of gender inequality and violence in the sex industry, the general inaction to prosecute the criminal offenses that result from these harms, and the trafficking itself is enough to hold governments liable under these international law obligations.

An Example: Article 4 European Convention on Human Rights (ECHR) and Positive Obligations

The "due diligence" aspect of state obligations has been well developed under European law, supported since 2005 by the obligation in Article 6 of the Council of Europe Convention on Action against Trafficking in Human Beings requiring Member States to "discourage the demand that fosters all forms of exploitation of persons, especially women and children, that leads to trafficking." In the case of *Siliadin v. France*, the **ECtHR** held that States have positive obligations under Article 4 of the ECHR in relation to slavery. Article 4 requires Member States to penalize and prosecute effectively any act aimed at maintaining a person in a situation of slavery, servitude, or forced or compulsory labor (*C.N. v. the United Kingdom*, paragraph 66; *Siliadin v. France*, paragraph 112; *C.N. and V. v. France*, paragraph 105), clearly covering women who are held in prostitution (see also *Osman v. UK*, paragraph 115; in relation to rape, see *MC v. Bulgaria*). In order to comply with this obligation, Member States are required to put in place a legislative and administrative framework to prohibit and punish such acts (*Rantsev v. Cyprus and Russia*, paragraph 285). The Court also stated that both the Palermo Protocol and the Council of Europe Convention on Trafficking refer to the requirement for a comprehensive approach to combat trafficking: this includes measures to prevent trafficking and to protect victims (at paragraph 285).

The **ECtHR** has, therefore, developed case law that obligates the State to go out and actively find the trafficking, not just wait for cases to appear before it and then effectively investigate and prosecute (*C.N. v. the United Kingdom*, paragraph 69; *Rantsev v. Cyprus and Russia*, paragraph 288; *X and Y v. the Netherlands*). Thus, a positive obligation to take operational measures arises where it can be demonstrated that the State authorities were aware, or ought to have been aware, of circumstances giving rise to a credible suspicion that an identified individual had been or was at real and immediate risk of slavery/trafficking. If this is the case, there will be a violation of its obligations where the State fails to take appropriate measures within the scope of its powers to remove the individual from that situation or risk (*Rantsev v. Cyprus and Russia*, paragraph 286; *C.N. v. the United Kingdom*, paragraph 67).

In the context of this chapter, this means the continued harm caused by the sex industry to women/girls in prostitution because where "trafficking is the method and means of delivery, prostitution is the end game" (Turner 2012, p. 33).

It is the position of this chapter that these positive duties, not only in relation to State action but also in relation to inaction, when it comes to harms caused by third parties, not only should be, but in fact are, the prevention obligations of international law in relation to human trafficking for the purposes of sexual exploitation in the sex industry across the globe (see Box 6.6). Currently, these obligations are not being met.

BOX 6.6   CANADA: NATIONAL ACTION PLAN TO COMBAT HUMAN TRAFFICKING 2012 (EXCERPT)

The Government's view is that prostitution victimizes the vulnerable and that demand for sexual services can be a contributing cause of human trafficking. Prevention is a critical component in responding to human trafficking. The Government of Canada (2012) recognizes the importance of developing holistic strategies that address the root causes and risk factors that can lead to human trafficking and related forms of exploitation and that will assist in reducing the levels of victimization and the harms associated with it. Successful prevention strategies must be developed and implemented at all stages of the prevention continuum, from awareness raising to prevention of revictimization.

ACTION HIGHLIGHTS

- Promote training for frontline service providers
- Support and develop new human trafficking awareness campaigns within Canada
- Provide assistance to communities to identify people and places most at risk
- Distribute awareness materials at Canadian embassies and high commissions abroad
- Strengthen Child Protection Systems within the Canadian International Development Agency's programs targeting children and youth

Source: http://www.publicsafety.gc.ca/cnt/rsrcs/pblctns/ntnl-ctn -pln-cmbt/index-eng.aspx (see also Roots 2013).

If the crime of human trafficking is found, then State obligations arise to prosecute it. A State that does nothing to prevent trafficking or willfully shuts its eyes to the fact that the prostitution system and the sex industry are a fertile ground for trafficking to flourish is not fulfilling its obligations under both international and domestic trafficking and criminal laws.

Preventing Trafficking in the Sex Industry: The "Swedish"/"Nordic" Model

Debates over what the best strategies are to prevent trafficking are ongoing (Bruckmueller and Schumann 2012, p. 114; Cho et al. 2013; Rietig 2015; Todres 2010). In terms of trafficking for the purpose of sexual exploitation, one course is the legalization of prostitution. This is not a new argument but brought back to the limelight after the legalization policy shift by Amnesty International, one of the world's leading human rights organizations, in the summer of 2015 (Amnesty International 2015). Some nonabolitionists, including the Amnesty International in their new policy,* have argued that prostitution should be seen as work and made safer with the legalization of prostitution and the sex industry in general. In this context, forced prostitution could be a form of forced labor and should be treated as such. The choices and autonomy of the individual undertaking the sex work are not the business of governments and in fact undermine women's equality and their human rights (Spencer and Broad 2012) (see Box 6.7).

The rationale for this policy initiative is the minimization of possible harm (abuse, violence, rape, etc.) to women who are in prostitution alongside a crime prevention strategy (Cho et al. 2013; Spapens and Rijken 2015, p. 157). This approach exists, for instance, in parts of Australia, the Netherlands, and Germany. Minimization, it is claimed, is a rational "solution" to a profession that will not go away, but helps those who work in it.

Minimization of harm does not mean eradication. Abolitionists[†] and many feminist NGOs have argued that prostitution is a form of violence against women and girls of and by itself, as well as a harmful practice, and as such seriously undermines the goal of a gender-equal society. The decriminalization of prostitution, including pimps, brothel owners, and buyers, is seen as a direct violation of several international conventions (the Palermo

---

* For example, the English Collective of Prostitutes.
† Generally, it is accepted that there are three broad different policy regimes: abolitionism, prohibitionism, and regulation. Abolitionism favors criminalizing the demand side, prohibitionists favor making prostitution illegal, and regulationists favor legalizing prostitution and the state regulating the market (maybe for health reasons). All three vary depending on countries. See Jakobsson and Kotsadam (2013, section 2) and Limoncelli (2010) for an overview of the differing debates.

**BOX 6.7   ARGUMENTS IN FAVOR
OF LEGALIZATION OF PROSTITUTION**

Jo Bindman and Jo Doezema argue in *Redefining Prostitution as Sex Work on the International Agenda* that "The designation of prostitution as a special human rights issue, a violation in itself, emphasises the distinction between prostitution and other forms of female or low-status labour… however exploitative they are. It thus reinforces the marginal, and therefore vulnerable, position of the women and men involved in prostitution. By dismissing the entire sex industry as abusive, it also obscures the particular problems and violations of international norms within the industry which are of concern to sex workers."

Thus, anything but legal status for sex workers leads to marginalization and abuses: "even in the many countries where prostitution itself is not illegal, sex workers cannot secure the minimum basic standards which other workers have acquired as far as conditions of work or their personal safety are concerned. It also means that the police frequently fail to take action to help the significant minority among prostitutes who really are victims of slavery" (http://www.walnet.org/csis/papers/redefining.html#1; accessed February 25, 2016).

Prostitution in Germany is regulated by law (introduced in 2002 and amended), and as a result, prostitution is regarded as a "regular job" subject to tax payment and retirement schemes.

Protocol, the 1949 Convention on the Suppression of the Trafficking in Persons and of the Exploitation of the Prostitution of Others, **CEDAW**, **DEVAW**, the UN General Recommendation 19 on Violence Against Women, and other international legal instruments that recognize prostitution as harm; EVAW 2014; Tyler 2012). This is because what some call the sex trade is "a system of commercial sexualized exploitation" that is part of the history of "patriarchal oppression, racism, colonialism, slavery, genocide and cultural acceptance of violence and discrimination primarily against women, who are overwhelmingly of colour, in poverty, with absence of choice and who have suffered sexualized and economic violence, incest, repetitive rapes, torture, homelessness, and socio-cultural marginalization." Thus, prostitution cannot be categorized as "sex" or "work," but rather is a form of gender-based violence and discrimination that is propagated by a multi–billion-dollar commercial sex trade. In addition, many hold the view that it is impossible to fight human trafficking for the purposes of sexual exploitation without criminalizing demand and other aspects of the sex industry because a legalized sex industry provides the means by which trafficking can and does flourish (Hughes 2000, p. 651; Jakobsson and Kotsadam 2013, p. 88). This is a rational strategy in order to eradicate harm, rather than simply to minimize it. In addition, most instances of sex trafficking are part of organized crime. As such, "the administrative authorities can play an important role" in fighting these criminal gangs as "they often require the use of the legitimate infrastructure (buildings, zones, licences). Denying criminals access to this infrastructure can therefore be very effective. Other public authorities, for example the Tax and Customs Administration, may also be able to intervene. In some instances, this is also true of private institutions, such as banks (Aronowitz, Theuermann, and Tyurykanova 2010)" (quoted in Spapens and Rijken 2015, p. 161).

This is a growing movement. Several governments have accepted the abolitionist view and consequently have passed legislation as a prevention strategy that criminalizes demand. Even the Netherlands has thought about criminalizing men who buy sex from under 21-year-olds (Spapens and Rijken 2015, p. 165). Introduced in 1998, the so-called Kvinnofrid law, more commonly referred to as the "Swedish" or "Nordic" Model, is a set of laws and policies that penalizes the demand for commercial sex while decriminalizing individuals in prostitution and providing them with support services, including help for those who wish to exit prostitution. The Nordic Model has two main goals: to curb the demand for commercial sex that fuels sex trafficking and to promote equality between men and women. It is seen as part of a state's obligation in relation to one of the four Ps: prevention. Research suggests that it has reduced the demand for sexual services, the number of women in street prostitution, and the level of human trafficking for the purpose of sexual exploitation.

Sweden as a Good Practice Example

In 1998, Sweden passed a law that criminalized the buying of sex and decriminalized the act of selling sex (Erikson 2012; Erkberg 2004; Jyrkinen 2012; Kelly et al. 2009). Sweden's approach is underpinned by the principle that gender inequality and sexual exploitation, including sex trafficking, cannot be combated effectively as long as it is considered acceptable to purchase access to another human being's body (see Box 6.8). It is especially the case when the person is often more vulnerable and disadvantaged and there is no equality of bargaining. As part of this prevention strategy, the Swedish government also established several exit programs for those who wanted to leave prostitution and provided comprehensive social services for victims of exploitation. This is vitally important for the women. It is also a key part in recognizing the gender inequality in the situation women find themselves in. Introducing the Sex Buyer law is being debated in the United Kingdom at

**BOX 6.8   SWEDISH AND NORWEGIAN ASSESSMENT
OF THE EFFECT OF THE NORDIC MODEL**

According to the National Criminal Police, it is clear that the ban on the purchase of sexual services acts as a barrier to human traffickers and procurers considering establishing themselves in Sweden.

A reduced market and increased law enforcement posit larger risks for human traffickers... The law has thus affected important pull factors and reduced the extent of human trafficking in Norway in comparison to a situation without a law (both quoted in *Report of the Commission on the Sex Buyer Law* 2016, p. 1).

the moment. A key recommendation is to harness existing service provision "into multi-agency, holistic support that enables women to leave commercial sexual exploitation" through national and local strategies and tailored provision (Commission on the Sex Buyer Law 2016, p. 2).

The Swedish Ministry of Justice report has stated that since the introduction of the law, street prostitution has decreased (while increasing in neighboring countries where no such measures existed; see also Europol 2014) and Sweden has consequently become a hostile destination for pimps and traffickers (police report having intercepted communications from traffickers declaring that Sweden is a "bad market"; Ekberg 2004; Jakobsson and Kotsadam 2013, p. 101; Swedish Ministry of Justice 2010). Significantly in terms of prevention, the law influenced attitudes toward the purchase of sex: from 1996 (before the law) until 2008, the number of male sex buyers decreased from 13.6% to 7.9% (Claude 2010), partly because Swedish men fear being arrested and taken to open court (Jakobsson and Kotsadam 2013; Swedish Police 2016), alongside a change in attitude (70% of the public support the law; Swedish Police Presentation at launch of Commission on the Sex Buyer Law, February 24, 2016). It is also one of the only regimes that can claim to have implemented the section in the Palermo Protocol on addressing demand (Kelly et al. 2009). Norway introduced a similar law in 2009, and since its introduction, the prostitution trade has shrunk. Systematic field observations of the street prostitution in Oslo reveal that it has declined by 40%–65% since the law was adopted (VISTA ANALYSE 2014).

Iceland passed similar laws in 2009, and in December 2014, Northern Ireland became the first country in the United Kingdom to do so. Canada also adopted a law in this spirit in November 2014. In the last few years, Nordic Model–style legislation has also been discussed in the parliaments of France, Ireland, Scotland, England, and Wales (Bennett 2016). In early 2014, the European Parliaments and the Council of Europe both adopted nonbinding resolutions recommending Member States to consider the Nordic Model.

Conclusion

This chapter has argued that States that have ratified the Palermo Protocol have international law obligations in relation to human trafficking, regardless of whether it is perpetuated by the State itself or third parties. If States are serious about fulfilling these obligations and preventing trafficking for the purposes of sexual exploitation, then better prevention strategies are required. Human trafficking is complex, and while anti–human trafficking strategies are innovative, so are the traffickers. It is, therefore, strategic (and obligatory) for all governments and civil society in general (Kara 2009, p. 201, pointing out that "the key steps might prove antagonistic to the global economic system that these governments have erected"; Kaye and Winterdyk 2012, p. 72) to invest in prevention: from anti-trafficking awareness raising (secondary prevention) to training sessions for public officials, religious, business, and community leaders, and the youth (primary prevention). There are obvious advantages to prevention work in that it has the potential to keep people safe from abuse and it saves us the financial and emotional cost and effort of rescuing, rehabilitating and reintegrating victims, and ultimately prosecuting criminals/traffickers, which, to date, has been costly and with nominal results. Given the complexity and relative magnitude of the problem, prevention also requires capacity building—partnership building. Prevention work also includes providing alternatives to the world's "social ills that drive human trafficking" (Britton and Dean 2014; Chuang 2006) and progressing further than the human rights paradigm (Ross 2014). Criminalizing the demand side of sexual services (prostitution) as part of the wider sex-trade industry alongside public education and exit alternatives is one such strategy that has been employed successfully in Sweden and other States in order to tackle the root causes of trafficking, including violence against women and gender inequality. Predictably, three of the top four countries with the highest level of gender equality have adopted the Nordic Model (World Economic Forum 2013).* This is an example of a hybrid (Britton and Dean 2014, p. 314)/ holistic approach. It is time that more states take up the call to end the harm caused by the sex (trafficking) industry and criminalize the demand that fuels the market for trafficked women and girls. This is one aspect in the holistic approach the four Ps demand in order to tackle human trafficking effectively.

---

* Iceland is 1, Norway is 3, and Sweden is 4.

Glossary of Key Terms

CEDAW: Convention on the Elimination of All Forms of Discrimination against Women, UN

DEVAW: Declaration on the Elimination of Violence against Women, UN

ECtHR: European Court of Human Rights

EVAW: End Violence against Women Coalition, UK

GDP: Gross Domestic Product

ILO: International Labour Organization

Sex workers: Women, men, and transgendered people who receive money or goods in exchange for sexual services, and who consciously define those activities as income generating even if they do not consider sex work as their occupation.

TIP Report: Trafficking in Persons Report

Discussion Questions

1. What are the primary causes of human trafficking?
2. What are the normative instruments and policies to tackle human trafficking in your country?
3. Does crime control alone work to eradicate human trafficking or do we need a human rights approach as well? Give reasons.
4. How do NGOs, civil society, and businesses deal with the issue?
5. What are the harms of prostitution and the sex industry?
6. What is the link between sex trafficking and prostitution?
7. What solutions have been presented to eradicate human trafficking?

Recommended Web Links

U.S. TIP Reports. These provide useful data on how more than 150 countries are dealing with human trafficking, from laws to policies and what further steps are required. It is produced by the U.S. State Department each year. http://www.state.gov/j/tip/rls/tiprpt/

Huda, S. (2006). Integration of the Human Rights of Women and a Gender Perspective, 42, *Commission on Human Rights*, U.N. Doc. E/CN.4/2006/62. The first international statement by the UN Special Rapporteur on Violence of Women that highlights the link between prostitution and human trafficking. http://www.refworld.org/docid/48abd53dd.html

Global Report on Trafficking in Persons 2014. https://www.unodc.org/documents/data-and-analysis/glotip/GLOTIP_2014_full_report.pdf

A National Overview of Prostitution and Sex Trafficking Demand Reduction Efforts. 2012. The National Institute of Justice Office of Justice Programs, U.S. Department of Justice. https://www.ncjrs.gov /pdffiles1/nij/grants/238796.pdf

Hughes, D. (2004). *Best Practices to Address the Demand Side of Sex Trafficking*. http://www.popcenter.org/problems/trafficked_women /PDFs/Hughes_2004a.pdf

Acknowledgments

The author would like to thank John Winterdyk and Professor Phil Rumney for extremely helpful comments on earlier drafts and their patience.

References

All-Party Parliamentary Group (APPG) on Prostitution and the Global Sex Trade. (2014). *Shifting the Burden: Inquiry to Assess the Operation of the Current Legal Settlement on Prostitution in England and Wales*. Parliament. https://appg prostitution.files.wordpress.com/2014/04/shifting-the-burden1.pdf (accessed February 25, 2016).

Amnesty International. (2015). *Q & A: Policy to Protect the Human Rights of Sex Workers*. https://www.amnesty.org/en/qa-policy-to-protect-the-human-rights-of -sex-workers/ (accessed February 21, 2016).

Annison, R. (2013). *Hidden in Plain Sight*. Anti-Trafficking Monitoring Group. http://www.ecpat.org.uk/sites/default/files/atmg_hidden_in_plain_sight.pdf (accessed February 17, 2016).

Aronowitz, A., Theuermann, G., and Tyurykanova, E. (2010). *Analysing the Business Model of Trafficking in Human Beings to Better Prevent the Crime*. OSCE.

Atak, I., and Simeon, J. (2014). Mapping the legal boundaries of international refugee law and criminal justice. *Journal of International Criminal Justice* 12: 1019–1038.

Bachelet, M. (2012). Fighting Human Trafficking: Partnership and Innovation to End Violence against Women and Children. United Nations General Assembly Interactive Dialogue, April 3, 2012.

Bennett, C. (2016). Criminalize the sex buyers, not the prostitutes. *The Guardian*. http://www.theguardian.com/commentisfree/2016/feb/21/sex-trade-prostitution -criminalise-sex-buyers (accessed February 21, 2016).

Bindman, J., and Doezema, J. (1997). Redefining Prostitution as Sex Work on the International Agenda. http://www.walnet.org/csis/papers/redefining.html#1 (accessed February 25, 2016).

Britton, H., and Dean, L. (2014). Policy responses to human trafficking in Southern Africa: Domesticating international norms. *Human Rights Review* 15: 305–328.

Bruckmueller, K., and Schumann, S. (2012). Crime control versus social work approaches in the context of the "3P" paradigm. In *Human Trafficking: Exploring the International Nature, Concerns, and Complexities*, eds. J. Winterdyk, B. Perrin, and P. Reichel, 103–127. Boca Raton, FL: CRC Press.

Chicago Law School and Cornell Law School. (2015). *India's Human Trafficking Laws and Policies the UN Trafficking Protocol: Achieving Clarity.* http://www.jgu.edu.in/chlet/pdf/Indias-Human-Trafficking-Laws-Report-Book_Feb-2015.pdf (accessed February 17, 2016).

Cho, S.-Y., Dreher, A., and Neumayer, E. (2013). Does legalized prostitution increase human trafficking? *World Development* 41: 67–82.

Chuang, J. (2006). Beyond a snapshot: Preventing human trafficking in the global economy. *Indiana Journal of Global Legal Studies* 13(1): 137–163.

Clapham, A. (2006). *Human Rights Obligations of Non-State Actors.* Oxford, UK: Oxford University Press.

Claude, K. (2010). *Targeting the Sex Buyer.* The Swedish Institute. http://www.si.se/upload/Human%20Trafficking/Targeting%20the%20sex%20buyer.pdf (accessed November 1, 2015).

C.N. and V. v. France. Application No. 67724/09. Judgment of 11.10.2012.

Commission on the Sex Buyer Law. (2016). *How to Implement the Sex Buyer Law in the UK.* All-Party Parliamentary Group on the Global Sex Trade. http://enddemand.uk/wp-content/uploads/2016/02/Report-How-to-implement-the-Sex-Buyer-Law-in-the-UK-2016.pdf (accessed February 25, 2016).

Elliott, J. (2015). *The Role of Consent in Human Trafficking.* Abingdon, London and New York: Routledge.

End Violence against Women Coalition. (March 2014). *Submission to Amnesty International's Global Policy Consultation on Sex Work.* http://www.endviolenceagainstwomen.org.uk/data/files/resources/62/EVAW-Submission-on-Amnesty-consultation-FINAL.pdf (accessed October 4, 2015).

Erikson, J. (2012). The "various" problems of prostitution—A dynamic frame analysis of Swedish Prostitution Policy. In *Prostitution, Harm and Gender Inequality*, ed. M. Coy, 159–180. Ashgate.

Erkberg, G. (2004). The Swedish law that prohibits the purchase of sexual services. *Violence Against Women* 10(10): 1187–1287.

Ertürk, Y. (2006). *The Due Diligence Standard as a Tool for the Elimination of Violence against Women.* Report of the Special Rapporteur on violence against women, its causes and consequences.

European Union Agency for Fundamental Rights. (2009). *Child Trafficking in the European Union. Challenges, Perspectives and Good Practices.* Luxembourg: Office for Official Publications of the European Communities. Available at http://fra.europa.eu/sites/default/files/fra_uploads/529-Pub_Child_Trafficking_09_en.pdf (accessed February 21, 2016).

Europol. (2014). *Situation Report. Trafficking in Human Beings in the EU.* The Hague. Netherlands. Available at http://ec.europa.eu/anti-trafficking/sites/antitrafficking/files/situational_report_trafficking_in_human_beings-_europol.pdf (accessed March 1, 2016).

EUROSTAT. (2015). *Trafficking in Human Beings.* Available at https://ec.europa.eu/anti-trafficking/sites/antitrafficking/files/eurostat_report_on_trafficking_in_human_beings_-_2015_edition.pdf (accessed February 21, 2016).

EVAW Consultation Response on Sex Work to Amnesty International. Available at https://amnestyaction.wordpress.com/2015/10/21/submission-to-amnesty-internationals-global-policy-consultation-on-sex-work/ (accessed January 3, 2016).

Farley, M. (2004). Bad for the body, bad for the heart: Prostitution harms women even if legalized or decriminalized. *Violence against Women* 10(10): 1087–1125.

Farley, M., Cotton, A., Lynne, J., Zubeck, S., Spiwak, F., Reyes, M.E., Alvarez, D., and Sezgin, U. (2003). Prostitution and trafficking in nine countries. Update on violence and posttraumatic stress. *Journal of Trauma Practice* 2(3/4): 33–74.

Fernandes v. Brazil. Case 12.051, Report No. 54/01, OEA/Ser.L/V/II.111 Doc. 20 rev. at 704 (2000).

Finkel, R., and Finkel, M.L. (2015). The 'dirty downside' of global sporting events: Focus on human trafficking for sexual exploitation. *Public Health* 129(1): 17–22.

Fosson, G. (2011). The Serbian Government's response to human trafficking. *European Journal of Crime, Criminal Law and Criminal Justice* 19: 183–198.

Gallagher, A.T. (2001). Human rights and the new UN protocols on trafficking and migrant smuggling: A preliminary analysis. *Human Rights Quarterly* 23: 975–1004.

Gallagher, A.T. (2010). *The International Law of Human Trafficking.* Cambridge, New York: Cambridge University Press.

Godinez Cruz v. Honduras. Inter-American Court of Human Rights (ser. C) No. 5 of January 20, 1989.

Government of Canada. (2012). National Action Plan to Combat Human Trafficking. http://www.publicsafety.gc.ca/cnt/rsrcs/pblctns/ntnl-ctn-pln-cmbt/index-eng .aspx (accessed February 21, 2016).

Grahn-Farley, M. (2011). Examining Janet Halley's critique of rape as torture. In *Feminist Perspectives on Contemporary International Law*, eds. S. Kouvo and Z. Pearson, 121. Oxford, UK: Hart Publishing.

Huda, S. (2006). Integration of the Human Rights of Women and a Gender Perspective, 42, *Commission on Human Rights*, U.N. Doc. E/CN.4/2006/62.

Hughes, D. (2000). The "Natasha" trade: The transnational shadow market of trafficking in women. *Journal of International Affairs* 53(2): 625–651.

International Labour Organisation. (2012). Geneva. http://www.ilo.org/global /topics/forced-labour/lang—en/index.htm (accessed January 5, 2016).

International Labour Organisation. (2015). Geneva. http://www.ilo.org/global /topics/forced-labour/lang—en/index.htm (accessed January 5, 2016).

Jakobsson, N., and Kotsadam, A. (2013). The Law and economics of international sex slavery: Prostitution laws and trafficking for sexual exploitation. *European Journal of Law and Economics* 35: 87–107.

Jeffreys, S. (2009). *The Industrial Vagina: The Political Economy of the Global Sex Trade.* New York: Routledge.

Jeffreys, S. (2012). Beyond "agency" and "choice" in theorizing prostitution. In *Prostitution, Harm and Gender Inequality*, ed. M. Coy, 69–87. Abingdon, UK: Ashgate.

Jyrkinen, M. (2012). McSexualization of bodies, sex and sexualities: Mainstreaming the commodification of gendered inequalities. In *Prostitution, Harm and Gender Inequality*, ed. M. Coy, 13–32. Abingdon, UK: Ashgate.

Kara, S. (2009). *Sex Trafficking: Inside the Business of Modern Slavery.* New York: Columbia University Press.

Kaye, J., and Winterdyk, J. (2012). Explaining human trafficking. In *Human Trafficking: Exploring the International Nature, Concerns, and Complexities*, eds. J. Winterdyk, B. Perrin, and P. Reichel, 57–78. Boca Raton, FL: CRC Press.

Kelly, L., Coy, M., and Davenport, R. (2009). *Shifting Sands: A Comparison of Prostitution Regimes across Nine Countries*. Child and Woman Abuse Studies Unit, London Metropolitan University.

Kendall, V.M. (2011). Greasing the palm: An argument for an increased focus on public corruption in the fight against international human trafficking. *Cornell International Law Journal* 44: 33–47.

Laczko, F., and Danailova-Trainor, G. (2009). *Trafficking in Persons and Human Development: Towards a More Integrated Policy Response*. UNDP Research Paper 2009/51.

Leishman, M. (2007). Human trafficking and sexual slavery: Australia's response. *Australian Feminist Law Journal* 27: 193–218.

Lim, L.L. (1998). *The Sex Factor. The Economic and Social Bases of Prostitution in Southeast Asia*. Geneva: International Labour Office.

Limoncelli, S.A. (2010). *The Politics of Trafficking*. Stanford: Stanford University Press.

Macleod, J., Farley, M., Anderson, L., and Golding, J. (2008). *Challenging Men's Demand for Prostitution in Scotland*. http://www.prostitutionresearch.com/pdfs /ChallengingDemandScotland.pdf (accessed October 5, 2015).

MC v. Bulgaria. (2005). 40 EHRR 20.

Milivojevic, S., and Segrave, M. (2012). Evaluating responses to human trafficking: A review of international, regional, and national counter-trafficking mechanisms. In *Human Trafficking: Exploring the International Nature, Concerns, and Complexities*, eds. J. Winterdyk, B. Perrin, and P. Reichel, 234–263. Boca Raton, FL: CRC Press.

NHS Scotland. (2009). 'Commercial Sexual Exploitation', available at http://www .gbv.scot.nhs.uk/wp-content/uploads/2009/12/GBV_Commercial-Sexual Exploitation-A4-81.pdf. Quoted in Prostitution Law Reform (Scotland) Bill. Available at http://www.scottish.parliament.uk/S4_MembersBills/2015-09-3_Pros titution_Law_Reform_Bill_consultation_-_final.pdf (accessed February 17, 2016).

Obokata, T. (2006). *Trafficking of Human Beings from a Human Rights Perspective: Towards a Holistic Approach*. Leiden: Martinus Nijhoff Publishers.

Osman v. UK. Application No. 23452/94. Judgment of 28.10.98.

Rantsev v. Cyprus and Russia. Application No. 25965/04. Judgment of 10.05.2010.

Rietig, V. (2015). Prevent, protect, and prosecute human trafficking in Mexico: Policy and practical recommendations. *International Migration* 53(4): 9–24.

Rijken, C. (2013). Trafficking in human beings for labour exploitation: Cooperation in an integrated approach. *European Journal of Crime, Criminal Law and Criminal Justice* 21: 9–35.

Roots, K. (2013). Trafficking or pimping? Human trafficking legislation and its implications. *Canadian Journal of Law and Society* 21: 21–41.

Ross, M. (2014). A diamond in the rough: The transnational duty to prevent human trafficking in the protocol. *Duke Journal of Gender, Law & Policy* 21: 325–368.

Samarasinghe, V., and Burton, B. (2007). Strategising prevention: A critical review of local initiatives to prevent female sex trafficking. *Development in Practice* 17(1): 51–64.

Seelke, C.R. (2015). *Trafficking in Persons in Latin America and the Caribbean*. Congressional Research Service. RL33200.

SERAC and CESR v. Nigeria. 2002. ACHPR Comm. No 155/96.

Siliadin v. France. Application No. 73316/01. Judgment of 26.10.2005.

Smith, C.J., and Kangaspunta, K. (2012). Defining human trafficking and its nuances in a cultural context. In *Human Trafficking: Exploring the International Nature, Concerns, and Complexities*, eds. J. Winterdyk, B. Perrin, and P. Reichel, 19–39. Boca Raton, FL: CRC Press.

Smolin, D.M. (2006). Child laundering: How the intercountry adoption system legitimizes and incentivizes the practice of buying, trafficking, kidnapping and stealing children. *Wayne Law Review* 52(113): 115–200.

Spapens, T., and Rijken, C. (2015). The fight against human trafficking in the Amsterdam red light district. *International Journal of Comparative and Applied Criminal Justice*. 39(2): 155–168.

Spencer, J., and Broad, R. (2012). The 'Groundhog Day' of the human trafficking for sexual exploitation debate: New directions in criminological understanding. *European Journal of Criminal Policy Research* 18: 269–281.

Swedish Ministry of Justice. (2010). *English Summary of the Evaluation of the Ban on Purchase of Sexual Services (1999–2008)*.

Swedish Police Presentation at the launch of the Sex Buyer Report, UK, May 2016.

Todres, J. (2010). Taking prevention seriously: Developing a comprehensive response to child trafficking and sexual exploitation. *Vanderbilt Journal of Transnational Law* 43(1): 1–56.

Turner, J. (2012). Means of delivery: The trafficking of women into prostitution, harms and human rights discourse. In *Prostitution, Harm and Gender Inequality*, ed. M. Coy, 33–52. Abingdon, UK: Ashgate.

Tyler, M. (2012). Theorizing harm through the sex of prostitution. In *Prostitution, Harm and Gender Inequality*, ed. M. Coy, 87–101. Abingdon, UK: Ashgate.

United Nations. *The Protocol to Prevent, Suppress and Punish Trafficking in Persons, Especially Women and Children*. United Nations Treaty Series, Vol. 2237: 319; Doc. A/55/383.

United Nations Office on Drugs and Crime. (2014). *Global Report on Trafficking in Persons 2014*. New York. Available at https://www.unodc.org/documents/data-and-analysis/glotip/GLOTIP_2014_full_report.pdf (accessed February 21, 2016).

UNODC. (2009). Global Report on Trafficking in Persons. UN.

U.S. Trafficking in Persons Reports. (2012). http://www.state.gov/j/tip/rls/tiprpt/ (accessed November 12, 2015).

U.S. Trafficking in Persons Reports. (2015). http://www.state.gov/j/tip/rls/tiprpt/ (accessed November 12, 2015).

Velásquez Rodríguez Case. Judgment of 29 July 1988. Inter-American Court of Human Rights (Ser. C) No. 4 (1988).

VISTA ANALYSE. (2014). *Evaluering av forbudet mot kjøp av seksuelle tjenester*. Rapport nummer 2014/30.

Wilson, S. (2015). *Violated*. London: Harper Element.

Winterdyk, J., Perrin, B., and Reichel, P. (eds.). (2012). *Human Trafficking: Exploring the International Nature, Concerns, and Complexities*. Boca Raton: CRC Press.

Winterdyk, J., and Reichel, R. (2010). Introduction to special issue human trafficking: Issues and perspectives. *European Journal of Criminology* 7(1): 5–10.

World Economic Forum. (2013). *The Global Gender Gap Report*. http://www.weforum.org/issues/global-gender-gap (accessed November 12, 2015).

X and Y v. the Netherlands. (1986). 8 EHRR 235.

Community Crime Prevention and Punishment

7

HELMUT KURY

Contents

Learning Outcomes
After reading this chapter, you should be able to

- Understand historical response mechanisms to crime and how various societies have resolved social conflict
- Recognize the background circumstances and developments behind the progression from crime prevention measures by communities to an organization of the "problem" by the state
- Understand the factors that dominate crime policy today (especially the role of media) and how and why much modern crime policy has come to be of a symbolic nature
- Appreciate the negative effects of harsh punishment, especially imprisonment (prisonization)
- Trace the rediscovery of Community Crime Prevention measures in Western industrialized countries over the past several decades
- Understand what Community Crime Prevention is, how it is defined, and how effective it is in reducing crime and deviant behavior

Introduction

> ... he quitted the fortification a very different man from the man he was when he entered it... 'I entered the fortification', he said, 'as an erring man, and I left it—a villain... I had lost every body and everything... I had nothing more to lose and nothing more to guard. I no more needed any good quality, because none believed I could have any.
>
> **Friedrich Schiller**
> *Der Verbrecher aus verlorener Ehre (1786; 1964, pp. 9–11)*

In more or less all countries and throughout all centuries, punishment has been, and still is, symbolized as the "natural" reaction to crime and deviant behavior. In the past, if this punishment did not bring about the desired result, the "treatment" was intensified: more of the same or more severe punishment. In the Middle Ages, for example, humankind was very creative in finding new and cruel punishments to fight crime. Eisner (2001, p. 83) found in his comparative research about severe crimes (killings) in five European regions (England, the Netherlands and Belgium, Scandinavia, Germany and Switzerland, and Italy) that the crime rate—despite the cruel punishment for deviants in the 13th and 14th centuries—was around 25 times higher than today. Thus, one could conclude that severe punishment certainly had no preventive effect at that time. Five hundred years ago, Thomas Morus (1516; 1992, p. 51) disclosed a dinner conversation, at the Cardinal-Archbishop of Canterbury's residence, in which an English lawyer highly commended the harsh execution of justice upon thieves, who at the time, as he said, were hanged so fast that there were sometimes 20 on a single gallows. He added that he could not in any way fathom how it came to pass that, though few escaped, there were still so many who escaped the long arm of the law and continued to commit crimes. This early example of extremely severe punishment clearly illustrates the dilemma of punishment as being its questionable efficiency in preventing crime. New international research has, in the meantime, clearly shown the short- and long-term effects of punishment to be an ineffective but more expensive response to deviant behavior when compared to other, less harsh, alternatives.

This background chapter presents new results about the (non)efficacy of "classical" penal punishment, especially prison sentences. The development of more "modern" forms is discussed, within a framework of reactions to crime and deviant behavior, and the advantages of Community Crime Prevention measures are illustrated. Different forms and iterations of this framework for responding to crime are presented. A final discussion on the background of the rich body of literature on the topic and the effect on crime prevention rounds out the chapter (Death Penalty Information 2016; Kury 2001).

Punishment and Crime Prevention—
The Historical Development

Advocates of alternatives to "classical" punishment, such as Community Crime Prevention, mediation, or restitution, often refer to historical examples. The United Nations (2006, p. 99) points out that "those initiatives often draw upon traditional and indigenous forms of justice which view crime as fundamentally harmful to people." For example, Frühauf (1988, p. 8) discusses the history of restitution and shows that it is one of the most interesting topics in the history of punishment. Indeed, preindustrial sanctioning systems predate the origins of written laws (see also Hagemann 2011). For example, the Code of Hammurabi, developed approximately 1700 BC, is one of the oldest handed-down law books and describes, beside severe forms of punishment, many regulations about restitution for the victims by the offenders in the instance of theft, bodily harm, or even in the context of killings. Broader and more detailed are the measures of victim restitution outlined in the laws of the Hetties, which date back to before 1300 BC. Clearly, alternative approaches to reducing crime-based conflicts in societies have a long and, arguably, successful history.

Frühauf (1988, p. 11) notes that regulated systems of restitution existed in most cultural regions, citing examples from antiquity, the Islamic penal system, and those of other highly developed cultures and tribes. Punishment and restitution are also mentioned throughout the bible (see Burnside 2007). Indeed, Sharpe (2007, p. 26) points out that "reparation has been a vehicle for justice throughout human history." Frühauf (1988, p. 13ff.) also presents an overview of the development of restitution in the German legal system over the last five centuries, including novel solutions for dealing with crime in the community. Since the 5th century AD, different nations wrote more and more laws in this regard. The punishment of offenders in the community by restitution was at that time seen as normative (p. 17). The offender was pressured to provide restitution for the damage caused by his or her criminal act, but in subsequent centuries, the principle of restitution was increasingly replaced by harsher forms of punishment.

With the establishment of kingdoms, the distribution of power between the state and tribes was fundamentally changed (Frühauf 1988). The kingdoms, wanting to ensure that their jurisdiction extended throughout their respective domains, were in favor of abolishing the old ways of regulating laws and conflicts in communities. This was the beginning of a fundamental change in the means of social control. As the rulers of these new kingdoms established generalized penal systems and laws, the influence of the local population and their communities diminished. The establishment of state penal laws and procedures at the beginning of the Middle Ages meant that formerly private conflicts were turned into public conflicts (Rössner 1998). The concept of restitution no longer fit into this new concept of state-centered authoritarian punishment. The potential for restoration of the social balance (i.e., social network theory), damaged by the criminal act, was taken away from the community to be instead managed by means of a special relationship between state power and the offender. Exclusion and separation of the offender rather than inclusion and integration became the goal. The conflict, as well as the cooperation in solving and reducing it, was taken away from the victim (Christie 1977). As Bullock (2014, p. 3) emphasizes when discussing the situation in Great Britain: "[p]rior to the establishment of a professional police service in 1829 crime control was the outcome of the social structures and social relations embedded in communities, characterised by 'volunteer' citizen patrols and private policing."

With the advent of the state, punishment came to mean absolute power: with the use of the death penalty in particular, the shift toward sovereign power and the enforcement of authoritarian penal laws became clear-cut (Frühauf 1988). During this time, the concept of "Friedensgeld" (payment of the victim) also began to be widely used to deal with lesser crimes. Such fines then became an income stream for the state. This was the beginning of a problem that continues to this day. Frühauf (1988, p. 45) discusses an all-around "fiscalization" of penal law against a backdrop of the massive financial interests that began with the emergence of kingdoms and the state (see Box 7.1). Fines were, and still are, an important source of income for the state; the topic of restitution for victims as a state responsibility has regained some attention only in recent years. Frühauf (1988, p. 59) points out that the regulation and control of justice in a society by the state is the most effective way to control the social behavior of its citizens despite new problems that have arisen as a result of such regulation. Overall, we have more justice and more equal treatment of all penal cases. In this regard, this development—which began in Middle Ages—has also been a significant driver of justice in society.

The replacement of community jurisdiction with state-centered authoritarian punishment also characterizes the colonization of North America. State-centered punishment was used to subjugate Native Americans, many of whom, in turn, used their traditional approaches to law violations as forms of resistance. Many indigenous cultures all over the world have a heritage of justice systems based in mediation, restitution, and restoration, for instance, the Chinese I Ching, the Maori, African tribal societies, or North American Indians (see Kury and Kuhlmann 2016). Christie (2009, p. 196) points out: "First among the growth factors for interest in restorative justice has been that highly industrialized societies have been increasingly interested in and aware of their roots, examples being the Maori in New Zealand, North American Indians, or Eskimos or Inuit in the far north. The culture of the original inhabitants has attracted more and more attention. Maybe there was

BOX 7.1   CRIME AND CRIME CONTROL
IN ANCIENT SOCIETIES

Crime in ancient societies was much more common than today, especially street crime. This was attributed to both the general living conditions and a lack of crime control. Poverty was widespread and robbery and theft were common. Traveling between towns was very unsafe. As Hinckeldey (1980, p. 103ff.) points out: "the imposition of the death penalty in ancient times was not only to atone for the crime itself, but particularly to serve as a deterrent to neutralise further such behaviour." The death penalty was particularly used for crimes like homicide, infanticide, arson, theft, embezzlement, robbery, fraud, or sexual assault. Executions were also conducted in a variety of cruel and unusual ways, including live burial (Leder 1986). Despite this, the level of crime—reported and unreported—remained very high, even though the methods used to ascertain information about criminal behavior, especially torture, were unreliable.

The normal preventive measure during these ancient times was thus harsh punishment, in many cases, the death penalty, accompanied by torture before execution. This goes back to the Bible, which, in many cases, recommends this punishment (see Buggle 1992, p. 70ff.). Buggle points out (1992, p. 68): "Violence as a means of controlling behaviour by adding physical pain and suffering to physical destruction (or even the threat of these measures) is… characteristic of the Biblical attitude towards deviant behaviour (sin)." For example, the Old Testament (Dtn. 22; 13, 14, 20, 21) defines the death penalty for sexual contact before marriage: if a man finds out that his wife had sexual intercourse before the marriage, he should take her to the front of her father's house where she shall be stoned to death by the men of the city. This punishment displays particular cruelty in that the act should occur in front of the house of her parents and would only be used against women/girls. During the Middle Ages, much barbarity was also carried out through the religiously motivated execution of "witches": this is remembered nowadays through the term *witch hunt*, which is often used to describe authoritarian repression (Behringer 1988; Hasler 1982).

something of value there after all? One of their values increasingly deemed useful for modernity has been seen to be their ways of solving internal conflicts, with the emphasis on creating peace rather than civil war."

With the activity of crime control being handled by the state since the late 1800s, this topic increasingly became a subject for the government, especially in democratic countries where politicians have to be elected. With the increasing role of the media in society, the discussion of crime, fear of crime, and security was intensified (Shapland 2009). In election campaigns, crime and inner security became a crucial topic: promises to increase criminal punishments began to be used to win elections. "Crime control policies frequently emphasize harsh punishment as elected officials both produce and respond to punitive public sentiments (…). That is, elected officials do not simply respond to the punitive will of the electorate; they help create that will by capitalizing on the fear of crime and on the anxieties about social order that lay beneath the surface of crime control debates" (Miller 2001, p. 4). The "solutions" of the governments very often concentrate on harsher punishment for offenders, based on what politicians know that citizens "want to hear." Concerning the situation in the United States, Miller (2001, p. 44) emphasizes that "the dominant theme of federal policymaking has been punitive; it limits the range of possibilities for community involvement in crime prevention."

Miller (2001, p. 21) continues that "research on federal crime control strategies reveals that the primary emphasis is on punishment and that symbolic politics is routine." Most federal crime initiatives in the United States "tend to be primarily about punishing criminals and those that involve community members tend to focus on a narrow, opportunity-reduction version of crime prevention" (Miller 2001, p. 21). As Scheingold (1991) shows, simplistic law and order politics seem less likely to be successful at a local political level. This might have to do with the actual experience that local residents have with crime. Thus, "while national crime control politics pushes policy agendas towards punishment and law enforcement, local urban politics may present an opportunity for tapping into more nuanced public sentiment that goes beyond simple law enforcement solutions … at the same time that the national agenda appears receptive to punitive policymaking, community policing, which some would characterize as a less punitive form of policing, has flourished on the local/municipal level. Alternatives to incarceration for non-violent and/or first-time offenders, such as drug courts, are also popular and appear to be proliferating on local agendas" (Miller 2001, p. 6). "[T]he research illustrates that residents of a high-crime minority neighbourhood can view crime prevention in substantially different terms than policymakers at both the national and local municipal levels" (p. 3).

The **Commission on Law Enforcement and the Administration of Justice**, established by President Lyndon Johnson in 1965, advocated for broad social programs and addressed the social background of criminal behavior, especially unemployment and poverty; federal crime control strategies focused especially on punishment and incarceration instead of preventive social measures (President's Commission on Law Enforcement and Administration of Justice 1967; see Box 7.2). As Schneider (2015, p. 248)

**BOX 7.2   THE COMMISSION ON LAW ENFORCEMENT
AND THE ADMINISTRATION OF JUSTICE**

The President's Commission on Law Enforcement and Administration
of Justice was appointed by President Johnson in 1965. The Commission's
task was to study the American criminal justice system and make suggestions for preventing crime more effectively. President Johnson pointed
out in his "Special Message to the Congress on Law Enforcement and
the Administration of Justice" on March 8, 1965 (Johnson 1965) that
"Crime has become a malignant enemy in America's midst. Since 1940
the crime rate in this country has doubled. It has increased five times as
fast as our population since 1958. In dollars, the **cost of crime** runs to
tens of billions annually. The human costs are simply not measurable.
The problems run deep and will not yield to quick and easy answers.
We must identify and eliminate the causes of criminal activity whether
they lie in the environment around us or deep in the nature of individual men. This is a major purpose of all we are doing in combatting
poverty and improving education, health, welfare, housing, and recrea-
tion." He pointed out not only the role of institutions of law enforcement, such as the police, the courts, and the correctional agencies, but
also the role of the individual: "Law enforcement cannot succeed without the sustained—and informed—interest of all citizens ... The long-
run solution to the view of crime is jobs, education and hope. This is
a goal to which this country is now committed ... We must, in short,
understand that the reasons for the growth of crime are many and complicated. We must accept hard facts at every turn. But like the related
problems of poverty and of education, we must face them squarely if
we are to succeed. And we must succeed." Johnson considered the state
to have a special responsibility in fighting organized crime, narcot-
ics, and gun sales but noted that "whatever we may do to strengthen
federal law enforcement, the principal enforcement responsibility still
rests on state and local governments—and that has become a very large
burden indeed." The final report of the Commission was issued in 1967
(President's Commission 1967; see also McGarrell 1988). The report
recommended a range of reforms, for example, "that police agencies
establish community relations units and citizen advisory committees,
improving training on community relations, expand the recruitment
of minorities, increase training and education opportunities, adopt
policies limiting the use of firearms by officers, and dozens of other
suggestions designed to improve the relationships between police and
communities" (Maguire and Wells 2002, p. 35; see also Giles 2002).

Several suggestions related to the poor treatment of juvenile offenders. Hence, the Commission provided evidence of "disenchantment with the experience of the juvenile court" (President's Commission 1967, p. 17) and emphasized (p. 69) that "[i]nstitutions tend to isolate offenders from society, both physically and psychologically, cutting them off from schools, jobs, families and other supportive influences and increasing the probability that the label of criminal will be indelibly impressed upon them." The Commission therefore recommended that community-based correctional alternatives to institutionalization should be considered, especially for juvenile offenders. "At the same time, the U.S. Department of Justice published 'The Challenge of Crime in a Free Society' (1967), also questioning the policy of incarceration for nonviolent juvenile offenders" (Hess 2010, p. 49). The issues that were raised by the Commission and others "indicated a need to integrate rather than isolate offenders. The resulting community-based correctional programs, such as probation, foster care and group homes, represented attempts to respond to these issues by normalizing social contacts, reducing the stigma attached to being institutionalized and providing opportunities for jobs and schooling. The President's Commission also strongly endorsed diversion for status offenders and minor delinquent offenses. In addition, the Commission recommended establishing a national youth service bureau and local or community youth service bureaus to assist the police and courts in diverting youths from the juvenile justice system" (Hess 2010, p. 49f.).

points out, this was the foundation of Community Crime Prevention. "Until Congress passed the Omnibus Crime Control and Safe Streets Act in 1968, the federal government played only a minimal role in crime fighting activities" (Miller 2001, p. 22; Krislov and White 1977). During the crime problems in the 1960s, the federal government was more and more involved. This was the beginning of an increasing symbolic "punitive politics" that led to an increased prison rate from the 1970s that has lasted until today. Punitive politics was supported by reports about the failed results of rehabilitation or, in short, the "nothing works" message (Lipton et al. 1975; Martinson 1974).

President Johnson's Commission also suggested introducing "Community Programs" and funds were to be set aside for this. "However, while the President's crime commission report called for an active and involved citizenry, most of the money was directed towards reaction to crime, rather than dealing with its origins and much of the community involvement funding appears to have been directed at crime awareness and avoidance strategies.

This, the community involvement was largely confined to controlling criminal behaviour by making crimes harder to commit, rather than preventing criminality in the first place" (Miller 2001, p. 27f.). In the 1970s, there "emerged a number of community-based alternatives that sought to provide fairly intensive supervision in combination with a number of other intervention programmes primarily as an alternative to custody. Developing initially in the U.S. and the UK in the late 1970s (…), they became relatively common internationally during the course of the 1980s" (Newburn and Souhami 2005, p. 358).

Interestingly, developments in Canada during the same period were much more rehabilitative and nonpunitive. Roberts and Sprott (2008, p. 55) emphasize that "although Canada is economically tied and geographically proximate to the United States, punishment policies have taken a very different course in this country." The authors discuss the reasons for this at a sociopolitical level (p. 66): "It is apparent that the federal government has elected to ignore, to a large degree, the punitive element of public attitudes reflected in public opinion polls." Also, Winterdyk and King (2011, p. 108) point out that "[n]otwithstanding a few exceptions, the Canadian government has traditionally not supported the punitive attitudes of the general public." Canada's sentencing policy has relied more on the use of conditional release, so that "instead of serving the entire length of their sentence in institutional custody (i.e., prison), most offenders move into a sophisticated system of community corrections" (p. 110). Schneider (2015, p. 249) emphasizes that "[i]n their 1993 report on crime prevention, the Canadian Standing Committee on Justice and the Solicitor General recommended that future federal crime and control policies be premised on the belief that 'crime occurs in communities and priorities concerning crime prevention are best determined at the local level'" (Parliament of Canada 1993, p. 33). In the years after this report, there was a "renewed focus on early childhood and the challenge of making a strong collective commitment to our young children" (Hertzman 2002, p. 1).

In Australia, the National Community Crime Prevention Programme was established in 2004. In England and Wales, under the New Labour Government, a major national crime prevention strategy was known as the "Safer Communities Initiative." In Germany, the discussion about community crime prevention began in the early 1990s. At that time, pilot projects were started, driven also by the increasing discussion about fear of crime, a topic more often discussed after the reunification of Germany where opinion polls pointed at a large degree of anxiety among the general population (Dölling et al. 2003). As a result, the German government funded Community Crime Prevention initiatives, and with the support of local police departments, a number of new projects began during the 1990s (Obergfell-Fuchs and Kury 2003).

Is Punishment (Imprisonment) a Good Way to Prevent Crime?

The political strategy to fight criminal behavior in the United States through harsh sentences has led to the country having the highest incarceration rate worldwide; a lot of money is thus ineffectively being spent in an aid to reduce crime, as prison is by far the most expensive sanction among all crime control measures (Wright 2010). For example, Trevena and Weatherburn (2015, p. 12) emphasize that, in the case of Australia, "it costs about 10 times more to keep an offender in prison for a day than to keep an offender on some form of community corrections order." In their research project, the authors demonstrate that by using "propensity score matching … to compare time to reconviction among 3,960 matched pairs of offenders, in which one of each pair received a prison sentence of 12 months or less and the other received a suspended sentence of two years or less," there were "no significant differences … between the matched prison and suspended sentence groups in the time to first new offence … These results suggest that short custodial sentences exert no more deterrent effect than comparable community orders" (p. 1). Other studies and reviews on the specific deterrent effects of prison come to similar results (see, e.g., Dölling et al. 2011; Nagin et al. 2009). Werminck et al. (2010) could demonstrate in their large study in the Netherlands that recidivism was significantly higher for people who went to prison: the difference could still be seen after eight years of follow-up. Farrington et al. (1994) compared crime and punishment trends in the United States, England, and Sweden: as the authors failed to find an effect of severity, it was concluded that the varying degrees of punitiveness in the sentencing policies had no positive outcomes on crime prevention (Wright 2010, p. 5).

Criminal behavior is seen in society today above all as individual misbehavior, influenced especially by the U.S. discussion and point of view. Miller (2001, p. 5f.) emphasizes that "the conception of individual fault and wrongdoing is at the heart of American ideas of criminality and leads to particular policy solutions." The role and responsibility of society are denied in public discussions and referred to only in critical criminological literature (Goffman 2014). "The appeal of an emphasis upon the pathologies of criminals and the utility of punishing them lies partly in what it negates: the tracing of crime to pathological social conditions" (Edelman 1988, p. 28).

Meanwhile, a large number of international studies have shown the counterproductive effects of imprisonment, at least in the form of imprisonment that is mainly practiced today. "There is no indication that harsher or more intensive punishments lead to greater public safety and peace. On the contrary, the more the public policy relies exclusively on repression and punishment, the more this will lead to more imprisonment, more humane and financial costs, less ethics, less public safety and a lower quality of social life" (Walgrave 2008, p. 54; see also the meta-analysis by Dölling et al. 2011). Wright (2003, p. 17) points out that "[p]unitive sanctions are not very effective in deterring offenders, but once the offence has been committed, they deter them from admitting their actions." Braithwaite (2005, p. 285) agrees when he writes "Criminal justice with its commitment to punishment is intrinsically the major obstruction to good communication, because it encourages cultures of denial" (see also Kury and Kuhlmann 2016).

In the 1960s and 1970s, **deterrence theory** was increasingly called into question. Scholarly research generally concludes that increasing the severity of penalties will have little, if any, effect on crime (Spohn and Holleran 2002, pp. 329–330; Wright 2010). Research could show more and more that incarceration not only has no positive effect on recidivism but, in many cases, also has a negative one, a **prisonization** effect. Prisons are "total institutions" that create a "Society of Captives" that can have serious problems for the goal of rehabilitation, even after their release (Clemmer 1940; Goffman 1961; Ortmann 1993; Sykes 1958). The negative dynamic between prisoners and staff was clearly illustrated by Zimbardo (2007) in his well-known "Stanford Prison Experiment."

As Wright (2010, p. 9) points out: "existing evidence does not support any significant public safety benefits of the practice of increasing the severity of sentences by imposing longer prison terms. In fact, research findings imply that increasingly lengthy prison terms are counterproductive … As a result, such policies are not justifiable based on their ability to deter" (Wright 2010, p. 9). Rather, there is ample evidence that imprisonment deteriorates the income and housing situation of former prisoners (see Weijters and More 2015). The problem is that "stable accommodation after release from prison and a satisfying job are very important factors that reduce the risk of recidivism," which ultimately has to do with successful reintegration in the community (Weijters and More 2015, p. 46). Griffiths et al. (2007, p. 39) further point out that "[i]n recognition of the fact that nearly all offenders will return to the community, there has been an emphasis among community leaders and politicians on managing the release and reintegration of offenders into the community."

Such findings have led to a critique of the "classical" sanctioning of offenders and the gradual move (from the late 1960s onward) to assess "theories, strategies, activities, and programs that can be classified as crime prevention" (Schneider 2015, p. 5). Indeed, crime prevention has now become an "important arena where criminological knowledge is produced" (Hope and Karstedt 2003, p. 480).

Community and Crime Prevention

As Friday (2003, p. 370) emphasizes: "One of the most significant developments in the field of criminal justice in recent years has been the emergence
of a wide range of restorative justice/community justice programs" (see also,
United Nations 2006). While the first inklings of this movement could be
seen in the United States as far back as the 1950s, it was not until 1977 that
17 states established special **Community Crime Prevention** programs that
were mostly organized as "Crime Watch" initiatives (Ward 1998, p. 22; see
also Doleschal 1984). In the West, community involvement soon became "an
essential ingredient of crime prevention in all kinds of partnerships involving municipalities, the police, schools, health and social services, and the private sector" (Griffiths et al. 2007, p. 31; see also Shaw 2006). As Ward (1998,
p. 22) notes, these programs mostly included three components:

1. Reduction of the opportunity of crime, for example, by environmental design or patrols of citizens
2. Improving the responsiveness of the criminal justice system
3. Providing assistance to local citizens by social programs that divert
   them from engaging in criminal behavior

One important advantage of Community Crime Prevention is that these
programs do not concentrate on punishing the offender but instead follow a
procedure that seeks to produce a "fair outcome for the accused, satisfaction
for the victim or harmony in the community to which both the offender and
victim belong" (Friday 2003, p. 371). Nowadays, it is largely taken for granted
that communities have an important role to play in preventing crime and
fostering community safety (Jamieson 2008). Nevertheless, there is no generally accepted definition of (community) crime prevention but rather a "number of philosophies, strategies, programs, and practices that could potentially
be classified as crime prevention" (Schneider 2015, p. 5).

Community Crime Prevention is seen today as one category of prevention that relies on especially informal social control. The dislocation
of responsibility for crime prevention from the government to the community brings informal forms of control into the foreground. Schneider
(2015, p. 21) points out that "[c]ommunity crime prevention in particular
is concerned with reinforcing or modifying the individual and collective
behaviours of local residents to produce or strengthen a local social environment that can informally regulate itself, including the regulation and
prevention of criminal, delinquent, disorderly, and uncivil behaviour."
These initiatives have increasingly been discussed as a positive alternative to formal classical approaches to social control organized by the state
(Schneider 2015).

Crime prevention targets not just criminal behavior but also fear of crime and disorder. Fear of crime, in particular, has been an important and often politicized topic in recent decades. Politicians have responded to what they feel is public alarm by talking about a "war on crime" (Shapland 2009, p. 140), and the topic of "security" has been increasingly bandied about (especially in reaction to media reports) (Hestermann 2010, 2016). Yet, criminological research has shown that the high rate of fearful people revealed by many surveys has to do with poorly defined concepts and questions, meaning the true level of "fear" is notably lower and that the official rates are largely over-estimation (Farrall et al. 1997, 2000).

Schneider (2015, pp. 27, 239) defines Community Crime Prevention as "[t]he mobilization of neighbourhood residents based on two different (yet complimentary) approaches: (i) the community defence approach (in which residents work together to prevent crime, primarily through opportunity reduction measures) and (ii) the community development approach (in which the causes and aggravating factors that promote crime and criminality locally are addressed through social, economic, and physical development)" (see Box 7.3). According to him, "a dominant etiological theory of crime upon which Community Crime Prevention is premised is that the loss of the socially cohesive community within advanced Western societies has contributed to crime and disorder" (p. 38). Meanwhile, Welsh and Hoshi (2006, p. 165) characterize "community-based crime prevention" as a combination of situational crime prevention and developmental approaches.

As Schneider (2015, p. 241) points out, "Community Crime Prevention fundamentally depends on the integration of people into a community through a socialization process that involves the inculcation of shared norms and values and the creation of an individual and collective consciousness that serves as the foundation for a communal approach to controlling, deterring, and preventing crime and criminal behaviour." For Sherman (1997b), communities are the central institution for crime prevention, the stage on which all other institutions perform. He emphasizes (Sherman 1997a, p. 5) that a very important condition for success is "adequate support for the practice in related settings. Schools cannot succeed without supportive families, labour markets cannot succeed without well-policed safe streets, and police cannot succeed without community participation in the labour market." Hence, the focus of the criminal behavior shifts away from the individual to the community. Therefore, a socially cohesive community will produce informal social control so the opportunity for crime and deviant behavior will be reduced.

The United Nations defines Community Crime Prevention as any initiative that seeks to "change local conditions that influence offending, victimization and insecurity caused by crime, by leveraging initiatives, expertise and commitment of community members" (United Nations Office on Drugs and Crime 2010, p. 13). Schneider (2015, p. 239) points out in this context that

BOX 7.3   CRIME PREVENTION PROGRAMS

One of the most discussed programs is the **"Weed and Seed" Program** (Miller 2001; Sherman 1997b, p. 3-35f.), which was announced by President George Bush in 1992 and sponsored by the Department of Justice. "The advantages of the Weed and Seed program are: the offender is immediately removed from the streets, and the public immediately sees that these law enforcement efforts are effective; the offender is met with swift justice; and those convicted serve longer sentences mandated by federal law and are prevented from committing further criminal acts for years to come" (Miller 2001, p. 1). "Perhaps most importantly, Weed and Seed coupled efforts with seeding monies to help rebuild neighbourhoods" (p. 3). Miller (2001, p. 167ff.) notes that at the first Western Regional Conference about the program in 1999, a "successful Weed and Seed program in Seattle [was presented] and... praised... for its efforts in bringing community members into the process" (p. 157). However, she also emphasizes that the Seattle program's success is more complex as the "community level crime control perspectives in Seattle are less punitive and more oriented towards crime's root causes than those that were presented in the original Weed and Seed Program goals originating with the Justice Department" (p. 170). Thus, "opportunity reduction strategies were less prominent in the Seattle Weed and Seed experience" (p. 172). The priorities were seen in Seattle in a different way compared to the program presented by the government. Crime prevention was not to have to do with police but in broader concerns, such as economic development. This is precisely the reason that governing through crime control strategies proliferate: they do not involve broad social and economic development programs and they fund existing police programs that strengthen police authority and visibility. The study "suggests that order maintenance strategies are all too easily absorbed into a governance strategy that promotes crime control as a means of exerting state authority" (p. 173). As Sherman (1997b, p. 3-35) points out, the evaluation of the initial Weed and Seed target area in Kansas City "found a 49 percent reduction in gun crime and a statistically significant reduction in homicide." The author emphasizes (pp. 3-35/36): "The most challenging theoretical element for any inner-city crime prevention program is raising the community rate of adult labour force participation... Labour force programs have suffered from a lack of focus on the Weed and Seed strategy, scattering resources across individuals spread out over many disparate communities. More recent private and public efforts to change community labour markets, rather than personal labour skills, fit right into Weed and Seed… [as] they can easily become an integral part of its multi-risk factor reduction strategy, coupling high enforcement with greater opportunity."

Sherman (1997b, pp. 3-36/38) gives a short overview of additional programs, such as the "V Community Prevention Program," the "Gang Prevention and Intervention," the "JUMP: Juvenile Mentoring Program," and the "STOP Formula Grants to Combat Violence Against Women."

In Germany, Community Crime Prevention has traditionally concentrated on police supervision and intervention, though in recent years, more focus has been given to supporting families with problems at a community level. Support is also provided to social workers, psychologists, and other such professionals. The involvement of police in community-oriented prevention has also changed the way police deal with citizens: the police are interested in engaging with citizens and they are consequently now seen as a helping institution (Feltes 2003).

"this broad definition is reflective of the lack of consensus in the academic and professional literature on both the definition of community prevention and the types of initiatives that fall within it." Ward (1998) speaks about "Community Education and Crime Prevention" and defines the topic as a "philosophy, process, and program comprised of three overriding and interrelated elements: community empowerment, community problem-solving, and the effort to involve all community members in the pursuit of lifelong learning."

As Schneider (2015) emphasizes, the community and neighborhood have become a central point for crime prevention for at least three reasons: (1) Crime prevention is located in the community, acknowledging that the citizens play an important role in maintaining order in a free society and therefore should be encouraged to accept more responsibility for crime prevention; (2) Many crimes are committed in residential neighborhoods and these crimes can have the effect of destabilization of these neighborhoods, which in turn has the effect of increasing criminal behavior as can be seen in big cities (Goffman 2014); and (3) "The primacy of the neighbourhood and the community cuts across all other approaches to crime prevention. Situational prevention measures involve managing the physical environment of the local neighbourhood. Most developmental approaches to crime prevention take place at the neighbourhood level, whether concerned with the local physical, social, or socioeconomic infrastructure. Most crime prevention initiatives work best when there is a strong sense of local social cohesion (i.e., a sense of community)" (p. 242) (also see Jacobs 1961, p. 31f.).

The strong influence of individual living conditions in communities was already pointed out in the 1930s in the **Chicago Area Project**. On the basis of this project, Shaw and McKay (1942) formulated their theoretical foundation of Community Crime Prevention (see also Goffman 2014) (see Box 7.4). "As a result of this social pathology and the weakening of local informal social controls, children and young people were ineffectually socialized, which gave rise to delinquency" (Schneider 2015, p. 244). In this context, the regular use and abuse of alcohol and other drugs has been seen in these subgroups since the 1980s, which itself also leads to criminal behavior. This abuse occurs "in socially disorganized areas with few legitimate economic opportunities and strained informal social controls, conditions associated with increased rates of predatory and expressive violent crimes" (Fagan and Chin 1990, p. 13). The rise of these problems was one reason for the United States' "War on Drugs" and the ensuing rise in **punitiveness** and, consequently, prison rates (Ferdinand 2006). "Though the [War on Drug's] agenda had little connection to actual rates of drug use, it deployed powerful symbolic language and aggressive law enforcement tactics ... The public's punitive attitudes appear to be more latent and contingent than one might think, given broad public support for long prison terms and the death penalty" (Miller 2001, p. 5; see also Beckett 1997; Tonry 1995). Miller (2001, p. 6f.) emphasizes, "when local community involvement in crime control is encouraged, the punitive emphasis might be muted and the individual-responsibility rhetoric might give way to more structural explanations and... towards different solutions." In other words, the more people are involved in Community Crime Prevention, the more they are informed about the nature and characteristics of criminal behavior, which, in turn, decreases overall punitiveness (see Roberts 1992; Roberts and Hough 2002; Sato 2014).

Is Community Crime Prevention Effective?

A broad range of research findings on the influence of living conditions in communities on behaviors of children and juveniles and later adults exist; many of these have been collected in large-scale empirical projects in the United States, for example, the "Perry Preschool Project" (Schweinhart 2004), the "Elmira Prenatal/Early Infancy Project" (Eckenrode et al. 1998), or the "Seattle Social Development Project" (Hawkins et al. 1999). Increased risk factors were found in these studies, including low levels of parental supervision, inconsistent discipline, child maltreatment, parental alcohol or drug abuse, and so on (Homel 2005, p. 74). The basic idea of this approach [crime prevention] is very simple: "Identify the key risk factors for offending and implement prevention methods designed to counteract them" (Farrington 2002, p. 660). Such measures to reduce crime appear to work, as longitudinal

BOX 7.4   THE CHICAGO AREA PROJECT

The Chicago Area Project was established by Clifford Shaw, a sociologist from the University of Chicago, "who believed every neighbourhood could reduce juvenile delinquency by improving community life" (Chicago Area Project 2016). The project is now considered to be a "legendary experiment in community-based delinquency prevention during the 1930s and 1940s" (Schlossman and Sedlak 1983a, p. v). On the basis of a report by Burgess et al. (1937), Schlossmann and Sedlak (1983a, p. iiif.) provide a succinct summary of the Chicago Area Project (see also Schlossman and Sedlak 1983b): "(1) The Chicago Area Project is a program which seeks to discover by actual demonstration and measurement a procedure for the treatment of delinquents and the prevention of delinquency ... the distinctive emphasis in the Project is to achieve the fullest possible neighbourhood participation ... All of the activities in the program are carried on with a view to making the neighbourhood conscious of the problems of delinquency, collectively interested in the welfare of its children, and active in promoting programs for such improvements of the community environment as will develop in the children interests and habits of a constructive and socially desirable character ... (contrasted with the methods employed by traditional, casework-oriented social agencies) the Area Project emphasizes the development of a program for the neighbourhood as a whole, as against a circumscribed institutional setup; (2) the Area Project stresses the autonomy of the actual residents of the neighbourhood in planning and operating the program as contrasted with the traditional organizations in which control is vested in lay and professional persons who reside in or represent the interests of the more privileged communities; (3) the Area Project places great emphasis upon the training and utilization of neighbourhood leaders as contrasted with the general practice in which dependence is largely placed upon professionally trained leaders recruited from sources outside of the local neighbourhood; (4) the Area Project seeks to utilize to the maximum established neighbourhood institutions, particularly such natural social groupings as churches, societies, and clubs, rather than to create new institutions which embody the morale and sentiments of the more conventional communities; (5) the activities program in the Area Project is regarded primarily as a device for enlisting the active participation of local residents in a constructive community enterprise and creating and crystallizing neighbourhood sentiment with regard to the task of promoting the welfare of children and the social and physical improvement of the community as a whole; and (6) finally, an essential aspect of the Area Project is the emphasis which it places upon the task of evaluating the effectiveness of its procedure in constructively modifying the pattern of community life and thus effecting a reduction in delinquency and other related problems."

studies have shown that help for neglected children and cooperation with parents shows a positive effect, for example, in the Montreal Prevention Project (Tremblay et al. 1995). The earlier the intervention begins in the development of children, the more positive are the results, but lifelong learning is possible and an important factor (Homel 2005, p. 84). Early interventions are additionally much cheaper than later interventions (Aos 2003).

The discussion about the success of Community Crime Prevention is mixed. Hughes and Edwards (2005) show that most evaluations of crime prevention programs have tended to focus on general program success while overlooking the relative impact on those who participate in the program. In doing so, there is a risk of overgeneralizing the results. Community Crime Prevention is defined and understood in different countries in different ways; hence, cultural backgrounds and setting must be taken into account (Karstedt 2004). In discussing the success of Community Crime Prevention research, Schneider (2015, p. 276) summarizes as follows: "Research and project evaluations have shown that applied Community Crime Prevention models have fallen short of the expectations set by their theoretical prescriptions. A host of empirical studies indicate that various Community Crime Prevention projects have had only modest or no impact on crime and fear or crime." The reviews of programs by Rosenbaum (1988), Hope (1995), and Sherman (1997c) show that "[e]ach of these authors has reached similar conclusions: a review of Community Crime Prevention program evaluations finds generally little evidence that local, collective crime prevention programs have achieved their desired impact" (Schneider 2015, p. 276).

Schneider (2015, p. 282) concludes: "Despite the attractiveness and benefits of Community Crime Prevention, research indicates that many projects fail to reach both their substantive goals (i.e., a reduction in or prevention of crime) and their process-oriented objectives (e.g., widespread participation, social interaction, etc.). This is especially true in socially disadvantaged neighbourhoods, which are most in need of crime prevention initiatives. Participants in Community Crime Prevention initiatives tend to be in the middle- or upper-income range, well-educated, white, middle-aged, longer-term, home-owning residents who are socially integrated and committed to their neighbourhood." Sherman (1997b, p. 3-32) summarizes in his overview by noting: "[b]y the criteria used in this report, there are no community based programs of 'proven effectiveness' by scientific standards to show with reasonable certainty that they 'work' in certain kinds of settings. There are programs for which we can conclude the evidence shows with reasonable certainty that they do not work, at least in the settings where they have been evaluated. But even these programs might be found effective even if varied in significant ways and rigorously evaluated in terms of their outcomes. Moreover, there is both empirical evidence and theoretical reason to conclude that some programs are promising enough to merit further replication and evaluation." Thus, it seems that more intensive initiatives should be implemented and that stronger contacts and motivation initiatives in subgroups are required (see, e.g., Goffman 2014).

Tilley (2005, p. 6) points out another possibly problematic side of special Community Crime Prevention programs such as neighborhood or citizen watch: the displacement of crime to other parts of the community. This is especially relevant if programs are very specific and not too far-reaching. Tonry (2004) also points out that in the experience of England, the more people are reminded about crime topics, the more they have a tendency to become fearful.

Conclusion and Discussion

Given rising criticism about the punitive treatment of offenders, especially imprisonment and the costs associated with it, "alternative" forms of community-based methods to reduce conflicts and restore peace have been rediscovered and increasingly debated in recent decades. Indeed, empirical research findings from the 1960s onward clearly demonstrate that imprisonment is not only less effective in preventing crime than Community Crime Prevention but also much more expensive. The focus on alternative methods to reduce both crime and imprisonment "has come about because current policies and practices in criminal justice have not proven especially effective in reducing crime and in offering citizens' confidence in and support from their legal authorities" (Friday 2003, p. 370).

The underlying reasons behind much criminal behavior can be seen especially in families and communities. Imprisonment rates can be reduced without increasing problems with security if long-term imprisonment is primarily reserved for dangerous offenders. Nondangerous offenders should be excluded from society for as short a time as possible as imprisonment has strong negative side effects that research on prisonization clearly demonstrates. Community treatment offers victims, offenders, and the broader community an active role in the resolution of conflicts. This is in stark contrast to the punitive model that in fact increases the problems caused by crime.

An additional positive side effect of community treatment is that these measures not only help reduce crime but also are much cheaper (Raynor 2002, p. 1198). As Farrington (2002, p. 662) emphasizes: "[A]n important development in the 1990s was the increasing use of cost-benefit analysis in evaluation crime prevention programmes," which demonstrate that early intervention programs in families and communities save money (Aos 2003). As Raynor (2002, p. 1195) stresses: "Community penalties clearly have a future: they are such an important part of our sentencing system that it is not possible to imagine their disappearance under any reasonable probable or foreseeable set of criminal justice policies." While the political climate can of course change from time to time because of unforeseeable events, in Western democratic societies, the research on this topic is so overwhelming that the overall direction of reform cannot be deviated from (Kury 2015).

What criminal behavior actually is remains, of course, a complex question: "criminality" is defined in different countries/societies differently, such that a given crime at a given time in one country cannot automatically be considered a crime in another country. This creates additional problems in preventing crime. Hope and Karstedt (2003, p. 479) emphasize that cultural aspects have to be considered, a problem that must be seen, for example, in dealing with the huge number of refugees in the past few years in western European countries, especially Germany. These people come from different cultures with different attitudes to deviant behavior. To integrate these people in society, Hope and Karstedt (2003) point out that all relevant partners, especially the members of the community, have to cooperate.

Many authors criticize the missing theoretical concepts behind Community Crime Prevention initiatives and accompanying research: "Crime prevention remains a vague concept that can mean different things to different people" (Schneider 2015, p. 6). Community Crime Prevention works, but there are many different programs and no unique theoretically founded model (Friday 2003). In fact, all too often, evaluations of crime prevention initiatives are instituted in a theoretical vacuum, and for many evaluations, there is limited, if any, attention paid to the assumptions underlying the prevention program (Holcomb and Lab 2003). Arguably, the underpinnings of such programs are very often political as they are initiatives designed to escape media pressure after severe crimes. Accordingly, these programs often have a symbolic nature and, when the media reporting ceases, so too does their interest to politicians.

Schneider (2015, p. 282) discusses another important problem of Community Crime Prevention initiatives when he emphasizes that "[d]espite the attractiveness and benefits of Community Crime Prevention, research indicates that many projects fail to reach both their substantive goals (i.e., a reduction in or prevention of crime) and their process-oriented objectives (e.g., widespread participation, social interaction, etc.). This is especially true in socially disadvantaged neighbourhoods that are most in need of crime prevention initiatives. Participation in Community Crime Prevention initiatives tend to be in the middle- or upper-income range, well-educated, white, middle-aged, longer-term, home-owning residents who are socially integrated and committed to their neighbourhood." Community Crime Prevention is most important and also most effective with the most disadvantaged members of a community who experience personal difficulties with income, housing, jobs, education, and behavioral issues (such as substance abuse). That said, greater engagement and experience are required to motivate these groups to participate in programs. This necessitates a great deal of motivation on the part of researchers and project organizers, though as the example of the Chicago Area Projects demonstrates, this is far from impossible (Coates 1987; see also Goffman 2014).

Another problem of Community Crime Prevention is that programs do not concentrate on crime generally but only specific parts. For example, Community Crime Prevention does not focus on economic crimes, corruption, graft, or international crimes. Community Crime Prevention instead concentrates on criminal behavior that can be handled in families and neighborhoods, that is, criminal behavior that creates fear of crime and insecurity.

Despite the aforementioned shortcomings, a broad range of scientific literature nevertheless attests to the positive effects of Community Crime Prevention. Hope and Karstedt (2003, p. 481) suggest that future research should concentrate not only on "'what works' but why it works; particularly why it should work (or not) in terms of criminological theory." In this way, Community Crime Prevention brings both the "problem" and the "solution" back to the core: assessing deviant behavior and determining the environments that support and negate it.

Glossary of Key Terms

Chicago Area Project: One of the earliest and most widely known Community Crime Prevention initiatives, begun by Clifford Shaw in the 1930s. The Chicago Area Project remains active to this day and concentrates on improving overall community life and well-being, especially for children and adolescents. Neighborhood participation and the inclusion of citizens in community structures and organizations are of particular importance.

Commission on Law Enforcement and Administration of Justice: Established in 1965 by President Lyndon Johnson in the United States. The Commission suggested a range of broad social programs for crime prevention and addressed the social background of deviant behavior, focusing particularly on the reduction of unemployment, poverty, and punitive punishment. The Commission's finding (1967) are often considered the foundation stone of Community Crime Prevention in the United States.

Community Crime Prevention: The concept of preventing crime by bringing conflicts back to the roots of families and communities. In past millennia, this was the most common way of preventing crime. However, with the advent of the modern state, efforts were made to institutionalize conflicts and punishments, thereby removing conflicts from their background.

Costs of Crime: Strongly crime and reaction dependent. The human costs for victims cannot be measured. An important development in the evaluation of crime prevention programs occurred with the increased use of cost-benefit analyses from the 1990s onward.

Deterrence Theory: A theory that proposes severe forms of punishment to deter criminal conduct. In the 1960s and 1970s, criminological research showed that the deterrent effect of punishment only had a marginal or even no effect on (severe) crimes.

Prisonization: The adaptation of prisoners to the prison culture, a negative effect of imprisonment. Imprisonment should have, like other sanctions, a resocialization effect that supports the change of offenders into that of law-abiding citizens. As a "total institution," prisons do not generally support the inclusion of released offenders in society but rather they support inclusion in the prison community, especially in cases of long-term incarceration.

Punitiveness: While not an entirely clear concept, it concentrates on attitudes toward punishment especially about attitudes toward offenders. The discussion about punitiveness can be differentiated into three aspects and is empirically measured on at least three levels: the attitude of the public or persons dealing with crime, such as judges, prison officials, or social workers about (severe) punishment (this is on an individual level and can be proved by polls); punitiveness as a general kind of discussion in a society (e.g., in the media, as a macroperspective); and punitiveness on the level of dealing with crime and offenders at an official level of the penal system (sanctioning).

Weed and Seed Program: A crime prevention initiative announced by President George H.W. Bush in 1992. The program was carried out in different cities and concentrated on young offenders. Offenders were immediately removed from the streets, thereby demonstrating to the public the effectiveness of law enforcement efforts. Money was also provided to rebuild neighborhoods.

Discussion Questions

1. Community Crime Prevention has, historically speaking, a long and successful history. However, it has fallen out of use in the modern state-sanctioned justice system. Do you think that it is important to revitalize this concept today?
2. After reading about the different elements of Community Crime Prevention, which special aspects of the concept should be realized today to prevent crime? Which aspects might not be so important?
3. Should Community Crime Prevention initiatives be offered to offenders during their imprisonment and, if so, how can this be done? What are the opportunities and problems that may arise from prison-based initiatives?
4. Why do countries handle crime and punishment differently? For example, why does Canada have a much lower imprisonment rate than the United States and, at the same time, a lower rate of violent crimes?
5. What should be done to realize more effective crime prevention programs in society, such as Community Crime Prevention, which are cheaper and no less effective than harsh sanctions?

Suggested Reading

Bullock, K. (2014). *Citizens, Community and Crime Control*. Basingstoke, UK: Palgrave Macmillan.

Knepper, P. (2009). *Urban Crime Prevention, Surveillance and Restorative Justice. Effects of Social Technologies*. Boca Raton, FL: CRC Press.

Kury, H., Redo, S., and Shea, E. (Eds.). (2016). *Women and Children as Victims and Offenders: Background–Prevention–Reintegration. Suggestions for Succeeding Generations*. Berlin–Dordrecht–Heidelberg–New York: Springer.

Schneider, S. (2015). *Crime Prevention. Theory and Practice* (2nd ed.). Boca Raton, FL: CRC Press.

Recommended Web Links

https://www.unodc.org/pdf/criminal_justice/06-56290_Ebook.pdf

Website of United Nations Office on Drugs and Crime: Handbook on Restorative Justice Programmes. The text presents a good overview about main topics of (Community) Crime Prevention from an international, UN perspective and also gives definitions of different terms and concepts.

https://www.crimesolutions.gov/TopicDetails.aspx?ID=10
    Website of the National Institute of Justice—NIJ about "Crime &
    Crime Prevention." There are a lot of links to literature about the
    topic of Community Crime Prevention.
http://www.asca.net/system/assets/attachments/1463/Deterrence_Briefing
    _.pdf?1290182850
    Website of the "Sentencing Project." The website presents infor-
    mation about the effect of deterrence.
http://www.rand.org/content/dam/rand/pubs/notes/2005/N1944.pdf
    Website with a text on the Chicago Area Project. The text gives an
    overview about the Chicago Area Project, including its background
    and development.

References

Aos, S. (2003). Cost and benefits of criminal justice and prevention programs. In:
    Kury, H., Obergfell-Fuchs, J. (Eds.), *Crime Prevention. New Approaches*. Mainz,
    Germany: Weisser Ring, 413–442.
Beckett, K. (1997). *Making Crime Pay: Law and Order in Contemporary American
    Politics*. New York: Oxford University Press.
Behringer, W. (Ed.). (1988). *Hexen und Hexenprozesse in Deutschland*. Munich,
    Germany: Deutscher Taschenbuch Verlag.
Braithwaite, J. (2005). Between proportionality and impunity: Confrontation–truth–
    prevention. *Criminology* 43: 283–306.
Buggle, F. (1992). *Denn sie wissen nicht, was sie glauben. Oder warum man redlicher-
    weise nicht mehr Christ sein kann*. Reinbek, Germany: Rowohlt.
Bullock, K. (2014). *Citizens, Community and Crime Control*. Basingstoke/Hampshire,
    New York.
Burgess, E., Lohman, J., and Shaw, C. (1937). The Chicago Area Project. Yearbook of
    the National Probation Association, 8–10.
Burnside, J. (2007). Retribution and restoration in biblical texts. In: Johnstone, G., Van
    Ness, D.W. (Eds.), *Handbook of Restorative Justice*. Cullompton: Willan, 132–148.
Chicago Area Project. (2016). Strengthening neighborhoods, helping young people.
    http://www.chicagoareaproject.org/about-us.
Christie, N. (1977). Conflicts as property. *British Journal of Criminology* 17: 1–26.
Christie, N. (2009). Restorative justice: Five dangers ahead. In: Knepper, P., Doak,
    J., Shapland, J. (Eds.), *Urban Crime Prevention, Surveillance, and Restorative
    Justice. Effects of Social Technologies*. London, New York: CRC Press, 195–203.
Clemmer, D. (1940). *The Prison Community*. Boston: Christopher Pub. House.
Coates, R. (1987). Social service and citizen involvement. In: Johnson, E. (Ed.), *Handbook
    on Crime and Delinquency Prevention*. Westport, CT: Greenwood Press.
Death Penalty Information Center (DPIC). (2016). Facts about the death penalty.
    Washington, DC. http://www.deathpenaltyinfo.org/documents/FactSheet.pdf.
Doleschal, E. (1984). *Prevention of Crime and Delinquency*. Davis, CA: International
    Dialogue Press.

Dölling, D., Entorf, H., Hermann, D., and Rupp, T. (2011). Meta-analysis of empirical studies on deterrence. In: Kury, H., Shea, E. (Eds.), *Punitivity—International Developments. Vol. 3: Punitiveness and Punishment*. Bochum, Germany: Dr. Brockmeyer, 315–378.

Dölling, D., Feltes, T., Heinz, W., and Kury, H. (Eds.). (2003). *Kommunale Kriminalprävention*. Holzkirchen/Obb.: Felix Verlag.

Eckenrode, J., Olds, D., Henderson, C.R., Kitzman, H., Luckey, D., Pettitt, L.M., Sidora, K., Morris, P., Powers, J., and Cole, R. (1998). Long-term effects of nurse home visitation on children's criminal and anti-social behaviour. *Journal of the American Medical Association* 208: 1302.

Edelman, M. (1988). *Constructing the Political Spectacle*. Chicago: University of Chicago Press.

Eisner, M. (2001). Individuelle Gewalt und Modernisierung in Europa, 1200–2000. In: Albrecht, G., Backes, O., Kühnel, W. (Eds.), *Gewaltkriminalität zwischen Mythos und Realität*. Frankfurt/M., Germany: Suhrkamp, 71–100.

Fagan, J., and Chin, K.L. (1990). Violence as regulation and social control in the distribution of crack. In: De La Rosa, M., Lambert, E.Y., Gropper, B. (Eds.), *Drugs and Violence: Causes, Correlates and Consequences*. Washington, DC: National Institute on Drug Abuse Monograph Services No. 103, 8–43.

Farrall, S., Bannister, J., Ditton, J., and Gilchrist, E. (1997). Questioning the measurement of the 'fear of crime.' Findings from a major methodological study. *British Journal of Criminology* 37: 658–679.

Farrall, S., Bannister, J., Ditton, J., and Gilchrist, E. (2000). Social psychology and the fear of crime: Re-examining a speculative model. *British Journal of Criminology* 40: 399–413.

Farrington, D.P. (2002). Developmental criminology and risk-focused prevention. In: Maguire, M., Morgan, R., Reiner, R. (Eds.), *The Oxford Handbook of Criminology*. Oxford, UK: Oxford University Press, 657–701.

Farrington, D., Langan, P., and Wikstrom, P.-O.H. (1994). Changes in crime and punishment in America, England and Sweden between the 1980s and the 1990s. *Studies in Crime Prevention*, 3: 104–131.

Feltes, T. (2003). Kommunale Kriminalprävention: Studien zur Viktimisierung, Verbrechensfurcht und Polizeibewertung als Ansätze zu einer Neuorientierung der Polizeiarbeit. In: Dölling, D., Feltes, T., Heinz, W., and Kury, H. (Eds.), *Kommunale Kriminalprävention—Analysen und Perspektiven*. Holzkirchen/ Obb., Germany: Felix Verlag, 5–13.

Ferdinand, T.N. (2006). Why is American criminal justice so flawed? In: Obergfell-Fuchs, J., Brandenstein, M. (Eds.), *Nationale und internationale Entwicklungen in der Kriminologie. Festschrift für Helmut Kury zum 65. Geburtstag*. Frankfurt/M., Germany: Verlag für Polizeiwissenschaft, 471–483.

Friday, P.C. (2003). Community-based restorative justice: The impact on crime. In: Kury, H., and Obergfell-Fuchs, J. (Eds.), *Crime Prevention. New Approaches*. Mainz, Germany: Weisser Ring, 370–389.

Frühauf, L. (1988). *Wiedergutmachung zwischen Täter und Opfer. Eine neue Alternative in der strafrechtlichen Sanktionspraxis*. Gelsenkirchen: Verlag Dr. Mannhold.

Giles, H. (Ed.). (2002). *Law Enforcement, Communication and Community*. Amsterdam/ Philadelphia: John Benjamins Publishing Company.

Goffman, A. (2014). *On the Run: Fugitive Life in an American City*. Chicago: The University of Chicago Press.

Goffman, E. (1961). *Asylums*. Essays on the social situation of mental patients and other inmates. Garden City, NY: Doubleday.

Griffiths, C.T., Dandurand, Y., and Murdoch, D. (2007). *The Social Reintegration of Offenders and Crime Prevention*. The International Centre for Criminal Law Reform and Criminal Justice Policy (ICCLR). Research Report: 2007-2. Ottawa, Ontario/Canada: National Crime Prevention Centre (NCPC).

Hagemann, O. (2011). Restorative justice: Concept, ideas and impediments. In: Lummer, R., Hagemann, O., Tein, J. (Eds.), *Restorative Justice—A European and Schleswig-Holsteinian Perspective*. Schleswig-Holstein Association for Social Responsibility in Criminal Justice; Victim and Offender Treatment, Schriftenreihe Soziale Strafrechtspflege, Band 1, 34–59 and 151–178. http://www.cepprobation.org/uploaded_files/RJ_Band1.pdf.

Hasler, E. (1982). *Anna Göldin—Letzte Hexe*. Solothurn, Düsseldorf: Benziger Verlag.

Hawkins, D.J., Catalano, R., Kosterman, R., Abbot, R., and Hill, K. (1999). Preventing adolescent health-risk behaviours by strengthening protection during childhood. *Archives of Paediatrics and Adolescent* Medicine 153: 226–234.

Hertzman, C. (2002). *An Early Child Development Strategy for Australia? Lessons from Canada*. Brisbane: Queensland Government Commission for Children and Young People.

Hess, K.M. (2010). *Juvenile Justice*. Belmont, CA: Wadsworth.

Hestermann, T. (2010). *Fernsehgewalt und die Einschaltquote. Welches Publikumsbild Fernsehschaffende leitet, wenn sie über Gewaltkriminalität berichten*. Baden-Baden, Germany: Nomos.

Hestermann, T. (2016). Violence against children sells very well. Reporting crime in the media and attitudes to punishment. In: Kury, H., Redo, S., and Shea, E. (Eds.), *Women and Children as Victims and Offenders: Background, Prevention, Reintegration. Suggestions for Succeeding Generations*. Heidelberg, New York: Springer.

Hinckeldey, C. (1980). *Strafjustiz in alter Zeit*. Rothenburg o.d.T., Germany: Mittelalterliches Kriminalmuseum.

Holcomb, J., and Lab, S.P. (2003). Evaluation: Building knowledge for crime prevention. In: Kury, H., and Obergfell-Fuchs, J. (Eds.), *Crime Prevention. New Approaches*. Mainz, Germany: Weisser Ring, 443–457.

Homel, R. (2005). Developmental crime prevention. In: Tilley, N. (Ed.), *Handbook of Crime Prevention and Community Safety*. Portland, OR: Willan Publishing, 71–106.

Hope, T. (1995). Community crime prevention. In: Tonry, M., and Farrington, D. (Eds.), *Building a Saver Society: Strategic Approaches to Crime Prevention*. Chicago: University of Chicago Press, 21–89.

Hope, T., and Karstedt, S. (2003). Towards a new social crime prevention. In: Kury, H., and Obergfell-Fuchs, J. (Eds.), *Crime Prevention. New Approaches*. Mainz, Germany: Weisser Ring, 461–489.

Hughes, G., and Edwards, A. (2005). Crime prevention in context. In: Tilley, Nick (Ed.), *Handbook of Crime Prevention and Community Safety*. Portland, OR: Willan Publishing, 14–34.

Jacobs, J. (1961). *The Death and Life of Great American*. Chicago: Random.

Jamieson, W. (2008). Factors related to successful mobilization of communities for crime prevention: In: Hastings, R., and Bania, M. (Eds.), *Towards More Comprehensive Approaches to Prevention and Safety*. University of Ottawa, Ontario, Canada: Institute for the Prevention of Crime.

Johnson, L.B. (1965). Special Message to the Congress on Law Enforcement and the Administration of Justice. Washington, DC: The American Presidency Project. Retrieved from http://www.presidency.ucsb.edu/ws/?pid=26800.

Karstedt, S. (2004). Durkheim, Tarde and beyond: The global travel of crime policies. In: Newburn, T., and Sparks, R. (Eds.), *Criminal Justice and Political Cultures*. Cullompton, UK: Willan Publishing.

Krislov, S., and White, S.O. (1977). Understanding crime: An evaluation of the National Institute of Law Enforcement and Criminal Justice. Committee on Research on Law Enforcement and Criminal Justice, Assembly of Behavioral and Social Sciences, National Research Council.

Kury, H. (2001). Das Dunkelfeld der Kriminalität. Oder: Selektionsmechanismen und andere Verfälschungsstrukturen. *Kriminalistik* 55: 74–84.

Kury, H. (2015). Härtere Strafen—Oder mehr Alternativen? Was ist die bessere Kriminalprävention. In: Bannenberg, B., Brettel, H., Freund, G., Meier, B.-D., Remschmidt, H., and Safferling, C. (Eds.), *Über allem: Menschlichkeit*. Festschrift für Dieter Rössner. Baden-Baden, Germany: Nomos, 240–258.

Kury, H., and Kuhlmann, A. (2016). *More Severe Punishment—Or More Alternatives? Mediation in Western Countries*. Mokslo darbei Kriminologijos Studijos.

Leder, K.B. (1986). *Die Todesstrafe. Ursprung, Geschichte, Opfer*. Munich, Germany: Deutscher Taschenbuch Verlag.

Lipton, D., Martinson, R., and Wilks, J. (1975). *The Effectiveness of Correctional Treatment. A Survey of Treatment Evaluation Studies*. London: Praeger Publishers.

Maguire, E.R., and Wells, W. (2002). Community policing as communication reform. In: Giles, H. (Ed.), *Law Enforcement, Communication and Community*. Amsterdam/Philadelphia: John Benjamins Publishing Company, 33–66.

Martinson, R. (1974). What works?—Questions and answers about prison reform. *The Public Interest* 35: 22–54.

McGarrell, E.F. (1988). *Juvenile Correctional Reform. Two Decades of Policy and Procedural Change*. Albany, NY: State University of New York Press.

Miller, L.L. (2001). *The Politics of Community Crime Prevention. Implementing Operation Weed and Seed in Seattle*. Aldershot, Burlington USA: Ashgate.

Morus, T. (1516; 1992). *Utopia*. Frankfurt/M., Germany: Insel Verlag.

Nagin, D., Cullen, F., and Jonson, C. (2009). Imprisonment and re-offending. In: Tonry, M. (Ed.), *Crime and Justice: An Annual Review of Research*, Chicago: University of Chicago Press, 38: 115–200.

Newburn, T., and Souhami, A. (2005). Youth diversion. In: Tilley, N. (Ed.), *Handbook of Crime Prevention and Community Safety*. Portland, OR: Willan Publishing, 355–384.

Obergfell-Fuchs, J., and Kury, H. (2003). Opfererfahrungen, Kriminalitätsfurcht und Vorstellungen zur Prävention von Kriminalität—Stand der Forschung. In: Dölling, D., Feltes, T., Heinz, W., Kury, H. (Eds.), *Kommunale Kriminalprävention*. Holzkirchen/Obb., Germany: Felix Verlag, 32–55.

Ortmann, R. (1993). Prisonisierung. In: Kaiser, G., Kerner, H.-J., Sack, F., and Schellhoss, H. (Eds.), *Kleines Kriminologisches Wörterbuch.* Heidelberg, 401–409.

Parliament of Canada (1993). Crime Prevention in Canada: Toward a National Strategy. Standing Committee on Justice and the Solicitor General, Twelfth report. Ottawa, Ontario, Canada: Queen's Printer for Canada.

President's Commission on Law Enforcement and Administration of Justice (1967). The Challenge of Crime in a Free Society. Washington, DC: United States Government Printing Office. Retrieved from https://www.ncjrs.gov/pdffiles1/nij/42.pdf.

Raynor, P. (2002). Community penalties. Probation, punishment, and 'what works.' In: Maguire, M., Morgan, R., Reiner, R. (Eds.), *The Oxford Handbook of Criminology.* Oxford, UK: Oxford University Press, 1168–1205.

Roberts, J.V. (1992). Public opinion, crime, and criminal justice. In: Tonry, M. (Ed.), *Crime and Justice: A Review of Research.* Chicago: University of Chicago Press, 16: 99–180.

Roberts, J.V., and Hough, M. (Eds.). (2002). Changing attitudes to punishment: Public opinion, crime and justice. Cullompton, UK: Willan.

Roberts, J., and Sprott, J.B. (2008). Exploring the differences between punitive and moderate penal policies in the United States and Canada. In: Kury, H., and Ferdinand, T.N. (Eds.), *International Perspectives on Punitivity.* Bochum, Germany: Universitätsverlag Brockmeyer, 55–77.

Rosenbaum, D. (1988). Community crime prevention: A review and synthesis of the literature. *Justice Quarterly* 5: 323–395.

Rössner, D. (1998). Die Universalität des Wiedergutmachungsgedankens im Strafrecht. In: Schwind, H.-D., Kube, E., and Kühne, H.-H. (Hrsg.), *Festschrift für Hans Joachim Schneider zum 70. Geburtstag am 14. November 1998.* Kriminologie an der Schwelle zum 21. Jahrhundert. Berlin, 877–896.

Sato, M. (2014). *The Death Penalty in Japan. Will the Public Tolerate Abolition?* Wiesbaden, Germany: Springer VS.

Scheingold, S. (1991). *The Politics of Street Crime.* Philadelphia: Temple University Press.

Schiller, F. (1786; 1964). *Der Verbrecher aus verlorener Ehre.* Stuttgart, Germany: Philipp Reclam.

Schlossman, S., and Sedlak, M. (1983a). The Chicago Area Project revisited. The National Institute of Education. Santo Monica: The Rand Corporation. Retrieved from http://www.rand.org/content/dam/rand/pubs/notes/2005/N1944.pdf.

Schlossman, S., and Sedlak, M. (1983b). The Chicago Area Project Revisited. *Crime & Delinquency* 29: 398–462.

Schneider, S. (2015). *Crime Prevention. Theory and Practice.* London, New York: CRC Press.

Schweinhart, L.J. (2004). *The High/Scope Perry Preschool Study through Age 40: Summary, Conclusions, and Frequently Asked Questions.* Ypsilanti, MI: High/Scope Educational Research Foundation.

Shapland, J. (2009). Key elements of restorative justice alongside adult criminal justice. In: Knepper, P., Doak, J., and Shapland, J. (Eds.), *Urban Crime Prevention, Surveillance, and Restorative Justice. Effects of Social Technologies.* London, New York: CRC Press, 123–147.

Sharpe, S. (2007). The idea of reparation. In: Johnstone, G., and Van Ness, D.W. (Eds.), *Handbook of Restorative Justice.* Cullompton, UK: Willan, 24–40.

Shaw, C.T., and McKay, H.D. (1942). *Juvenile Delinquency and Urban Areas*. Chicago: University of Chicago Press.

Shaw, M. (2006). Communities in Action for Crime Prevention. Background Paper. Canberra: International Centre for the Prevention of Crime. Retrieved from http://ww.crime-prevention-intl.org/publications/pub_174_1.pdf?PHPSESSID =379e20fefdf5c7e5781f0be1fbd647b1.

Sherman, L.W. (1997a). Thinking about crime prevention. In: Sherman, L.W., Gottfredson, D., MacKenzie, D., Eck, J., Reuter, P., and Bushway, S. (Eds.), *Preventing Crime: What Works, What Doesn't, What's Promising. A Report to the United States Congress*. Washington, DC: National Institute of Justice, Chap. 2. Retrieved from https://www.ncjrs.gov/works/.

Sherman, L.W. (1997b). Communities and crime prevention. In: Sherman, L.W., Gottfredson, D., MacKenzie, D., Eck, J., Reuter, P., and Bushway, S. (Eds.), *Preventing Crime: What Works, What Doesn't, What's Promising. A Report to the United States Congress*. Washington, DC: National Institute of Justice, Chap. 3. Retrieved from https://www.ncjrs.gov/works/.

Sherman, L.W. (1997c). Policing for crime prevention. In: Sherman, L.W., Gottfredson, D., MacKenzie, D., Eck, J., Reuter, P., and Bushway, S. (Eds.), *Preventing Crime: What Works, What Doesn't, What's Promising. A Report to the United States Congress*. Washington, DC: National Institute of Justice, Chap. 8. Retrieved from https://www.ncjrs.gov/works/.

Spohn, C., and Holleran, D. (2002). The effect of imprisonment on recidivism rates of felony offenders: A focus on drug offenders. *Criminology* 40: 329–358.

Sykes, G.M. (1958). *The Society of Captives: A Study of a Maximum Security Prison*. Princeton, NJ: Princeton University Press.

Tilley, N. (2005). Introduction: Thinking realistically about crime prevention. In: Tilley, N. (Ed.), *Handbook of Crime Prevention and Community Safety*. Portland, OR: Willan Publishing, 3–13.

Tonry, M. (1995). *Malign Neglect*. New York: Oxford University Press.

Tonry, M. (2004). *Punishment and Politics: Evidence and Emulation in the Making of English Crime Control Policy*. Cullompton, UK: Willan Publishing.

Tremblay, R.E., Pagani-Kurtz, L., Masse, L.C., Vitaro, F., Pihl, R.O. (1995). A Bimodal Preventive Intervention for Disruptive Kindergarten Boys: Its Impact through Mid-Adolescence. *Journal of Consulting and Clinical Psychology* 63(4): 560–568.

Trevena, J., and Weatherburn, D. (2015). Does the first prison sentence reduce the risk of further offending? Sydney: NSW Bureau of Crime Statistics and Research, Crime and Justice Bulletin 187.

United Nations Office on Drugs and Crime (2006). *Handbook on Restorative Justice Programmes*. Criminal Justice Handbook Series. New York, Vienna: United Nations. Retrieved from https://www.unodc.org/pdf/criminal_justice/06-56290 _Ebook.pdf.

United Nations Office on Drugs and Crime (2010). *Handbook on the Crime Prevention Guidelines: Making Them Work*. Vienna, Austria: United Nations Office on Drugs and Crime. Retrieved from http://www.unodc.org/pdf/criminal_justice /Handbook_on_Crime_Prevention_Guidelines_-_Making_them_work.pdf.

Walgrave, L. (2008). *Restorative Justice, Self-interest and Responsible Citizenship*. Cullompton, UK: Willan.

Ward, C.S. (1998). *Community Education and Crime Prevention. Confronting Foreground and Background Causes of Criminal Behavior.* Westport, CT: Bergin & Garvey.

Weijters, G., and More, A. (2015). Comparing income and housing of former prisoners after imprisonment with their situation before imprisonment. *European Journal of Criminal Policy and Research* 21: 35–48.

Welsh, B.C., and Hoshi, A. (2006). Communities and crime prevention. In: Sherman, L.W., Farrington, D.P., Welsh, B.C., and MacKenzie, D.L. (Eds.), *Evidence-Based Crime Prevention.* New York: Routledge, 165–197.

Werminck, H., Blokland, A., Nieuwbeerta, P., Nagin, D., and Tollenaar, N. (2010). Comparing the effects of community service and short-term imprisonment on recidivism: A matched samples approach. *Journal of Experimental Criminology* 6: 325–349.

Winterdyk, J., and King, D. (2011). Perspective on punitiveness for adult offenders: Contrasting Canada and the United States. In: Kury, H., and Shea, E. (Eds.), *Punitivity. International Developments. Vol. 3: Punitiveness and Punishment.* Bochum: Universitätsverlag Dr. Brockmeyer, 101–130.

Wright, M. (2003). Is it time to question the concept of punishment? In: Walgrave, L. (Ed.), *Repositioning Restorative Justice.* Cullompton, UK: Willan, 3–23.

Wright, V. (2010). Deterrence in criminal justice: Evaluating certainty vs. severity of punishment. Washington, DC: The Sentencing Project. Retrieved from http://www.asca.net/system/assets/attachments/1463/Deterrence_Briefing_.pdf?1290182850.

Zimbardo, P. (2007). *The Lucifer Effect—Understanding How Good People Turn Evil.* Philip G. Zimbardo, Inc.

Social Crime Prevention
Concepts, Developments, and Challenges

8

MATJAŽ AMBROŽ
GORAZD MEŠKO
BENJAMIN FLANDER

Contents

Learning Outcomes
After reading this chapter, you should be able to understand the

- Concept of social crime prevention
- Key developments in social crime prevention
- Role of root causes of crime in planning for social prevention
- Importance of preventive activities that depend on inclusive social policy (family support, education, employment, etc.)
- Challenges for the concept of social crime prevention in times of globalization, individualization, and neo-liberalism

Introduction

> What all this means is that real social crime prevention, like the prevention of
> other social ills, is now more than ever dependent on our capacity to build …
> movements for social action and social change. These … should be commit-
> ted to the long-rage effort to replace a society based increasingly on the least
> inspiring of human values with one based on the principles of social solidarity
> and contributive justice.
>
> **E. Currie**
> *1996, p. 354*

Social crime prevention (SCP) can be linked to the social control theory
of crime (Hirschi 1969), which asserts that the strength and durability of
an individual's bonds or commitments to society serve to diminish his or
her propensity for deviant behavior. Unlike the more traditional example
of **situational crime prevention** (Clarke 1996; Jeffery 1971; Newman 1972;
also see Chapter 14 in this volume), SCP is based on an assumption that real
changes regarding diminishing deviancy and crime rates can be achieved
mainly through solving social problems, such as social inequality, a low educational level, structural unemployment, poor employment opportunities,
discrimination, poverty, and social exclusion (Meško 2002). Attempting to
achieve its goals, SCP is concerned with measures aimed at tackling the root
causes of crime and the predisposition of individuals to offend (Crawford
and Traynor 2012; Graham and Bennet 1995). SCP programs and initiatives
focus on individuals, groups and communities, and (potential) victims of
crime (Meško 2002). Such programs minimize the risk for individuals, be
they (potential) offenders or victims of crime, and contribute to the reinforcement of resilient communities. Usually, adherents of SCP criticize other
preventive approaches and programs for wrongly addressing the root causes
of crime while dealing only with its symptoms (see Box 8.1).

In this chapter, we will first attempt to conceptualize SCP and outline
briefly the key developments of the concept. While highlighting the post-
war period, we will argue that contemporary trends in crime prevention are
somewhat ambivalent. On the one hand, governments promote measures that
undoubtedly emphasize control and surveillance; on the other hand, they
have not abandoned traditional SCP initiatives and programs, although these
enjoy less political support than in the 1970s (Baillergeau and Hebberecht
2012). In the core sections, we will address the role of the social root causes
of crime in planning for SCP and systemize the social prevention approaches
by identifying six common areas of social policy (i.e., urban, health, family,
education, youth, and employment), where prudent management of society's
principal structures and institutions may help prevent criminal behavior
(Meško 2002). We will sketch the crime prevention potential of each of these

BOX 8.1   A SHIFT IN PARADIGM

It is widely acknowledged that the last four decades have seen an expansion in crime reduction initiatives focused on prevention rather than the traditional means of prosecution, punishment, and repression. The ascent of crime prevention represents a major paradigm shift in criminal justice and crime control, fundamentally altering the way in which society manages crime and structures social relations (Tuck 1988, cited in Crawford 2007, p. 867). This shift to a preventive mentality took place in most western countries as well as in the post-communist European countries. Among different approaches to crime prevention, SCP gained a lot of attention in western and particularly European countries until the end of the 1970s and even at the beginning of the 1980s. Afterward, in academic debate as well as in crime and social policies, the concept of SCP has taken a less important role, as—with the processes of globalization, individualization, and neo-liberalism—actively promoting welfare for all has ceased to be a central ambition of rulers and policymakers. With the rapid economic, political, social, and cultural changes that have taken place during the last decade, it is difficult to make a prognosis about the future development of SCP (Baillergeau and Hebberecht 2012).

areas of policy and conclude by addressing the primary challenges associated with the implementation of SCP programs and initiatives.

Defining and Conceptualizing SCP

For a number of reasons, defining SCP is a challenging task. One of the reasons stems from the problem of defining and operationalizing what is meant by **crime prevention**. Almost no discussion about "crime prevention" fails to mention that crime prevention is an ill-defined concept that leaves room for a certain ambiguity (Groenemeyer and Schmidt 2012; also see Bennet 1989; Crawford 1998; Gilling 2009). Even the task of crime prevention is not clear and subject to dispute, while, sometimes, the term is classified as a form of crime reduction (Groenemeyer and Schmidt 2012); in other cases, victim protection and reducing fear of crime and feelings of insecurity (Meško et al. 2008) also fall under the umbrella of crime prevention.

Another difficulty, when defining SCP, lies in the fact that the use of the term is quite generic and often used to describe anything that is not repressive. Also, in criminological literature, "social crime prevention" often overlaps with terms/concepts such as structural crime prevention, **developmental**

crime prevention, risk-focused crime prevention, **community crime prevention**, and—somewhat confusingly—**community safety** (see, e.g., Crawford and Traynor 2012, pp. 65–66; de Maillard and Germain 2012, p. 109). The boundaries between these concepts of and approaches to crime prevention are rather porous. Finally, it is not an easy task to delineate what SCP is and what it is not because its measures sometimes overlap with programs and interventions in the field of social policy, to the extent that SCP programs have been criticized for "a criminalisation of social policy" mainly because of their name (Crawford 1997, p. 228; Groenemeyer and Schmidt 2012, p. 122). In this case, programs that focus on the improvement of quality of life are much more readily accepted than ones that include social "crime" prevention (see Box 8.2).

Brantingham and Faust (1976) introduced a now widely accepted conceptual model that defines the three levels of crime prevention (see Chapter 1). While primary prevention entails initiatives and programs directed at general populations, secondary prevention involves work with individuals, groups, or places identified as "at risk" because of some predisposing factor,

---

BOX 8.2   WHAT IS SCP?

Preventive strategies, which utilize an SCP perspective, aim to modify social environments and, consequently, influence offenders' motivations, preferably with planned and coordinated multiagency approaches (Crawford and Traynor 2012). Hence, SCP primarily centers on interventions that seek to strengthen socialization agents such as informal control (e.g., family, peers, school, etc.), education, employment, and support schemes for ex-convicts in order to minimize opportunities to (re)offend (see Crawford and Traynor 2012; Groenemeyer and Schmidt 2012; Meško et al. 2012). Similarly, Crawford and Traynor (2012, p. 65) assert that SCP incorporates interventions aimed at reducing individual motivations to offend via their social environments and institutions of socialization and altering social relationships and the social environment through a collective focus on communities, neighborhoods, and social networks. In contrast to situational prevention, which involves the management, design, or manipulation of the immediate physical environment aimed at reducing the opportunities for specific crimes (Clarke 1996; Jeffery 1971; Newman 1972), the concept of SCP comprises "inclusive" measures that target the social causes of crime rather than those concerned with the mechanical reduction of opportunities or with deterrence (Young 2001). In the broader social context, SCP—primarily focusing on interventions that seek to affect and target social processes and collective relationships— aims at providing an alternative to the dissuasive or repressive effects of the criminal justice system (Crawford and Traynor 2012, p. 65).

and tertiary prevention is directed toward preventing the recurrence of criminal events, by targeting known offenders, victims, or places that are already part of the crime pattern (Crawford 2007). The concept of SCP includes measures and interventions at all three levels of prevention of crime inside and outside the criminal justice system. Within the criminal justice system, SCP is aimed at ensuring individual and general preventive effects on known as well as potential offenders. Outside the criminal justice system, a social crime-preventive effect is expected from the economic, urban, educational, social, and cultural policies implemented as part of general social policies in different segments of society (see Hebberecht 2012, p. 38).

As stated above, the boundaries between SCP and various concepts of crime prevention, which are closely related to it, are rather vague. Developmental crime prevention, for example, focuses largely on an individual's childhood development and the opportunities present at critical junctures during life course, to prevent the onset of offending in the early years. The developmental crime prevention programs, targeted at children and young people, as well as their parents, identified as "at risk" of offending, have been named by van Dijk and de Waard (2009, pp. 137–138) "secondary offender-oriented crime prevention" (also see Crawford and Traynor 2012, p. 67). These "early intervention" programs have been sometimes classified as a part of SCP and vice versa. More importantly, attention should also be focused on the fact that, under certain (e.g., undesirable) circumstances, developmental crime prevention is an ambivalent model of crime prevention. While providing parental support might help young members of "at-risk" families to avoid embarking on criminal careers, developmental crime prevention carries the risk of stigmatizing them, which may result in exclusion and compromise the inclusive potential of SCP (Baillergeau and Hebberecht 2012).

Since about the 1970s, in academic debate as well as in crime policies, the concept of SCP has been rather marginalized. While neo-liberal conservatives have criticized SCP efforts within the functioning of the criminal justice system for their lack of deterrent effect on criminal behavior, the radical left has provided a critique of the controlling and disciplinary effects of SCP programs (Hebberecht 2012). In the vast majority of European countries and North America, different prevention strategies such as "community safety," "community crime prevention," "situational prevention," and "social safety" have all been given far more attention than SCP. On many occasions, in addition to situational schemes of crime prevention, countries have introduced more repressive and punitive policies (Crawford and Traynor 2012; de Maillard and Germain 2012; Hebberecht 2012; Kerezsi 2012; Peršak 2004; Petrovec 2004; Šelih 2004). We will address the key post-war developments in SCP in more detail in The Historical Context: A Brief Sketch of the Key Post-War Developments in SCP, relying mostly on a comprehensive survey by Baillergeau and Hebberecht (2012).

The Historical Context: A Brief Sketch
of the Key Post-War Developments in SCP

After World War II, until the end of the 1970s, the concept of SCP as a policy aimed at preventing economic and social marginalization and exclusion gained attention in several European countries. Initially, the concept was incorporated in the educational, public housing, and social policies carried out in the context of the developing social welfare state (Baillergeau and Hebberecht 2012). In the functioning of criminal justice systems, emphasis was given to the reintegration and rehabilitation of convicted offenders and juvenile delinquents. While the 1960s and 1970s are considered the "golden age" of SCP, even during the 1980s, there were several attempts at applying this concept as a policy aimed at preventing the marginalization and exclusion of vulnerable social groups and their members (see Baillergeau and Hebberecht 2012; Meško et al. 2012; Šelih 2004; Selmini 2012).

The research carried out primarily by French sociologists and socialist-oriented policymakers helped develop a so-called French SCP model (Baillergeau and Hebberecht 2012). Founded on the elaboration of an urban and structural view of SCP and in state-driven policies aimed at changing structural conditions for young people at risk of crime in various fields such as education, leisure, and labor, this model was exported to a significant number of other European countries and even to other continents. Another model developed throughout this period was the Nordic model. On the basis of the ideas of Scandinavian critical criminologists such as Nils Christie and the Scandinavian concept and practice of welfarism, this model involved social and educational programs aimed at eliminating or reducing the social causes of crime (Baillergeau and Hebberecht 2012). The third model of the 1980s, identified by Baillergeau and Hebberecht (2012) as the prevalent alternative to situational crime prevention in the United Kingdom and other Anglophone countries, was the community crime prevention model, relying primarily on affirmative action aimed at young people in socially deprived areas (also see Crawford 1997, 1998, 2007; Crawford and Traynor 2012).

Until the end of the 1980s, SCP was also at the peak of its development in some post-communist countries. In Slovenia, for example, the idea of SCP was somehow integrated into the socialist state's welfare programs and activities. This period was characterized by a crime policy that was devoted to resocialization and rehabilitation practices and a critical examination of the role of the police in society. During the democratization process of the second half of the 1980s, SCP was still a part of crime policy and crime response practices (Meško et al. 2012). In Hungary, a political and professional environment had also emerged during the 1980s that clearly encouraged the idea of the prevention-oriented transformation of crime control and a complex system of crime prevention, which included SCP initiatives and programs (Kerezsi 2012).

At the end of the 1980s, in Great Britain and in a number of continental European countries, the trend toward SCP started to lose its appeal and momentum. The neo-liberal–inspired "first turn in SCP" (Hughes 2007) of the 1980s redirected the focus to crime prevention and control through the deterrent effects of the criminal justice system and situational crime prevention, which aimed to reduce opportunities to commit crime. These new developments played a central role in the crime policies of the Conservative administration of the then Prime Minister Margaret Thatcher (Crawford 2009; Hughes 2007). According to Baillergeau and Hebberecht (2012), under British influence, the "preventive turn" took place in the Netherlands, Belgium, France, and Italy, among others. The dismantling of the social welfare state in these and the vast majority of other European countries was, however, less pronounced than in the United Kingdom and the United States, their role model countries. In most of these countries, SCP policy, nevertheless, remained an integral part of broader social policies. Their respective crime control policies became more flexible and reactive to real and immediate social needs. For example, while the Nordic countries, which were equally influenced by neo-liberal ideas, also introduced situational crime prevention strategies, post-war SCP efforts remained the leading force within the their social and criminal policies. As Baillergeau and Hebberecht (2012, pp. 26–27) have put it, throughout the Nordic countries, the concept of the welfare state was maintained, albeit not to the same extent in all of them.

While recognizing that punitiveness has become a dominant feature of penal policy in the vast majority of democratic countries since the beginning of the 1990s (see Garland 2001; Green 2009; King and Maruna 2006; Lappi-Seppälä 2008; Pratt 2006, 2008), some criminologists have concluded that, simultaneously, the "second turn in SCP" happened. Baillergeau and Hebberecht (2012) assert that this second turn was the result of an adaptation of the reconfigured SCP of the 1980s to a new wave of neo-liberal situational crime prevention policies developed, initially, in Great Britain, the Netherlands, and Belgium. While this second turn took the form of "an integrated administrative crime prevention policy" (Hebberecht 2012, p. 40) in the Netherlands and Belgium, in England and Wales, it was realized by implementing the concept of "community safety" (Crawford 2007, p. 889). The SCP reconfiguration reached its fullest development in the security and safety policy of UK Prime Minister Tony Blair's New Labor government between 1997 and 2007.

The second turn in SCP also influenced developments in crime prevention in France, Germany, Italy, Spain, Belgium, Portugal, Greece, and some other "old" European democracies (see Castro et al. 2012; de Maillard and Germain 2012; Selmini 2012; Vidali 2012), as well as in some post-communist

BOX 8.3   TOWARD A MORE AUTHORITARIAN CONCEPT OF CRIME PREVENTION

The latest reconfigurations in SCP policies toward a more individualized, control-oriented, and authoritarian "community safety" crime prevention model in the vast majority of European countries prioritize, among other things, the fight against antisocial behavior and public disorder. These policies incorporate measures aimed at reducing individual motivations to offend via their institutions of socialization through the focus on communities, neighborhoods, and social networks. According to Baillergeau and Hebberecht (2012), this neo-classicist and neo-positivist approach to SCP ties in with the individual positivist perspective prevalent in the second half of the 19th century.

Central and Eastern European countries (see Kerezsi 2012; Petrovec 2004; Šelih 2004). In Hungary, the prevention-oriented transformations were interrupted by the change of political regime in 1989, such that the idea of a complex crime prevention system was taken off the agenda up until the mid-1990s (Kerezsi 2012, p. 184). In contrast, it was not until the late 1990s that Slovenia underwent a "turn" toward a more punitive stance and a withdrawal from the past "inclusive" orientation in crime prevention practices (Meško et al. 2012, pp. 303–305). According to Baillergeau and Hebberecht (2012, p. 29), the transfer of the new western "safety and security" policy to the post-socialist countries was realized partly by initiatives of the European Crime Prevention Network (EUCPN), which was set up by the European Union (EU), and by incorporation of EU law into their domestic legal systems (see Box 8.3).

The current era of rising **penal excess** (Pratt 2008) and focus on other crime prevention models notwithstanding, SCP programs and initiatives are still advocated by criminologists and social scientists and play a role in official social and crime policies in various countries across the world (see the Measures of SCP section). It is, however, impossible to predict how crime prevention will develop in the future and what faith will be retained in SCP. As Winterdyk asserts in the Introduction to this volume, the one thing that is reasonably certain is that crime prevention will continue to undergo constant (and at times rapid) change.

The Social Root Causes of Crime and SCP

SCP focuses on the "root causes" of crime, especially the factors that contribute to delinquency, drug abuse, and adolescent problems. On the basis of the premise that crime is caused by the social ills of society, the SCP model focuses on developing programs and policies to improve the health, family life, education, housing, work opportunities, and neighborhood activities of potential offenders (Rosenbaum et al. 1988). In general terms, social factors that contribute to delinquency and crime are neighborhood instability and change, rapid turnover of households, decline of the labor market, loss of services and transport, and visible deterioration of buildings as well as radical physical alteration, such as demolition and construction of housing stock (Knepper 2007, pp. 60–61).

Searching for the social root causes of crime, the social disorganization theory refers to the inability of a community structure to realize the common values of its residents and maintain effective social controls. In terms of this theory, social organization and disorganization are different ends of the same continuum with respect to systematic networks of community social control (Sampson and Groves 1989). Sampson and Groves (1989) introduced the term *collective efficacy*, which they defined as the neighborhood's ability to maintain order in public spaces. **Collective efficacy** is implemented when neighborhood residents act to maintain public order by complaining to the authorities or by organizing neighborhood watch programs. The residents take such actions only when social cohesion and mutual trust in the neighborhood are high. Housing ownership has been identified by the adherents of the social disorganization theory as a relevant variable in high levels of crime in specific areas (see Mazerolle et al. 2011, p. 134).

According to Robert Merton's *strain theory*, many people cannot access a legitimate means to achieve material success, which is a highly valued goal in western (e.g., capitalist) society. This is regarded in Merton's theory as an incentive to commit crime (Baillergeau and Hebberecht 2012). Similarly, the *relative deprivation theory* asserts that crime occurs because of "the excess of expectations over opportunities" (Lea and Young 1996, p. 140), and according to the *conflict theory*, the root causes of crime originate from "people's natural tendency to pursue economic self-interest in a high-conflict world" (see Arrigo and Bernard 2002, p. 255). A more radical perspective on the social root causes of crime and their role in planning for SCP is advocated by the (neo-Marxist) *critical criminological theory*. This theory focuses on the social structure of capitalism and the inequitable distribution of economic wealth across society (Arrigo and Bernard 2002). Accordingly, crime is a rational response to class-based inequalities and disproportionate acquisition and/ or the accumulation of capital. In the opinion of these critics, changes in the social structure will result in changes in the tendency to pursue self-interest, leading to a more consensual and safe society. Crime could be eliminated, or reduced, through SCP if SCP was part of a political struggle for social empowerment and justice (Arrigo and Bernard 2002; Hulsman 1996). SCP is also a central concept in the writings of critical left-wing realists (Currie 1988;

Lea 1997, cited in Baillergeau and Hebberecht 2012, p. 24; Young 1991), who claim that crime is a product of institutions and community structures.

Hence, different criminological theories provide different explanations for the root causes of crime and propose different SCP approaches for their elimination or reduction. In the following sections, we will attempt—beyond any specific criminological theory of the root causes of crime—to systemize the most common SCP approaches in different areas of social policy and conclude by addressing the primary challenges associated with their implementation.

Measures of SCP

As stated above, SCP is "a vast, loosely defined terrain without clear-cut boundaries" (Rosenbaum et al. 1988, p. 202). Many initiatives, measures, and projects may fall within its scope, without necessarily bearing the direct crime prevention label (Baillergeau 2012). Indeed, the preventive potential of initiatives such as family support, employment, and housing shall be "enhanced and celebrated without requiring specific interventions to be overly labelled (and stigmatized) as 'crime prevention'" (Sutton et al. 2008, p. 46).

There have been several attempts at systemizing SCP approaches. Basically, six areas of social policy can be identified, where judicious management of principal structures and institutions may help prevent criminal behavior: urban, health, family, education, youth, and employment policy. Although these areas of social policy often partially overlap, we will, for reasons of clarity and transparency, sketch the crime-preventive potential of each of them separately, relying on a comprehensive study by Graham and Bennet (1995).

In general, large and overpopulated cities tend to suffer from higher crime rates than planned, low-density urban environments (Graham and Bennet 1995). In many cases, it will be difficult, if not impossible, to manipulate density of population in certain environments, yet improving the spatial organization of existing urban populations should be encouraged in order to minimize segregation along class, race, or other grounds (see Box 8.4). For example, a plausible but expensive option includes **neighborhood renewal programs** as a contribution to the improvement of living conditions in deprived neighborhoods. A good example can be currently seen in Australia, where neighborhood renewal programs bring together the resources and ideas of residents, governments, businesses, and community groups to tackle disadvantage in areas with disproportionate concentrations of public housing (Human Services 2015; for similar programs in the Netherlands, see Baillergeau 2012). In some welfare states, such as Norway, they stress the importance of granting access to the housing market with affordable,

BOX 8.4   EMPOWERMENT OF COMMUNITIES

SCP seeks to empower communities to deal with social issues that lead to crime and address fears of crime and perceptions of unsafe environments. According to Human Services (2015), neighborhood renewal programs are not only about improving public housing estates; rather, they are "transforming whole streets and neighborhoods—creating vibrant places where people want to live." Thus, the declared goals go beyond enhancing housing conditions and include, inter alia, increasing access to services, improving government responsiveness, promoting health and well-being and increasing people's pride and participation in their community.

subsidized loans, since without sufficient capital to buy a home, the alternative is a poor and expensive rental market (Egge and Gundhus 2012).

An accessible health care system also plays an important role within SCP, since health problems, most notably substance abuse and mental disorders, might be seen as risk factors for criminality (Meško et al. 2012). Insofar as physical and mental disabilities may lead to greater feelings of alienation and exclusion (Graham and Bennet 1995), national and local policies and programs for ensuring the social integration of such vulnerable groups should be encouraged. As regards drug and other psychoactive substance use, harm reduction programs are of special importance. A well-known example in the EU has been the OKANA program (European Monitoring Centre for Drugs and Drug Addiction 2015), aiming at harm reduction at both an individual level (reducing the exclusion of drug users from health care services) and a social level (decreasing the incidence of infectious diseases and reduction of drug-related delinquency).

Families as primary units of socialization and social integration play an important role in the prevention of delinquent behavior. *Dysfunctional family relations* (e.g., child neglect; a persistent atmosphere of conflict or a disruptive family setting; and parents involved in criminal behavior or substance abuse) are identified as increasing the risk of offending. Such troubled relations may be influenced by external factors such as unemployment, low income, or inappropriate housing that can adversely affect parents' capacity to bring up their children effectively. In Canada, home visits to assist "at risk" mothers with parenting skills helped decrease the percentage of children who were later handed over to child protection authorities from 25% to just 2.3% (Canadian Council on Social Development 2015). Another example of a good parenting support program can be found in Belgium (European Platform for Investing in Children 2015a). This program was formally adopted in 2007 as a government policy through a government decree. The decree describes parenting support as "easily accessible, basic parenting support to parents and persons with childcare responsibilities." The decree specifies multiple levels of parenting support, such as local- and regional-level support, the provision of services through parenting "workshops," the organization of parenting support coordinators, provincial parenting support centers, and a center for obtaining expert advice in parenting matters.

Education policy is also an important part of the SCP perspective, since children and young people spend a great deal of their formative years in various educational establishments. Schools therefore offer a promising focus of intervention and innovation and as institutions are more easily targeted than, for example, the family (Graham and Bennet 1995). Research has shown that children who drop out from school or behave disruptively when they are there are more likely to get involved in criminal offending (Thronberry et al. 1985). Therefore, policies that help prevent dropping out from schools and improve the ability of children and youngsters to handle conflicting situations in a constructive manner must be welcomed, such as social learning programs and antibullying programs (see, e.g., Harlan et al. 2015). Schools are places where young people can engage in a wide range of activities, foster their talents, acquire work experience, and, in so doing, develop a sense of commitment and strengthen self-esteem. One successful example is Germany's dual educational system, which connects apprenticeships in companies and schools. This model provides for a successful transition of German youth from school to work and helps keep youth unemployment relatively low (Dynot 2015).

Youth policy is strongly interwoven with school and family policies, yet its main target is the time that young people spend outside schools and family environments. The chief idea has been that youngsters have to be offered an alternative to "pointless hanging around" by providing them with diverse forms of leisure, sports, and cultural activity, while at the same time ensuring some degree of supervision over them. This idea has been implemented through various forms of youth work or street work, which encompass a variety of activities and incentives. One example is the "street workers" in the Netherlands (Baillergeau 2012, p. 245), whose task is to guide young people to fruitful alternative ways of using their spare time by (1) getting them enrolled in activities provided by neighborhood centers (sport, music, and similar activities); (2) providing them with guidance toward relevant agencies such as debt clearance support, work experience programs, and similar programs; and (3) getting them enrolled in some specific projects through which young people will "discover talents" and gain new skills. Thus, Dutch street work does not focus primarily on the "problems" caused by young people but rather emphasizes their "talents" that need to be fostered. When it concerns projects such as organizing a music festival, the involvement of young people occurs at all levels: project definition, fundraising, applications for authorizations, publicity, approaching guest artists for performance scheduling, practicalities, and project evaluation. An important achievement with regard to such projects is that their involvement provides young people with new skills that are regarded as equally valuable for their curriculum vitae as for job applications (see Box 8.5).

Although the influence of *unemployment* on crime can hardly be isolated from other socioeconomic factors, such as education, income distribution, housing conditions, and relative deprivation, there is evidence that suggests that young males are more likely to commit offenses during periods of unemployment, owing to lack of income, boredom, demoralization, and the destabilization of the family unit (Graham and Bennet 1995). This problem can be addressed through different social measures that may also help prevent or reduce crime. Besides granting opportunities for gaining formal qualifications and technical skills, trainings and retraining programs may help young unemployed people to cope with the quickly changing needs of the labor market. The "Ecce ama!" program might serve as an example. This is run by a private human services organization in Belgium, which is targeting low-income families with training modules to prepare low-skilled men and women for jobs in the childcare sector (European Platform for Investing in Children 2015b).

One should, however, be realistic about what can be achieved. Even with comprehensive retraining programs, it is difficult to imagine that full employment rates can be reached in the foreseeable future. The creation of new jobs may be one of the possible ways of addressing the problem. Quite ironically, the private crime prevention industry, which basically relies on situational crime prevention and has little to do with its "social sibling," has in the past

---

**BOX 8.5   AN EXAMPLE FROM SLOVENIA—
OVERCOMING A SOCIAL CONFLICT**

Another promising example is a Slovenian project aimed at overcoming tensions between Roma and non-Roma communities in Slovenia. Six Roma and six non-Roma young people have participated in the project by shooting 15 short documentaries on the life of young people from the Roma minority. Through active participation and peer education and with the help of skilled mentors, they have gained basic knowledge of video production. The films have been broadcast on public TV channels in Slovenia and in other European countries (Education and Culture DG 2015).

decades offered various posts, such as security guard, that have been interesting and accessible to otherwise hardly employable men. Unfortunately, such newly created jobs are often precarious in their nature and rarely offer steady and long-term employment, which is, anyway, especially for young people, a vanishing prospect in most western societies.

Problems and Evaluation

As with any other social activity, SCP can face a gap between policy and practice. Unrealistic expectations about what can be achieved may lead to disappointment ("nothing works"), resulting in budget cuts, abandonment of programs, and shifts to situational approaches (see Baillergeau 2012, pp. 247–248), as well as to a variety of unintended results of preventive measures owing to bad science, bad planning, and implementation failure (Grabosky 1996). Therefore, it seems crucial that policymakers do not expect too much from short-term projects, but bear in mind that, as already mentioned, inclusive societies are generally less burdened with crime. In any case, we should be wary of the "utopian dream that every form of 'deviant energy' can and should be transformed into socially acceptable activity" (Sutton et al. 2008, p. 36).

One of the difficulties with SCP is that its effectiveness is often difficult to measure. It is impossible to estimate, for example, how many criminal offenses have been prevented by a specific measure, if any at all. Lack of accurate measurement might be considered as a weakness, especially after the rise of evidence-based criminology, the "academic sibling of what works movement" (Clear and Frost 2009, p. 20). Nevertheless, even without directly measurable effects, it is evident that there is less crime in countries with smaller social class differences, good integration, and equal opportunities (Egge and Gundhus 2012).

Another challenge with SCP is that it does not address all types of crimes or possible offenders. Rather, SCP is usually linked with the prevention of "conventional crime" such as street crime (violence), property crime, and public nuisance (Meško 2002). The basic aim of SCP is to enhance opportunities for those who are socially disadvantaged, providing them with legitimate means to improve their social status. This is not enough, because if crime prevention focuses only on crimes committed by the disadvantaged, it will fail to address the array of crime committed by people who hold significant social, economic, or political power (e.g., crimes of the powerful, corporate crime, and white collar crime) (see Meško et al. 2012, p. 315).

At the risk of blurring boundaries between SCP and other concepts such as developmental crime prevention, community crime prevention, and so on, SCP faces the dilemma of whether it should focus on individuals or social structures and institutions. While SCP initiatives have recently become more and more based on individual and family interventions in some countries, one may wonder about the ambition of these initiatives to address the structural causes of crime (see Baillergeau and Hebberecht 2012). Although a targeted, person-oriented approach, which focuses on individuals and families at risk of committing crime, might appear more cost-effective, policymakers should be aware that ignoring the structural causes of crime has long-term negative effects and that special support to individuals provided outside the context of normal life runs the risk of stigmatizing recipients (Sutton et al. 2008).

Summary

According to Rosenbaum et al. (1998), the challenges of SCP in the 21st century are related to the political will for long-term investment, clear responsibility for crime prevention ("everyone's but no one's responsibility"), labeling and new widening (focusing on specific groups of people), victim blaming (tension between individual responsibilities and structural determinants), assuring proper evaluations, and implementation failure. Besides these specific challenges, one general trend in crime prevention has to be borne in mind: many researchers have shifted from SCP to a more positivist developmental crime prevention (see, e.g., Lab 1997, 2000). Perhaps this is a sign that SCP was an idea related to the welfare state and started diminishing with the advent of liberal and neo-liberal policies that pay more attention to situational factors than social ones for crime and delinquent behavior.

As noted earlier in this chapter, after the 1980s, SCP has also been increasingly challenged by the populist demand for harsher punishment. Indeed, the "law and order" message is far easier to sell to the mass media and the public than SCP (Sutton et al. 2008, p. 34). In some cases, instead of preventing crime through social policy, one can even speak of "criminalizing social problems," which refers to the criminalization of behaviors that were once considered to be expressions of social deprivation and marginality such as begging, vagrancy, drinking in public spaces, or street prostitution (for the United Kingdom, see Crawford and Traynor 2012; for Italy, see Selmini 2012). It is very doubtful whether such criminalization can help in solving social tensions in the long run.

The authors of this chapter are convinced that SCP can still offer a fruitful alternative to punitive and situational approaches in the future; instead of advocating this or that specific program, they think that, in the future, priority has to be given to a universalistic approach to SCP that fosters an inclusive society. SCP is now more than ever dependent on our capacity to challenge those forces dimming the life chances of vast numbers of people, to build movements for social action and social change, and to replace a society based increasingly on the least inspiring of human values with one based on the principles of social solidarity (Currie 1996). One possible model of such an inclusive society is the Nordic model, based on a proactive state and guided by the principles of equality of opportunity, including a supportive labor market policy and a broad range of social services and benefits that are delivered on the basis of uniform rules of eligibility (Egge and Gundhus 2012). A key to successful SCP can be therefore seen in efforts for the more equitable distribution of wealth, rather than sporadic "humanitarian" programs for the disadvantaged, which are often no more than crumbs from the table of an unjust society.

Glossary of Key Terms

Collective efficacy: involves the neighborhood's ability to maintain order in public spaces. Collective efficacy is implemented when neighborhood residents act to maintain public order by complaining to the authorities or by organizing neighborhood watch programs. The residents take such actions only when social cohesion and mutual trust in the neighborhood are high.

Community crime prevention: refers to strategies and programs that target changes in community infrastructure, culture, or the physical environment in order to reduce crime. Community-based crime prevention programs include those that operate within the community and involve community residents actively working with their local government agencies to address issues contributing to crime, delinquency, and disorder.

Developmental crime prevention: focuses largely on an individual's childhood development and the opportunities present in critical junctures during life course, to prevent the onset of offending in the early years. The developmental crime prevention programs are targeted at children and young people, as well as their parents, identified as "at risk" of offending.

Neighborhood renewal programs: are strategic, usually government-funded improvements of neighborhoods, public places, sidewalks, streetlights, and other public infrastructure intended to make people feel better and safer. Improvements may also include increasing access to services, improving government responsiveness, and promoting health and well-being.

Situational crime prevention: involves the management design or manipulation of the immediate physical environment aimed to reduce the spatial opportunities for specific crimes.

Social crime prevention: incorporates "inclusive" interventions and measures aimed at tackling the root causes of crime and the dispositions of individuals to offend. It is based on an assumption that real changes regarding diminishing deviancy and crime rates can be achieved mainly through solving social problems, such as social inequality, a low education level, structural unemployment, poor employment opportunities, discrimination, poverty, and social exclusion.

Social policy: refers, in broad terms, to public policy that relates to social issues. More particularly, it refers to guidelines, principles, legislation and activities that affect the citizen's living conditions and quality of life.

Social root causes of crime: are social factors that contribute to delinquency and crime (such as social discrimination and inequality, neighborhood instability and change, rapid turnover of households, decline of labor market, loss of services and transportation, visible deterioration of buildings, and radical physical alteration, such as demolition and construction of housing stock, etc.).

Discussion Questions

1. What is social crime prevention?
2. Can you briefly outline the key historical developments of the concept of social crime prevention?
3. How would you assess the contemporary trends in crime prevention in general and social crime prevention in particular?
4. What is the role of the social root causes of crime in planning for social crime prevention?
5. Which are the most common social crime prevention approaches in different areas of social policy?
6. Can you briefly describe the primary challenges associated with the practical implementation of social crime prevention measures?

Suggested Reading

Baillergeau, E., and P. Hebberecht (Eds.) (2012). *Social Crime Prevention in Late Modern Europe. A Comparative Perspective*. Brussels: VUBPress Brussels University Press.

Canadian Council on Social Development. (2015). *Children and Youth Crime Prevention through Social Development*. http://www.ccsd.ca/resources/Crime Prevention/sd.htm.

Crawford, A. (1998). *Crime Prevention and Community Safety. Politics, Policies and Practices*. London: Longman.

Sutton, A., Cherney, A., and White, R. (2008). *Crime Prevention: Principles, Perspectives and Practices*. Oxford, UK: Oxford University Press.

Recommended Web Links

European Social Policy Network: http://ec.europa.eu/social/main
.jsp?catId=1135&langId=en

This is the website of the European Social Policy Network (ESPN).
Established in 2014, ESPN provides information, analysis, and
expertise on the EU's social policies. The website is maintained by
the European Commission's DG for employment, social affairs, and
inclusion.

EUCPN: http://eucpn.org/search/knowledge-center/social%20prevention

This website accumulates and evaluates the EUCPN information
on crime prevention activities in EU member states. The EUCPN
contributes to developing local and national strategies on crime
prevention and promotes crime prevention activities by organizing
meetings, seminars, and conferences.

ICPC: http://www.crime-prevention-intl.org/en/welcome.html

This is the website of the International Centre for the Prevention
of Crime (ICPC). ICPC is a global nongovernmental organization
located in Montreal, Canada. It is a unique international forum and
resource center dedicated to the exchange of ideas and knowledge on
crime prevention and community safety.

Social policies:

- http://www.sgi-network.org/2015/Policy_Performance/Social
_Policies
- http://www.durban.gov.za/City_Government/safer_cities/Pages
/Social-Crime-Prevention.aspx
- http://efus.eu/files/fileadmin/efus/pdf/national_strat_crime
_prevention.pdf
- http://www.prevention-commerce.com/pcepr.asp
- http://www.ccsd.ca/resources/CrimePrevention/sd.htm
- http://www.communitiesthatcare.net/how-ctc-works/social
-development-strategy/
- http://www.aic.gov.au/publications/current%20series/rpp/100
-120/rpp120/07_approaches.html

These websites provide multiple sources of information on social
policies and crime prevention through social development in different regions and countries.

References

Arrigo, B.A., and Bernard, T.J. (2002). Postmodern criminology in relation to radical
and conflict criminology. In *Criminological Theories, Bridging the Past to the
Future*, ed. S. Cote, 250–257. London: Sage Publications.

Baillergeau, E. (2012). Social crime prevention in the Netherlands in the 2000s: A marginalised bit enduring line in crime reduction. In *Social Crime Prevention in Late Modern Europe: A Comparative Perspective*, ed. P. Hebberect, and E. Baillergeau, 235–254. Brussels: VUBPress.

Baillergeau, E., and Hebberecht, P. (2012). Social crime prevention in late modern Europe. Towards a comparative analyses. In *Social Crime Prevention in Late Modern Europe. A Comparative Perspective*, eds. P. Hebberecht and E. Baillergeau, 21–36. Brussels: VUBPress Brussels University Press.

Bennet, T. (1989). Crime prevention. In *The Handbook of Crime and Punishment*, ed. M. Tonry, 369–402. New York: Oxford University Press.

Brantingham, P.J., and Faust, F.L. (1976). A conceptual model of crime prevention. *Crime and Delinquency* 22(3): 284–296.

Canadian Council on Social Development. 2015. *Children and Youth Crime Prevention through Social Development*. http://www.ccsd.ca/resources/CrimePrevention /sd.htm.

Castro, J., Cardoso, C.S., and da Agra, C. (2012). Social crime prevention in Portugal. In *Social Crime Prevention in Late Modern Europe. A Comparative Perspective*, eds. P. Hebberecht and E. Baillergeau, 279–301. Brussels: VUBPress Brussels University Press.

Clarke, R.V.G. (1996). 'Situational' crime prevention: Theory and practice. In *Criminological Perspectives. A Reader*, ed. J. Muncie, E. McLaughlin, and M. Langan, 332–342. London: Sage Publications.

Clear, T.R., and Frost, N.A. (2009). Criminology and public policy. In *21st Century Criminology: A Reference Handbook, Volume 1*, ed. M.J. Miller, 18–27. London: Sage.

Crawford, A. (1997). *The Local Governance of Crime. Appeals to Community and Partnerships*. Oxford, UK: Oxford University Press.

Crawford, A. (1998). *Crime Prevention and Community Safety. Politics, Policies and Practices*. London: Longman.

Crawford, A. (2007). Crime prevention and community safety. In *The Oxford Handbook of Criminology* (4th ed.), eds. M. Maguire, R. Morgan, and R. Reiner, 866–909. Oxford, UK: Oxford University Press.

Crawford, A. (2009). *Crime Prevention Policies in Comparative Perspective*. Cullompton, UK: Willan Publishing.

Crawford, A., and Traynor, P. (2012). La prevention de la délinquance chez les Anglais: From community-based strategies to early intervention with young people. In *Social Crime Prevention in Late Modern Europe. A Comparative Perspective*, eds. P. Hebberecht and E. Baillergeau, 63–101. Brussels: VUBPress Brussels University Press.

Currie, E. (1988). Two visions of community crime prevention. In *Communities and Crime Reduction*, ed. T. Hope and M. Shaw, 280–286. London: HMSO.

Currie, E. (1996). Social crime prevention strategies in a market society. In *Criminological Perspectives. A Reader*, eds. J. Muncie, E. McLaughlin, and M. Langan, 343–354. London: Sage Publications.

de Maillard, J., and Germain, S. (2012). Social prevention in France. Erasure, permanence, regeneration? In *Social Crime Prevention in Late Modern Europe. A Comparative Perspective*, eds. P. Hebberecht and E. Baillergeau, 103–120. Brussels: VUBPress Brussels University Press.

Dynot. (2015). *The German Education System*. Retrieved from http://www.dynot.net /index.php?option=com_content&task=view&id=39&Itemid=73.

Edgeworth, B. (2003). *Law, Modernity, Postmodernity. Legal Change in the Contracting State*. London: Ashgate.

Education and Culture DG. (2015). *Good Practice in the Youth Field*. Retrieved from http://ec.europa.eu/youth/policy/youth_strategy/documents/youth -participation-brochure_en.pdf.

Egge, M., and Gundhus, H.I. (2012). Social crime prevention in Norway. In *Social Crime Prevention in Late Modern Europe: A Comparative Perspective*, eds. P. Hebberect, and E. Baillergeau, 255–277. Brussels: VUBPress.

European Monitoring Centre for Drugs and Drug Addiction. (2015). *Direct Aid and Support Unit of OKANA*. Retrieved from http://www.emcdda.europa.eu/html .cfm/index52035EN.html?project_id=2647&tab=overview.

European Platform for Investing in Children. (2015a). *Belgium: Leader in Pre-school Education*. Retrieved from http://europa.eu/epic/countries/belgium /index_en.htm.

European Platform for Investing in Children. (2015b). *Ecce Ama!: Child Care in Learning Networks*. Retrieved from http://europa.eu/epic/practices-that-work /practice-user-registry/practices/ecce-ama_en.htm.

Garland, D. (2001). *The Culture of Control: Crime and Social Order in Contemporary Society*. Oxford, UK: Clarendon Press.

Gilling, D. (2009). Crime prevention. In *Criminal Justice*, eds. A. Hucklesby and A. Wahidin, 11–36. Oxford, UK: Oxford University Press.

Grabosky, P. (1996). *Unintended Consequences of Crime Prevention*. Retrieved from http://www.popcenter.org/library/crimeprevention/volume_05/02_Grabosky .pdf.

Graham, J., and Bennett, T. (1995). *Crime Prevention Strategies in Europe and North America*. Helsinki: HEUNI.

Green, D.A. (2009). Feeding wolves: Punitiveness and culture. *European Journal of Criminology* 6(517): 517–536.

Groenemeyer, A., and Schmidt, H. (2012). Social crime prevention in Germany. Balancing social policy and crime policy? In *Social Crime Prevention in Late Modern Europe. A Comparative Perspective*, eds. P. Hebberecht and E. Baillergeau, 121–150. Brussels: VUBPress Brussels University Press.

Harlan, L., Limber, S.P., and Olweus, D. (2015). Bullying in U.S. schools: 2014 status report. Retrieved from http://olweus.sites.clemson.edu/documents/Bullying%20 in%20US%20Schools--2014%20Status%20Report.pdf.

Hebberecht, P. (2012). The turns in social crime prevention in Belgian crime prevention policy since the 1980s. In *Social Crime Prevention in Late Modern Europe. A Comparative Perspective*, eds. P. Hebberecht and E. Baillergeau, 37–62. Brussels: VUBPress Brussels University Press.

Hirschi, T. (1969). *Causes of Delinquency*. Berkeley, CA: University of California Press.

Hope, T. (1995). Community crime prevention. *Crime and Justice* 19: 31–89.

Hughes, G. (2007). *The Politics of Crime and Community*. Basingstoke, UK: Palgrave MacMillan.

Hulsman, L.H.C. (1996). Critical criminology and the concept of crime. In *Criminological Perspectives. A Reader*, eds. J. Muncie, E. McLaughlin, and M. Langan, 299–303. London: Sage Publications.

Human Services. (2015). *Neighbourhood Renewal*. Retrieved from http://www
.dhs.vic.gov.au/about-the-department/plans,-programs-and-projects
/projects-and-initiatives/housing-and-accommodation/neighbourhood-renewal.

Jeffery, C.R. (1971). *Crime Prevention through Environmental Design*. Beverly Hills,
CA: Sage.

Kerezsi, K. (2012). 'Grandpa's fashion in the New Year'—Innovative theoreti-
cal thoughts vs. simplistic crime prevention practices in Hungary. In *Social
Crime Prevention in Late Modern Europe. A Comparative Perspective*, eds.
P. Hebberecht and E. Baillergeau, 181–208. Brussels: VUBPress Brussels
University Press.

King, A., and Maruna, S. (2006). The function of fiction for a punitive public. In
Captured by the Media: Prison Discourse in Popular Culture, ed. P. Mason,
16–30. Cullompton, Devon, UK: Willan Publishing.

Knepper, P. (2007). *Criminology and Social Policy*. Los Angeles: Sage.

Lab, S.P. (1997). *Crime Prevention: Approaches, Practices and Evaluations*. 3rd ed.
Cincinnati: Anderson Publishing Company.

Lab, S.P. (2000). *Crime Prevention: Approaches, Practices and Evaluations*, 4th ed.
Cincinnati: Anderson Publishing Company.

Lab, S.P. (2014). *Crime Prevention: Approaches, Practices and Evaluations*, 8th ed.
Amsterdam: Anderson Publishing Company.

Lappi-Seppälä, T. (2008). Trust, welfare, and political culture: Explaining differences
in national penal policies. *Crime and Justice: A Review of Research* 37: 313–387.

Lea, J. (1997). From Integration to Exclusion: The Development of Crime Prevention
Policy in the United Kingdom. Retrieved from http://www.bunker8.pwp.blue
yonder.co.uk/misc/polis.htm.

Lea, J., and Young, J. (1996). Relative deprivation. In *Criminological Perspectives. A
Reader*, eds. J. Muncie, E. McLaughlin, and M. Langan, 136–144. London: Sage
Publications.

Mazerolle, L., McBroom, L., and Rombouts, S. (2011). Compstat in Australia: An
analysis of the spatial and temporal impact. *Journal of Criminal Justice* 39(2):
128–136.

Meško, G. (2000). Pogledi na preprečevanje kriminalitete v poznomodernih družbah
[Aspects of crime prevention in the late modern societies]. In *Prvi slovenski
Dnevi varstvoslovja*, ed. M. Pagon, 295–306. Ljubljana, Slovenia: Visoka polici-
jsko-varnostna šola.

Meško, G. (2002). *Osnove preprečevanja kriminalitete [Basics of Crime Prevention]*.
Ljubljana, Slovenia: Visoka policijsko-varnostna šola.

Meško, G., Fallshore, M., Muratbegovic, E., and Fields, C.B. (2008). Fear of crime in
two post-socialist capital cities—Ljubljana, Slovenia and Sarajevo, Bosnia and
Herzegovina. *Journal of Criminal Justice* 36(6): 546–553.

Meško, G, Kanduč, Z., and Jere, M. (2012). Social crime prevention in Slovenia—
Recent developments. In *Social Crime Prevention in Late Modern Europe.
A Comparative Perspective*, eds. P. Hebberecht and E. Baillergeau, 303–319.
Brussels: VUBPress Brussels University Press.

Newman, O. (1972). *Defensible Space: Crime Prevention through Urban Design*. New
York: MacMillan.

Pease, K. (1997). Crime prevention. In *The Oxford Handbook of Criminology*, eds. M.
Maguire, R. Morgan, and R. Reiner, 963–996. Oxford, UK: Clarendon Press.

Peršak, N. (2004). Nekateri problematični konceptualni vidiki in popularni miti sodobnih smeri prevencije [Some conceptual problems with new forms of crime prevention]. In *Preprečevanje kriminalitete. Teorija, praksa in dileme* [*Crime Prevention—Theory, Practice and Dilemmas*], ed. G. Meško, 82–98. Ljubljana, Slovenia: Inštitut za kriminologijo pri Pravni fakulteti v Ljubljani.

Petrovec, D. (2004). Temna prihodnost kriminalitetne politike [The dark future of criminal policy]. In *Preprečevanje kriminalitete. Teorija, praksa in dileme* [*Crime Prevention—Theory, Practice and Dilemmas*], ed. G. Meško, 99–106. Ljubljana, Slovenia: Inštitut za kriminologijo pri Pravni fakulteti v Ljubljani.

Pratt, J. (2006). *Penal Populism*. London: Routledge.

Pratt, J. (2008). Scandinavian exceptionalism in an era of penal excess. *British Journal of Criminology* 48(2): 119–137.

Rosenbaum, D.P., Lurigio, A.J., and Davis, R.C. (1998). *The Prevention of Crime: Social and Situational Strategies*. Canada: Wadsworth Publishing Company.

Sampson, R.J., and W. B. Groves. (1989). Community structure and crime: Testing social disorganisation theory. *The American Journal of Sociology* 94(4): 774–802.

Selmini, R. (2012). Social crime prevention in Italy: A never-ending story? In *Social Crime Prevention in Late Modern Europe. A Comparative Perspective*, eds. P. Hebberecht and E. Baillergeau, 209–233. Brussels: VUBPress Brussels University Press.

Sutton, A., Cherney, A., and White, R. (2008). *Crime Prevention: Principles, Perspectives and Practices*. Oxford, UK: Oxford University Press.

Šelih, A. (2004). Preprečevanje kriminalitete—razvoj in dileme [Crime prevention—Development and dilemmas]. In *Preprečevanje kriminalitete. Teorija, praksa in dileme* [*Crime Prevention—Theory, Practice and Dilemmas*], ed. G. Meško, 19–30. Ljubljana, Slovenia: Inštitut za kriminologijo pri Pravni fakulteti v Ljubljani.

Thronberry, T.P., Moore, M., and Christenson, R.L (1985). The effect of dropping out of high school on subsequent criminal behavior, *Criminology* 23(1): 3–18.

Tuck, M. (1988). *Crime Prevention: A Shift in Concept*. Home Office Research and Planning Unit Research Bulletin, No. 24, London, Home Office.

van Dijk, J., and J. de Waard. (2009). Forty years of crime prevention in the Dutch polder. In *Crime Prevention Policies in Comparative Perspective*, ed. A. Crawford, 130–152. Cullompton, UK: Willan Publishing.

Vidali, S. (2012). Social crime prevention in Greece. In *Social Crime Prevention in Late Modern Europe. A Comparative Perspective*, eds. P. Hebberecht and E. Baillergeau, 151–180. Brussels: VUBPress Brussels University Press.

Young, J. (1991). Left realism and the priorities of crime control. In *The Politics of Crime Control*, eds. K. Stenson and D. Cowell, 146–160. London: Sage.

Young, J. (2001). Social crime prevention. In *The Sage Dictionary of Criminology*, eds. E. McLaughlin and J. Muncie, 272. London: Sage.

Restorative Justice and Crime Prevention

Constructive Alternative or Soft Option?

9

RICHARD GRIMES*
SCOTT WALSH†

Contents

Learning Outcomes

After reading this chapter, you should be able to

- Explain the rationale for a restorative justice program in the context of criminal or antisocial behavior
- Describe the principal features of a restorative justice program in terms of its structure and operational logistics
- Identify the potential relevant stakeholders in community restorative justice initiatives
- With reference to a relevant evidence base, critically evaluate the impact restorative justice can have in terms of crime prevention/reduction

---

* Richard Grimes was, until April 2016, Director of Clinical Programmes at York Law School, the University of York. He is now an independent consultant specialising in legal education reform and access to justice.
† Scott Walsh was a team member on the NACRO (Preston) Restorative Justice Team and is now acting manager of Restorative Justice Foundation, UK.

Introduction

Restorative justice is one of the most talked about developments in the field of crime and justice. Its advocates and practitioners argue that state punishment—society's customary response to crime—neither meets the needs of crime victims nor prevents reoffending. In its place, they suggest, should be restorative justice in which families and communities of offenders are encouraged to take responsibility for the consequences of their actions.....

G. Johnstone
2011

Discourage litigation. Persuade your neighbors to compromise whenever you can. Point out to them how the nominal winner is often a real loser—in.... expenses, and waste of time.

A. Lincoln
1850

Restorative justice (RJ), as both concept and practice, has featured in criminal justice systems worldwide for many years, even though it may not always have been recognized or termed as such. The fundamental characteristic of RJ in the context of crime prevention is addressing offending and antisocial behavior by considering the position of the victim, the offender, and the wider community, where possible through interparty dialogue.

This chapter looks briefly at the definition and significance of RJ and asks, and seeks to answer, two basic questions: (1) Is RJ a viable alternative to other means of criminal justice disposal? (2) How can RJ be delivered to maximize its crime prevention potential?

This contribution draws on the experience of the two authors from different but complementary standpoints. The discussion is located in relevant and contemporary literature. Specific examples are given through a case study of RJ programs whose design, delivery, and impact have been developed and assessed.

Against this background of theory applied to practice, the chapter endeavors to highlight the relevance of RJ to varying stakeholder interests in an international context showing what each may have to gain (or "pay") as a participant in or party affected by RJ processes.

The chapter concludes by and posing questions for both the reader and practitioner to dwell on including examining the part RJ can play in shaping an effective crime prevention strategy.

What Is RJ and Why Use It?

Simply put, and in a criminal justice context, RJ

gives victims the chance to meet or communicate with their offenders to explain the real impact of the crime—it empowers victims by giving them a voice. It also holds offenders to account for what they have done and helps them to take responsibility and make amends.

The source of this quotation goes on to say that RJ

is about victims and offenders communicating within a controlled environment to talk about the harm that has been caused and finding a way to repair that harm.*

We suggest that RJ is more than this in a philosophical sense but that this definition is a helpful starting point.

If RJ involves bringing those affected together (and this may include a multitude of interested and affected parties) with a view to addressing unacceptable actions, mitigating against future violations and possibly attempting to deal with grievances, how do we know that RJ may have something to offer?

Space here does not permit a detailed citation or account of the relevant research but this is easily accessed elsewhere. While not every research finding is conclusive about the impact on reoffending rates, two common denominators run through the results. At the very least, those going through RJ processes are no more likely to reoffend than those who do not (and indeed in many instances are less likely to) and the cost to the state of RJ intervention (even where programs are state sponsored) is considerably less than disposal through the formal criminal justice system. These conclusions are consistent across different research and in different jurisdictions. For a summary of research findings concerning the key performance indicators of RJ in a criminal justice setting, see Grimes (2012).[†]

According to a 2004–2008 **Ministry of Justice** (UK) evaluation of RJ schemes, reoffending rates after RJ intervention fell by a significant amount (27% in one study and 14% in another). Victim participation and satisfaction rates were very high—more than 50% and 80%, respectively (Shapland et al. 2011).[‡] For every £1 (approximately US$1.50) spent on RJ programs, an estimated £9 (approximately US$13.50) was saved. Further, an estimated £400 less (US$600) per case is spent on police time, when compared with issuing an offender with a caution or reprimand—and considerably more on staffing and related costs if the offender were to be prosecuted through the courts (Shewan 2010).[§]

---

* Taken from the Restorative Justice Council (UK) website available at http://restorative justice.org.uk/criminal-justice.html (accessed June 15, 2015).
† A further account addressing reoffending, victim satisfaction, benefits to criminal justice agencies and associated monetary savings can be found in Johnstone (2011, pp. 18–21).
‡ The actual reports referred to were released in four stages by the Ministry of Justice and the website cited at the end of this chapter will give access.
§ *Further*, an estimated savings of £7050 (US$10,500) per offender is made if a case is taken through RJ and not through the courts (see Matrix Evidence 2009).

Given the above, we suggest that this is potentially (and likely to be) a positive outcome across a number of indicators and will serve a variety of stakeholder interests.

A Case Study

Let us now look at RJ on the ground. Take this example:

> I am 49 years old and married with two children, living in the north of England. I would like to explain how I entered the world of restorative justice and to do so we must return to my youth and what I now call my "wilder days." My first introduction to the British criminal justice system was back in 1984. As a teenager, going out drinking with friends and getting into trouble seemed to be very "normal." It was not long before one night the police raided a pub that we were in, I remember taking offence to what seemed their heavy-handed approach and ended up in court facing charges of disturbing the peace and assault. Although I was only fined, I did spend two nights in the police station; my first of many.

And more…

> By 1988 I travelled to Europe for work and adventure but constantly found myself in one scrape or another, usually resulting in being arrested and spending the night in cells. In 1989 I was offered some landscaping work in Holland but, as usual, my attitude landed me in trouble when a friend and I were involved in a fight and accused of stealing a car. This was now a lot more serious and we faced trial being remanded in prison for two months. However, just before the case came to court the charges were dropped on a technicality.

Were lessons learned from these brushes with the law? Apparently not:

> Back in the UK I still had a somewhat care-free attitude towards life in general and I pretty much had a total disregard for everybody I came across. By 1995 I was making my living by smuggling cigarettes from Europe to the UK. It was only a matter of time before I found myself in trouble again. Even though by 1995 I was married and had two small children my selfishness and immature approach to life remained.
>
> Shortly after this, trying to recoup my losses in a poorly thought out smuggling scam, I found myself in London with a gang who seemed hell-bent on ruining their life's faster than mine. In a drunken state I was persuaded to hold up a money exchange booth with an imitation firearm. Although I did not know it at the time, this would be a defining moment for me. I escaped from the scene of the crime without any cash but knowing I had been recognised. After taking legal advice I handed myself into the police and ended up in Brixton prison, staring at up to 15 years behind bars. I was taken to the Old Bailey (the historic and principal

criminal court in London). Although I intended to plead guilty from the outset when the prosecution read out the charges and the details of the case against me (including how I had threatened the clerk with the gun) I realised how much I must have frightened him. I then looked up at the public gallery and saw that the clerk I had held up was actually there! What was clear was how upset and distressed the man looked. It was something that I had not even considered before— how frightened must he have been and what an on-going impact my actions had had on him. I was later given a 5-year jail term. Although I felt hard done to and full of self-pity I could not get the image of the clerk out of my mind. I was also beginning to feel really bad about the effect on my family.

It is interesting and important to note that at this stage, remorse is clearly setting in as is the recognition of the wider and lasting impact of our offender's behavior. The account of these events and developments continues:

After being in prison for about 3 months I was reading through my court papers one morning and remembered the clerk and how distressed he had looked. I had had no intention of targeting him or hurting him personally, but when I analysed it more I began to put myself in his shoes—I realised that he was not to know I would not harm him. I decided I would write to him to explain my thoughts and apologise for my actions. I contacted my solicitor to ask him for assistance in sending the letter, which he did. I did not hear anything back for around a month and just when I had given up hope of receiving a reply I was handed a letter one morning—it was from the clerk. I was humbled to read that he accepted my apology. It was a very kind letter filled with empathy and understanding and he even wished me well on my eventual release and for the future. We carried on writing to each other for a couple of years before finally losing contact. Although I did not know it this was my entry into the world of restorative justice (RJ).

These facts and feelings were real and are the direct experience of Scott, one of the authors of this chapter.

Encouraged by the response of the victim, Scott made a conscious decision to attempt to turn over a new leaf. Part of this was to take up education again—something that had been sadly neglected in his past. On release from prison and with the help of his family, Scott found work and began to study. In 2004, after a few short-term jobs (it's tough getting work with a criminal record), Scott read an advertisement for a youth court facilitator course run by the local **youth offending team** (YOT), so he applied and was accepted on to the course, which was basically about RJ and one-to-one mediation. He got through the course with flying colors but, unfortunately, on completion, he was told that because of his criminal record, he could not work with the YOT. He was, instead, invited to volunteer with a national charity (National Association for the Care and Resettlement of Offenders [**NACRO**]) that works with offenders, particularly those under 21 and in trouble for the first time.

Although this was not paid work, Scott enjoyed volunteering and was delighted to be offered a part-time post after a short time at the first national RJ center in Preston, UK. Call it a commitment to make amends or a sense of belonging, but Scott had clearly found his niche. At this early stage, the project used peer panels (copying a model found in the United States*) where law students sit on a panel effectively in judgment of offenders. The peer panels focus on low-level crimes in communities and schools. The rationale is based, in part, on the need to reduce the high cost of running actual court cases,[†] as well as being designed to lower reoffending rates on the presumption that being judged by your peers might be more effective than more formal judicial proceedings. It was also felt that this would be great education and training for law students to be directly involved in the preparation and running of the panels. Using law students not only made sense in terms of building capacity for the program but also provided a point for the "hands-on" education of the students themselves. This "learning by doing" model is sometimes referred to as **clinical legal education**. The concept of learning through the application of theory to practice is an increasingly common feature in law schools in the United Kingdom and much further afield (see Bloch 2011; Carney et al. 2014).

A panel would be made up of four student peers with a lead advocate "chairing" proceedings.

The offender has allegations read to him or her and responsibility has to be accepted—in other words, like a guilty plea but without the formal consequences of a criminal record or legally enforceable penalty. The panel then considers any mitigating circumstance and decides on the outcome. This could be, for example, a letter of apology or a direction to attend anger management sessions.

The program started with some adverse publicity. The press printed headlines such as "students to punish kids" and "panels let offenders off the hook." This did not go down well. Local councils, who had helped fund the scheme, and the police were getting very agitated about how little progress was being made. The councils had expected to save money by reducing human resource input and cutting the cost caused by antisocial behavior.

Although the peer panel project produced some interesting results in terms of outcomes and compliance, the team was somewhat disappointed with the results, largely because of the number of offenders who refused to take part or who did not agree to comply with the sanctions imposed. In reality, the panel members were sitting much like a bench of judges would

---

* See the Teen Court model as developed by the NGO Global Youth Justice and pioneered by Scott Peterson. http://www.globalyouthjustice.org.html (accessed September 1, 2015).
† The methodology used in the Teen Court can be followed at http://www.globalyouthjustice .org/About_us.html (accessed September 1, 2015). For a wider discussion of the U.S. approach to youth crime, see Bartollas and Miller (2013).

do—hearing the facts, taking into account personal circumstances, and passing a sentence (albeit one that was not legally enforceable).

The contrast between the claims of success for the U.S. peer panel model and the relative lack of success of the UK pilot was very evident. In the UK scheme, student peers did not seem to fully appreciate that purpose of the initiative—resolving problems rather than punishing offenders. There were also issues with reliability with student peers often being unavailable for panel sessions. This suggests that the induction and training had not worked effectively. Offenders also showed a marked (and perhaps understandable) resistance to be effectively judged by their peers. There were possibly many reasons for this, including the perception by the offenders (and, in many cases, the fact) that the student peers were often from very different and relatively privileged backgrounds. Anecdotal evidence suggests that some of the offenders' parents shared the same viewpoint.

There may also be important cultural differences. In the United States, the public are perhaps (and at the risk of generalization) more respectful of law enforcement than in Britain, with the consequence that participation in and compliance with the process and outcomes may be more likely. In addition, some U.S. States have adopted the peer panel system and embedded this into statutory law, clearly adding perceived legitimacy and weight to the process. The perceived failure of the peer panel scheme within a UK context was perhaps more down to cultural difference and public perception than simply bad publicity and poor training.

The project team therefore called a meeting to discuss the future of the initiative and, if appropriate, how to make improvements. It was clear that a rethink would have to take place. The project manager (who had set up the peer panels before Scott's involvement) then reviewed the program and said perhaps the project should focus on reparation and concentrate on victim and offender conferencing instead. Students could still be involved but in a less judgmental way (both in a procedural and moral sense). In consultation with a victim support nongovernmental organization (NGO), it was suggested that the team should look at a more established European model of RJ, which involved the victim from the outset, which the peer panel scheme had not. In their research, the Preston team found that the Dutch legal system had long taken the victim's situation into account when dealing with crime in general and juvenile crime in particular and was heavily influenced by the reported experience of RJ programs in the Netherlands when redesigning the UK program. An account of developments around RJ in that part of the world can be found elsewhere (Groenhuijsen 2010). With the help of the (then) RJ Council in the United Kingdom, a new scheme was devised involving victims from the start of the process. Students would still be involved, but more as facilitators, rather than adjudicators, in a multiparty discussion of who did what and why and how to move forward. Another important consideration was that the victims were now asked in advance what outcome (including details of possible reparation) they would be prepared to accept.

Both research and experience suggest that active participant engagement is critical to the success of any RJ model—one-to-one mediation run by a facilitator followed by interparty conferencing, bringing victim and offender together to discuss what had taken place and why, and what might be done by way of reparation. On the whole, this approach was well received by all those involved. In a little over two years, Scott personally facilitated more than 50 RJ conferences. He was then offered a full-time contract on the project.

Under this alternative model, the students were there to simply guide proceedings, letting the process itself work, with the victim on an equal footing with the offender in terms of participation. The facilitation, although central to the process, could be compared to the role of a good soccer referee, regulating proceedings but only intervening where necessary. That said, the facilitators did not have red cards to wave!

The concept of acknowledging responsibility and (possibly) offering reparation facilitated through a meeting or "conference" is sometimes referred to as the Wagga Wagga model, named after the Australian town where the idea is said to have been pioneered. A discussion of this and the notion of blameworthiness (coupled with a willingness to address ways of moving forward) are discussed at length by Johnston in his previously cited book on RJ, under the heading "Shame apology and forgiveness" (Johnstone 2011).

Before looking at the wider implications of this one case study, we will first describe how it operated and what the outcomes were.

Most of the referrals to the newly designed RJ program concerned young offenders who had committed relatively low-level, first-time crimes, ranging from minor shoplifting to various forms of antisocial behavior. There was some initial negative feedback from the public and clearly this needed to be addressed. The Borough Council were helping in the funding, and as this involved spending funds generated from local taxes, it was particularly important that the public were involved in discussions around the aims and benefits of RJ and took a degree of ownership of the initiative. Considerable effort went into promoting the scheme through public meetings and press releases.

Referrals started to come from the police, YOTs, local councils, schools, and even local business in shoplifting cases. Some of these matters may not have been a priority for the RJ team (who were, because of community demands, more focused on street crime and antisocial behavior than on relatively minor dishonesty offenses). However, in order to get relevant "buy-in" from the whole community, a wide range of offending was encompassed. The focus, however, was on youth offenders. It was felt that this would be more likely to have the maximum impact effect. Those invited to take part in the scheme were those considered to have committed the relevant offenses (but were not necessarily otherwise facing formal prosecution).

Preparation was and is an integral part of the process. After a referral is received, prompt contact is needed, first with the victim and then, second, with the offender. It is very important that everyone, including the victim, knows exactly what the process will be if they are to take part. This is important to convince likely participants of the value of the initiative (hence increasing actual participant numbers) and is required to manage expectations and to ensure, as far as possible, an effective process and meaningful outcome. Home visits by two members of the team always took place, to both victim and offender. Timing is also important so that action is taken and is seen to be taken promptly when events are still fresh in peoples' minds and consequences can be seen to flow from the behavior involved.

To give a flavor for the type of cases handled in the early days of the amended Preston RJ project, Scott provides this example:

> Three boys were referred by the local YOT. They had been at a haulage company yard late at night they had started a small fire. Things had got out of hand and there was a lot of damage to a building and a storage unit. After the one to one meetings a conference took place that was attended by the boys, their parents, the owner of the business, the fire service, and representatives from the local YOT. The owner spoke about how he was a local employee and in future young lads like the boys could be looking for work or apprenticeships there. The meeting went well (as evidenced by the active and constructive participation of all) and the boys eventually apologised and agreed to go on a hard-hitting fire safety course. We later received letters from the boys' parents and grandparents thanking us for running the conference and saying we had helped to turn the boys' lives around.
>
> RJ sessions in shoplifting cases from local traders always seemed to have positive results. Once young people realised that they were stealing from a small business in their own community and that it was not a harmless crime their attitude really changed. We also had quite a few bullying cases including some early online abuse.

After about two years and the initial success of the project, referral numbers however started to fall and the "failure" rate in terms of further offenses and related problems occurring began to rise, albeit not significantly. Victim satisfaction was also less than hoped for with around 50% not reporting favorably on the conferencing experience. Keeping records, whatever the results, remains a very important part of research and development. The team knew they had to improve the project. First, the training package for facilitators was changed to put more emphasis on role-play and preparation. Facilitators clearly needed and valued hands-on practical experience before getting involved in the conferencing process.

Knowing the area and its problems well, Scott suggested to the project team that they could run RJ conferences to help in neighborhood disputes.

Management agreed and once further training (on mediation) was completed, the project was soon running at least one neighborhood dispute case per week. Outcomes again were tracked, and this time, the RJ community-based intervention had an immediate and significant impact (as measured by the level of further problems and incidents reported to the team or the police). Reoffending/antisocial behavior decreased by more than 80%. That said, setting up and running the sessions proved to be very testing and challenging. Winning hearts and minds was part of the battle. While this comes from just one example of RJ in practice, we suggest that it has wider implications as will be seen later in the chapter.

Later in the project, a large number of referrals involving antisocial behavior incidents on housing estates in the local area were received. These problems were taking up significant amounts of police and housing authority time and causing great distress in the neighborhood—particularly among the older residents. The first background report stated that up to 15 youths had been involved in more than 90 reported incidents over a three-month period. It was obvious that a one-to-one approach would be impossible when dealing with such large numbers. Scott suggested that the project should run a multiparty conference inviting all stakeholders—victims, offenders, residents, local authority, school, and law enforcement agencies. The first referral was made in late 2008 with more than 15 offenders named. An action plan was drawn up and it was now vital, more than ever, to get the public fully on board. Scott and his team visited every victim for a one-to-one discussion so that the RJ process could be explained in detail, including how the RJ conference would work and what the benefits might be, including possible reparation. With careful handling and appropriate reassurance, 18 victims agreed to participate in the first conference. Scott then visited the offenders, again individually, inviting them to volunteer to attend the conference. Some parents were hesitant, but 14 offenders eventually agreed to attend the conference. Scott confesses that, by this point in his career, he knew every trick in the book to encourage offenders to attend, without of course now breaking any rules! First, it was important to get the police to back the scheme up with the pointed comment that if offenders did not take the RJ path, then they could be taken to court. Second, work was needed with the parents, many of whom rented their homes from the Council. They were told that Council representatives would be attending and their absence would be noted! In some circumstances (and legally), tenants can be evicted if found responsible for criminal or antisocial behavior.

With all the parties agreeing to attend the meeting, the RJ team then planned the multioffender conference in detail—looking after parties on arrival, working out where everyone would sit, and deciding who would speak and when. The team invited representatives from as many different organizations as possible including the police, the housing department, the local YOT, residents and tenants' associations, shopkeepers, and the local schools. As attendance was entirely voluntary, the guest list could be drawn as widely as was necessary. No one had to come (even if consequences for offenders not coming could follow). On the night, 37 people attended. After setting out the ground rules—no raised voices and respect shown for all—the conference started, first with the offenders being asked why they thought they were at the meeting. Some were not as forthcoming as others, but the skilled and well-prepared facilitators managed to tease out of them the reasons why they thought that they had been asked to come. The victims were less than polite at the start! Clearly, there was anger and resentment involved. However, it was interesting how quickly the offenders started to open up, acknowledging that what they had done had caused problems to local residents and effectively admitting their wrongdoings. As the proceedings progressed and started to gain credibility in the eyes of participants, the victims gave moving and powerful testimonies as to how they had been harmed and the extent of the upset caused. With relatively little direct input from other stakeholders, the offenders and victims talked for well over an hour. As in all RJ conferences, it is wise to meet the victims first to seek out what "punishment" or reparation they would be satisfied with. Scott knew beforehand that the majority of victims only expected an apology and said that they would be happy with that. This is not what happened though. Of their own volition, the offenders went into a separate room to speak about how they could make amends and returned to say they would all send a letter of apology, that they would ask residents when it would be acceptable for them to play on the streets and that they wanted to know what they could do to clear up any mess or damaged caused. They also offered to try to raise money between themselves to run a community "clear-up" day followed by a barbecue. These offers were totally unprompted by the conference team. At the end of the meeting, everyone broke out into applause. The RJ team was, of course, delighted with this outcome but were even more pleased when, three months later, the police informed a drop in reported crime and antisocial behavior on the estate of more than 90%.*

The RJ team also kept other statistics. Using the multiparty conferencing technique, it consistently found that around 80% of sessions were successful as evidenced by victim responses to exit questionnaires, reparation agreements that were carried out, and reductions in reoffending rates as reported

---

* While this reported drop in offending appears high, this may be explained by the very specific and local focus of the project and in any event is consistent with significant levels of crime reduction reported elsewhere. In a relatively recent meta-analysis, the reconviction rates was found, on average, to be 46% across a range of projects evaluated, significantly less than reoffending rates where formal criminal justice disposal had been used. See Wilcox and Hoyle (2004).

by the police.* Compliance with such agreements has been found in other studies, suggesting a more universal significance.†

In the space of 18 months, with a team of 3 employed staff and 25 volunteers, the team handled 300 referrals, of which 180 (60%) resulted in face-to-face meetings between victim and offender. The other cases either proved unsuitable for conferencing or, for various reasons, did not proceed to a meeting where reparation proved possible.

The independent evaluation team has also conducted a cost analysis and has come to the conclusion that the RJ process costs on average around £500 (approximately US$750) per case for those cases that go to a full conference. The follow-up costs are estimated at £400 (approximately US$600) per case. Dealing with such cases by way of police reprimand or court hearing is said to be considerably more costly and a significant savings seems to be made by using RJ.

Reports of the success of this model must have traveled far, because a few months later, the Preston RJ team were invited to London to receive a Ministry of Justice Youth Crime Prevention Award—using RJ to tackle antisocial behavior. The award was presented to the team by the then Home Secretary (government minister responsible for security and related home affairs) who, interestingly enough, Scott had met on a visit during his prison years when the minister was an opposition parliamentarian! Nomination for this prestigious award had come through the local police force.

However, as is often the case in the not-for-profit sector, it was not long before it became clear that funding for the project was under threat—as part of a wider cutback in government spending. NACRO applied for a separate grant for Scott to run a peer mentoring project working with offenders who had followed the RJ path. With his background, this was thought to be a great opportunity to work with young offenders and team them up with positive mentors who could help steer them onto a better course. Scott knew that mentoring alone would probably not be enough and that offenders may need to have more of an understanding of how the justice system works, so he contacted what has turned out to be his co-author of this chapter, Richard Grimes. Richard had been running a very successful **Street Law** (legal literacy/awareness) program and Scott invited him to come to NACRO and talk about how Street Law could help and to run a pilot training session with the staff and young people. This turned out to be

---

* High satisfaction rates have also been found among victims of crime after participation in the RJ process. In one study, 85% reported that they were satisfied with the outcome (Shapland et al. 2007).
† Agreements that were reached through RJ were fully or partially completed in 88% of cases (Shapland et al. 2006).

a very positive experience that gave Scott and his team a real understanding of how to teach young offenders about the legal process and justice system including role-play (which the young offenders really enjoyed—especially when they had to act out court scenarios where they were the judges!). Unfortunately, the grant bid was not successful, and before these new skills could be put into practice, NACRO sadly had to bring the project and the entire RJ program to a close. The team members including Scott were all made redundant.

Scott continues to tell this in his own words:

> This was now 2011 and I was out of work again but I was determined that I would carry on with restorative justice if possible. Thankfully Richard and I had kept in touch with each other and he invited me to run a training session for his law students on restorative justice. The students showed a positive interest in all aspects and we managed to complete the first stage of their induction to being RJ facilitators. Richard was keen to help me stay focused on my career and wanted to build a structure that might take this work forward. Together, and with the help of a retired senior police officer, we formed the Restorative Justice Foundation (RJF) with a view to gain funding so that we could run our own RJ projects. This body is now up and running and we continue to explore funding options but if anything the financial situation is now worse than it was when the NACRO project finished. Bringing together my practical experience and the academic resources and interests at one of the UK's most respected universities makes real sense. We are continuing to work with the York University's law students helping prepare the next generation of RJ practitioners.
>
> In 2014 I was invited by the European Restorative Forum to lecture at their conference at Queens University in Belfast. It looks like RJ has now become a mechanism in the global tool kit to tackle youth crime.

Scott continues to work on RJ initiatives despite the constant struggle for sustainable funding.

The Issues Arising and Some Questions for Discussion

In this chapter, we have attempted to outline the nature and benefits of a restorative approach to addressing criminal and antisocial behavior, albeit from a UK perspective. What does this all mean in a wider, international context?

The roots of RJ have been variously ascribed to different countries, cultures, and traditions. This approach to problem recognition and possible resolution is not unique, is not of recent origin, or is not necessarily known by the tag "restorative justice."

In their edited book on the global RJ picture, Galaway and Hudson include several contributions that examine the history and current place of a restorative approach to justice. Pratt, for example, looks at the Maori tradition for dispute resolution in New Zealand (Pratt 1996). Yazzie and Zion (1996) look at justice in the Navajo tradition in the first Nation/Native American culture.

Findlay also takes a similar (and perhaps understandably critical) position, establishing the importance of restorative approaches to dispute resolution in a pre- and postcolonial context (Findlay 2000).

At the risk of sounding dismissive of and insensitive to cultural, political, religious, and ethnic differences (not something we intend), we suggest that none of this really matters. What is important is the process and the principles upon which constructive approaches to addressing and resolving conflict are founded.

Dialogue is perhaps the most important. How can we expect the difficulties presented by offending behavior to be tackled in every sense—crime prevention among them—if there is no discourse? The evidence, at least in an RJ setting, suggests that the more you involve those concerned, the greater the likelihood is of a positive outcome in terms of the satisfaction of the parties, the chance of reparation being made, and the probability of a reduction in the cause of the problem—for example, evidenced by offending and reoffending rates (Sherman and Strang 2007).*

Alongside this overall principle, however, are a set of concerns and challenges as well as potential benefits. For the sake of brevity, we will set these out as bullet points:

- Managing expectations is critical to both individual case success and program credibility. As the old adage goes, you only get one chance to make a first impression! Expectations can be those of direct participants in the process including victim and offender or those of an agency with a vested interest in the outcome, such as criminal justice/enforcement representatives and funders. This point can also be applied to public perception and the sociopolitical world in which opinion is shaped and policy and law are formed.

---

* Not only does this meta-analysis examine key findings in RJ research, for example, the impact of RJ on reconviction and offending rates, but it looks at projects in a wide variety of comparable countries including Australia, Canada, the United Kingdom, and the United States, involving adult offenders, youths, and the wider community. The conclusions, while guarded in the sense that none of the results are conclusive, are that RJ works with a significant impact and in different contexts with a degree of consistency in its outcomes to the extent that it could be the basis for a promising strategy for addressing current problems in global criminal justice systems.

- One of the cornerstones of RJ, at least in the literature and in our experience, is that it is a voluntary process and impact is presumably more likely to be profound if people engage willingly. How does this square with a more formalized process where RJ may (this is under debate in the United Kingdom) be recognized and even insisted upon as part of (or an alternative to) the judicial process?

- Even where RJ may not be formalized, is the veiled threat of legal proceedings—take part in RJ or you may be prosecuted—contrary to the ethos of a restorative approach? This in turn raises some fundamental questions about due process, human rights, and civil liberties. Are "offenders" given the opportunity to defend themselves and the protection others might have under the criminal justice system?

- Significant claims are made for the value of RJ in terms of reoffending rates, victim and other participant's satisfaction, and cost savings to the State and other parties. While research findings do variously support these claims, there is considerable inconsistency in the results, and there are methodological questions about how these findings have been obtained and whether like is being compared with like. Clearly, more and appropriately robust research is needed to ensure that we fully understand the impact of RJ.

- There are many common denominators in both the research settings and results produced none the least being that a person is no more likely to reoffend having been through the RJ process and the cost of conducted RJ is significantly lower than most other forms of disposal including police cautions.

- One major issue that is seldom discussed is the significance of a criminal record, particularly for a young person. Much has been written in the criminology literature of the impact of stigmatization on offenders and the alienation this can produce along with an accelerated "career" course in crime (e.g., McGrath 2009). We submit that using techniques such as RJ not only can address unacceptable behavior but also can avoid labeling an offender at a relatively early stage of his or her life.

- For the purposes of this chapter, there is an educational dimension, which we turn to below.

RJ as Education

We have suggested throughout this chapter that RJ is as much about changing attitudes as it is addressing specific problems. This raises the important consideration of educating all involved.

We mention this for two reasons. In the case study set out above, the term *Street Law* was used. By this, we mean awareness-raising of a range of everyday rights and responsibilities (hence, reference to the street). Legal literacy programs have been around for many years in different guises from formal education courses with a legal content at school and university to more community-based awareness-raising campaigns such as those forged by the early community law center movement in the United Kingdom.

The Street Law program in particular began in the United States in the early 1970s when a group of students from Georgetown University, Washington, DC, took the idea into local schools to better prepare pupils there for real-life encounters with the law. As the case study implies, the use of legal literacy work within or as an adjunct to RJ sessions can provide valuable buy-in from participants and may give a useful grounding in some basic legal issues. This initiative now features in many countries worldwide.*

The educational theme, however, has another dimension. One project that the authors of this chapter have developed has been to involve law students in the RJ process—first, after requisite training, as volunteers in the face-to-face meetings and conferences associated with RJ cases, and, second, as deliverers of Street Law–styled sessions. For a law student to have to explain the law and the legal process to a lay audience is a significant opportunity to demonstrate the extent of their own understanding of the theory as well as the practice. The workings of such a model are explained in detail elsewhere (Grimes 2012).

The involvement of law students in pro bono and related legal service activity, as seen above, is often referred to as clinical legal education. The prevalence of law school–based clinics is growing and highly significant. In the United Kingdom alone, over the past 20 years, the number of law schools engaging in clinical work has grown rapidly, with now more than 70% of UK law schools taking part in this type of activity (Carney et al. 2014). The international perspective is well set out in Bloch's edited volume referred to above (Bloch 2011).

The educational dimension, therefore, might yet be another example of RJ and associated activity being the win/win situation suggested by one of our opening quotations and might be a matter of outcome as well.

Conclusion

In the Introduction to this book, an equation accounting for the commission of crime is set out. This is expressed as: Crime = skills + motivation + opportunity. Without disagreeing with this, we suggest a similar formulation but from the crime prevention/reduction perspective.

---

* For an overall view of this model and development, see Grimes et al. (2010).

The "skills" component is embedded in the philosophy, design, and training that underpin an effective restorative program. The "motivational" aspect draws on the relative success of RJ initiatives including, in particular, the satisfaction expressed by victims and offenders in both process and, in many instances, outcomes.

The "opportunity" needed for restorative practices is perhaps more challenging. As in all things, particularly in the access to and administration of justice context, there are resource implications. Every aspect of the RJ process from the one-on-one meetings through to the conference session(s) and on to the follow-up and monitoring work needs to be paid for and organized. There have been a number of local and national initiatives to help fund RJ at home and abroad. Some of these have emanated from projects run through local police forces and criminal justice agencies. Others have stemmed from direct government funding, for example, through the Ministry of Justice. As research findings have discovered, the cost of RJ is likely to be significantly less than disposal through the court system. Nonetheless, the resourcing of RJ schemes remains an obstacle and can frustrate otherwise available opportunities.

While sending out a clear message in this chapter that RJ has considerable potential, internationally, to reduce and prevent criminal acts, none of this is without its challenges, finance apart. There is a lobby that takes a critical stance, for example, on the constitutional position of those involved in the RJ process, pointing out, for example, that the right exists under the European Convention of Human Rights (and now under domestic law in the United Kingdom by virtue of the Human Rights Act 1998) to a fair hearing "by an independent and impartial tribunal." An RJ conference is not that, in the sense of being an independent judicial proceeding. Additionally, the potential influence of the victim in terms of the case outcome may introduce an element of bias.*

We maintain, however, that the evidence in favor of a greater expansion of RJ options and a carefully structured evaluation process is convincing none the least given the cost and other implications of formal criminal justice disposals. When one goes on to consider the philosophical issues around restorative principles and constructive outcomes to dispute resolution, we believe that, in such a troubled world, the case becomes compelling.

If the relevance and success of RJ hinge on effective communication and a cooperative spirit, so does its future. Closer collaboration is needed between all those with a vested interest in addressing and resolving conflict. Starting from home, is this time for a national (UK) task force on restorative approaches that can feed into the wider, global scene?

---

* See, for example, Ashworth (2002, 2003).

Glossary of Terms

Clinical legal education: Credit-bearing modules or extracurricular activity in which law students apply theory to practice in real or simulated cases under the supervision of suitably qualified personnel and are given the structured opportunity to reflect on that experience. The word *clinical* is taken from the medical world, but in legal education terms, the patient becomes the client.

Ministry of Justice: The government department in the United Kingdom for a range of legal issues including access to justice and the legal process. The Home Office is a separate body within the UK government with other law- and security-related functions.

National Association for the Care and Resettlement of Offenders (NACRO): A charitable NGO in the United Kingdom that aims to assist those convicted of criminal offenses

Restorative justice (RJ): A model of dispute resolution in which those responsible for criminal or antisocial activity are encouraged (or in some jurisdictions required) to meet with the victims of their actions in order to address their behavior and to attempt to make reparation for it. This is commonly conducted through meetings or conferences of offenders, victims, and possibly other interested parties.

Street Law: A legal literacy program in which law students (and possibly others) present, in an interactive format, material on legal rights and responsibilities to community-based groups such as those in schools and prisons with the aim of raising awareness. The topics for presentation are selected by the group in question, thus giving a degree of relevance and ownership—see www.streetlaw.org (accessed September 9, 2015).

Youth offending team: The multiparty agency with statutory and additional responsibilities for addressing youth crime in England and Wales. YOTs typically include representatives from local authority social services departments, the probation service, and education providers.

Discussion Questions

1. Is RJ a credible and sustainable means of resolution/disposal in the crime reduction/prevention context?
2. If so, does it need to operate alongside but independent of, or within, the statutory criminal justice framework?
3. Does RJ have global relevance, and if so, what factors need to be taken into account to reflect social, cultural, and other relevant characteristics?

4. What strategies, resources, and policies are needed if RJ is to be supported and developed?
5. What are the limits of RJ? Could it be used on the international stage—perhaps to defuse serious conflict situations such as where there is an act or threat of "terrorism" (e.g., the terrorist events in Paris in November 2015)?

Suggested Reading

Gavrielides, T., and Artinopoulou, V. (Eds.). (2013). *Reconstructing Restorative Justice Philosophy*. Ashgate

This book takes bold steps in forming much-needed philosophical foundations for RJ through deconstructing and reconstructing various models of thinking. It challenges current debates through the consideration and integration of various disciplines such as law, criminology, philosophy, and human rights into RJ theory, resulting in the development of new and stimulating arguments.

Sullivan, D. (Ed.). (2007). *Handbook of Restorative Justice: A Global Perspective*. Routledge International Handbooks

The Handbook of Restorative Justice is a collection of original, cutting-edge essays that offer an insightful and critical assessment of the theory, principles, and practices of RJ around the globe.

Zehr, H. (2015). *The Little Book of Restorative Justice: Revised and Updated*. Justice and Peacebuilding Paperback

Howard Zehr is well known worldwide for his pioneering work in transforming understandings of justice. Here, he proposes workable principles and practices for making RJ possible in this revised and updated edition of his seminal book on the movement.

Recommended Web Links

www.restorativejustice4schools.co.uk/

An interesting UK-focused website on RJ in a school setting.

www.restorativejustice.org/

A clearinghouse of information including research tools, bibliographies, training, tutorials, and expert articles on RJ.

www.ousd.org/restorativejustice

A case study of one school where RJ is central to operations. It addresses responses to student misconduct, with the goal of repairing harm and restoring relationships between those affected.

http://www.homeoffice.gov.uk/

The website of the UK government department responsible for law and order. This site has a wealth of information covering, among other things, the criminal justice system. It includes a range of reports including those on RJ.

http://restorativejustice.org.uk/

The website for the umbrella support and accreditation organization on RJ in the United Kingdom and site of the NGO that promotes and supports RJ initiatives more generally. It includes background information of RJ in the United Kingdom and other countries and contains a register of accredited RJ practitioners. It also has details of training programs for those interested in developing RJ-related skills.

References

Ashworth, A. (2002). Responsibilities, rights and restorative justice. *British Journal of Criminology* 42(3): 578–595.

Ashworth, A. (2003). Is restorative justice the way forward for criminal justice? In *Restorative Justice Critical Issues*, ed. E. Mclaughlin. Bath, UK: Open University.

Bartollas, C., and Miller, S. (2013). *Juvenile Justice in America*. Upper Saddle River, NJ: Prentice Hall.

Bazemore, G., and Stinchcomb, J. (2004). Civic engagement model of re-entry: Involving community service and restorative justice. *Fed. Probation* 68(2): 14–24.

Bloch, F. (ed.). (2011). *The Global Clinical Movement: Educating Lawyers for Social Justice*. New York: OUP.

Carney, D., Dignan, F., Grimes, R., Kelly, G., and Parker, P. (2014). *The LawWorks Law School Pro Bono and Clinic Report*. London: LexisNexis.

Findlay, M. (2000). Decolonising restoration and justice: Restoration in transitional cultures. *Howard Journal of Criminal Justice* 39(4): 398–411.

Grimes, R. (2012). Justice, Education and Human Rights: Partnerships, Policies and Progress in the UK, In *Rights & Restoration within Youth Justice*, ed. T. Gavrielides, 257. Whitby, ON, Canada: de Sitter Publications.

Grimes, R., O'Brien, E., McQuoid-Mason, D., and Zimmer, J. (2010). Street law and social justice education. In *The Global Clinical Movement: Educating Lawyers for Social Justice*, ed. F. Bloch, 225. New York: OUP.

Groenhuijsen, M.S. (2010). Herstelrecht in Nederland: een slachtofferperspectief. *Tijdschrift voor herstelrecht* 10(4): 53–62.

Johnstone, G. (2011). *Restorative Justice: Ideas, Values, Debates*. London: Routledge.

Lincoln, A. (1850). Notes for a law lecture. In *The Collected Works of Abraham Lincoln*, ed. R.P. Basler 1953. Volume II, 81. New Brunswick: Rutgers University Press.

Matrix Evidence. (2009). *Economic Analysis of Interventions for Young Adult Offenders*. London: Barrow Cadbury.

McGrath, A. (2009). Offenders' perceptions of the sentencing process: A study of deterrence and stigmatisation in the New South Wales Children's Court. *Australian and New Zealand Journal of Criminology* 42(1): 24–46.

Pratt, J. (1996). Colonization, power and silence: A history of indigenous justice in New Zealand society. In *Restorative Justice: International Perspectives*, ed. B. Galaway and J. Hudson, 137. Monsey, NY: Criminal Justice Press.

Shapland, J., Atkinson, A., Atkinson, H., Chapman, B., Colledge, E., Dignan, J., Howes, M., Johnstone, J., Robinson, G., and Sorsby, A. (2006). *Restorative Justice in Practice: The Second Report from the Evaluation of Three Schemes,* University of Sheffield Centre for Criminological Research Occasional Paper 2, Sheffield, UK: University of Sheffield, Faculty of Law.

Shapland, J., Atkinson, A., Atkinson, H., Chapman, B., Dignan, J., Howes, M., Johnstone, J., Robinson, G., and Sorsby, A. (2007). *Restorative Justice: The Views of Victims and Offenders*, Ministry of Justice Research Series 3/07, London: Ministry of Justice.

Shapland, J., Robinson, G., and Sorsby, A. (2011). *Restorative Justice in Practice.* London: Routledge.

Sherman, L.W., and Strang, H. (2007). *Restorative Justice: The Evidence*. London: Smith Institute.

Shewan, G. (2010). The business case for restorative justice and policing. In *A New Way of Doing Justice*. Restorative Justice Council. Retrieved from http://www.restorativejustice.org.uk/assets.html.

Wilcox, A., and Hoyle, C. (2004). *The National Evaluation of Youth Justice Board's Restorative Justice Projects.* London: Youth Justice Board.

Yazzie, R., and Zion, J. (1996). Navajo restorative justice: The law of equality and justice. In *Restorative Justice: International Perspectives*, ed. B. Galaway and J. Hudson, 157. Monsey, NY: Criminal Justice Press.

Prevention of Femicide

10

MICHAEL PLATZER

Contents

Learning Outcomes
After reading this chapter, you should be able to

- List the different forms of femicide
- Realize the challenges in combating femicide
- Identify the different strategies in preventing and prosecuting femicide
- Appreciate the limitations of a criminal justice response
- Understand the difficulties of overcoming structural discrimination against women, social and religious realities, and the widespread impunity for these crimes

Introduction

> Violence against women and girls, in all its many forms, shames us all. To end
> this serious crime, we must all work in a spirit of partnership and cooperation
> to change laws, change perceptions and change behaviours. If not, we will
> continue to see this violent crime undermine our efforts to build better, more
> inclusive societies.
>
> **Yury Fedotov**
> *UNODC Executive Director (2015, p. 47)*

Domestic violence (see Chapter 5) and sexual assault have been well documented for some time now (General Assembly Resolution 68/191), but the
brutality of the other extreme forms of violence against women and girls
has until recently received virtually no attention from national governments,
let alone the international community. However, the growing number of
shocking acts perpetrated against women has been exposed by the media
and nongovernmental organizations, and this has led the United Nations
and State governments to draft laws and develop intervention and prevention strategies.

The United Nations defines **femicide** as the gender-related killings of
women and girls. According to the Special Rapporteur on violence against
women, its causes, and consequences, Mrs. Rashida Manjoo, these crimes are
not new forms of violence against women, but only the most extreme manifestations of existing forms of gender-based violence (Manjoo 2012). They can
be the result of direct acts such as intimate partner violence (see Chapter 5),
honor-related killings, dowry-related killings, sex-selective abortions, witch
hunting, sexual orientation murders, armed conflict–related killings, and ethnic and indigenous identity killings. In all these cases of murder, a female
is the victim and perpetrators are invariably males, although female family
members may also be involved. We will explore these relationships below.

The indirect category includes deaths from harmful practices such as
female genital mutilation (FGM), poorly conducted or clandestine abortions,
high maternal mortality, deaths linked to human trafficking, drug dealing,
organized crime- and gang-related activities, the death of girls or women
from simple neglect (through starvation or ill-treatment), and deliberate
acts of omission on the part of the State. In these cases, defendants may be
more difficult to identify. There may be patterns of structural discrimination,
institutional factors, and political, legal, and societal realities, which allow
for impunity, non-action, or discriminatory treatment of offenders (Civil
Society Organizations 2014).

Where women (usually also poorly educated) are treated like chat-
tels and subjugated by men, they are often powerless to defend against ill-
treatment, beatings, torture, sexual abuse, rape, and degrading treatment. As

Shalhoub-Kevorkian (2002, p. 81) has observed, women who are subjected to continuous violence or living under insufferable conditions of gender-based discrimination are always on "death row," always in fear of execution.

The term *femicide* has been used in the English language since the beginning of the 19th century to describe the killings of women (Wharton 1848). In the 1970s, feminists described "the murders by men motivated by hatred, contempt, pleasure, or ownership of women by men" as femicide (Caputi and Russell 1990). Later, all sexist killings were included, from misogynist killings and sadistic murders to those socially constructed as a "right to do so"—I did it because I could.

In 2010, the General Assembly adopted the updated Model Strategies and Practical Measures on the Elimination of Violence against Women in the Field of Crime Prevention and Criminal Justice (Resolution 65/228, annex). These emphasized the rapid investigation and prosecution of incidents and the preclusion of the defense of "honor" and or "provocation." In many countries, for "crimes of passion," penalties are reduced because of so-called provocation by women (going out with another man, adultery, indecently attired, verbal abuse by the woman toward her partner in a domestic situation). In the Middle East, the entire family might be excused for committing an act of femicide because the woman brought shame upon the relatives through her "loose morals" or behavior. It is said that femicide is the least-punished crime in the world (Femicide IV 2015, preface). In South Asia, female infanticide, the neglect and starvation of the girl child, and dowry-related deaths are accepted practices in many communities (Kumari 2014).

In the 1990s, international attention focused on the horrific crimes of kidnapping, rape, mutilation, and murders of young women by criminal gangs took place in Mexico, El Salvador, and Guatemala (Manjoo 2012, paragraph 24). As it proved difficult to identify any clear motives for the crimes or to identify the perpetrators, activists in Mexico adopted the term *feminicidio* to hold the State responsible for the negligence, omission of preventive actions, lack of pursuit of the perpetrators, tolerance of such crimes, and even proven corruption of the authorities. Different Latin American states hold different crimes to fall under the definition of feminicide (Civil Society Organizations 2014).

In almost all jurisdictions, domestic violence or partner violence that leads to the death of a mother, child, grandmother, or mother-in-law is considered to be femicide and will be prosecuted (see Chapter 5). One of the main reasons for this is that the culprit(s) is (are) easily identified. For these crimes, there is a considerable body of literature and existing institutions (special units) to deal with intimate partner violence. The United Nations Office on Drugs and Crime (UNODC) has produced three excellent publications: the *Handbook on Effective Police Responses to Violence against Women*, the *Handbook on Effective Prosecution Responses to Violence against*

Women, and *Strengthening Crime Prevention and Criminal Justice Responses to Violence against Women.**

UN-Women and the High Commissioner for Human Rights have developed a Latin American model protocol for the investigation of gender-related killings of women, which is endorsed by a number of regional and international bodies. Although the prevention of domestic murder can range from stopping a recurrence of violence, sensitizing the police and judicial authorities, providing shelters to women at risk, community-based interventions, harsher penalties that can have a preventive impact, media campaigns, programs for boys and men to respect girls and women, and so on, most of these measures cannot be used for the other forms of femicide.† We will now examine specific forms of femicide that are not related to intimate partner violence.

Honor-Related Killings

Murder to "cleanse the family honor" is committed with high levels of impunity, although the perpetrator(s) may be known to the authorities. These killings range from the Sahara to the Himalayas in Muslim communities, but have also occurred in other regions of the world in immigrant communities (Manjoo 2012, paragraphs 43–50). Cases have been prosecuted in the United Kingdom and Germany (Oberwittler 2011) and have been rising in Canada (Canada Department of Justice 2016). The United Nations Population Fund has estimated that an estimated 5000 women are murdered by family members each year. **Honor killings** (also referred to as "shame killing") can take many horrific forms: stoning, flogging, hanging, disfiguration by acid burns, even forced suicide (i.e., the victim is forced into committing suicide to avoid an alternative option the victim perceives as being even worse). Some of these acts are sanctioned by the local community, religious leaders, or local authorities. Despite communications from UN Human Rights Mandate holders to prevent such barbaric executions (in the cases of 30 women sentenced to death by stoning in Iran), none were stopped. The Special Rapporteur on Violence against Women has raised concerns about the phenomenon of self-immolation, reported in Afghanistan and the Islamic Republic of Iran, whereby young women set themselves on fire because they feel they are "dishonoring" the family (Manjoo 2012).

The UN Special Rapporteur on extrajudicial, summary, or arbitrary executions has reported that these honor-related crimes often go unreported, are

---

* Available at http://www.unodc.org.
† Available at http://www.unodc.org/documents/justice and prison reform/Protocolo Latinamerico De Investigacion.pdf.

rarely investigated, and are punished far less than equivalent violent crimes. In migrant communities where a femicide is investigated, an underage male relative will often be offered up to the authorities as he cannot be given a long prison sentence.

In response to these and related concerns, the Secretary-General has presented a series of recommendations in relation to the criminalization of such acts and urged that those participating in, facilitating, or encouraging such killings, or threatening women and girls in the name of honor should be punished (see A/57/169 §32).

Although often unreported, this form of femicide is observed by the international media with massive protest campaigns but without an effective result (Kishwar 2005). Even in countries that have a well-developed criminal justice system, these femicides are hidden within the community.*

Dowry-Related Deaths

The dowry is an ancient custom but continues to be expected in parts of Asia, North Africa, and the Balkans. However, disputes over the amount of the transfer of wealth and dowry-related violence are most often seen in the South Asian region (Agnes 2011). All the countries in the region have banned dowries: India in 1961, Pakistan in 1976, Bangladesh in 1980, and Nepal in 2009. However, the dowry has remained an indispensable part of weddings and, in fact, the demands for more money or expensive gifts (cars, washing machines, televisions, furniture, and down payments on apartments) have increased in recent years (Kumari 2014), as has the pressure from the groom's family to extract a higher bride price, through harassment, threats, "accidents" (exploding stoves), acid attacks, torture, forced suicide, and even burning the bride if the transfer of gifts is not enough. Even after the wedding, the greed of the in-laws may not be sated. Young women may also be targeted for spurning a suitor or for rejecting proposals of marriage (Natarajan 2015). The Government of Bangladesh has enacted two laws against acid violence. Despite the heavy penalties for acid attacks, which can lead to blindness, disfigurement, and death of women, these outrages continue. The World Health Organization estimates that, each year, 195,000 deaths result from burns and approximately 10 million serious injuries. In India alone, approximately 200,000 deaths are annually caused by burns. Of course, not all are intentional but certainly many are attributed to domestic disputes (as very few men are affected) but the law enforcement system rarely investigates acid or burn attacks. In India, the National Crime Records Bureau reports that,

---

* See report of Special Rapporteur on extra-judicial summary or arbitrary executions (2010), E/CN.4/2003, 2000, paragraph 78.

in 1 year, there were 1948 convictions and 3876 acquittals for dowry deaths (Kumari 2014).

The Commission on the Elimination of Discrimination against Women and the Committee on the Rights of the Child have regularly condemned these practices. However, experts argue that there is a need to address the underlying cultural concerns, such as the subordinate status of women within their natal and marital homes, issues of lack of property ownership, the control of women's sexuality, the stigma attached to divorce, and the lack of support after she is married (Madhu 2012).

Burning of Widows

In India, the ancient practice of "sati," the burning alive of a widow on her husband's funeral pyre, continues with the assistance of the family and community (Banerji 2016). The practice was initially tolerated by British colonial officials and then banned by Queen Victoria in 1861. Because of recent public incidents, the Sati Prevention Act of 1988 was passed, which further criminalized any form of aiding, abetting, and glorifying of sati. Nonetheless, in the 21st century, incidents continue to come to public attention. Observers now explain these suicides as similar to those of a widow's grief and her rapid death after the loss of her husband, which has been noticed in other societies, but others state that those who commit sati are often "childless or old and face miserable impoverished lives" owing to the loss of personal support (Inamdar 1983).

Killings of Women Attributed to Accusations of Sorcery/Witchcraft

The belief in witchcraft and sorcery is ancient but is still practiced in the third millennium. Reports of the killing of "suspected" witches for casting evil spells have been confirmed in Burkina Faso, Congo, Ghana, Kenya, India, Malawi, Nepal, Nigeria, Papua New Guinea, Saudi Arabia, Sierra Leone, South Africa, and Tanzania (Sajor 2011). In Tanzania, approximately 500 older women are murdered each year following accusations of witchcraft. In the Congo, between 25,000 and 50,000 children have been accused of witchcraft and thrown out of their homes to live on the street. In Ghana, there are at least six witch camps where women suspected of being witches can flee for safety. In Kenya, a mob in 2008 burnt to death 11 people accused of witchcraft. In Nigeria, 15,000 children have been accused of witchcraft and 1000 were murdered. These usually unpunished crimes include violent murders, physical mutilation, kidnapping, "disappearances," and women being driven out of the community together with their children. In addition, in many cases, these women are also subjected to exorcism ceremonies involving public beatings and abuse by shamans or village elders, and in the majority of cases, younger women are at a higher risk of accusation of witchcraft (Manjoo 2012). Husbands simply wish to be rid of their spouses.

In India, dalit (lower caste) women are accused of being a "dayan" (a witch) or of practicing "banamathi," and then physical violence is employed to take possession of their family lands or to keep them under economic subjugation, sexual exploitation, and gender control (Chen 2016).

Similarly, in Nepal, in the southern Teral region, elderly women, widows, destitute women, and women of low caste are often targeted and deprived of their property rights or victimized to settle a personal vendetta (Schnoebelen 2009). Similar accounting of torture and murder of women accused of witchcraft in Papua New Guinea have also been reported. Despite efforts to curb such practices, sorcery allegations against women have been increasing, particularly in the Highlands region. Victims of such attacks and murders are mainly widows or other vulnerable elderly women who do not have children or relatives to protect them, women born out of wedlock, or women who do not have any standing in the family.

In conclusion, accusations of sorcery are primarily economically motivated, for the purpose of taking over land or possessions of the accused witch. Those who torture or kill are almost exclusively men and usually are biologically related to the victim. Accusations of sorcery are a convenient disguise for premeditated killings based on greed, envy, rivalry, revenge, a personal dislike for another, or targeting women from other tribes, strangers, or the most vulnerable (Reiterer 2012).

Killings of Aboriginal and Indigenous Women

Aboriginal and indigenous women and girls experience extremely high levels of violence as a result of the social, cultural, and economic discrimination against indigenous women. A negative legacy of colonialism, genocide, and historic racist government policies and the consequences of economic policies have driven an alarming number of these women into extremely vulnerable situations. In Central America, poor young indigenous women have been forced to migrate, and then pressed into low-skilled and low-paid jobs, mainly in assembly factories, domestic service, and the sex trade and prostitution under exploitative conditions (Manjoo 2012).

During the 36-year civil war (1960–1996) in Guatemala, the military and paramilitary force undertook systematic attacks against Mayan women. It is estimated that 100,000 to 200,000 people were killed during the conflict. However, the Peace Accord afforded immunity to the perpetrators of sexual violence against women and girls older than 12 years. Thus, the Spanish colonial legacy of violating indigenous women has been perpetuated (The Commission for Historical Clarification 2012).

Canada had many discriminatory laws against aboriginal women and children until 1985.* This has had an intergenerational impact and contributed to a legacy of violence, abuse, and impunity (McIvor and Day 2011). According to Amnesty International (2009), a young aboriginal woman is five times more likely than other Canadian women of the same age to die of violence.† Aboriginal women and girls are more likely to be killed by a stranger than non-aboriginal women. Approximately 50% of such murders remain unsolved (Native Women's Association of Canada 2010), and the numbers are rising. The Committee on the Elimination of Discrimination against Women has expressed its concern that "hundreds of cases involving aboriginal women have gone missing or been murdered in the past two decades have neither been fully investigated nor attracted priority attention, with the perpetrators remaining unpunished" (CEDAW 2008).

Similarly, in Australia, violence against aboriginal women is egregious because of the use of weapons, firearms, knives, hammers, stones, and sticks. Recent reports indicate that aboriginal women are at far greater risk of being victims of murder, rape, and other assaults than non-aboriginal women. However, aboriginal women are reluctant to expose these acts of violence, if committed by aboriginal men, in order to prevent further denigration of their communities (Andrew 1997). The Committee on the Elimination on the Elimination of Discrimination against Women has reported that "indigenous women and girls face the highest levels of violence, especially at home where indigenous women are 35 times more likely to be hospitalized as a result of family violence-related assaults than non-indigenous females" (CEDAW 2010).

Space does not allow for extended coverage of other countries, where a notable number of indigenous people are treated in a violent manner not only by dominant European cultures but also by other stronger indigenous tribes or other ethnic groups. These tensions have led to tribal wars, where women are captured, raped, and enslaved. This topic will be covered in a subsequent section on targeting women in conflict.

Extreme Forms of Violent Killings of Women

Femicide is also associated with gangs, organized crime, drug dealers, human trafficking, drug dealing, prostitution, and extortion rackets. This

---

* See https://www.youtube/watch?v=nPqaL7J4F10.
† http://amnesty.ca/our-work/campaigns/no-more-stolen-sisters

phenomenon is particularly grizzly in Mexico and Central America. In one year, rates of female homicide increased by 141% in Guatemala to more than 166% in Honduras (Prieto-Carron et al. 2007).

In 1993, international media began to cover the discovery of mutilated bodies of raped and murdered women on wastelands outside of the city of Ciudad Juarez, in Mexico. The patterns of killings included abduction and disappearances for a few days; torture and sexual assault by groups of men; murder and mutilation, particularly of the sexual organs and breasts; decapitation; and naked body parts being left on public display or dumped in empty wastelands of the city (Monarrez 2009). In the worst cases, parts of the bodies are scattered throughout different areas of the city, with messages written on the bodies or on papers pinned to the bodies. These horrific crimes had the purpose of establishing territorial boundaries for gangs, or demonstrating their power in certain regions and what might happen if people did not cooperate, with women being considered waste material. Gangs known as "maras" have created an internal control of a local area for arms trade, drug trafficking, and prostitution and have provided private security for criminal cartels, rich businessmen, and elite personalities (see Segato 2004).

Often, the clients of human smuggling or cognizant human trafficking are poorly treated, particularly if the entire operation is endangered. Women must regularly pay for their travel in the form of sex. At the end of the journey, when women are delivered to brothels, domestic servitude, or the *macquilas*, the period of their exploitation or brutalization may only have begun.

Killings in the Context of Armed Conflict

During armed conflict (e.g., civil wars, insurrections, and international wars), women experience all forms of physical, sexual, and psychological violence, perpetrated by both State and non-State actors, including unlawful killings, this despite International Humanitarian Law and national criminal laws (Secretary-General's Report 2015). Such violence is often used as a weapon of war, targeting women to frighten their husbands and the communities to which they belong. They suffer from torture, rape, sexual mutilations, and summary executions (Manjoo 2012). These women may be part of resistance movements or may be suspected of collaboration, but often women and girls are selected randomly. The Special Rapporteur on the situation of human rights defenders has stated that women who challenge oppressive governments or their policies are more at risk of suffering from violence, as they are perceived as challenging accepted sociocultural norms and stereotypes about femininity and the role of women in society (Sekaggya 2010).

For example, in Afghanistan, women's rights defenders are regularly threatened and political activists have been assassinated, and their killers are not brought to justice (UN Assistance Mission in Afghanistan 2010). The Taliban interpretation of Sharia law is used to justify harsher punishments for women seen associating with men outside their immediate families. A common means of intimidation and control of local communities is the use of "night letters," threatening letters pasted onto a door or in the mosque by insurgent groups for girls not to go to school, or for women not to leave their homes and go to work or speak to men outside their own family (UN Assistance Mission in Afghanistan 2010).

In the 45-year-long civil war in Colombia, women community leaders fighting for their rights have been the main targets of gender-related killings. These women are especially vulnerable if they promote land rights and the rights of the most marginalized groups, such as indigenous people, ethnic and religious minorities, and trade unionists. Outspoken women are murder targets by both Colombian state forces and illegal armed groups. Gender-specific intimidation of women defenders includes targeting of their children and families as a way to stop their human rights work (Colombia Human Rights Network 2002).

Killings as a Result of Sexual Orientation and Gender Identity

Lesbians, gay, transsexual, and transgender persons are targeted in many countries because they do not conform to stereotypes of gender sexuality and have become the victims of homophobic crimes, including murder. This violence, motivated by hatred and prejudice, is exercised with complete impunity and often exceeds other types of hate crimes (Human Rights First 2008). Law enforcement officers and custodial officials often look away when such violence occurs in the community or in prisons. These killings often occur in public places and are known as "social cleansing"; at other times, the mob breaks into private homes. At the same time, blackmailers take advantage of these fears and extort money from the victim. The Human Rights Council has expressed its concern in a resolution about the increasing violence and killing of lesbian, gay, bisexual, and transgender persons and the impunity surrounding these crimes (Human Rights Council 2010).

The Inter-American Commission on Human Rights has held several hearings regarding the situation of violence and discrimination against sexual minorities in some countries of the Caribbean, Central America, and South America. Civil society organizations have expressed great concern about the increasing number of homophobic crimes.

Female Infanticide and Abortions

Sex-selective abortions, although illegal, have become widespread throughout the world through technological advances like scanning machines that can be transported on the back of motorcycles to a home or examination room (see Figure 10.1).

This new technology is of great concern in countries where families prefer boys, and as a result, the country has a skewed gender balance against women. Boys are favored because of inheritance traditions and the heavy dowries that must be paid for the marriage of daughters (see above). This results in secondary social problems and increased sexual violence against women by the oversupply of unattached men and the phenomenon of purchasing brides from different countries. The husband will frequently have no linguistic or cultural affinity with his wife and resort to beating her because he has no way to communicate with her (Banerji 2016).

Because of the strong preference for boys, baby girls are suffocated, drowned, starved, simply neglected, or exposed to the cold or other harsh elements (Russell 2001). In India, for example, it is estimated that 1 million female selective abortions occur annually, such that 100 million women are "missing" from its population (Allahbadia 2002). The preadolescent mortality rate of girls under 5 years old is 21% higher than that for boys of the same age in India. Sex ratio statistics are worsening, and this negative trend is spreading to neighboring villages, to cities, and to other regions in India; scholars have referred to the "masculinization of the country" (Gerdes 2014).

The Challenge

Embedded Social Attitudes

In view of the embedded discrimination against women, the position of women in the family, inheritance laws, economic discrimination, and cultural attitudes, it may be difficult to prevent and let alone successfully prosecute perpetrators of femicide. Lack of access to justice, police corruption, blaming the victim, and a culture of machismo discourage victims from coming forward. In other words, femicide has evolved into a state crime owing to the inability to prevent, protect, and guarantee the lives of women. Some feminists speak about "feminicide" or **gendercide**, stating that the whole political, economic, police, judicial, and family is rigged against women (Diana Russell argues for a new "Femicide" convention or that these patterns of killings should be condemned under the UN Convention of Genocide). The fact that impunity is almost universal reinforces the notion that prosecutions alone will not make a notable difference for the vast majority of women who risk being victims of

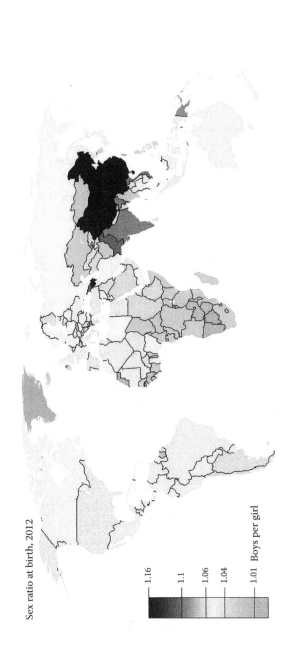

Figure 10.1 Gender ratio at birth, 2012. (From Tracy Hunter, "2012 Birth Sex Ratio World Map," *Wikimedia Commons.* https://commons.wikimedia.org/wiki/File:2012_Birth_Sex_Ratio_World_Map.jpg.)

femicide. To combat patriarchal ideologies, lessen the absolute power of men who now control women, and improve the status of women, there are long-term projects for the education of men and empowerment of women, as well as awareness-raising campaigns. As UNESCO proclaims, "Women and girls who are educated have greater awareness of their rights, and greater confidence and freedom to make decisions that affect their lives, improve their own and their children's health and chances of survival" (UNESCO 2013).

What Is to Be Done?

In a background paper prepared by the UNODC for the Expert Group on gender-related killing of women and girls, it is stated that violence against women can be stopped and prevented only through efforts to challenge social norms and stereotypes that support and condone male domination and control over women and by strengthening women's economic and social authority (UNODC 2014).

Too often, existing laws and law enforcement mechanisms are limited to intimate partner or domestic violence. While most of the crimes listed here could be prosecuted as murder or attempted murder, seldom are enough resources devoted to these crimes (UNODC 2014). The killing of women accused of sorcery/witchcraft, prenatal sex selection, girl neglect, female infanticide, dowry-related murders, and target killing of women in conflicts will require different approaches as the community may condone or accept these types of killings. Within a prevention framework, educational programs and awareness raising may, in fact, not prove very effective in the short term. Similarly, empowering women who are victims may also not work as they may be frightened, be in a vulnerable minority, be children (or unborn girls), or be dead. The greatest hope for changing attitudes are local campaigns, outside pressure, modernization, education of women, and the prosecution of blatant offenders. Rita Banerji (2009) has launched an effective "50 million missing" awareness campaign in India to draw attention to female feticide, infanticide, and dowry murders through workshops, statistical analyses, lectures, and public demonstrations asking people not to look away—for which she has received many awards and international support (see Box 10.1).

Criminalization and allocation of sufficient law enforcement, investigation, and judicial resources are, of course, necessary first steps. Holding the perpetrators accountable may serve as a specific and possibly general deterrent. The successful prosecution of the gang rapists and murderers of Jyoti Singh in 2012 led to mass demonstrations and demands to prosecute such cases much more expeditiously (Delhi Gang Rape 2012). Frequent patrols, situational crime prevention, and dedicated officials to combat the various forms of femicide as well as offices to provide information, shelter, and protection of

BOX 10.1   THE 50 MILLION MISSING CAMPAIGN

Launched in 2008 in India, the campaign is now a global initiative to end female genocide in India. As noted on their website (see https://genderbytes.wordpress.com/about/), "it is the largest, grassroots movement to end the genocide of women, and is supported in more than 203 countries." The campaign has three basic objectives:

1. Raise public awareness
2. Lobby international acknowledgment of genocide
3. Lobby for the time-bound action to end this genocide

Uniquely, the organization does not raise operational funds but relies entirely on volunteer support although donations are welcome. The rationale provided on their website states: *The reason for this policy is to keep the campaign free of certain restraints that often come about through donor dependency.*

women at risk are needed practical measures (Platzer 2016). The assistance to victims should be provided as early as possible in order to avoid the victim being further denigrated; femicide is often described as the last stage in a continuum of violence. Some countries have established programs to protect women from specific forms of violence, such as trafficking in persons or FGM. In Bangladesh, the Acid Control Act provides for medical treatment and a rehabilitation center for victims of acid attacks, and in many countries, intersectoral frameworks of governmental and nongovernmental agencies have been set up to deal with diverse forms of violence against women. The report of the Secretary-General on Action Taken by Member States lists preventive measures, victim issues, criminal responses, and data analysis in connection with gender-related killing of women (Secretary-General's Report 2015).

In cases where aboriginal people, ethnic groups, castes, minorities, or races have been particularly affected, reparations or special programs might be considered (see Box 10.2). The legacy of slavery of Africans or the mistreatment of Native Americans has never been properly addressed in terms of destruction of families, rape, alcoholism, and deliberate policies to humiliate the male members of the community (Joseph 2014). Reparations might also be conceived for the larger system of gender hierarchy and institutionalized violence, which can only be fully grasped when seen in the broader structural context. In this context, "transformative" reparations aspire to subvert instead of reinforcing pre-existing patterns of cross-cutting structural subordination, gender hierarchies, systematic, marginalization, and structural inequalities (Manjoo 2012).

BOX 10.2   CANADA'S TRUTH AND RECONCILIATION (TRC)

Started in June of 2008 and completed in December of 2016, the mandate of the TRC was to inform all Canadians about what happened in Indian Residential Schools (IRS). In the report, it is estimated that some 4000 children died while in the care of the IRS. The Commission was led by Murray Sinclair, Manitoba's first aboriginal associate chief justice; the Commission documented the stories and accountings of numerous survivors, families, communities, and anyone personally affected by the IRS experience.

Upon its completion, the TRC report identified 94 "Calls to Action" to "redress the legacy of residential schools and advance the process of Canadian reconciliation." These were divided into two main categories: *Legacy*, which included the categories of child welfare, education health, justice, and language and culture, and *Reconciliation*, which included almost 20 subcategories ranging from Settlement agreement parties and the United Nations Declaration on the Rights of Indigenous Peoples to Newcomers to Canada.

For further details on this historic inquiry, see http://www.trc.ca/websites/trcinstitution/index.php?p=905.

Of course, practical proactive technical assistance and exchange of good practices can be of use. In Papua New Guinea, for example, the Office of the High Commissioner for Human Rights, together with Oxfam, has provided technical assistance to the government to end killings of individuals accused of sorcery and witchcraft. UNFPA works around the world to address various forms of harmful practices that can result in gender-related killings, including infanticide and sex-selective abortions. Such approaches entail great sensitivity to local, cultural, religious, and traditional beliefs and behaviors, while never losing sight of the imperative of adhering to the principle of the universal human rights. UNFPA runs programs in 156 countries to support the implementation of legislation of long-term measures to enhance gender equality. UN-Women (2015) has, for example, carried out an analysis of penal codes and civil laws with a view of identifying elements that discriminate against women and supporting decision makers in addressing all forms of violence against women, including femicide. UN Peacekeeping operations have provided technical advice to operationalize a special court for the prosecution of sexual and gender-based violence in Liberia and to assist the transitional authorities in the Central African Republic in establishing a special court to address the most serious crimes, including gender-based violence (UNODC 2015).

The UNODC (2015) has prepared a booklet: "Recommendations for Action Against Gender-Related Killing of Women and Girls." The specific recommendation on investigation and prosecution include the following: (1) address risk factors for lethal violence (firearms, presence of gangs); (2) take action with due diligence and without delay; (3) ensure protection (witness protection, shelters) and access to justice (legal aid, language support services); (4) avoid secondary victimization (testimonial aids, victim assistance); (5) integrated, multidisciplinary, and gender-sensitive approach (close collaboration, information sharing among institutions); (6) specialized units with sufficient resources; (7) manuals, training, and protocols; (8) enhance forensic investigations, DNA databases, centers for missing persons; (9) monitor and sanction officials who do not exercise due diligence; and (10) ensure appropriate sanctions for perpetrators.

With respect to *victim support*, the booklet emphasizes that the needs of women in vulnerable conditions be addressed, including the elderly, rural women, indigenous women, foreign women, immigrants, women in irregular situations, victims of human trafficking, children of victims of violence, women with disabilities, and women in armed conflict. Hence, within a preventive context, the role of civil society is important both in advocacy and in filling the gaps in governmental assistance (UNODC 2015).

With regard to *prevention*: UNODC underlines the importance of promoting changes in social norms and attitudes harmful to women through early and continuous educational programs and awareness raising, quick accessible protection and restraining orders, frequent police patrols and women's urban safety audits, regulating possession of firearms by violent offenders, criminalizing all forms of violence against women, rehabilitation and re-education of perpetrators, analyzing indirect forms of gender-related killing, and collecting and publishing data and information regularly and transparently.

With respect to the *due diligence* obligations of States: they must conduct effective investigations of the crime, and prosecute and sanction acts of violence perpetrated by the State or private actors, especially when these acts demonstrate a pattern of systematic violence toward women. A holistic approach for the elimination of all forms of violence against all women requires that systematic discrimination, oppression, and marginalization of women be addressed at the political, operative, judicial, and administrative levels (UNODC 2014). In order to eliminate the customary practices based on the inferiority of women and stereotyped roles for men and women, social and cultural patterns of conduct of men and women must change (Manjoo 2012). UNODC also advocates data collection and evaluation programs to build a knowledge base on what works to prevent violence against women.

Consistent with the classical school of criminology and deterrence theory, formal responses to any form of femicide should be swift and certain, and the response should be proportionate to the gravity of the offense. For femicide such as targeting women in war, or the signature murders by criminal gangs, the deaths caused by human trafficking or through traditional harmful practices, it may be complicated to identify the persons ultimately responsible; however, efforts should be made with all the resources that the state authorities can muster. The fact that the victim is a prostitute, from a lower class, an indigenous woman, or even an enemy should not deter investigation or prosecution (Domazetoska et al. 2014).

In 2015, the Secretary-General submitted a report: *Action against gender-related killing of women and girls*, through the Commission Crime Prevention and Criminal Justice to the General Assembly. In this document, preventive measures undertaken by Member States are listed. Action plans, public awareness raising, and education campaigns to address violence against women, situational prevention (i.e., increased patrols and more rapid responses), and broader initiatives aimed at eliminating gender inequality, gender based discrimination, and other root causes of violence against women are described. For example, in Germany, the Second Action Plan to combat violence against women encompasses 130 measures and programs to be implemented together with nongovernmental services and state institutions. Other countries (e.g., Spain and the United Kingdom) have specific laws to combat intimate partner violence, FGM, or honor-related killings. In addition, many countries have victim support programs for the survivors of lethal violence and also for family members who have suffered the loss of their mothers, wife, or daughter. "Panic buttons," hotlines, dedicated response teams, shelters, rehabilitation centers for victims of acid attacks and traumatic injuries, and special training programs for law enforcement officers are other positive examples of national practices.

In conclusion, the Secretariat recommends the ratification of a number of International Conventions and their follow-up mechanisms; the dissemination of the Latin American model for the investigation of gender-related killings of women; a review and updating of national laws; assessing the effectiveness of laws; training programs and awareness campaigns; identifying gender stereotyping, sexual misconduct, and discrimination in institutions; promotion of women in law enforcement and legal professions; gender-sensitive budget policies; better coordination among services and with civil society organizations; and improvement of data collection.

What Can Be Done to Prevent Extreme Violence against Girls?

Children regardless of gender represent a vulnerable demographic of the population; however, female children in many parts of the world are at greater risk than are their male counterparts for many of the same reasons women are. A girl child is essentially defenseless in a family that hides starvation, beatings, and sexual abuse by fathers, older brothers, or relatives; even worse, she suffers from public female gender sexual mutilation; endures "breast ironing," scarring, and other body mutilations; is promised in marriage at an early age; is sold into prostitution and domestic servitude; and is forced to work in agricultural and manufacturing enterprises with little or no compensation. Usually denied an education, she is abused by her natal family and is again beaten in the forced marriage by her elderly husband, mother-in-law, and other wives of her husband. Because of such circumstances or simple poverty, she flees the home, lives on the street, begs, commits petty crimes, prostitutes herself, and often joins a gang or is exploited by a criminal organization. She is then subjected to be trafficked abroad for prostitution, pornography, forced labor, or domestic indenture.

Young girls are particularly vulnerable in conflict zones to depredations by the combatants, often kidnapped by armed groups, and forced into "marriage" with a soldier to provide him sex, food, and ancillary services (Amnesty International 2014). Even UN peacekeepers have taken advantage of girls under the age of consent, in exchange for food or small sums of money. This phenomenon has risen to new levels of depravity through kidnapping of girls from schools by armed groups (Boku Haram kidnapped 274 Christian schoolgirls in 2014, most of whom have not been heard from since) (UNHRC 2015) and, similarly, the recent revelations about slave auctions of captured women and girls by the Islamic State terrorists in Syria and Iraq. The worst thing is that when wives and girls are liberated, they are often not welcomed back by their families and community (Human Rights Watch 2014). The children of raped women are also rejected by even their own mothers (UNICEF and International Alert 2016).

Girls fleeing war are particularly vulnerable to being targeted, sexually assaulted, and enslaved by the warring parties. In addition, they risk being abused by smugglers, traffickers, and older boys and men in the refugee camps. Sexual abuse of minorities, unaccompanied minors, and "virgins" is common in camps, including the establishment of unofficial brothels. The situation can of course be worse en route, sleeping in open fields, in parks, in slum housing, or outside of the shelters organized by UNHCR or government agencies. It is estimated that 10,000 refugee children in the recent Syrian crisis are at the mercy of traffickers and fellow travelers (Rape and domestic violence follow Syrian women into refugee camps 2013). If unaccompanied, they have no family members to protect them. Sometimes, parents allow their children to be abused for a little money, packet of cigarettes, or food. Parents even sell their daughters to rich Arabs from the Gulf and Saudi Arabia for a marriage lasting only a few months. In fact, bridal shops and "marriage bureaus" are established inside or near the large refugee camps in Lebanon, Jordan, and Turkey, where 14-year-old girls are sold to old men. UN peacekeepers have been found guilty of sexually abusing adolescents for such exchanges of food for sex (Problem of sexual abuse by peacekeepers now openly recognized 2006).

Many of the same recommendations that have been proposed above, where criminal justice systems are supposed to be functioning, should be tried in practice. However, when law enforcement officers are molesting or raping street/homeless children, guardians in juvenile homes violating girls, or UN officials abusing adolescents, some major system reforms must be pursued and persons abusing their authorities must be disciplined and punished. Such a widespread pattern of abuses in conflict situations should be considered war crimes and the officers should be sanctioned, with no time limits even after the conflict has ceased. The violators should be brought to trial, in national or military courts as has been done in Guatemala (Guatemala: Rape sentences [360 years for two officers] in landmark military trial for murder, rape, and sexual enslavement of indigenous women 2016). If the national courts are unable to bring the violators to trial, international tribunals can hold individuals responsible for such war crimes. The practice of attaching child protection officers and human rights officers to the UN peacekeeping operations has proven very useful but must be expanded and more resources must be dedicated to such teams.

The report of the Secretary-General on conflict-related violence* made 21 recommendations to Member States, including broad intervention and *prevention* recommendations to promote gender equality, women's empowerment, and national responsibility, as well as very specific actions to the Security Council to include conflict sexual violence in the work of relevant sanctions committees, refer cases to the International Criminal Court, use field visits to solicit the views of women's organizations and survivors, and give due consideration, in planning UN missions, to the warning signs of sexual violence in relation to elections, civil strife, forced displacements, or expulsions. The report also urged an accelerated deployment of Women's Protection Advisers and Gender Advisers as well as funding for monitoring teams for conflict sexual violence, particularly in relation to the Central African Republic, Libya, Mali, Myanmar, and South Sudan. Furthermore, the Secretary-General encouraged multisectoral (i.e., health, psychosocial, livelihood, shelter, reintegration) support for individuals released from situations of abduction, forced marriage, trafficking, and sexual slavery as well as engagement with faith-based leaders to counter religious justifications for violence and reduce the stigma faced by survivors. The Secretary-General praised the roles of civil society

* S/2015.

and women's organizations in community-level protection and of journalists and human rights defenders in reporting these hidden crimes and changing social norms. Among several other supportive comments, the Secretary-General encouraged private sector actors to make specific commitments to ensure that proceeds acquired (e.g., "blood diamonds," weapons) do not fund armed groups that perpetuate conflict-related sexual violence.

Capacity Building through Partnership Building

The Secretary-General's boldest statement has been that conflict-related sexual violence should be considered grounds for the recognition of refugee status and that sexual violence is a tactic to induce displacement.

On October 13, 2015, the Security Council held a thematic discussion on Women, Peace, and Security. A record 110 countries spoke on this topic. The Secretary-General called for particular attention for the most vulnerable women, such as those facing the compound disadvantage of gender and ethnicity, and indigenous women, who suffer from multiple forms of discrimination, especially in times of conflict. He specifically mentioned that "groups such as Daesh and Boko Haram have mercilessly targeted women and girls," noting that the systematic killings, torture, rape, and sexual slavery against Yazidi women amount to war crimes, crimes against humanity, and genocide (UN Press Release 2015).

Security Council Resolution

Resolution (S/2242) urged the Secretary-General to introduce gender perspectives to address accountability deficits throughout all stages of mission planning, implementation, and drawdown; to double the number of women in peacekeeping operations; and to invite civil society and women's organizations to brief regarding country-specific situations. To address the continued charges of sexual exploitation and abuse by UN peacekeepers, the Security Council urged that troop-contributing countries provide "robust" predeployment training, conduct swift and thorough investigation of uniformed personnel, and, if appropriate, prosecute offenders (Ledererer 2016).

On March 11, 2016, the Security Council adopted a second resolution (2272), specifically relating to the steps to combat sexual exploitation by UN peacekeepers, whereby whole contingents would be repatriated if it appeared there were systemic violations by troop-contributing countries, but no actions appeared to be taken. Moreover, countries would still be responsible for pursuing cases against its personnel for criminal actions.

Child Sexual Abuse by UN Peacekeepers

In Bosnia, forced prostitution was associated with the arrival of the UN peacekeepers in 1993. However, the human rights officers who exposed the direct involvement of the UN peacekeeping force in the procurement of sex slaves for a local brothel in Bosnia were at first disciplined by the United Nations itself (Vulliamy 2012). UN employees in the Democratic Republic of the Congo have been accused of the sexual abuse of girls, as have UN troops in Haiti, Sudan, and Central Africa (Caplan 2012; Cox 2016; Deardon 2016; A Tale of Horror at the United Nations 2016). Similarly, Save the Children and UNICEF revealed that 8 out of 10 minor girls admitted to regularly being raped and forced into sexual acts by UN soldiers in the Ivory Coast (UN sex abuse sackings in Burundi 2016). In Haiti, an investigative report highlighted the brutal raping of a mentally handicapped child over a five-year period. This was reported to the Pakistan UN commander, who decided to handle the case himself. Apparently, the UN officer was hoping the case would disappear, "since he was also abusing the child" (Laville 2015; Newman 2016). In the Security Council, U.S. Ambassador Samantha Powers questioned why the only punishment for the abuse was a nine-day suspension by the Canadian police investigation (Geoffrey 2016).

Ironically, the problem of sexual abuse by peacekeepers was discussed 10 years earlier in the UN Security Council. The Undersecretary for Peacekeeping Operations then admitted that not all troop contingents or staff on the ground fully supported all aspects of the "zero tolerance" policy particularly as it pertained to prostitution. Prince Zeid Ra'ad Zeid Al-Hussein, the Adviser on Sexual Exploitation and Abuse in UN Peacekeeping Operations, said that allegations being lodged against UN peacekeeping personnel remained high and unacceptably so. It was difficult to change a "culture of dismissiveness, long developed within ourselves, in own countries, and in the mission areas" (Problem of sexual abuse by peacekeepers now openly recognized 2006) (see Box 10.3).

Now, for the first time since the European refugee crisis began, some 60% of the migrants crossing into Macedonia from Greece are women and children. The unaccompanied minors, mainly adolescents aged 15 to 17 years old, have fled from Syria, Afghanistan, and Iraq. UNICEF has stressed that effective guardianship programs for children on the move are needed every step of the way. UNHCR has expressed regret that many European states are in fact reducing available legal avenues, suggesting that some countries are prioritizing keeping refugees and migrants out over finding realistic solutions to their staying (Europe's restrictive measures… 2016; Flemming 2016).

The UN-Women Executive Director at the end of 16 days of activism against gender-based violence, "Oranging our world," which started with the 2015 International Day, said that less than half of existing domestic violence

BOX 10.3   INTERNATIONAL DAY FOR THE ELIMINATION OF VIOLENCE AGAINST WOMEN

Each year, the Secretary-General issues a statement on November 25 on the atrocity crimes committed against women and girls not only in the conflict zones but also in the home. Mr. Ban spoke clearly about the plight of women and girls living in conditions of armed conflict, who suffer various forms of violence, sexual assault, sexual slavery, and trafficking. Violent extremists are perverting religious teachings to justify the mass subjugation and abuse of women. These are not random acts of violence but rather systematic efforts to deny women's freedoms and control their bodies. Roughly half of today's 60 million forcibly displaced people are women. Many who flee war and violence are often exploited by unscrupulous smugglers and frequently suffer gender discrimination and xenophobia in host societies. Those who are too young, too old, or too frail to make the risky journey are left behind, even more vulnerable without those who have left (Secretary-General's Message for International Day for the Elimination of Violence against Women 2015).

laws are being enforced. Mrs. Mlambo-Ngcuka stressed that gender-based violence is rooted in discrimination, unequal power relations, pervasive social norms, attitudes, and beliefs, and that it occurs in every country in the world. She noted that the international community needs to make sure leaders do not send mixed messages. She called for men and boys to be active in advancing gender equality. The Executive Director spoke of FGM and child marriage and that "girls are bearing the brunt of the violence that is perpetrated against women and girls around the world" (We must focus on changing attitudes 2015).

The UN Framework to Underpin Action to Prevent Violence against Women was launched in New York in December 2015 by UN-Women, ILO, UNDP, UNESCO, UNFPA, WHO, and the Office of High Commissioner for Rights (UN-Women 2015). At the same time, the UN Joint Global Programme on Essential Services for Women and Girls Subject to Violence—a collaborative efforts of UN Women, UNFPA, WHO, UNODC, and UNDP—was launched in Istanbul (UNFPA 2013). Both documents describe the need for multisectoral services for survivors. However, the reality is that less than 40% of the women who experience violence seek help. The Executive Director of UNFPA, Dr. Babatunde Osotimehin on the 20th anniversary of the Beijing Declaration, said that "there is no country in the world, where women and girls live free from violence." At this same conference, "Violence against Women: Building on Progress to Accelerate Change," held in Istanbul on December 9–10, 2015, Phumzile Mlambo-Ngcuka, the Executive Director of

UN Women, admitted that "violence against women and girls remains one of the most widespread and tolerated violations of human rights—but it is not inevitable, we can prevent it. We are here today to say that enough is enough." The conference ended with a "We can make it happen," agreed by 16 countries, experts, and nongovernmental organizations (Zero tolerance a must to end violence against women and girls 2015).

The Secretary-General's own Plan of Action to Prevent Violent Extremism was presented to the General Assembly in January to a mixed reaction (General Assembly decides to take more time in considering Secretary-General's proposed action plan for preventing violent extremism 2016). Ban's seven-point plan of action called for dialogue to prevent conflicts, strengthening good governance, promoting human rights and the rule of law, engaging communities, empowering youth, ensuring gender equality and empowering women, improving education and increasing jobs, and strategic communications that also harnesses the Internet and social media—all very good crime prevention strategies; however, in lawless territories, this may prove difficult. The United Kingdom Representative Matthew Rycroft called it pragmatic and comprehensive and said its recommendations could be the basis of national action plans based on respect for human rights and the rule of law. The U.S. Ambassador Michele J. Sison (2016) added:

> addressing the conditions conducive to terrorism and implementing a human rights based counterterrorism programs within the rule of law are critical. ... We must find ways to prevent people from being radicalized in the first place.

Sison praised the "All-of-UN" approach, whereby all its various agencies, offices, missions, and programs advance the goals. She also underscored the importance of involving a diverse range of government and nongovernmental stakeholders in the development and implementation of such plans—local governments, the private sector, youth, women, religious and educational leaders, and civil society. However, the General Assembly did not adopt the Plan because there were strong differences as to whether issues such as "foreign occupation" and "self-determination" should be included. Nevertheless, it is expected that the discussion will continue on and efforts will likely be made to more clearly define the lack of clarity around such concepts as "terrorism," "violent extremism," and the intended meaning of "aggression" in the plan.

Conclusion

In this chapter, attention has clearly been drawn to the many forms of femicide through the work of the Special Rapporteurs, the Committee on the Elimination of Discrimination against the Women, the Child Rights

Committee, the Human Rights Council, the Commission of the Status of the Women, the Commission on Crime Prevention and Criminal Justice, the General Assembly, and now the Security Council—thanks to the UN Secretariat, women's rights organizations, national advocacy groups, and academic associations such as the Academic Council on the United Nations System.

Many useful situational crime prevention techniques described above can stop extreme violence against women and girls and provide multisectoral services to those who survive these heinous assaults and those to their dependents. Yet, despite the initiatives of the United Nations, other international organizations and national efforts, the necessary societal changes in attitude toward these crimes have not evolved much in the past decades. According to the evidence available, femicide has been increasing rather than declining. Although steps have been taken to properly document the extent of these crimes, it is clear that more reliable and valid data are needed to inform policymakers—this is the major point of the last resolution from UN Crime Commission. However, the long-term education and women empowerment programs will probably make the biggest difference. In the meantime, all criminal justice tools to investigate and prosecute all killings of women and girls should be pursued to the maximum extent possible. It is also clear that actions, not mere hortatory statements, are needed. Partnerships with religious leaders and organizations, women's groups, a variety of donors, community leadership, media, civil society, the various UN agencies, governmental structures, financial institutions, the military, police, judiciary, and respected persons need to be mobilized against entrenched prejudices, violent extremism, and the worst forms of femicide.

Glossary of Key Terms

Femicide: The killing of women because of their gender (women can also be the murderer); a sexual/gender hate crime; includes female infanticide, sex selective feticide, dowry deaths, bride burning, witchcraft killing, targeting women in war, killing as a result of intimate partner violence, lesbiscide, honor killing, stoning, violence against prostitutes, and misogynist murders. Feminists have also included the immediate stages before the murder and argue that sexist attitudes that condone these killings be included, as well as such horrific practices as acid throwing, breast ironing, child or forced marriages, FGM, mass sexual assaults, sexual slavery, gang rape, and extreme forms of domestic violence.

Feminicide: The non-actions of a governmental body that fail to prevent the killings and therefore are to be sanctioned.

Gendercide: Often used as synonymous with femicide, but feminists argue that killing a man involves a completely different set of motivations.

Gender-related killings: The preferred United Nations term; it also covers the above forms as these extreme forms of violence often lead to suicide, and violence prevention techniques can be employed for all these extreme forms of battery and assault.

Genocide: The systematic killing of a group of people. Feminists argue that the systematic violence and killing of women amounts to genocide (the killing of a targeted group of people) and therefore the sanctions from the Genocide Convention should apply.

Honor killing (or "shame killing"): The intentional killing of a member of a family (usually female) by other members. It is usually attributed to the belief that the victim has brought shame or dishonor upon the family or has violated the principles of a community or a religion, usually for reasons such as refusing to enter an arranged marriage.

Infanticide: Although common during the Roman Empire, today, it is the intentional killing of unwanted (usually female) babies.

Discussion Questions

1. What is the most widespread form of femicide? Which forms exist in your country?
2. What can be done against extreme violence against girls?
3. To what extent can states (and who?) be held responsible for the killing of women in their jurisdiction?
4. What is the difference between women being killed in a war and gendercide?
5. To what extent should a woman's wishes be taken into account in the withdrawal of a complaint in domestic violence, violence among indigenous peoples, and trafficking cases?
6. What extenuating circumstances would you allow to be considered in the killing of a woman? Underage relative? Provocation? Part of group decision? Following orders?

Suggested Reading

Academic Council on the United Nations System, Vienna Liaison Office (2013), Femicide Volume 1, "A Global Issue That Demands Action" (contains the papers of November 25, 2012 Symposium, Latin American Protocol for investigation of extreme violence against women, and Manjoo report to Human

Rights Council), also available at http://acuns.org/femicide-a-global-issue-that-demands-action/ or http://bit.ly/2ckPQch.

Academic Council on the United Nations System, Vienna Liaison Office (2014), Femicide Volume II (contains General Assembly Resolution 68/19; High Level Meeting, New York, October 18; Symposium on Forced Marriage, Violence Against Migrant Women, and the Istanbul Convention), available at http://acuns.org/femicide-volume-ii-a-global-issue-that-demands-action/ also at http://bit.ly/2cZvegP.

Academic Council on the United Nations System, Vienna Liaison Office (2015), Femicide Volume III (contains Symposium "Targeting Women in War" Vienna, November 25, 2014; UNODC Expert Group on Gender-related Killings of Women and Girls, Bangkok, November 13, 2014), available at http://acuns.org/feminicide-volume-iii-targeting-of-women-in-conflict/ also at http://bit.ly/2ciwUps.

Academic Council on the United Nations System, Vienna Liaison Office (2015), Femicide Volume IV (contains General Assembly Resolution 70/176; Secretary General Report: Taking Action Against Gender Related Killing of Women and Girls; Security Council Report of Secretary General: Conflict-related Sexual Violence; articles on honour killings, dowry deaths, acid attacks, sex selective foeticide, sexual violence and torture), available at http://acuns.org/femicide-a-global-issue-that-demands-action-volume-iv/ also http://acuns.org/bit.ly/2cyWtUy.

Academic Council on the United Nations System, Vienna Liaison Office (2016), Femicide Volume V (contains High Level Meeting on Femicide, New York, October 16, 2015; Security Council Review session on Women, Peace and Security; Documents on Violence against Women in Conflict; Extremist and Terrorist Groups Targeting Women and Girls), http://acuns.org/femicide-a-global-issue-that-demands-action-volume-v/ ISBN:978-3-200-03012-1.

Ambassador Michele J. Sison. (Febuary 12, 2016). Remarks to the UN General Assembly on the Secretary's Plan of Action to Prevent Violent Extremism. Retrieved from http://usstate.gov/remarks.

Fedotov, Y. (2015). Part 11: 24th session commission on crime prevention and criminal justice. *Femicide: A Global Issue That Demands Action—Vol. IV.* Vienna, Austria: Academic Council of the United Nations.

Shalhoub-Kevorkian, N. (2002). *Re-examining Feminicide: Breaking the Silence and Crossing Scientific Borders.* SIGNS, University of Chicago Press.

Recommended Web Links

www.facebook/femicide/news provides updated news about femicide and gender-related violence worldwide.

WHO (2009) Violence prevention: The evidence. This report presents seven briefings on violence prevention and the available evidence on their impact. http://apps.who.int/iris/bitstream/10665/77936/1/9789241500845_eng.pdf?ua=1.

References

Agnes, F. (October 12, 2011). Gender-based killings: A South Asian perspective. Paper prepared for Expert Group Meeting, United Nations, New York.

Allahbadia, G. (2002). The 50 million missing women. *Journal of Assisted Reproduction and Genetics*, 19(9): 411–416.

Amnesty International. (September 2009). No More Stolen Sisters: The Need for a Comprehensive Response to Discrimination and Violence against Aboriginal Women. Retrieved from www.amnesty.org/document.

Amnesty International. (2014). Escape from Hell: Torture, Sexual Slavery in Islamic State Captivity. Retrieved from www.amnesty.org/documents.

Andrew, P. (1997). Violence against aboriginal women in Australia: Possibilities for redress within the international human rights framework. *Albany Law Review* 60: 917.

A Tale of Horror at the United Nations. (February 17, 2016). The *New York Times*. New York: The International *New York Times*, http://www.nytimes.com/2016/02/17/opinion/a-tale-of-horror-at-the United Nations.html.

Banerji R. (2016). Karva Chauth: A Womanly Celebration of Cultural Misogyny. *Huffington Post*, 15 March. Retrieved from http://www.huffingtonpost.in/rita-banerji-/karva-chauth-a-womanly-ce_b_8429386.html.

Banerji, R.R. (October 2009). Female genocide in India and the 50 million missing campaign. *Intersections: Gender and Sexuality in Asia and the Pacific* (22).

Canada Department of Justice. (2016). Preliminary Examination of So-called "Honour killings" in Canada. Retrieved from www.justice.ca/eng/rp-pr/cj-jp/fv-vf/hk-ch/p2.html.

Caplan, G. (2012). Peacekeepers gone wild: How much more abuse will the UN ignore in Congo. *The Globe and Mail*, August 3. www.theglobeandmail.com/news/politics/second-reading/peace-how-much-more-abuse-will-the-un-ignore-in-congo-/article 4462151/.

Caputi, J., and Russell, D.E.H. (1990). Femicide: Speaking the unspeakable. *The World of Women* (1)2: 34–37.

CEDAW. (2008). Committee, Concluding Observations: Canada, UN DOC. CEDAW /C/CAN/CO/.

CEDAW. (2010). Committee, Concluding Observations to Australia, UN DOC. CEDAW /C/AUL/CO/7.

Chen, M.A. (2016). Widowhood and ageing in India. United Nations Research Institute for Social Development case study. Retrieved from http://www.unrisd/website/projects.

Civil Society Organizations. (May 2014). Information on gender-related killings of women and girls provided to the Commission on Crime Prevention and Criminal Justice, United Nations—E/CN.15/2014/Conference room paper no. 5.

Colombia Human Rights Network. (2002). Urgent Appeal, May 3. Retrieved from http://colhrnet.igc.org/newitems/may02/ai_urgent_appeal_3may02.htm.

Cox, J. (April 1, 2016). French peacekeeping troops tied young girls and forced them to have sex with dogs. *The Sun (UK)*.

Croll, E. (1980). *Feminism and Socialism in China*. New York: Schocken Books.

Delhi Gang Rape. (2012). Retrieved from Wikipedia, en.wikipedia.org/wiki/2012_Delhi -gang-rape.

Deardon, L. (March 31, 2016). French troops accused of forcing girls into beastiality in CAR. *Indenpendent (UK)*.

Domazetoska, S., Platzer, M., and Plaku, G. (2014). Combating femicide in Latin America. In *Femicide II*. Vienna, Austria: ACUNS.

Europe's restrictive measures draw UN concern as refugee and migrant influx continues. (2016). UN News Centre. Retrieved from http://www.un.org/apps/news /story.asp?NewsID=53217#.V_lu4iTNxf0.

Femicide: A global issue that demands action. Volume IV. (2015). Retrieved from http://acuns.org/wp-content/uploads/2016/07/FemicideVol-IV.pdf.

Flemming, M. (February 12, 2016). UNHCR concerned over increasing restrictive measures. Palais des Nations, Geneva: UNHCR Press Release.

General Assembly decides to take more time in considering Secretary-General's proposed action plan for preventing violent extremism. (February 12, 2016). General Assembly Meetings Coverage. Retrieved from http://www.un.org /press/en/2016/ga11760.doc.htm.

Geoffrey, Y. (March 10, 2016). U.S. official blasts UN over response to sexual abuse by peacekeepers. Retrieved from http://www.theglobalandmail.com/news.

Gerdes, N. (2014). A case of femicide: Sex-selective feticide in India. In *Femicide II*. Vienna, Austria: ACUNS.

Guatemala: Rape sentences (360 years for 2 officers) in landmark military trial for murder, rape, and sexual enslavement of indigenous women. (February 27, 2016). London: BBC News.

Human Rights Council. (2010). Resolution 17/19. Human rights, sexual orientation, and gender identity.

Human Rights Watch. (2014). Those Terrible Weeks in Their Camp. Boko Haram Violence against Women and Girls in North East Nigeria. Retrieved from http:// www.hrw.org/sites/default/files/reports/nigeria 1014web.pd.

Human Rights First. (2008). Hate Crime Survey, "Violence Based on Sexual Orientation and Gender Identity Bias," p. 125. Retrieved from http://www.human rightsfirst.org/sites/default/files/FD-081103-hate-crime-survey-2008.pdf.

Inamdar, S.C. (1983). A suicide by self-immolation: Psychological perspectives. *International Journal of Social Psychiatry* 29: 130–133.

Joseph, J. (2014). Intimate femicides in the U.S.: The Black Experience. In *Femicide II*. Vienna, Austria: ACUNS.

Kishwar, M. (2005). Destined to Fail-Inherent Flaws in the Anti-Dowry Legislation. Manushi, (148), May–June, pp. 3–12.

Kumari, R. (2014). The case of dowry deaths in India. In *Femicide III*. Vienna, Austria: ACUNS.

Laville, S. (2015). UN aid worker suspended for leaking report on child abuse by French troops. London: *The Guardian*. Retrieved from www.theguard ian.com/world/2015/apr/29/un-aid-worker-suspended-leaking-report -child-abuse-french-troops-car.

Lederer, E. (2016, 12 March). UN Adopts First Resolution Tackling Sex Abuse by UN peacekeepers. Associated Press, ABC News, UN News Centre.

Madhu, K. (2012). *Off the Beaten Track: Rethinking Gender Justice for Indian Women*. Oxford, UK: Oxford University Press.

Manjoo, R. (2012). Report of the Special Rapporteur on Violence against Women, Its Causes and Consequences, to the Human Rights Council, May 23, 2012, A/HRC/20/16.

McIvor, S., and Day, S. (October 12, 2011). Gender-Motivated Killings of Aboriginal Women and Girls Canada. Prepared for UN Expert Group Meeting on Gender-Motivated Killings of Women, New York.

Natarajan, M. (2015). Understanding and preventing burn and acid attacks on women. In *Femicide IV*. Vienna, Austria: ACUNS.

Native Women's Association of Canada. (2010). What Their Stories Tell Us: Research Findings from the Sisters in Spirit initiative. Retrieved from http://www.nwac .ca/sites/default/files/imce/2010-NWAC-SIS-Report-EN.pdf.

Newman, A. (June 18, 2015). Sex abuse by UN peace troops becoming global scandal. *The New American*.

Oberwittler, D. (2011). Ehrenmorde in Deutschland 1996–2005. Eine Untersuchung auf der Basis von Prozessakten. Cologne, Wolters Kluwer Deutschland [in German].

Platzer, M. (2016). The Right to a Safe City for Women and Girls. In *Women and Children as Victims and* Offenders, eds. H. Kury and S. Redo. New York: Springer Verlag.

Preventing gender-biased sex selection. (2011). An Inter-Agency Statement by OHCHR, UNFPA, UNICEF, UN-Women, and WHO. Geneva, Switzerland. Retrieved from http://www.who.int/reproductivehealth/publications/gender -rights/9789241501460/en/.

Prieto-Carron, M., Thomson, M., and Macdonald, M. (2007). No more killings! Women respond to femicides in Central America. *Handbook on Gender and Development*, 15(1). Oxford, UK: Routledge.

Problem of sexual abuse by peacekeepers now openly recognized. (February 23, 2006). United Nations: Security Council Press Release, SC/864, New York.

Rape and domestic violence follow Syrian Women into refugee camps. (July 25, 2013). London: *The Guardian*. Retrieved from http://www.theguardian.com/world /2013/jul/25/rape-violence-syria-women-refugee-camp.

Reiterer, J.A. (2012). *Hexenkind*. Cologne, Germany: Bastei Lubbe.

Russell, D. (ed.). (2001). *Femicide in Global Perspective*. New York: Teachers College Press.

Sajor, I. (October 12, 2011). Gender-Motivated Killings of Women Accused of Sorcery and Witchcraft, a Form of Femicide: Papua New Guinea Case. Paper prepared for Expert Group Meeting, New York.

Schnoebelen, J. (2009). Witchcraft allegations, refugee protection and human rights: A review of new evidence. New Issues in Refugee Research, Research Paper No. 169, Policy Development and Evaluation Service, UNHCR, Geneva.

Secretary-General's Message for International Day for the Elimination of Violence against Women. (November 25, 2015). Retrieved from http://www.un.org/end violenceday/2015/sgmessage.

Secretary-General's Report. (March 2015). Conflict-related sexual violence, S/2015/203.

Segato, R. (2004). Territorio, soberania y crimenes de sequndo Estado: La escritura en el cuerpo de las mujeres asinadas en Ciudad Juarez. Serie Antropologica, 362, Departament de Antropologia da Universidade de Brasilia, Brazil.

Sekaggya, M. (2010). Report of the UN Special Rapporteur on the situation of human rights defenders. Mission to Colombia. United Nations. A/HRC/13/22/Add.3.

Sen, A. (2003). Missing women revisited. *British Medical Journal* 327: 1297–1298.

Shalhoub-Kevorkian, N. (2002). *Re-examining Feminicide: Breaking the Silence and Crossing Scientific Borders.* SIGNS, The University of Chicago Press.

Special Rapporteur on extra-judicial, summary, or arbitrary executions (2010), Philip Alston, Mission Report to Colombia., United Nations. A/HRC/14/24/Add.2.

The Commission for Historical Clarification (Comision para el Esclarciemto Historico). (1999). *La Violencia Sexual contra La Mujer* 3(41), Guatemala City.

UN Assistance Mission in Afghanistan. (2010). Harmful Traditional Practices and Implementation of the Law on Elimination of Violence against Women in Afghanistan. Kabul, and Office of the High Commissioner for Human Rights, Geneva, December 9, 2010.

UN Press Release. (October 13, 2015). SC/12076, p. 3. Security Council Unanimously Adopts Resolution 2242 (2015) to improve implementation of Landmark Text on Women, Peace, Security Agenda. Retrieved from http://www.un.org/press /en/2015/sc12076.doc.htm.

UN sex abuse sackings in Burundi, BBC. (2016). Retrieved from http://news.bbc.co .uk/2/hi/africa/4697465.stm.

UNESCO. (2013). Education Transforms Lives: Education for All Global Monitoring Report. Paris.

UNHCR concerned at reports of sexual violence against refugee women and children. (October 23, 2015). Retrieved from http://www.unhcr.org.

UNICEF and International Alert. (2016). Report, Bad Blood: Perception of Children born of conflict sexual violence and women and girls associated with Boko Haram in northeastern Nigeria. UNICEF, New York. Retrieved from http:// www.international-alert.org/sites/files/Nigeria_Bad Blood_EN_2016.pdf.

UNODC. (2015). Recommendations for Action Against Gender Related Killing of Women and Girls. Retrieved from http://www.unodc.org/documents/justice -and-prisons-reform/GRK_ebook.pdf.

UNODC Secretariat. (2014). Gender-related killing of women and girls: Promising practices, challenges and practical recommendations. Background paper prepared for Expert Group on the gender-related killing of women and girls, Bangkok, November 11–13, 2014 UNODC/CCPCJ/EG.8/2014/2.

UN-Women. (2015). A framework to underpin action to prevent violence against women. Retrieved from http://www.unwomen.org/publications.

Vulliamy, E. (January 15, 2012). Has the UN learned lessons of Bosnian Sex Slavery? *The Guardian.* Retrieved from http://www.theguardian.com/world/2012/jan/15 /bosnia-sex-trafficking-whistleblower.

We must focus on changing attitudes. (December 9, 2015). Retrieved from http:// www.unwomen.org news/ed-speech in Istanbul.

Wharton, J.S.S. (1848). *The Law Lexicon, or Dictionary of Jurisprudence.* London: Spettigue and Farrance.

Zero tolerance a must to end violence against women and girls. (December 9, 2015). Retrieved from http://www.unwomen.org/news/zero-tolerance.

Terrorism Crime Prevention Policies in Liberal Democracies

Challenges, Dilemmas, and Options

11

RAYMOND R. CORRADO
IRWIN M. COHEN
GARTH DAVIES

Contents

Learning Outcomes
After reading this chapter, you should be able to

- Identify why terrorism differs from all other types of serious crimes
- Identify the intelligence lead framework of the prevention of terrorism
- Identify why the end of the Cold War resulted in fundamental changes in counterterrorism strategies
- Identify the key issues in terrorism identification and monitoring technologies

- Identify the legal and moral issues associated with extreme counter-terrorism strategies/programs
- Identify the unique crime prevention policy aspects of jihadist terrorism threats
- Identify the commonalties and differences in the intelligence/police frameworks and strategies among certain liberal democracies

Introduction

> Terrorism has evolved into a new phase… [The San Bernardino shootings by radical Jihadists] was an act of terrorism designed to kill innocent people. As we've become better at preventing complex multifaceted attacks like 9/11, terrorists turns to less complicated acts of violence like the mass shootings that are all too common in our society.*
>
> **President Barack Obama**
> *2015*

Julian Assange, co-founder and editor-in-chief of *Wikileaks*, and Edward Snowden, a former private defense intelligence contractor now (in 2016) in exile in Moscow, both revealed the enormity and complexity of the hyper-secret policies and structures that the United States and its allies, such as Canada and Germany, have instituted to prevent terrorist attacks in their countries (see Figures 11.1 and 11.2, Tables 11.1 and 11.2). These disclosures shocked many citizens in **liberal democracies**, and the resulting intense and often angry political debates on how best to respond and prevent domestic and international terrorism remain largely unresolved. Several policy themes emerged, focusing on a number of key issues, such as the legality of certain countries' counterterrorism policies, the depth and scope of these secret policies, the role of these policies in preventing terrorist acts, the effect of counterterrorism structures and policies on citizen's privacy, and the nature or profile of terrorist threats. Despite the absence of any systematic research that might provide definitive answers to these policy issues and questions, this chapter will explore the largely case-based, country, and historical information to address these critical issues.

It can be argued that the tragic events of September 11, 2001 (also referred to as 9/11) marked a critical historical juncture that signified the failure of traditional antiterrorism policies in liberal democracies. Before 9/11, many theorists had become somewhat optimistic that most of the notorious terrorist organizations that dominated the second half of the 20th century were in

---

* Quote from President Barack Obama, in response to the threat of terrorism in the United States in response to the San Bernardino mass shootings: http://www.nasdaq.com/article/terrorist-threat-has-entered-a-new-phase-obama-says-20151206-00071#ixzz3wabXXjsJ.

Figure 11.1 The United Kingdom counterterrorism structure. (Created by Maike Knoechelmann.)

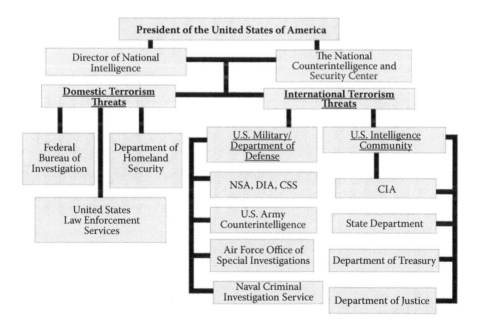

Figure 11.2 The United States of America counterterrorism structure. (Created by Maike Knoechelmann.)

Table 11.1 Country Comparison of Special Pre-Radicalization Programs

Special Pre-Radicalization Programs	United Kingdom	United States of America	Israel	Canada
Community	The counterterrorism local profile (CTLP) is provided to local authorities Channel, a multi-agency program to identify and help people at risk of radicalization	Special grants distributed by U.S. embassies to local communities in conflict zones to prevent individuals from joining extremist groups or militias	N/A	Family support group Hayat Canada: supports spouses, parents, and siblings of radicalized individuals Muslim community programs: moderate teaching of Islam, i.e., the Islam care center
Prison	The Al Furqan program using imams to teach prisoners moderate Islam The healthy identities intervention: psychotherapy to identify causes of radicalization	Counterinsurgency in the wire program in Iraqi prisons: teach reading, writing, agriculture, textiles, and Iraqi politics Re-integration in Afghani prisons: learn to read, write, banking, and farming	Spokesmen positions for Fatah, Islamic Jihad, and Hamas prison members to address issues High school classes are offered in prison; once a year the Palestinian matriculation exam can be taken	Few prison imams provide support to Muslim prisoners and teach moderate Islam to prevent radicalization or to deradicalize
Secondary education	The department of education does extensive checks on independent schools and their teachings	N/A	N/A	N/A
Higher education	Support of national union of students to educate about the risk of extremist speakers	N/A	N/A	N/A

Note: Created by Maike Knoechelmann.

Table 11.2 Country Comparison of Special Post-Radicalization Programs

Special Post-Radicalization Programs	United Kingdom	United States of America	Israel	Canada
Domestic security agencies	Deportation of foreign nationals upon suspicion of engagement in terrorist activity Cyclamen: detect and deter the importation of nuclear and radiological material The counterterrorism Internet referral unit: assess and remove illicit Internet content CCTV cameras	The nationwide suspicious activity reporting initiative: train local law enforcement to detect suspicious behavior FBI counterterrorism fly team: trained agents ready to fly to scenes of terrorism abroad and at home Bio watch system: detect the release of bio agents counterterrorism street cameras	Shin Bet Yamas unit: eliminates terrorist threats such as the leadership, suicide bombers, and bomb makers Shin Bet interrogation torture methods Yaman unit (border police) rescues hostages but is also engaged in evacuation of civilians from terror incidents The west bank barrier	RCMP: INSETS/NSESS teams collect, share, and analyze information and intelligence that concern threats to national security and criminal extremism/terrorism Enforcement information index: system administered by CBSA that alerts immigration and customs officers about suspected and known terrorists
International security agencies	Communication data (CD): identify who has communicated, when, with whom, and where (can be used as evidence in court)	CIA: collects Humint through agents and covert operations abroad PII: investigation into terrorist attacks	Mossad: conducts espionage overseas, its agents often receive diplomatic covers -> Kidon: assassins executing terrorists targets overseas	CSIS threat assessment unit: evaluations about the scope of a variety of threats posed by individuals and groups in Canada and abroad

(Continued)

Table 11.2 (Continued) Country Comparison of Special Post-Radicalization Programs

Special Post-Radicalization Programs	United Kingdom	United States of America	Israel	Canada
Air travel/public transport	The rollout of biometric residence permits to all non-European economic area (non-EEA) nationals seeking to stay in the UK for more than six months. Increase in emergency service communication capacity at key London undeground stations and increase in police patrols	Advanced imaging technology (AIT): full body scanners at every U.S. airport Pre-departure vetting: high risk passengers if likely inadmissible to U.S. may not board the plane. Secure flight: TSA prescreens 100% of passengers against government watchlist	Risk assessment profiling interviews by highly trained former military (behavior, background). Every checked piece of luggage is x-rayed/ put into pressure chamber to detect explosives. El Al airline: missile defense systems on commercial planes	Full body scanners. Passenger behavior observation (PBO): focuses on identifying irregular or suspicious behavior. The minister of public safety may direct an air carrier to deny an individual suspected of terrorism transportation and to administer additional screening
Financial oversight	Can deny public funds to any extremist, violent organization safer giving: community guidance to sponsors of extremist charities	Counterterrorism finance (CTF): delivery of assistance and training to foreign governments battling terror financing and money laundering	Israel money laundering and terror financing prohibition authority (IMPA): financial intelligence unit to prevent terror financing	The charities directorate of the Canada revenue agency has oversight over money transfers to charities in and outside of Canada

Note: Created by Maike Knoechelmann.

sharp decline, primarily because of the demise of the former Soviet Union in 1991 (Wilcox 2002). The unexpected dissolution of this key Cold War empire (commonly considered the period between 1947 and 1991), which played such an essential historical role in both state and anti-state terrorism globally, into independent republics became identified with the end of anti-state secular ideological terror movements (LaFree et al. 2015). In other words, the end of the Cold War between the United States and the Soviet Union resulted in the end of their respective sponsorship of ideologically affiliated anti-state and state terrorist organizations, such as the Red Brigades in Italy (circa 1970–1984); military dictatorships, such as the Pinochet regime in Chile (circa 1973–1990); and the apartheid government in the Republic of South Africa (circa 1984–1994). Of course, **terrorism** was to continue as a major policy issue for certain former multiethnic colonial countries with developing economies in Africa, such as the Republic of the Congo and Rwanda, as well as for several newly emerging or re-emerging countries, such as Serbia and Croatia, Afghanistan, and Sri Lanka. In effect, it was theorized that terrorism largely would be confined to countries undergoing fundamental political and economic transitions (Cohen and Corrado 2005). In contrast, liberal democracies with advanced industrial economies were expected to have few "major" terrorist movements, and even certain non-liberal democracies with dramatically and rapidly industrializing economies, such as the Republic of Korea (South Korea) and the Republic of China, would experience less state terrorism (Cohen and Corrado 2005). Nonetheless, isolated and episodic terrorist threats in liberal democracies would continue in the form of anti-state terrorist groups focused on traditional, largely single issues, including race, abortion, animal rights, economic justice/poverty, and the environment. Also, the construct of terrorism would come to be used to describe informal state-related acts involving police and correctional authorities acting against minority individuals (Cohen and Corrado 2005). For example, in Canada, there is the controversial assertion that aboriginal individuals have been subjected to systematic discriminatory police treatment, such as arbitrary arrest and violence. For example, in Saskatoon, Saskatchewan, certain members of the city police force were involved in an apparent informal policy of arresting aboriginal individuals for drunkenness or disorderly conduct and then driving them to the outskirts of the city in the middle of extreme winters and abandoning them without proper clothing or assistance. This police practice was known as "starlight tours." However, three aboriginal men—Rodney Naistus, Lawrence Wegner, and Neil Stonechild—died from hypothermia ("Starlight Tours" from CBC News Online July 2, 2004. Retrieved February 15, 2010). In the United States, there were numerous cases of police using deadly force against mainly Black teenage males such Michael Brown in Ferguson Missouri in 2014 (www.washingtonpost.com/news/storyline/wp/2014/08/12/why-the -police-shooting-riots-in-ferguson-mo-had-little-to-do-with-ferguson/) and

Laquan McDonald in Chicago in 2015 (see www.cbsnews.com/...brief-troubled -life-of-laquan-mcdonald), which resulted in riots, protests, and U.S. federal agencies investigations of police use of deadly force and systematic law enforcement discrimination/punishment.

Despite several devastating acts of terrorism toward the end of the last century in liberal democratic counties, such as the Air India (Flight 182) bombings of mainly Canadian citizens (268 of 329 people killed) and residents on June 22, 1985, and the Oklahoma federal building truck bombing on April 19, 1995, both anti-state and state terrorism acts were predicted to decline sharply in the new millennium. There was even restrained optimism that another long-standing major source of state and anti-state terrorism, the Israeli–Palestinian/ Arab conflict, would diminish with the 1993 Oslo Accords, facilitating an eventual "Two State Solution" (i.e., Arab states formal recognition of Israel and creation of an independent Palestinian state) (Kepel 2004). Also, even though the withdrawal of the Soviet troops from Afghanistan in 1989 resulted in the emergence of Al-Qaeda as a new focal point of terrorism in South Asia and the Middle East in the 1990s, this transnational organization initially appeared limited to these regions. Even the failed (although six people were killed and injured more than a thousand) first attempt to destroy the World Trade Center with a truck bomb in New York on February 26, 1993, brought no overwhelming new policy reaction to an apparent emerging international terrorist threat. Despite the audacity of a direct attack on the U.S. mainland, this incident appeared to be relatively crudely planned and executed, rather than a harbinger of the far more sophisticated attempts that were to follow.

This historical context is important in understanding the enormous counterterrorism intelligence shock that occurred when **Al-Qaeda** succeeded in destroying the World Trade Center and striking against the Pentagon in Washington, DC, in 2001. It is this colossal intelligence failure among the U.S. counterterrorism agencies and the intelligence institutions of its allies that set the stage for the type of terrorism crime prevention policies over the last 15 years and into the foreseeable future. As will be evident, the broader antiterrorism policies emerging since 9/11 are directed not only to organizations, such Al-Qaeda and the **Islamic State** (IS), but also to a broad range of terrorist threats, including those associated with the novel cyberterrorism engaged in by an array of countries, including China, Israel, Russia, and the United States. At the same time, these policies must continue to address the threat posed by traditional and issue terrorist organization, including racist neo-Fascist types and anarchists, along with antiabortion and animal rights groups.

A main theme of this chapter is that, unlike previous historical periods, terrorism crime prevention policies in liberal democracies are confronting diverse forms of terrorist crimes, as well as unprecedentedly complex and rapidly evolving, highly technology-based types of attacks. Given this, liberal democratic crime prevention policies require a global perspective that involves international laws concerning acceptable practices, cross-national/ regional intelligence sharing, joint nation disruptive tactics, and long-term strategic planning to diminish the political, economic, and social risk factors that facilitate the persistence of most forms of terrorism.

Not surprisingly, in the aftermath of 9/11, all liberal democracies have developed common domestic-focused terrorism crime prevention policy approaches with the overwhelming concentration of resources and efforts on multiple forms of national and international intelligence gathering, even for traditional issue terrorism, such as animal rights and environmental issues (see, e.g., Lum et al. 2006). As such, the focus of this chapter is on national domestic anti-state terrorism crime prevention policies in liberal democracies.

Intelligence-Focused Terrorism Crime Prevention Policies and the Emergence of Secular Ideologies

Terrorism differs from most types of crime, not only because of its explicit political motivation, but because it occurs infrequently, yet has the potential to be catastrophic in terms of its numbers of victims, extremely pervasive and long-lasting fear reactions, structural economic costs (e.g., business security, target hardening of transportation facilities), extensive intelligence/ police/criminal justice budget resources, threats to individual civil rights (e.g., privacy, freedom of thought and speech), and discrimination resulting from threat stereotyping of individuals from vulnerable ethnic or ideological groups.

In comparison to other threat-creating crimes, such as gang violence, serial murder, sexual offending, and arson, terrorism typically exhibits an even lower base rate that requires novel and rapidly evolving policies based on intelligence. Of course, there are overlapping or shared strategies, such as the use of informants, wire tapping, and surveillance for all types of serious crimes; however, the differences in prevention policies between violent conventional offences and terrorism are fundamental (see, e.g., Forst 2009). Most serious crimes have obvious geographic foci or "hotspot" where these crimes are most likely to occur (see Chapter 14). Terrorism, while involving the careful selection of targets, can be seen, by the public, as a much more random act. In addition, serious criminal or violent offenders typically have extensive criminal histories, including many negative police contacts and long criminal records. In addition, these types of offenders often associate with other known offenders, engage in opportunistic or impulsive crimes, victimize each other as often as "innocent" victims, and are disproportionately from socially and economically disadvantaged neighborhoods and families. There are exceptions to the impulsive/opportunistic characteristic, such as when organized crime and serious serial criminality are involved; however, these types of offenders typically exhibit impulsivity or opportunistic criminality in their other criminal acts (Hoffman 2006). Although terrorist groups engage in traditional crimes, such as credit card, fraud, kidnapping, and bank robberies to fund their activities, and the distinction between this traditional criminal profile and the terrorist individual profiles can be blurred substantially for the criminal first/then terrorist type, politically motivated individuals who engage in anti-state terrorism in liberal democratic contexts typically engage in extensive planning, which demands emotional discipline, group-based organization, and quick behavioral adjustment in reaction to unanticipated obstacles or the activities of the state.

Recognizing the distinction between a conventional offender and a convictional one, contemporary **counterterrorist** intelligence institutions can be traced back to the French Revolution of 1789–1799. The Republican radical government that replaced the French monarchy and aristocratic government instituted state terrorism primarily in order to preempt reactionary domestic political enemies from reinstituting the monarchy (Tackett 2015). This immediate threat was compounded since foreign monarchies formally had coalesced to invade the nascent Republic of France. Given that the typical institutions for protecting public order, namely, the police and the military, were focused on the "street" threats and foreign armies, a clandestine civilian intelligence group was formed to obtain information on individuals and groups engaged in counterrevolutionary activities, especially those with links to enemy countries (Hibbert 2012). This government needs to gather intelligence information that was seen as critical in order to plan and execute disruptive police and military actions against enemy agents and groups. Another intelligence challenge was related to a broader political motivation, to identify French citizens and foreigners who were potential ideological enemies, rather than just enemy agents. Because opposition to the radical Republican ideology of the revolutionary government was so widespread, this expanded intelligence objective required informants be located even at the neighborhood/small town/village levels (Cohen and Corrado 2005).

The roots of political violence throughout the 19th century can also be traced to other secular-based political ideologies that emerged to challenge the traditionally dominant models of monarchy, aristocracy, theology-based kingdoms, or empires. These ideologies included the Republican, **liberal democracy** ideology first evident in the creation of the United States, socialism, anarchism, and communism. In emerging industrial countries, especially those in Europe and North America, political groups advocating violence and terrorist tactics against the state to force the implementation of their ideologies began to arise. Importantly, international ideological organizations were created to assist national movements. Concurrently, by the end of the 19th century, the entire globe had been colonized and divided into a series of European- and Asian-dominated empires that engaged in economic competition and expansion, as well as espionage and wars. Colonialism also gave rise to nationalist political movements within many of these territories (Chatterjee 1986). These groups were especially inspired by the successful Republican model first evident in the United States in the 18th century and then in France in the 19th century. Also, violence in the form of guerrilla groups (armies holding territories) and terrorist tactics (small clandestine organizations engaged in targeted acts of violence) was employed at different stages in the anticolonial movements.

By the late 19th century, and during the initial two decades of the 20th century, secular ideological terrorists,* in particular **anarchists**, perpetrated bombings and the assassination of key political figures in the United States, throughout Europe, and in Russia (Hoffman 2006). Violence was also being committed by **ethnic–nationalist terrorists** opposed to the European Empires (e.g., Serbian nationalist assassination on June 28, 1914, of Austria–Hungarian Empire's Archduke Ferdinand and his wife in Sarajevo in Bosnia-Herzegovina). In other words, an array of terrorist organizations threatened both liberal democracies and authoritarian regimes during this period before The Great War (i.e., World War 1) and throughout the subsequent decade. It appeared that these terrorist groups intensified their violence in rapidly evolving industrial economies and urban societies, which raised the need for novel government counterterrorism policies to prevent the perpetuation of this form of political crime. In response, all these countries and empires developed counterterrorist policies that were primarily suppression or target hardening oriented and specific agencies to implement them. Several counterterrorism models emerged, largely dependent on the type of national political system, such as whether countries/empires were liberal democracies, authoritarian monarchies, or dictatorships, and whether a country's colonies were involved.

The British Model for the Prevention of Terrorism: An Evolving Historical Perspective

Until the middle of the 20th century, the British Empire was the largest territory internationally. Therefore, the United Kingdom, arguably, more than any other liberal democracy, has experienced the longest and most prominent counterterrorism policy challenges. Not surprisingly, in 1909, it became the first liberal democracy to initiate the contemporary intelligence-based model of counterterrorism. This model is still evident in most liberal democratic countries. Even after undergoing several structural iterations, this

---

* According to Gregg (2014), unlike conventional forms of terrorism, religiously motivated terrorism can be defined as the threat or use of force with the purpose of influencing or coercing governments or populations toward saliently religious goals.

model constitutes one of the longest continues series of policies in response to the evolving forms and profiles of terrorism over the 20th century and the initial decade and a half of the 21st century.

The Secret Service Bureau was created in 1909 to coordinate two key agencies: the Secret Service (MI5—Military Intelligence, Section 5) that was focused on domestic intelligence and the Secret Intelligence Service (MI6—Military Intelligence, Section 6) that was designed to target foreign intelligence (see Figure 11.1). Originally, the primary concern was to counter the extensive German espionage network that had infiltrated the United Kingdom and its colonies, including, most importantly, the increasingly rebellious Ireland (Andrew 2009). Irish nationalist violence emerged in the middle of the 19th century and episodically intensified until it metastasized into guerilla and terrorist organizations, such as **Irish Republican Army** (IRA).

Terrorism by Irish Nationalists and British forms of state terrorism ultimately contributed to the creation of the Catholic Irish Free State in 1922 and the Protestant-dominated Ulster region of Northern Ireland (Valiulis 1992). The latter remained part of the United Kingdom and became the basis for the resurgence of the IRA terrorism and Ulster Protestant terrorist organizations in the late 1960s and early 1970s. For the next 20 years, terrorism intensified in Northern Ireland and spread throughout the United Kingdom. From the 1970s to the late 1990s, counterterrorism primary became a key focus of MI5 in conjunction with metropolitan police forces in mainland Britain (Andrew 2009). Because the IRA's financial and other resources, such as weapons procurement, involved citizens from foreign countries, MI6 was also involved in counterterrorism policies. Of note, since the Good Friday Agreement on Friday, April 10, 1998, only a small breakaway faction of the IRA has continued sporadic terrorist acts (McKearney 2011).

However, after World War I (WWI), MI5 and MI6 concentrated first on international communist espionage threats and subsequently British Fascist and German Nazi espionage and sabotage threats. This initial post-WWI intelligence policy focus reflected the threat posed by the then newly created (1917) Union of Soviet Socialist Republics (USSR). This threat in large part moved beyond traditional espionage to possible USSR infiltration and funding of anti-British government movements involving socialist-focused and communist union organizations that had begun to disrupt the British economy with widespread and general strikes. Therefore, MI5 and MI6 had to coordinate closely concerning the linkages between domestic violence, industrial sabotage, and the USSR's traditional espionage functions. In addition, immediately after WWI, the United Kingdom established a highly secret communications monitoring agency now identified as the Government Communications Headquarters (GCHQ). It coordinates with Britain's Joint Intelligence Committee and the intelligence agencies responsible for implementing counterterrorism policies (Davies 2011).

The British model regarding the prevention of terrorism is premised on the frequent historical connections between domestic terrorist organizations and international/transnational terrorist organizations, including foreign government–sponsored or –directed terrorist groups. In the United Kingdom and in many other liberal democracies, the need for specialized intelligence and coordination with domestic police forces to preempt or disrupt planned terrorist acts and to arrest and prosecute terrorists that are governed by extensive, if often highly controversial, national legislation. Historically, this legislation has attempted to balance the civil rights of British citizens against intelligence and police intrusions into their lives with the need to implement effective anti-state terrorist policies. In contrast, in international contexts, intelligence and disruptive tactics are typically dependent on the type of political system of a particular targeted country. For example, MI6 usually employs more cooperative policies when operating in allied European liberal democracies and in the United States, compared to more clandestine operations in the extremely dangerous intelligence contexts of the Russian Federation, Iran, Saudi Arabia, or Egypt (Dorril 2002).

As mentioned above, the United Kingdom has remained a major international political power. This global position of power partly explains the use of specialized domestic- and foreign-focused agencies, policies, and national intelligence and counterterrorism laws. These laws have evolved primarily because of changing international and national political contexts, military and intelligence technologies, and globalization trends, such as changing immigration profiles and access to global transportation, and United Nations–based International Law regarding human rights, genocide, terrorism, asylum, and torture (see, e.g., the UN Convention Against Torture and Other Cruel, Inhuman, or Degrading Treatment or Punishment, 1987, and the UN Convention on the Prevention and Punishment of the Crime of Genocide 1948).

The counterterrorism policy challenge in the United Kingdom and other liberal democracies involves the delicate balance of civil liberties and national security. MI5's mandate, for example, resulted in its agents and informants infiltrating traditional domestic civil institutions, such as universities, media, unions, and religious institutions. In other words, right from their initiation, British intelligence agencies, whether preventing espionage, general violence, or targeted terrorist acts, were and still are faced with the potential of violating civil rights and even criminal laws (Wright and Kreissl 2014). The latter situations arise most explicitly when agents, or informants, establish their credibility within the targeted organization by initiating, organizing, or engaging in serious criminal acts. The construct "agent provocateur" refers to the subcategory of such acts where the illegal act likely would not have occurred without the agent's involvement.

The second historical policy challenge involves MI6 activities in foreign countries. The main issues involve not espionage, but "disruptive acts," especially those that result in the arrest, torture, or death of agents and innocent

BOX 11.1   CYBERTERRORISM, THREATS, AND CYBERSECURITY

The growth of technology not only has many advantages but, increasingly, also poses numerous potential threats to people, governments, and those agencies or organizations that rely on it. This is clearly evident in the increasing trend in the growth of cybercrimes globally (e.g., Skipwire in 2012; Paypal in 2010; Titan Rain in 2004, etc.). Not only has cyberterrorism become a major global concern in recent years, but international efforts to combat or prevent cyberattackers and cyberterrorists are becoming increasingly more challenging as their techniques and strategies continually evolve.

The first ever reported cyberterrorist attack took place in the year 1982 where the 414s broke into 60 computer systems at institutions ranging from the Los Alamos Laboratories to Manhattan's Memorial Sloan–Kettering Cancer Center and served to demonstrate the destructive power of cyber(terrorist) attacks. Since then, cyberattacks have become one of the most powerful and destructive forms of terrorist attacks. Cyberspace is today an arena for the myriad of computing devices and virtually no corner of the world does not have some kind of Internet access. Compounded by the presence of autonomous bodies, numerous technological developments posit not merely new advances but also new threats. In fact, it is estimated that by the end of 2020, online devices are projected to outnumber human users by a ratio of 6:1.

Cyberterrorists are made not born. They typically enter into cyberterrorism because (1) they are attracted toward the terrorist organizations because of their ideologies and support systems, (2) they are trained technological persons and professional hackers who are then hired by terrorist organizations, (3) they represent a new group of individuals who join together to achieve certain goals or a few frustrated individuals try to create damages against the society, or (4) they are individuals who would like to experiment and show off their capabilities to the world.

Some of the main forms of cyber threats include data theft, destruction of E-Governance, E-sources, and E-resources; Distributed Denial of Services Attack (DDSA); network damage and disruptions; and the most recent version of cloud computing and security threats. Cloud computing is the result of evolution and adoption of existing technologies and paradigms. The goal of cloud computing is to allow users to take benefit from all of these technologies, without the need for deep knowledge or expertise with each one of them.

The ability to prevent **cyberterrorism** lies with the ability to safely secure cyberspace. One of the primary prevention strategies is the principle of target hardening. For the case of cybercrime prevention, target hardening may be done using various technologies and products (e.g., firewalls, applying cryptology, and intrusion detection) and procedures to protect the information technology assets owned or operated by an individual or organization. Drawing on target hardening concept, there are five technological aspects that are considered important when preventing cyberterrorism incidents. They include the following: (1) strengthening the intelligence gathering, applying technology for effectively evaluating and acting on intelligence; (2) securing SCADA systems for managing critical physical and telecommunications infrastructures; (3) upgrading the security of the information assets; (4) forming emergency response teams in every State of a country; and (5) developing disaster management techniques.

Despite the proliferation of cyberattacks and cyberterrorism, the key to combatting and preventing its cancerous spread is cooperation from everyone. It is also increasingly important to raise the awareness of all issues to help counter such threats. In so doing, it will build public capacity to build and work in a safer and more secure environment for all.

victims, and involvement in "regime change," such as the involvement of MI6 in Iran in the 1953 Mordad coup that replaced the democratically elected government of Prime Minister Mohammad Mosaddegh with Mohammad Reza Shah Pahlavi. This event remains a key rationale for the current Iranian theocratic government's use of state terrorism in Iran, its support of espionage, and the use of its agents and those of its proxy guerilla/terrorist organizations, such as Hezbollah, against targets in other countries (Kinzer 2003). Both MI6 and the U.S. Central Intelligence Agency (CIA) were directed by their respective governments to undertake this regime change for strategic political and economic reasons that stemmed from the Cold War. In addition, British and American regimes and multinational oil corporations were concerned over the control and prices, which were influenced significantly by Iran's vast oil and gas reserves (Roosevelt 1979).

Since 9/11, there is little doubt that terrorism crime prevention policies and related programs in the United Kingdom, and in most other liberal democracies, have included a major, if not primary, focus on **jihadist terrorism** threats (see Box 11.1). As will be evident, part of the ongoing policy challenges has been the considerable difficulty of intelligence agencies to sufficiently understand jihadist terrorism and, consequently, anticipate and implement effective counterterrorism programs. While the United States experienced the single most destructive jihadist terrorist attack in 2001, the United Kingdom has had to deal with more persistent and diverse jihadist terrorism threats. Among European countries, the United Kingdom has large Muslim populations from the Middle East, Africa, and, most notably, its former colonies in South Asia. These Muslim citizens and residents span multiple generations, increasingly including those who were born and raised in Britain. Importantly, many of these individuals and their families retain their ethnic/religious cultural values and traditions, maintain contact with their ancestral countries and relatives, travel back and forth to these countries, and identify, empathize, and sympathize with negative political and social dilemmas, such as poverty, persistent political violence, and civil or guerilla wars in their ancestral homelands (see, e.g., Gerges 2007).

Anti-Jihadist Terrorism Policies

Western intelligence agencies were aware of Al-Qaeda (translation: "The Base," "The Fundamental") since it was formed in 1988 to coordinate Arab mujahedeen fighters drawn to Pakistan and Afghanistan to fight the Soviet army's occupation of the latter country. Again, the Cold War context is vital to understand why the threat of jihadist terrorist organizations was underestimated up to 9/11. For example, an internal British Security Service's 1994 study of the "Origins of Terrorism" concluded that transitional Islamist terrorism was not a serious threat and was only a "potent force when allied to national interests" (Andrew 2009, p. 799). In other words, only when countries, such as Iran, choose to utilize these Islamist terrorist organizations did it become a threat to the United Kingdom. By the end of 1995, MI5 reported to the heads of the special branches that

> ...suggestions in the press of a worldwide Islamic extremist network poised to launch terrorist attacks against the West are greatly exaggerated... The contact between Islamic extremists in various countries appears to be largely opportunistic at present and seems unlikely to result in the emergence of a potent transnational force.

> **C.M. Andrew**
> *2009, p. 801*

However, in the same year, the British Security Service opened a permanent file on Osama bin Laden because "No matter where you look in studying Islamic Extremism from Kashmir to Algeria, the name bin Laden seems to crop up" (as quoted in Andrew 2009, p. 801). Rather than being recognized as Al-Qaeda's primary planner and leader, bin Laden was seen principally as a financier of Islamists terrorism (CIA 1996). The turning point occurred in

1998, when Al-Qaeda suicide bomb trucks destroyed the American embassies in Nairobi, Kenya, and Dar es Salaam, Tanzania. By 1999, a Security Service Report included intelligence indicating that, under bin Laden's direction, Al-Qaeda had planned bomb, missile, and biological toxin attacks, as well as kidnappings and hijackings against American targets (Andrew 2009). Equally disconcerting, these attacks were planned across most of the globe, including the United Kingdom (Andrew 2009). At the same time, a fundamental policy and intelligence challenge was the possibility that Al-Qaeda was conducting a disinformation campaign of fear among Western governments and citizens. Yet, as early as 1998–1999, the G9 Branch of the British Security Service created by MI5,* responsible for Middle Eastern counterterrorism, raised the possibility of racialization nearly 15 years before it became a major policy challenge:

> In recent years, we have given much thought to how to identify those in the UK who develop extreme Islamic views and to deter them from subsequently becoming involved in terrorism. The challenge for us is to find ways of predicting the associations and conditioning factors in the UK which convert young Muslims into extremists, but to do so in a way which does not exacerbate religious and racial sentiments. In short, we need to understand how individuals who are attracted by militant Islam at home become terrorist or potential terrorists when overseas, and to find ways of undermining that connection.
>
> **C.M. Andrew**
> *2009, p. 805*

The primary importance of Islamic counterterrorism was reflected in part by the appointment of the G8 Branch's counterterrorism leading analyst, Jonathan Evans, to the position of Director General of the Security Branch in 2007. After the 9/11 attacks, a major counterterrorism concern was preventing Al-Qaeda from obtaining fissionable material for a "dirty" nuclear bomb, or biological or chemical weapons. The obvious immediacy was the enormous damage and subsequent fear and chaos that would follow such an attack. The economic costs of not only the damage caused by destroying the World Trade Center buildings, but subsequent and still continuing security measures were estimated to be in the trillions of dollars. These costs have been borne primarily by the United States but also affect all countries with transportation and trade links to the United States and allied countries (Bloomberg and Hess 2009; Blunk et al. 2006; Yerger 2011). In effect, in comparison to any other crime prevention policy, counterterrorism has had to address the most exorbitant economic costs and manage the greatest public fear challenges (see, e.g., Bjorgo 2013; Mackay and Jevan 2012).

---

* In 1991, MI5 established T Branch to handle Irish and domestic terrorism.

Interagency Intelligence Integration

After 9/11, more than any other period historically, MI5 and MI6 collaborated closely and willingly despite the long-standing differences in organizational cultures and rivalries (Andrews 2009). Other countries similarly exhibited difficulties in coordinating their responses to real and imagined terrorist threats. For example, America's Federal 9/11 Commission Report cited the lack of collaboration between the Federal Bureau of Investigation (FBI) and the CIA as a central contributing factor to the successful attacks (Kean and Hamilton 2004). The legislation that created the massive U.S. Department of Homeland Security was designed to force such collaboration and coordination between domestic and foreign intelligence agencies, as well as other federal agencies involved with potential security roles, such as Defence Intelligence, Coast Guard, U.S. Customs, Transport Security Agency, and Drug Enforcement Agency (see Figure 11.2). In addition, intelligence collaboration among the FBI and state and local police agencies was institutionalized.

While the Al-Qaeda cells in the 9/11 attacks were in the United States before the attack, police in these cities and states were unaware of their potential presence. For example, a North Carolina State Trooper had stopped a car with one Al-Qaeda cell driving to the Boston area from Florida for a traffic violation, but was unaware of impending attacks somewhere in the United States, despite increasing CIA and FBI intelligence to that effect (Britain 2015). An important part of the multilevel integrative terrorism crime prevention policy strategy, therefore, is the utilization of information and intelligence from local government, police, and service agencies that engage in daily contact with the public. For example, daily postal services or weekly garbage collection services typically involve workers who observe routine behaviors and are in the position to identify unusual or suspicious incidents that might add up to a pattern when linked to other information already in the terrorist national information base (Cohen and Corrado 2005).

For example, sanitation workers in the British city of Birmingham noticed large empty bottles used to possibly mix toxic ingredients needed for the production of biological weapons, such as niacin. This strategy of incorporating a broad array of "first responders" and the general public in gathering information has become routine for major public events (see, e.g., the Suspicious Incident Reporting system of the Royal Canadian Mounted Police [RCMP]; RCMP 2011), such as the Olympics, where the concentration of large crowds provide "soft targets" for both traditional bomb attacks and chemical or biological attacks. In the United Kingdom, in 2003, according to then Director General of MI5, Jonathan Evans, it was a "tip-off from a member of the public that provided critical information that instigated the largest initial counter-terrorism operation in the UK intelligence-police operation CREVICE. It was directed at a network of five jihadists involved in planning bomb attacks in public places, including shopping centres, pubs, and night clubs where mass casualties were inevitable" (Andrews 2009, p. 817).

Regarding intelligence and disruptive crime prevention strategies, the jihadist threat was diffused, as the Muslim population in the United Kingdom was not only substantial (1.55 million in 2001 and 2.71 million in 2011, constituting 5% of the population) but also concentrated in major metropolitan regions, primarily in England (approximately 2.6 million), with far fewer in Scotland (approximately 77,000) (Muslim Council of Britain 2015) and Wales (approximately 48,000) (Office for National Statistics 2012a,b). In comparison, the Muslim population in Canada was less than 1 million. In addition, densely populated English cities are relatively close to one another geographically and are linked by an array of easily accessed transportation systems, including motorways, rail, and airplanes. This combination of relative density of ethnic population and transportation networks enhances the capabilities of even a relatively small jihadi cell and greatly complicates the efforts of police and intelligence services to identify and monitor all potential threats. In response to this distribution of potential terrorist cells and the recruitment of individuals, the British Security Service further developed their regionalization strategy by setting up regional offices in all of the major population regions in the United Kingdom. This policy relies on close cooperation with local police forces for intelligence gathering, as well as the assessment of leads by the Joint Terrorism Intelligence Analysis Centre (JTAC) established in 2003 in London (see Figure 11.1).

In order to protect the Critical National Infrastructure (CNI) and corporations, as well as evaluate threat information from the public, the JTAC coordinated with the National Infrastructure Security Co-ordination Centre (NISCC) to issue "E" threats or potentially devastating virus programs, particularly for media and businesses. Another MI5 component, the National Security Advice Center (NSAC), was initiated in 2004 to provide the program's advice beyond CNI clients to the local governments, medium and small businesses, and the general public. In 2007, the NISCC and NASC services were combined into the more integrated institution, the interdepartmental Centre for the Protection of the National Infrastructure (CPNI) (Andrews 2009). In effect, a key counterterrorism policy trend in the initial decade of this century has been the ever-increasing coordination of vast amounts of potential terrorist threat information from an array of sources, including the traditional and new intelligence and police agencies, as well as local governments, businesses, media, and the public. Importantly, this policy also includes the targeted dissemination of threat information and specific terrorism prevention programs to key sections of British society. This strategy for attempting to prevent terrorism further reflects the ability of terrorists to shift victim target locations continuously in response to various attempts at "target hardening." For example, as airport screening technologies and surveillance programs increased over the last several decades, terrorist targets shifted to the far more vulnerable transportation systems, such as trains and buses.

Antiterrorism intelligence has also been bolstered by the use of closed-circuit television cameras (**CCTVs**) in public places. CCTV has been utilized directly and routinely by local police forces, particularly in the United Kingdom in its major cities, and its use has now spread to more than 100 countries and regions as part of comprehensive urban public safety strategies (Kruegle 2007). While the focus of CCTV is typically street crimes, rather than the tracking potential or actual terrorists, this technology did provide identification of the individuals involved in the cell that carried out the July 7, 2007, London Tube and bus bombings that killed 52 riders and injured hundreds (BBC News July 2008). Advances in **facial recognition technology** will increase the importance of CCTV in the monitoring, disruption, and prevention of soft target attacks, particularly in large and densely populated cities, such as London and New York. The New York City Police Department's (NYPD) large counterterrorism unit has focused its CCTVs in the financial district in lower Manhattan because of its obvious symbolic association with the 9/11 destruction of the World Trade Center and the continued presence of numerous Wall Street international banking and securities exchange institutions. Like the broad CCTV coverage in much of London's business districts, tourist sites, and transit, the NYPD plans to extend its CCTV coverage throughout Manhattan (Francescani, June 2013, Reuters Online).

Another counterterrorism intelligence component that has developed exponentially is **network analysis technology**. This analytical and visualization software technology has been implemented by police forces, intelligence agencies, and the military to connect offenders operating in group structures, such as organized crime, terrorists, and spies. This technology allows agencies to identify potential networks of terrorists based on various contact types among members, such as phone call, e-mails, travel, financial transactions, family, friendships, previous criminal partnerships, and relationship patterns, such as frequency timing, length, and location of contacts. Again, Snowden and *Wikileaks* exposed the vastness of the scale of tracking by key American intelligence and monitoring agencies under the direction of the National Security Agency.

In response to the relatively new phenomenon involving the radicalization of youth to engage in terrorist acts and join jihadist military groups abroad via the Internet, counterintelligence agencies have relied on innovative algorithm software program methods to "crawl" through massive amounts of Internet communications to assist in identifying potential jihadist recruits. Moreover, the now standard array of intelligence-based counterterrorism programs have expanded enormously (Counter-terrorism intelligence, policy and theory since 9/11. *Terrorism and Political Violence.* 27(2): 2015; Newton Lee, *Counterterrorism and Cybersecurity: Total Information Awareness* (Second Edition), Switzerland: Springer International Publishing, 2015). First, the logging of mail has become virtually all-encompassing. For example, in the United States, every piece of mail, 160 billion pieces in 2012, has its exterior photographed and archived under the Mail Isolation and Control Tracking program, and this database is available, under certain legally specified conditions, to intelligence and police agencies. Second, the traditional wire tapping of phones has expanded through the use of speech to text programs and social network analysis. The infiltration of smartphones with new tracking device technologies has similarly expanded this intelligence method. Third, Internet tracking, including the unresolved controversies surrounding access to data sources, such as those maintained by multinational phone companies, and social networking companies, such as Google and Facebook, has allowed for unprecedented access to information about members of the public. Fourth, the data mining of financial transactions is increasingly being facilitated through the use of "big data" analytic techniques. Fifth, in addition to CCTV, airborne surveillance technologies, such as drones, are being used to identify individuals and vehicles in locations and over time. At the same time, agencies still engage in traditional covert operations, such as the undercover infiltration of "activist" groups potentially associated with terrorist cells, or with support functions, such as recruitment or financing.

Finally, there has been a notable rise in the number of strength of links between national and foreign intelligence agencies. Historically, these programs have gone beyond intelligence gathering and engaged in disruptive activities designed to stop terrorist attacks, to degrade them, or to retaliate through a variety of strategies discussed below.

Foreign Intelligence and Disruptive Programs

While the focus of counterterrorism programs has shifted at different times between domestic and foreign concerns, it is domestically that much of the focus has been placed in liberal democracies. In the United Kingdom, Andrews (2009), in his official history of MI5, stated that "SIS (Security Intelligence Service, MI6) disruption campaigns against terrorism groups abroad (almost 50% greater in 2006 than in 2005) also made an increasing contribution to counterterrorism. In total, 10% of the members of the Security Service CT (counterterrorism) teams were SIS officers. By 2007, over one-third of GCHQ's effort was devoted to counter terrorism" (Andrews 2009, p. 824).

In contrast, while Canada's major intelligence agency, the Canadian Security Intelligence Service (CSIS), has some foreign intelligence capacity, along with the Canadian Armed Services and the Canadian Security Establishment (see Figure 11.3), it apparently devotes few resources to foreign operations, particularly any involving disruptive antiterrorist targets. In fact, before the passage of the Anti-Terrorism Act in 2015, CSIS did not have the mandate to participate in foreign operations (Bronskill 2015). Instead, CSIS tends to rely on its close connections with the CIA, MI6, and other allied foreign intelligence agencies for information relevant to foreign-based terror threats to Canada (Government of Canada 2013). Domestically, in contrast, a special counterterrorism section, the National Security Criminal Investigations Program, under the RCMP, engages in disruptive operations in Canada.

There also have been several notorious cases where CSIS and the RCMP were accused of coordinating with the FBI and the CIA to engage in disruptive operations, such as the rendition of Canadian citizen Mahar Arar (1970–) in collaboration with the United States to government national security services in Damascus, Syria. Arar was detained in September 2002 at John F. Kennedy International Airport in New York while in transit from Tunis on his way home to Ottawa, Canada. He was subject to torture during

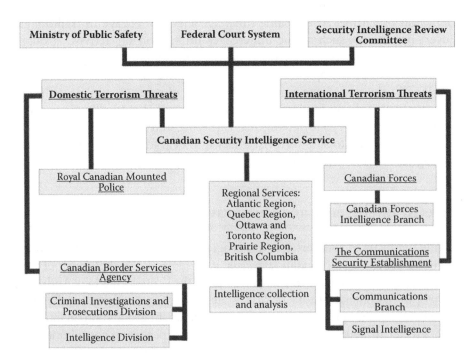

Figure 11.3 Canada's counterterrorism structure. (Created by Maike Knoechelmann.)

his one-year imprisonment in Syria, yet he subsequently was vindicated of any terrorism involvement by a Canadian federal commission and received a $10.5 million financial settlement from the Canadian government (*Dark Days: The Story of Four Canadians Tortured in the Name of Fighting Terror* by Kerry Pither. ISBN 978-0-670-06853-1).

With the major exception of the United States and several of its allies in Eastern Europe, such as Poland and Romania, the use of torture to prevent terrorist acts by liberal democratic countries has generally been denied. There are ongoing political controversies in the United States about its extensive use of waterboarding and extreme deprivation techniques, such as constant loud music, sleep disruption, verbal and physical threats, and cultural humiliation, against arrested or captured Al-Qaeda members, and the rendition of terrorist suspects to countries that use torture against accused jihadists, such as Egypt (Senate Select Committee on Intelligence 2014). The use of these types of techniques reflects the desperation that liberal democratic governments face in trying to prevent a major terrorism crime by obtaining actionable and relevant information in a timely fashion in order to prevent an attack. In addition to the issue of the national and international legality of the use of torture as part of any antiterrorism policies, there are fundamental intelligence concerns about the validity or usefulness of the information extracted (Schiemann 2015). While some people, such as former U.S. Vice President Dick Cheney, maintain that torture has prevented major attacks in the United States and remains a necessary and effective part of counterterrorism strategies (Shane 2014), others argue that there is little evidence to support the notion that torture-based information has prevented any major terrorist attacks (Arrigo and Wagner 2007; Schiemann 2012).

Other strategies, such as the use of major military interventions, such as the invasion of Iraq and Afghanistan, and the use of airstrikes in Syria, are also believed to be essential in countering jihadist terrorism. For example, the former Canadian government led by Prime Minister Stephen Harper argued that the use of Canadian fighter jets in attacking IS military targets in Syria and Iraq was essential in preventing or mitigating jihadist terrorist threats in Canada (*Toronto Star*, March 14, 2015). In contrast, the Parliamentary opposition leaders, Tom Mulcair of the New Democratic Party and Justin Trudeau of the Liberal Party, rejected this counterterrorism tactic because they considered it ineffective and not authorized in international law by either the United Nations or the North Atlantic Treaty Organization, both of which Canada is a member.

Similarly, there is an intense controversy concerning the use of targeted killing against terrorists through the use of drones (see Tables 11.3 and 11.4). Again, drone attacks are an integral part of the counter jihadist strategy used by the United States and Israel, which claim that it is justified by both international self-defense laws and U.S. law (Council on Foreign Relations 2013).

Table 11.3   Controversies Surrounding Targeted Killings

For Targeted Killing	Against Targeted Killing
Drones	**Drones**
Drones are prohibited weapons under international humanitarian law because they may cause, or have the effect of causing, necessarily indiscriminate killings of civilians	Given the accuracy of drones, the use of this technology is not necessarily different from the use of other weapons such as guns, armed helicopters, or gunships that fire missiles
Drones	**Drones**
Legal under international humanitarian law and illegal under human rights law	Illegal under international humanitarian law and human rights law
New category between combatant and civilian must be introduced: unlawful combatant, a civilian engaging in unlawful military action which becomes a legitimate target	Civilians may not become legitimate targets
Armed conflict can be state vs. state or state vs. non-state actor (terrorist group) because non-state actors these days can have effective armies with sophisticated weapons	Armed conflict legally only occurs state vs. state and therefore human rights law applies when dealing with a terrorist group

Note: Created by Maike Knoechelmann.

Since 2009, the United States has successfully targeted four of its citizens abroad, including most notoriously Anwar al-Awlaki and his son in 2013 in Yemen. Al-Awlaki was one of the purported leaders of Al-Qaeda in the Arab Peninsula and was renowned for his sophisticated use of the Internet for disseminating the jihadist message to recruit Western members to implement terrorist attacks against American targets (Brachman and Levine 2011). According to American political leaders, drone assassinations of jihadists are justified because their leaders and members constitute a persistent and direct terrorist threat to the safety of American citizens and property. In effect, drone strikes remove lay leaders from their propaganda and terrorist planning roles, and, therefore, are also essential to proactive/preventive counterterrorism policies (Council on Foreign Relations 2012).

In contrast to the above primary counterterrorism policies, there is little debate concerning the use of the more secondary-level prevention strategy that focuses on extensive passenger and baggage screening and no-fly passenger lists for all airliners leaving from and destined to the United States. While the safety of the airplane and passengers can be considered a primary strategy, the denial of transportation to training camps or terrorist planning meetings are secondary prevention. However, the relatively recent phenomenon of IS using the Internet to recruit youth in Western countries to travel to Syria and Iraq has resulted in the need for additional travel restrictions and

Table 11.4   Countries Using Targeted Killings

Targeted Killing Policy	The Russian Federation	Israel	The United States of America
Official declaration of use	2006	November 2000	November 2002
Government policy	May be employed as a counterterrorism measure. When conducted abroad, the president needs approval from the federation council	Israeli security forces may employ targeted killing operations in self-defense against actors that the Palestinian authority is unwilling or unable to stop, investigate, and prosecute	The CIA is not required to identify its target by name; rather, targeting decisions may be based on surveillance and pattern of life assessments. Targeted killings are part of the fight against Al-Qaeda
Legality	Based on a 2006 national counter-terrorism law, principle of self-defense (UN charter) and IHL	Based on a 2006 Israeli supreme court ruling, principle of self-defense (UN charter) and IHL	Principle of self-defense (UN charter), IHL, U.S. national law
Employed where?	Mostly Chechnya but also most recently Syria	Gaza Strip, West Bank, Lebanon, and Syria	Afghanistan, Iraq, Pakistan, Yemen, and Syria

Note: Created by Maike Knoechelmann.

related policies for those identified as a risk for terrorism, such as confiscating passports and de-radicalization programs. Again, the history of post-9/11 terrorism crime prevention policies is characterized by frequent adjustments to the structure of intelligence and police agencies, domestic and international laws, and policies related to programs directed at key community institutions, such as mosques, schools, and families at risk for radicalization because of the persistency of organizational change among radical Muslim nationalist and jihadist terrorist organizations.

Arguably, one trend is the apparent increase in the level of religious ideological extremism and terrorist violence not only against enemy combatants and noncombatant children, women, and the elderly, but also within their own organizations, such as targeting rivals perceived as disloyal members and religious apostate (see, e.g., Gregg 2014). As mentioned above, the most recent policy challenge in liberal democracies is the surprising "success" of IS in attracting adolescents and young adults from Western countries to support and participate in the creation and sustenance of the **Caliphate**, and to engage in terrorist attacks in their homelands and in their countries of origins in the West. Part of this counterterrorism policy challenge involves the "home-grown" individual or small group of terrorists. Unlike the typical pattern of the previous decades of recruitment (systematic intelligence-based screening), training (usually in jihadist training camps), and planning by senior terrorist operations' leaders, current jihadist terrorist organizations often simply provide the motivation or inspiration to plan and carry out terrorist attacks.

The Jihadist Radicalization Challenge and Prevention

The (current) civil war in Syria began in 2011 as the Arab Spring movement against secular, largely military-based or backed dictatorships spread from Tunisia in 2010 across North Africa and into the Middle East (Gilsinan 2015). Importantly, the IS has recruited its members from Syria, as well as from an array of Arab and non-Arab foreign countries, including Western democracies. The surprise for western intelligence agencies was the IS's leadership's ability to adapt quickly to military contingencies, such as the weakness of the Syrian government's military in eastern and northern Syria and the Iraqi military's weakness in their Sunni regions to restructure their military and political organizational structure. This reorganization has involved integrating largely foreign recruits with Syrian and Iraqi members into highly mobile battle units. The Caliphate has become an integral part of IS's recruitment strategy globally because the Salafi extreme orthodox religious doctrine mandates that all Muslims must reside in a Caliphate-structured society. The IS appeal to youth, in particular, is that Western liberal democratic values and societies are completely anathema to their ideological interpretation of Islam. In effect, Muslims are required to both defend Islam against contemporary Western "Crusaders" and partake in the original 6th-century lifestyle promulgated by Mohammed in the Koran and subsequent related sacred and inspired teachings (Nimer 2002). The latter focuses on traditional religious-defined communal entities involving the primacy of the extended family rigid gender roles, strict morality, and the dominance of the theocratic political structure over all aspects of the members of the Caliphate. Unlike any prevention programs directed at traditional crimes, the unique challenge in responding to jihadist radicalization threat requires that the radical fundamentalist religious message be responded to in a somewhat similar religious theme, such as the notion that the jihadist/Salafi perspective is not justified and allowed according to the authentic interpretation of Muslim religious text and teachings. A second program theme involves responding to the identity and social needs of youth and young adults in highly competitive, individualized, aspiritual, sexualized, and materialistic liberal democratic societies. In other words, the inability to successfully integrate young Muslims into the dominant culture of Western societies, or their unwillingness to integrate, will continue to pose significant terrorism prevention challenges. The apparent success of this recruitment/ radicalization policy has been widely reported in the international media (cnn.com/2015/02/25/middleeast/isis-kids-propaganda/index.html).

Conclusion

On January 7, 2015, two brothers attacked the offices of Charlie Hebdo, a weekly newspaper in Paris, killing 11 people and injuring another 11 people. The gunmen identified themselves as being members of the Al-Qaeda in Yemen (Schmitt et al. 2015). On November 13, 2015, a number of well-coordinated terror attacks were perpetrated in Paris and Saint-Denis, France, killing 130 and injuring nearly 400 others (Nossiter and Gladstone 2015). The IS claimed responsibility for this attack and, it appears, that the attack was planned and executed by a cell from Brussels. Finally, on December 2, 2015, a husband and wife attacked a holiday party by the Department of Health in San Bernardino, California. In this attack, 14 people were killed and another 22 were injured. At the time of this writing, it is believed that this was a lone-wolf, but Islamic extremist-inspired attack (Nossiter et al. 2015). What these three attacks demonstrate is that each geographic region has its own unique challenges with jihadist extremism and that the various forms of this type of terrorism is changing at such a rapid rate that it is very difficult for terrorism prevention policies to keep pace.

When comparing terrorism prevention programs to traditional strategies designed to deter and respond to conventional crimes, it is vital to keep in mind that terrorism is enormously complex and has no generally accepted universal definition not only because of the nature of the acts being perpetrated but also because of the primacy of political themes (see Table 11.5).

Given that there are so many different acts that are defined as acts of terrorism, so many difficult groups that are labeled terrorists, and so many different goals that terrorists are trying to achieve, it is not surprising that it is extremely difficult to develop policies that are effective against all terrorist groups everywhere. However, one policy constant is the central role that specialized intelligence agencies have had, typically, in coordination with specialized police counterterrorism units. In other words, while the type of profile of terrorist organizations changes, and the strategies and tactics change substantially, the institutional framework for attempting to prevent terrorism largely remains the same. Of course, even among liberal democracies, counterterrorism policies reflect the peculiar domestic political and broader geopolitical circumstances of each liberal democracy. For obvious historical reasons, beyond the scope of this chapter to discuss, the United

Table 11.5 Debate on the Need for an International Terrorism Definition

For an International Definition	Against an International Definition
Needed because terrorism is a form of war (war is a continuation of politics just as terrorism)	Not needed because terrorism is a form of criminality
Needed to create consensus among states. Otherwise, one's man's terrorist is another man's freedom fighter	Not needed. Every country can have their own definition and deal with terrorism on their own
Needed to create international laws to fight terrorism	Not needed. National laws will suffice
Needed to create specific terrorism laws because of its political nature	Not needed. Form of criminality; therefore, national crime legislation can be applied
Needed to create international cooperation among states to beat the Jihadi terrorist network	Not needed for international cooperation Case-by-case strategy
Needed for extradition laws, stopping incitement, and stopping funding, and this will affect the terrorists' behavior	Not needed because those laws can be created through state-to-state negotiation and basing itself on existing national laws and the terrorist will not obey any laws whether they are established internationally through a definition or through national legislation
Not having a definition creates gray zones in which terrorism can operate	Criminalizing certain crimes that overlap with terrorism will suffice to punish and prevent terrorism
Not having a definition increases the chances of political manipulation, which can lead to state-sponsored terrorism	Even with a definition, certain states will continue to sponsor terrorism and deny their involvement

Source: From Ganor, B. (2007). The Counter-Terrorism Puzzle: A Guide for Decision-Makers.
Note: Created by Maike Knoechelmann.

States and Israel, for example, have had the most comprehensive institutional structures, including major military strategies to respond to an array of terrorist threats since the second half of the 20th century. However, the United States does not provide an adequate model of terrorism prevention for others to follow because of the sheer enormity of the counterterrorism complex. In effect, the United States is an anomaly among Western democracies. In contrast, the United Kingdom's model is arguably a better reflection of the approach typically taken in Europe and Canada.

In assessing the effectiveness of the prevention of terrorism policies, it is necessary to first identify the specific types of terrorist threat profiles that each country confronts, understanding that specific terrorist threat types are often directed at all liberal democracies, even though a particular country might experience the actual terror attack. Second, the criterion for the effectiveness of crime prevention policies is deceptively simple, namely, the absence of terrorist attacks. Nonetheless, terrorism is fundamentally distinguished from other serious crimes because of its catastrophic potential harm, which, like major earthquakes, requires both short-term and long-term prevention and mitigation policies. For example, all liberal democratic nations have long implemented short-term "target hardening" programs for obvious major government and infrastructure facilities, but few have sufficiently anticipated and prepared for an organized and complex terrorist strategy, such as hijacking multiple airplanes and crashing them into major buildings. Because the profile of potential novel terrorist acts can evolve quickly, long-term projections of such threats have become routine in intelligence agency planning.

Regarding counterterrorism policy parallels with other types of crime prevention, it is not surprising that several of the key strategies utilized against organized crime are very similar to those used against terror groups. The strategies against the latter are intelligence-led and involve integrated multipolice, multijurisdictional, and multiagency coordination and cooperation. Nonetheless, while the drug cartels can threaten the political integrity of countries indirectly through corruption and extensive civil violence, and directly, on occasion, by cooperating with ideological terrorist organizations, their primary criminal objective is monetary and not political. In contrast, while some terror groups are interested in changing a specific policy in a particular region, others are interested in completely restructuring the political, economic, and social structure of a state, while others are focused on imposing their religious views upon the entire world. Western democracies are challenged with preventing all of these forms of terrorism, while walking the delicate balance of effective counterterrorism and the rule of law.

Glossary of Key Terms

Al-Qaeda: Established by Osama bin Laden in the late 1980s, Al-Qaeda is a Salafi jihadist group motivated by the principles of Wahhabism. Its ideology is based on using armed conflict to spread Islam and to rid the Muslim world of any Western influence and implement an Islamic Caliphate under Sharia law.

Anarchism: A political ideology that promotes self-governed societies without the formal institutions of the state.

Caliphate: A form of Islamic government.

Counterterrorism: The strategies, tactics, and initiatives that governments use to respond to and prevent terrorism.

Cyberterrorism: The FBI defines cyberterrorism as a "premeditated, politically motivated attack against information, computer systems, computer programs, and data which results in violence against non-combatant targets by sub-national groups or clandestine agents."

Ethnic–nationalist terrorism: Politically motivated violence based on ethnicity or a desire to create a state based on ethnic criteria and is frequently produced by the discriminatory practices of the majority against an identifiable ethnic group. Some of the more well-known ethnic nationalist terrorist groups include Le Front de Liberation de Quebec (FLQ) in Quebec, the Basque Homeland and Freedom (ETA) in Spain, the Irish Republican Army (IRA) in Ireland, and the Sikh separatist movement in India.

Facial recognition technology: Applications used to identify a person from a digital image or a video source by comparing the image to those in a facial database.

Islamic State: Founded by al-Zarqawi in 1999, Islamic State is a political and military group that wants to impose its version on Sunni Wahhabi Islam. The Islamic State promotes a strict adherence to Sharia law and the overthrow of all regimes to be replaced by the Islamic State.

Jihadist terrorism: Acts of terrorism committed by Muslims who hold particular interpretations of the Quran and other Islamic teachings as the motivations or justifications for violence.

Liberal democracy: A political ideology characterized by multiparty elections, the rule of law, separation of powers between different branches of government, and a focus on human rights, civil liberties, and political freedoms. Examples of liberal democracies include the United States of America, Canada, and the United Kingdom.

Network analysis technology: Computer applications designed to find and visually display links between people, places, and objects in time and space.

Terrorism: Politically motivated, systematic violence or the threat of violence that is designed to instill extreme fear in an audience that is distinct from the immediate victim(s) of the violence.

Discussion Questions

1. How effective do you think the various countries' terrorism prevention strategies have been?
2. What terrorism prevention strategies would be most successful in responding to Islamic fundamentalist terror?
3. What role should citizens and communities play in preventing terrorism?
4. What is the utility of a policy of targeted killing?
5. What role, if any, should the use of torture play in terrorism prevention strategies?

6. In what way, if any, have terrorism prevention policies contributed to the rise of Islamic fundamentalist terrorism?
7. In what ways is terrorism in the 21st century different from terrorism in the early and mid-20th century?

Recommended Web Links

http://www.nctc.gov/
> National Counterterrorism Center (NCTC)
> NCTC serves as the primary organization in the U.S. government for integrating and analyzing all intelligence pertaining to terrorism possessed or acquired by the U.S. government (except purely domestic terrorism). This website features a wide variety of counterterrorism resources, a timeline of terrorist events, terrorist profiles, and materials related to methods and tactics.

http://www.publicsafety.gc.ca/cnt/ntnl-scrt/index-en.aspx
> Public Safety Canada/National Security
> Public Safety Canada functions as a centralized hub for coordinating work in counterterrorism, critical infrastructure, cybersecurity, and transportation security. This website outlines Canada's counterterrorism strategy, contains links to several important reports, such as the annual Public Report on the Terrorist Threat to Canada, and presents Canada's strategy for countering violent extremism.

http://www.rand.org/topics/terrorism-and-homeland-security.html
> RAND
> RAND is a world leader in research on terrorism, counterterrorism, counterinsurgency, disaster management, and homeland security. This website includes an extensive archive of articles on a wide range of topics.

http://www.tsas.ca/
> Canadian Network for Research on Terrorism, Security, and Society (TSAS)
> TSAS engages in policy-relevant research and dissemination in terrorism, security, and society. This website features a virtual library of important publications and timely working papers.

References

Ali, S. (2015). British Muslims in Numbers: A Demographic, Socio-Economic, and Health Profile of Muslims in Britain Drawing on the 2011 Census. Published by the Muslim Council of Britain.

Andrew, C.M. (2009). *Defend the Realm: The Authorized History of MI5*. New York: Alfred A. Knopf.

Arrigo, J.M., and Wagner, R.V. (2007). Psychologists and military interrogators rethink the psychology of torture. *Peace and Conflict: Journal of Peace Psychology* 13(4): 393–398. doi:10.1080/10781910701665550.

BBC News. (July, 2008). What happened. Retrieved from http://news.bbc.co.uk/2 /shared/spl/hi/uk/05/london_blasts/what_happened/html/.

Bjorgo, T. (2013). *Strategies for Preventing Terrorism*. New York: Palgrave Macmillan Pub.

Bloomberg, S.B., and Hess, G.D. (2009). Estimating the macroeconomic consequence of 9/11. *Peace Economics, Peace Science and Public Policy* 15(2): 7–24. doi:10.2202/1554-8597.1167.

Blunk, S.S., Clark, D.E., and McGibany, J.M. (2006). Evaluating the long-run impacts of the 9/11 terrorist attacks on U.S. domestic airline travel. *Applied Economics* 38(4): 363–370.

Brachman, J.M., and Levine, A.N. (2011). You too can be Awlaki. *Fletcher F. World Affairs* 35: 25.

Britain, V. (2015). The Senate Intelligence Committee Report on Torture.

Bronskill, J. (2015, October 25). Expanded CSIS mandate under C-51 raises accountability concerns. *The Globe and Mail*. Retrieved from http://www .theglobeandmail.com/news/national/expanded-csis-mandate-under-c -51-raises-accountability-concerns/article26967021/.

Central Intelligence Agency. (1996). Report on *Osama Bin Laden: Islamic extremist financier*. The Central Intelligence Agency.

Chatterjee, P. (1986). *Nationalist Thought and the Colonial World: A Derivative Discourse?* London: Zed Books for the United Nations University.

Cohen, I.M., and Corrado, R.R. (2005). State torture in the contemporary world. *International Journal of Comparative Sociology* 46(1–2): 103–131.

Council on Foreign Relations. (2013). *Target Killings*. http://www.cfr.org/counter terrorism/targeted-killings/p9627.

Davies, P.H. (2011). Twilight of Britain's Joint Intelligence Committee? *International Journal of Intelligence and Counterintelligence* 24(3): 427–446.

Dorril, S. (2002). *MI6: Inside the Covert World of Her Majesty's Secret Intelligence Service*. Simon and Schuster.

Forst, B. (2009). *Terrorism, Crime, and Public Policy*. Cambridge, UK: Oxford University Press.

Gerges, F.A. (2007). *Journey of the Jihadist: Inside Muslim Militancy*. Orlando, FL: Harcourt Books.

Gilsinan, K. (2015, October 29). The confused person's guide to the Syrian civil war. *The Atlantic*. Retrieved from http://www.theatlantic.com/international/archive /2015/10/syrian-civil-war-guide-isis/410746/.

Government of Canada. (2013). *Building Resilience against Terrorism: Canada's Counter-terrorism Strategy*. 2nd edition. Her Majesty the Queen in Right of Canada.

Gregg, H.S. (2014). Defining religious and secular terrorism. *Perspectives on Terrorism* 8(2). Retrieved from http://www.terrorismanalysts.com/pt/index.php/pot/article /view/336/html.

Hibbert, C. (2012). *The Days of the French Revolution*. New York: Harper Perennial.

Hoffman, B. (2006). *Inside Terrorism*. New York: Columbia University Press.

Kean, T.H., and Hamilton, L. (2004). *The 9/11 Commission Report: Final Report of the National Commission on Terrorist Attacks upon the United States*. Washington, DC: National Commission on Terrorist Attacks upon the United States. Retrieved from http://www.9-11commission.gov/report/911Report.pdf.

Kepel, G. (2004). *The War for Muslim Minds: Islam and the West*. London: Belknap Press.

Kinzer, S. (2003). *All the Shah's Men: An American Coup and the Roots of Middle East Terror*. Hoboken, NJ: John Wiley & Sons.

Kruegle, H. (2007). *CCTV Surveillance: Video Practice and Technology*. 2nd ed. Burlington, MA: Butterworth-Heinemann.

LaFree, G., Dugan, L., and Mille, E. (2015). *Putting Terrorism in Context: Lessons from the Global Terrorism Database*. New York: Routledge.

Lum, C., Kennedy, L.W., and Sherley, A.J. (2006). The effectiveness of counter-terrorism strategies. Oslo, Norway: Campbell Systemic Review.

Mackay, D.A., and Jevan, K. (eds.). (2012). *Crime Prevention*. Burlington, MA: Jones and Bartlett Pub. Chapter 6.

McKearney, T. (2011). *The Provisional IRA: From Insurrection to Parliament*. London: Pluto Press.

Nimer, M. (2002). *The North American Muslim Resource Guide: Muslim Community Life in the United States and Canada*. New York: Routledge.

Nossiter, A., Breeden, A., and Bennhold, K. (2015, November 14). Three Teams of Coordinated Attackers Carried Out Assault on Paris, Officials Say; Holland Blames ISIS. *New York Times*. Retrieved from http://www.nytimes.com/2015/11/15/world/europe/paris-terrorist-attacks.html.

Nossiter, A., and Gladstone, R. (2015, November 13). Paris attacks kill dozens in night of deadly terror. *New York Times*. Retrieved from http://www.nytimes.com/2015/paris%202015/Paris%20Attacks%20Kill%20Dozens%20in%20Night%20of%20Deadly%20Terror%20-%20The%20New%20York%20Times.html.

Office for National Statistics. (2012a). 2011 Census: Key Statistics for England and Wales, March 2011. Office for National Statistics. Retrieved from http://www.ons.gov.uk/ons/dcp171778_290685.pdf.

Office for National Statistics. (2012b). Report on *Religion in England and Wales 2011*. Office for National Statistics. Retrieved from http://www.ons.gov.uk/ons/dcp171776_290510.pdf.

Roosevelt, K. (1979). *Countercoup, the Struggle for the Control of Iran*. New York: McGraw-Hill Companies.

Royal Canadian Mounted Police. (2011). Report on *The RCMP and Canada's National Security*. RCMP. Retrieved from http://www.rcmp-grc.gc.ca/nsci-ecsn/nsci-ecsn-eng.htm.

Schiemann, J.W. (2012). Interrogational torture: Or how good guys get bad information with ugly methods. *Political Research Quarterly* 65(1): 3–19.

Schiemann, J.W. (2015). *Does Torture Work?* New York: Oxford University Press.

Schmitt, E., Mazzetti, M., and Callimachijan, R. (2015, January 15). Disputed claims over Al-Qaeda's role in Paris attacks. *New York Times*. Retrieved from http://www.nytimes.com/2015/01/15/world/europe/al-qaeda-in-the-arabian-peninsula-charlie-hebdo.html?_r=0.

Senate Select Committee on Intelligence. (2014). *Committee Study of the Central Intelligence Agency's Detention and Interrogation Program*. https://www.gpo.gov/fdsys/pkg/CRPT-113srpt288/pdf/CRPT-113srpt288.pdf.

Shane, S. (2014). Backing C.I.A., Cheney Revisits Torture Debate from Bush Era. *New York Times*, December 14, 2014. http://www.nytimes.com/2014/12/15/us/politics /cheney-senate-report-on-torture.html?_r=0.

Tackett, T., Revolution (France: 1789–1799), and Reign of Terror (France: 1793–1794). (2015). *The Coming of the Terror in the French Revolution*. Cambridge, MA: The Belknap Press of Harvard University Press.

Wilcox, P.C. Jr. (2002). United States. In *Combating Terrorism: Strategies of Ten Countries*, ed. Y. Alexander, 23–61. Ann Arbor, MI: University of Michigan Press.

Wright, D., and Kreissl, R. (2014). European responses to the Snowden revelations. In *Surveillance in Europe*, eds. D. Wright and R. Kreissl, 6–50. London: Routledge.

Yerger, D.B. (2011). The economic costs of 9/11 on the U.S. *Phi Kappa Phi Forum* 91(3): 12.

Valiulis, M.G. (1992). *Portrait of a Revolutionary: General Richard Mulcahy and the Founding of the Irish Free State*. Blackrock (Co. Dublin): Irish Academic Press.

The Criminalization of Poverty

12

JOHN ROOK
SAMANTHA SEXSMITH

Contents

Learning Outcomes

After reading this chapter, you should be able to

- Define poverty
- Identify and understand the relationship between poverty and crime
- Identify policies and legislation contributing to the perpetuation of poverty and crime
- Understand and explain the cyclical nature of poverty and crime
- Identify policy gaps or policy alternatives to address underlying contributors to crime that lead to solutions

Introduction

Poverty is the parent of revolution and crime.

Aristotle

Which came first, the chicken or the egg? When analyzing the relationship between poverty and crime, one is faced with a similar paradigm. This chapter will bring to light the cyclical nature of poverty as it relates to crime and crime as it relates to poverty. We will also consider some solutions that have been attempted to destigmatize a person whose crime is not violent but is survival or biological.

Is it a crime to be poor? After reading this chapter, you should be able to formulate an answer to this question. This cursory overview will explore a number of elements contributing to poverty and crime in industrialized countries. With a heavy focus on Canada and the United States, you will learn about society's use of tools to control and police the actions of poor people. You will learn how these tools, while belonging to a crime prevention model, do not prevent crime at all. It will be demonstrated that rather than addressing the social issues leading to the commission of crime, the criminal justice or conservative responses to crime perpetuate the cycle of crime for those living in poverty. While this chapter will touch on the relationship between poverty and crime, the relationship is complex and there are numerous additional elements to be considered. We hope that this brief chapter will provide insight into the issues of **poverty**, and will aid in the creation of solutions (i.e., crime prevention) that will save society from chaos and make our world a better place for all.

Absolute poverty is...

A condition characterized by severe deprivation of basic human needs, including food, safe drinking water, sanitation facilities, health, shelter, education and information. It depends not only on income but also on access to services.

Overall poverty takes various forms, including

A lack of income and productive resources to ensure sustainable livelihoods; hunger and malnutrition; ill health; limited or lack of access to education and other basic services; increased morbidity and mortality from illness; homelessness and inadequate housing; unsafe environments and social discrimination and exclusion. It is also characterized by lack of participation in decision making in civil, social, and cultural life. It occurs in all countries: as mass poverty in many developing countries, pockets of poverty amid wealth in developed countries, loss of livelihoods as a result of economic recession, sudden poverty as a result of disaster or conflict, the poverty of low-wage workers, and the utter destitution of people who fall outside family support systems, social institutions, and safety nets.

These are relative definitions of poverty, which see poverty in terms of minimum acceptable standards of living within the society in which a particular person lives (United Nations 1995).

The Criminalization of Poverty

From the early 1800s to the early 1900s in several countries including the United Kingdom and the United States of America, people unable to afford homes were sent to live in poorhouses. Poorhouses were created to reform the character of poor people and to repress pauperism (Wagner 2005). In keeping with a conservative or criminal justice model of crime prevention, it was thought that the threat of being pushed to the outskirts of society would deter individuals from begging or applying for social assistance from the government (Katz 1996). Inhabitants of poorhouses (see Box 12.1) worked in difficult conditions until they were discharged or eventually died (Wagner 2005). An 1856 New York State Senate review of poorhouses reported that these institutions were miserable, poorly managed, and underfunded, and that they did not achieve the goals that led to their creation (Katz 1996). The banishment of

BOX 12.1   A DAY IN A POORHOUSE...

At the crack of dawn each morning, a rising bell was rung. Roll call was conducted in each area of the poorhouse to ensure that none of its residents (often referred to as inmates) had escaped during the night. Each hour of the day was strictly scheduled, with one hour allotted for recreational activity. Poorhouses operated under a lengthy list of rules and procedures. This list was posted publicly and read aloud each week so that those who were illiterate would not have an excuse to disobey them. Food items were withheld from those who broke the rules, and in more serious cases, disobeyers faced periods of solitary confinement. Each inmate was assigned a job where the work hours were long and the work was physically demanding. Conditions inside workhouses varied among institutions, but for the most part were unsanitary and cramped. Sleeping spaces were small, and the inmate's toilet facilities were contaminated and disease ridden. Just once a week, inmates were bathed and the men were shaved.

While residing in a poorhouse, inmates were not allowed to leave without permission. An inmate could discharge him or herself, but was likely to land in prison as a result of continued pauperism. Most inmates in poorhouses left only as a result of their death (Higginbotham 2016).

individuals who could not afford a home effectively made it criminal or deviant to be poor in this time. While poor people are no longer banished to physical locations, to be poor is still treated as criminal in many ways today.

Since the early 1960s, major cities in industrialized countries have seen a substantial increase in the number of people living in poverty and without appropriate housing (Schafer 1998). As a result, legislation has been adopted to control the issue of panhandling and begging. Individuals without housing frequently receive sanctions for sitting, sleeping, lying, or relieving themselves in public spaces (FEANTSA 2015). Cities across the United States, Canada, and Europe have criminalized the life-sustaining activities of poor people to minimize the public nuisance associated with this type of behavior (Schafer 1998). These laws apply primarily to the actions of homeless people and serve to perpetuate crime rather than prevent it.

Legislation criminalizing the everyday actions of poor people contributes to a cycle of poverty and crime rather than the prevention of crime. Homeless advocates often note that people are fined or arrested for doing things in public space that most of us are able to do in private space. Those receiving sanctions do not typically have the funds to pay fines, and failure to do so can result in the issue of warrants or criminal records (Bryant 2014; Roebuck 2008). Such actions by the police, while following approved bylaws, force people further into poverty and place a large financial burden on the police and the justice system as a whole. With a criminal record or unpaid fines, individuals experience further difficulty in finding a job or being accepted into social or emergency housing (Roebuck 2008). Without housing or income comes desperation, which can lead to criminal measures for survival (Chesney-Lind and Shelden 2004). And so, the cycle continues.

Canada—A Case in Point

The Government of Canada's National Crime Prevention Strategy explicitly recognizes the relationship between poverty and crime (Jamieson and Hart 2003). In coordination with the Caledon Institute of Social Policy, the Government of Canada released a Compendium of Promising Crime Prevention Practices in Canada in 2003. The prevention strategies mentioned in the report were designed using a social model of crime prevention, as they had recognized crime as being a product of a social problem (White 2005). The compendium identified preventive methods geared specifically to the unique issues in the community in which they are to be implemented (Jamieson and Hart 2003).

The National Crime Prevention Strategy in Canada demonstrates commitment and innovation on part of the government in the development of social programming to prevent crime in its communities.

While social programming exists, there are policies and legislation in place that perpetuate rather than prevent crime among those experiencing poverty. Rather than addressing the issues leading to the breakdown of society, a conservative or criminal justice prevention model appears to be preferred in practice when addressing the criminal actions of poor people. Notably, 2 of 10 Canadian provinces have adopted legislation in an effort to regulate activities of citizens at the local level. This legislation is counterproductive as it treats those living in poverty as criminals, rather than providing those in need with the resources necessary to eliminate criminal behavior. In response to an increase in visible homelessness, the province of Ontario enacted the Safe Streets Act (SSA) and amended the Highway Traffic Act to regulate activities on roadways (Gaetz 2014). The SSA and other amendments made it illegal to offer window-cleaning services on highways (also referred to as "squeegeeing"), restricted panhandlers from conducting business in certain areas, and banned people from engaging in aggressive panhandling (SSA 1999). Critics argue that the SSA disproportionately targets vulnerable populations (Bryant 2014). It is argued that the Act is too vague in its language, as it defines aggressive panhandling as "a manner that is likely to cause a reasonable person to be concerned for his or her safety or security" (Bryant 2014). While the Act attempts to define the aggressive nature of panhandling, it fails to determine what constitutes a "reasonable person." It is argued that most people have their own standards for what is compromising to their safety, and that the vagueness of the Act provides too much discretion to police officers (Bryant 2014). The SSA was challenged in the Ontario Supreme Court in 2005, but the court upheld the validity of the legislation (Gaetz 2014). The Ontario Court of Appeal affirmed the Act on a constitutional challenge, and the Supreme Court of Canada denied the application for further review (Gaetz 2014).

Steven Gaetz of York University studied the effects of the SSA on enforcement trends in Toronto. The number of tickets issued under the SSA rose from 710 in 2000 to more than 15,000 tickets issued in 2010, equating to an increase of 2147% (Gaetz 2014). Of the tickets issued in 2010, 20% were for aggressive solicitation, while 80% were for non-aggressive acts of solicitation, such as approaching those waiting in line at an institution where cash can be withdrawn. Gaetz's research indicates that nearly all of the tickets issued under the SSA were distributed to homeless individuals, the majority of which are not able to pay the fines (Gaetz 2014). It is estimated that implementing the SSA cost the Toronto Police Services $936,019 CDN in administration costs between 2000 and 2010, while only $8086 CDN in fines were collected (Gaetz 2014). Fines issued under the SSA are up to $500 for a first offense and increased to $1000 with a chance of imprisonment for secondary and tertiary offenses (Gaetz 2014). The debt and involvement in the criminal justice system that result from tickets issued under the SSA can lead to difficulty for individuals in securing jobs or appropriate housing, which may perpetuate homelessness (Bryant 2014).

The province of British Columbia, in Western Canada, adopted its own version of the SSA, which is a verbatim replica of the legislation in Ontario (SSA 2004). British Columbia's SSA has been met with similar criticisms as in Ontario. Many have questioned the ability of the Act to achieve its stated goals. It is argued that the Act targets the poor and the mentally ill and that treatment addressing the root causes of panhandling would be a more effective solution than sanctions (Young 2007).

While only two Canadian provinces have enacted laws related to panhandling, it is typical of cities to adopt laws to regulate local activities. The content and the degree to which laws are enforced vary among Canadian cities. The City of Calgary bylaws, for example, prohibit panhandlers from soliciting for money near any institution where cash can be withdrawn, near transit stops, or within enclosed pedestrian walkways (The City of Calgary 2015). The City additionally limits panhandling to the hours of 8 a.m. to 8 p.m. and defines the nature upon which panhandlers can legally approach or engage with the person they are soliciting (The City of Calgary 2015). The laws in Calgary differ from those in Quebec City that outwardly prohibit begging on streets or in any public venue (Young 2007). These laws differ still from the laws in Victoria, which allow for a panhandler to approach an individual one time to solicit money legally, but consider a second approach to be aggressive panhandling and attach a fine to those who engage in this type of behavior (Young 2007). From these examples, it is clear that crime prevention is not achieved from these bylaws. It could be argued that the bylaws are not an effective control mechanism, as the same people are constantly being targeted by the police. A more effective crime prevention strategy could require the police to direct repeat offenders to support services.

The United States of America—A Case in Point

> Doubling the conviction rate in this country would do more to cure crime in America than quadrupling the funds for [Hubert] Humphrey's war on poverty.
>
> **Richard Nixon**
> *38th President of the United States of America*

Beginning in the 1960s, decision makers in the United States increased their utilization of punitive measures as a means to prevent street-level crime. Street-level crime at this time was characterized by drug crime and other crimes committed most often by those living in poverty (Beckett and Sasson 2004). This tough-on-crime mentality represents a tendency to use a conservative or criminal justice crime prevention model. In the 1980s, poverty and homelessness presented as major political and social issues in the

United States. In response to a growing need, a greater number of homeless shelters were opened and generous social assistance was offered to those unable to adequately provide for themselves (Knapp 1991). This provision of social assistance to reduce poverty appeared to signify a shift toward a social model of crime prevention. However, between 1980 and 1990, the number of people without adequate housing in America grew from several hundred thousand to several million (Knapp 1991). At this time, the provision of social assistance slowed, and the law became less tolerant of the actions of homeless people and punitive methods of crime prevention emerged once again (Knapp 1991).

Roughly, 76% of American cities had implemented panhandling bans to varying degrees (Dwoskin 2007). These bans make it illegal to beg for money or panhandle in designated areas throughout American cities. These actions of lawmakers and policymakers would appear to speak to suppression as opposed to positive crime intervention built on fundamental crime prevention strategies. Anti-panhandling laws have been challenged in courts in the United States, with plaintiffs arguing that these laws violate the constitutional rights of homeless people (Dwoskin 2007). To make requests for charity illegal for some and not for others is argued to be discrimination based on observable characteristics (Dwoskin 2007). In August of 1989, the New York City Transit Authority adopted legal revisions prohibiting persons from panhandling in subway stations in New York City (Young v. New York City Transit Authority). The new provisions still allowed for the solicitation of money by organized charities, artists, and public speakers (Dwoskin 2007). In 1990, two homeless men brought action upon the New York Transit System, claiming that New York Penal Law section 240.35(1) infringed upon their right to free speech as protected under the First Amendment of the Constitution. The two men argued that their asking for money was no different than charitable requests for funds (Knapp 1991). The Appeals court rebutted that begging is more "conduct" than it is "speech," as begging is not expressive in nature and has the potential to be dangerous (Knapp 1991). The Appeals court further stated that even if begging were communication worthy of First Amendment protection, the revisions adopted by the Transit Authority were not discriminatory, as they were implemented to fulfill a government purpose. The government purpose argued in this case was the protection of the safety of subway riders from the potential danger of panhandling (Dwoskin 2007). The outcome of the Young v. NYC TA case sets precedent to allow for the punishment of beggars, and the infringement of the constitutional rights of homeless and poor people (Dwoskin 2007). The decision of the court signaled that it was acceptable to criminalize poverty in New York City, by treating the poor differently under the law than citizens who are not poor. This is not crime prevention but a method of behavior control for unwanted activities.

In a similar 1992 Miami Federal Court Case, plaintiffs filed an action against the city on behalf of themselves and approximately 6000 other homeless individuals living in Miami (Miami Law 1992). The plaintiffs sought to dispute the city's policy requiring police to arrest homeless people for engaging in life-sustaining activities in public (Miami Law 1992). They argued that this policy was a clear violation of multiple amendment rights under the U.S. Constitution. The Miami Federal Court ruled in favor of the plaintiffs, stating that the city could not arrest individuals for engaging in life-sustaining activities that they had no other place to conduct (Miami Law 1992). The court's decision led to the allotment of more shelter beds in the City of Miami. However, in light of an increase in the number of homeless individuals, there are not enough shelter beds in Miami to accommodate the needs of the entire population today. As a result, the everyday actions of the homeless in public spaces are still treated as deviant and are often met with resistance (Miami Law 1992). This is an excellent example of a potential solution that was not designed as a universal option.

In 2009, the National Coalition for the Homeless surveyed 235 cities in the United States in regard to their response to homelessness. Of the 235 cities surveyed, 30% had legislation in place making it illegal to sit or lay down in certain areas, 47% restricted begging in public areas, and 23% had prohibited begging of any kind citywide (National Coalition for the Homeless 2009). Additionally, 33% of the surveyed cities prohibited camping in certain areas, with 17% having a citywide camping prohibition (National Coalition for the Homeless 2009). The survey indicated that the creation of this type of legislation is on the rise. Over the three-year duration of the study, cities saw an increase in laws concerning begging, loitering, and camping in certain city areas (National Coalition for the Homeless 2009).

Europe—A Case in Point

> Like slavery and apartheid, poverty is not natural. It is man-made and it can
> be overcome and eradicated by the actions of human beings.
>
> **Nelson Mandela**

At a United Nations assembly meeting to discuss crime prevention and international drug control, a representative of the European Union spoke to European strategies to curb crime rates among those living in poverty. The strategies discussed included information sharing, an increase in law enforcement, and capacity building in countries to rehabilitate, treat, and socially reintegrate offenders and drug users back into society (United Nations 2005). The choice to use both an increase in law enforcement and methods to treat offenders in the community demonstrates a European use of social methods of crime prevention, as well as more traditional criminal justice methods of deterrence.

At the national level, many European countries have signaled a commitment to address the social causes of crime in their communities. In line with the social model of prevention, laws criminalizing beggars and the homeless were repealed in many Western European societies in the 1960s and 1970s (Doherty et al. 2008). In 1993, Belgium repealed an Act prohibiting vagrancy, and replaced the Act with a new law stating that homeless people should instead be treated in centers designed to address the root causes of poverty and to help people reintegrate into society (Doherty et al. 2008). Similar legislation criminalizing homeless people in Norway and France was also repealed in the late 1990s and early 2000s (Doherty et al. 2008).

Despite the repeal of national legislation, local governments in Europe have introduced legislation that deters begging, loitering, and other activities frequently associated with homeless people and people living in poverty, demonstrating the use of punitive preventive methods (Doherty et al. 2008). Under the City Management and Cleanliness Regulation, the Vilnius City Council in Lithuania strictly prohibits begging and providing beggars with money (FEANTSA 2015). The Act additionally forbids the creation of temporary shelter under balconies or apartment buildings (FEANTSA 2015). In Slovenia, the Law on Protection of Public Peace and Order prohibits begging and rough sleeping in public spaces. Individuals who engage in these activities are given fines, and failure to pay these fines may result in imprisonment or alternative punishment (FEANTSA 2015). Meanwhile, in the Netherlands, many local authorities have imposed regulations to control public space by requiring homeless people to enter accommodation centers in order to be eligible to receive certain benefits (FEANTSA 2015). Legislation similar to this exists at the local level in many other Western European cities, most notably in Ireland, Denmark, and Austria (see Doherty et al. 2008).

Those with Lower Incomes Are More Likely to Be Arrested

The rich get richer... and the poor get prison.

J. Riemen
2013

Decades of statistics from countries around the world indicate that young low-income males are the most likely population to be arrested and incarcerated (National Council of Welfare 2000). However, studies dating back to the 1960s reveal that criminal behavior is not exclusively linked to low income. An American study administered surveys to participants from a variety of backgrounds in an effort to reveal their criminal histories. The results from the survey indicated that the majority of all male participants had committed crimes (National Council of Welfare 2000). In a similar study, Canadian criminologist Marc Leblanc surveyed more than 3000 Montreal participants from various socioeconomic backgrounds. The study determined that more than 90% of respondents had committed delinquent acts in the past year. The most common acts included vandalism, operating a motor vehicle while under the influence of alcohol, shoplifting, and taking minor drugs such as marijuana. Roughly 9% had committed crimes of a more serious nature (National Council of Welfare 2000). Children of professional parents were as likely to have reported committing a crime as children of parents with low-status jobs, indicating that committing a crime is not strongly correlated with low socioeconomic status (National Council of Welfare 2000). This suggests that low-income individuals are no more likely than their high-income counterparts to commit crimes, but are rather more likely to be arrested, tried, and incarcerated for the delinquent acts they have committed (see Table 12.1).

Using a data set from the American Bureau of Justice Statistics, the Prison Policy Initiative of Massachusetts compared the pre-incarceration incomes of incarcerated American adults to the incomes of the non-incarcerated adults. The study findings determined that in 2014 dollars, incarcerated Americans had a median annual income of $16,185 before their incarceration (Rabuy and Kopf 2015). This median salary is 41% less than the median salary of non-incarcerated individuals of similar age. The comparison supports

Table 12.1 Prisons of Poverty: A Comparison of Salaries and Education

	Incarcerated (Prior)		Non-Incarcerated	
	Men	Women	Men	Women
Average income				
All	$19,650	$13,890	$41,250	$23,745
White	$21,975	$15,480	$47,505	$26,130
Hispanic	$19,740	$11,820	$30,000	$15,000
Black	$17,625	$12,735	$31,425	$24,225
Average education level				
High school or more	20.4%	21.6%	83.4%	83.4%
Some postsecondary or more	8.8%	11.2%	51.6%	48.6%
Postsecondary graduate or more	2.3%	3.1%	27.5%	23.1%

Source: Adapted from Day, J., and Curry, A. (1998). *Educational Attainment in the United States: March 1997.* Washington, DC: The Census Bureau; Harlow, C.W. (2003). *Bureau of Justice Statistics Special Report: Education and Correctional Populations.* Washington, DC: U.S. Department of Justice; and Rabuy, B., and Kopf, D. (2015). Prisons of poverty: Uncovering the pre-incarceration incomes of the imprisoned. *Prison Policy Initiatives.*

the hypothesis that those with lower incomes are more likely to be arrested for a crime than those with higher incomes. Alternatively, some have argued that this disparity in median incomes is a product of race. It is argued that there is a high proportion of Hispanic and African-American prisoners in American prisons and, on average, individuals of these racial categories tend to earn lower salaries than whites. When controlling for race, those who were imprisoned still earned significantly less before incarceration than those who were not (Rabuy and Kopf 2015). A comparison of salaries is summarized in Table 12.1.

Studies further indicate that police tend to use a heavier-handed approach in low-income areas where they expect crime to occur (National Council of Welfare 2000). This may increase the chance of arrest for individuals residing in these areas. There is a greater likelihood of charges being laid for a crime in low-income areas than there is for the same crime being committed in middle- to high-income areas (National Council of Welfare 2000). A study in St. John's, Newfoundland found that police officers had mental images of various sections of town, which affected the way that they administered their police work. The areas that had greater police presence and higher service calls were generally interpreted by officers as "trouble areas" (National Council of Welfare 2000). When local police officers patrolled these areas, they approached situations with an increased level of suspicion and concern (National Council of Welfare 2000). Police attitudes can lead to different policing practices and may therefore affect crime rates in various communities. Police officers may seek arrests in low-income communities more frequently than in middle- to high-income communities, thus skewing the arrested population to include a higher number of low-income people (National Council of Welfare 2000).

In many low-income areas, quality relationships, functional families, quality education including high school and college, appropriate mentors, and good relationships with police are missing (BladeRunners 2016). Programs such as BladeRunners, an aboriginal youth employment program in Vancouver, Canada, is an example of an attempt to rectify these significant gaps in low-income communities. Community-based policing and drug treatment courts are designed to address the need for quality relationships and fair treatment.

Homelessness and Prison

Research indicates that the relationship between homelessness and incarceration is cyclical. Those with lower income are more likely to be arrested than those of similar age with higher or more stable income (National Council of Welfare 2007). A circumstance of imprisonment can intensify a situation of poverty and homelessness for someone dealing with poverty prior to their involvement with the criminal justice system. Individuals not yet living in poverty may experience it for the first time as a direct result of coming into conflict with the law (National Council of Welfare 2007).

Involvement with the criminal justice system increases one's risk of experiencing poverty and **homelessness**. Those who have been incarcerated for a significant length of time are unlikely to have the financial resources necessary to rent an apartment at market price (Rodriguez and Brown 2003). When offenders are released from prison, common policies and procedures in the application process for social housing allow for the legal discrimination against previously incarcerated individuals. Landlords require applicants to disclose their criminal history on application forms. Corporations and organizations remain within their right to deny housing to people with criminal histories involving drugs or violence (Rodriguez and Brown 2003).

At any given time in the United States, 30%–50% of those on parole in Los Angeles and San Francisco are homeless (Rodriguez and Brown 2003). In New York City, 20% of previous inmates released from city jails are released to situations of homelessness or unstable housing (Rodriguez and Brown 2003). This raises some significant issues for parole officers and other legal officials tasked with providing community supports to clients. Caseworkers and legal officials must be in contact with ex-offenders in order to assist them with supports related to successful re-entry. Without the proper supports in place, ex-offenders have a heightened chance of reoffending (Rodriguez and Brown 2003). One solution is for agencies to lease apartments from landlords using a Master Lease Agreement and to sublet the apartment to the person who has been released from prison. This means that the agency shares responsibility for the state of the unit and for the payment of rent. Where this has occurred, the chance for success is higher.

Common policies and procedures additionally hinder an ex-offender's ability to secure employment. Much like the application process for social housing, employers often require that applicants disclose any criminal offense for which they have not been pardoned on their original application form (Raphael and Winter-Ebmer 2001). Given the choice between a candidate with a criminal background and one without, employers are within their legal right to choose to hire the employee who has not been involved with the justice system (Raphael and Winter-Ebmer 2001).

For ex-offenders experiencing homelessness, a lack of a fixed address can contribute to the difficulty experienced in securing employment. Employers may have a difficult time coordinating with a candidate to interview or hire them. Without a fixed address or telephone number, employers do not have a method to contact individuals, overall reducing the chance that they will be able to coordinate potential training or employment (Raphael and Winter-Ebmer 2001). If an individual is unable to secure employment, they may not

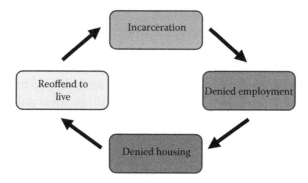

Figure 12.1 The cycle of crime, poverty, and recidivism. (Courtesy of Dr. John Rook.)

have the source of income necessary to afford housing. Through community integration agencies such as the John Howard and Elizabeth Fry Societies, former inmates are supported to live successful in society and to find housing and employment. It is common that a lack of a legitimate source of income can result in a return to criminal activity as a means to generate income. This presents another contributor to the cyclical relationship between poverty and crime (Raphael and Winter-Ebmer 2001) (see Figure 12.1).

Given our knowledge of the relationship between crime and homelessness, we are presented with an opportunity to break the cycle and prevent future crime. Using punitive measures as a way to deter future crimes has not shown to be an effective way to reduce recidivism (Raphael and Winter-Ebmer 2001). Alternative preventive methods addressing the social issues leading to homelessness are likely to have a larger impact in reducing crime rates in a community.

Pay-to-Stay Fees

Prisons, penitentiaries, and other institutions in the United States who have opted to use the **"Pay to Stay"** model charge fees to inmates for daily programs, services, and functions (Eisen 2014). The Pay-to-Stay model obliges incarcerated offenders to pay a portion of what it costs the state to feed and house them. While an inmate is incarcerated, fees are collected from their commissary (American Civil Liberties Union of Ohio 2015). Once released from prison, debts are handled by external collection agencies that deal directly with the previously incarcerated individual until the amount is paid in full (American Civil Liberties Union of Ohio 2015).

Pay-to-Stay fees emerged as a result of a financial and political need in the United States. The number of incarcerated Americans grew significantly following an increase in the general population and the introduction of tough-on-crime legislation. From 1980 to 2008, the number of people incarcerated in the United States increased from roughly 500,000 to 2.3 million (Eisen 2014). This growth in the prison population resulted in an increased cost of incarceration for governments and taxpayers. As a means to offset some of these rising costs, Pay-to-Stay policies were created to allow offenders to bear some of the financial burden (Eisen 2014). These policies were also formulated with the intent to serve as a **deterrent**, as they are punitive in nature and seek to punish offenders for their criminal behavior.

If Pay-to-Stay fees operated in practice as they do in theory, their implementation would serve to deter and prevent crime. However, research indicates that this is not the case. Incarcerated individuals are rarely able to pay off their fees before exiting prison and typically leave prison having accumulated a large amount of debt, making it more difficult to succeed in their communities. Without the ability to successfully reintegrate into society, individuals face an increased risk of recidivism (American Civil Liberties Union of Ohio 2015). With a return to prison, inmates will accumulate further debt that is unlikely to ever be paid off in its entirety (Eisen 2014). If an individual does not reoffend, they are often unable to achieve adequate employment, affordable housing, or a good credit rating as a result of increased debt (Eisen 2014). As such, formerly incarcerated people remain a burden on taxpayers, as they may require social assistance for the duration of their lives (Eisen 2014). Rather than reducing the chance of recidivism, Pay-to-Stay policies attach low-income people to the criminal justice system for an extended duration of time (American Civil Liberties Union of Ohio 2015). Hence, from a crime prevention perspective, Pay-to-Stay policies are highly counterproductive.

Crimes of Survival

If an individual experiencing poverty is unable to achieve their basic needs, this can result in the commission of a crime in order to survive (Chesney-Lind and Shelden 2004). Research indicates that the longer a person is without adequate food, shelter, and protection, the greater the chance that they will resort to crime in order to secure their basic needs (Roebuck 2008). Crimes of an economic nature most often occur out of desperation and a lack of options for those without the material means to survive, and society's reaction to survival crimes is often punitive in nature (Roebuck 2008). Given our knowledge of the motivation behind crimes of this nature, it appears as if a social model of crime prevention would be more effective than the use of criminal justice measures. Rather than using legal sanctions to address crimes of an economic nature, it is more effective to address the issue that individuals do not have the material means to survive. Given the availability of resources, an individual would have less of a motive to commit a survival crime. Some factors relating to survival crimes are discussed in the following section.

Property Crimes

People who are poor are more likely to commit crimes against property rather than against people (Roebuck 2008). As property crimes are often a needs-based response to economic scarcity, changes in the rates of poverty and unemployment have a statistically significant effect on crime rates (Roebuck 2008). A study of youth living in poverty in Toronto determined that serious incidents of theft increased when youth were unable to find shelter (McCarthy and Hagan 1992). The study further indicated that minor incidents of theft increased with increased levels of hunger (McCarthy and Hagan 1992). Research indicates that long periods of unemployment and homelessness are strongly related to an increase in incidents of property crime (Roebuck 2008).

Drug Crimes

Homelessness and drug use are strongly related, as drug use among the homeless population is prevalent (McCarthy and Hagan 1992). McCarthy and Hagan determined that 30% to 40% of the studied homeless population abused alcohol, and 10% to 30% abused other substances. While there is a clear relationship between drug use and homelessness, the relationship is not one-directional. While drug use can lead to homelessness, homelessness may additionally lead to drug use. When an individual is living on the street, their chance of substance abuse increases (McCarthy and Hagan 1992). This may be as a result of the street lifestyle or a possible coping mechanism for the hardships associated with homelessness. McCarthy and Hagan additionally argue that those who use drugs are more likely to sell them. Their research states that the longer an individual has been without a legitimate means to generate income, the greater the chance that they will become involved in the selling and trafficking of drugs.

Sex Work

Survival sex refers to prostitution or sex work engaged in by a person as a result of an extreme need (Chettiar et al. 2010). A study in Vancouver, Canada, determined that youth living on the street are becoming increasingly engaged in survival sex as a means to generate income (Chettiar et al. 2010). The study included a sample of 560 youth. The results determined that 11% of all participants had engaged in survival sex in the past six months. It is estimated that the prevalence of survival sex among adults is even higher than among youth. The study found a strong relationship between survival sex and drug use, with the use of non-injection crack and crystal methamphetamines increasing the chances that an individual would engage in sex for money (Chettiar et al. 2010). Belonging to the female sex and being of aboriginal ethnicity were factors also strongly correlated with sex work.

McCarthy and Hagan's research indicates similar findings in the United States as those in Vancouver. Their research determined a strong relationship between poverty and prostitution. The study indicated that acts of prostitution were significantly linked to unemployment and difficulty in finding suitable shelter. Instances of trading sex for money increased with prolonged experiences of homelessness and unemployment (McCarthy and Hagan 1992). McCarthy and Hagan estimated that roughly one in three youth living on the streets has some experience selling sex as a commodity for survival.

A study conducted in Montreal highlighted the prevalence of survival sex among male street youth in Canada (Haley et al. 2004). Participants were recruited from a pool of street active youth aged 14–23 who were able to provide informed consent to participate. Of the 542 male participants recruited, 27.7% disclosed their involvement in survival sex as a means to generate income (Haley et al. 2004). These numbers indicate that the realm of sex work is not necessarily dominated by one gender; rather, rates vary based on the unique characteristics of the homeless population at hand.

Women and Crime

The rate of incarcerated women in industrialized countries has increased in recent decades, despite overall declining crime rates (Gelb 2003). In the United States, the female incarceration rate was roughly 8 per 100,000 women in the early 1950s. This rate increased to double digits in 1977 and reached 51 per 100,000 by the late 1990s (Currie 1998). In Australia, between the years of 1995 and 2002, the number of women incarcerated increased from 12.0 per 100,000 in 1995 to 19.2 per 100,000 in 2002 (Gelb 2003). Similarly, in Canada, the proportion of women charged with crimes has increased over the past three decades. In 1979, women accounted for 15% of all adults charged with a Criminal Code offense. By 2009, women were accountable for more than one-fifth (or 21%) of adults charged (Mahon 2015).

The boom in women's imprisonment is largely attributed to the circumstances of poverty that many women face today. Steffensmeier (1996) argues that an increase in female crime comes as a result of higher levels of divorce, a higher number of female-headed households, an increase in the cost of living, and an increase in responsibility for children. Of the incarcerated women in Canada, 75% have a junior high education or less, 40% are functionally illiterate, and 80% were unemployed at the time of arrest (Walsh et al. 2012). Women are paid less than men for comparable positions, are denied access to high-paying positions, and have limited access to social resources such as affordable daycare (Walsh et al. 2012). In relation to these social circumstances, female offenders most commonly commit crimes related to their economic survival (Balfour 2008). According to Statistics Canada, nearly half (47%) of accused females were accused of a property crime (Kong and AuCoin 2009), such as theft or fraud. Female offenders are most likely commit a theft in Canada, and are accused at a rate of 291/100,000 females. Two-thirds of thefts (66%) involving a female were incidents of shoplifting. When held in comparison to their male counterparts, females were additionally more likely to be incarcerated for drug possession and prostitution (Kong and AuCoin 2009). These crimes are material in nature and are likely to occur as a direct or indirect result of experiencing poverty (Walsh et al. 2012).

Indigenous Peoples and Crime

In 2011, the National Household Survey revealed that indigenous peoples make up 4.3% of the general Canadian population. This percentage signifies an increase from 3.3% of the population in 2001 and 2.8% in 1996 (Statistics Canada 2011). While indigenous peoples compose 4.3% of the general population, they are overrepresented in Canadian prisons. Statistics Canada data indicate that in 2010/2011, 27% of adults in provincial custody and 20% of adults in federal custody were indigenous peoples. In all provinces and territories, the representation of indigenous adults in correctional services exceeds their representation in the general population (Perreault 2009). This has been a long-standing issue. As early as 1989, reports by the Royal Commission expressed concerns regarding the number of aboriginal people in the correctional system (Perreault 2009). To address the issue of overrepresentation, amendments to the Criminal Code were adopted in 1996, requiring judges to consider all other sanctions before imposing a sentence of imprisonment on an indigenous offender (Statistics Canada 2011). This measure does not appear to have been effective in reducing the number of these offenders in prison. The Correctional Service of Canada determined that indigenous offenders were more likely than non-indigenous offenders to be serving their sentence in an institution than they were to be serving their sentence in the community on supervision (Correctional Service of Canada 2013).

Research indicates that the socioeconomic background of indigenous peoples provides an explanation for their overrepresentation in Canadian prisons (Perreault 2009). According to the 2006 Census, 38% of indigenous peoples aged 20 years and older had not completed high school, compared to 19% of non-indigenous peoples. In the same year, the unemployment rate among indigenous peoples was 14%, compared to 6% of the general population (Perreault 2009). Data from various Canadian provinces demonstrate a strong correlation between education, employment, and risk factors for incarceration (Perreault 2009). Evidence additionally points to a strong relationship between socioeconomic disadvantage and criminal behavior (Correctional Service of Canada 2013). In Canada, a large proportion of the aboriginal population suffer from being economically disadvantaged (Correctional Service of Canada 2013). It has been determined that inadequate educational opportunities, unemployment, poverty, poor living conditions, intergenerational alcohol abuse, and domestic violence all contribute to indigenous peoples coming into conflict with the law (Correctional Service of Canada 2013).

Similarly, indigenous peoples are overrepresented in custody in Australia. In 1992, there were roughly 2200 indigenous peoples in prisons in Australia. The 1991 Australian census determined that there were only 159,705 indigenous peoples over the age of 15 in the total Australian population. These numbers indicate that an indigenous person is 14 times more likely to be imprisoned than a non-indigenous person (Walker and McDonald 1995). Australian data indicate that at the time of arrest, two-thirds of people were unemployed. The overrepresentation of this population in Australian prisons is explained with international research indicating that problems of violence and petty crimes are associated with social problems (Walker and McDonald 1995).

Alternatives to Criminalizing Poverty: Preventive Methods

The discussion above has highlighted the problems associated with poverty and resultant crime. Overall, the decision to introduce policies and legislation as discussed above has resulted in the oppression of people living in poverty rather than the prevention of crime. Get-tough policies are not supported by the bulk of sociological research, which suggests that the severity of a punishment does not have a specific deterrent effect (Beckett and Sasson 2004). Rather than criminalizing the behavior of those experiencing poverty, we believe, and research suggests, that it is more effective to address the causes of poverty that lead to the commission of the crime (Beckett and Sasson 2004).

The United Nations General Assembly recognizes crime as being both a cause and a consequence of society (United Nations 2005). As such, addressing the contributors to poverty will in turn address the issue of poverty crime in society. Rather than addressing crimes committed by those living in a state of poverty with a criminal justice response, it is more effective to utilize a social model of crime prevention. By working to alleviate poverty using the social model of crime prevention, communities and neighborhoods will be strengthened, and the issues related to crime will be addressed. Below, we will discuss some alternative methods that can be used in place of criminal justice responses to deter and prevent crime.

Early Intervention Strategies

Early intervention strategies are a prevention tactic rather than a crime management tactic, as they are focused on addressing the underlying causes of crime and victimization (Begin 1995). These types of programs are typically utilized as a means to target at-risk children in low-income, at-risk communities early in life as a way to reduce their chance of criminal involvement in adolescence and adulthood (Begin 1995). Programs appear in varying forms and are implemented within a range of settings depending on the severity of antisocial behavior.

To see an early intervention program in practice, it is possible to look at the effects of the Montreal Longitudinal Experimental Study. The study was designed and implemented in Montreal, Quebec, in response to calls for the investment of public monies in a proactive approach to the prevention of youth crime (Begin 1995). Researchers from the University of Montreal had an interest in determining how the early onset of antisocial behavior and inadequate parenting could lead to delinquent behavior among children from economically disadvantaged families. In the spring of 1984, teachers working in schools in the low-income areas of Montreal were asked to review and rate the behavior of their students between the ages of 7 and 9. Following the results of these ratings, boys from 53 schools across Montreal were selected to participate in the study (Begin 1995). The boys were randomly separated into three groups: the treatment group, the observation group, and the no-contact group created to control for the effects of the study (Begin 1995). The intervention for the treatment group involved many different actors and included parenting training groups as well as education regarding social skills for the children (Begin 1995).

Following the treatment, both teachers and parents annually rated the behavior of the boys from the ages of 9–12. Ratings were provided in the following categories: educational achievement, fighting behavior, overall school behavior, delinquent behavior, and the overall perception of antisocial behavior (Begin 1995). The results of the study determined that when compared to the untreated participants, boys who had received treatment exhibited less aggressive behavior in school, performed better academically on average, and experienced fewer difficulties adjusting to new situations (Begin 1995). Those belonging to the treatment group additionally had fewer teacher-reported acts of delinquency at the three-year follow-up period posttreatment (Begin 1995). The researchers of the study additionally asked the boys from each of the three groups to complete a self-reported survey three years after the completion of treatment. Results from this survey indicated that 62% of the untreated boys had committed delinquent acts such as trespassing (compared to 40% of those who had been treated) and 20% had committed acts of theft (compared to 7% of those who had been treated) (Begin 1995). This study clearly demonstrates that strong relationships via parenting are an excellent determining factor of future success or failure.

To understand the effects of early childhood intervention on criminal behavior in an American context, it is useful to look at the effects of the Perry Preschool Project. The Perry Preschool Project, piloted in 1962, involved the provision of preschool intervention to three- and four-year African-American children who were living in poverty and were thought to be at risk of high school failure (Schweinhart 2003). Seventy-five percent of the participants were enrolled in the program for two years (ages 3 and 4), and 25% participated for only one year (at the age of 4) (Schweinhart 2003). The program cost roughly $11,300 per child, with a child-to-teacher ratio of 6:1 (Schweinhart 2003). The daily curriculum of the program focused on active learning and challenged the young students to develop skills related to decision making and problem solving (Schweinhart 2003). Teachers additionally paid weekly visits to the parents of participants as a means to involve the parents in the educational process and to ensure that the curriculum was also being implemented at home (Schweinhart 2003).

The effects of the program were evaluated using a randomized controlled trial of 128 students, with 64 participants receiving the intervention and 64 receiving no treatment (Schweinhart 2003). Both groups received follow-up assessments at predetermined checkpoints until the final assessments, which were completed at the age of 40. The results of the final assessment revealed that those belonging to the treatment group had been arrested a significantly lower number of times than their counterparts and were far less likely to have been arrested for violent crimes (Schweinhart 2003). The impact of the project on the criminal behavior of participants is summarized in Figure 12.2.

From this study, it is clear that skill development and parental support are predictors of success. The study does not make an economic claim, but it can be posited that the $11,300 cost per child is insignificant to the costs of future incarceration should the child not have been in the program.

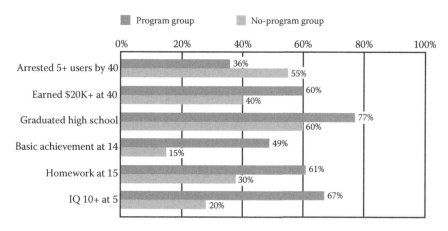

Figure 12.2 Perry Preschool Project: effects of early childhood intervention. (From Schweinhart, L.J. (2003). Benefits, Costs, and Explanation of the HighScope Perry Preschool Program. Paper presented at the Meeting of the Society for Research in Child Development. Tampa, FL, p. 10.)

Community and Drug Courts

Community and drug courts are used as alternatives to traditional criminal justice proceedings for crimes committed by those living in poverty in many industrialized countries. These courts were created with the intent to prevent future criminal behavior by imposing meaningful sanctions on offenders, to help offenders address the problems at the root of their criminal behavior, and to repair the harm done in communities where crimes occur (Lee 2000). The use of extrajudicial courts signifies a shift toward addressing the societal contributors to crimes committed by people from disadvantaged backgrounds (Lee 2000).

The emergence of crack cocaine had a substantial impact on the administration of justice in the 1980s. The large-scale use of this drug resulted in an unprecedented number of arrests and prosecutions of drug offenders in the United States (Ashcroft et al. 2003). With the sudden influx of offenders into the system, the courts were unable to keep up with their increased caseloads (Ashcroft et al. 2003). Frustrations began to emerge with the cyclical nature of drug cases, as the same offenders continued to appear in court repeatedly. As a result, jurisdictions began to analyze the relationship between the criminal justice system and the issue of substance abuse. It was at this time that the idea of treatment-oriented criminal processing emerged, and specialized community drug courts were created (Ashcroft et al. 2003). A high prevalence of drug use subsequently made its way north in the early 1990s, affecting the administration of justice in Canada (Latimer et al. 2006).

Drug courts involve a range of multidisciplinary actors, including but not limited to treatment professionals, social workers, defense attorneys, prosecutors, and community corrections. Support and input from the community are additionally welcomed in proceedings. Multidisciplinary teams work together as a means to address the root causes of drug crimes and to increase the chance of successful reintegration into their communities (Office of Justice Programs 2015). Drug treatment courts ultimately aim to reduce the commission of drug crimes by offenders with substance abuse problems through the use of court-monitored treatment and community service support (Office of Justice Programs 2015).

Drug courts are frequently used as an alternative to traditional courts today. As of June 2014, there were more than 3400 drug courts operating in the United States (Office of Justice Programs 2015). In Canada, the first formal drug court was established in Toronto in 1998, with a second court opening not long after in Vancouver in 2001 (Latimer et al. 2006). As a result of Canada's Drug Strategy, the number of drug courts was expanded (Latimer et al. 2006). In 2005, the federal government announced that additional funding would be allotted for the creation of four additional courts in Regina, Edmonton, Winnipeg, and Ottawa (Latimer et al. 2006). In addition to federally funded drug courts, various Canadian municipalities operate drug courts of their own. For example, the Calgary Drug Treatment Court opened its doors in 2007 to provide a community-based alternative to incarceration for addictions-driven crimes committed by Calgary's citizens (Calgary Drug Treatment Court 2016).

To evaluate the ability of drug courts to achieve their desired goals, a meta-analysis was conducted by the Research and Statistics division of the Government of Canada. The division analyzed 54 studies that had been performed over the past 20 years. Of the studies used in the analysis, 50 were conducted in the United States, 2 were from Canada, and the remaining 2 occurred in Australia. The study included data on more than 17,000 offenders participating in 66 individual drug treatment programs. Findings from the study determined that the use of drug courts resulted in lower recidivism rates among program participants when held in comparison to comparable probationers (Latimer et al. 2006). More specifically, drug treatment courts appeared to reduce recidivism rates by 14%. The study additionally indicated that treatment services provided for one year to 18 months had a stronger correlation to reduced recidivism rates than did longer or shorter programs (Latimer et al. 2006) (see Box 12.2).

BOX 12.2   POVERTY AND PREJUDICE

How much of the relationship between poverty and crime can be attributed to prejudicial attitudes on behalf of citizens, legal actors, or policy officials? To begin to deconstruct this question, it is useful to complete this yes or no quiz to determine your own attitude toward those experiencing poverty and homelessness. What would it mean for society if those with the power to make decisions answered yes to any of these questions?

- Do we assume we know a person's life story by looking at them?
- Do we assume we know how a person got into trouble?
- Do we assume they are criminals, lazy, or miserable?
- When we see two homeless people talking together in private, do we assume they are up to no good?
- When we see a homeless person working on two or more bikes, do we think they have stolen them?
- When we see a homeless person pushing a shopping cart, do we assume they stole it from a grocery store?
- Do we think homeless people need just one thing to help them? (e.g., food, a place in a shelter, a kick in the butt, a listening ear?)
- Do we assume that all homeless people want to live like us? Or that they all want to be homeless?
- Do we assume that all homeless people are addicts?
- Do we look down on a homeless person doing something that wouldn't be considered "bad" if they did it in their own personal apartment? (e.g., drinking a beer, having sex with their girlfriend, sleeping)
- If we saw a homeless person on our property, is our impulse to call the police to get rid of them?
- Do we want to take care of homeless people, assuming they can't help themselves?
- Do we assume all homeless people are mean? Or dangerous?
- Do we assume all the homeless people are friendly? Or looking for help? (Kimes 2015)

Concluding Thoughts

In this cursory overview, it is clear that there is a direct connection between poverty and crime. We have seen that the criminalization of people in poverty is universal. We have also seen that poverty crime is often survival crime. We have shown that subgroups in our society are more susceptible to survival crime than the general population. Having had the opportunity to reflect on this relationship, we now have an opportunity to address it and to prevent crime committed among people living in poverty. We hope that whatever you choose as your profession, this overview has given you a sense of our most vulnerable people. Our desire is that you seek to understand the root causes of poverty so that you are able to treat vulnerable people with dignity and respect.

Glossary of Key Terms

Absolute Poverty is... A condition characterized by severe deprivation of basic human needs, including food, safe drinking water, sanitation facilities, health, shelter, education, and information. It depends not only on income but also on access to services.

Deterrence... Whether through preventive patrol by police officers or through stiff prison sentences for violent offenders, is the principal mechanism through which the central feature of criminal justice, the exercise of state authority, works—it is hoped—to diminish offending and to enhance public safety (Kennedy 2009).

Homelessness describes... The situation of an individual or family without stable, permanent, appropriate housing, or the immediate prospect, means and ability of acquiring it. It is the result of systemic or societal barriers, a lack of affordable and appropriate housing, the individual/household's financial, mental, cognitive, behavioural or physical challenges, and/or racism and discrimination. Most people do not choose to be homeless, and the experience is generally negative, unpleasant, stressful and distressing (The Canadian Observatory on Homelessness 2012).

Overall poverty takes various forms, including... A lack of income and productive resources to ensure sustainable livelihoods; hunger and malnutrition; ill health; limited or lack of access to education and other basic services; increased morbidity and mortality from illness; homelessness and inadequate housing; unsafe environments and social discrimination and exclusion. It is also characterized by lack of participation in decision making and in civil, social, and cultural life. It occurs in all countries: as mass poverty in many developing countries, pockets of poverty amid wealth in developed countries, loss of livelihoods as a result of economic recession, sudden poverty as a result of disaster or conflict, the poverty of low-wage workers, and the utter destitution of people who fall outside family support systems, social institutions, and safety nets (United Nations 1995).

Discussion Questions

1. Is homelessness a crime? Is a criminal justice response the best response to homelessness? What might be some alternate policy options to prevent the "undesirable" actions of people living in poverty?
2. Do you think that the provision of a guaranteed annual income would affect the rate at which survival crimes are committed? Could a guaranteed annual income be used as a crime prevention technique?
3. Drug courts are used to divert people living in poverty from the criminal justice system. Can you think of any additional policy options that might similarly achieve this?
4. What is the thought process of somebody committing a survival crime? What sets someone who commits a crime apart from someone who does not commit a crime in similar circumstances?

Recommended Web Links

http://www.publications.gc.ca/site/archivee-archived.html?url=http://www.publications.gc.ca/collections/Collection/HS4-31-2007E.pdf

http://tamarackcommunity.ca/cities_reducing_poverty.html?gclid=COK20J3SsssCFQyNaQodxpMO8g and/or http://plancanada.ca/5-ways-to-end-poverty

http://www.one.org/canada/

http://www.gmfc.org/en/action-within-the-movement/gmc-actions/actions-by-imperatives/10-fight-poverty-invest-in-children/current-actions/411-global-call-to-action-against-poverty

endpoverty2015.org

References

American Civil Liberties Union of Ohio. (2015). *In Jail and in Debt: Ohio's Pay-to-Stay Fees*. ACLU.

Ashcroft, J. et al. (2003). *Juvenile Drug Courts: Strategies in Practice*. U.S. Department of Justice.

Balfour, G. (2008). Falling between the cracks of retributive and restorative justice: The victimization and punishment of aboriginal women. *Feminist Criminology* 3(2): 101–120.

Balfour, G., and Comack, E. (2006). *Criminalizing Women: Gender and (In)justice in Neo-Liberal Times*. Halifax, NS, Canada: Fernwood Publishing.

Beckett, K., and Sasson, T. (2004). *The Politics of Injustice: Crime and Punishment in America* (2nd Ed.). Thousand Oaks CA: Sage Publications Inc.

Begin, P. (1995). Delinquency Prevention: The Montreal Longitudinal Study. Parliamentary Research Branch: Political and Social Affairs Division. Retrieved from http://publications.gc.ca/Collection-R/LoPBdP/MR/mr132-e.htm.

BladeRunners. (2016). City of Vancouver Youth Social Policy. Retrieved from http://www.vancouveryouth.ca/node/558.

Bryant, M. (2014). The case against the Safe Streets Act, 1999. *The Homeless Hub.* Retrieved from http://homelesshub.ca/blog/case-against-safe-streets-act-1999.

Calgary Drug Treatment Court. (2016). About CDTC. Retrieved from http://calgarydrugtreatmentcourt.org/about-us//.

Chesney-Lind, M., and Shelden R.G. (2004). *Girls, Delinquency and Juvenile Justice* (3rd Ed.). Belmont CA: Wadsworth.

Chettiar, J. et al. (2010). Survival sex work involvement among street-involved youth who use drugs in a Canadian setting. *Journal of Public Health* 32(3): 322–327.

Correctional Service of Canada. (2013). Demographic Overview of Aboriginal People in Canada and Aboriginal Offenders in Federal Corrections. Retrieved from http://www.csc-scc.gc.ca/aboriginal/002003-1008-eng.shtml.

Currie, E. (1998). Crime and Punishment in America: Assessing the Prison Experiment. The *New York Times.* Retrieved from http://www.nytimes.com/books/first/c/currie-crime.html.

Day, J., and Curry, A. (1998). *Educational Attainment in the United States: March 1997.* Washington, DC: The Census Bureau.

Doherty, J. et al. (2008). Homelessness and Exclusion: Regulating Public Space in European Cities. *Surveillance and Society* 5(3): 290–314.

Dwoskin, E. (2007). Panhandling in Subways and the First Amendment: Young v. New York City Transit Authority. Columbia University. Retrieved from http://archive.helvidius.org/2007/2007_Dwoskin.pdf.

Eisen, L.B. (2014). Paying for your time: How charging inmates fees behind bars may violate excessive fines clause. *Journal of Public Interest Law* 14: 319–340.

FEANTSA. (2015). Fighting Against the Criminalization of Homelessness and Poverty in Europe. Poverty is Not a Crime.

Gaetz, S. (2014). It's time to repeal the Safe Streets Act! *The Homeless Hub.*

Gelb, K. (2003). *Women in Prison—Why Is the Rate of Incarceration Increasing?* Australian Bureau of Statistics.

Haley, N. et al. (2004). HIV risk profile of male street youth involved in survival sex. *Journal of Sexually Transmitted Infections* 80(6): 526–530.

Harlow, C.W. (2003). *Bureau of Justice Statistics Special Report: Education and Correctional Populations.* Washington, DC: U.S. Department of Justice.

Higginbotham, P. (2016). The Workhouse: The Story of an Institution. Retrieved from http://www.workhouses.org.uk.

Jamieson, W., and Hart, L. (2003). *Compendium of Promising Crime Prevention Practices in Canada.* Caledon Institute of Social Policy.

Katz, M.B. (1996). *In the Shadow of the Poorhouse: A Social History of Welfare in America.* Basic Books.

Kennedy, D.M. (2009). *Deterrence and Crime Prevention: Reconsidering the Prospect of Sanction.* Abingdon, Oxon: Routledge Taylor & Francis Group, 8.

Kimes, S. 2015. Breaking Down Hobo-phobia. *The Radical Reformer.* Retrieved from http://stevesbasics.blogspot.ca/2015/04/breaking-down-hobo-phobia.html?m=0.

Knapp, C.F. (1991). Statutory restriction of panhandling in light of Young v. New York City Transit: Are states begging out of First Amendment proscriptions? *Iowa Law Review* 405.

Kong, R., and AuCoin, K. (2009). *Female Offenders in Canada.* Statistics Canada.

Latimer, J., Morton-Bourgon, K., and Chretien, J. (2006). *A Meta-Analytic Examination of Drug Treatment Courts: Do They Reduce Recidivism?* Department of Justice Canada: Research and Statistics Division.

Lawston, J. (2008). Women, the criminal justice system and incarceration: Processes of power, silence and resistance. *Journal of the National Women's Studies Association* 20(2).

Lee, E. (2000). *Community Courts: an Evolving Model.* U.S. Department of Justice Office of Justice Programs.

Mahon, T.H. (2015). *Women and the Criminal Justice System.* Statistics Canada.

McCarthy, B., and Hagan, J. Mean streets: The theoretical significance of situational delinquency among homeless youth. *The American Journal of Sociology* 98(3): 597–627.

Miami Law. (1992). Pottinger v. City of Miami. Retrieved from http://osaka.law.miami.edu/~schnably/pottinger/pottinger.html.

National Coalition for the Homeless. (2009). Homes Not Handcuffs: The Criminalization of Homelessness in U.S. Cities. Retrieved from http://www.nationalhomeless.org/factsheets/criminalization.html.

National Council of Welfare. (2000). *Justice and the Poor.* National Council of Welfare Publication.

National Council of Welfare. (2007). Solving Poverty: Four Cornerstones of a Workable National Strategy for Canada. *National Council of Welfare Reports* 126(1).

Office of Justice Programs. (2015). *Drug Courts.* National Institute of Justice.

Perreault, S. (2009). *The Incarceration of Aboriginal People in Adult Correctional Services.* Statistics Canada.

Rabuy, B., and Kopf, D. (2015). Prisons of poverty: Uncovering the pre-incarceration incomes of the imprisoned. *Prison Policy Initiatives.*

Raphael, S., and Winter-Ebmer, R. (2001). Identifying the effect of unemployment on crime. *The Journal of Law and Economics* 44(1): 259–283.

Rodriguez, N., and Brown, B. (2003). *Preventing Homelessness among People Leaving Prison.* Vera Institute of Justice.

Roebuck, B. (2008). *Homelessness, Victimization and Crime: Knowledge and Actionable Recommendations.* University of Ottawa: Institute for the Prevention of Crime.

Rossman, S.B. et al. (2011). The multi-site adult drug court evaluation: The drug court experience. *Urban Institute Justice Policy Center.* 3: 7–130.

Safe Streets Act. (1999). Legislative Assembly of Ontario. 37:1 Bill 8.

Safe Streets Act. (2004). Queens Printer British Columbia. Chapter 75.

Schafer, A. (1998). Down and Out in Winnipeg and Toronto: The Ethics of Legislating against Panhandling. *Caledon Institute of Social Policy.* Retrieved from www.caledoninst.org/Publications/PDF/345ENG.pdf.

Schweinhart, L.J. (2003). Benefits, Costs, and Explanation of the HighScope Perry Preschool Program. Paper presented at the Meeting of the Society for Research in Child Development. Tampa, Florida.

Statistics Canada (2011). Aboriginal Peoples in Canada: First Nations People, Metis and Inuit. Retrieved from http://www12.statcan.gc.ca/nhs-enm/2011/as-sa/99 -011-x/99-011-x2011001-eng.cfm.

Steffensmeier, D. (1996). Gender and Crime: Toward a Gendered Theory of Female Offending. *Annual Review of Sociology*. 22: 459–487.

The Canadian Observatory on Homelessness. (2012). Canadian Definition of Home-lessness. *The Canadian Observatory of Homelessness Working Group*, 1.

The City of Calgary. (2015). Bylaw of the City of Calgary to Regulate Panhandling. Bylaw Number 3M99.

United Nations. (1995). *The World Summit for Social Development: Programme of Action*. Department of Social and Economic Affairs.

United Nations. (2005). Crime Is Both Cause, Consequence of Poverty, Third Committee Told As It Begins Discussion of Crime Prevention, International Drug Control. General Assembly, Third Committee. Retrieved from http:// www.un.org/press/en/2005/gashc3817.doc.htm.

Wagner, D. (2005). *The Poorhouse: America's Forgotten Institution*. Rowman and Littlefield Publishers.

Walker, J., and McDonald, D. (1995). *The Over-Representation of Indigenous Peoples in Custody in Australia*. Australian Institute of Criminology.

Walsh, C.A. et al. (2012). Aboriginal women's voices: Breaking the cycle of home-lessness and incarceration. *Pimatisiwin: A Journal of Aboriginal and Indigenous Community Health* 11(3): 377–394.

White, R. (2005). *Situating Crime Prevention: Models, Methods and Political Perspec-tives*. University of Melbourne. 97–113.

Young, D. (2007). *Prohibitions on Panhandling Engage Charter Rights*. University of Alberta. Retrieved from http://ualawccsprod.srv.ualberta.ca/ccs/index.php /constitutional-issues/25-other/357-prohibitions-on-panhandling-engage -charter-rights.

Preventing Corporate Crime

13

MIKE B. BEKE

Contents

Learning Outcomes
After reading this chapter, you should be able to better understand

- Concepts of corporate crime
- Causes of corporate crime
- Theories of corporate crime prevention
- Interventions to reduce corporate crime
- The role of sanctions to respond to corporate crime

Introduction

A company may in many ways be likened to a human body. It has a brain and nerve centre which controls what it does. It also has hands which hold the tools and act in accordance with directions from the centre. Some of the people in the company are mere servants and agents who are nothing more than hands to do the work and cannot be said to represent the mind or will. Others are directors and managers who represent the directing mind and will of the company, and control what it does. The state of mind of these managers is the state of mind of the company and is treated by the law as such (Lord Denning 1957).

345

When thinking about corporate crime prevention, there are two major ideas that one needs to bear in mind. First, as detections of corporate crimes (with environmental, financial, labor, or unfair trade practices) increase, so will criminal prosecutions against companies, leading to major impacts for a corporation and its members. Second, it is also becomes increasingly obvious that discourses and practices of crime prevention in general are greatly needed (Alvesalo et al. 2006). However, there is little research on the specific topic of corporate crime prevention. This is possibly attributed to the overall complexity of the subject, its interconnectedness to law and public policy, and a lack of reliable data (Vaughan 2007).

This chapter aims to offer a presentation of the main theories explaining and preventing what is sometimes referred to as **"white-collar crime,"** often seen as "the conduct of a corporation, or of employees acting on behalf of a corporation, which is proscribed and punishable by law" (Braithwaite 1984, p. 6). Specifically the chapter addresses some important questions in this field (see also Simpson et al. 2014):

 a. Is the "skills-motivation-opportunities" model applicable to corporate crimes?
 b. Do the elaborated theories on crime prevention in general or white-collar crime in particular (e.g., deterrence and compliance) apply to corporate crime?
 c. What kinds of interventions diminish the incentives for corporate crime?
 d. Do interventions lead to different effects based on the type of offense?
 e. Can criminal sanctions on corporations play a role in future crime prevention?

Concept of Corporate Crime

From a criminological perspective, corporate crime includes crime committed by a business or individuals acting on behalf of a business, and the concept closely interlinks with other types of crime, such as organized crime, white-collar crime, and state-corporate crime (Friedrichs 2010, p. 5). These types of crimes share one important commonality, namely, that they necessitate a debate on how best to address the behavior associated with the crimes. Different forms of corporate crime can include corporate violence, corporate theft, corporate financial manipulation, and corporate political corruption or meddling (see Box 13.1). Kagan and Scholz (1983, p. 288) categorize corporate offenders as "amoral calculators, who break laws to maximize profit; political citizens, who disagree in principle with regulatory rules or laws; and the organizational incompetent, whose lawbreaking is a product of mismanagement and incompetence."

BOX 13.1   VIOLENT AND NONVIOLENT CORPORATE CRIME

Since the initial introduction of the concept of white-collar crime by Edwin H. Sutherland (1883–1950), a variety of closely related concepts have been discussed by criminologists, that is, corporate crime, occupational crime, governmental crime, state-corporate crime, contrepreneurial crime, and so on. Despite being divided over the definition of these concepts, criminologists who study white-collar crime generally agree that it occurs in a legitimate occupational context, it is motivated by economic gain or occupational success, and it is not characterized by direct, intentional violence (Friedrichs 2010, p. 5). Types of corporate crimes can be violent, for example, when workers or consumers are exposed to harmful conditions or products (Friedrichs 2010, pp. 64–77). High-profile public scandals concern toxic waste or air pollution cases, food or pharmaceutical product scams, and unsafe automobiles. Common types of corporate violence against workers can concern poor health and safety conditions on the work floor, which can have fatal consequences. Nonviolent corporate crimes include abuse of power, fraud, and economic exploitation (Friedrichs 2010, pp. 77–91). Prevalent types of corporate fraud concerns trade restraints, financial manipulation, copyright violations, unfair labor practices, and so on. Abuse of power includes corruption of political processes through, for example, bribery. Corporate crimes against the public could take the form of tax evasion or unfair obtaining of public contracts. Nonviolent corporate crimes directed at consumers include price fixing or manipulation, false advertising, and so on. Against employees, forms of nonviolent crimes include economic exploitation, theft from employees, or corporate surveillance. Finally, corporate crimes can also affect other competitors, for example, through monopolistic practices, corporate espionage, and theft of trade secrets.

It is perhaps no surprise that given the diversity and complexity of what constitutes corporate crime and who are corporate offenders, countries differ in how they choose to regulate corporate offenses through criminal or civil law. In addition, citizens might perceive acts by companies and their employees as criminal without these legally being characterized as such. In other words, certain forms of legal corporate behavior could also be considered unethical or immoral. Debates on the ethics of corporate behavior and how to respond to criminal behavior especially became relevant during the recent global economic and financial crisis (Huisman 2011). These debates were evident during the formation of grassroots movements, such as the Occupy Wall Street Movement in the United States (see, e.g., http://occupywallst .org/) or the 15-M Movement in Spain (see, e.g., http://www.movimiento15m .org/). With the financial and economic crisis, fueled by risky behavior in the financial and banking sectors and corruption scandals involving public money, the call for less corporate power and the criminalization of corporate offenders increased. The crisis exposed the fine line between legal corporate behavior and perceived immoral corporate behavior. Byrne (2007) describes how corrupt behavior can be seen as the deterioration of self-regulated behavior and that the legal response to this helps society to determine right from wrong. However, that response focuses on the legality of behavior rather than on the morality. When behavior does not self-regulate because of low morality, and falls within the boundaries of the law, legal forms of corruption could occur (see Box 13.2). Kaufmann (2006) warns that these forms of corruption might even be more prevalent than illegal forms of behavior.

The concept of corporate crime arguably originates from the introduction of the concept of **white-collar crime** in the late 1930s by one of the most influential American sociologists and criminologists, Edwin H. Sutherland (1883–1950). Since he introduced the term into literature, numerous scholars have debated the definition of white-collar crime. Sutherland (1940, p. 1) talked about "crime in the upper or white-collar class, composed of respectable or at least respected business and professional men." He also

BOX 13.2 BALANCING BETWEEN LEGALITY AND ILLEGALITY

Karstedt (2015) discusses that society changed since the first debates about white-collar crime. The rise of the middle class during the second half of the last century resulted in today's middle class representing the center of contemporary society. This group now represents the core of shared beliefs and norms. Changes in consumption, finances and banking, and in particular the use of the Internet are believed to have increased the number of "ordinary people" committing white-collar crimes. Karstedt and Farral (2006, p. 1011) point to the gray zone of legality and morality, seen, for example, in the fine line between a gift and a bribe, or aggressive tax planning and illegal tax evasion. They also point out that the public shares moral intuitions that allow for widely held justifications, that is, "everybody does it," and for uninhibited discussions of such behavior among relatives and friends. What strikes Karstedt and Farral is that the middle classes are offending and victimized at the same time.

referred to the "violation of delegated or implied trust." Besides pointing to the damage of white-collar crime, Sutherland importantly advocated for the recognition of white-collar crime as a "real" crime and warned for the influence of upper classes on the formulation of criminal laws as well as the means white-collar criminals have at their disposal to minimize chances of conviction. Sutherland exposed the fact that crime was occurring not only solely among the lower social and economic classes but also from persons in higher classes like the business sector. The broad definition of white-collar criminals is narrowed down when speaking of corporate crime, which links the criminal behavior to companies as well as the economic system. Corporate crime, according to Clinard and Quinney (1973, p. 188), can be defined as "offenses committed by corporate officials for their corporation and the offenses of the corporation itself." It distinguishes itself from occupational crime in the sense that it concerns mostly crime in the economic interest of the company and involving executives from the corporation or the corporation itself. **Occupational crime** goes beyond the scope and refers mostly to crimes committed by persons when exercising the duties of their job. Corporate crime can involve different types of criminal acts that are generally characterized by low detection from law enforcement or the public because the illegal activities often take place within the framework of legal activities. In fact, offenders and victims are not clearly identifiable, given that corporations embody a collective of individuals, for example, the public, the employees, or other companies (Etzioni and Mitchell 2007).

A historical examination of the development of corporate crime reveals that the legislative response to forms of corporate behavior predominantly included legal controls, often implemented after scandals surfaced of cases involving "bribery, fraud, stock manipulation, predation against competitors, price gouging, exploitation of labor, and maintenance of unsafe working conditions" (Friedrichs 2010, p. 61). In order to ensure compliance with the legal controls, sanctioning measures were put in place, aimed at minimizing the harms caused by corporate crime, depending on the jurisdiction and the type of crime. These measures included the use of fines and sometimes imprisonment. For example, if we look at the crime of corporate manslaughter and homicide, the Sentencing Guidelines in the United Kingdom recommend a fine to be no less than GBP 500,000. However, the United Kingdom sets no limit on the amount that can be fined to companies. Ancillary sentences can include a publicity order compelling the company to publish the conviction in a public media forum or a remedial order forcing companies to rectify breaches identified within a case (Provisions 9 and 10). The French Penal Code (Articles 221–227) states that legal persons convicted for corporate manslaughter can be fined or have other sanctions imposed, such as judicial supervision or publicity orders. On the basis of available data in France, fines imposed in 2008 ranged between EUR 21,000 and EUR 150,000. Germany's administrative fines for corporate manslaughter (Ordnungswidrigkeiten) can reach up to EUR 1 million (see Box 13.3).

While crime prevention approaches differ from country to country, there is a general tendency to rely on formal legal responses as a sanctioning means to corporate crime and to serve as a quasi-regulatory measure

BOX 13.3   CORPORATE CRIMINAL LIABILITY

A challenge facing corporate crime prevention is legal accountability. Looking for ways on how to attribute responsibility to those causing crime, countries have attempted through their respective legal systems to govern risk-creating business activities. Countries started at different speeds with introducing industrial safety legislation in the 19th century, which performed in line with the industrial developments in countries and the need for functional laws to deal with issues concerning the physical workplace (i.e., working hours, sanitary conditions). In the 20th century, laws were developed to pursue social change in which employers were forced to manage safety risks. Also, internal compliance was promoted to deal with health and safety while, at the same time, inspection and enforcement systems were set up. Regulatory law instead of criminal law was used to deal with a legal response to severe health and safety offenses. Not until the last decades, countries started shifting toward criminal law to deal with forms of corporate violence against workers. England and Wales introduced in 2007 the offense of corporate manslaughter, which allows for imposing liabilities to corporations. However, legal traditions differ when looking at issues such as criminal liability. Other common-law jurisdictions such as Australia, Canada, and the United States have pursued initiatives to legally criminalize corporations. Mainland European countries with civil law traditions have, for a long time, resisted the corporate criminal liability, strictly seeing criminal law to be applicable to natural persons. However, initiatives to deal with corporate crime, that is, on issues such as bribery, from the European Union (EU), United Nations, and the Organisation for Economic Co-operation and Development (OECD) have pressured countries to converge. Today, several countries have pioneered in Europe with measures to address corporate liability, for example, the Netherlands, Denmark, and France. Countries that followed were Austria, Belgium, Estonia, Finland, Lithuania, Luxembourg, Portugal, Romania, and Slovenia. Italy and Spain indirectly adopted corporate liability, bypassing this way any limitations within their legal systems. Germany, Sweden, and the Czech Republic have not adopted corporate criminal liability and continue to apply administrative liability.

(Middleton 2005). An important factor explaining this approach is that conventional crime is perceived as destructive and opposite to socially desired behavior. Corporate crime, on the other hand, closely interacts with behavior that is productive and desirable from a social and economic point of view (Friedrichs 2010, p. 61). This is particularly evident when looking at **corruption** cases that challenge decision makers to undo investments that were based on criminal transactions. For example, Jiménez (2009) compiled data on corruption cases concerning urban planning in the Spanish coastal areas. The importance of tourism in those areas weighs heavily on the decision of judges to order the destruction of hotels that are built through corrupt practices (i.e., with illegally obtained building permits). In times of high unemployment, the destruction of hotels would mean the destruction of jobs, which, in the eyes of politicians and the public, is likely undesired.

Causes of Corporate Crime

Most explanations of corporate crime tend to emphasize the differences in circumstances or opportunities. Gobert and Punch (2003) note that the company often provides the context, opportunities, means, and incentives for criminal behavior. For example, active lobbying by companies or donations to legislators or political action committees give reason to believe that companies aim to control the legal and regulatory environment in which they operate. Opportunities to deviate are often created when a business environment constantly tries to expose new market opportunities created by regulatory weaknesses (Gobert and Punch 2007, p. 299). While conventional crimes are considered more accessible for larger groups of people (e.g., a group of young people on the street), often require a limited skill set or amount of planning, and can be rather opportunistic in nature (Maguire 1997), corporate crimes are often restricted to a small set of "white-collar" executives that are in a select position within the company and society to exploit unique opportunities (Clinard and Yeager 1980; Gobert and Punch 2007). Arguably, Sutherland's (1947) social processing theory of differential association can apply to both conventional and corporate crime, suggesting that white-collar workers operate in an environment that provides learning opportunities for lawbreaking behavior. Whether a person adopts these criminal behaviors depends on factors such as the intensity, frequency, and duration of contact with others who demonstrate those behaviors, creating environments for these criminal techniques to be learned. Furthermore, the social process theory of operant learning of the American psychologist B.F. Skinner (1904–1990) also applies to the concept of these learned criminal behaviors. Skinner's theory refers to a deviant behavior that is learned and continues if there are no negative consequences, such as a punishment that outweighs the positive results. In the corporate setting, the positive incentives of economic gain and the approval of peers can often outweigh the negative consequences of deviant behavior. Negative consequences can break a pattern of deviant behavior.

The operant learning theory can also be linked to repeat offenders because the absence of identifiable consequences (i.e., punishment) can lead to operant behavior. In addition, if corporate crime goes unnoticed, this offers reason to believe that the pattern will not be broken and behavior does not self-regulate. On the other hand, a limitation to the social learning and process theories, according to Goode (2008), is that learning criminal behavior through the interaction with others does not address the behavior of corporate criminals that act on an individual basis. Nor does it address the fact that corporate criminals might behave in accordance with the law in other walks of life. According to Geis and Goff (1986), however, the theory does not address the structural origin or cause of criminal behavior, but rather focuses on the process of involvement in such behavior.

This brings us to the theory of **anomie** developed by Robert Merton (1957), which builds on Émile Durkheim's concept of anomie referring to the social instability caused by the erosion of standards and values. Merton cites societal situations in which material success is valued, but the means to achieve that success is not equally accessible. As a consequence, some in society will pursue material success through criminal behavior. This has been observed in the former Soviet states in Eastern Europe that made the transition from communism to free market–based economies (Novolselec et al. 2015, p. 565). The upheaval in those countries led to opportunities to plunder public assets, and in combination with a total lack of regulation or control, white-collar criminals enriched themselves in "innovative" ways (e.g., through corruption, fraud, or embezzlement). Anomie could explain why corporations resort to illegal means to achieve goals that cannot be achieved legally. However, Merton's theory is challenged by the fact that white-collar criminals often do have the means to achieve their goals and therefore fall outside the scope of his explanation, which is more suited for explaining the crimes committed by those of a lower socioeconomic status looking to move up.

The **economic (general) strain theory** has been used to explain behavior of corporations that, under the pressure of economic competition, resort to criminal activities. Apart from the need to survive economically, Robert Agnew's (1992) strain theory explains the emotional factors that may drive criminal behavior, such as when companies resort to crime owing to the stress they experience from competitors. Finally, Lilly et al. (2011) refer to a breakdown of conventional behavior in times of rapid social change (see Box 13.4).

BOX 13.4   DUTCH REAL ESTATE FRAUD

In 2012, the Dutch courts convicted 11 defendants and four companies in the biggest fraud trial in Dutch history. The so-called Ivy Case involved widespread real estate fraud committed by executives holding leading positions in semipublic and commercial companies. According to van de Bunt and van Wingerde (2015), the case received considerable media attention because of its size, time frame (fraudulent practices took place for almost 10 years), and the fact that it went unnoticed for a long time. Van de Bunt et al. (2011, p. 53) explain how this case was a product of its time and place. The economic boom in the 1980s and 1990s, in combination with the general belief and support in privatization and the power of market forces, particularly caused economic optimism. This translated into willingness of banks to finance real estate projects up until the moment the crisis started in 2008. Van de Bunt et al. characterize the case as an example of anomie but also subscribe to Hansen and Mohavedi's (2010, p. 367) explanation of personal greed, a selfish pursuit of self-interest.

This leads us to the debate concerning the question of why normal counteracting forces in the business environment do not prevent persons from committing crimes. Grasham Sykes and David Matza (1957) remind us that offenders are generally accepting of social norms and values but deviate under certain circumstances, and in this way, people rationalize criminal behavior based on positive self-perception. Sykes and Matza's **techniques of neutralization** follow the differential association patterns established by Sutherland and distinguish five types: denial of responsibility, denial of substantial harm, denial of victimization, condemnation of law enforcement, and invocation of higher principles. Techniques of neutralization are in a sense counter to the theory of delinquent subculture, which argues that criminals have their own values and rules that differ from the rest of society (Vaughan 2007). While their focus is primarily on conventional crime, Steven Box (1983) reviewed the corporate environment and argued that offenders often denied responsibility by claiming ambiguity in the law, arguing that the act was accidental or the blame belonged to third parties. In addition, Box notes that corporate offenders argue that their acts are economically beneficial and therefore deny that any victims exist as a result of their behavior. Alternatively, corporations might criticize the law and law enforcement by claiming that those forces go against free market principles. Finally, Box argues that corporate offenders might use the neutralization technique of invoking "higher loyalties," by affirming their duties to service the needs of the corporation and its stockholders. Engaging in such neutralization techniques serves to facilitate the creation of subculture of behavior that, according to Shover and Hochstetler (2006), can be described as a culture of noncompliance, although the type of rationalization used by offenders might differ per offense type. Cloward and Ohlin (1960) present the differential opportunity theory, which sees criminal behavior as a function of the structure of opportunity. Toward this end, the Australian criminologist John Braithwaite (1992) added that corporate criminals markedly have, in addition, the skills to create such opportunities. This touches upon the concept that corporate crime is a response to a situation in which the benefits of crime outweigh behaving within the boundaries of the law. In turn, this reflects on the regulatory arms that aim to ensure corporate compliance. This environment adds to the socialization of opportunities that influence criminal opportunity in the face of threatened punishment.

Control theorists use a different lens to explain corporate and conventional criminal behavior. Their focus shifts to investigating why persons *do not* commit a crime despite the available opportunities. The social control theory of the esteemed American sociologist Travis Hirschi has been used to explain how persons with a strong attachment to others, a commitment to achievement, involvement in conventional activities, and a belief in moral validity of rules are restrained from engaging in criminal activity. However, in a culture of noncompliance, the belief component can be challenged. If criminal behavior is an underlying part of the business culture, the moral rationality of the law is constantly violated. In addition, people—both corporate offenders and the general public—perceive the gravity of violent and economic crimes differently. As discussed earlier in this chapter, the line between illegal and unethical behavior is often blurred. Hirschi, together with Gottfredson, later developed the **theory of self-control**, arguing that low self-control causes a person to commit crimes (Hirschi and Gottfredson 1989). Conversely, Charles Tittle (1995) adds to this by stating that too much control can lead to crime and therefore control should be balanced. Tittle's **control balance ratio** refers to the amount of exercised control versus the amount of imposed control. Both a surplus and a deficit could cause criminal behavior (Piquero et al. 2005).

In summary, we should also address the **economic theory of crime** in which the **rational choice model** embodies a commonly accepted explanation of human criminal behavior (Clarke and Felson 1993; Hirschi 1986). Criminal offenders plan and reason, adapt to circumstances, and weigh benefits against costs, and a combination of the low likelihood of sanctions with the higher likelihood of expected gains increases the instances of criminal behavior. The rational choice model for criminal justice originates in the work of Italian nobleman Cesare Beccaria (1764), as well as the English philosopher Jeremy Benthem (1789), who developed the utilitarian view that people engage in a calculus to maximize profits and minimize pain. More recent use of the model comes from Gary Becker (1968) who argues that there is no difference between criminal or noncriminal behavior and that the main reason to choose one or the other relates to the cost–benefit analysis. A subtype of the rational choice model is deterrence, which argues that criminal behavior is inhibited because of the possible punishment that is associated with it. While deterrence in the time of Beccaria and Bentham solely meant the threat of legal punishment, modern-day deterrence also looks at informal types of deterrents. Formal punishments include fines and imprisonment while informal punishments could include shame and feelings of guilt and embarrassment.

Deterrence and Compliance

Although each of the aforementioned theories offer an explanation as to why corporate crimes occur, they vary in scope and testability (i.e., two fundamental criteria for a "good" theory). As a result, it is clear that no one theory can address and solve all types of corporate crimes. As Vaughan (2015) points out: "in the historical trajectory of theories of cause in the sociology of crime and deviance [...], each theory of cause suggested a particular strategy of control that targeted the causal elements identified in that theory." Regardless of this, Vaughan does note that strategies to control corporate crime should target the causes of the problem, whereas responses should address social control, opportunistic structures, or cognitive states (Friedrichs 2010, p. 347). In addition, the response to corporate crime, as with most crimes, runs the gambit of being preventive in orientation, creating regulatory controls, or attempting to apply punitive sanctions against corporate offenders. Friedrichs (2010, p. 347) sums up that the approach against corporate crime should include a variety of measures, which together aim to reduce the motivation for committing the act, address the conditions that provide the opportunity to act, and promote a moral climate that does not tolerate such behavior.

As mentioned in the Introduction, the dominant legal response to corporate crime is regulatory rather than penal. An important reason for this has to do with the perception that corporate behavior (and crime) is closely associated with productivity and activities considered socially and economically desirable—especially in a capitalist-based market or neo-liberal enterprise. Responding in a punitive manner could create an unintended effect of harming productivity. As Friedrichs (2010, p. 283), among others, has observed, an important difference between regulatory versus penal enforcement is that the former has a "lower profile and is less likely to involve an adversarial confrontation between two parties," a preferred option for decision makers owing to the political sensitivity with which corporate (bad or good) behavior is addressed. Orbach (2012, p. 6) defines regulation as a "government intervention in the private domain or a legal rule that implements such intervention," which implies that regulations intend to shape behavior. Nevertheless, while rules and regulations may be designed to shape behavior, there is evidence to support that there is a virtual inverse correlation between the number of laws a country has and the amount of crime it has. An example of this can be seen in the legislative framework against corruption in European countries. For example, the European Commission noted in its 2014 European Anticorruption Report that Spain's anti-corruption legal framework was largely in place and that law enforcement made good progress in investigating corrupt practices (European Commission 2014, p. 14). Despite that, the country has seen large-scale corruption cases in recent years, revealing the corruption of public funds and the financing of political parties. Two particularly vulnerable sectors are public procurement and urban planning. The reporting of the European Commission, as well as other international bodies such as GRECO, exposes deficiencies in the implementation of legislation and more general deficiencies in checks and balances. The same is seen for laws aiming to prevent **money laundering**. Regulations can address the functioning of the market, for example, by preventing the formation of **corporate cartels** or preventing public procurement fraud. In addition, they can be used to address labor issues, such as the exploitation of workers. The enforcement of regulation violations can differ owing to the assessment of whether a specific action is considered compliant or noncompliant with regulations. When enforcing regulations, enforcers are often confronted with the decision to focus on compliance, or deterrence. Depending on the type of behavior, one or the other approach might be preferred or expected in accordance to the law. Deciding on this approach can hold a degree of discretion by the decision maker (Van de Bunt and Huisman 2007). For example, a government labor safety inspector may have a rulebook that stipulates which criteria are needed before a case can be named a violation. However, such a rulebook cannot be expected to provide an answer to every situation, meaning that the decision ultimately depends on the perception of the inspector. At the same time, the decision of the inspector has consequences, in that it could result in criminal investigation (and prosecution) into the doings of a corporation or directly result in an administrative penalty. In other words, the inspector has a degree of decision-making power, which without the proper control lends itself to possible abuse (Soudry 2007).

Frank (1984) distinguishes different policing styles adopted by regulatory agencies and differentiates those into persuading and cooperating and those prosecuting and punishing. The dividing line between these styles is not always clear as regulatory agencies often adopt a joint approach including persuasion and prosecution. In addition, such an approach can vary based on the problems encountered when implementing the regulation.

Important factors include the political climate in which the regulatory agency operates, the public and agency's opinion of the regulated company, and the potential damage of noncompliance. According to Simpson (2002), the typical responses to corporate and conventional types of crime tend to overlap. People perceive environmental crime as most severe, followed by worker's health and safety crimes, **price fixing**, and finally **insider trading** (see Box 13.5). Concerning sanctions, Simpson highlights that the public prefers more severe sanctions when the offender is a company as opposed to a single individual, although such attitudes vary "by the degree of harm and the culpability of the act" (2002, p. 4). The same is noted for criminal justice authorities that, according to Benson and Cullen (1998), perceive corporate

---

BOX 13.5   CORPORATE INTEGRITY

The call for businesses to operate in an ethical manner is increasingly reaffirmed not only on the national level through its legal system but also on the international level through conventions such as the 1999 OECD Anti-Bribery Convention and the United National Convention against Corruption. High media visibility of corruption or fraud scandals, such as the Siemens bribery case or the recent Volkswagen CO_2 emissions scandals, has made companies aware of risks to their reputation. Public pressure in combination with risks of financial sanctions are arguably compelling reasons for companies to act ethically and take proper measures to ensure compliance. An example of corporate self-regulation integrated into a business model is corporate social responsibility (CSR). With CSR, a company can monitor and enforce compliance with the law, as well as ethical standards or national and international norms. Self-regulation to prevent corporate crime is a contested approach as opponents might argue that this is a form of window dressing to the outside world. Proponents might argue that this fits into long-term business strategies aiming for sustainability and are therefore desirable. Regardless of the desirability of self-regulation of the business sector, research on its effects is contested. For example, Orlitzky et al. (2003) conducted a meta-analysis of 52 studies and found that corporate social performance is likely to positively affect financial performance. However, this does not necessarily imply that it prevents criminal behavior from occurring, especially if we take in account rational choice models in which corporations might decide based on maximizing profits. In fact, Hong and Liskovich (2016) point out that socially responsible companies could receive more lenient settlements from prosecutors after being caught bribing.

crime differently as a function of community characteristics. For example, prosecutors in more urban areas often perceive corporate crime as a "very serious" or "somewhat serious" problem (1998, p. 51). While a criminal justice response is seen as a strong deterrent for corporate crime (especially with possible imprisonment) and widely used, Simpson raises the question of whether criminal law has the capacity to prevent and control corporate crime (2002, p. 9). The threat of criminal punishment ignores other potential kinds of control that deter persons from criminal behavior, such as "threats to reputation, current and future employment, access to competitive resources (e.g., bids, contracts), friendship networks or associations, and family attachments" (Simpson 2002, p. 9).

As early as 1975, Christopher Stone argued that criminal law will fail to address corporate crime given it is not flexible enough "to adjust to and permeate dynamic business organizations" (1975, p. 93). Various reasons why this does not have the desired effect are "limited liability, the lack of congruence between the incentives of top executives and the incentives of 'the corporation,' the organisation's proclivity to buffer itself against external, especially legal threats" (Stone 1975, p. 93). Stone presents a set of alternatives to criminal law, by approaching corporate crime primarily by focusing on liability questions and enhancing CSR. He also argues that laws or profit making partially dictate corporate behavior.

Finally, globalization and the integration of economies place corporate crime prevention in a different perspective. For example, the LIBOR scandal included fraudulent practices by banks concerning the manipulation of short-term interest rates, involving approximately USD 350 trillion in derivatives, making it a financial scam of epic proportions. The cross-border element of corporate crime is and has become ever more important when discussing deterrence and compliance, especially considering that corporations have been increasingly operating across borders since the 1970s (Braithwaite and Drahos 2000). This poses different challenges to classical deterrence models at the national level that assume that sanctioning risks and consequences are bigger than the benefits from criminal behavior. First of all, different enforcement of national models could shift the problem from one jurisdiction to the next, as offenders might migrate to jurisdictions where enforcement of deterrence models is weaker. For example, anticorruption watchdogs see the bribery of foreign officials in less developed countries by corporations from more developed countries as a form of corporate crime owing to the uneven enforcement of law (see, e.g., Transparency International reports on the implementation of the OECD Anti-Bribery Convention). Second, corporations operating in multiple jurisdictions can more easily hide activities and complicate law enforcement because of the complexity of company structures (van Wingerde 2015). There are many instances of corporations using shell companies in different jurisdictions

BOX 13.6   DUMPING TOXIC WASTE

The 2006 *Probo Koala* case is an example that highlights the challenges of using deterrence models for corporate crime. The case involved the toxic waste dump in Ivory Coast, involving the *Probo Koala* vessel that was Korean-built, Greek-owned, Panama-registered, and chartered by a Dutch-based oil and commodity shipping company. In Europe, this has been one of the largest European environmental scandals to date. It took six years before the criminal sentences were imposed, which shows the legal complexities characterizing corporate environmental crime (Nelken 2002). The *Probo Koala* case exposed various difficulties, such as the ambiguous nature of the product waste (van Wingerde 2015). While waste product can be defined as hazardous waste based on the origin of the product in some jurisdictions, in others, this is viewed differently depending on the use, that is, as fuel. A second challenge concerns different views on the composition of the waste and its effect on health. Different interpretations immediately complicate efforts to determine responsibility, especially when multiple stakeholders are involved, coming from different countries. Finally, van Wingerde points out that the ambivalent response to corporate environmental crime, that is, criminal or civil, added to the ambiguity of the case. The difficulty of collecting sufficient evidence for criminal prosecution and the challenge to ascertain responsibility can result in out-of-court settlement.

for various reasons, including tax evasion (see, e.g., the 2016 Panama Papers scandal) and the dumping of toxic waste (Box 13.6).

Reducing Corporate Crime Risks

Etzioni and Mitchell (2007) remark that the literature on preventing corporate crime highlights the importance of fostering a culture of respect for the law within businesses and creating internal controls to prevent misbehavior. For example, business schools have a role to play in preventing corporate crime by educating future corporate executives. However, incorporating ethics into the curriculum is not necessarily straightforward as definitions and values can differ. Friedrichs (2010) emphasizes the conditions when looking at crime prevention such as time, place, offender, and victim, although the identification of offenders arguably does not have the same priority in corporate crime as it has in conventional crime. The fact that corporate crime is often hidden within normal, or legal business, procedures makes a case for first focusing on ensuring that the crime itself can be detected. As mentioned above, techniques can be formal (e.g., through law enforcement) or informal (e.g., through company compliance systems).

Two techniques that can be used are monitoring systems that red flag possible irregularities or safety mechanisms such as compliance systems that strengthen control within business processes. The interesting contemporary element in these techniques is the use of new technologies that allow for the real-time surveillance of complex processes (see, e.g., Goldstein and Dyson 2013). For example, the use of open data on public procurement can be used not only by law enforcement but also by normal citizens to identify anomalies in public spending (see, e.g., http://www.open-contracting.org/ or http:// monitoring.transparency-usa.org/). The use of compliance systems including codes of conduct, or whistleblower channels, also supports workers that want to advocate corporate responsibility in the interest of the public. Repeatedly, citizens are asked and motivated to report suspicious behavior of companies, for example, relating to tax evasion or pollution. Such techniques are not uncommon in cases of conventional crimes, for example, through neighborhood watch schemes (Alvesalo et al. 2006).

A distinction can be made between so-called **command-and-control strategies** and self-regulation approaches (Simpson et al. 2013, p. 232). Concerning the former, here, the authorities dictate the terms of compliance, which often also includes specific formal sanctions in cases of noncompliance. Imposing severe sanctions as a deterrent for crime is a frequently chosen approach in responses to conventional crimes. However, Cohen (2000) argues that the severe punishment of corporate crime alone does not work without also ensuring proper inspection, and Simpson (2002) argues that inspection frequency is more important than severe sanctioning. In other words, reducing the risk of corporate crime should be addressed by detection strategies in combination with punishment (see Box 13.7).

Self-regulation can be seen as a complementary system to command-and-control strategies enforced by the authorities (Simpson et al. 2013, p. 232). Corporations can set up compliance systems, establish ethical guidelines, and adopt informal sanctioning structures. The objective of self-regulation is to reduce crime opportunities, although this departs from the assertion that the corporations themselves are best placed to detect and deter crime. The difficulty with self-regulation is that its effect is dependent on internal accountability structures (Soudry 2007). Specifically, in order for structures within a corporation to be able to reduce crime, an adequate balance of power is needed. A common example is a workers' union that monitors safety conditions at the workplace, and therefore the organization of trade unions creates a way to hold management accountable for its actions.

BOX 13.7   BLOWING THE WHISTLE

Whistleblowing is most commonly defined as the "disclosure by organization members (former or current) of illegal, immoral or illegitimate practices under the control of their employees, to persons or organizations that may be able to effect action" (Near and Miceli 1985, p. 4). Kölbel (2015) presents a comparative overview of legal frameworks in Europe to deal with whistleblowing. He highlights how systems differ between countries—with Anglo-American countries notably having institutionalized systems. The anti-corruption movement Transparency International considers whistleblowing a direct method of exposing corruption. However, the organization highlights that whistleblowers commonly face retaliation, such as harassment, firing, blacklisting, threats, and even physical violence. Aside from this, the functioning of the whistleblower mechanism is challenged by the fear of retaliation (Kölbel 2015), which raises the question as to whether people should be legally protected from this.

The government can play a role in enforcing self-regulation, but the concept does not necessarily rely on formal regulation. Braithwaite (1989) talks about the **family model of crime control** in which workers, when confronted with crime opportunities, make a decision based on not only their understanding of right and wrong but also the impact of the behavior on their reputations. This, in other words, challenges rational choice assumptions that views offenders as persons that weigh costs against benefits. Self-regulation can thus be seen as a form of organizational social responsibility in combination with the norms and values of individual workers.

Reputational damage or negative publicity can be a deterrent for criminal behavior and also a motivator for companies to strengthen internal corporate crime prevention mechanisms (see, e.g., the Siemens case in Box 13.9). Corporations could suffer from negative consequences from allegations, let alone from formal investigations and prosecution cases. It could have an effect on the public image, on the market price of corporation, and even stock prices or sales (Orlitzky et al. 2003). The question of whether the stigma associated with criminal behavior weighs equally for both conventional and corporate offenders, and therefore reducing crime, is uncertain. The labeling theory provides some insight into the process of how society responds to perceived crime (Schur 1971). Corporate criminals arguably differ in the fact that individuals and corporations have the means to avoid negative labeling or, at the very least, influence the degree of stigmatization that comes with being labeled a criminal. This is particularly visible in bribery settlement cases where companies are willing to pay large sums of money in order to avoid legal prosecution (Hong and Liskovich 2016). Often, an important part of settlement negotiations concerns the question of whether corporations can settle without acknowledging wrongdoing (see, e.g., http://www.reuters .com/article/us-ibm-sec-idUSBRE96O1FB20130726). This has partially to do with the desire of corporations to not be stigmatized as corrupt.

Effects of Interventions

Types of interventions against corporate crime might have different effects depending on the characteristics of the offense type. Apart from the nature of the crime (e.g., corruption, fraud, violence, etc.), there are also other relevant characteristics such as the type of victims (e.g., consumers, employees, the public or other corporations, etc.) and the type of corporation (e.g., big, small, local, international, private or semipublic, etc.) (Friedrichs 2010).

Responses to "violence" committed by corporations could require different approaches as compared to responses for "abuse of power" committed by corporations, although there is a systemic element embedded when trying to understand the causes of crimes in both types of offenses. For example, the illegal dumping of toxic waste can be the (opportunistic) behavior of a specific individual, but penalizing that person might not address the more systemic problem, which is the need to dispose of toxic waste in a responsible manner. Arguably, the risk potential for corporate crime increases in a business environment that is driven by maximizing profits. Thus, responding to the dumping of toxic waste by imprisonment might deter individuals from repeating their crimes, but it does not guarantee that others do not repeat crimes as long as the systemic conditions that have facilitated and driven this behavior remain the same. The same argument could be made for responses to abuse of power, such as fraud and corruption by corporations.

An **abuse of power** differs from more conventional types of crime in the sense that damage is difficult to determine and evidence of criminal behavior is difficult to detect. Most importantly, an abuse of power can go blatantly unnoticed. Also, in this case, the conditions in which corporations operate create a climate in which the abuse of power can occur. For example, **rational choice institutionalism** explains how the preferences of individuals are determined by the institutional context in which their choices are made (Zald 1987). The corporation functions as a structure that provides incentives and disincentives for certain choices based on its formal and informal rules. Companies are not only the cause of certain behavior but also an effect of behavior. In other words, companies are shaped according to the needs of the participating actors. The **bargaining model of bribery** described by Fisman and Gatti (2002) shows how an abuse of power can go unnoticed and remain a secret between the corrupted and the corruptor. It considers that a bargaining situation occurs between a corporation and a public official. The former is confronted with a number of regulatory requirements that bear certain costs. Such regulatory requirements could be, for example, upholding labor and environmental standards. The company could either comply with these requirements or pay a bribe in order to avoid them (see Box 13.8). The public official might be in a position to skew the regulation without inflicting any costs to the company. In other words, a bribe agreement between the public official and the corporation benefits both parties. At the same time, breaking the agreement disadvantages both parties, making bribery—especially when not consisting of money—particularly difficult to detect.

In order to target specific interventions intended to prevent opportunistic corporate criminal behavior, it is important to consider the conditions under which corrupt and fraudulent behavior by corporations takes place. The father of the Transparency International Corruption Perception Index, Johann Graf Lambsdorff (2002), details how corporations make corrupt deals. He describes how criminals first seek the appropriate partner and subsequently design an enforceable contract that will minimize opportunistic behavior during and after the corrupt transaction. The latter is of special importance as it refers to the increasing interdependence between the bribed public official and the corporation. It also explains why crimes relating to the abuse of power can go unnoticed as long as both parties stick to the agreement. At the same time, this helps us better understand what measures to take in order to address the problem.

The process of seeking an adequate partner in crime, engaging this person, and agreeing on a "workable" arrangement is difficult (Lambsdorff 2002). The partner needs to possess the abilities to actually deliver the required goods or services, and in practice, there can be a sense of public and political sensitivity toward the output of the activity (e.g., public procurement activities). In addition, simply approaching a partner can expose one to accusations, especially when offering a bribe that does not outweigh the risk of accepting the bribe. At the same time, for the person offering the bribe, the costs associated with the bribe should not outweigh the expected gains. The specific conditions described here arguably provide for an environment more perceptive to preventive than to reactive measures, given that corruption often goes undetected, and when detected, it is difficult to expose and prove (see Box 13.9).

Taking preventive measures such as establishing whistleblower channels and ensuring whistleblower protection provides a safe environment for persons to come forward about undue corporate behavior. In addition, another element to take into account is that corruption can be linked to opportunistic behavior in which trust between stakeholders is important. Transparency and accountability measures are important and widely advocated to reduce the risk of abuse of power and facilitate a business culture less perceptive to criminal behavior.

BOX 13.8 COLLECTIVE ACTION

The U4 Anti-Corruption Resource Centre (U4) and the international anti-corruption movement Transparency International (TI) (2015) define collective action as "actions undertaken by individuals and/or groups toward a collective purpose or goal" and highlight the growing support for such initiatives in order to fight abuse of power. According to the organizations, lack of political will undermines the effectiveness of top-down anti-corruption approaches. Mungiu-Pippidi (2013) argues that failure of many approaches to date is attributed to the top-down approach. Instead, a combination with bottom-up is advocated to increase sustainability of reform and ensure that change occurs at all levels of society. Collective action hinges toward social learning theories in which the relevance of social or group dynamics to influence one's decisions is important. Trust in others and the real or perceived behavior of others influences the way one looks at deviant behavior. If corruption is seen as normal in a certain context, it also facilitates such behavior. Collective action initiatives could break patterns when, for example, people stop bribing (supply) with the consequence that asking (demand) will become more difficult.

Various types of collective action are identified by U4 and TI, ranging from individualistic to collectivistic, normative to nonnormative, and punishable to unpunishable. A further differentiation between persuasive and confrontational forms of collective action refers to those actions aiming to solve internal issues, that is, through lobbying or petitioning, versus those that directly target other parties, that is, through demonstrations. A collective action tool used by TI is the Integrity Pact (IP). This tool was developed in the 1990s to improve procurement processes. By applying a collaborative approach, the tool aims to establish a level playing field in a contracting process. This is ensured by encouraging companies to refrain from bribery, committing government agencies to prevent corruption, and following transparent procedures. An IP includes key criteria for anti-corruption in public procurement, such as transparency, professionalism, and accountability. Applied since the 1990s, a solid sample of cases is available for review, covering many countries across the world. The characteristics of each case differ, requiring the IP model to be flexible in order to be an effective anti-corruption tool. At this stage, experience with IPs shows that four main elements are crucial (see TI's IP Guide): political will of the authorities, transparency and professionalism throughout the contracting process, external independent monitoring, and a participatory/multi-stakeholder involvement.

BOX 13.9   THE SUPPLY SIDE OF CORRUPTION

Between 2001 and 2007, the German industrial giant Siemens allegedly embezzled an estimated EUR 1.3 billion. Investigations exposed structural corruption at the company, in particular in the telecommunications and power generation divisions, and regional offices abroad. Funds were used to bribe foreign officials. Siemens pled guilty to having violated the U.S. Foreign Corrupt Practices Act and settled for roughly EUR 1 billion. The characteristics of this case are especially interesting because it includes large amounts of money, a major economic operator on the global level, and a form of corruption (bribery) that proves to be highly resilient against anti-corruption laws (Weismann 2007). More importantly, corruption research tends to focus on the demand side of bribery, that is, looking at the public sector and governance issues, while in this case, the bribing of foreign officials by a renowned company sheds light on the supply side of corrupt practices. In his *Handbook of White-Collar and Corporate Crime in Europe*, Klinkhammer (2015) presents an interesting case study on the Siemens scandal. The case study focuses on the supply side of corrupt practices and discusses, inter alia, what the social structure of offenders reveals about individual offenders, what motivated their actions, and whether these were indicative of organizational cultures or strain.

The Future of Preventing Corporate Crime

The final section of this chapter is meant to initiate debate by discussing the relevance of criminal sanctions to prevent corporate crime in today's postmodern and globalized world. Friedrichs (2015) notes how the study of white-collar crime calls for the attention of many different academic disciplines (including criminology, political science, history, economics, psychology, sociology, managerial sciences, etc.). Since the first discovery of white-collar crime by Edwin Sutherland, society and technology have changed, and with those advancements, new forms of white-collar crime emerged. According to Friedrichs, agencies of social control and regulation are facing challenges to deal with the new forms of corporate crime and the increasingly powerful globally operating corporations. We have seen some examples of corporate crime and globalization, such as financial crime, already in this chapter. Another important example of this is cybercrime, which is increasingly considered by international organizations as a threat to public safety, especially when it is linked to terrorism.

Cybercrime is a quite recent phenomenon surfacing in the late 1990s and its evolution has been very fast and continuous (see Chapter 15 in this volume). Currently, the scale of cybercriminal activity represents a considerable challenge to law enforcement agencies and the total cost of cybercrime to society is considered quite significant. A report by McAfee in 2014 estimates that the annual cost to the global economy from cybercrime is around EUR 400 billion. A study conducted by the Ponemon Institute in 2014 for HP Enterprise Security finds that the cost of cybercrime has increased 95% over the last four years. With billions of people accessing the Internet worldwide on a daily basis, the exposed risks are increasingly affecting citizens, businesses, and governments. The EU and the United States represent key targets because of their advanced Internet infrastructure and increasingly Internet-based economies and payment systems.

A Eurobarometer report on cybersecurity from 2015 shows that 63% of the European Internet users are concerned about being a victim of bank card or online banking fraud, 60% are concerned about having their social media or e-mail account hacked, 56% are concerned about online fraud, and 66% are concerned about discovering malicious software on their devices. In Europe, key challenges need to be addressed with the harmonization of national legislation, enhanced law enforcement, and improved international cooperation. European regulations aim to adapt to globalization challenges by harmonizing criminal law across EU Member States. This includes establishing minimum rules and sanctions concerning the definition of criminal offenses and improving cooperation between competent authorities.

Key challenges for law enforcement lie ahead in defining national approaches to computer-related crimes. This includes fraud and forgery, child pornography, copyright infringements, and security breaches. Countries are challenged with establishing national procedures for detecting, investigating, and prosecuting such crimes. In addition, the need for collecting electronic evidence and establishing an effective system for international cooperation poses challenges against the backdrop of creating mutual legal frameworks, tools, and cooperation between disparate authorities.

Friedrichs (2015) observes that developments do have an effect on the control and regulation of corporate crime and challenges whether existing regulatory mechanisms are equipped to cope with the globalized world or not. As an example, Friedrichs points out that international financial institutions were established to regulate international finance but failed to do so in light of scandals as discussed above. Apart from enforcement challenges, a next step in the context of a globalized world would be to look at whether criminal sanctions are relevant when dealing with corporate crime. First, the potential deterrent effect of criminal sanctions might weigh less on corporate offenders as these can be powerful and this way reduce the severity and likelihood of a criminal sanction. For example, we have seen the complexity of criminally prosecuting the 2006 *Probo Koala* case involving the illegal dumping of toxic waste off the Ivory Coast, with the consequence that authorities resort to out-of-court settlements. In addition, a secondary effect of criminal sanctions, such as reputational damage, can be of importance. We have also seen that this is an incentive for companies to initiate CSR programs.

Glossary of Terms

Anomie: refers to social instability caused by the erosion of standards and values. In a society where material success is valued but the means to achieve that success is not equally accessible, some will pursue this through criminal behavior.

Bargaining model of bribery: refers to a situation in which a company is required to deal with a number of bureaucratic regulations, which bear costs. The enforcer of the regulations can either force the company to comply or pay a bribe to circumvent these regulations. In order for the latter to happen, the costs of a joint agreement between the company and the official need to be lower than the costs of complying with the regulation.

Command-and-control strategy: is a form of direct regulation of activities by rules that stipulate what is considered illegal and legal.

Compliance: refers to the objective of organizations to ensure that they are aware of and take steps to comply with the rules and regulations.

Control balance ratio: pertains to the amount of exercised control versus the amount of imposed control. Control balance suggests that crime is more likely to occur when people are more controlled than controlling, as well as when people are more controlling than controlled. Control ratios could influence motivation, provocation, opportunity, and constraint.

Corporate cartels: involve agreements between competing companies to control prices or exclude other companies from entering the market. A public cartel refers to the involvement of a government to enforce the agreement. Private cartels only involve private-sector stakeholders, which often are regulated through antitrust laws.

Corporate crime: pertains to the crimes committed by the corporation or by corporate officials, mostly in the economic interest of the corporation. It distinguishes itself from occupational crime, which refers more to crimes committed by persons when exercising their job.

Corporate criminal liability: refers to the liability imposed upon a corporation for the crime committed by any natural person.

Corruption: can be defined as the abuse of power for private gain. This definition includes three elements: corrupt acts occur in the private and public sector; there is abuse of power held by a public institution or private organization; the "corrupted" and the "corruptor" benefit from the corrupt act.

Economic theory of crime: adopts a rational choice model in explaining human criminal behavior. Criminal offenders plan and reason, adapt to circumstances, and weigh benefits against costs, and a combination of the low likelihood of sanctions with the higher likelihood of expected gains increases the instances of criminal behavior.

Family model of crime control: is a model in which workers, when confronted with crime opportunities, make a decision based on their understanding of right and wrong, as well as the impact of such behavior on their reputation.

Insider trading: refers often to trading of stocks or other securities by individuals with access to restricted/non-public information about the company. Insider trading is often considered illegal and an unfair practice.

Money laundering: is the term used to describe the process that criminals use to transform the proceeds of crime into legitimate money or other assets.

Price fixing: refers to an agreement between participants on the same side in a market to maintain market conditions or to buy or sell at a fixed price.

Rational choice institutionalism: represents a theoretical approach to studying institutions. It argues that actors use institutions to maximize their utility but are facing rule-based constraints provided by the institutional environment that influences their behavior. Institutions are created in an attempt to reduce transaction costs of collective activity.

Self-regulation: to prevent corporate crime refers to the process whereby organizations monitor their own adherence to standards. These standards can be legal or ethical in nature.

Techniques of neutralization: are a series of methods by which people temporarily turn off certain values that would normally prohibit them from committing crimes. Five main neutralization techniques are denial of responsibility, denial of substantial harm, denial of victimization, condemnation of law enforcement, and the appeal to higher loyalties.

White-collar crime: can be defined as illegal or unethical behavior of a corporation, or of employees, which are often of high or respectable status and acting on behalf of the corporation.

Discussion Questions

1. Discuss which of the theories presented appear to offer the greatest explanatory model for preventing white-collar/corporate crime.
2. Which kinds of interventions diminish the risk of corporate crime? Explain.

3. Do interventions have different effects by offense type?
4. Can criminal sanctions applied to corporations play a role in crime prevention?
5. What will be the effect of new forms of globalized corporate crime on crime prevention?

Suggested Reading

Erp, J.G. (2015). *The Routledge Handbook of White-Collar and Corporate Crime in Europe.*

Pontell, H.N., and Geis, G. (2007). *International Handbook of White-Collar and Corporate Crime.* New York: Springer.

Recommended Web Links

U4 Anti-Corruption Resource Centre—http://www.u4.no/

The website of the U4 Anti-Corruption Resource Centre provides applied research material ranging from private- to public-sector corruption, development aid and corruption, and anti-corruption initiatives in the justice sector. Apart from publications, the website also provides audiovisual material as well as links to other resources and recommended reading material

Transparency International—http://www.transparency.org/

The website of the anti-corruption watchdog Transparency International provides information on the organization's activities and publications. Documentation can be found on corruption per country and topic (i.e., private sector), as well as the yearly Corruption Perception Index, which is considered one of the main tools to measure the level of corruption around the world.

European Commission DG Home Affairs—http://ec.europa.eu/dgs/home-affairs/

The website of the European Commission, Directorate-General on Migration and Home Affairs provides information on EU policies relating issues such as organized crime and human trafficking. This includes resources on types of crime, such as cybercrime, corruption, and money laundering. In addition, the website addresses EU initiatives to prevent crime, conduct financial investigation, and deal with confiscation and asset recovery.

OECD—http://www.oecd.org/

The website of the OECD has dedicated sections on bribery and corruption, as well as corporate governance. The former include information on the OECD Anti-Bribery Convention, including information on its implementation per country. The website also provides resources on tax and crime. The section on corporate governance includes sets of guidelines for multinational enterprises to promote responsible business conduct.

UNODC—https://www.unodc.org/unodc/index.html?ref=menutop

The United Nations Office on Drugs and Crime (UNODC) presents resources on a variety of topics such as corruption, crime prevention and criminal justice, fraudulent medicines, and money laundering. The website also contains detailed information on the United Nations Convention against Corruption, which is seen as one of the most important legal instruments against corruption.

WEF—https://www.weforum.org/

The World Economic Forum (WEF) website presents information in relation to the Partnering against Corruption Initiative (PACI). PACI brings businesses together and promotes corporate citizenship. The website includes various sector-specific publications, for example, on urban and development industries, as well as information on the Business 20 group that brings together business leaders from the world's leading economies.

Acknowledgments

I would like to especially thank my colleague and friend Joel Troge for his valuable input on this chapter. Also, I extend a notable thank you to Professor John Winterdyk for his patience and guidance and feedback throughout the process of finalizing the work.

References

Agnew, R. (1992). Foundation for a general strain theory of crime and delinquency. *Criminology* 30(1): 47–87.

Alvesalo, A., Tombs, S., Virta, E., and Whyte, D. (2006). Re-imagining crime prevention: Controlling corporate crime? *Crime, Law and Social Change* 45(1): 1–25.

Benson, M., and Cullen, F. (1998). *Combatting Corporate Crime: Local Prosecutors at Work*. Boston: Northeastern University Press.

Box, S. (1983). *Power, Crime and Mystification*. London: Travistock.

Braithwaite, J. (1984). *Corporate Crime in the Pharmaceutical Industry*. London: Routledge & Kegan Paul.

Braithwaite, J. (1989). Criminological theory and organizational crime. *Justice Quarterly* 6: 333–358.

Braithwaite, J. (1992). Poverty, power, white-collar crime and the paradoxes of criminological theory. *Australian & New Zealand Journal of Criminology* 24(1): 40–58.

Braithwaite, J., and Drahos, P. (2000). *Global Business Regulation*. Cambridge, UK: Cambridge University Press.

Byrne, E. (2007). *The Moral and Legal Development of Corruption: Nineteenth and Twentieth Century Corruption in Ireland*. PhD Thesis, University of Limerick.

Clarke, R.V., and Felson, M. (1993). Introduction: Criminology, routine activity, and rational choice (from *Routine Activity and Rational Choice: Advances in Criminological Theory*, Vol. 5, pp. 1–14, 1993, Ronald V. Clarke and Marcus Felson, eds.—see NCJ-159998).

Clinard, M., and Quinney, R. (1973). *Criminal Behavior Systems: A Typology*. New York: Holt, Rinehart and Winston.

Clinard, M., and Yeager, P. (1980). *Corporate Crime*. New York: Free Press.

Cloward, R., and Ohlin, L. (1960). *Delinquency and Opportunity: A Theory of Delinquent Gangs*. Glencoe, IL: Free Press.

Etzioni, A., and Mitchell, D. (2007). Corporate Crime. In *International Handbook of White-Collar and Corporate Crime*, eds. H.N. Pontell and G. Geis. New York: Springer.

European Commission. (2014). Spain to the EU Anti-corruption Report. http://ec.europa.eu/dgs/home-affairs/what-we-do/policies/organized-crime-and-human-trafficking/corruption/anti-corruption-report/docs/2014_acr_spain_chapter_en.pdf.

Frank, N. (1984). Policing Corporate Crime: A Typology of Enforcement Styles. Justice Quarterly, 1(2) (1984): 235–251. Published by Taylor & Francis Ltd.

Friedrichs, D.O. (2010). *Trusted Criminals: White Collar Crime in Contemporary Society*, 4th Edition. Belmont, CA: Wadsworth Pub. Co.

Friedrichs, D.O. (2015). White-collar crime in Europe—American reflections. In The Routledge handbook of white-collar and corporate crime in Europe, eds. Van Erp et al. sOxon: Routledge.

Geis, G., and Goff, C. (1986). Edwin H. Sutherland's white-collar crime in America: An essay in *historical* criminology. *Criminal Justice History* 7: 1–31.

Gobert, J., and Punch, M. (2003). *Rethinking Corporate Crime*. London: Butterworths/LexisNexis.

Gobert, J., and Punch, M. (2007). Because they can—Motivations and intent of white-collar criminals. In *International Handbook of White-Collar and Corporate Crime*, eds. H. Pontell and G. Geis. New York: Springer.

Goldstein, B., Dyson, L. (2013). Beyond Transparency: Open Data and the Future of Civic Innovation. San Francisco: Code for America Press.

Goode, E. (2008). *Out of Control: Assessing the General Theory of Crime*. Stanford, CA: Stanford Social Sciences.

Hansen, L.L., and Movahedi, S. (2010). Wall Street scandals: The myth of individual greed. *Sociological Forum* 25(2): 367–374.

Hirschi, T. (1986). On the compatibility of rational choice and social control theories of crime (from *Reasoning Criminal*, pp. 105–118, 1986, Derek B. Cornish and Ronal V. Clarke, eds.—see NCJ-102282).

Hirschi, T., and Gottfredson, M. (1989). The significance of white-collar crime for a general theory of crime. *Criminology* 27: 359–371.

Hong, H.G., and Liskovich, I. (2016). Crime, Punishment and the Value of Corporate Social Responsibility. Available at SSRN: http://ssrn.com/abstract=2492202.

Huisman, W. (2011). Corporate crime and crisis: Causation scenarios. In *Economic Crisis and Crime (Sociology of Crime, Law and Deviance, Volume 16)*, ed. M. Deflem, 107–125. Emerald Group Publishing Limited.

Jiménez, F. (2009). Building boom and political corruption in Spain. *South European Society and Politics*, 14(3): 255–272.

Kagan, R.A., and Scholz, J.T. (1983). The criminology of the corporation and regulatory enforcement strategies. In *Enforcing regulation*, eds. K. Hawkins and J. Thomas. Boston: Kluwer-Nijhoff Publishers.

Karstedt, S., and Farrall, S. (2006). The moral economy of everyday crime: Markets, consumers and citizens. *British Journal of Criminology* 46(6): 1011–1036.

Karstedt, S. (2015). Charting Europe's moral economies: Citizens, consumers and the crimes of everyday life. In *The Routledge Handbook of White-Collar and Corporate Crime in Europe*, eds. J. Erp et al.

Kaufmann, D. (2006). *Corruption, Governance and Security*. World Economic Forum: Global Competitiveness Report 2004/2005.

Klinkhammer, J. (2015). Varieties of corruption in the shadow of Siemens: A modus operandi study of corporate crime on the supply side of corrupt transactions. In *The Routledge Handbook of White-Collar and Corporate Crime in Europe*, eds. J. Erp et al.

Kölbel, R. (2015). Whistleblowing in Europe: Regulatory frameworks and empirical research. In *The Routledge handbook of white-collar and corporate crime in Europe*, eds. Van Erp et al. Oxon: Routledge.

Lilly, J., Cullen, F., and Ball, R. (2011). *Criminological Theory: Context and Consequences*. Thousand Oaks, CA: SAGE Publications.

Maguire, M. (1997). Crime statistics, patterns, and trends: Changing perceptions and their implications. In *The Oxford Handbook of Criminology*, eds. M. Maguire et al. Oxford, UK: Clarendon Press.

Merton, R. (1957). Social theory and anomie. *American Sociological Review* 3: 672–682.

Middleton D. J. (2005), 'The Legal and Regulatory Response to Solicitors Involved in Serious Fraud Is Regulatory Action More Effective than Criminal Prosecution?', *British Journal of Criminology*, 45, 810–36.

Mungiu-Pippidi, A. (2013). Controlling corruption through collective action. *Journal of Democracy* 24(1).

Near, J.P., and Miceli, M.P.J. (1985). *Business ethics* 4: 1. doi:10.1007/BF00382668.

Nelken, D. (2002). White-collar crime. In *The Oxford Handbook of Criminology*, eds. M. Maguire, R. Morgan, and R. Reiner. Oxford, UK: Oxford University Press, pp. 844–877.

Novolselec, P., Roksandic Vidlicka, S., and Marsavelski, A. (2015). Retroactive prosecution of transitional economic crimes in Croatia. In *The Routledge Handbook of White-Collar and Corporate Crime in Europe*, eds. J. Erp et al.

Orbach, B. (2012). What Is Regulation? Yale Journal on Regulation Online 1 (2012); Arizona Legal Studies Discussion Paper No. 12–27. Available at SSRN: http://ssrn.com/abstract=2143385.

Orlitzky, M., Schmidt, F.L., and Rynes, S. (2003). Corporate Social and Financial Performance: A Meta-Analysis.

Piquero, N.L., Exum, M.L., and Simpson, S.S. (2005). Integrating the desire-for-control and rational choice in a corporate crime context. *Justice Quarterly* 22: 251–280.

Schur, E.M. (1971). Labeling deviant behaviour-Its sociological implications. New York: Harper & Row.

Shover, N., and Hochstetler, A. (2006). *Choosing White-Collar Crime.* Cambridge, UK: Cambridge University Press.

Simpson, S. (2002). Corporate Crime, Law, and Social Control. Cambridge Studies in Criminology.

Simpson, S., Gibbs, C., Rorie, M., Slocum, L.A., Cohen, M.A., and Vandenbergh, M. (2013). An empirical assessment of corporate environmental crime-control strategies. *Journal of Criminal Law and Criminology* 231. Retrieved from http://scholarlycommons.law.northwestern.edu/jclc/vol103/iss1/5.

Simpson S.S., Rorie, M., Alper, M., and Schell-Busey, N. (2014). *Corporate Crime Deterrence: A Systematic Review Campbell Systematic Reviews* 4. doi: 10.4073/csr .2014.4.

Simpson, S., Rorie, M., Alper, M.E., Schell-Busey, N., Laufer, W., and Smith, N.C. (2014). *Corporate Crime Deterrence: A Systematic Review.*

Soudry, O. (2007). A principal-agent analysis of accountability in public procurement (http://www.ippa.org/IPPC2/BOOK/Chapter_19.pdf).

Stone, C.D. (1975). Where the Law Ends. New York: Harper and Row.

Sutherland, E.H. (1940). The White-collar criminal. *American Sociological Review* 5: 1–12. DOI: 10.2307/2083937.

Sutherland, E.H. (1947). Principles of criminology (4th ed.). Philadelphia: Lippincott.

Sutherland, E.H. (1949). *White Collar Crime.* New York: Dryden.

Sykes, G., and Matza, D. (1957). Techniques of neutralization: A theory of delinquency. *American Sociological Review* 22(6): 664–670.

Tittle, C. (1995). *Control Balance: Toward a General Theory of Deviance.* Boulder, CO: Westview.

Van de Bunt, H.G., and Huisman, W. (2007). Organizational crime in the Netherlands. *Crime & Justice* 32: 477–493.

Van de Bunt, H., and van Wingerde, K. (2015). 'We are all going to be rich': Case study of the Dutch real estate fraud case. In *The Routledge Handbook of White-Collar and Corporate Crime in Europe*, eds. J. Erp et al.

Van de Bunt, H.G., Holvast, N.L., Huisman, K., Meerts, C., Mein, A.G., and van Wingerde, C.G. (2011). Bestuurlijke rapportage vastgoedfraudezaak 'Klimop'. Eindrapportage doi: 10.13140/RG.2.1.2548.6327.

Van Wingerde, K. (2015). The limits of environmental regulation in a globalized economy: Lessons from the Probo Koala case. In *The Routledge Handbook of White-Collar and Corporate Crime in Europe*, eds. J. Erp et al.

Vaughan, D. (2007). Beyond macro- and micro-levels of analysis, organizations, and the cultural fix. In *International Handbook of White-Collar and Corporate Crime*, eds. H.N. Pontell and G. Geis.

Weismann, A. (2007). Rethinking criminal corporate liability. *Indiana Law Journal* 82(2).

Zald, M. (1987). The new institutionalism in economics. *American Journal of Sociology* 93: 701–708.

Crime Prevention through Environmental Design (CPTED)

14

J. BRYAN KINNEY
ELLIOTT MANN
JOHN A. WINTERDYK

Contents

Learning Outcomes

After reading this chapter, you should understand

- The fundamental principles of Crime Prevention through Environmental Design (CPTED)
- The differences between first- and second-generation CPTED
- The ways by which CPTED is implemented on an international scale
- The challenges associated with measuring/evaluating the impact of CPTED initiatives

Introduction

> Criminal behavior is a biological–psychological–sociological response to an environmental situation which makes crime profitable…. If we engineer the environment in such a way as to make the cost factor in the commission of a crime greater than the potential gain, the behavior will not occur.
>
> **C. Ray**
> *1921–2007*

The previous entries in this text set out something of the variety of responses to the challenge of preventing crime. The reader will recognize that there are several different approaches that one can take in this regard. Some will prefer, or otherwise focus on, increased efforts to manage known offenders, while some others will look to the strengthening of social structures to prevent children and youth from becoming offenders in the first place. It is common to hear calls for the criminal justice system to take crime problems more seriously. The basis of this notion of taking crime seriously often includes an admonishment or at least a firm prodding to start with addressing so-called root causes of crime, or to perhaps reap the crime rate dropping gains of focusing on repeat or "prolific" offenders. The following statement is from a 2008 Home Office (United Kingdom) document, the "Youth Crime Action Plan." The statement is taken from the Minister's Foreword to the planning document:

> On [the issue of] prevention we will address the root causes of crime … but also in a much more targeted and individual way: spotting problems early and intervening to stop them getting out of control. We know that the vast majority of young people are well behaved and that it is a minority we really need to focus on—around 5 per cent who commit half of all youth crime. Increasingly we know how to identify these young people early on—in particular how they tend to come from a small number of vulnerable families with complex problems. On support, we will offer non-negotiable intervention to the families at

greatest risk of serious offending. These are the families whose children are disrupting our classrooms—or worse, roaming the streets committing crime.

Home Office
2008, p. 1

Both of these prevention objectives take the offender as the primary unit of focus. Much of the research and theorizing in criminology and sociology of crime tends to follow this general view: that offenses are committed by individuals and that these individuals require some form of correction, be it (re)training, therapy, or punishment. Our focus in this chapter takes the crime event as the central issue (an event that has spatial, temporal, and situational aspects) rather than as a case involving people (i.e., victims, offenders, witnesses, etc.). The distinction is an important one; once we (i.e., police, academics, or practitioners) begin to view crime as a complex setting, we can broaden our theoretical thinking about social and geographic settings, rather than limiting ourselves to people and their relation to the law (Brantingham and Brantingham 1984; Brantingham and Faust 1976). **Environmental criminology** is an example of one orientation that takes this wider view as a starting point for the study of crime events. Environmental criminology is primarily interested in the dynamic interaction between people and their surroundings (Rossmo 2000, p. 111). The use of **Crime Prevention through Environmental Design** (CPTED) as a tool for crime prevention focuses the influence of the built environment on human behavior and interaction. This chapter will provide an overview of the core CPTED principles and will examine the implementation of CPTED within an international context.

Emerging support for the introduction of CPTED on an international scale has begun to reinvigorate a theory and practice that has undergone much fragmentation and dissimilation over the past few decades. CPTED, as a theory and practice, incorporates both the theoretical elements of criminological theories with the practical policymaking applications in cities and neighborhoods around the world. CPTED has been adopted and reformed by city planners, state governments, and academics to the extent that there exists a vast array of literature on this method as a tool for increasing crime prevention and building safer environments. This chapter will briefly discuss the history and development of CPTED as a theory and tool for crime prevention. The focus on this chapter will be the international implementation of CPTED and a look at the successes of CPTED outside of developed nations.

CPTED has undergone many changes in the decades since its inception, and perhaps most notable is the movement from its original use as a theory that invokes a "**fortress mentality**" to one that encompasses a range of social considerations and policy implications. Through its evolution as a theory and practice, CPTED is not restricted to the changes in the physical environment. It encompasses changes in the social environment by changing human behaviors, whether this includes promoting the legitimate use of a given space or deterring illegitimate users within an environment (Schneider 2015).

One of the challenges that come with the implementation of CPTED is the measurement of success of these implementations. At the neighborhood level, for example, success may be measured by an empirical decrease in crime rates or by a qualitative measurement of the views of residents within the neighborhood. At the micro level, when measuring the success of CPTED for a new building development, success may also be measured by increased feelings of safety among legitimate users of the space. This chapter will discuss these methods for measuring the successful implementation of CPTED, as well as the challenges of measuring success.

Defensible Space and the Concept of CPTED

From a contemporary point of view, the works of Newman (1972) and Jeffery (1971) serve as the primary catalysts for what would become new approach for creating safer environments that provided less opportunity for crime. These early efforts have since grown into a multidimensional discipline that encompasses structural, social, and policy implications. Newman's *Defensible Space* advocates the "restructuring of residential developments" in order to aid control by the individuals who live there (Newman 1972, p. 204). Newman's influential book proposed alternative means by which to restructure the residential environments so that they may become livable and controlled by a community of individuals with a common terrain (Newman 1972, p. 2). Newman essentially tried to define a strategy for architects and planners that would reduce crime through the building of barriers and territorial markers, delineating private and semiprivate space, while decreasing semipublic and public spaces within an environment (Brantingham and Brantingham 1993, p. 13). In his book, Newman examines the ineffectual design of New York housing projects and explores ways in which to lower crime rates and deviance through specific optimized design features (Newman 1972, p. 204). This "defensible space" theory outlined four elements intended to encourage residents to take ownership of their neighborhood: territoriality, natural surveillance, image, and milieu (Lersch and Hart 2011, pp. 164–165) (see Box 14.1). These elements of Newman's theory formed the basis of what would eventually be "Crime Prevention through Environmental Design."

BOX 14.1   OSCAR NEWMAN

Oscar Newman (1935–2004) is widely recognized as having coined the term *defensible space*, which C. Ray Jeffery (1921–2007) later built upon and applied the concept to crime prevention through the phrase he coined—Crime Prevention through Environmental Design (CPTED).

Newman was by profession an international known architect and city planner who, in the early 1970s, had his book *Creating Defensible Space* published by the U.S. Department of Housing and Urban Development. The book was an expansion of his earlier books *Defensible Space* and *Community of Interest*, which helped inform housing policies around the world.

On the back cover of *Defensible Space*, Clark Whelton states: "…the most important book about urban living since Jane Jacob's book: *The Death and Life of Great American Cities.*" Jacob's book was published in 1961, and in the book, among other issues, she raised concern that modern urban renewal did not take into account the needs of most its citizens.

Newman was instrumental in setting up the not-for-profit corporation, Institute for Community Design Analysis. The main objective of the Institute was to assist residential communities in reducing crime and improve social stability through physically restricting housing and building and the surrounding environment.

In 1995, he was named Man-of-the-Year by "Law Enforcement News." A *google track* search of "defensible space" in 2016 showed that the term is no longer widely used but rather CPTED and environmental design have become the in vogue terminology.

First-Generation CPTED

In the early 1970s, alongside the development of "defensible space," C. Ray Jeffery coined the term *Crime Prevention through Environmental Design* (CPTED) (Andresen 2014; Lersch and Hart 2011). Reacting to the works of Jane Jacobs (1961) and writing contemporaneously with Newman (1972), Jeffery proposed an interdisciplinary approach to examine ways to make built environments safer and less inviting for potential offenders (Schneider and Kitchen 2007, p. 23).

CPTED contains six primary dimensions within the overarching schema that aim to create safer spaces and places.

1. Territoriality
2. Image Management

3. Legitimate Activity Support
4. Target hardening
5. Access Control
6. Surveillance

The overarching principle of **geographical juxtaposition** envelops the six dimensions. We will next discuss each of the key dimensions below.

Territoriality

Territoriality involves the use of the physical environment to create clear zones of territorial control and influence that define ownership of space (Reynald 2015, p. 74). The concept of territoriality seeks to promote a sense of ownership within a space and discourages the presence of illegitimate users of a space (Cozens and Love 2015, p. 4). Examples of territoriality may include signage or barriers that delineate the intended use of spaces, well-maintained landscaping, or clearly marked entry points and exits (Cozens 2014, p. 21).

Image Management

The concept of image management seeks to promote a positive likeness of the built environment to ensure the continued legitimate use and proper functioning of that environment (Cozens and Love 2015, p. 4). The aim of this concept is to design a space such that it produces positive emotionally driven behavioral effects (Cozens 2014). Examples of image management may include the routine repair and maintenance of a space, regular landscaping and removal of vandalism, and the maintenance of street lamps, locks, and other design features.

Legitimate Activity Support

The use of design features and signage to encourage acceptable behavior within a space is the aim of legitimate activity support. This concept attempts to both promote the legitimate use of a space and discourage the illegitimate uses of a space that may include social or physical disorder (Reynald 2015, p. 80). The rationale for this concept is closely bound to that of surveillance, as the congregation of legitimate users in a space provides more capable guardians who may observe, intervene, or report illegitimate activities (Cozens 2014). Examples of legitimate activity support may include the location of playgrounds in areas with high surveillance or visibility, placing ATM or bus stops in areas where other users are likely to congregate.

Target Hardening

Target hardening is one of the keystone components of first-generation CPTED as its intention is to deny access to a target through physical or artificial barriers (Crowe and Fennelly 2013, p. 26). Target hardening aims to reduce opportunities for crime and disorder within a space by utilizing secure features such as fences, locks, barriers, or security doors. While a long-standing component of CPTED theory, there is disagreement as to the efficacy of target hardening as a legitimate component of modern CPTED theory, because of the concerns of "fortressification" of spaces and the development of a fortress mentality (Cozens and Love 2015, p. 5).

Access Control

The concept of access control is closely linked to the concept of target hardening, though there are distinct differences between these two concepts. While target hardening aims to improve the secured design features of a space, access control specifically aims to reduce criminal opportunity by controlling the flow of traffic to and from a given space (Cozens and Love 2015, p. 5; Reynald 2015, p. 78). Access control strategies may include limiting entrances and exits to buildings, streets, or reducing the number of entrances and exits to a neighborhood or public space. The zoning of areas as unrestricted, or restricted through the use of signage, fencing, or pathway color is another method of access control (Cozens 2014, p. 24).

Surveillance

The concept of surveillance stems from the works of both Newman (1972) and Jacobs (1962), who argued that more "eyes on the street" will result in fewer opportunities for crime and disorder to occur (Cozens and Love 2015, p. 4). This key element of CPTED theory states that natural surveillance is considered a form of *guardianship* that increases the potential of detection, intervention, and prosecution of criminal behaviors (Cozens and Love 2015).

Geographical Juxtaposition

The concept of **geographical juxtaposition** encapsulates the six aforementioned concepts of CPTED within the scope of the built environment as a place within a given space—sometimes referred to as "safe zones" (see, e.g., Wortley and Mazerolle 2011). Geographical juxtaposition is the capacity for crime in one space to influence levels of crime in adjacent areas (Cozens 2014, p. 26).

Second-Generation CPTED

Second-generation CPTED was labeled and created by Saville and Cleveland in 1997, and expanded on the theory of first-generation CPTED by including the consideration of social factors in addition to physical characteristics of the built environment (Saville and Cleveland 2008, p. 80). On the basis of Jane Jacobs' original design of community orderliness, this **second generation of CPTED** accounts for the social environment within a space and promotes a "community CPTED" approach (see Box 14.2). This approach extends beyond physical design to encompass community participation through social programs and cohesion to promote self-policing within the community (Cozens and Love 2015, p. 5). There are four main principles of second-generation CPTED in addition to the core principles of first-generation CPTED. These principles include social cohesion, community connectivity, community culture, and threshold capacity.

Social Cohesion

Social cohesion is the core principle of second-generation CPTED, whereby the aim is to enhance relationships between neighborhood residents in order

---

BOX 14.2   SCHOOLS-SECURED DESIGN

In many corners of the world, there have being growing concerns about the safety of students while attending school. Such dramatic incidents as March 13, 1996, in Dunblane, Scotland (16 deaths); April 28–29, 1996, in Port Arthur, Tasmania, Australia (35 deaths); April 20, 1999, in Littleton, Colorado, USA (14 deaths); April 26, 2002, in Erfurt, Germany (16 deaths); November 7, 2007, in Tuusula, Finland (8 deaths); and December 14, 2012, in Newtown, Connecticut, USA (26 deaths), among numerous others, have raised public concern about the safety not only of students but also of staff.

Although more conventional safety barriers such as high fences, walls, or other effective barriers have become more commonplace, they have arguably created an environment that is less welcoming and more militaristic or fortress-like in appearance. However, the UK-based company "Secured by Design," which was established in 1989, represents the new generation of CPTED by focusing on the design and security for residential dwellings, commercial premises, and car parks through both convention target hardening/physical products as well as incorporating second-generation processes to promote public, commercial, and individual safety (see http://www.securedbydesign.com /about-secured-by-design/).

to build a sustainable neighborhood and community (Saville 2009, p. 395; Saville and Cleveland 2008, p. 95). Furthermore, social cohesion aims to create an environment that appreciates the differences and similarities between people groups within that community (Cozens 2014, p. 86). Within social cohesion, there are two subgroups: *social glue* and *positive esteem*. Social glue denotes strategies that improve feelings of community responsibility within a street or block. Positive esteem refers to the characteristics that individuals require in order for social cohesion to occur (Saville and Cleveland 2008, p. 82). These individual characteristics may include conflict resolution or self-confidence skills.

Community Connectivity

A neighborhood with a high level of community connectivity is one that fosters enhanced community togetherness with positive relations with external agencies, or sources. Connections within the community form the basis of activities and programs that link outside agencies to the community. Examples of enhanced community togetherness may include formal activities with outside groups, organizations, or other neighborhoods, or adequate transport facilities that link the neighborhood to outside areas. The benefit of having a tight-knit community with a high degree of togetherness is that well-integrated communities are more empowered, and they develop a stronger sense of place (Cozens 2014, p. 86).

Community Culture

The aim of community culture as a principle of second-generation CPTED is to implement programs tailored to fostering an acceptance of differing cultural views within the community. This may include gender-based programs such as violence against women, or the prevalence of special places, festivals, or events. Placing an importance on community culture promotes a unique sense of pride and distinctiveness, which serves to further strengthen community ties and influence positive behaviors (Cozens 2014, p. 86).

Threshold Capacity

It is helpful to view neighborhoods as ecosystems with a finite capacity for certain land use and activities. When a community moves toward community imbalance through poor allocation of space or resources within the social ecology of the environment, this is a breach of the threshold capacity in that environment. Some characteristics of capacity may include human-scale, land-use density and maximum diversity, as well as minimal congestion and maximum intensity of use (Cozens 2008, p. 170; Saville and Cleveland 2008, p. 84). A breach of the threshold capacity in an environment is referred to as the tipping point, whereby the functioning of a neighborhood may change significantly (Cozens 2014, p. 87).

CPTED on an International Scale

CPTED as a crime prevention tool has sparked the creation of many similar crime prevention initiatives that are based on the core elements of first- and second-generation CPTED. Many of these new programs are rebranded and adopted by city governments, architects, city planners, and police forces with varying degrees of success (Schneider and Kitchen 2002). Examples of related CPTED interventions and experiments within North America include "Safe Cities" in Toronto; "Riverside Park" in Fort Lauderdale, Florida; "Safer City Task Force" in Vancouver; "Neighborhoods to Standard" in Houston, Texas; and most notably "Five Oaks" in Dayton, Ohio (Schneider and Kitchen 2002, p. 158). CPTED initiatives in Europe include **Secured by Design** in the United Kingdom (see Box 14.2), The Dutch Label Police Housing program in the Netherlands, **Designing Out Crime** in the United Kingdom and Australia, and various other CPTED implementations based on the Western model of first- and second-generation CPTED (Cozens and Love 2015; Crowe and Fennelly 2013; Saville 2009; Schneider and Kitchen 2007). These combined efforts suggest that the CPTED of Jeffery and Newman, approximately two academic generations past, continues to be a vital research stream and has the potential to reach the "real world" of policy and planning.

City Revitalization in South Korea

CPTED has shown to be successful when implemented during the design process of new housing developments, communities, or neighborhoods. However, the implementation of CPTED within existing developments or neighborhoods requires a consideration of the preexisting physical and social structure of the location. Seoul, South Korea, is one example of a city that has begun to integrate the principles of CPTED within preexisting older neighborhoods and commercial development projects. New developments within Seoul already employ CPTED features into their design; however, one of the challenges still faced by developers and city planners is the implementation of CPTED principles within older neighborhoods. While new neighborhood developments within Seoul incorporate CPTED in order to create safer environments, Mayor Park Won Soon of Seoul, South Korea, aimed to integrate social elements from second-generation CPTED in order to revitalize older neighborhoods (Thorpe and Gamman 2013, p. 211). One of the challenges for implementing CPTED in older neighborhoods is the preexisting social environment that may not be as receptive to innovative new design features aimed at reducing fear of crime and levels of crime within these neighborhoods.

Led by the Design Policy Department of Seoul Metropolitan Government, CPTED principles were implemented through an integration of multiple social drivers (Thorpe and Gamman 2013, p. 207). Mayor Park and his colleagues applied an approach that reframed crime problems in order to deliver crime prevention outcomes without being strictly crime led. This process was done by engaging multiple actors and focusing on the well-being that is required by community members, while focusing on crime problems that citizens want to see less of. By using a social design approach, the program team integrated CPTED crime reduction methods while focusing on the role of social innovation in order to address the needs of citizens (Thorpe and Gamman 2013, p. 220). One activity that addressed the concerns of residents was the development of a "fear of crime map," which indicated the areas within the neighborhood residents were more fearful of criminal activity. This community consultation led to the development of volunteer "safe houses" within the community, which provided refuge for residents experiencing crime or fear of crime on the street. Thorpe and Gamman report encouragingly that the reporting of crime fosters community togetherness and territorial management through safe houses where residents can seek help. While the efficacy of this implementation has yet to be realized, the use of second-generation CPTED in the revitalization of older neighborhoods exudes an optimistic outlook for the integration of second-generation CPTED around the world.

Ha et al. (2015), however, provide empirical evidence in support of first-generation CPTED interventions in reducing residential burglary in a suburb of Seoul, South Korea. The authors compare two townships along two dimensions: perception of crime problems and police-recorded burglaries. For both dimensions, CPTED/secured by design (SBD) complexes in Pangyo New Town fared better than their non-SBD counterparts in Yatap Town (Ha et al. 2015, pp. 506–507, Tables 1–3). In terms of raw burglary rates, the SBD complexes experienced rates (per 100,000 persons) of approximately one-half of the non-SBD study area (between 177 and 282 per 100,000 compared to between 345 and 527 per 100,000 persons, respectively). Despite the weaknesses entailed in the design (small counts of raw burglaries—approximately 120–150 cases in Pangyo [SBD] and 245–283 in Yatap [non-SBD] over a three-year period), the results are suggestive of an impact; however, it is important to continue to test whether these possible patterns persists.

CPTED in Sub-Saharan Africa

While CPTED has traditionally been implemented in developed nations, second-generation CPTED may also be well suited for use in developing countries within the bounds of the cultural dynamics and infrastructure of the nation. It can be argued that the concept of CPTED is increasingly important now on an international scale, as more than half the world's population is now urbanized and many parts of the developing world are seeing increased urbanization (Cozens and Love 2015, p. 1). While areas with low social cohesion and empty public spaces may preclude legitimate community engagement, areas that have a preexisting high level of social cohesion may be more receptive to the implementation of second-generation CPTED principles (Saville 2009). Unlike the Western world, there exists little research on the implementation of CPTED within developing areas such as Sub-Saharan Africa. Ghana is one nation within Africa that is undergoing a drastic shift from rural to urban areas, although this transition has been encumbered by poor infrastructure and higher fear of crime within the general public. In 2015, the Safe and Inclusive Cities (SAIC) global research program examined two cities in Ghana in order to compare the relative levels of fear of crime and actual crime incidents in an effort to develop intervention measures to reduce crime and fear of crime. With the limited policing and increased levels of crime, many Ghanian neighborhoods have responded by using traditional target hardening measures to ensure safety and a decreased fear of crime (Owusu et al. 2015).

The SAIC research program is a global research program aiming to address gaps in knowledge and understanding of the social and physical drivers behind violence within the urban landscape in an attempt to develop interventions to address these issues. The cities of Accra and Kumasi were included in the study by SAIC because of the marked increase in crime in these cities since 1990. The period of high crime has been associated with increasing urbanization within metropolitan areas in both Accra and Kumasi. In addition to other drivers, part of the rapid growth in urbanization has been driven by the influx of global capital, which has grown because of the urban middle class and has produced soaring income disparity, and subsequently an increase in poverty and slums (Owusu et al. 2015). Interview and focus group data suggest that while lower-income areas reported fewer target hardening or other prevention measures, these areas did not see rises in serious forms of robbery/burglary; however, more affluent areas with more classical target hardening measures (e.g., strengthened access controls, etc.) saw relative increases. The authors suggest that a likely explanation flows from a consideration of Cohen and Felson's routine activity theory—and that the target environment is simply too rich to be deterred—especially when such affluence is so proximate to concentrated poverty.

Police Label Secure Housing in the Netherlands

After the 1997 international conference on "Crime and Urban Insecurity in Europe," it was determined that crime, fear of crime, and lack of urban security were major problems affecting the general public in Europe. This conference concluded that it should be the mandate of local and regional law enforcement agencies to develop integrated crime reduction plans with increased public involvement (Stummvoll 2012; van Soomeren and Woldendorp 1997). The UK approach to designing out crime initiated the Dutch police force to develop the Police Label Secure Housing program (Jongejan and Woldendorp 2013, p. 31). The primary objective of this program is to reduce both crime and the public's fear of crime through environmental design, architectural changes, and target hardening measures (Crowe and Fennelly 2013, p. 256). This program aimed to reduce crime and fear of crime by improving communication between developers, architects and planners, and the police (Stummvoll 2012). The Dutch Label Secure Housing project was initiated by the policy labeled "Society and Crime" within the Netherlands, and was issued in 1985 with three main directions (Stummvoll 2012):

1. Modifying the physical design of urban environments, ensuring that surveillance of potential offenders is facilitated and opportunities for crime are reduced
2. Re-introducing in all vulnerable environments (shopping malls, public transport, and high-rise buildings) individuals who, as a part of their job, exercise surveillance
3. Strengthening the bond between the younger generations and society, particularly through the family, school, leisure activities, and employment (pp. 385–386)

When housing developers or planners choose to apply the Police Label Secure Housing initiative, the project and surrounding environment must meet certain criteria as stipulated by the label itself. The label can then be used after the police have made an assessment and granted permission (Crowe and Fennelly 2013). Since the implementation of this housing standard, the risk of dwellings being burgled has dropped by 95% for new estates and 80% in preexisting environments (Jongejan and Woldendorp 2013). While largely based on the principles of first-generation CPTED, the implementation of this housing standard has proven successful within the Netherlands and shows promise for implementation in nations outside of Europe.

The Dutch Police Label Secure Housing has been labeled a success since its initial implementation in 1994 (see Jongejan and Woldendorp 2013; van Soomeren and Woldendorp 1997). It was so successful in the late 1990s that many local planning firms and authorities adopted its policy into their design guidelines. From an architectural and structural standpoint, the implementation of this housing label provides a model of the success of

CPTED in both new developments and preexisting housing developments. While this is an example of a long-standing successful implementation of CPTED, it is important to note that its success is contingent upon a city infrastructure that supports the communication and integration between community stakeholders, city planners, architects, and law enforcement representatives (see Box 14.3).

BOX 14.3   SECOND GENERATION AND THE AUSTRALIAN "SCHOOL EXPERIMENT"

Graduating from high school is usually accompanied by students having a major celebration shortly before the school year ends. In Australia, holding major parties and performing various "rite of passage" activities (e.g., doing drugs, drinking, or engaging in any assortment of risky peer-pressured behavior) are also more commonly known as "leavers." There is considerable risk to the young persons who participate in the activity, and researchers have used first- and second-generation crime prevention strategies to try to curb the risky behavior.

In addition to using standard CPTED practices, Letch et al. (2011) used second-generation CPTED methods and techniques to try to curb the risky behavior. Using a school on Rottnest Island, in the southwestern part of Australia, not far from Perth, the research found that using first-generation CPTED techniques (e.g., target hardening, setting of physical barriers, use of closed-circuit television [CCTV] cameras, and increasing natural surveillance) by authority figures was less effective than trying to build a sense of social cohesion and to facilitate and promote a "stronger sense of threshold" (p. 43). Another strategy the researchers introduced to enrich the second-generation measures was strategically added lighting and pathway lighting, which was found to improve sense of security and safety.

The research team concluded that while first-generation strategies had some benefit, they found that second-generation CPTED strategies that focus on building social cohesion were more effective. Furthermore, Letch et al. noted that when first- and second-generation CPTED strategies were combined, the effect was even greater. The study served to show that by employing first- and second-generation CPTED techniques, the community could continue to retain some of its local events and thereby enliven the sense of community already established on the island.

Crime Prevention through Urban Design and Planning (CP-UDP)

The European Cooperation in Science and Technology (COST) was created as an intergovernmental collaboration between 35 member countries across Europe. This framework combines Pan-European funding for a network of scientists and researchers across all science and technology fields, labeled as "COST Actions" (COST Action TU1203 2014a). One such action, labeled TU1203, has been branded Crime Prevention through Urban Design and Planning (CP-UDP) and is an action based on the principles of CPTED for creating safer built environments.

One of the more recent case studies conducted by the CP-UDP action was of a neighborhood in Barcelona, Spain, in 2014. The focus of the study was a neighborhood historically characterized by problematic architectural design that consisted of high-density, high-rise housing in an outlying area of Barcelona. This study examined whether the architectural design within this neighborhood alone was a key catalyst for crime and disorder in the 1980s. Historically, the neighborhood of Bellvitge has been characterized as having a high frequency of drug-using residents and rampant crime and disorder. This case study examined the improvements, renovations, and changes that transformed this neighborhood into the thriving high-density residential area that it is today, showing significantly lower rates of crime and disorder. Many first- and second-generation CPTED principles were applied to this neighborhood in the 1990s and early 2000s, including the paving of streets and walkways, the creation of meeting places for residents, the regeneration of the natural areas, and the introduction of small playgrounds between housing units to promote legitimate use of the given space. However, it was noted that, today, the neighborhood of Bellvitge still carries a reputation as a neighborhood with crime and disorder, reminiscent of the crisis during the 1980s. This case study concludes that architectural design was not solely responsible for crime and disorder within this neighborhood; rather, they were the result of an interplay between multiple social drivers and other extraneous factors in addition to architectural design. This study postulates that the study of crime and disorder in the built environment requires an examination of architectural design, community policing, investment in developing infrastructure, and social services and community support (COST Action TU1203 2014a, p. 10).

Another case study conducted by CP-UDP focused on the Bijlmermeer in Amsterdam, which shared similar characteristics to the high-rise trouble in Barcelona, although this case study produced drastically different results. As a by-product of crime and drug-related disorder in the 1970s within Amsterdam, the neighborhood of Bijlmermeer located near the city center became ridden with drug-related crime and disorder (COST Action TU1203 2014b). Applying the principles of first-generation CPTED in order to find a solution for the rampant crime and disorder within the neighborhood, safe design features were employed between 1985 and the early 1990s. These measures were aimed at renovating the existing built environment in order to promote a sense of territoriality, ownership of space, natural surveillance, and access control measures all in an effort to build "people-friendly" cities.

After more than 3000 apartments were demolished in 1991, the city employed a second phase approach based on the principles of spatial renewal and social renewal, with the inclusion of community policing measures. The second phase approach involved the construction of 7200 new low-rise and four-floor-high dwellings, using the existing space available. Ground floors of these high-rises were replaced with studios and small businesses in order to enhance the feeling of security and promote legitimate use of the previously unused space. The primary roads in Bijlmermeer were also lowered in order to accommodate various types of traffic while retaining function as residential throughways. In addition to the introduction of these physical measures, first-generation CPTED-like measures were implemented within building blocks that were not renovated, such as the inclusion of CCTV cameras within high-density neighborhoods.

Equally as important as the spatial renewal within the area was the social renewal, which addressed the social environment existing within Bijlmermeer. Unemployed individuals were involved in construction projects within the area and were given neighborhood watch duties in semipublic areas of the block. Furthermore, migrants who were lacking education received training in Dutch language and culture, as a component of a national and municipal program. These aspects of social renewal were implemented in order to work on the socioeconomic degradation of Bijlmermeer, and many of these measures proved to have long-term success.

While the measures implemented in Bellvitge and Bijlmermeer were quite different in nature, both cases exemplify the implementation of physical and social renewal drawing on both first- and second-generation CPTED (COST Action TU1203 2014b). Despite the vastly different measures used in both cases, the effects of these measures had positive outcomes and resulted in decreasing crime rates and fear of crime in both cases (see Box 14.4).

BOX 14.4   AN INNOVATIVE CPTED "TWIST"

There are numerous CPTED initiatives that can be found globally (see useful links). One innovative program and movement in Canada is found in Red Deer, Alberta. The concept and movement was created by Lorne Daniel from Victoria, British Columbia, in Canada and has gradually spread across the country. The movement is known as "Rethink Urban." Operating since the early 2012, Rethink Urban is fundamentally based on CPTED principles, but it builds on reducing crime and improving the quality of urban living by creative placemaking and community engagement through what the Red Deer executive director Steve Woolich has operationalized as the SafeGrowth methodology. Some of the successful initiatives have included setting up a piano in a walking area for anyone to use and encourage social and communal interaction. Other initiatives have included providing opportunities for troubled youth to create art or murals on buildings to enliven the neighborhood or brighten otherwise drab alleyways. Community members have even been invited to come up with creative ways to create signage that is designed to reduce/limit traffic flow.

The initiative focuses on three main elements:

- **"Engagement**—ways of connecting with one another that are meaningful, positive and productive
- **Place and Spaces**—taking a close look at the design details that make a difference between venues for crime and safe, stimulating urban environments
- **Creative Change**—from pop-up parks to street pianos, we look at quick catalysts for transforming downtowns, plazas and other public space."

See: http://rethinkurban.com/about/.

Managing Expectations

Because of the complex nature of CPTED projects, an evaluation of their success is contingent upon a thorough examination of all the factors that may influence potential outcomes, within the context of each project (Cozens and Love 2015). Furthermore, the expectations for each CPTED project must not exceed the initial intended outcome that justified the implementation of CPTED in the first place. For example, the expected outcomes of CPTED principles applied in a city park compared to the outcomes of second-generation CPTED integrated within a residential area are similar insofar as a reduction in crime and fear of crime is anticipated. However, the way in which these results will be achieved may be uniquely based on the context of the project itself. As evidenced by the differences between first- and second-generation CPTED, a project implementing first-generation CPTED should expect to see results based primarily on the physical and structural enhancements. A second-generation CPTED project should expect to see results based on the physical and structural improvements, as well as increased community connectivity and social cohesion within the context of the project. Both the Ghanian (Owusu et al. 2015) and South Korean (Ha et al. 2015) studies include a mix of both social perceptions and the best available crime event records and, in this respect, can be seen as representing second-generation approaches. However, the directly observable "results" of these projects is difficult to capture empirically. When studied, the social reactions to CPTED improvements are typically positive and can be interpreted as evidence of changing attitudes toward generalized fear/worry/concern about crime and disorder. Care must be taken, however, as not all cities or communities will respond in ways traditionally expected, as seen by Owusu et al. in Ghana. There, the CPTED improvements and the influx international corporations aid groups, and an unusually brisk establishment of cellular phone service and usage was thought to contribute to massive increases in crimes reported to police in some of the areas with strong economic and social capital indicators.

A renovation of a city park may include such additions as improved lighting, clear delineation between borders and edges on pathways and entrances, improved signage, enhanced playgrounds, and trimmed shrubs and trees for improving natural surveillance. All of these first-generation CPTED principles serve the common goal of improving territoriality by creating incentive for the space to be utilized by legitimate users, while deterring the use of the space from illegitimate users. Furthermore, these enhancing features increase a level of ownership within the park, which will provide more opportunities for potential crime or disorder to be seen and reported. With regard to measuring the expectations of CPTED as implemented within a city park, the expected outcome must be intrinsically linked to the features that were improved upon within the park. Clearly defined borders and edges and clearer signage make it more likely that users will recognize the intended uses of spaces such as green spaces, pathways, and playgrounds. The expected outcome of improved lighting will be a reduction in fear of crime, despite mixed results in the criminology literature with regard to reductions in actual crime incidences as a result of improved lighting. Enhanced playgrounds will provide legitimate users of the space more of an incentive to utilize the space for its intended use and will further dissuade illegitimate users. Finally, the trimming of shrubs and trees in accordance with recommended CPTED guidelines for maximum sightlines will allow increased natural surveillance and in turn improve territorial management and reduce the potential opportunities for crime and disorder within the space.

The implementation of second-generation CPTED with a focus on social cohesion within the social environment of the space allows for the consideration of many more factors above and beyond the physical and structural innovations of first-generation CPTED. As made evident by Saville (2009), expectations of second-generation CPTED principles must also be tied to their initial outcomes.

Measuring and Evaluating CPTED Impacts

Measuring the successful implementation of CPTED programs is challenging when presented only with official police data as the measure for crime rates. Because the principles of CPTED are so intrinsically linked to qualitative measures of the public's fear and perception of crime, official crime data are not sufficient for gauging the successful implementation of CPTED. While the traditional method of employing CPTED on the built environment invokes a type of "fortress mentality," second-generation CPTED remains an attractive method for designing safe built environments for policymakers, city planners, and state governments around the world. One of the important considerations when looking at the propagation of CPTED on a global scale is the extent that the success of this approach can be measured. Empirically, the success of CPTED can be measured by localized decreases in crime through official crime statistics. This method of measurement is not without errors, though, as decreases in crime may be caused by other external factors.

Just as the implementation of CPTED is based on the feedback, views, and concerns of neighborhood residents, stakeholders, or citizens, perhaps the successful implementation of CPTED is best measured by using a combination of qualitative and quantitative measures in order to adequately measure its effectiveness. Literature on the successes of CPTED around the world suggest that the successful implementation of this place-based crime prevention technique must not rely solely on structural changes to the built environment; it should rely on social practices enumerated by the second generation of CPTED as well. However, it should be noted that the physical environment is much easier to measure than social factors such as the sense of community and the extent that neighbors care about the happenings within their neighborhood (Cozens and Love 2015).

As social cohesion and community togetherness are such integral components of second-generation CPTED, planners and practitioners need to look for ways to formally embed such opportunities into regular and ongoing functions (see, e.g., Brantingham et al. 2005). For example, community meetings with city planners, developers, or law enforcement representatives will serve to enhance community togetherness and provide an opportunity for community members to voice their concerns. Furthermore, meetings with law enforcement representatives indicate the inherent interest of law enforcement in the happenings within that community and, as such, provide reassurance for community members. One of the secondary benefits of holding community meetings as a part of a second-generation CPTED project is the ability for city planners and law enforcement representatives to measure the relative success of the CPTED implementations as perceived by community members. Such a measurement may be gathered simply through oral discourse with community members, anonymous comments, or a brief survey after a community meeting with city planners or law enforcement representatives. This qualitative measurement of success coupled with official police statistics provides a twofold measure of success that can be applied to a variety of first- or second-generation CPTED projects and initiatives.

Crime Displacement

One of the primary criticisms of CPTED programs is the fear of **crime displacement**, whereby offenders may simply move to a more suitable location to commit crimes. However, measuring the extent of crime displacement generally requires an assessment of changes outside of the scope of the CPTED project (Cozens and Love 2015, p. 10). It has also been argued that CPTED initiatives may create a "halo effect" whereby the crime reduction effects of the CPTED project are diffused beyond the boundaries of the project. Taylor (2002) describes how the diffusion of the positive effects of CPTED may outweigh any effects of crime displacement as a result of the CPTED initiative. Clarke (1997, p. 30–33) warns against a general trend in the early (pre-1990s) tendency in the crime prevention literature to assume that crime prevented is merely crime displaced. Instead, he suggests that crime and place researchers use the concept of displacement as guide to interpretation of likely effects, including the possibility of intended and unintended consequences (see also Clarke 2005). For Clarke, displacement represents a way to systematically consider the likely intended and unintended outcomes for crime prevention interventions.

Future Directions and Considerations for Taking CPTED Seriously

CPTED has become something of a familiar term since its beginning statements in the early 1970s. Like many commonly used terms, CPTED, as a concept, is prone to misunderstandings and misuse. This chapter offers a re-introduction to the earlier works on preventing crime and disorder through the manipulation of the built environment. Jeffery (1971) takes the view that this environment is complex but can be used to mediate the ways in which individual users of a particular space behave. If done with prevention of specific acts in mind, local areas/spaces can be organized to make noncriminal uses of space the most "fit" response for most individuals, most of the time. Oscar Newman (1972) represents a more deterministic view, however, one in which residents and users of spaces are not only sensitive, but also respond, to architectural cues. Building design, in this view, offers a powerful opportunity to control behavior directly by deflecting unwanted behavior and encouraging sanctioned, pro-social options.

CPTED raises interesting issues for anyone interested in what "causes" crime, or what can be done to reduce or even prevent its occurrence. Newman's conceptualization of "defensible space" is a natural starting point to explore the promise of CPTED and to consider the criminological theories that are typically used to interpret its effects and motivations, primarily via routine activities, rational choice, and crime pattern theories. CPTED also invites us to consider a range of social issues regarding human nature, and its ability to be altered through internal (endogenous) and or external (exogenous) factors. The CPTED approach is also subject to critiques, particularly those involving "displacement" or that target hardening successes are merely won at the expense of one's nearby neighbor who couldn't afford to employ similar techniques. There is also a tempting thread regarding the possible damaging impact of CPTED—that, as an approach, it is overreliant on technology (e.g., lighting, surveillance, better locks, etc.) and that we are simply inviting a technological arms race. Such a development, it is argued, can lead to economic ruin and unequal access to business or residential spaces. Critical scholars (see, e.g., a particularly cogent discussion of this by Parnaby 2006) are also worried that CPTED engenders a new form of professionals with the ability to push/pull economic and social development through controlling access to and regulation/governance of city and area planning. Still, others see the bulk of CPTED efforts (e.g., gates, bars on windows, signage warning of crime problems, etc.) as causing exaggerated fear and general mistrust and, in the process, doing more harm than good. Crime prevention efforts will always be open to such critiques, but that good research, planning, and evaluations of interventions can reduce these concerns—particularly when applied in specific, situationally focused environments (Brantingham et al. 2005; Clarke 2005).

Governments in North America and in the United Kingdom are quick to point to the "crime drop" as clear evidence that their policies work and are working. Police chiefs and leaders do the same. What is the role, if any, for CPTED in this debate? There is room here for CPTED studies (and crime prevention at large) to provide context to this discussion. Police seem to be busier than ever despite the reported crime drop. Crime prevention research can help document the work that police, planners, residents, and nonprofit groups do—often without publicity. Some of this activity is captured in the "gray literature"—that which is found only in unpublished work. There is real value in capturing this gray literature and encouraging its findings to be examined and published more widely. Yet, it seems as though the social sciences—at least in terms of the study of crime and its prevention—is trending away from such a scheme. There is a recent call for crime prevention programs to be evaluated with more scientific rigor (see Eckblom and Pease 1995). While the approach taken here is that crime prevention efforts (CPTED included) should be assessed as critically and as systematically as possible and using the best available evidence, it is short sighted to disregard "studies" that do not stem from a randomized controlled trial design. We see the pursuit of randomized control studies as laudable, but not always practical. While not ideal, case studies can still provide value, such as showing "promising" results, or even something akin to a "best practice," to the wider research community. Once promising practices are identified, perhaps then we, as a research community, can begin to lobby for the resources and political appetite necessary to endure more rigorous designs.

Glossary of Terms

CPTED: Crime Prevention through Environmental Design is a technique that aims reduce/prevent crime by modifying the physical environment/space through design that will reduce opportunities for crime and nuisance activity.

CP-UDP: Crime Prevention through Urban Design and Planning is a partnership and action plan for designing safer cities in Europe. Designed by the European Cooperation in Science and Technology (COST), this action attempts to contribute to the existing knowledge on urban planning and safe design and has a large focus on the training of young people.

Crime displacement: A concept used to describe the risk of crime prevention initiatives. The result of a crime prevention initiative can trigger the relocation of crime (or criminals).

Designing out crime: CPTED-based scheme within Australia and throughout Europe.

Environmental criminology (EC): Considered part of the Positivist School of criminological thought, EC focuses on criminal patterns within particular built environments and analyzes the impacts of these external variables on people's behavior.

Fortress mentality: An excessively fearful attitude often activated by a primary focus on target hardening with little attention given to other design factors such as openness, access control, or aesthetic design.

Geographic juxtaposition: A concept used with first-generation CPTED, which includes six key schemes that can be used to improve safety and prevention crime.

Second-generation CPTED: Introduced in 1997, second-generation CPTED accounts for the social environment within a space and promotes a "community CPTED" approach. The technique focuses on four main elements that adapt CPTED to prospective offender individuality.

Secured by design: One of the largest adaptations of CPTED launched in 1989 within the United Kingdom and based on the principles of physical security, surveillance, territoriality, and management and maintenance.

Discussion Questions

1. What are the practical benefits of using CPTED principles?
2. What are the main differences between first-generation CPTED and second-generation CPTED? How might they compare with emerging trends in CPTED?
3. What are some of the challenges faced by city planners, state governments, and law enforcement agencies when implementing CPTED programs?
4. What are some of the challenges of measuring the success of CPTED initiatives?
5. In your living environment, based on what was discussed in this chapter, how might you improve "territorial reinforcement"? How might you control for possible crime displacement?
6. CPTED assumes that criminals are "rational thinkers." Discuss the merits of this perspective.
7. How might CPTED be applied to other themes covered in this book (e.g., terrorism, domestic violence, corporate crime, etc.)?

Suggested Reading

Atlas, R.L. (2013). *21st Century Security and CPTED* (2nd ed.). Boca Raton, FL: CRC Press.

This edited collection "includes the latest theory, knowledge, and practice of CPTED as it relates to the current security threats facing the modern world: theft, violent crime, terrorism, gang activity, and school and workplace violence."

Brantingham, P., and Brantingham, P. (1993). Nodes, paths and edges: Considerations on the complexity of crime and the physical environment. *Journal of Environmental Psychology*, 13(1), 3–28. http://dx.doi.org/10.1016/S0272-4944(05)80212-9.

This classic environmental criminology article by Paul and Patricia Brantingham outlines research on the relationship between the physical environment and crime, as mediated through action spaces and individual opportunity.

Crowe, T.D. (revised by R.J. Fennelly). (2013). *Crime Prevention through Environmental Design* (3rd ed.).

The book offers a practical, yet comprehensive guide to implementing CPTED principles in a range of urban-based settings with a focus on architectural design, space management, and urban planning.

Jacobs, J. (1961). *The Death and Life of Great American Cities* (Revised Ed. 1993). New York: Modern Library.

This book exemplifies much of the research that Jane Jacobs produced, which paved the way for modern CPTED research.

Lab, S. (2014). *Crime Prevention: Approaches Practices, and Evaluations* (8th ed.) Waltham, MA: Anderson Publishing.

This, the 8th edition, is a classic introductory text for the wider field of crime prevention, and provides an efficient discussion of the connecting theory and research.

Newman, O. (1976). *Defensible Space: Crime Prevention through Urban Design*. New York: Collier Books.

Along with Jacobs (1961), this book began the theory of "Defensible Spaces" and provided a foundation for the development of CPTED as a theory and practical tool.

Security Journal. Although not an exclusive CPTED-based journal, the journal regularly includes articles on CPTED related studies.

Recommended Web Links

http://www.cpted.net

The International CPTED Association promotes and supports the local implementation of CPTED principles for community and development projects that aim to create safer environments.

http://www.designagainstcrime.com/

The Design against Crime (DAC) research center provides resources and information for designing socially useful spaces that reduce opportunities for criminal behavior.

http://www.crdi.ca/EN/AboutUs/Pages/default.aspx

With its headquarters based in Canada, the organization includes the program SAIC. SAIC is a "global research program that documents the links between urban violence, poverty, and inequalities" and among other strategies also uses CPTED principles.

http://costtu1203.eu/

COST Action TU1203: Crime Prevention through Urban Design and Planning. This page provides a conduit to the European efforts to integrate science and technology into urban planning.

http://www.popcenter.org/tools/cpted/PDFs/NCPC.pdf

Although many countries have similar sites, this site is a comprehensive guidebook for CPTED practices in Singapore.

http://www.unodc.org/unodc/en/frontpage/2011/August/unodc-and
-unhabitat-release-guidelines-to-help-prevent-crime-in-urban
-areas.html

The United Nations website for the UNODC and UN-Habitat release guidelines to help prevent crime in urban areas. A rich source for CPTED and related crime prevention strategies.

References

Andresen, M. (2014). *Environmental Criminology: Evolution, Theory, and Practice.* New York: Routledge.

Armitage, R., and Monchuk, L. (2011). Sustaining the crime reduction impact of designing out crime: Re-evaluating the Secured by Design scheme 10 years on. *Security Journal* 24(4): 320–343. Retrieved from http://dx.doi.org/10.1057/sj.2010.6.

Armitage, R., Monchuk, L., and Rogerson, M. (2011). It looks good, but what is it like to live there? Exploring the impact of innovative housing design on crime. *European Journal of Criminal Policy and Research* 17(1): 29–54. Retrieved from http://dx.doi.org/10.1007/s10610-010-9133-8.

Atlas, R. (2008). *21st Century Security and CPTED.* Boca Raton, FL: Auerbach.

Brantingham P., and Brantingham P. (1984). *Patterns in Crime.* New York, Macmillan/McGraw Hill.

Brantingham, P., and Brantingham, P., (1993). Nodes, paths and edges: Considerations on the complexity of crime and the physical environment. *Journal of Environmental Psychology* 13(1): 3–28. Retrieved from http://dx.doi.org/10.1016/S0272-4944(05)80212-9.

Brantingham P., Brantingham, P., and Taylor, W. (2005). Situational crime prevention as a key component in embedded crime prevention. *Canadian Journal of Criminology and Criminal Justice* 47(2): 271–292.

Brantingham. P., and Faust, F. (1976). A conceptual model of crime prevention. *Crime and Delinquency* (July): 284–296.

Clarke, R. (1997). Introduction. In *Situational Crime Prevention: Successful Case Studies,* 2e, ed. R. Clark, 1–45. New York: Harrow and Heston.

Clarke, R. (2005). Seven misconceptions of situational crime prevention. In *Handbook of Crime Prevention and Community Safety,* 39–70. Portland, OR: Willan Publishing.

COST Action TU1203. (2014a). *Publications on CP-UDP: A European Bibliographic Overview across the Language Barriers—Including Some Questions on Terminology.* Retrieved from http://costtu1203.eu/wp-content/uploads/2014/10/01.-Publications-on-CP-UDP-A-European-bibliography.pdf.

COST Action TU1203. (2014b). *High-Rise in Trouble: The Bijlmermeer in Amsterdam.* Retrieved from http://costtu1203.eu/wp-content/uploads/2014/12/High-rise-in-trouble-DSP-report.pdf.

Cozens, P. (2008). Crime prevention through environmental design. In *Environmental Criminology and Crime Analysis*, eds. R. Wortley and L. Mazerolle, 153–177. Portland, OR: Willan Publishing.

Cozens, P. (2014). *Think Crime! Using Evidence, Theory and Crime Prevention through Environmental Design (CPTED) for Planning Safer Cities*. Quinn Rocks, Western Australia: Praxis Education.

Cozens, P., and Love, T. (2015). A review and current status of Crime Prevention through Environmental Design (CPTED). *Journal of Planning Literature* 30(4): 393–412. Retrieved from http://dx.doi.org/10.1177/0885412215595440.

Crowe, T., and Fennelly, P. (2013). *Crime Prevention through Environmental Design* (3rd ed.). Amsterdam, Netherlands: Elsevier.

Eckblom, P., and Pease, K. (1995). Evaluating crime prevention. *Crime and Justice* 19: 585–662.

Ha, T., Oh, G., and Park, H. (2015). A comparative analysis of defensible space in CPTED housing and non-CPTED housing. *International Journal of Law, Crime and Justice* 43: 496–511.

Home Office. (2008). Youth Crime Action Plan. Retrieved from http://webar chive.nationalarchives.gov.uk/+/http:/www.justice.gov.uk/publications/docs /youth-crime-action-plan.pdf [ISBN: 978-1-84726-752-8; document number CDSD 15].

Jacobs, J. (1961). *The Death and Life of Great American Cities*. New York: Random Press.

Jeffery, C.R. (1971). *Crime Prevention through Environmental Design*. Beverly Hills, CA: Sage Publications, Inc.

Jongejan, A., and Woldendorp, T. (2013). A successful CPTED approach: The Dutch 'Police Label Secure Housing.' *Built Environment* 39(1): 31–48.

Kang, S.-J., Kim, D.-J., Lee, K.-H., and Lee, S.-J. (2014). Application and assessment of crime risk based on crime prevention through environmental design. *International Review for Spatial Planning and Sustainable Development* 2(1): 63–78.

Letch, J., McGlinn, E., Bell, J.F., Downing, E., and Cook, D.M. (2011). An exploration of 1st and 2nd generation CPTED for end of year school leavers at Rottnest Island. Perth, Australia: Edith Cowen University—Australian Security Intelligence Conference. Retrieved from http://ro.ecu.edu.au/cgi/viewcontent .cgi?article=1012&context=asi.

Naghibi, M., Faizi, M., Khakzand, M., and Fattahi, M. (2015). Achievement to physical characteristics of security in residential neighbourhoods. *Procedia—Social and Behavioral Sciences* 201: 265–274. Retrieved from http://dx.doi.org/10.1016/j .sbspro.2015.08.175.

Newman, O. (1972). *Defensible Space: Crime Prevention through Urban Design*. New York: Macmillan.

Owusu, G., Wrigley-Asante, C., Oteng-Ababio, M., and Owusu, A. (2015). Crime prevention through environmental design (CPTED) and built-environmental manifestations in Accra and Kumasi, Ghana. *Crime Prevention and Community Safety* 17(4): 249–269. Retrieved from http://dx.doi.org/10.1057/cpsc.2015.8.

Parnaby, P. (2006). Crime prevention through environmental design: Discourses of risk, social control, and a neo-liberal context. *Canadian Journal of Criminology and Criminal Justice* 48(1): 1–29.

Reynald, D. (2015). Environmental design and crime events. *Journal of Contemporary Criminal Justice* 31(1): 71–89. http://dx.doi.org/10.1177/1043986214552618.

Rossmo, K. (2000). *Geographical Profiling.* Boca Raton, FL: CRC Press.

Saville, G. (2009). SafeGrowth: Moving forward in neighbourhood development. *Built Environment* 35(3): 386–402.

Saville, G., and Cleveland, G. (2008). Second-generation CPTED: The rise and fall of opportunity theory. In *21st Century Security and CPTED,* ed. R. Atlas, 79–90. Boca Raton, FL: Taylor & Francis Group.

Schneider, R. (2015). *Crime Prevention* (2nd ed.). Boca Raton, FL: CRC Press.

Schneider, R., and Kitchen, T. (2002). *Planning for Crime Prevention: A Transatlantic Perspective.* London: Routledge.

Schneider, R., and Kitchen, T. (2007). *Crime Prevention and the Built Environment.* London: Routledge.

Stummvoll, G. (2012). Governance through norms and standards: The normative force behind design-led crime prevention. *Criminology & Criminal Justice* 12(4): 377–396. Retrieved from http://dx.doi.org/10.1177/1748895812452280.

Taylor, R. (2002). Crime prevention through environmental design (CPTED): Yes, no, maybe, unknowable and all of the above. In *Handbook of Environmental Psychology,* eds. R. Bechtel, and A. Churchman. New York: John Wiley & Sons.

Thorpe, A., and Gamman, L. (2013). Walking with Park: Exploring the 'Reframing' and Integration of CPTED principles in neighbourhood regeneration in Seoul, South Korea. *Crime Prevention and Community Safety* 15: 207–222. Retrieved from http://dx.doi.org/10.1057/cpsc.2013.6.

van Soomeren, P., and Woldendorp, T. (1997). CPTED in the Netherlands. 2nd Annual International CPTED Association Conference, Orlando, Florida.

Wortley, S., and Mazwerolle, L. (eds.). (2011). *Environmental Criminology and Crime Analysis.* New York: Routledge.

Crime Prevention and the Victims— Lessons Learned from Victimology

15

RITA HAVERKAMP
MICHAEL KILCHLING

Contents

Learning Outcomes
After reading this chapter, you should understand

- That in crime prevention, as in criminal policy in general, victims and offenders are addressed as completely different populations
- That the legal and political attributions are based on stereotypical assumptions (labels)
- How empirical research has shown that there is often significant overlap on the individual level between the two groups, victims and offenders
- That both groups, victims and offenders, share similar characteristics. The same groups are at increased risk for becoming a victim or an offender

- That the overlap can be explained by a variety of traditional criminological theories
- That, besides conventional procedural justice mechanisms, restorative justice is an important instrument to focus on and deal with aspects of the conflict between parties that cannot be addressed through conventional criminal proceedings
- That more focused empirical research is needed in order to systematically analyze victim experiences by offenders as well as offending patterns of victims in order to provide the necessary evidence for more reality-oriented crime prevention programs.

Introduction

Offenders that merge with the victims make for bad offenders, just as victims that merge with offenders make for bad victims.

Nils Christie
1986, p. 25

Until fairly recently, the offending victim or the victimized offender have been neglected figures in victimology, though researchers have been well aware of the nexus between offending and victimization (Mendelsohn 1956, p. 99; von Hentig 1948, p. 383 et seq.; Wolfgang 1958, p. 337). So far, neither research focusing on offending and reoffending nor victimization surveys address the full spectrum of life experiences. Although it can be concluded from such research that the actual status of victims and offenders is often altering and, furthermore, that victim and offender roles are often blurring or even overlapping (see Box 15.1), the two groups are systematically separated in empirical research.

While it had been a relatively undisputed state of knowledge during the so-called era of rehabilitation (e.g., Campbell 2005) that many offenders have been subject to violence in their childhood or youth, the interest for the interdependency of victimization and offending more or less completely disappeared—as a consequence of the punitive shift in criminal policy according to which considering past victimizing events in sentencing appeared to be too offender-friendly. The same is true in regard to violent victimization of prisoners—that is, offenders or, more precisely, ex-offenders—while imprisoned. This latter example underlines that the victim–offender nexus always carries a political component: in the current popular discourse about crime, offenders are perceived as bad and victims are perceived as good (see Tonry 2004). Such dichotomist "good–bad" labels do not care for nuances. Even more in crime prevention, the impact of real victimization is often ignored or "overlooked." This is somewhat surprising since early victimology literature

BOX 15.1   VICTIM–OFFENDER OVERLAP IN LIFE PERSPECTIVE—CATEGORIES AND EXAMPLES

- **Occasional overlap of victim and offender roles**
  - Interchanging roles in a concrete crime scenario
  - For example, excessive self-defense
  - For example, provoking behavior resulting into row (formal roles often coincidental: the one setting the first punch will be considered as the offender, no matter whether the [alleged] victim has initiated the escalation)
- **Situational role changes**
  - Individuals acting alternately as offenders and victims
  - For example, longitudinal gang or group rivalries
- **Victim–offender sequence, nonrecurring**
  - Offending after one-time or multiple prior victimization
  - For example, revenge, retaliation
- **Victim–offender career**
  - Multiple offending after one-time or multiple prior victimization
  - For example, serial property or violent crimes
  - For example, domestic violence, harassment
  - For example, (political) radicalization
- **Offender–victim sequence, double role**
  - Offenders/ex-offenders victimized
  - For example, (hard) drug users pickpocketed, ripped off, or mugged
  - For example, gang/mafia members "disciplined" or killed
  - For example, prisoners exposed to inmate violence

Kilchling 2014
Current State of the International Discussion on Victims' Experiences in and Victims' Expectations towards the Criminal Justice System

already stressed that crime prevention must originate with the victim (see Schneider 1982, p. 15). Nevertheless, quite regularly, the main focus of crime prevention still continues to evolve around the offender(s) and potential offender(s), and on situational and environmental attributes (see Chapter 14). Victims, on the other hand, are only dealt with as a virtual dimension at best, that is, as potential victims whose victimization ought to be prevented.

This issue has different theoretical and practical characteristics that will be examined in this chapter from a victimological perspective. The notion of an *ideal victim* will be given special attention so as to illustrate how this limited perspective hampers to give victims a place in contemporary theories of prevention (see, e.g., Christie 1986, and see below). This might be one reason, why individual—or special—prevention is still dealing with offenders almost exclusively. As a result of this mainstream approach, offending or reoffending resulting from negative victim experience has long been beyond conventional criminological interest and inquiry. Therefore, an overview of the victim–offender overlap and existing victim research will be presented to provide a basis for an integration of the victim and the victimized offender in crime prevention in practice. The starting point will be one of the main findings in international literature, that is, the desire of victims for procedural justice, which, as a significant component, includes options for participation as well as for compensation. There can be no doubt that the frustration of such expectations can have significant impact for crime prevention initiatives.

Victimization

Whereas victimology takes an interest in getting more information about the interplay of becoming a victim and an offender, in crime prevention, the distinction between victim and offender roles still prevails. This inclination might be based on ideas of the ideal victim (see Box 15.2).

BOX 15.2   VICTIMS AND OFFENDERS IN EARLY VICTIMOLOGY

Benjamin Mendelsohn (1900–1998), often considered as the forefather of victimology, started the systematic scientific study of victims of crime in 1937. Since then, **victimology** has been established as a scientific discipline covering subjects such as the extent and prevalence of victimization, the process of victimization, effects and consequences of victimization, needs of victims, victims' rights, and fear of crime.

Recognizing the dynamics of victimization, Mendelsohn portrayed offender and victim as a "penal couple" (1956, p. 99) while **Hans von Hentig** (1887–1974), victimology's second forefather, addressed them as "partners" in crime (1948, p. 383).

Despite these early insights into the manifold connections of victimhood and offending, it remains true what **Ezzat E. Fattah** (1929–) from Simon Fraser University, in Canada, has emphasized more than two decades ago: There have been very few endeavors to [systematically] link victimological and criminological theories (1991, p. 346).

The "Ideal Victim"

The concept of an **ideal victim** is based on an innocent, defenseless victim without complicity in the crime (e.g., Skogan and Maxfield 1981, p. 257 et seq.) or personal connections, direct or indirect, to crime or criminals. Christie's (1986, p. 19 et seq.) famous stereotype of the "ideal victim" consists of the following six attributes: first, a weak victim (female, sick, old, or young); second, taking part in a respectable activity; third, a blameless victim; fourth, a large and evil offender; fifth, an unknown and not related perpetrator; and sixth, a successfully elicit victim status. Thus, the ideal victim is perceived as innocent (Walklate 2007, p. 28) and as vulnerable as possible (Smolej 2010, p. 70). While elderly women and small children reflect this generic narrative, young men and marginalized groups (e.g., homeless and drug addicts) face difficulties in conferring the status of being a victim and are often withheld of being worthy of sympathy and compassion (Greer 2007, p. 22).

This one-dimensional image evokes a simplified and artificial perspective on the victim and fosters a "hierarchy of victimhood" in media, the police, and the judicial system (Carrabine et al. 2004). The status of ideal victim on top of the hierarchy implies various benefits concerning financial compensation and emotional support on a broad level from closest relatives and friends to victim aid organizations, and right up to the public (Jägervi 2014, p. 73). Moreover, media attention and legislative campaigns allow for remarkable change to criminal justice policy and practice (Greer 2004) by enacting laws often named after specific child victims (McAlinden 2014, p. 180). At the very end, the "undeserved" or "rejected victim" is located and is denied of his or her legitimate victim status (Greer 2007, p. 22) or even attributed offender status (Strobl 2004, p. 296). Demographic characteristics (e.g., gender, race, and respectability) decide upon the levels of media interest and especially the ascription of being an ideal victim (Greer 2007, p. 23). Stereotypical attributes can also be found in victim compensation schemes. By way of example, the German law is limited to blameless victims of violence who cooperate with the police (section 1, paragraph 2 of the German Victim Compensation Act; see Kaiser and Kilchling 1996, p. 275, Strobl 2004, p. 298); even family members of an offender who had been killed are not eligible to receive state compensation although they clearly qualify, according to the common victimological categories, as indirect victims (Kaiser and Kilchling 1996; for a survey on legislation in other European countries, see Greer 1996). However, unlike in case of socially acknowledged victims, their legitimate victim status is occasionally rejected because they do not want to fulfill the victim role and its obligations (e.g., helplessness, in need of professional services, etc.) (Strobl 2004, p. 296).

It seems probable that the generic picture of an ideal victim may influence crime prevention in practice, as yet, largely unexplored demand (Dignan

2005, p. 17). At any rate, the question remains open, "to which [extent] Christie's stereotypical ideal victim image is confirmed or confounded by empirical data, and the possibly contrasting light that these may shed on the 'actual' identity of victims and their attributes" (Dignan 2005, p. 18).

Victimization Surveys

Representative victim surveys such as the American Crime Victimization Survey (**NCVS**), the British Crime Survey (**BCS**), or the International Crime Victims Survey (**ICVS**) are an essential source to gather more knowledge about victimization apart from criminal justice databases as well as perceptions of victims concerning victimization and its consequences (for an overview, see Bradford and MacQueen 2015). Substantial attention should be given to the demographic information derived from victim surveys owing to methodological weaknesses. Certain restrictions leave out significant target groups who are vulnerable to becoming a victim. On the one hand, juvenile victims (under the age of 16), victims in (closed) institutions, homeless victims, and victims from ethnic minorities are rarely addressed (Dignan 2005, p. 18). On the other hand, a limited range of the so-called **standard offenses** surveyed excludes various categories of victims (see Box 15.3).

BOX 15.3 "STANDARD" OFFENSES COVERED IN VICTIM SURVEYS

1. Household crimes:
   - Theft of car
   - Theft from car
   - Car vandalism
   - Motorcycle theft
   - Bicycle theft
   - Burglary
   - Attempted burglary
2. Personal crimes:
   - Robbery
   - Theft of personal property
   - Sexual incidents
   - Assaults/threats

van Kesteren et al. 2014
The International Crime Victims Surveys: A retrospective

Data sets concentrate mainly on conventional crime to which the general public is exposed (assault, burglary, or vehicle theft), but often ignore new forms of offenses (Internet crime) and victim complicit crimes (e.g., offenses connected with drug or alcohol abuse) (Dignan 2005, p. 18; Pérez Cepeda et al. 2013, p. 19). Less serious common offenses are usually overfocused because the frequently applied telephone interview methods do not allow for asking questions pertaining to such topics as severe sexual assaults with respect to the willingness of the victim to reveal such sensitive information (Stanko 1998, p. 45) and for a host of ethical concerns (e.g., deepening of **secondary victimization**) (Schwartz 2000, p. 827). Additionally, serious offenses occur rarely, and the small samples pose problems in making estimates (Schwartz 2000, p. 820). Further common shortcomings are related to the respondents because they may tend to both underreport and overreport victimization (i.e., telescoping effect, etc.) (Schwartz 2000, p. 821). However, victim surveys provide important insights to the vulnerability of various groups of victims concerning particular offenses (Dignan 2005, p. 18).

One well-known worldwide data set is the **ICVS** (Box 15.4) that was built after the Dutch, British, and Swiss national surveys and has been carried out in five subsequent sweeps, thereof the last round in 2010 (van

---

BOX 15.4   THE INTERNATIONAL CRIME VICTIMS SURVEY

The ICVS is the world's most comprehensive and, in terms of sample size, the world's largest victimization survey. It was initiated in 1987 by a group of European criminologists. It is administered by an international research consortium. Its concept has been comparative from the beginning on.

Up until 2016, five waves have been completed. The first survey took place in 1989 with 14 participating countries (mainly Europe, plus Australia, Canada, and the United States). The second ICVS wave was conducted in 1992 (plus New Zealand). The third wave (1996–1997) involved 12 industrialized nations and 15 developing nations. The fourth wave was administered in 2000 in 47 countries. The fifth round (2004–2005) includes some 30 states representing Africa, North and Latin America, Asia, Europe, and Oceania. Currently, a sixth wave is in process.

Since its start-up, some 320,000 citizens have been interviewed in the course of the ICVS so far. Meanwhile the database covers information from more than 325,000 individual respondents from 78 countries.

To access more information on the survey, visit: http://www.unicri .it/services/library_documentation/publications/icvs/.

Kesteren et al. 2014, p. 50). Despite different design features and small samples interviewed (2000 per country) (van Dijk 2012, p. 25), the survey is widely accepted for enabling more reliable comparisons across countries (e.g., Lewis 2012, p. 9). The findings confirm that juvenile age is a risk-enhancing factor (van Kesteren et al. 2014, p. 53). Apart from the significant increased risk of victimization for young women concerning sexual incidents, young men aged 16 to 24 run the highest risk of becoming a victim. In contrast, elderly people are affected the least by crime, so that seniority serves as a risk-reducing and protective factor (van Kesteren et al. 2014, p. 53). Repeat victimization across and within crime types amounts to 40% of all crime for the 11 standard crime types in 17 industrialized countries according to analyses of the 2000 **ICVS** data set (Farrell et al. 2005). After further analyses, repeat victims tend to express less satisfaction with their treatment by the police, show less trust in their neighbors, and have a lower propensity to inform the police about another victimization (van Dijk 2001, p. 33 et seq.). As a result, it has turned out that repeat victimization is a predictor of future victimization (van Kesteren et al. 2014, p. 53). Besides, this subgroup seems to be remarkably underreported in victim surveys (Genn 1988, p. 90). The reason for this is the frame of reference in questionnaires that has an upper limit of the number of offenses as well as the need for specified information on each incident occurred (Dignan 2005, p. 19). However, this approach is not able to encompass "chronic" victims who regularly experience offenses and tend to live in deprived residential districts in the United Kingdom and the United States according to other studies (Hough 1986, p. 118 et seq.; Skogan 1981). As a consequence, crime prevention should take into account multiple victims and develop particular programs of prevention and victim care for them (van Kesteren et al. 2014, p. 55).

Key findings from victim surveys bring to light that boys and men are usually more susceptible of becoming a victim than girls and women, except of sexual offenses, as well as young people in comparison to elderly people (Fox et al. 2009, p. 24; Scott 2003, p. 203). However, victimization surveys constantly disclose that **fear of crime** is more widespread among female and elderly populations than among male and young populations (Fox et al. 2009, p. 25; Scott 2003, p. 203). This victimization-fear paradox is explained, inter alia, with increased perceptions of personal vulnerability with regard to physical strength (Hale 1996, p. 95 et seq.). However, a higher level of fear of crime among female and elderly people is even in accordance with the idea of the ideal victim in contrast to survey data on the likelihood of victimization. The connection between fear of crime and the legitimate victim status might also affect crime prevention because the focus lies upon groups who feel and seem to be more vulnerable of becoming a victim. However, the victim–offender separation obscures the view of looking at the social interaction and intertwining between victims and offenders (Dignan 2005, p. 20).

Victims' Expectations and Criminal Justice

It has been recognized for some time now that the victim—like the offender—needs rehabilitation: besides their coping with the direct consequences of the crime, that is, the material, psychical, and social harm, victims have to be reintegrated into the social environment, the families, and the job (e.g., Schneider 1982, p. 28). The criminal justice system plays a major role within the coping processes after victimization. Prevention of **(primary) victimization, secondary victimization, tertiary victimization,** and **revictimization** (new, repeat primary victimization) (see Box 15.5) are key components of a victim-oriented criminal policy (e.g., Haverkamp 2015, 2016).

Besides concrete measures of victim protection aiming at reducing anger and anxiety toward the offender and his or her adjacencies, including lawyers, adequate treatment of the victim by all actors on the different levels of the criminal justice system, from the early stages of the penal procedures onward, is considered to be of utmost importance (Goodey 2005, p. 121

BOX 15.5   CATEGORIES OF VICTIMIZATION

- **Primary victimization**
  - Immediate victimizing event (crime), causing material, physical, or psychological (emotional) harm
  - *One-time or repeat (revictimization, serial/multiple re-victimization ↻)*
- **Secondary victimization**
  - Consolidation of primary damages and consequences
  - Retraumatization
  - *Reinforced or fortified through relatives and social vicinity*
  - *Reinforced or fortified through instances of social control (police, criminal justice system)*
  - *Reinforced or fortified through media*
- **Tertiary victimization**
  - Longitudinal effects of primary and secondary victimization

Haverkamp 2015
The victim perspective in crime prevention—part 1

et seq.; Schneider 1982, p. 27 et seq.). The latter is usually referred to as **procedural justice** (e.g., Shapland et al. 1985; Wemmers 1996); it can be differentiated into several segments: voice, respect and recognition, and just outcome (Wemmers 2011, p. 74 et seq.). Where restitution cannot be claimed from offenders, state compensation schemes are provided as an additional instrument to fill this gap. In civil law jurisdictions, active participation of the victim as a party to the proceedings is an additional important component that has an impact on victim satisfaction (see Kury and Kilchling 2011). Adversarial (common law) systems provide more indirect options such as victim impact statements (**VIS**) or victim personal statements (**VPS**) in order to give victims a voice; since such instruments provide for a passive role, at most their benefit is, however, disputed (e.g., Crawford and Goodey 2000; Erez et al. 2011; Pemberton and Reynaers 2011).

Restorative justice approaches are internationally recognized for their increased potential for addressing interests and needs of the victims and for providing opportunities for repairing the harm they suffered, also in cases of serious victimization (e.g., Van Camp 2014; also see Chapter 9 in this volume). Since the frame of reference in restorative justice settings, in contrast to the formal criminal justice perspective with its limited focus on the actual crime and its consequences, includes the (deeper) conflict between the parties and its background (e.g., Galaway and Hudson 1996), such practices may have de-escalating effects in regard to the dynamics, especially in cases with a victim–offender overlap. Unfortunately, evaluation of restorative justice programs are based on similar methods to that of criminal penalties; that is, it is focused on re-arrest or reoffending of defendants who participate in the programs, and on satisfaction of the victims (e.g., McCold 2003, p. 95 et seq.). Hence, following the mainstream approach of recidivism research, potential subsequent offending of victims has not been systematically inquired yet.

Empirical research on **procedural justice** has shown that objective factors—involvement of the victim and effective compensation of material and nonmaterial damages—as well as subjective factors (in particular the individual experience of fair treatment and the perception of having received fair compensation) have a significant impact (e.g., Kilchling 1995; Wemmers 1996). Failure to satisfy one or more of these expectations has a potential to seriously affect victims' trust in justice and in the legal order as a whole, and to fuel negative emotions or even retaliatory thoughts toward both the actual counterpart (the offender) and the criminal justice system and society as a whole. Increased punitiveness of victims who reported dissatisfaction related to negative experiences with the criminal justice system (Kilchling 1995, p. 174 et seq.) may be seen as an indicator for such precarious processes.

Victim–Offender Overlap

With this background in mind, it is not surprising that, in contrast to the bipolar concept of fixed role expectations toward the victim and the perpetrator, we can observe that victims not infrequently become offenders, and vice versa (e.g., Gottfredson 1981, p. 722 et seq.; Lauritsen et al. 1991, p. 267). This victim–offender overlap has been well documented empirically (Jennings et al. 2012), but the etiology of the phenomenon remains elusive (Berg et al. 2012, p. 360; Lauritsen and Laub 2007, p. 62). Since the beginning of the 21st century, the victim–offender overlap has come to the fore in research by addressing various mechanisms of the association between victimization and offending (e.g., genetic factors: Barnes and Beaver 2012; bullying: DeCamp and Newby 2015; behavioral economics: Entorf 2013; cyberbullying: Marcum et al. 2014; intimate partner violence: Muftić et al. 2012; Skubak Tillyer and Wright 2013).

Theoretical Approaches

In the late 1990s, criminological theory captured attention to explain victimization (Schreck and Stewart 2012, p. 51). The victim–offender lap raised awareness among researchers that offending and victimization might develop from the same processes and thus they use different general categories of criminological theories, including theories of lifestyle, routine activity, subculture of violence, strain, and self-control (Daigle and Muftić 2016, p. 43 et seq.; Schreck et al. 2008, p. 874). Although the theories shed light on the causes of becoming both an offender and a victim, distinctive characteristics only applying either for criminality or for victimization remain largely concealed (Schreck et al. 2008, p. 874).

According to the lifestyle theory, differences in lifestyles provide for variations in victimization risk (Hindelang et al. 1978, p. 241 et seq.). As a consequence, individuals with more risky lifestyles tend to expose themselves to situations that bear more opportunities of becoming a victim. The risk of being subjected to crime is also affected by demographic and social characteristics such as sex, age, occupation, ethnicity, and social group. Besides, victims, as well as perpetrators, exhibit a comparable sociodemographic profile because of related lifestyle features (Hindelang et al. 1978, p. 79). This is why factors such as age, leisure activities, and residential proximity to crime are linked with both offending and victimization (Sampson and Lauritsen 1990, p. 132). Substance use characterizes not only risky lifestyles but also a factor linked to both victimization and offending (van Gelder et al. 2015, p. 655).

Related to the lifestyle theory is the routine activity theory that high-lights three elements for the likelihood that an offense is committed: a moti-vated offender, a suitable victim, and no capable guardian converging at a given time and place (Cohen and Felson 1979; Cohen et al. 1981). The risk of becoming a victim is influenced by how daily routines are organized. A delinquent lifestyle, seen as an exposure to the violation of law, may enhance the likelihood of violent victimization (Fattah 1991, p. 126 et seq.). Therefore, the prevalence of victimization can heighten when daily routines fulfill the aforementioned three factors. In this sense, unstructured and unobserved social activity allows for a greater probability of becoming both a victim and an offender (Schreck et al. 2008, p. 875).

Subcultural theories of crime emphasize a circle of violence between offenders and victims (Singer 1981). Within subcultures of violence, offend-ers inflict violence on their victims who then attack their former perpetra-tor as an act of retaliation. According to the "code of the street" (Anderson 1999, p. 59), violence belongs inseparable to an individual's identity, self-respect, and honor. Retaliatory violence occurs because a violent affront is understood as a sign of disrespect. In particular, groups, such as gangs, internalize norms that support the use of force in conflicts (Sampson and Wilson 1990, p. 50). Individuals switch the role of an offender and a victim in disorganized areas where norms of violence are widely accepted (Schreck et al. 2008, p. 876).

Meanwhile, according to the general strain theory, victimization is seen as a type of strain that would lead to a greater level of offending (Agnew 2002, p. 606). An effect on delinquency has experienced not only physical victim-ization but also vicarious and anticipated physical victimization. While vicarious strain results from witnessing the victimization of close others, anticipated strain is based on feeling unsafe and thus expecting to become a victim of serious violence with a high probability of occurrence (Agnew 2002, p. 627). These cases have an impact on anger/frustration, which, in turn, increases the risk for (violent) offending (Agnew 2002, p. 629).

Originally, the general theory of crime referred to the offender whose low self-control causes deviance or crime owing to failed socialization (Gottfredson and Hirschi 1990, p. 97). More recently, however, this theoretical perspective has been extended to explain victimization (e.g., Schreck 1999). Six character-istics of low self-control are conducive to victimization and offending, which means shortsightedness, self-centeredness, anger, low diligence, preference for physical over mental tasks, and risk or sensation-seeking behavior. The vul-nerability to become a victim derives from a lack of respect for consequences and other negative events such as history of broken relationships and failure at work associated with low self-control (Schreck et al. 2008, p. 876).

According to any of these theoretical approaches, it is evident that it is a plausible assumption that the risk groups—prone to become either a victim or an offender (or both)—are more or less the same. This confirms the conceptual interpretation of criminalization and victimization as a process of interaction (Schneider 1982, p. 13).

Research Findings

Research on the victim–offender overlap (for an overview, see Jennings et al. 2012; Lauritsen and Laub 2007) has pointed out a strong correlation between the two, and the phenomenon has been one of the most robust empirical relations in criminology (e.g., van Gelder et al. 2015, p. 654). On the basis of prior work, it is also known that the relationship varies substantially across types of offenses and is stronger for violent offenses than property offenses (Jennings et al. 2012, p. 22). Empirical findings suggest that previous violence seems to predict more strongly offending than victimization (Jennings et al. 2012; Kühlhorn 1990, p. 23) and offending is connected to a greater risk of becoming a victim (Lauritsen and Laub 2007, p. 59). Nonetheless, the association has been confirmed across time and place, and for various subgroups regardless of the type of data used as well as demographic correlates and lifestyle characteristics (Lauritsen and Laub 2007, p. 260).

Most empirical studies such as, for example, the International Self-Report Delinquency Studies (**ISRD**) include adolescents, school-based samples of children, high school or college students, parolees, psychiatric patients, or known offenders and their victims (Entorf 2013, p. 8; Jennings et al. 2012, p. 18). Surveys based on relatively large samples from relevant subpopulations were carried out in America (e.g., Barnes and Beaver 2012; Klevens et al. 2002) and more general samples in Europe (Entorf 2013; Matz 2007; Sparks et al. 1977; Wittebrood and Nieuwbeerta 1999). Other qualitative studies are built on narrative in-depth interviews with perpetrators (Jacobs and Wright 2010; Jacques and Wright 2008). Whereas more general data might fail to identify specific interrelations between offenders and victims, the small number of interviews bounds the external validity and statistical interference (Entorf 2013, p. 8).

Previous research focused on how victims and offenders resemble and on how the association between being a victim and an offender could be explained (van Gelder et al. 2015, p. 668). Thereby, many studies concentrate on demographic and neighborhood characteristics (Berg et al. 2012), routine activities and risky lifestyles (Lauritsen et al. 1991; Smith and Ecob 2007), subcultures of violence (Matsuda et al. 2013), and low self-control (Flexon et al. 2015). To a lesser extent, socio-psychological characteristics that influence the onset, development, and outcome of violent interactions are explored (van Gelder et al. 2015, p. 668). Only recently, some studies take an interest in disentangling victim and offender roles by identifying differences between victims, offenders, and victim–offenders (Broidy et al. 2006; Schreck et al. 2008; van Gelder et al. 2015).

Most of the earlier research on the topic revealed shared common demographic characteristics between victims and offenders (von Hentig 1948, p. 383) that were validated, such as age, race, gender, and marital status (Lauritsen et al. 1991, p. 265 et seq.). A good deal of evidence hints at some impact of lifestyle factors and routine activities for both offending and victimization (Maldonaldo-Molina et al. 2010, p. 1198 f.; Mustaine and Tewksbury 2000, p. 357), although there are a few researches that examine the factors explaining differential exposure to lifestyle features and routine activities (Barnes and Beaver 2012, p. 5). Subcultural explanations arouse increased interest regarding studies on neighborhood, culture, and gang membership (Pyrooz et al. 2013, p. 316). The influence of the neighborhood context has not yet been adequately clarified because of a few studies with contradicting findings (Posick and Zimmerman 2015, p. 1433). According to this, the victim–offender overlap is either strong (Berg et al. 2012) or weak (Wright and Fagan 2013) in more disadvantaged neighborhoods. Studies on retaliatory offending show that gang membership (Pyrooz et al. 2013) enhances subsequent victimization as well as negative emotionality, with anger as its most pronounced factor (Maschi et al. 2008). The research base toward the impact of low self-control on the relationship of being an offender and a victim remains thin and is partially supported (Flexon et al. 2015, p. 16; Schreck 1999, p. 648; van Gelder et al. 2015, p. 668).

Meanwhile, Lauritsen and Laub (2007, p. 62) stressed that "violent offending remained the strongest predictor of victimization [...]. If we want to identify the mechanism underlying the relationship between offending and victimization, [...] we must consider various biological and psychological measures that capture aspects of personality and decision-making capacities and assess how these individual differences in tandem with specific types of social environments may be linked to differential proneness in victimization." Furthermore, instead of focusing on similarities between victims and offenders, scholars (Schreck et al. 2008, p. 873) recommend a shift in research on the victim–offender overlap: In order to justify for specialized theories of criminality and victimization, differentiations between victims, offenders, and victim–offender should be addressed to a greater extent by researchers (e.g., Broidy et al. 2006; Mustaine and Tewksburry 2000; van Gelder et al. 2015).

Implications for Crime Prevention

More knowledge about the process underlying the victim–offender overlap might also have an impact on crime prevention (Berg and Felson 2016, p. 16). In particular, programs that address violence are based on the distinction between victims and offenders. This separation disregards the needs of victim–offenders in victim assistance programs owing to the focus on the ideal victim (Schreck et al. 2008, p. 894). In contrast, programs that are directed toward offenders could better meet the claim to relate experiences as a victim, especially when it comes to incidents in the childhood (Schreck et al. 2008, p. 894).

The claim to take into account psychological constructs could be misleading because the wrong conclusion as blaming the victim could be drawn (van Gelder et al. 2015, p. 668). Apart from this, empirical results might hint at certain psychological traits that heighten the vulnerability and likelihood of becoming a victim (van Gelder et al. 2015, p. 668); this applies in particular to the neglected figure of the victim–offender in crime prevention. The integration of empirical findings about the association could contribute to improve the effectiveness of both victim and offender programs (Schreck et al. 2008, p. 894). As an example, Lauritsen and Laub (2007, p. 69) introduce an evaluation of crime prevention strategies for a subgroup of victims to show them ways to diminish their risk of future victimization (Davis and Smith 1994). Although participants learned more about crime prevention and took more precautions than victims without undergoing a specific training, the researchers could not find a significant effect on revictimization. The researchers concluded that this might be caused by false assumptions on which the program has been based (Davis and Smith 1994, p. 66). Therefore, Lauritsen and Laub (2007, p. 70) wonder if the consideration of the victim–offender overlap might have contributed to change the result.

It is not only the victim–offender overlap relationship but also the differentiation between victims, offenders, and victim–offenders that should be borne in mind when specific interventions for these groups are developed in order to address their different needs (van Gelder et al. 2015, p. 668). Concerning victim–offenders, programs should be tailored in a way that they reduce both the risk of offending and victimization (Costello 2010, p. 611). Broidy et al. (2006, p. 27) refine that "violence reduction efforts may be able to target individuals following violent victimization and utilize proactive strategies (e.g., counseling, anger management, mental health assessment/treatment, drug/alcohol abuse treatment, or job training/placement services) to reduce the likelihood of future offending, rather than relying solely on the reactive strategies that typically follow offending (e.g. arrest or incarceration)."

Summary and Implications

Although having a comparatively robust history, the victimology–crime prevention nexus within a criminological context remains a relative understudied area. However, as illustrated throughout this chapter, crime prevention programs mostly lack a comprehensive approach that considers the obvious links between victimization and offending in a more systematic manner. We have demonstrated that victims and offenders have more in common than public opinion and mainstream policies would acknowledge. In particular, the following findings and implications became evident:

- "Research has established that victims of crime are disproportionately male, young, and members of racial and ethnic minority groups" (Schreck 1999, p. 633). This finding is in contrast to the image of the ideal victim, which mostly is a stereotype.
- Since the early years of victimology, the interpersonal dynamics of victimization are a well-known phenomenon. Benjamin Mendelsohn portrayed offender and victim as a "penal couple" (1956, p. 99) while Hans von Hentig addressed them as "partners" in crime (1948, p. 383).
- To date, the victim–offender remains a blind spot in crime prevention, though long known in victimology; practice of crime prevention ignores the upcoming results of different empirical studies.
- "As for individual likelihood of victimization, many of the same risk factors apply as those identified for offenders" (Rubin et al. 2008, p. 7).
- "In fact, not unlike offending rates, victimization rates are highest among young, minority, males and are inflated in socially disorganized areas, leading to the suggestion that offenders and victims are, in fact, overlapping populations" (Broidy et al. 2006, p. 23).
- A variety of diverse categories of victim–offender overlap can be identified, all based on, or related to, victim experiences of offenders or on situational involvement of victims in criminogenic situations or criminal activities.
- Disappointment by victims based on negative experience with the criminal justice system can also have a potential to stimulate victim–offender escalation.
- Delivery of procedural justice is an important precondition of victim satisfaction.
- Restorative justice, with its broader focus on the conflict between parties, may have de-escalating effect in regard to the dynamics of victim–offender overlap.
- More research is needed (Costello 2010, p. 611), in particular offender victimization surveys (Jennings et al. 2012).
- There is a further need to gain more information on the nature of victimization and the nature of offending (Jennings et al. 2012).
- In addition, more information about the complexity of relationships between specific types of offending behaviors and victimization experiences is required (Jennings et al. 2012).

- There is also a lack of panel data (Entorf 2013, p. 24).
- In the area of crime prevention, the connection between the victimization and the offending perspective has to be recognized in order to raise more awareness.
- Secondary victimization should not be underestimated in its criminogenic effect; actually, the impact of the phenomenon is not sufficiently evaluated.
- The design of prevention programs should always address offenders as victims, and vice versa, in order to overcome the artificial divide between the two groups.

Glossary of Key Terms

BCS (the British Crime Survey): Regular representative survey on criminal victimization in England and Wales conducted on behalf of the British Home Office (Office for National Statistics) since 1982.

Fear of crime: Important area of victimological research. It focuses on citizens' perception of the risk of becoming a victim of crime, and on feelings, thoughts, and behaviors about the personal risk of criminal victimization. Fear of crime includes affective, cognitive, and behavioral aspects.

ICVS (the International Crime Victims Survey): Initiated by a group of European researchers in 1987, the ICVS developed to become the world's most comprehensive and, in terms of sample size, the world's largest victimization survey (see Box 15.4).

Ideal victim: A term introduced by Nils Christie in 1986 that refers to a victim (i.e., person or category of individuals) who will not be judged to have precipitated the crime against them in any way.

ISRD (the International Self-Report Delinquency Study): The ISRD project is an international collaborative study, which repeatedly collects self-reported data on juvenile delinquency and victimization. The first study was conducted in 13 countries (ISRD-1: 1992–1993), the second one was extended to 31 countries (ISRD-2: 2005–2007), and the third one includes 34 countries (ISRD-3: 2012–2015).

NCVS (the American Crime Victimization Survey): Since 1973, the NCVS is conducted annually by the U.S. Census Bureau for the Bureau of Justice Statistics. Persons aged 12 or older from a nationally representative sample of households in the United States are asked about victimizations, characteristics of the crime, whether and why the crime was reported to police (or why not), and victim experiences with the criminal justice system.

Procedural justice: Working term for assessing the treatment of individuals by the agencies of the criminal justice system. It has been developed as an adequate parameter for the treatment of victims, as a parallel to the fair trial principles that relate to the treatment of defendants.

Restorative justice: Alternative model of conflict resolution with a special emphasis on inclusion, communication, restoration, and restitution. Developed first in Canada in the 1970s (Kitchener, Ontario), it has been internationally recognized and promoted by institutions as renowned as the United Nations and the Council of Europe. There are a variety of models in practice such as victim–offender mediation, family group conferencing, peace circles, and so on (also see Chapter 9).

Standard offenses: Internationally standardized offense categories covered in most national and international victimization surveys (see Box 15.3).

Victimization (primary [direct] victimization, secondary victimization, tertiary victimization, revictimization): Different categories of victimization (see Box 15.5).

Victim impact statement (VIS), victim personal statement (VPS): Victim impact statement is a procedural instrument introduced in common law systems providing crime victims an opportunity to articulate, in their own words, about how a crime has affected them. It has been introduced in jurisdictions in which the adversarial process system does not provide formal participant or party status to the victim (e.g., United States, Canada, and Australia).

Victim–offender overlap: Personal interconnection between victim role and offender role that can become prevalent in different forms and scenarios (see Box 15.1).

Discussion Questions

1. How can the popular perception of the "ideal victim" be explained? Why can the ideal victim be considered an artificial rather than a reality-based construct?
2. What can empirical data obtained through victimization surveys (e.g., NCVS, BCS, and ICVS) tell us about the reality of victimization? What are the major challenges of such surveys in terms of methodology and representativeness?
3. What different situations of overlap, or linkages, between victimization and offending can be identified? How might these be

categorized? What additional concrete examples of crimes that may potentially precede or follow victimization can be thought of?

4. Which of the theoretical approaches discussed in this chapter can explain the similarities of, and connections between, victim and offender populations? What might be the strengths and shortcomings of each approach? In regard to which aspects do you think they can supplement each other?

5. Which individuals, or groups, run the highest risks of offending or reoffending, or being victimized or revictimized?

6. What is procedural justice? What is the impact of procedural justice for crime victims?

7. What should be the relevance of victims in the context of crime prevention? How best might their needs be assessed?

Recommended Web Links

ICVS data with further methodological background and country-related info as well as a comprehensive list of related publications are available at www.wp.unil.ch/icvs/; www.unicri.it/services/library _documentation/publications/icvs/.

In **Canada**, victimization data are collected as part of the General Social Survey. Most recent data about criminal victimization in Canada in 2014 are available at www.statcan.gc.ca/pub/85-002-x/2015001 /article/14241-eng.htm.

Comparative data from **ISRD** studies 1–3 and additional methodological background info are available at www.northeastern.edu/isrd/.

Rich information about the concepts and practices of restorative justice can be found in the UN Handbook on Restorative Justice Programmes, which is available for free of charge download at www. unodc.org/pdf/criminal_justice/06-56290_Ebook.pdf.

Acknowledgment

Special thanks go to Ms. Ines Hohendorf for her valuable support.

References

Agnew, R. (2002). Experienced, vicarious, and anticipated strain: An exploratory study on physical victimization and delinquency. *Justice Quarterly*, 19, pp. 603–632.

Anderson, E. (1999). *Code of the Street: Decency, Violence, and the Moral Life of the Inner City*. New York: W.W. Norton.

Barnes, J.C., and Beaver, K.M. (2012). Extending research on the victim–offender overlap: Evidence from a genetically informative analysis. *Journal of Interpersonal Violence*, pp. 1–23.

Berg, M.T., and Felson, R.B. (2016). Why are offenders victimized so often? In: C.A. Cuevas and C.M. Rennison (eds.), *The Wiley Handbook on the Psychology of Violence*. Chichester, UK: John Wiley & Sons Ltd., pp. 49–66.

Berg, M.T., Stewart, E.A., Schreck, C.J., and Simons, R.L. (2012). The victim–offender overlap in context: Examining the role of neighborhood street culture. *Criminology*, 50, pp. 359–390.

Bradford, B., and MacQueen, S. (2015). Victimization surveys: Tolls for research and policy; sites of contest and debates. In: M. Tonry (ed.), *Oxford Handbooks Online: Criminology and Criminal Justice*. Oxford, UK: Oxford University Press.

Broidy, L.M., Daday, J.K., Crandall, C.S., Sklar, D.P., and Jost, P.F. (2006). Exploring demographic, structural, and behavioral overlap among homicide offenders and victims. *Homicide Studies*, 10, pp. 155–180.

Campbell, K.M. (2005). Rehabilitation theory. In: M. Bosworth (ed.), *Encyclopedia of Prisons & Correctional Facilities*. Thousand Oaks, CA: Sage, pp. 831–834.

Carrabine, E., Inganski, P., Lee, M., Plummer, K., and South, N. (2004). *Criminology. A Sociological Introduction*. New York: Routledge.

Christie, N. (1986). The ideal victim. In: E.A. Fattah (ed.), *From Crime Policy to Victim Policy. Reorienting the Justice System*. New York: St. Martin's Press, pp. 17–30.

Cohen, L.E., and Felson, M. (1979). Social change and crime rate trends: A routine activities approach. *American Sociological Review*, 44, pp. 588–608.

Cohen, L.E., Kluegel, J.R., and Land, K.C. (1981). Social inequality and predatory criminal victimization: An exposition and test of a formal theory. *American Sociological Review*, 46, pp. 505–524.

Costello, A. (2010). Offending and victimization. In: B.N. Fisher & S.P. Lab (eds.), *Encyclopedia of Victimology and Crime Prevention*. Los Angeles: Sage Publications, pp. 610–612.

Crawford, A., and Goodey, J. (eds.) (2000). *Integrating a Victim Perspective in Criminal Justice: International Debates*. Aldershot, UK: Dartmouth.

Daigle, L.E., and Muftić, L.R. (2016). *Victimology*. Los Angeles: Sage Publications.

Davis, R.C., and Smith, B. (1994). Teaching victims crime prevention skills: Can individuals lower their risk of crime? *Criminal Justice Review*, 19, pp. 56–68.

DeCamp, W., and Newby, B. (2015). From bullied to deviant: The victim–offender overlap among bullying victims. *Youth Violence and Juvenile Violence*, 13, pp. 3–17.

Dignan, J. (2005). *Understanding Victims and Restorative Justice*. New York: Open University Press.

Entorf, H. (2013). *Criminal Victims, Victimized Criminals, or Both? A Deeper Look at the Victim–Offender Overlap*. http://ftp.iza.org/dp7686.pdf, 03.03.2016.

Erez, E., Ibarra, P.R., and Downs, D.M. (2011). Victim welfare and participation reforms in the United States: A therapeutic jurisprudence perspective. In: E. Erez, M. Kilchling and J.A.M. Wemmers (eds.), *Therapeutic Jurisprudence and Victim Participation in Justice. International Perspectives*. Durham, NC: Carolina Academic Press, pp. 15–39.

Farrell, G., Tseloni, A., and Pease, K. (2005). Repeat victimization in the ICVS and NCVS. *Crime Prevention and Community Safety: An International Journal*, 7, pp. 7–18.

Fattah, E.A. (1991). *Understanding Criminal Victimization*. Scarborough, Ontario: Prentice-Hall Canada.

Flexon, J.L., Meldrum, R.C., and Piquero, A.R. (2015). Low self-control and the victim–offender overlap: A gendered analysis. *Journal of Interpersonal Violence*, pp. 1–25.

Fox, K.A., Nobles, M.R., and Piquero, A.R. (2009). Gender, crime victimization and fear of crime. *Security Journal*, 22, pp. 24–39.

Galaway, B., and Hudson, J. (eds.) (1996). *Restorative Justice: International Perspectives*. Amsterdam: Kugler.

Genn, H. (1988). Multiple victimization. In: M. Maguire and J. Pointing (eds.), *Victims of Crime: A New Deal?* Philadelphia: Open University Press, pp. 90–100.

Goodey, J. (2005). *Victims and Victimology. Research, Policy and Practice*. Harlow etc.: Pearson Education Ltd.

Gottfredson, M.R. (1981). On the etiology of criminal victimization. *Journal of Criminal Law and Criminology*, 72, pp. 714–726.

Gottfredson, M.R., and Hirschi, T. (1990). *A General Theory of Crime*. Stanford, CA: Stanford University Press.

Greer, C. (2004). Crime, media and community: Grief and virtual engagement in late modernity. In: J. Ferrell, K. Hayward, W. Morrison and M. Presdee (eds.), *Cultural Criminology Unleashed*. London: Cavendish, pp. 109–118.

Greer, C. (2007). News media, victims and crime. In: P. Davies, P. Francis and C. Greer (eds.), *Victims, Crime and Society*. London: Sage, pp. 20–49.

Greer, D. (ed.) (1996). *Compensating Crime Victims. A European Survey*. Freiburg i.Br., Germany: Edition iuscrim.

Hale, C. (1996). Fear of crime: A review of the literature. *International Review of Victimology*, 4, pp. 79–150.

Haverkamp, R. (2015). Die Opferperspektive in der Kriminalprävention (Teil 1)—Begriffsverständnis, Opfererfassung und Opfergefährdung [The victim perspective in crime prevention—part 1]. *Forum Kriminalprävention*, 4, pp. 45–50.

Haverkamp, R. (2016). Die Opferperspektive in der Kriminalprävention (Teil 2)—Rechtlicher Rahmen, praktische Ansätze und mediales Interesse [The victim perspective in crime prevention—part 2]. *Forum Kriminalprävention*, 1, pp. 45–50.

Hindelang, M.J., Gottfredson, M.R., and Garofalo, J. (1978). *Victims of Personal Crime: An Empirical Foundation for a Theory of Personal Victimization*. Cambridge, MA: Ballinger.

Hough, M. (1986). Victims of violent crime: Findings from the first British crime survey. In: E.A. Fattah (ed.), *From Crime Policy to Victim Policy*. Basingstoke, UK: Macmillan, pp. 117–132.

Jacobs, B.A., and Wright, R. (2010). Bounded rationality, retaliation, and the spread of urban violence. *Journal of Interpersonal Violence*, 25, pp. 1739–1766.

Jacques, S., and Wright, R. (2008). The victimization-termination link. *Criminology*, 46, pp. 1009–1038.

Jägervi, L. (2014). Who wants to be an ideal victim? A narrative analysis of crime victims' self-presentation. *Journal of Scandinavian Studies in Criminology and Crime Prevention*, 15, pp. 73–88.

Jennings, W.G., Piquero, A.R., and Reingle, J.M. (2012). On the overlap between victimization and offending: A review of the literature. *Aggression and Violent Behavior*, 17, pp. 16–26.

Kaiser, M., and Kilchling, M. (1996). Germany. In: Greer, Desmond (ed.), *Compensating Crime Victims. A European Survey*, Freiburg i.Br., Germany: Edition iuscrim, pp. 255–297.

Kilchling, M. (1995). Opferinteressen und Strafverfolgung [Interests of the Victim and Public Prosecution]. Freiburg i.Br., Germany: Edition iuscrim.

Kilchling, M. (2014). Stand der internationalen Diskussion zu Opfererfahrungen und Opfererwartungen in der Kriminaljustiz [Current State of the International Discussion on Victims' Experiences in and Victims' Expectations towards the Criminal Justice System]. Unpublished Conference Paper. 24th Opferforum Mainz, November 2014.

Klevens, J., Duque, L.F., and Ramirez, C. (2002). The victim–offender overlap and routine activities: Results from a cross-sectional study in Bogota, Colombia. *Journal of Interpersonal Violence*, 17, pp. 206–216.

Kühlhorn, E. (1990). Victims and offenders of criminal violence. *Journal of Quantitative Criminology*, 6, 51–59.

Kury, H., and Kilchling, M. (2011). Accessory prosecution in Germany: Legislation and implementation. In: E. Erez, M. Kilchling and J.A.M. Wemmers (eds.), *Therapeutic Jurisprudence and Victim Participation in Justice. International Perspectives*. Durham, NC: Carolina Academic Press, pp. 41–65.

Lauritsen, J.L., and Laub, J.H. (2007). Understanding the link between victimization and offending: New reflections on an old idea. In: M. Hough & M. Maxfield (eds.). *Surveying Crime in the 21st Century: Commemorating the 25th Anniversary of the British Crime Survey*. Monsey, NY: Criminal Justice Press, pp. 55–76.

Lauritsen, J.L., Sampson, R.J., and Laub, J.H. (1991). The link between offending and victimization among adolescents. *Criminology*, 29, pp. 265–292.

Lewis, C. (2012). Crime and justice statistics collected by international agencies. *European Journal on Criminal Policy and Research*, 18, pp. 5–21.

Maldonaldo-Molina, M., Jennings, W.G., Tobler, A.L., Piquero, A.R., and Canino, G. (2010). Assessing the victim–offender overlap among Puerto Rico youth. *Journal of Criminal Justice*, 38, pp. 1191–1201.

Marcum, C.D., Higgins, G.E., Freiburger, T.L., and Ricketts, M.L. (2014). Exploration of the cyberbullying victim/offender overlap by sex. *American Journal of Criminal Justice*, 39, pp. 538–548.

Maschi, T., Bradley, C.A., and Morgen, K. (2008). Unraveling the link between trauma and delinquency: The mediating role of negative affect and delinquent peer exposure. *Youth Violence and Juvenile Justice*, 6, pp. 136–157.

Matsuda, K.N., Melde, C., Taylor, T.J., Freng, A., and Esbensen, F.-A. (2013). Gang membership and adherence to the 'code of the street.' *Justice Quarterly*, 30, pp. 440–468.

Matz, D. (2007). Development and key results from the first two waves of the offending crime and justice survey. In: M. Hough and M. Maxfield (eds.), *Surveying Crime in the 21st Century: Commemorating the 25th Anniversary of the British Crime Survey*. Monsey, NY: Criminal Justice Press, pp. 77–98.

McAlinden, A.-M. (2014). Deconstructing victim and offender identities in discourses on child sexual abuse. *British Journal of Criminology*, 54, pp. 180–198.

McCold, P. (2003). A survey of assessment research on mediation and conferencing. In: L. Walgrave (ed.). *Repositioning Restorative Justice*. Cullompton and Portland, OR: Willan Publishing, pp. 67–120.

Mendelsohn, B. (1956). Une nouvelle branche de la science bio-psych-sociale: la victimologie. Etudes Internationales de Psycho-Sociologie Criminelle [today: *Revue Internationale de Criminologie*], 10, pp. 95–109.

Muftić, L.R., Finn, M.A., and Marsh, E.A. (2012). The victim–offender overlap, intimate partner violence, and sex: Assessing differences among victims, offenders, and victim–offenders. *Crime & Delinquency*, 61, pp. 899–926.

Mustaine, E.E., and Tewksbury, R. (2000). Comparing the lifestyles of victims, offenders, and victim–offenders: A routine activity theory assessment of similarities and differences for criminal incident participants. *Sociological Focus*, 33, pp. 339–362.

Pemberton, A., and Reynaers, S. (2011). The controversial nature of victim participation: Therapeutic benefits in victim impact statements. In: E. Erez, M. Kilchling and J.A.M. Wemmers (eds.), *Therapeutic Jurisprudence and Victim Participation in Justice. International Perspectives.* Durham, NC: Carolina Academic Press, pp. 229–248.

Pérez Cepeda, A., Benito Sánchez, D., Haverkamp, R., Viuhko, M., Yordanova, M., Markov, D., Doichinova, M., Joutsen, M., and Jokinen, A. (2013). Review of existing efforts to describe trends at European level. In: S. Maffei and L. Markopoulou (eds.), *Fiducia New European Crimes and Trust-Based Policy.* Greece: EPLO.

Posick, C., and Zimmerman, G.M. (2015). Person-in-context: Insights on contextual variation and in the victim–offender overlap across schools. *Journal of Interpersonal Violence*, 30, pp. 1432–1455.

Pyrooz, D.C., Moule, R.K. Jr., and Decker, S.H. (2013). The contribution of gang membership to the victim–offender overlap. *Journal of Research in Crime and Delinquency*, 51, pp. 315–348.

Rubin, J., Gallo, F., and Coutts, A. (2008). *Violent crime. Risk models, effective interventions and risk management.* Cambridge: Rand Europe.

Sampson, R.J., and Lauritsen, J.L. (1990). Deviant lifestyles, proximity to crime and the offender–victim link in personal violence. *Journal of Research in Crime and Delinquency*, 27, pp. 110–139.

Sampson, R.J., and Wilson, W.J. (1990). Toward a theory of race, crime, and urban inequality. In: J. Hagan and R.D. Peterson (eds.). *Crime and Inequality.* Palo Alto, CA: Stanford University Press, pp. 37–56.

Schneider, H.J. (1982). The present situation of victimology in the world. In: H.J. Schneider (ed.), *The Victim in International Perspective.* Berlin/New York: de Gruyter, pp. 11–46.

Schreck, C.J. (1999). Criminal victimization and low self-control: An extension and test of a general theory of crime. *Justice Quarterly*, 16, pp. 633–654.

Schreck, C.J., and Stewart, E.A. (2012). The victim–offender overlap and its implications for juvenile justice. In: B.C. Feld and D.M. Bishop (eds.), *Juvenile Crime and Juvenile Justice.* Oxford, UK: Oxford University Press, pp. 47–69.

Schreck, C.J., Stewart, E.A., and Osgood, D.W. (2008). A reappraisal of the overlap of violent offenders and victims. *Criminology*, 46, pp. 871–906.

Schwartz, M.D. (2000). Methodological issues in the use of survey data for measuring and characterizing violence against women. *Violence Against Women*, 6, pp. 815–838.

Scott, H. (2003). Stranger danger: Explaining women's fear of crime. *Western Criminology Review*, 4, pp. 203–214.

Shapland, J., Willmore, J., and Duff, P. (1985). *Victims in the Criminal Justice System.* Aldershot, UK: Gower Publishing.

Singer, S.I. (1981). Homogenous victim–offender populations: A review and some research implications. *Journal of Criminal Law and Criminology*, 72, pp. 779–788.

Skogan, W.G. (1981). *Issues in the Measurement of Victimization*. Washington DC: U.S. Department of Justice, Bureau of Justice.

Skogan, W.G., and Maxfield, M.G. (1981). *Coping with Crime. Individual and Neighborhood Reactions*. Beverly Hills, CA: Sage Publications.

Skubak Tillyer, M., and Wright, E.M. (2013). Intimate partner violence and the victim–offender overlap. *Journal of Research in Crime and Delinquency*, pp. 1–27.

Smith, D.J., and Ecob, R. (2007). An investigation into causal links between victimization and offending in adolescents. *The British Journal of Sociology*, 58, pp. 633–659.

Smolej, M. (2010). Constructing ideal victims? Violence narratives in Finnish crime-appeal programming. *Crime Media Culture*, 6, pp. 69–85.

Sparks, R.F., Genn, H.G., and Dodd, D.J. (1977). *Surveying Victims*. New York: Wiley.

Stanko, E.A. (1988). Hidden violence against women. In: M. Maguire and J. Pointing (eds.), *Victims of Crime: A New Deal?* Philadelphia: Open University Press, pp. 40–46.

Strobl, R. (2004). Constructing the victim: Theoretical reflections and empirical examples. *International Review of Victimology*, 11, pp. 295–311.

Tonry, M. (2004). *Thinking about Crime: Sense and Sensibility on American Penal Culture*. New York: Oxford University Press.

Van Camp. T. (2014). *Victims of Violence and Restorative Justice Practices. Finding a Voice*. London/New York: Routledge.

van Dijk, J.J. (2001). Attitudes of the victim and repeat victims towards the police. Results of the International Crime Victims Survey. In: G. Farrell and K. Pease (eds.), *Repeat Victimization*. Monsey, NY: Criminal Justice Press, pp. 27–52.

van Dijk, J.J. (2012). The International Crime Victims Survey. Latest results and prospects. *Criminology in Europe*, 3, pp. 24–33.

van Gelder, J.-L., Averdijk, M., Eisner, M., and Ribaud, D. (2015). Unpacking the victim–offender overlap: On role differentiation and socio-psychological characteristics. *Journal of Quantitative Criminology*, 31, pp. 653–675.

van Kesteren, J., van Dijk, J.J., and Mayhew, P. (2014). The International Crime Victims Surveys: A retrospective. *International Review of Victimology*, 20, pp. 49–69.

von Hentig, H. (1948). *The Criminal and His Victim: Studies in the Sociobiology of Crime*. Edition 1967, New Haven, CT: Yale University Press.

Walklate, S. (2007). *Imagining the Victim of Crime*. Maidenhead, England: Open University Press.

Wemmers, J.A.M. (1996). *Victims in the Criminal Justice System*. Amsterdam: Kugler.

Wemmers, J.A.M. (2011). Victims in the criminal justice system and therapeutic jurisprudence: A Canadian perspective. In: E. Erez, M. Kilchling and J.J.M. Wemmers (eds.), *Therapeutic Jurisprudence and Victim Participation in Justice. International Perspectives*. Durham, NC: Carolina Academic Press, pp. 67–85.

Wittebrood, K., and Nieuwbeerta, P. (1999). Wages of sin? The link between offending, lifestyle and violent victimization. *European Journal of Criminal Policy and Research*, 7, pp. 63–80.

Wolfgang, M.E. (1958). *Patterns in Criminal Homicide*. New York: Wiley.

Wright, E.M., and Fagan, A.A. (2013). The cycle of violence in context: Exploring the moderating roles of neighborhood disadvantage and cultural norms. *Criminology*, 51, pp. 217–249.

The Politics of Crime Prevention

16

MARGARET SHAW

Contents

Learning Outcomes
After reading this chapter, you should be able to

- Understand the political nature of crime prevention policy decision-making
- Describe and understand the evolution of crime prevention internationally, and the ways it is being entrenched in many government policies
- Access some international examples of successful crime prevention strategies especially at the city level
- Understand the importance of international standards in crime prevention, and some of the challenges for the development of prevention in the future

Introduction

However we dress, wherever we go, Yes means Yes and No means No!*
Since the Harper Government first came to office, the security and prosperity of Canadians has been our priority.†

---

*One of the chants used by women during "Take Back the Night" marches in North America in the 1970s.
† http://daily.pm.gc.ca/en/content/your-canada/strong-canada#sthash.X9H1XSiL.dpuf

These two very disparate quotations underline the very political nature of policies that try to improve the lives of women and men in all societies. The first is a chant initially used on marches organized by women's groups in the United States and Canada in the 1970s, to protest the lack of public action on sexual violence against women, especially in public spaces. It was part of a powerful social movement that helped persuade governments that they should put in place legislation and policies to help prevent such violence. The second quotation is taken from the website of the Canadian federal government in 2015. The Conservative party, under former Prime Minister Steven Harper, had been in power from 2005 until its defeat in October 2015, and the statement clearly reflected his view that the most important priorities were the economy, and tough legislation and criminal justice responses to deter and punish offenders, which, at times, was to the detriment of the rights of individuals.

Modern approaches to crime prevention and community safety have emerged and evolved for more than a quarter of a century. What has been termed by one observer as "the preventive turn" (Crawford 2009b) initially emerged in North America and some European countries and spread very rapidly across countries in many regions of the world. National and local crime prevention strategies now incorporate—and try to live up to—a number of international norms and standards adopted by the United Nations. These lay out the principles on which countries and local governments should develop comprehensive strategies to promote safe cities and communities and the characteristics of good strategies (UNODC 2010). They are about understanding how crime and violence arise—their so-called root causes—and implementing a range of strategic policies and programs that will help reduce those root causes and promote healthier societies. These international standards have drawn on the accumulated research and knowledge of the viability and effectiveness of crime prevention.

As other sections of this book have underlined, relying on the justice system to respond to crime and violence, after it occurs, is much more complex and costly than prevention. The costs of the criminal justice system, including policing, the courts, and correctional systems, are exceedingly high. The social and economic impacts of crime on victims and their families, on individual offenders and their families, as well as society as a whole are enormous, affecting physical and mental health, education, and work.

The growth of interest in crime prevention can be seen in the expanding network of cities and countries working with the European Forum on Urban Security (EFUS) and the International Centre for the Prevention of Crime (ICPC), both of which were established in the early 1990s to promote crime prevention and community safety. Work to reduce violence against women and promote women's safety in urban settings has also been expanding over the past 12 years especially with projects initiated by nongovernment organizations (NGOs) such as Women in Cities International, based in Montreal, Red Mujer Y Habitat in Latin America, and Jagori in Delhi, as well as UN Habitat, the World Bank, and the World Health Organization (WHO). In 2010, UN Women launched a global program on safe cities for women and girls, modeled in part on the work of those organizations.

Prevention has become in many ways "mainstreamed" in international discourse. In a series of regional studies, UNODC has demonstrated that safe cities and communities are essential for the social and economic growth of a country (e.g., UNODC 2005). A number of other international organizations including the World Bank and WHO now recognize that safety and violence reduction are essential prerequisites for development, and making cities inclusive, safe, resilient, and sustainable is one of the new Sustainable Development Goals adopted by the United Nations General Assembly in October 2015.

Yet, despite the high ideals adopted internationally, the decision by a government to develop and implement crime prevention policies is always a political one and, thus, still vulnerable.

How Political Are National Crime Prevention Policies?

A linear history of the evolution of crime prevention can throw light on the knowledge accumulated and on changes in perspectives or approaches, but it does not help elucidate the political and social currents that helped create those changes. The work of the British criminologist and sociologist Paul Rock has thrown considerable light on the very complex ways in which government policies come into being. Far from originating entirely from government or party offices, they are often the product of a mix of social movements and changing values, nongovernment advocacy, new research, and, in many cases, the energies of significant individuals within government and outside (moral entrepreneurs) who help raise and push the issues. This is well demonstrated in Rock's seminal study "A View from the Shadows," on the development of Canadian Federal government policy to support victims of crime in the 1980s (Rock 1987). Rock shows the intricate range of interests, individuals, and groups involved in the development of that policy, many of whom saw themselves as the "prime mover" of the new victims' legislation, when in reality, they all helped enable the new policy.

In relation to federal policy on crime prevention in Canada, this gradually emerged after a House of Commons Committee Report on Crime Prevention (Horner Report 1993). In 1994, the new Liberal government established the initial National Strategy on Community Safety and Crime Prevention and appointed a National Council to develop it (Leonard et al. 2005). In 1997, the National Strategy on Crime Prevention was finally put in place, backed by four main funding streams encouraging a wide range of social and community prevention projects and partnerships, including the prevention of crime and violence affecting youth, women, and the elderly. The National Crime Prevention Centre (NCPC) was established at the same time within the Ministry of Justice to administer the program.

While NCPC and a national strategy on crime prevention continued to be funded under the successive Conservative governments that took office from 2006 to 2015, the focus of the strategy changed. Under that government, it became narrower and more targeted to high crime areas and individuals, and to "at risk" youth, especially youth gangs and aboriginal youth. It also became less "risky," requiring those receiving funding to implement established, replicated programs that have been found to be effective elsewhere, rather than also encouraging innovation. In part, this change of focus reflected the experience gained in the first 10 years of the National Strategy, as well as increasing interest—common to many governments—in evidence-based approaches that reflect "value for money" (see Chapter 19). However, the change in the focus of the strategy also reflected the Conservative government's agenda of being "tough on crime" and fiscally conservative. It is, nevertheless, a tribute to the strength of crime prevention experience and knowledge that it has continued to be accepted as a component of Canadian government policy.

In the United Kingdom, an analysis of the development of national crime prevention policy in the 1980s and 1990s provides a very detailed case study of the political nature of its development (Koch 1998). It shows the strong influence of the ideology of the ruling Conservative party and especially their conception of crime prevention, which included a focus on policing, and on situational and target hardening strategies (see Chapter 14), rather than on social or community approaches (see Chapter 8). The influence of a small group of key NGOs and key individuals was also notable, but governments are also influenced by what they think their supporters want, by specific events, and by strong public reactions, and may modify their policies as a result. In a case study of the privatization of policing in the United Kingdom, for example, Adam White examines the impact of government cost-cutting policies that led to stringent cuts to police budgets in 2010 (White 2015). Some police authorities outsourced many of their functions to private companies, in one case causing a strong reaction from the public, which led to modification of the privatization trend. White concludes that the development of such policies under a specific government is "not logical or inevitable, but contingent and unpredictable" (White 2015, p. 286).

The political influence of government views is also well illustrated in a comparative study conducted in 2007 of the crime prevention strategies that have emerged in European countries (Crawford 2009a). These clearly demonstrate how different governments opted for approaches that fitted their world view—a heavy emphasis on situational prevention and CCTV in England, rather than on programs to tackle the social exclusion generating violence; social prevention and mediation in France; and an emphasis on evaluation and evidence in Sweden. Within the United Kingdom, there were very evident differences in the emphasis given to crime prevention policy in Scotland, Northern Ireland, Wales, and England (Henry 2009). In Wales, for example, there has been an emphasis on the social task of developing community safety partnerships to deliver crime prevention, while in England, they were given the more specific and narrower title of crime reduction partnerships, emphasizing a greater criminal justice role in prevention. Scotland, with more devolved powers and its own justice system, has on the whole demonstrated a strong commitment to social welfare and social justice in its crime prevention policies (Henry 2009).

As Adam Crawford notes (2009b), prevention policy is also influenced by regional or local movements or circumstances and, in some cases, can be triggered by serious events such as youth riots or a series of domestic homicides. The success of one city's approach to prevention may be copied by, or inspire, other cities or even the national government. Outside Europe, this has certainly been the case in countries such as Colombia and Brazil. The crime prevention strategy developed by the Brazilian city of Diadema near Sao Paulo at the beginning of the 2000s in response to their high rate of homicide and violence proved to be very successful (Shaw and Travers 2007). The approach—a 10-point local strategy and the establishment of a city department to oversee and manage its implementation—became the blueprint for PRONASCI, the national program for public safety with citizenship, launched by the Brazilian government in 2007 (Shaw and Carli 2011). What is also relevant here is that the initial Diadema initiative was itself inspired by successful crime prevention initiatives in a number of U.S. cities, including New York and Boston (see Box 16.1).

The political pressures on policymakers in relation to crime and criminal justice policy are very strong. This relates especially to public perceptions of crime and how it should be dealt with, as Welsh and Farrington (2012) have highlighted. Crime prevention policies are sometimes portrayed (falsely) as "soft on crime," something that all politicians are reluctant to be perceived as. In fact, as the American criminologist Lawrence Sherman and his colleagues (1996) pointed out, in their seminal review of "what works" in preventing crime, "crime prevention programs are neither 'hard' nor 'soft' by definition; the central question is whether any program or institutional practice results in fewer criminal events than would otherwise occur" (see also Roberts and Hastings 2012). There are also myths, which are again false, about the punitive nature of public attitudes toward offenders, which may lead policymakers to favor more punitive policies. Yet, given a choice of alternatives, public surveys in a number of countries

BOX 16.1   CITY OF DIADEMA, BRAZIL: 10-POINT CRIME PREVENTION STRATEGY

- The creation of a Municipal Department of Social Policies and Public Security; mapping all criminal activity
- The integration of all police forces in the city (municipal, military, and civil regional)
- New law enforcing the closure of all establishments selling alcohol from 11 p.m. to 6 a.m.
- Launching the municipal council for the safety and the prevention of crime
- Increasing the municipal police force by 70% and establishing "The Neighbourhood Angels"
- Establishing "The Young Apprentice Project"
- Social and environmental policies including *favela* and school projects
- The installation of surveillance cameras
- Inspections and law enforcement operations
- Launching three major campaigns:
  - Disarmament of firearms campaign
  - Children's disarmament of toy guns campaign
  - Drugs and alcohol awareness campaign

De Filippi Junior 2007
Shaw and Travers (2007, pp. 92–98)

have consistently shown that the public prefers public funds to be spent, for example, on prevention or rehabilitation programs rather than on tougher prisons (Roberts and Hough 2005).

The *sustainability* of crime prevention policies is similarly affected by a number of factors. As Crawford (2009b) notes, stated government policies are not always followed through with the necessary administrative supports or funding, so that what a government says it will do is not always found to have taken place or been well monitored.

National governments are influenced not only by changing attitudes and understanding of the benefits of prevention policies but also by economic factors that may force some to curtail programs when the economy weakens. As noted above, in the United Kingdom, the Conservative government made extensive budget cuts in 2010, including cutting 20% of the police budget, which has affected their ability to sustain community policing and other prevention initiatives since that time (White 2015).

In addition, the life of a government, whether it is national, federal, regional, or local, is often quite short, commonly four years. This means that politicians want to see concrete and rapid results from the policies they introduce and for the public money invested—they have short time horizons. Unfortunately, many crime prevention programs, especially long-term developmental prevention programs, and those that involve multiple interventions in a community, can take a long time to clearly demonstrate their social and economic benefits, and their effectiveness in reducing crime and violence. Governments need to be convinced of the value of investing in such interventions. Changes of government can also affect the sustainability of a policy. A new government that replaces one that had established good prevention policies may have a very different agenda and world view. They may very specifically wish to dissociate themselves from prior policies, cut their funding, or end programs initiated by their rivals and predecessors to please their political "base" or because of competition for scarce financial resources.

How Political Is the Role of Local Government in Crime Prevention?

A very strong component of the 1995 and 2002 UN Guidelines on crime prevention is the crucial role of mayors at the local government level. While national governments have an important leadership role in setting out national strategies and funding mechanisms to encourage and foster local action, it is at the local level that crime primarily affects individuals and communities, and where action on the ground is needed. A recent study of the role of local government in crime prevention in Australia provides a valuable picture of the variety of ways in which city governments tackle prevention in relation to the specific problems experienced in their communities and some of the challenges they face (Homel and Fuller 2015).

While crime prevention policies developed by national governments are clearly influenced by how those governments understand crime and violence issues, and position themselves in terms of social and economic policies, this is even more evident at the local level. Some city mayors may want to promote the economy and the business community in their city; others may be more concerned about social and economic inequalities. Thus, some cities have undertaken urban redevelopments that they hope will encourage businesses and improve safety by moving slum populations, itinerants, or street vendors out of city centers, to be replaced by new apartments, offices, and shopping complexes. In so doing, they increase inequalities and exclusion and increase the risks of exploitation and violence for those displaced. More thoughtful and very successful approaches that incorporate the needs of squatters or street traders as well as others have been used, for example,

BOX 16.2   URBAN REGENERATION AS A CRIME PREVENTION STRATEGY: CASE STUDY OF WARWICK JUNCTION, DURBAN, SOUTH AFRICA

CONTEXT

Warwick Junction, located in eThekwini municipality (formerly Durban) in South Africa, is a transit hub on the periphery of the central business district, which includes the main city bus and train stations and taxi ranks. An estimated 300,000 citizens, visitors, and commuters pass through the area each day. During the apartheid era, Black and Indian buses, prohibited from entering the city center, had to stop on the Junction. It became the main site for informal trading in the municipality, including some 500 traders selling herbal cures and providing survival support to their urban and rural communities. By 1996, the area was in considerable urban decay and there were serious problems of crime and order maintenance. The expanding taxi trade and informal traders were using the streets and pavements to trade, and living in unsanitary conditions, often sleeping on the streets. The area gave rise to considerable environmental, safety, health, and planning concerns.

GOALS

- Improve the safety and security and overall quality of life of the Warwick Junction area
- Promote citizen and community empowerment through organized participation in decision making with the city administration
- Upgrade cleanliness and the quality of the physical environment
- Increase trading, employment, and investment opportunities

DESCRIPTION

The Warwick Junction Urban Renewal Project began in 1997. It is a multiagency holistic redevelopment initiative that turned a problematic area into a vibrant business center and a popular tourist attraction. Rather than clear the informal traders out of the area, the city administration recognized the importance of the informal economy and decided to work with them, and other key stakeholders, by negotiating to improve their conditions in a participatory way. It chose to locate the project office at the Junction rather than at the City Hall.

A derelict warehouse was converted into a community hall for this purpose and to enable project teams, community members, and city representatives to meet and discuss issues, and to serve as a base for developing the consultation process with stakeholders. An umbrella traders' street committee was established to enable them to discuss their needs and space requirements. The city then identified a section of elevated city highway that had never been utilized. By constructing a bridge and pedestrian access, they were able to create a purpose-built and functional Herb Traders Market. The more limited space necessitated negotiations among the informal traders themselves, which were carefully conducted by the traders over a process of months. Each trader now had a formal rental arrangement and individual kiosk. Multipurpose centers were also created for street traders to carry out their business activities. The overall costs for the development of the market, infrastructure, and services were approximately US$500,000.

Subsequent developments included the construction of other market areas, with night lock-ups for goods, and regular cleaning by the city. The project has also revamped streets and improved lighting and sanitation in the area. To deal with the traffic congestion caused by the huge growth in private taxis, the city has created taxi ranks and holding areas. The Inner Thekwini Regeneration and Urban Management Programme (iTRUMP) has since absorbed the Warwick Junction project as one district within its Programme. This expanded Programme uses many of the prior lessons learned, particularly that of area-based management, which has also been institutionalized as a local government function within the eThekwini Municipality. From this work, five urban regeneration strategies can be identified as having made a positive contribution to crime prevention.

OUTCOMES

Since the implementation of the Warwick Junction Renewal Project, there has been a marked improvement in trading, commuter safety, and living conditions. Crime rates have declined from 50 violent deaths in the Warwick Junction area in 1997 to a recorded 6 in 2002, in part attributed to the work of the traders who formed an organization, Traders Against Crime, using conflict resolution to resolve disputes. The annual turnover of the Herb Traders Market has increased enormously. Apart from the area becoming a major tourist attraction, an employment chain of an estimated 14,000 jobs in Durban has been created.

Nevertheless, residents in the area are still concerned about the level of safety and security. The city has now launched iTRUMP to apply similar processes to other inner-city areas.

PARTNERS

City Council, Traders Association

Dobson, R.
Urban regeneration as a crime prevention strategy:
The experience of Warwick Junction, eThekwini (Durban),
South Africa, in Shaw and Travers (2007)

in Warwick Junction in Durban, South Africa (see Box 16.2), and the city of Solo in Indonesia (Burnell 2013; Dobson and Skinner 2009). Similarly, the use of a social urbanism approach in Medellin, Colombia, has contributed to major reductions in crime and violence, by recognizing the needs of poor and poorly served communities, reducing inequalities, and improving the lives of those communities (Calderon 2012; Perez 2010) (see Box 16.3).

At the international level, UN Habitat has had a Safer Cities Programme since 1996. From the start, the program provided support to cities to improve their safety, grounded in the 1995 and 2002 UN Guidelines on prevention. They helped cities undertake safety audits; develop their prevention strategies, using a range of social, educational, and situational crime prevention approaches; and focus on the most vulnerable places and people, especially young people and women and girls. Initially developed at the request of African mayors, the program has now worked with some 70 cities around the world.

Since 1996, the Safer Cities Programme has benefited from the experience gained and the trials and challenges of developing strategic prevention at the city level, and its concept of safer cities has evolved. It has evolved into a broader notion of a safe city as one concerned not only with crime and violence but also with human or urban security—encompassing social integration, poverty, housing tenure, and environmental safety. The program also demonstrates the importance of partnerships at the city level, and the necessity of using a multidimensional approach with city government working in a participatory way with civil society, a wide range of institutions, the business and private sector, and NGOs. Developing safer cities entails not only urban planning but also good governance and management. In 2012, UN Habitat launched the Global Network on Safe Cities (GNSC) to provide a collaborative basis for cities to exchange knowledge and experience and good practices (see Chapter 17).

What has become clear since the mid- to late 1990s, therefore, is that while the leadership of mayors and recognition of their responsibilities are essential for the development of urban crime prevention, a lot of other sectors, institutions, and people are also essential to that development. The experiences of other cities can be very helpful in demonstrating good, and less successful, strategies. The GNSC includes a steering committee of mayors

BOX 16.3   VIOLENCE PREVENTION AND URBAN GOVERNANCE IN MEDELLÍN, COLOMBIA

Parts of Latin America have seen considerable delegation of powers to municipalities, as a result of democratic reform and policies of decentralization,* which has facilitated some of the most sustained examples of successful reductions in violence, through innovation in urban governance, often with key mayoral figures at their helm standing outside mainstream national politics. Cities such as Bogotá and Medellín in Colombia have seen spectacular reductions in homicide rates through various municipal programs over the long term involving a mixture of police reform, conflict resolution, urban regeneration, and social development/prevention.

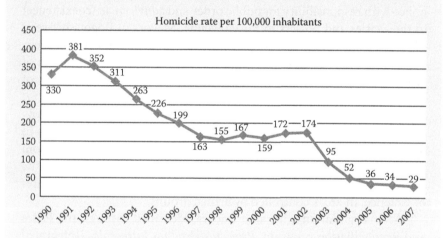

Homicide rate per 100,000 inhabitants

Medellín, for example, experienced the highest rate of homicide in the world at 381 per 100,000 in 1991, which though halving over the next 10 years, remained one of the highest rates of homicide globally. A central problem for the city was the control exerted over many areas of the city by armed groups of drug traffickers, paramilitary groups, guerrilla groups, and organized territorial protection. As one mayor put it, "during those years in Medellín there was an absence of the state... and various criminal groups were able to exert territorial control and

* Satterthwaite, D. (2009) What role for mayors in good city governance? *Environment and Urbanization* 21: 3–17.

violence in the majority of areas."* However, between 2002 and 2007, rates in the city fell from 174 to 29 per 100,000, which is a startling achievement (see the graph).

Although the various projects and initiatives undertaken in these cities make it impossible to ascribe one reason for these falls, these achievements are characterized by the key role of their mayors in initiating local analysis of violence problems, multisector partnerships, and investing in the institutionalization of urban security policies sustainable over the longer term, largely removing them from electoral politics, which, though supporting criminal justice agencies, emphasized the prevention of violence rather than law enforcement.

Mayors in Colombia have been elected since 1988, and in 1991, decentralization reforms led to new powers for mayors as chiefs of police with responsibility for public order and *convivencia* (coexistence) in their cities and powers to raise revenue. Mayors in Bogotá between 1994 and 2000 used these powers to institutionalize their role in security provision through local regulation to control the consumption of alcohol and carrying of guns in public spaces, through the creation of a multiagency Security Council (based on French models of a *contrat de sécurité*), and a long-term strategy covering all aspects of the governance of security from prevention to the judicial system.[†] Mayors in Medellin were slower to use their powers to address security but from 2002 began to take steps to institutionalize responsibility, echoing the Bogota model, and focused their attention on areas with highest rates of violence, in areas controlled by armed groups.

After negotiation with area leaders, identified through the Peace and Reconciliation program, *Projectos Urbanos Intregrales* (Integrated Urban Projects), the city undertook large-scale investment to provide public services to informal settlements on the mountainsides surrounding the city, particularly transport, education, housing, and green space.[‡] These were presented as an investment in the city as a whole,

---

* Quoted in Acerco Velásquez, H. and Cardona, S. (2009) Medellín, Bogotá: Del autoritarismo y anarquía a la garantía civilista de los derechos ciudadanos. Mejoría de la seguridad ciudadana: 5 (Available at: http://www.convivenciayseguridad ciudadana.com/contenido/images/stories/medell%EDn%2C%20bogota%2C%20 seguridad.pdf).

† Acerco Velásquez, H. and Cardona, S. (2009) *Medellín, Bogotá: Del autoritarismo y anarquía a la garantía civilista de los derechos ciudadanos. Mejoría de la seguridad ciudadana.*

‡ UN Habitat and Universidad Alberto Hurtado (2009) *Guía para la Prevención Local: Hacia Políticas de Cohesión Social y Seguridad Ciudadana.* Nairobi: UN Habitat.

stressing solidarity and the need to reduce inequality and promote opportunity.* Key to this was the ability of the municipality to work with civil society organizations, whose presence in and knowledge of their neighborhoods, as well as their legitimacy within them, having sustained their independence from armed groups in preceding years, gave the local authority a means to establish contact with communities.

ICPC 2010, pp. 108–109

* Dávila, J. (2009) Being a mayor: The view from four Colombian cities. *Environment and Urbanization* 21: 37–56.

from across the world and is developing a range of good practices, tools, and technical supports for cities. These include a compilation of 100 good prevention practices in cities around the world (ICPC 2015). In addition, as noted earlier in this chapter, a new set of UN Guidelines on Safer Cities is expected to be adopted in 2016 to accompany the existing 1995 and 2002 guidelines on crime prevention. They are likely to provide more detailed guidance on implementation and evaluation, building on recent knowledge, including mainstreaming gender in prevention, the use of peacebuilding, good data gathering, and "smart" technologies.

At a symposium on The Flexible City in 2013, Michele Acuto cautioned that while mayors are seen as powerful, their powers can be quite limited, which affects their ability to enact change (Acuto 2013). They need solid funding and the support of a network of institutions and actors, as well as some devolved powers. He refers to what he terms "the geography of responsibilities" for change and policy development in cities, which is itself "always changing."

He also noted that "'city-to-city' learning is entirely political." Those interested in the benefits of prevention rather than repression will be influenced by the experiences of other cities and chose to examine their approaches. As discussed above in this chapter, this has been quite evident in Latin American countries, and among cities in the European Union, as the ongoing work of the European Forum for Urban Security (EFUS) and the European Institute for Crime Prevention and Control (HEUNI) illustrates.

Balancing the Role of Governments and the Private Sector in Crime Prevention—Social Financing

Governments have long understood that crime prevention strategies need the support of civil society and the business and private sector, and in many countries, there have been specific attempts to encourage cooperation, for example, by offering funding for partnership projects. Civil society and private sector involvement forms a core part of the UN guidelines on prevention. Indeed, the role of the private sector in crime prevention was one of the topics discussed at the 13th UN Congress on Crime Prevention and Criminal Justice. The 13th Congress, an event held every five years, and bringing together all member states of the UN, took place in Doha, Qatar, in April 2015 (UNODC 2015). Workshop 4, one of the official workshops at the Congress, which showcase developments in good practices, was on the role of the public in crime prevention.

Within the business sector, what is often referred to as "corporate social responsibility"—encouraging employees to undertake community activities, or contribute to programs to reduce poverty or inequalities—has also existed for many years. Private-sector involvement in local crime prevention programs has included sponsoring sports programs for young people living in deprived areas, or families and children. Such involvement is seen as a good thing in its own right by many companies, and also helps provide them with good advertising (ICPC 2011). Such projects are usually quite localized, however, and do not aim to replace government intervention. They are part of the multiple partnership approach to crime prevention that enriches local and community involvement in the social and economic problems which help to foster crime and violence. It becomes a shared responsibility. In recent years, in this area of prevention as well, there has been an evolution in approaches. More recent examples of public–private partnerships (PPPs) include private companies funding prevention research programs, for example, or NGOs working in the field, or supporting city-wide programs for job training, (see Box 16.4). In other words, they work with prevention experts and communities in a more constructive and collaborative way, rather than just to "feel good" or advertise their name (ICPC 2011).

In recent years, the political nature of government crime prevention policy has been underlined by increasing economic pressures (see Chapters 17 and 18 as well). Governments at all levels have been searching for ways to reduce the costs of programs and service provision. This has resulted in cuts to programs or the outsourcing of jobs—previously undertaken by state or city employees—to the private sector. In terms of funding social programs, one development has been the increase in interest in the topic of "social financing." This has occurred in the United Kingdom, Belgium, Australia, the United States, and Canada, among other countries.

Social financing, including social impact bonds and "payment by results" approaches, have been seen by a number of governments as a way of reducing their involvement in service provision and "difficult social problems" by getting the private sector to invest money in social programs (see Chapter 19). If a program is successful, the investors will receive a return—a

BOX 16.4   EXAMPLES OF INNOVATIVE PRIVATE-PUBLIC CRIME PREVENTION PARTNERSHIPS (PPPS)

- **Cybercap**—Montreal, Canada. Training in multimedia for young people at risk/ex-offenders and their families. PPPs with Microsoft, Ubisoft, Radio Canada, TSQ Television, Quebec banks, who fund and provide computers, materials, internships, etc.
- **SulAmerica Peace Parks**—Brazil. The insurance company SulAmerica works with local youth at risk and their communities, and in high-risk areas to recover public spaces. Encourages employees to become corporate volunteers.
- **Bogota Como Vamos?**—Colombia. Partnership with publishing house El Tempio, Corona Foundation, and Bogota Chamber of Commerce to organize a permanent discussion forum to promote improved and effective local public safety policies, and public accountability.
- **Encuestas de Victimization**—Peru. Major mining and cement companies and Andean Development Corporation–funded development of national and urban victimization surveys—in Lima and its 35 municipalities, and 23 large cities + Cuidad Nuestra, Open Society Institute, and the Catholic University.
- **Prevention & Assistance to Survivors of Trafficking** (PAST)—India. PPPs between international organization on migration and businesses, chambers of commerce, Indian Industry Conference, governments, and civil society. Provided rehabilitation, training, employment opportunities, micro-credit, and support for survivors, as well as peer education training and awareness raising.

ICPC 2011

profit—on their investment. This usually involves a consortium of investors who work with NGOs with specialized expertise in an area. A number of national governments have begun to experiment with this model, especially after the UK government launched a large social financing pilot project in 2010. This project aimed to rehabilitate short-term prisoners on their release back into the community (Disley and Rubin 2014; Fox and Albertson 2011). The Peterborough Experiment, as it is named after one of the prisons involved, has been running for a period of four years, although with quite mixed results. The initial results after the first year seemed to promise a greatly reduced reconviction rate among the short-term prisoners, and thus a good investment, but subsequent results have not been so impressive. This means that investors will be unlikely to make a return on their investment in the long term.

While this approach to project financing is still being experimented with, including in relation to crime prevention, it is not necessarily the panacea that some governments hope for (see, e.g., Fox and Albertson op. cit.). How far can crime prevention projects expect to have large enough impacts to allow a return on investment? The cost savings from developmental crime prevention projects, for example, are real, but they take a long time to become apparent. Some other crime prevention projects will be easier to evaluate than others, and may offer results in a shorter period. Another concern is the extent to which projects can retain their innovative appeal, and the extent to which intervenors remain enthusiastic and fully engaged and able to maintain good results, even when they become scaled up or have "normal" ways of working. There are also concerns about the oversight and accountability of service provision when it is, in a sense, "privatized."

The Future of Prevention—Recognition on Multiple Fronts

Commenting on crime prevention 10 years ago, Peter Homel described it memorably "as 'a swan swimming in the surf', going up and down time and again, yet always re-emerging" (quoted in Shaw 2009, p. 234). It has to be continually interrogated and promoted. In a sense, while government investment in crime prevention remains a political choice, in many parts of the world, it has become an accepted approach on a wide range of political fronts, almost removing it from the political agenda. The range of similar and sometimes overlapping approaches have also emerged over the past 20 years, including the public health approach to violence reduction, urban regeneration, social urbanism, human security, and peacebuilding, and they all testify to the importance of prevention over reaction to social ills (Shaw 2009).

The growth of the Global Network of Safer Cities now supported by UN Habitat, the proposed new UN Guidelines for urban crime prevention to complement the existing guidelines, the World Bank Institute's e-learning Institute on crime prevention, the expanding range of cities and tools developed by ICPC, and EFUS among other international organizations, all illustrate the strength of crime prevention as an approach that provides viable alternatives to costly policies based on repression and reaction to crime and insecurity (see also ICPC 2015). The newly adopted UN Sustainable Development Goals also establish safe, inclusive, and accessible cities, and improving the safety of women and girls, as goals for all countries to work towards.

The challenges continue, nevertheless. One consistent concern is the failure of many crime prevention policies to invest in good monitoring and evaluation of those policies. Another is their failure to mainstream gender, to take account of the different experiences of boys and girls and women and men living in cities. Cities and countries need to ensure that they develop policies that take account of gender differences and collect disaggregated data, for example.

How prevention will fare in the future as cities and countries try to respond to the increasing movement of people to urban settings, whether fueled by war and conflict, environmental disasters, or poverty, also remains to be seen. In 2015, migration reached unprecedented and crisis levels in some parts of the world, bringing together peoples from many different cultural, ethnic, and religious backgrounds. In a review of global migration trends and their impacts on governments and cities, a 2014 international report shows how some cities and countries have responded to migrant communities and highlights good prevention practices that aid the integration of newcomers, reduce racism, and improve the overall social and economic health of all residents in those cities and communities (ICPC 2014). In fact, there is strong evidence, as the report underlines that migrants help reduce crime and violence in communities and contribute significantly to the economies and social life of their new countries. The roots of social and economic integration lie in the kinds of inclusive programs that crime prevention embraces, and about which there is increasing evidence of their value and effectiveness.

Thus, the demonstrable gains in the reduction of crime and violence, and improvements in social and economic prospects in cities in such countries as Indonesia, South Africa, Cote d'Ivoire, Colombia, and Brazil, among others, have convinced many that investing in crime prevention and community safety is both sound fiscal policy and good practice with many social and economic benefits beyond reductions in crime.

Glossary of Key Terms

Community safety: Community safety is a broader concept than "crime prevention." It refers to the sense of well-being and the quality of life of a community or neighborhood. It also suggests the collective nature of creating a safe community.

Human security: In relation to the city, the concept of human security includes not just protection from crime and violence and upholding the rule of law and human rights, but also economic and social justice and protection from environmental disasters.

Public–private partnerships (PPPs): In the crime prevention context, these are partnerships between the private sector, such as corporations or local businesses, and governments, community organizations, or the police, etc., providing co-funding to support specific projects or programs.

Social financing: A form of financing of public social programs by private investors, usually with the expectation that that investment will bring a profit or some kind of return to the investors.

Social impact bonds: One type of social financing where, for example, private investors contract with governments, investing in social problem interventions that expect to have a high impact on those problems. The private or nongovernment sector provides the services, and the investors receive a return on the bonds invested *if* results are better than expected.

Social urbanism: An approach to upgrading urban infrastructure in an integrated way that is based on participatory principles and approaches. Focusing on areas with a very poor quality of life, local communities are constantly consulted on their needs and concerns, to help improve services and conditions.

Discussion Questions

1. Why is crime prevention policy seen as a political issue?
2. What kinds of pressures do national governments face if they want to develop crime prevention policies?
3. How can national policies help local governments develop crime prevention policies?
4. What evidence is there that crime prevention policies are likely to continue to grow and become more accepted?
5. What are some of the challenges facing countries or cities in sustaining crime prevention policies?

Suggested Reading

Crawford, A. (ed.). (2009). *Crime Prevention Policies in Comparative Perspective.* Cullompton, Devon, UK: Willan Publishing.

ICPC. (2014). *Fourth International Report on Crime Prevention and Community Safety: Trends and Perspectives.* Montreal: International Centre for the Prevention of Crime.

Tilley, N. (ed.). (2005). *Handbook of Crime Prevention and Community Safety.* Cullompton, Devon: Willan Publishing.

UN HABITAT. (2007). Global Report on Human Settlements: Enhancing Urban Safety and Security. Nairobi, Kenya: UN HABITAT.

UNODC. (2010). *Handbook on the Crime Prevention Guidelines: Making Them Work.* Vienna: UNODC.

Welsh, B.C., and Farrington, D.P. (eds.). (2012). *The Oxford Handbook of Crime Prevention*. Oxford: University of Oxford Press.

Whitzman, C., Legacy, C., Andrew, C., Klodawsky, F., Shaw, M., and Viswanath, K. (eds.). (2013). *Building Inclusive Cities. Women's Safety and the Right to the City*. Abingdon, Oxford and New York: Earthscan, Routledge.

Recommended Web Links

EFUS: www.efus.eu/

ICPC: www.cipc-icpc.org

HEUNI (European Institute for Crime Prevention and Control): www .heuni.fi

NCPC: www.publicsafety.gc.ca

UN Habitat: Safer cities programme www.unhabitat.org/urban-initiatives /initiatives-programmes/safer-cities/

UNODC: www.unodc.org

WICI: www.femmesetvilles.org

World Bank Institute: www.einstitute.worldbank.org

References

Acuto, M. (2013). Presentation at *The Flexible City Symposium*, City-to-City Learning Session, Oxford University, October 2013. Online YouTube video. Retrieved from www.salford.ac.uk/builtenvironment.

Burnell, T. (2013). Presentation at *The Flexible City Symposium*, City-to-City Learning Session, Oxford University, October 2013. Online YouTube video. Retrieved from www.salford.ac.uk/builtenvironment.

Calderon, C. (2012). Social urbanism–Integrated and participatory urban upgrading in Medellin, Colombia. In Lawrence, Yildiz & Kellett (eds.). *Requalifying the Built Environment: Challenges and Responses*. Göttingen, Germany: Hogrefe Publishing.

Crawford, A. (ed.). (2009a). *Crime Prevention Policies in Comparative Perspective*. Cullompton, Devon, UK: Willan Publishing.

Crawford, A. (2009b). The preventive turn in Europe. In Crawford, A. (ed.). *Crime Prevention Policies in Comparative Perspective*. Cullompton, Devon, UK: Willan Publishing.

De Filippi Junior, J. (2007). The experience of the City of Diadema. In Shaw, M. and Travers, K. (eds.). *Strategies and Best Practices in Crime Prevention, in Particular in Relation to Urban Crime and Youth at Risk*. Montreal: International Centre for the Prevention of Crime.

Disley, E., and Rubin, J. (2014). *Phase 2 Report from the Payment by Results Social Impact Bond Pilot at HMP Peterborough*. London: RAND Europe, Ministry of Justice Analytical Series.

Dobson, R., and Skinner, C. (2009). *Working in Warwick. Including Streets Traders in Urban Plans*. Durban, South Africa: School of Development Studies, University of Kwazulu-Natal.

Fox, C., and Albertson, K. (2011). Payment by results and social impact bonds in the criminal justice sector: New challenges for the concept of evidence-based policy? *Criminology and Criminal Justice* 11(5): 395–413.

Henry, A. (2009). The development of community safety in Scotland: A different path? In Crawford, A. (ed.), *Crime Prevention Policies in Comparative Perspective*. Cullompton, Devon, UK: Willan Publishing.

Homel, P., and Fuller, G. (2015). Understanding the local government role in crime prevention. *Trends & Issues in Crime and Criminal Justice*. No. 505. Canberra, Australia: Australian Institute of Criminology.

Horner Report. (1993). Crime prevention in Canada: Toward a national strategy. *Twelfth Report of the Standing Committee on Justice and the Solicitor General*. Chairman Dr. Bob Horner M.P. February 1993. Ottawa: House of Commons.

ICPC. (2010). *International Report on Crime Prevention and Community Safety: Trends and Perspectives*. Montreal: International Centre for the Prevention of Crime.

ICPC. (2011). *Public Private Partnerships and Community Safety. Guide to Action*. Montreal, Washington, Bogota, Sao Paulo: ICPC, World Bank, Bogota Chamber of Commerce, Instituto Sou da Paz.

ICPC. (2014). *Fourth International Report on Crime Prevention and Community Safety: Trends and Perspectives*. Montreal: International Centre for the Prevention of Crime.

ICPC. (2015). *100 Promising Practices on Safer Cities*. Montreal: International Centre for the Prevention of Crime, in collaboration with The Global Network on Safer Cities (UN-Habitat) and EFUS.

Koch, B.C. (1998). *Politics of Crime Prevention*. Brookfield, VT: Ashgate.

Leonard, L. et al. (2005). Building safer communities. Lessons learned from Canada's National Strategy. *Canadian Journal of Criminology & Criminal Justice* 47(2): 233–250.

Perez, B. (2010). Social urbanism as a crime prevention strategy: The case of Medellin. In Shaw, M. and Carli, V. (eds.). *Practical Approaches to Urban Crime Prevention*. Montreal & Vienna: International Centre for the Prevention of Crime and UNODC.

Roberts, J.V., and Hastings, R. (2012). Public opinion and crime prevention: A review of international trends. In Welsh, B.C. & Farrington, D.P. (eds.). *Oxford Handbook of Crime Prevention*. Oxford, UK: University of Oxford Press.

Roberts, J.V., and Hough, M.J. (2005). *Understanding Public Attitudes to Criminal Justice*. Maidenhead, UK: Open University Press McGraw-Hill.

Rock, P. (1987). *A View from the Shadows. The Ministry of the Solicitor General and the Victims of Crime Initiative*. Oxford Socio-Legal Studies. Oxford, UK: Oxford University Press.

Shaw, M. (2009). International models of crime prevention. In Crawford, A. (ed.). *Crime Prevention Policies in Comparative Perspective*. Cullompton, Devon, UK: Willan Publishing.

Shaw, M., and Carli, V. (eds.). (2011). *Practical Approaches to Urban Crime Prevention*. Montreal & Vienna: International Centre for the Prevention of Crime and UNODC.

Shaw, M., and Travers, K. (eds.). (2007). *Strategies and Best Practices in Crime Prevention, in Particular in Relation to Urban Crime and Youth at Risk*. Montreal: International Centre for the Prevention of Crime.

Sherman, L., Gottfredson, D., Mackenzie, D., Eck, J., Reuter, P., and Bushway, J. (1996). *Preventing Crime: What Works, What Doesn't and What's Promising*. Washington, DC: U.S. Department of Justice, Office of Justice Programs.

UNODC. (2005). *Crime and Development in Africa*. Vienna, Austria: UNODC.

UNODC. (2010). *Handbook on the Crime Prevention Guidelines: Making Them Work*. Vienna: UNODC. Retrieved from http://www.unodc.org/documents/justice -and-prison-reform/crimeprevention/10-52410_Guidelines_eBook.pdf.

UNODC. (2015). See the *Report of Committee II—Workshop 4: Public contribution to crime prevention and raising awareness of criminal justice: Experiences and lessons learned*. A/CONF.222/L.4/Add.1 and the Workshop 4 *Background Paper* A/CONF.222/13 for the 13th UN Congress on Crime Prevention & Criminal Justice, April 12–19th Doha, Qatar. Retrieved from www.unodc/congress/en /documentation.html.

Welsh, B.C., and Farrington, D.P. (2012). The science and politics of crime prevention: Towards new crime policy. In Welsh, B.C. and Farrington, D.P. (eds.). *The Oxford Handbook of Crime Prevention*. Oxford, UK: University of Oxford Press.

White, A. (2015). The politics of police 'privatization': A multiple streams approach. *Criminology & Criminal Justice* 15(3): 283–299.

Smarter Crime Control
Putting Prevention Knowledge into Practice

17

IRVIN WALLER
VERONICA MARTINEZ SOLARES

Contents

Learning Outcomes
After reading this chapter, you should be able to

- Understand the prevalence and impact of street and intimate part-ner violence on both males and females as well as the costs to victims and society
- Get to know the easily accessible sources of the accumulated knowl-edge on effective and cost-effective prevention
- Recognize key governance processes and responsibility center to target investment into the areas and on risk factors that will prevent crime and violence across jurisdictions, including diagnosing risk factors and loca-tions, planning a comprehensive multisectoral strategy, developing the human capacity to implement the strategies, and evaluating outcomes
- Distinguish what basic elements are essential to putting prevention knowledge into practice, including funding, measurement of out-comes, quick wins, capacity development, and research
- Identify ways to encourage political will to implement, such as impor-tant groups and organizations that are advocating and promoting effective crime prevention, including communities of practice

Introduction

Smarter crime control is not about more or less policing or jails but about what is cost-effective in stopping victimization and husbanding taxes.

I. Waller
2014, p. 237

In 1985, the United Nations General Assembly (UNGA) adopted a land-mark resolution 40/34 on Basic Principles of Justice for Victims of Crime and Abuse of Power (UNGA 1985) where the governments of the world agreed for the first time to focus on the prevention of victimization and rights for victims of crime. This resolution recognized that crime is not just a violation against the state but is a violation of victims who suffer loss, injury, and trauma from the victimization. As a result, it called for a rebalancing of national policies from only punishing offenders to embracing significant efforts to prevent crime and support victims.

Today, we are able to put numbers to that victimization. We know, for example, that there are billions of men, women, and children who are victims of crime each year. We are able to demonstrate the impact of these crimes on the quality of life of the victims and how this leads to chronic disease. We even have an estimate that this diverts more than 5% of the world's GDP (Waller 2014).

At the same time, we have accumulated significant proven and evidence-based knowledge about what is effective and cost-effective in stopping inter-personal violence and the ways to implement it—**Smarter Crime Control** (Waller 2014). This knowledge is endorsed by some of the most prestigious organizations in the world, including the U.S. Department of Justice (DOJ) (2015), the World Health Organization (WHO) (2009a,b), and the World Bank (2012). The smart knowledge of how to implement this knowledge through "good governance" strategies is promoted by UN Habitat (Habitat, Safer Cities 2015a,b), the United Nations Office on Drugs and Crime (UNODC 2006a,b), and the WHO (2014).

In September 2015, world leaders committed to achieve 17 Sustainable Development Goals (SDGs) by 2030 in "Transforming Our World: The 2030 Agenda for Sustainable Development" (UNGA 2015) (also see Chapter 2). Among the more than 100 targets to achieve the SDGs, there are commitments to significantly reduce violence and homicides, halve traffic deaths, eliminate violence against women and children, make cities safer, and ensure equal access to justice for all.

The 17th goal identified what was essential for the implementation of the SDGs and their targets, including funding, development of human capacity, and measurement of outcomes. Importantly, the SDGs apply to both advanced and developing nations. The International Organization for Victim Assistance (2015) has proposed that 1/10 of 1% of the GDP be invested in harnessing this knowledge through those good governance strategies to achieve the violence reduction targets.

However, the challenge remains as to how to get national and local levels of government to make the shift to *smarter crime control*. Unfortunately, they continue to waste lives and taxes in reacting to crime through policing, courts, and incarceration that do little to prevent violence in the first place, or to respect the human rights of victims or, in many cases, offenders.

This chapter will address key issues relating to the implementation of *smarter crime control* that will reduce violence, save lives, and avoid wasted taxes. It will do this in five sections that will cover the following:

1. The prevalence and impact of street and intimate partner violence on both males and females as well as the costs of violence to victims and society
2. The easily accessible sources of the accumulated knowledge on effective and cost-effective prevention as well as the basis for their conclusions and what has been shown to be effective
3. The key governance processes and responsibility center to target investment into the areas and on risk factors that will prevent crime and violence across jurisdictions and cities, including diagnosing risk factors and locations, planning a comprehensive multisectoral strategy, developing the human capacity to implement the strategies, and evaluating outcomes
4. The basic elements that are essential to putting prevention knowledge into practice, including funding, measurement of outcomes, quick wins, capacity development, and research
5. Ways to encourage the political will to implement *smarter crime control*, such as the important groups and organizations that are advocating and promoting effective crime prevention, including cities in communities of practice

The Challenge of Interpersonal Crime and Violence

Interpersonal Violence and Crime Is Too Frequent, Damaging, and Costly

Sadly, criminal violence remains a deeply disturbing challenge in 2015. While homicide rates in many advanced nations have been steadily declining over the last 50 years, there are still epidemic rates of street violence in many countries in Latin America and some countries in Africa and elsewhere. Close to 500,000 persons will be killed each year in homicides—a rate of more than 1400 a day (UNODC 2006a,b).

The WHO defines rates of death above 10 per 100,000 as epidemic. There are more than 50 cities in the world that have these epidemic rates for homicide, including four cities in the most affluent country in the world—the United States. These are Baltimore, Detroit, New Orleans, and St Louis (Business Insider 2014). Further, in the United States, the national rate for homicides for black Americans is also epidemic at close to 20 per 100,000 and 12 times the rates of other advanced nations (FiveThirtyEight 2015).

Also disturbing are the rates of violence against women and girls across both advanced and developing nations. We do not know if these are increasing or decreasing, because we are not yet measuring rates consistently over time. Recently, the United States has innovated a state-of-the-art survey on Intimate Partner and Sexual Violence (CDCP 2010), which shows the following:

- Nearly 1 in 5 women (18.3%) and 1 in 71 men (1.4%) in the United States have been raped at some time in their lives.
- Approximately 1 in 4 women (24.3%) and 1 in 7 men (13.8%) have experienced severe physical violence by an intimate partner at some point in their lifetime.
- Victims of intimate partner and sexual violence in their lifetime were more likely than nonvictims to report frequent headaches, chronic pain, difficulty with sleeping, activity limitations, poor physical health, and poor mental health.
- Female victims of these forms of violence were also more likely than nonvictims to report having asthma, irritable bowel syndrome, and diabetes.

This survey is an important best practice for measuring risk and thus being able to measure whether we are achieving any change in **outcomes**. WHO and Fulu (2015) have used another best practice way of measuring such violence, including some of the reasons for the high levels of violence against women and girls (also see WHO 2015; Small Arms Survey 2012).

Worldwide, the WHO (2014) reports staggering rates of intimate partner and sexual violence, including the following:

- "A quarter of all adults report having been physically abused as children.
- One in five women reports having been sexually abused as a child.
- One in three women has been a victim of physical or sexual violence by an intimate partner at some point in her lifetime.
- One in 17 older adults reported abuse in the past month."

The WHO (2014) assesses the impact in the following terms:

Such violence contributes to lifelong ill health—particularly for women and children—and early death. Many leading causes of death such as heart disease, stroke, cancer and HIV/AIDS are the result of victims of violence adopting behaviours such as smoking, alcohol and drug misuse, and unsafe sex in an effort to cope with the psychological impact of violence. Violence also places a heavy strain on health and criminal justice systems, social and welfare services and the economic fabric of communities.

This strain on the individual and community is reiterated by Habitat, Safer Cities (2015a,b). Habitat points to the fact that "[h]igh crime levels affect all city dwellers, in particular the urban poor, and some groups are more vulnerable to specific forms of violence and insecurity (women, children, youth and the elderly). Crime destroys social cohesion and limits important investments in urban planning, infrastructure development and social program" (Habitat, Safer Cities 2015b).

Furthermore, high rates of violence cost economic development (World Bank 2012) and divert as much as 5% of the world GDP from sustainable development (Institute for Economics and Peace 2015)—often more than 15% of the GDP of developing countries.

Using only Repression Based on More Policing and Incarceration Is Ineffective and Costly in Tax and Human Terms

According to the WHO (2014), too many efforts to control crime are not using scientific methods or the agreed UN standards and norms (United Nations Office on Drugs and Crime 2006a,b) and thus are unnecessarily wasteful of human lives and scarce resources (Waller 2014).

By the standards of other affluent democracies such as Canada, England, or Germany, the United States is and indeed was always a heavy incarcerator, particularly of blacks. The American punitive incarceration rates have ballooned from the 1950s and 1960s at 200 per 100,000 to 700 per 100,000—levels unknown elsewhere today on this planet.

However, the U.S. spending spree on policing and incarceration does not come without a significant financial burden. U.S. taxpayers who often do not believe in big government spend a whopping $83 billion each year for its 2.2 million inmates, which account for approximately 20% of the world's incarcerated population. If the United States incarcerated at the German rate, it would save more than $70 billion in taxes annually. (Germany has an incarceration rate of 76 per 100,000 and the United States has 716 per 100,000.)

Various erudite organizations have assessed the contribution of this massive experiment to public safety in the United States. While the claims vary, few suggest a contribution in reduced violence from extraordinary rates of incarceration of more than 25%. However, this is not enough, as the United States still allows its homicide rates to be a multiple of two to three times those of other advanced nations and, as shown, its rates of violence generally are disturbing.

Careful analysis of the disparity in rates of incarceration for blacks versus whites—the rate for blacks is approximately six times the rate for whites—shows the multiple ways that racial bias is present in sentencing laws (Alexander 2010). However, the various nongovernmental organizations debating what to do about mass incarceration rarely refer to the equally and more disturbing disparity in rates of homicide for young men where the black rate is almost eight times that of whites (FiveThirtyEight 2015). If incarceration rates are to be reduced in the United States, then the focus must shift from policing problem places to solving the social problems and from efforts to arrest and incarcerate the way out of those social problems (Waller 2014).

Accumulation of Significant Evidence That Prevention Is the Effective Solution to Violence

What Are the Risk Factors for Violence?

Since the 1960s, we have accumulated significant knowledge about how various negative life experiences during the development of young boys from birth to adulthood correlate to persistent offending. These have come from large-scale studies of life course development involving thousands of young persons in many different countries.

These studies point to such **risk factors** as birth in relative poverty, inconsistent uncaring parenting, troublesome behavior in primary school, dropping out of school, and delinquent peers (Loeber and Farrington 2013; Waller 2014). Other important research has pointed to the importance of attachments for young persons to their family, school, or work (Hirschi 1971; Waller 1974).

In Mexico in 2014, a major and impressive national survey examined the distribution of these risk factors across the country as part of a strategy to focus social and situational prevention programs where they were most likely to prevent violence (Mexico INEGI 2014).

We also know the influence that access to guns and knives as well as alcohol and drugs have to rates of violence. In relation to violence against women and girls, gender values and disparities in income are just some of the well-established risk factors (WHO and Fulu 2015).

There is also an important literature about broader social risk factors. For instance, social protection policies reduce crime significantly even in situations of relative poverty. These policies enhance and protect human dignity by reducing impact of various job and family losses by providing benefits such as health care, unemployment insurance, pensions (including those associated with old age), support for survivors, an active labor market, and housing assistance (Rogers and Pridemore 2013). Research has also demonstrated that urban policies that deconcentrate poverty reduce crime (Cassidy et al. 2014).

What Prevents Violence by Tackling the Risk Factors

While the risk factor studies just show correlations, the preventive interventions tackling these risk factors prove that delinquency can be prevented, which suggests that these correlations are closer to causes.

Fortunately, since 1985, we have accumulated significant knowledge about risk factors that are linked to violence and what strategies prevent violence by tackling those risk factors. Further, this knowledge is endorsed by prestigious organizations (Waller 2014). Such scientific solutions are easily accessible. They are covered, for instance, on public websites such as that of the Centers for Disease Control and Prevention and the WHO—both of which consider rightly that endemic violence is as much of a public health challenge as a criminal justice one.

However, one of the most useful and informative sites is produced by the U.S. DOJ, aptly named crimesolutions.gov (US DOJ 2015). This was built on research results accumulated in the last 50 years in the United States and other countries, ranging from pre-crime prevention actions such as pre-school programs to criminal justice programs focusing on reentry. Many of the research studies cited involved random control trials that tested whether a particular innovative program reduced crime more than the traditional system such as reactive policing and court sentencing to incarceration. A program is rated "effective" only if there are enough reliable scientific studies to demonstrate it.

The DOJ site currently confirms the effectiveness in preventing crime of 83 out of 384 programs and 16 of a new category of 60 practices (US DOJ 2015). There are 234 rated as promising and 67 rated as ineffective. Most of the "effective" programs concern some type of pre-crime prevention rather than an action of the police, the courts, or a corrections system. More than half of the 83 successful programs tackle problems in families, or schools, or concern themselves with improving life skills through mentoring, substance abuse, or trauma treatment programs. This site also includes a new section on practices, where 16 are identified as effective and 23 are identified as promising. Among the practices, there are both social development strategies and problem-oriented policing practices, but these do not compare the positive results of investing in people through social development with the comparatively expensive and sometimes racially biased problem-oriented strategies such as stop and frisk.

Meanwhile, the WHO site points to similar pre-crime prevention focused on parenting and youth programs, as well as to control of weapons and alcohol, and changing attitudes to violence, particularly against women and children (WHO 2009a,b).

In Table 17.1, we present the main prevention measures that would contribute to the goal of reducing victims of crime by 50% within 10 years of implementation. This goal for the U.S. requires a reinvestment equal to 10% of expenditures on police, courts, and corrections (Waller 2014). Some of the targeted social development programs are based on the work of a number of rigorous scientific studies that constitute the "well-scrubbed lists of

Table 17.1   What Reinvestments Stop Violence Cost-Effectively?

		Reinvestment from Policing, Courts, and Incarceration in Billions
	Prevention through targeted social development	
1.1	Preschool and early parenting	$4
1.2	Life skill for 6- to 12-year-olds	$2
1.3	Outreach to street youth	$4
1.4	School life skills courses (relating to sex, alcohol, bullying, intervening, etc.)	$2
	Prevention through more effective police and justice	
2.1	Policing innovation (including focus on guns, traffic, alcohol, and more)	$2
2.2	Prevention through advancing standards for property and traffic safety	$2
3.1	Prevention through effective implementation	$2
4.1	City role in spearheading prevention	$1
4.2	Data to measure both less harm to victims (fewer, less serious injury, two less violence against women) and less waste of taxes	$2
4.3	Provide incentives to States to decarcerate (but ensure investment in effective prevention)	$5
	Total	$26

Source: Waller, I. (2014). *Smarter Crime Control: A Guide to Safer Futures for Citizens, Communities, and Politicians.* Lanham, MD: Rowman and Littlefield.

programs that have been proven to produce substantial reductions in crime, while saving taxpayers more than $10 in future correctional costs for every dollar expended" (Greenwood 2014).

Some design initiatives (such as installing a quality deadbolt or a seatbelt) require minimal investment, but the potential cost savings in lives is obviously much more (Waller 2014). Keep in mind that it is often not known whether these savings would be the same if the programs were implemented on a larger scale; in some cases, economies of scale might lower implementation costs (see Chapter 16).

Substantiating the targeted reinvestments listed above, the WHO (WHO and Kieselbach 2015) has recently identified a similar list but added to the deconcentration of poverty and spatial upgrading of urban areas. A similar list was identified by the WHO in its Global Status Report on Violence Prevention (WHO 2014, p. 27) and in their report on youth violence prevention (WHO and Kieselbach 2015).

On issues of the prevention of violence against women and girls (WHO and Fulu 2015), proposals include the following:

1. Enforce laws and implement national action plans that are holistic, evidence-based, and multisectoral and include operational actions, budgets, measurable target, capacity building, and system-strengthening strategies.
2. Invest in prevention and integrate efforts across sectors: address gender inequality, normalization of violence, and dominant models of masculinity and other drivers.
3. Strengthen the role of the health sector including training and institutional strengthening. Include other health initiatives, such as sexual and reproductive, adolescent, maternal, neonatal, and child health, mental health, HIV prevention, and substance abuse.
4. Invest in research and data collection including scale-up: national surveys to measure magnitude, consequences, and build evidence of what programs and policies are effective and how to scale-up (see Box 17.1).

BOX 17.1   EXAMPLES OF EFFECTIVE WAYS TO PREVENT VIOLENCE AGAINST WOMEN

In developing countries, violence against women has been reduced by the use of all-female police stations (United Nations Women 2015) and the combination of programs that integrate empowerment of women with coaching on ways to stop violence against women, such as IMAGE that combined microfinance and training on preventing violence against women.

Curriculum in schools can reduce sexual violence. Known as "The Fourth R" (US DOJ 2015), it was originally tested in a large-scale random control trial in Canada where the evaluators confirmed significant prevention of sexual violence. Since then, the program has received international recognition and some Canadian implementation, including now in a compulsory sex education program for the Province of Ontario.

Intervenor programs in universities are being encouraged in Canadian universities and by the Obama administration in U.S. universities. Established in 2008, *Green Dot* is an effective intervention program that encourages bystanders to intervene to stop potential incidents. *Green Dot* trains individuals as peers and cultural influencers in behaviors that help establish intolerance of violence as the norm. A five-year evaluation in schools showed a 50% reduction in sexual violence perpetration (University of Kentucky 2015). Arguably, this type of program could be cost-effectively placed on every university campus.

Benefits Include Less Harm to Victims, Better Human Development, and Less Need for Repressive Solutions

Strong evidence for a compelling business case is that if you invest in what is effective, you save lives, avoid loss of quality of life for victims, foster sustainable development, and avoid wasted resources—*an ounce of prevention is worth a pound of cure* (Waller 2014). Using tax revenue, for example, to invest in smart crime control and violence prevention would cut rates of violence, particularly affecting young black men, by as much as 50%, while reducing the need for so many police and unwarranted levels of incarceration (Waller 2014).

Growing Consensus on Importance of Governance Strategies That Are Multisectoral

Government Multisectoral Strategies

Among the governments to pioneer national multisectoral crime prevention strategies are England and Wales and France. The British included in their 1996 Crime and Disorder Act the creation of the Youth Justice Board that had a mandate to invest in preventing youth crime. One such action was to multiply youth inclusion projects into 72 different poor priority areas. These projects establish a center where outreach workers invite youth to come to play sports, use computers, and do homework and so also mentor. Overall, it is estimated that they produced a 26% decrease in crime, including nearly 50% in the lives of the young persons who got involved. This led to doubling the number of youth inclusion projects.

France followed a different trajectory starting in the 1980s with the creation of a comprehensive national crime prevention council that collaborated with six pioneer cities. Over time, the center of responsibility has shifted to an interministerial secretariat on the city that has provided a combination of funds for social investment in youth and mediation—creating thousands of mediator jobs for young persons who were unemployed. It has also supported the development of more than 300 local city-based crime prevention councils.

The Canadian-based International Centre for the Prevention of Crime (ICPC) has operated a clearinghouse for the exchange of advances and knowledge on national and local crime prevention strategies since 1996. In 2009, ICPC identified 57 countries that had some type of national crime prevention strategy. "Such strategies have usually adopted a multi-sector approach, and encouraged through funding, or in some cases required, local municipalities to undertake safety audits, develop and implement strategies, or establish their own local crime prevention councils" (ICPC 2014). While this is encouraging, few of these strategies are funded at a level where they are likely to make a significant difference to national rates of crime (see Box 17.2).

Even though national strategies are comprehensive, it is difficult to measure the impact in prevention terms. Generally, national crime prevention strategies coordinate national policies and funds local government strategies that include the following:

- "Socio-economic development and inclusion—the integration of crime prevention into relevant social and economic policies, and particular emphasis on at-risk communities, children, families and youth;
- Cooperation and partnerships across ministries and between authorities, community organizations, nongovernmental organizations, the business sector and private citizens;
- Sustainability and accountability—with adequate funding to establish and sustain programmes and their evaluation, and clear accountability for funding; and
- The use of a knowledge base—with strategies, policies and programmes based on a broad multidisciplinary foundation of knowledge and evidence about crime problems, their causes, and effective practices; ..." (ICPC 2014).

BOX 17.2   MEXICO AS A MODEL FOR EFFECTIVE NATIONAL VIOLENCE PREVENTION

Mexico has established an impressive National Program of Crime and Violence Prevention into which it has invested US$10 billion. This was achieved in part by a crime prevention law adopted in 2012 combined with major social investments in disadvantaged communities. The law created a national crime prevention center with responsibilities to promote prevention across Mexico, including in the municipalities. The major social investments are coming from the president's office.

In order to design more accurate, comprehensive, and efficient indicators, the National Survey on Social Cohesion and Crime Prevention 2014 "ECOPRED" was created to identify those people who concentrate the greatest number of risk factors in their lives as well those communities that have higher levels of disorganization and those environments in which certain opportunities for committing crime proliferate (Mexico 2015).

Local Comprehensive Community Safety Strategies

At the local level, an important consensus is developing around **comprehensive community safety strategies (CCSS)**. CCSS refers to strategies that achieve the prevention of crime and violence through multisectoral actions to tackle the risk factors that cause crime (UN Habitat, Safer Cities 2015a,b; Waller 2009). Typically, the strategy is led and coordinated by a **responsibility center** that promotes the strategy, brings together the different sectors around a diagnosis of the problems and thus a plan to tackle those problems, and oversees implementation and evaluation of the results. Figure 17.1 illustrates this strategy.

UN Habitat—Safer Cities Application of CCSSs

The main element of the Safer Cities (Habitat, Safer Cities 2015a,b) approach is to build a culture of urban prevention based on the comprehensive community safety strategy (CCSS). A key objective is to mainstream safety in the urban management and planning process. This includes the following:

- Implementing the principles of safe urban design in the conception, rehabilitation, and management of public spaces
- Providing professional police services to the population of all neighborhoods based on a community and problem-solving approach
- Addressing the root causes of crime by a range of support services and activities (housing, sports, culture, vocational training, microcredit, etc.) in particular for the most vulnerable groups, including women, children, youth, and minorities such as the disabled or marginalized ethnic groups
- Providing adequate assistance to the victims of crime

Figure 17.1 Comprehensive community safety strategies model. (Adapted from United Nations-Habitat. (2015). Safer Cities Program, Nairobi.)

- Undertaking awareness and information campaigns to promote tolerance and peaceful conflict resolution, to limit the circulation of light firearms, to fight sexism and stereotypes, and to counter the culture of violence in the media
- Fostering public engagement, participation, and community empowerment through local governance mechanisms, collaborative approaches, and partnerships
- Implementing policies, with the civil society, to empower women and to diminish and eradicate any kind of violence against them at home or in the public sphere

BOX 17.3   GLASGOW, SCOTLAND AS AN EXAMPLE OF SUCCESSFUL VIOLENCE REDUCTION

Glasgow (Glasgow 2015; Waller 2014) provides an impressive model for best practice that explicitly shows how a CCSS can succeed by combining enforcement *together with* prevention to greatly reduce urban and gang violence. Its action on prevention is much more comprehensive than U.S. gang prevention strategies such as Cure Violence or Boston (see Waller 2014), as it also includes some of the proven pre-crime prevention actions, as well as strategies that focus on reducing violence against women and limiting abuse of alcohol.

In 2007, the police service serving Glasgow instituted a public health strategy to diagnose ways to reduce knife and gang violence among young men. (Keep in mind that Scotland has had a tradition of having few handguns around, which was reinforced after the Dunblane mass shooting.) This strategy was committed to coordinating smart policing strategies with evidence-based investments to tackle those negative life experiences that are proven to lead to violence. Specifically, it included programs to help parents provide consistent and caring parenting and education, efforts to persuade victims of urban violence to change their lifestyles to avoid revictimization, enforcement targeted at persistent offenders, and measures to prevent young men from carrying knives in the first place.

Importantly, Glasgow also established a permanent violence reduction unit to take the lead on crime reduction. It is funded through the police department, so that the comprehensive initiative is able to continue in a sustained way. Preliminary analysis suggests that this initiative has cut violence in the targeted neighborhoods by 50% over only three years (Glasgow 2015; Waller 2014).

**BOX 17.4   BOGOTÁ AND RECIFE AS EXAMPLES
OF SUCCESSFUL VIOLENCE REDUCTION
IN HIGH-VIOLENCE COUNTRIES**

Two cities that have achieved remarkable reductions in violence through elements of the comprehensive community safety strategies are Bogotá in Colombia and Recife in Brazil. The Bogotá strategy started in the early 1990s and the Recife strategy began in the mid-2000s (Hoelscher and Nussio 2015).

In fact, Medellin, Bogotá, and Cali, Colombia, were paradigmatic of how to systematically reduce violence by investing in strengthening institutions of security and justice (National Plan for Community Policing by Quadrant, of the National Police of Colombia), but with a greater emphasis on prevention from many different fronts: from social approach to urban development and culture of legality.

The Pact for Life Program for Recife, of the Brazilian state of Pernambuco, focused on reducing homicide. It achieved a 40% reduction in the unintentional deaths and even larger for homicides from 2007 (year of implementation) to 2013.

In Box 17.3, we have highlighted the inspiring example of Glasgow from an advanced nation that has reduced violence by 50%. For the United States, we might have used the example of Minneapolis (Waller 2014). In Box 17.4, we have used two inspiring examples from high-violence countries of cities that have reduced violence by 50% or more.

Essential Supports for the Paradigm Shift to Effective Prevention

World leaders have adopted the Sustainable Development Goals at the UNGA (2015) and their underlying targets for both advanced and developing nations. As indicated earlier and discussed in greater detail in Chapter 2, it includes domestic resource mobilization and investment promotion; enhancing access to science, innovation, and knowledge; targeted capacity-building, particularly around national plans; multi-stakeholder partnerships that mobilize and share knowledge, expertise, technology, and financial resources, increasing significantly the availability of high-quality, timely, and reliable data disaggregated by income, gender, age, race, geographic location, and so on; and measurements of progress.

Effective Prevention Needs Funding

To achieve reductions, there must be adequate investment of funds in effective and cost-effective prevention. This requires political leadership as the investment is competing against the arguments for increasing spending on after the fact approaches. The best is a law to invest the equivalent of 10% of what is currently spent on policing, courts, and corrections. This ensures that funding goes to a new area that does not have the clout of the reactive systems. This amount is likely to produce significant results based on the studies of cost-effectiveness discussed earlier in this chapter (see Waller 2014).

Another way to invest in this new area is to invest as little as 1/10 of 1% of the GDP in the actions needed for the successful governance of the implementation of the strategies based on this knowledge. Waller's (2014) analysis shows how this would achieve a 50% reduction in the loss of human potential from violence by significantly reducing street violence and homicides, violence against women and children, and the penury of services for victims.

The *paradigm shift* must be accompanied by deliberate decarceration; the United States provides an extraordinary example of this, when large numbers of mentally ill patients—500,000—were released from institutions in the 1950s, 1960s, and 1970s. It achieved this through federal incentives. This will not work unless there is serious reinvestment in what works in community solutions. Thus, a rapid decarceration would require the investment in effective prevention that has been proposed above (Waller 2014).

Effective Prevention Needs Qualified Personnel to Apply It

The comprehensive community safety strategy model requires staff who are able to implement the various elements of the strategy. The coordinators of the responsibility center must be able to bring different sectors together to work on a diagnosis and then plan. Some of this can be learned on the job or from others who are prepared to mentor and coach, but some of it requires capacity development through education and training to bring staff up to specific standards.

To succeed in reducing violence across the world, political decision makers need access to the bottom lines from the conclusions, so that they can engage in evidence-based policy making.

Need to Advance Research and Development

Crimesolutions.gov shows the impressive results that have been obtained from research and testing. Most of their examples come from advanced nations. So much more is needed in other countries. There are already several institutes with the capacity to do more research and development in less advanced nations, including the Institute for Security Studies and the Human Sciences Research Council in South Africa. German and British overseas development agencies are just some that are taking some interest but much more is needed.

International Development Research Centre

The International Development Research Centre (IDRC) has invested in pioneering work to develop **effective violence prevention**, particularly in Latin America. In their recent book, de Boer and Gottsbacher (2016) include some remarkable successes in cities. These promising innovations are better than suffering from the economic, human, and democratic losses of continuing only more of the same. IDRC shows the type of work that remains to be done to develop and consolidate more knowledge of effective violence prevention and how to apply it in the context of Latin America and the Caribbean.

Measuring Outcomes Focuses Multisector Strategies on Results

It is difficult to get collaboration across different sectors and keep policymakers focused on preventing violence. A good measure of outcomes from hospital, death, or survey data provides a target for collaboration to be focused over time. What gets measured gets done! If we are to achieve a 50% reduction in street violence and violence against women and girls, then we need to measure the rates of violence over time.

We have some promising ways of doing this. It is well established that police data do not provide a reliable indicator. Hospital data might be used but surveys must be one part. For street violence, we can use victimization surveys and data on homicide deaths from medical examiners. For violence against women and girls, we have both the National Intimate Partner and Sexual Violence survey and the surveys used by Fulu (WHO and Fulu 2015).

Getting Political Action for the Essential Supports

This is a unique moment in human history. We can choose to contribute to the sustainable development goals by reducing interpersonal violence and improving victim assistance by 50% within the next 15 years. We have the knowledge endorsed by organizations such as the WHO and UN-Habitat to reach these targets. However, we need to make a significant shift from overreliance on the outdated retributive system to a modern evidence-based system of prevention and victim support. This is also a strategy that invests in the future of people.

Public Opinion and Victims Support
Social Investment in Prevention

Some naysayers claim that politicians cannot get ahead of their voters, but the reality is that the voters are ahead of the politicians. Surveys of victims show that they overwhelmingly want prevention and services, not punishment (Anderson 2015; Opportunity Agenda 2014; Waller 2011). This point is illustrated in Table 17.2.

Critical Events Can Shift Policy
to Evidence-Based Prevention Strategies

Some recent reforms to the juvenile justice system provide a promising example of how this shift can be accomplished. As crime rates go down, there are good reasons to cut back on funds going toward the reactive system. After years of having many more young offenders in custody per capita than any other affluent democracy, the United States has recently experienced a 50% drop in its juvenile incarceration rates (albeit to levels that are still high by international standards—but this is progress in avoiding the overuse of incarceration and saving taxpayers money). So less crime, less reaction to crime makes sense for juveniles. Why not for adults?

Several of the elements introduced that facilitated the drop in juvenile incarceration rates included the importance of a political champion that can set up a task force to propose a plan. To be cost-effective, the plan had to use evidence and proven programs. Shifting from a reactive model to a proactive model required a process of diagnosing the problem places as well as

Table 17.2 Preferred Approach to Lowering Crime

More money and efforts should go to attacking the social and economic problems that lead to crime through better education and job training.		More money and effort should go to deterring crime by improving law enforcement with more prisons, police, and judges.	
1989	61%	1989	32%
1990	57%	1990	36%
1992	65%	1992	26%
1994	54%	1994	40%
2000	68%	2000	27%
2003	69%	2003	29%
2006	65%	2006	31%
2010	64%	2010	32%

Source: Adapted from Hindelang Criminal Justice Research Center. (2015). *Sourcebook on Criminal Justice Statistics.* Albany: State University of New York. Retrieved from http://www.albany.edu/sourcebook/.

retraining professionals in the field. To ensure that taxes were available for this shift, deliberate efforts had to be made to limit the use of incarceration. Politically, the process had to make victims a priority—not only by preventing crime but also by ensuring that their needs were met with services and funds that were equivalent to what had been done for offenders.

In 2012, Mexico adopted the first "smart" piece of legislation to establish a national crime prevention center and services for victims. In the same year, public frustration boiled over into the presidential election campaign when the failure of policies that focused only on tough enforcement led to a shift in national priorities for the new president toward embracing violence prevention with funding supporting the action.

Intergovernmental Agencies Provide Collective Commitment for Action

The WHO has developed an injury prevention plan that focuses on violence prevention. It started with a Global Report on Health and Violence (WHO 2009a) and then a series of reports looking at cost-effectiveness, implementation, and the evidence. In 2014, the World Health Assembly adopted the historic resolution on "**Strengthening the role of the health system in addressing violence, in particular against women and girls, and against children.**"

In another first, UNDP, UNODC, and WHO collaborated on the first global survey of the status of violence prevention (WHO 2014). Their analysis focused on a short list of seven winning strategies focused on early childhood, youth, weapons, alcohol, violence against women, culture, and victim rights. It also assessed efforts for the good governance of violence prevention, including efforts to implement the winning strategies and measure outcomes such as reductions of deaths—not increases in arrests or prisoners. This effort calls on actions to scale up proven pre-crime prevention programs, ensure that existing laws are enforced, ensure that victim services are widely available and accessible, strengthen data collection and use, and set baselines and targets for violence prevention so that progress can be tracked.

UN Habitat has focused on its safer cities program and organizes meetings from time to time. These expand the use of comprehensive community safety strategies. Habitat III has a special session on safer cities in 2016.

Communities of Practice Provide Momentum for Action

International Centre for the Prevention of Crime

The ICPC is an international forum for national governments, local authorities, public agencies, specialized institutions, and nongovernment organizations to exchange experience, emerging knowledge, and policies and programs in crime prevention and community safety. It assists cities and countries to reduce delinquency, violent crime, and insecurity.

The ICPC helps put knowledge into action by making the knowledge base for strategic crime prevention and community safety better known and more accessible worldwide; encouraging the use of good practices and tools to produce community safety; fostering exchanges between countries and cities, criminal justice institutions, and community-based organizations; and providing technical assistance and training.

European Forum for Urban Safety

With a series of European conferences organized in the late 1980s by the Council of Europe group on Local and Regional Authorities, cities began to meet to explore a public safety agenda where the city and its citizens were at the center. At the conference in Barcelona, the cities got together to form the European Forum for Urban Safety (EFUS). In 1989 in Montreal and in 1991 in Paris, EFUS partnered with the United States Conference of Mayors and the Federation of Canadian Municipalities to organize major international conferences and develop manifestos or agendas for safer cities.

Over time, the EFUS has flourished with European Union and other funding and has fostered the creation of national forums in France, Italy, Spain, and Belgium. It continues to encourage the exchange of good practice around themes varying from homelessness to violence. It has also organized major international conferences that have produced their own manifestos. The most recent one put a strong emphasis on democracy and human rights and investing in prevention (European Forum for Urban Safety 2013).

African Forum for Urban Safety

Starting in 1997, considerable efforts were put into the implementation of the Safer Cities approach in a number of large urban centers in Africa. These projects have necessitated long and complex discussions and negotiations with the local authorities involved, national ministries, funding agencies, and other strategic partners. Nevertheless, comprehensive urban safety initiatives were rolled out in the following cities and countries:

- Johannesburg (South Africa), 1997
- Dar es Salaam (Tanzania), 1997
- Abidjan (Ivory Coast), 1998
- Durban (South Africa), 1999
- Antananarivo (Madagascar), 1999

- Bamako (Mali), 2000
- Nairobi (Kenya), 2001
- Yaounde (Cameroon), 2001
- Douala (Cameroon), 2003
- Ouagadougou (Burkina Faso), 2009

In almost all cases, the process involved the following:

- A project formulation phase
- The creation of a local coordination team
- A local safety diagnosis or victims' survey
- The mobilization and sensitization of municipal actors and other institutional and community partners
- The creation of a steering committee and of collaborative mechanisms
- The elaboration of an urban safety and crime prevention strategy
- The development and implementation of an action plan and targeted pilot projects
- The monitoring and evaluation of the project

In two cases (Tanzania and Ivory Coast), these initiatives opened the door for an extension of the Safer Cities approach to other cities within the country.

Developing Networks in North America

In the United States, the Institute for Prevention (2015) supports the Urban Network to Increase Thriving Youth (UNITY). UNITY builds support for effective, sustainable efforts to prevent violence before it occurs, so that urban youth can thrive in safe environments with ample opportunities and supportive relationships. It utilizes a public health, or prevention, approach to violence. Quality prevention incorporates data collection and analysis to pinpoint the populations and locations at greatest risk, identify risk and resilience factors, and develop and utilize effective strategies to prevent violence before it occurs, and to reduce the impact of risk factors and the reoccurrence of violence. This approach engages multiple sectors working in coordination with each other and with community members. Their efforts are twofold: support cities in developing, implementing, and evaluating effective and sustainable prevention efforts, and increase awareness of what is needed to prevent violence in the first place and build momentum for such approaches so that urban communities can have peaceful streets and thriving youth.

In Canada, the Canadian Municipal Network for Crime Prevention (Waller and Martínez Solares 2015) fosters a community of practice among Canadian municipalities to reduce and prevent crime and victimization, as well as enhance community safety. It will build and develop municipal capacity to harness evidence to prevent crime and to engage municipalities in comprehensive community safety strategies. This approach calls for municipal and community leadership, partnerships and coordination, strategic planning, public engagement, and targeted preventive programs. It supports intermunicipal coaching and mentoring, harnessing and disseminating of knowledge, mobilization and engagement of local stakeholders, and training of key municipal actors. It began with 15 municipalities across Canada in 2006, at the initiative of the Institute for the Prevention of Crime based at the University of Ottawa and with the financial assistance of the NCPC (National Crime Prevention Centre), to share experiences and knowledge and to develop tools to support their efforts to enhance community safety brings together (Canadian Municipal Network for Crime Prevention 2016; Public Safety Canada 2015).

Latin America Region

With the work of the UNODC, the WHO, the World Bank, the Inter-American Development Bank, and the Human Rights Council and also with the results of programs like Habitat and the United Nations Development, there is good news for Latin America.

The Declaration on Security in the Americas (2003) with its inalienable commitment to protect the human person, the dialogues of the Meeting of Ministers of Justice or Other Ministers or Attorneys General of the Americas and Reunion of Ministers Responsible for Public Security in the Americas increasingly placed systematic prevention within their agendas. The Declaration of San Salvador on Citizen Security in the Americas (2011) is the instrument that embodies the duty of governments on the matter.

A particularly hopeful innovation in Latin America is the collaboration between eight nations to develop and implement national strategies for effective violence prevention. The collaboration fosters the creation of a permanent office for violence prevention to develop a plan and ensure sustained reinvestment in evidence-based violence prevention across the key sectors. It is supported by EUROsociAL and inspired by EFUS (Martínez Solares et al. 2015).

The basic premise of all these efforts is, without a doubt, control, mitigate, and stop the violence.

Conclusion

Since 1985, when the UN General Assembly called for a shift to prevent violence and enhance principles of justice for victims, much has been achieved.

Some are celebrating the decline in rates of police-recorded crime to the rates of the 1960s. However, good news this may be, the bad news is that those rates were considered much too high in the 1960s and are still doing damage to the lives of victims measurable in trillions of dollars.

Some countries, particularly in Africa and Latin America, have seen a disappointing increase in violence and homicides. Further, we know how widespread violence against women and girls remains. Violence not only does significant harm to its victims but threatens human and economic development.

As shown throughout this chapter, there has been a rich accumulation of evidence on what prevents violence and supports victims. Such evidence serves to confirm that pre-crime prevention, particularly tackling social risk factors, can significantly reduce street violence, homicide, and violence against women and children. Investment in these strategies is much more cost-effective than standard police, court, and correctional strategies.

Significant progress has been made in implementing effective programs when they are based on a multisectoral approach based on diagnosing needs and evaluating outcomes. Some advanced nations are investing in these proven strategies. Leading cities in the advanced and developing world have demonstrated that violence can be significantly reduced, but much more is needed.

Implementation requires stable investments, ways to measure outcomes, capacity development, and continuing development of the knowledge bases. A shift in the war on drugs to prevention would also reduce violence and save money.

Furthermore, opinion polls show that the public is supportive of strategies that tackle social causes, though politicians are not following these opinions. Intergovernmental agencies as well as communities of practice such as cities are also supportive. The UN Agenda 2030 wants to "reduce significantly violence and related deaths everywhere, end violence against children and eliminate all violence against women and children by 2030." Some funding has come from foundations to fight for political changes consistent with these.

Future research requires evaluations to measure the extent to which countries are indeed investing in what is proven to work and the sustainable way to put them to work as well as monitoring outcomes through surveys or other techniques independent of the police.

Other research is needed to develop more knowledge about what prevents crime in different situations from the advanced nations. For example, IOVA (2015) called on the world community and particularly the 13th UN Congress on Crime Prevention and Criminal Justice to encourage Member States and UN Offices (jointly UNODC, WHO, UNDP, OCHR, UNHCR, and UN Habitat) in partnership with civil society to develop the business case and thus commit to four goals for Sustainable Development achievable by 2030:

1. Reduce the numbers of victims of intentional homicide by 50% as an indicator of reduction of interpersonal violence (UNODC indicator).
2. Reduce the number of women and children who are victims of violence by 25%.
3. Increase by 50% the number of victims of crime, abuse of power, and terrorism who demonstrably receive support, reparation, and rights consistent with international standards (international victimization surveys).
4. Invest 1/10 of 1% of the global GDP to the planning, training, development, implementation, and evaluation of the actions to achieve these goals (measured by Institute of Economics and Peace).

Glossary of Key Terms

Capacity development: refers to investing in the people who are needed to implement smarter crime control by advancing both their knowledge and their practical skills and experience.

Comprehensive Community Safety Strategy (CCSS): is a strategy that mobilizes different sectors around a diagnosis of the location and nature of risk factors leading to gaps in community safety. It requires a responsibility center to mobilize the sectors and coordinate their work. It must also measure outcomes and adjust the programming to improve outcomes. It is often the key to getting the funding needed to succeed.

Effective violence prevention: refers to strategies where scientific methods have been used to demonstrate that an intervention did indeed prevent violence. Some of these strategies involve random control trials. Others involve some type of comparative regression analysis.

Outcomes: has become important in violence prevention as it emphasizes the results of fewer victims or less harm to harms rather than processes such as arrests or length of sentences. Outcomes are often measured in surveys (e.g., victimization or intimate partner) to be independent of police or hospital data.

Responsibility center: is the key to providing leadership and coordination to comprehensive community safety strategies. A national crime prevention center, youth justice board, or violence reduction unit are examples of responsibility centers.

Risk factors: refer to situations that distinguish the likelihood of victimization from those that do not. Risk factors can be social, such as child abuse, poor parenting, or school dropout, or physical, such as presence of alcohol or guns.

Smarter crime control: refers to using evidence to invest in strategies that are more cost-effective in reducing crime. It is different from smart justice, which only embraces changes in the justice system. Acting smarter emphasizes changing the paradigm. It contrasts the prevention and evidence-based strategies with the costly and ineffective strategies that react to crime by using police and prisons, when they are not working to reduce crime.

Discussion Questions

1. How do we know that violence is not inevitable but preventable?
2. What are some of the early childhood and youth risk factors that have been targeted by pre-crime prevention to reduce violence? What are some examples of successful pre-crime prevention that targeted these risk factors and how do we know they were successful?
3. What is the role of problem-oriented policing and partnership policing in contributing to effective crime reduction? What are the dangers of hot spot policing in targeting minorities?
4. What are the key components of a governance strategy that would implement effective and cost-effective prevention in a jurisdiction such as a city, state, or nation? To what extent do Glasgow and Bogotá follow this governance strategy?
5. Why is it helpful, when trying to get adequate funding for what prevents violence, to fix it to a percentage of GDP or of what is currently spent in reacting to crime?
6. Why is the measurement of outcomes essential to success and particularly to multisectoral strategies?
7. What arguments or advocacy groups are most likely to influence a shift of significant funding into "Smarter Crime Control"? What can you do to contribute to this shift?

Suggested Further Reading

United Nations-Habitat. 2015. Safer Cities Program, Nairobi.
United States Department of Justice. 2015. Crimesolutions.gov. http://www.crime solutions.org.
Waller, I. (2014). *Smarter crime control: A guide to safer futures for citizens, communities, and politicians.* Lanham, Maryland: Rowman and Littlefield.
World Health Organization. (2015). Violence prevention milestones meetings. http://www.who.int/violence_injury_prevention/violence/7th_milestones_meeting/en/.

Acknowledgment

We acknowledge the research assistance of Paula Hirschman in finalizing the chapter.

References

Alexander, M. (2010). *The New Jim Crow: Mass Incarceration in the Age of Color-blindness*. New York: New Press.

Anderson, L. (2015). In California's experience, it isn't bigger prisons that crime victims want. Retrieved from http://www.penalreform.org/blog/in-californias-experience-it-isnt-bigger-prisons-that/#comment-149942.

Business Insider. (2014). 50 Most violent cities in the world. Retrieved from http://www.businessinsider.com/the-most-violent-cities-in-the-world-2014-11?op=1.

Cassidy, T., Inglis, G., Wiysonge, C., and Matzopoulos, R. (2014). A systematic review of the effects of poverty deconcentration and urban upgrading on youth violence. *Health & Place* 26: 78–87.

Centers for Disease Control and Prevention (CDCP). (2010). The National Intimate Partner and Sexual Violence Survey. *Injury Prevention & Control: Division of Violence Prevention*. Retrieved from http://azrapeprevention.org/sites/azrapeprevention.org/files/NISVS_Report_0.pdf.

de Boer, J., and Gottsbacher, M. (2016). *Vulnerability and Violence in Latin America and the Caribbean*. Cambridge University Press (in press).

European Forum for Urban Safety. (2013). Security, democracy and cities: Manifesto from Aubervilliers and St Denis, Paris. Retrieved from http://efus.eu/en/.

FiveThirtyEight. (2015). Black Americans are killed at 12 times the rate of people in other developed countries. Retrieved from http://fivethirtyeight.com/datalab/black-americans-are-killed-at-12-times-the-rate-of-people-in-other-developed-countries/.

Glasgow. (2015). *Violence Reduction Unit*. Retrieved from http://www.actiononviolence.org.uk/.

Greenwood, P. (2014). *Evidence Based Practice in Juvenile Justice: Progress, Challenges and Opportunities*. New York: Springer.

Habitat, Safer Cities. (2015a). Habitat III, Issue Papers 3—Safer Cities. Retrieved from http://unhabitat.org/issue-papers-and-policy-units/.

Habitat, Safer Cities. (2015b). Reviewing the role of local authorities in safety and security in Africa (Safer Cities+20): Towards the Africa agenda 2063, Africa Forum for Urban Safety (AFUS). First Technical Document on the First Conference 25th–27th November 2015.

Hindelang Criminal Justice Research Center. (2015). *Sourcebook on Criminal Justice Statistics*. Albany: State University of New York. Retrieved from http://www.albany.edu/sourcebook/.

Hirschi, T. (1971). *Causes of Delinquency*. Berkeley: University of California Press.

Hoelscher, K., and Nussio, E. (2015). Understanding unlikely successes in urban violence reduction. *Urban Studies*. Retrieved from http://dx.doi.org/10.2139/ssrn.2461064.

Institute for Economics and Peace. (2015). *Analyzing the Changing Dynamics of Peace in Mexico*. Washington, DC: Institute for Economics & Peace.

Institute for Prevention. (2015). Urban network to support thriving youth. Retrieved from http://www.preventioninstitute.org/unity.html.

International Centre for the Prevention of Crime. (2014). 4th International report on crime prevention and community safety: Trends and perspectives. Retrieved from http://www.crime-prevention-intl.org/uploads/media/ICPC_report_4.pdf.

International Organization for Victim Assistance. (2015). Retrieved from http://www.iovahelp.org/UNCrimeCongress.html.

Loeber, R., and Farrington, D. (2013). *Child Delinquents: Development, Intervention, and Service Needs*. Thousand Oaks, CA: Sage.

Martínez Solares, V., Aguilar, O., Gottsbacher, M., Mendoza, C., and Waller, I. (2015). Modelo Regional de Política Integral para la Prevención de la Violencia y el Delito. Bruselas: EUROsociAL, Proyectos Estratégicos Consultoría.

Mexico. (2015). Retrieved from http://embamex.sre.gob.mx/belgica/images /comunicadosegobsept2015.pdf.

Mexico INEGI. (2014). Encuesta de Cohesión Social para la Prevención de la Violencia y la Delincuencia, Secretaría de Gobernación, Política Nacional de Prevención Social de la Violencia y la Delincuencia.

Opportunity Agenda. (2014). An overview of public opinion and discourse on criminal justice. Retrieved from http://opportunityagenda.org/criminal_justice 3 September 2015.

Public Safety Canada. (2015). Policing research catalogue. Retrieved from http://www.publicsafety.gc.ca/cnt/cntrng-crm/plcng/cnmcs-plcng/rsrch-prtl /srch-eng.aspx.

Rogers, M.L., and Pridemore, W.A. (2013). The effect of poverty and social protection on national homicide rates: Direct and moderating effects. *Social Science Research* 42: 584–595.

Small Arms Survey. (2012). Femicide: A global problem. Retrieved from http://www.smallarmssurvey.org/fileadmin/docs/H-Research_Notes/SAS-Research -Note-14.pdf.

United Nations General Assembly. (1985). Resolution on basic principles of justice for victims of crime and abuse of power, 40/34.

United Nations General Assembly. (2015). Transforming our world: The 2030 agenda for sustainable development. Retrieved from https://sustainabledevelopment .un.org/content/documents/7891Transforming%20Our%20World.pdf.

United Nations-Habitat. (2015). Safer Cities Program, Nairobi.

United Nations Office on Drugs and Crime. (2006a). Guidelines for cooperation and technical assistance in the field of urban crime prevention, 1996, compendium of United Nations standards and norms in crime prevention and criminal justice. New York: United Nations.

United Nations Office on Drugs and Crime. (2006b). Guidelines for the prevention of crime, 2002, compendium of United Nations standards and norms in crime prevention and criminal justice. New York: United Nations.

United Nations Women. (2015). Virtual Knowledge Center to end violence against women and girls, New York. Retrieved from http://www.endvawnow.org/en /articles/1093-womens-police-stations-units.html.

United States Department of Justice. (2015). Crimesolutions.gov. http://www.crime
  solutions.gov

University of Kentucky. (2015). Green Dot effective at reducing sexual violence.
  Retrieved from http://uknow.uky.edu/content/green-dot-effective-reducing-sex
  ual-violence.

Waller, I. (1974). *Men Released from Prison*. Toronto: University of Toronto Press.

Waller, I. (2009). Making cities safer: Action briefs for municipal stakeholders.
  Ottawa: University of Ottawa. Retrieved from http://irvinwaller.org/wp-content
  /uploads/2010/12/IPC-Action-Briefs-full-text-en.pdf.

Waller, I. (2011). *Rights for Victims of Crime: Rebalancing Justice*. Lanham, MD:
  Rowman and Littlefield.

Waller, I. (2014). *Smarter Crime Control: A Guide to Safer Futures for Citizens,
  Communities, and Politicians*. Lanham, MD: Rowman and Littlefield.

Waller, I., and Martínez Solares, V. (2015). Derechos de las víctimas a treinta años
  de la Carta Magna de las Naciones Unidas: Acciones concretas en momentos
  críticos, Victimologia.

World Bank. (2012). World Development Report 2011. Washington, DC: World
  Bank.

World Health Assembly. (2014). Strengthening the role of the health system in
  addressing violence, in particular against women and girls, and against children. Geneva: 67th World Health Assembly.

World Health Organization. (2009a). Violence prevention: The evidence. Geneva:
  The World Health Organization.

World Health Organization. (2009b). Promoting gender equality to prevent violence
  against women. Geneva: World Health Organization.

World Health Organization. (2014). Global status report on violence prevention
  2014. Geneva: WHO, the United Nations Development Programme, and the
  United Nations Office on Drugs and Crime.

World Health Organization. (2015). 7th Violence prevention milestones meeting.
  Retrieved from http://www.who.int/violence_injury_prevention/violence
  /7th_milestones_meeting/en/.

World Health Organization, and Fulu, E. (2015). Preventing violence against
  women and girls: An overview of the evidence. World Health Organization
  Presentation by Emma Fulu. Retrieved from http://www.who.int/violence
  _injury_prevention/violence/7th_milestones_meeting/en/.

World Health Organization, and Kieselbach, B. (2015). Preventing youth violence:
  An overview of the evidence. World Health Organization Presentation by Berit
  Kieselbach. Retrieved from http://www.who.int/violence_injury_prevention
  /violence/7th_milestones_meeting/Kieselbach_youth_violence_prevention
  _manual.pdf?ua=1.

Safeguarding Sustainable Crime Prevention

18

The Rocky Case of the Netherlands

JAN VAN DIJK
PAUL VAN SOOMEREN
JAAP DE WAARD

Contents

Learning Outcomes

After reading this chapter, you should be able to

- Explain why crime prevention next to law enforcement and criminal justice requires special structures to be sustainable
- Describe the characteristics of the three phases in the institutionalization of crime prevention in the Netherlands since 1970
- Identify the two-dimensional typology of crime prevention promoted by the Directorate of Dutch Crime Prevention at the Ministry of Justice and distinguish between the nine different types of crime prevention

- Understand the factors that have led to the decline of special structures for crime prevention after 2000
- Understand the importance of public–private partnerships for sustainable crime prevention
- Understand the cyclical nature of crime, and why governments should maintain crime prevention structures in order to be prepared for the next crime cycle.

Introduction

The implementation of 'tried and tested' prevention practice however remains obstinately patchy and inconsistent. Why do we find it so difficult to replicate successful programmes? Why is it that we can't run programmes like say MacDonald's run their business?

Nigel Whiskin
Former CEO of Crime Concern, UK (Guestblog 08-18-2011 on www.waller.org)

In the opening lines of the 2002 UN Guidelines on Crime Prevention, this policy concept is introduced as an alternative, new approach to the problems of crime:

Effective, responsible crime prevention enhances the quality of life of all citizens. It has long-term benefits in terms of reducing the costs associated with the formal criminal justice system, as well as other social costs that result from crime. Crime prevention offers opportunities for a humane and more cost-effective approach to the problems of crime.

United Nations
2002

If war, in the famous words of Prussian general and military theorist Carl von Clauswitz (1780–1831),* is the continuation of diplomacy with other means, crime prevention, in the view of the UN Guidelines, is the opposite. It is the pursuance of the war on crime with nonpunitive, more benign means. This definition of crime prevention brings to the fore both its obvious political appeal—who would be opposed to a policy that is both more humane and more cost-effective than the conventional punishment of offenders?—and its fundamental operational challenge: which institution can ensure the implementation of this new policy replacing or supplementing law enforcement and criminal justice? Who are the natural ambassadors of this welcome alternative to the war on crime?

Although the initial drafts aimed at the imposition of due, normative principles on the branching out of criminal justice into the unchartered

---

* See https://en.wikipedia.org/wiki/Carl_von_Clausewitz.

BOX 18.1   HIGHLIGHTS OF CRIME PREVENTION INITIATIVES IN THE UNITED KINGDOM BETWEEN 1980 AND 2000

The following is a chronological sampling of some of the major crime prevention initiatives introduced during the Home Office's Safe Cities Program.

- 1980: Deployment of Crime Prevention officers by police forces and multiagency cooperation between police and local authority agencies
- 1887: Ministerial Group of Crime Prevention
- 1988: Safer Cities Programme established by Home Office Crime Prevention Unit ($n = 3600$ in 1990)
- 1989: Establishment of Crime Concern, cofounded by corporate world; Youth Action Groups projects ($n = 650$ in 1994)
- 1994: Safer Cities Programme relaunched as Single Regeneration Programme under responsibility of the Department of the Environment
- 1998: Crime and Disorder Bill of New Labour, introducing Anti-social Behavior Orders and Parenting Orders
- 2000: Zero tolerance policing

fields of crime prevention, the ultimate drafters of the guidelines appear to have been more concerned about the challenges facing the implementation of this new policy.* The largest part of the guidelines lay down not the normative principles of crime prevention but the ground rules for its sustainable implementation. This is unsurprising considering that around 2000, when the guidelines were finalized, major initiatives such as the French National Council of Crime Prevention, the U.S. National Crime Prevention Council, Crime Concern and the Safer Cities Programme in the UK (see Box 18.1), the Directorate of Crime Prevention at the Dutch Ministry of Justice, and the Permanent Secretariat of Crime Prevention at the Interior Ministry in Belgium, as well as the International Centre for Crime Prevention in Canada had all been downsized or, in the case of the Dutch Directorate, disbanded altogether. It is against this sobering background that the final drafters, many of whom had worked for one of the institutions just mentioned, included

---

* The drafters included, for example, Gloria Laycock (formerly Home Office UK), Irwin Waller (formerly ICPC, Canada), Leoluca Orlando (former, and present Mayor of Palermo), and Jan van Dijk (formerly Ministry of Justice, NL, and, at the time, director of the Centre of International Crime Prevention/UNODC in Vienna).

a mundane article like the following: "Crime prevention requires adequate resources, including funding for structures and activities, in order to be sustained."

In the terminology of the policy cycle, any new policy concept passes through the stages of Agenda Setting, Policy Formulation, Legitimization, Implementation, Evaluation, and, finally, Policy Maintenance, Succession, or Termination (Cairney 2013). Crime prevention policy in the Western world has gone rapidly through the stages of Agenda Setting and Policy Formulation around the mid-1980s, and duly acquired, around 1990, the necessary Political Legitimization. Policy Formulation soon followed in the form of adopted National Strategies or special laws.* In several Western countries, crime prevention subsequently moved into the stage of Implementation, by the establishment of one or more full-fledged organizations to take responsibility for delivery.† Finally, the stage of Evaluation seems to have been passed with honors around 2000 with the publication of several comprehensive and high-quality evaluation studies. Many forms of crime prevention were found to be both successful and cost-effective (see Chapter 19) and considerably more humane than conventional interventions to boot.‡ This was proven in particular for programs introducing situational crime prevention measures (Guerette 2009) or early interventions in at-risk families (Farrington and West 2003; Waller 2006).§ Crime prevention seemed destined to become a key permanent feature of counter crime policies.

The final question, then, is how the new policy of crime prevention fared in the final stage in the policy cycle, that of Policy Maintenance, Succession, or Termination? The implementation advice given in the UN Guidelines can, with hindsight, be read as the somewhat desperate plea of experts worrying that, without renewed political support, many of the new crime prevention programs, however favorably evaluated, might not be sustainable in the long run. Since the adoption of the UN Guidelines, crime prevention in the Western world has, in our estimation, seen more termination or succession of programs than their maintenance, leave alone their expansion. An

---

* A prime example of a law on crime prevention is the law of 1972 establishing the Swedish Council of Crime Prevention, which has been the model of similar legislation in other Scandinavian countries as well as in some Central and Eastern European countries.
† Examples were the National Council on Crime Prevention in France in 1983, the Interministerial Committee on Crime Prevention in the Netherlands in 1986 and the Safer Cities Programme in the United Kingdom in 1988.
‡ Examples are the studies of the Home Office Research Centre and the Police Research Group (Laycock and Heal 1989; Mayhew et al. 1976), the Research and Documentation Centre of the Dutch Ministry of Justice (van Dijk and de Waard 1991) and, in the United States, the Rand Corporation (Greenwood et al. 1996; Sherman et al. 1997) as well as the cost–benefit analyses by the Centre for Policy Analysis (Aos et al. 2001, 2004).
§ In the Netherlands, the costs and benefits of built-in devices to prevent household burglary and car theft have been favorably assessed by economists (Van Ours and Vollaard 2015; Vollaard and Van Ours 2011).

overview of experiences with crime prevention in a selection of European countries (Crawford 2009) conveys a picture of disintegration of support structures and decline of resources (see Box 18.2). The **European Crime Prevention Network** of the European Union (EU), meant as a powerhouse for crime prevention in the EU, seems, with the transfer of its secretariat from the Commission to the Belgium Ministry of the Interior in 2010, to have barely survived.

The international decline of crime prevention in so many countries begs the question which factors have propelled the sudden rise of crime prevention as a new policy concept in the 1980s and 1990s of the last century, and which factors have been instrumental in its subsequent stagnation or decline thereafter.

BOX 18.2   CRIMPREV INFO N°16BIS— COMPARATIVE MODELS OF CRIME PREVENTION AND DELIVERY: THEIR GENESIS, INFLUENCE, AND DEVELOPMENT

ADAM CRAWFORD (2008)

"There was some considerable consensus that the distinct models that preoccupied debate in the 1980s were less relevant today. Many countries appeared to have moved towards hybrid models, with a greater emphasis on pragmatism and evidence-based policy (at least at the level of rhetoric) and less emphasis on ideological fault-lines.

Many countries in their own developmental trajectories exhibited ambiguous shift and movements which could not be understood in terms of any unilinear trend. The strong influence of politics was evident in the paths taken within many jurisdictions.

The problem of political 'hyper-activity' was identified. There was a sense for some that there had been 'too much change' and that many of the initiatives had not been given sufficient time to bed down and produce long-term effects.

There were perceptions that in reflecting on developments, some of the optimism and early aspirations as to the impact of prevention policies on criminal justice systems had not been fully realised. However, some commentators remained optimistic about the future prospect for development.

There was some agreement that the delivery of holistic partnerships had proved particularly difficult to realise given the departmental boundaries between key organisations and agencies and reluctance on the part of some to participate in joint ventures."

In this chapter, we will examine this issue with an in-depth case study of the institutional history of crime prevention in the Netherlands between 1965 and 2015. We will document how crime prevention in the Netherlands went through the usual stages of the policy cycle between 1965 and 2015, and examine which factors have shaped its ever-changing arrangements. More specifically, we will try to identify which factors seem to have been responsible for the downfall of many of the support structures for crime prevention after 2000. Although aware of the idiosyncratic nature of much what has occurred in the Netherlands in this field, we will try to draw out some "lessons learned" that might be of interest to those committed to the promotion of crime prevention in other places in the world, now or in the future.

Police-Based Crime Prevention as a First Response to the Boom in Crime: 1970–1985

From 1960 onward, crime in the Netherlands continued to rise steeply for three decades. Police registrations show that the absolute numbers of recorded crime went up from 100,000 crimes per year in 1960 to well more than 1 million in 1985. Parallel to this upward trend in recorded crime, the percentages of recorded crimes cleared by the police went down from 70% in 1955 to 25% in 1985 (see Figure 18.1).

The rise of crime volume, and a call for law and order, emerged for the first time as a political issue in the national elections of 1971 (Beernink/CHU).

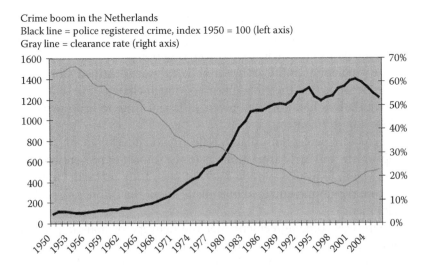

Crime boom in the Netherlands
Black line = police registered crime, index 1950 = 100 (left axis)
Gray line = clearance rate (right axis)

Figure 18.1 Trends in recorded crime and clearance rates in the Netherlands between 1950 and 2008.

At the same time, conventional law enforcement became the object of strident critiques from political parties of the New Left and from renowned criminologists. In response to widely shared concerns about a crisis in crime control, the Dutch Ministry of Justice first established a full-fledged research center, the Research and Documentation Centre in 1972. One of the first priorities of the center was the launch of a large-scale victimization survey in 1973 (Smit and van Dijk 2014; van Dijk and Steinmetz 1979). The main policy implication of the survey was that volume crime had become rampant and remained largely hidden from the police. The initial policy response from the Ministry of Justice to the boom in crime was the establishment in 1973 of a committee tasked to propose a set of priorities in the investigative efforts of the police (Commissie Verbaliseringsbeleid Misdrijven). The committee identified the types of crime that could possibly be given less attention by investigation departments of the police (e.g., shoplifting, vandalism, and bicycle theft). In the meantime, the Directorate of Police and several municipal police forces had taken up an interest in advising the public on target hardening against much occurring types of crime like vandalism and burglary. The Criminal Investigation Advisory Committee advised the Ministers of Justice and Interior that the country was in urgent need of more crime prevention policies and that the establishment of a national body for this purpose was desirable. Following this advice, the ministers adopted in 1970 the Police Crime Prevention Regulations, which provided the statutory basis for a national organization for the prevention of crime with a national office at the Ministry of Justice, a dozen regional offices, and local crime prevention units in the municipal police forces and the districts of the State Police. The national office developed special prevention concepts like Property Marking and Neighborhood Watch, which were then rolled out nationally through its regional and local bureaus. The organization also developed the first standards for household security. A key function of the organization was the transfer of knowledge through training courses, manuals, and a regular consultation structure (including work meetings at the national and regional levels). By the mid-1980s, several hundred police officers were active locally, regionally, or nationally in this police-based crime prevention structure.

Administrative Crime Prevention: Engaging Other Ministries and Local Authorities (1985–1995)

In the early 1980s, petty crime had, according to both police statistics and victimization surveys, continued to increase steeply and now gave rise to heated political debates among the mainstream political parties. In 1983, the center-right government established an Advisory Committee on Petty Crime, requested to come up with a set of recommendations to address the rise in crime.* In the winter of 1984, this committee published a report that heralded a new consensus among the main political parties, including the Labour Party, about both diagnosis and cure. While acknowledging victimization by crime as a serious social problem affecting broad sectors of society, the report rejected a mere expansion of the criminal justice system as a viable response to the problem of volume crime. Its key message was that juvenile delinquency and other forms of volume crime had grown from a weakening of informal social controls in an urbanized, consumerist, and secular society, and should primarily be tackled by reintroducing contemporary modes of informal or semiformal social control. Its recommendations were a strengthening of the national government's commitment to crime prevention, the involvement of intermediary structures such as schools and sports clubs, and businesses, and interagency cooperation at the central and local levels of government (van Dijk and Junger-Tas 1988). The new type of crime prevention that went far beyond police-based target hardening advice was called **administrative crime prevention**. It had gone from Agenda Setting to Legitimization within less than a year.

The recommendations of the "all-party" committee were favorably received by all main political parties and, within months, came to constitute the cornerstone of the government's anticrime policies as formulated in the White Paper "Samenleving en Criminaliteit" (*Society and Crime*) in 1985. Within months, the new concept of crime prevention went from Legitimization into the stage of Policy Formulation and even Implementation. As announced in the white paper, an Interministerial Committee for Crime Prevention was set up comprising high-level representatives of the Ministries of Justice and Interior and several other key ministries, under the chairmanship of the Secretary-General of the Prime Minister's office. It administered a fund of 25 million euros to permit local authorities to mount crime prevention programs in the period 1986–1990. Almost all larger towns appointed crime prevention coordinators to draft proposals for projects and to oversee their implementation. During the period 1986–1990, some 200 local projects were subsidized. Ten percent of the total budget was earmarked for independent evaluation, mainly by university-based research institutes (Willemse 1996).

Under a new, center-left administration, the secretariat of the Interministerial Committee was in 1989 upgraded to a full-fledged Directorate of Crime Prevention at the Ministry of Justice. The existing National Bureau

---

* The committee, established by Frits Korthals Altes, a minister of the VVD, was chaired by Hein Roethof, a former Member of Parliament of the Labour Party, known for his liberal ideas about crime control. Members included experts from different political parties, including the future, threefold Minister of Justice Ernst Hirsch Ballin (CDA) and Jaqueline Soetendorp (D'66), as well as Jan van Dijk, at the time head of the Research and Documentation Centre of the Ministry of Justice.

Table 18.1 Schematic Representation of the Different Types of Crime Prevention and Examples

	Primary General Application	Secondary Risk Groups At-Risk Neighborhoods	Tertiary Problem Groups Hot Places/Victims
Offender	• Teaching of norms • Truancy prevention • Support for disadvantaged groups	• Early intervention, for example, parenting support	• Reintegration • Alternative sanctions • Repeat offender projects
Situational	• Building regulations • In-built car security	• Caretakers in apartment buildings (concierges) • Neighborhood wardens, city guards, surveillance in industrial sites	• Policies and regulations in entertainment areas • Cameras at hotspots at crime primetime
Victim	• Awareness raising for schoolchildren • Self-defense training for girls and women	• Instructions for personnel of banks, shops (inoculation) • Neighborhood watch	• Prevention of repeat victimization • Victim support

Source: van Dijk, J.J.M., and de Waard, J. (1991). A two-dimensional typology of crime prevention projects: With a bibliography. *Criminal Justice Abstracts* 23: 483–503. Retrieved from https://pure.uvt.nl/portal/files/987925/TWO-DIME.PDF.

of the police-based crime prevention organization was incorporated in this Directorate.* The Directorate, consisting of 40 or more professional staff, disposed of an annual budget of 15 million euros to promote crime prevention programs. With this directorate, the implementation of the new policy had become institutionalized as a key governmental function.

The newly established Directorate consisted of departments for situational and offender-oriented crime prevention, respectively, and a small unit for supporting services for crime victims, including **Victim Support** Netherlands. Building on the well-known typology in preventive medicine, the Directorate distinguished between primary, secondary, and tertiary prevention (also see the Introduction in this volume). In addition to

---

* In 1992, the existing infrastructure of the police-based crime prevention organization was officially disbanded as part of a major reorganization setting up 25 regional police forces, replacing the municipal forces and the state police. It was felt that the regional police forces would need no support from a central unit in carrying out preventive activities. As will be discussed later, this decision has resulted in a radical decline of police-based crime prevention.

this dimension, the Directorate applied another threefold classification—offender-focused, victim-focused, and situational measures. Table 18.1 shows a schematic representation of the nine different types of crime prevention promoted by the Directorate with examples of concrete projects.

One of the key initial focuses of the directorate was the strengthening of semiformal social control or surveillance in the public and semipublic domain: City Guards, extra inspectors in public transport, and caretakers in crime-ridden high-rise apartment buildings (Hesseling 1995). An essential element of these projects was the joint tackling of three social problems: unemployment, crime, and resulting feelings of insecurity in the public domain (Willemse 1996). Building on the expertise on technical crime prevention within the Dutch police, the Police Label for Safe and Secure Housing was introduced, a sophisticated version of the UK Secured by Design label (Jongejan and Woldendorp 2013). The standardization of household security requirements would later result in the adoption of a set of minimum requirements in the Building Code (Vollaard and van Ours 2011) (see Box 18.3).

The new wave of administrative crime prevention was not exclusively situational or victim centered. Almost half of the funded projects were directed at potential or actual offenders. Pilot projects focused on reducing truancy

---

BOX 18.3   REGULATION OF BUILT-IN SECURITY IN THE NETHERLANDS

The Police Label for Safe and Secure Housing was incrementally developed by the police-based crime prevention organization. Certification was done by experts working for the local police. At present, this function is executed by the municipalities. Some municipalities urged project developers to adopt the measures—although they did not have the legal means to enforce their application. The Police Label exceeds the requirements of the Building Code 1999, by also encompassing burglary-proof garage doors, unobstructed views on parking lots, and no free access to back alleys.

The new Building Code regulating built-in home security came into force on January 1, 1999. As of that date, home builders can only obtain a building permit if they meet the legal requirements for built-in security. The criteria are spelled out in the law in great detail. Home builders are obliged to use certified burglary-proof locks and window and door frames. Certified materials can be identified by a hallmark showing two stars. The law prescribes which parts of the home need to be fitted with secured doors and windows, excluding those that cannot easily be reached by burglars.

and better achievements in secondary schools through improved record-ing systems and early contacting of parents (van Dijk and Junger-Tas 1988). Another signature program was the nationwide introduction of community service as diversionary option for minors (the so-called **HALT** option) (see Box 18.4). Minors arrested for minor crimes for the first time were referred to special agencies that arranged the carrying out of voluntary work after school hours or in the weekend, for example, cleaning the floor of the depart-ment store where they committed shoplifting or cleaning graffiti from bus-ses. Evaluation studies have shown favorable recidivism rates among former clients of the HALT bureaus (Van Hees 1998).

As part of its implementation strategy, the Directorate set up a database with current projects and their first results and launched a journal on crime prevention with a distribution among 20,000 practitioners. It also introduced an annual award for the most successful project, which later inspired the current Prevention Award of the EU. In 1992, the Directorate was given the additional task of screening companies with limited liability as a means to prevent infiltration of the legitimate economy by (associates of) organized

---

BOX 18.4   HALT PROGRAM—THE NETHERLANDS

Halt is a Dutch organization with a national network of offices that aims to prevent and combat juvenile crime. The crime prevention activities of Halt consist of advisory services, educational programs, and the development and implementation of crime prevention proj-ects. The activities are carried out at local and regional levels. Halt is also responsible for the enforcement of alternative punishment given to young people up to the age of 18. Approximately half of the juve-niles arrested by the Dutch police are referred to one of the Halt offices to undertake a Halt program. Juveniles aged 12 to 18 years, who have been apprehended by the police for vandalism, theft (e.g., shoplifting), or fireworks nuisance have a choice between the criminal justice system and the Halt program. If they decide to take the Halt program, they can right their wrongs while avoiding contact with criminal justice authori-ties. The Dutch Public Prosecution Service (OM) has laid down rules for the content and scope of the Halt program. The Halt program has a remarkable success rate: more than 90% of the juveniles complete the Halt program successfully. A successful Halt program requires that

- Juveniles and their parents accept such participation
- Juveniles comply in full with the arrangements
- Juveniles have no serious, underlying problems

crime groups. To this end, a database was set up of all Dutch limited companies, listing their board members and owners as well as records of past bankruptcies and criminal convictions (T.M.C. Asser Instituut 2000). In 1992, the Ministry of Justice institutionalized collaboration on crime prevention with the business world by setting up the National Platform of Crime Control. The platform launched several joint ventures, including the still existing Foundation Tackling Vehicle Crime.

Coalitions of the Willing: 1995–2015

In the mid-1990s, the Dutch government embarked on a general strategy of decentralization of responsibilities and budgets to local authorities. One of the areas where decentralization was found to be desirable was crime prevention. This resulted in the decision to transfer the responsibility for situational crime prevention from the newly established Directorate for Crime Prevention to the Ministry of the Interior. At the same time, the new government launched a new program on security, under the supervision of the Secretary of Interior, who was also responsible for urban renewal. The Ministry of the Interior had earlier introduced the concept of Integrated Security Policy, which broadened the subject matter to include, besides crime, road accidents, fires, and disasters, which had always been the responsibility of local government (Ministry of Interior 1994). Within the Ministry of Justice, the remaining functions of the Directorate on Crime Prevention were integrated into a new Directorate for Youth Policies and Crime Prevention, mainly tasked with the execution of sanctions for young offenders, including HALT.

Situational crime prevention continued to be supported in projects of the just mentioned National Platform. Modeled after the National Platform, a dozen larger cities established their own local platforms to promote public–private partnerships in crime prevention. To support these initiatives, a National Centre for Crime Prevention and Security was set up in 2004, co-funded by the business sector and the Ministries of Justice and the Interior. Its key tasks are gathering information and dissemination of best practices on tackling crime problems at the local level and in specific areas of the business sector. The Centre promotes, besides the Police Label for Safe and Secure Housing and the certification of safe entrepreneurship, the prevention of violence in the leisure industry. It also supports initiatives such as codes of ethics for companies and the prevention of employee theft.

A new trend in the discourse on crime and crime prevention since 2000 is the identification of so-called hardcore youth offenders. These are young persons, many of whom belonging to ethnic minorities, who chronically commit a variety of serious crimes including violent offenses (Van Gemert et al. 2008). In response to this new priority, crime prevention became more focused on tertiary offender-oriented prevention. In a project in Rotterdam, drug addicts highly active in crime were given vocational training and work experience during a two-year secured, in-house program as an alternative to a prison sentence (i.e., Strafrechtelijke Opvang Verslaafden). This project, initially cofounded with the city of Rotterdam, was later transformed in a nationwide program for habitual criminals. A new law introduced a special detention sentence of up to two years for highly active offenders. This project was found to have contributed significantly to the fall in drugs-related property crimes in the country (Vollaard 2013).

In several towns, experiments were initiated with **intensive probation supervision**. Young people who complete the program were offered jobs under the municipal employment schemes. The best-known project in Amsterdam, called New Perspectives, processed several hundred young people per year following a problem-oriented approach and achieved good results (Van Burik et al. 1999). This project was in 2013 remodeled in a more punitive mode by the Mayor of Amsterdam as the Project Top 600, targeting the most active young offenders in the city with a combination of sanctions and social services.

Several larger cities have established centers that bring together police, prosecutors, and municipal agencies responsible for youth work, social work, and health. These centers are called **Security Houses**. In 2015, 25 such centers were active, under the shared responsibility of the Public Prosecutor's Office and the municipalities, and co-funded by the Ministry of Security and Justice. One of the priority tasks of the Security Houses is the prevention of partner violence through risk assessments and the imposition of administrative eviction orders from the mayors for abusive partners.

Seen from a bird's eye view, the newer crime prevention initiatives are predominantly of a tertiary offender–based nature. At the same time, some situational crime prevention initiatives have been integrated into regular procedures, laws, and (building) codes. Victim Support Netherlands has evolved in a powerful national organization with a professional staff of several hundred and thousands of volunteers.* This organization supports more than 100,000 victims of crime annually and is one of the largest of its kind in the world.

The State of the Art in 2016

The "state of the art" of crime prevention governance in the Netherlands in 2016 shows, as in many other countries, a picture of institutional setbacks and fragmentation. At the level of the central government, the former Ministry of Justice, renamed Ministry of Security and Justice, has taken over

---

* See www.slachtofferhulp Nederland.

responsibility for the function of policing, which, since 2013, is executed by a unified National Police Force. This concentration offers, in theory, improved opportunities for the promotion of crime prevention. This opportunity has so far not been harnessed. Since 2010, the ministers responsible for the newly created mammoth ministry have presented themselves as champions of punitive criminal policies and their criminal policies have stressed repression over prevention. In fact, the very concept of crime prevention has not been mentioned in any of their policy plans, or in any of the regular annual plans of the Ministry of Security and Justice. Within the ministry, supervising the full range of law enforcement and criminal justice, no directorate carries crime prevention in its name.* Only the function of tertiary offender–oriented prevention is mentioned as one of the key tasks, namely, of the Directorate for Sanctions and Youth. Since the focus of this type of crime prevention is on the treatment of (persistent) offenders, it bears little resemblance to crime prevention proper, as defined in the United Nations Guidelines.

The recent and rapid demise of crime prevention as a distinct policy responsibility of the Ministry does not imply that no crime prevention initiatives are taken in practice. Arguably, elements of crime prevention have been mainstreamed into comprehensive crime control programs. Mention was already made of eviction orders for abusive partners to prevent partner violence. To prevent infiltration of the local economy by organized crime groups, legislation was passed in 2002, offering public bodies access to criminal records and investigative information (Law to Facilitate Integrity Checks of Companies by Public Bodies of 2002/BIBOB). Such administrative measures can be regarded as new forms of crime prevention. Also, situational crime prevention initiatives continue to be implemented. A nationwide program tackling the high impact crime of household burglary, for example, combines targeted criminal investigations with the promotion of high-quality security locks in social housing estates through a co-funding arrangement with housing associations.

Of the institutional structures for crime prevention, established in the 1990s, the National Platform for Crime Prevention is still active, though its highest echelon meets irregularly. Prevention of vehicle thefts continues to be promoted by the independent foundation established by the said Platform in 1996, and the Centre for Crime Prevention and Community Safety (CCV) continues to provide technical support, for example, by updating and promoting established instruments such as the security certification of houses and of commercial centers (see Box 18.5).

At the municipal level, the function of crime prevention coordinator, of which a hundred or so existed around 1990, has largely disappeared.

---

* See https://www.rijksoverheid.nl/ministeries/ministerie-van-veiligheid-en-justitie.

BOX 18.5   INTRODUCING THE CENTER FOR CRIME PREVENTION AND COMMUNITY SAFETY

The CCV develops and implements coherent instruments designed to enhance community safety. The CCV stimulates cooperation between public and private organizations to achieve a coordinated, integrated approach to crime prevention and reduction, and forms a bridge between policy and practice. The CCV manages and develops standards for fire alarm systems, CCTV, small fire extinguishers, public–private partnerships on business parks and shopping centers (Keurmerk Veilig Ondernemen), household security (Politiekeurmerk Veilig Wonen), sprinklers and watering systems, alarm systems, and alarm receiving centers.

By the certificate "Keurmerk Veilig Ondernemen," participants can demonstrate the effective management of their public–private partnership. By the cooperation of public and private parties, the social cohesion of these parties increases. This improves the security situation and thus the perceived safety of users of business parks and shopping centers. The evaluation by the certification body makes the collaboration that is entered into more binding. This leads to continuous initiatives to achieve the objectives of the public–private partnership.

For more information, see www.hetccv.nl.

Discernible units with a remit for crime prevention or urban security exist in Amsterdam and Rotterdam only. In both cities, various forms of crime prevention, such as the screening of companies, are important parts of the programs against organized crime groups infiltrating the local economy (Huisman and Nelen 2007).* These two cities also run special programs tackling high-intensive career criminals that combine punitive and rehabilitative measures. Interestingly, the concept of Neighborhood Watch, introduced in the 1980s, has recently reemerged as spontaneous, private initiatives (**Neighborhood Watch 2.0**) in many Dutch cities. The number is estimated to be 700 or more and has grown rapidly since 2010. In Tilburg, neighborhood groups have successfully piloted the use of WhatsApp groups as a surveillance tool. Tellingly, the organizational support for these citizens' initiatives lies with the municipality and not, as in the past, with the police (Lub 2016).

The police-based crime prevention organization, once comprising a hierarchical structure composed of hundreds of specialized officers, was formally dismantled in 1992. In 2006, the Council of Police Commissioners formally

---

* In Rotterdam, prosecutors have in 2015 taken the initiative to back up the fight against organized crime in Rotterdam South with awareness-raising drama classes in primary schools attended by pupils at risk to be recruited by criminal groups.

declared that crime prevention was no longer part of the core business of policing in the Netherlands. A head count in 2009 revealed that, nationwide, no more than a handful of police officers with crime prevention expertise were still in function. In one of the former districts, Hollands Midden, for example, the number went down from 11 in 1993 to 0.5 in 2012 (Van Nieuwaal and Beunders 2010). The annual Dutch victimization surveys confirm that the percentages of reporting victims who receive crime prevention advice from the police have significantly decreased (van Dijk et al. 2012b).* Proposals by the first two authors to concentrate crime prevention expertise within the newly established National Police fell on deaf ears, and in recent policy plans of the National Police, any reference to the concepts of crime prevention will be searched in vain. The Dutch police, once boasting a full-fledged crime prevention organization, have gone back to the basics of surveillance and criminal investigation. The refocusing on core functions of policing has not yet resulted in improved effectiveness of criminal investigation. Clearance rates of total crime have remained at an all-time low of 23%, and the proportion of court cases ending in acquittals because of poorly collected evidence has gone up.

To conclude, except for a few situational measures/approaches (e.g., police label, antiburglary requirements for residential housing, technical antitheft requirements for cars) which have been given a statutory basis, few of the support structures and programs of crime prevention, developed between 1975 and 1995, have been maintained. Most programs have been terminated and succeeded by more punitive programs of crime control. The once extensive structures for police-based crime prevention in the country have simply ceased to exist. Within the Ministry of Security and Justice, crime prevention is no longer promoted as a separate policy. Expertise on situational crime prevention implementation has been retained, thanks mainly to public–private partnerships with the business sector. In the largest Dutch cities, notably Amsterdam and Rotterdam, the tradition of crime prevention seems to have survived, but only in the narrow form of Security Houses, Top Hundred projects, and the integrity screening of companies.

Analysis and Lessons Learned

Our conclusion is that crime prevention, as a new type of policy, has been in decline in the Netherlands since 2000. This raises the pertinent question

---

* The provision of person-to-person crime prevention advice to households reporting a burglary is a proven crime prevention measure (Farrell and Pease 1993). The provision of advice to reporting victims of crimes on how to prevent repeat victimization has the potential to reduce crime and might be one of the most powerful opportunities to increase trust in the police.

what political factors have determined its rise and fall over the past five decades. A common interpretation of the decline of crime prevention is that this is caused by the so-called punitive turn in criminal policies in the 1990s (Garland 2001). In the case of the Netherlands, all ministers of justice since 2000, with a brief intermezzo between 2007 and 2009,* have indeed unequivocally advocated punitive responses to existing or perceived crime problems. In their election campaign of 2010, the conservative Liberal Party VVD campaigned for "More Blue in the Streets" and "Offenders Are Going to Pay." The two VVD politicians leading the new Ministry of Security and Justice between 2008 and 2015 projected an image of themselves as stern crime fighters. Whether this political rhetoric reflects a punitive turn in Dutch criminal policy seems doubtful. Careful analyses of trends in sentencing have shown that sentencing tariffs by the Dutch courts for key categories of crime have, for example, changed very little since 2003 (Berghuis 2015). It has often been argued that, in the final analysis, the only unambiguous indicator of the punitiveness of the criminal policies of a nation is its national prisoners rate. On this account, the Netherlands shows a remarkable trend. Since 2000, the prisoner rates went down from 130 per 100,000 inhabitants in 2005 to below 60 in 2015 (Aebi et al. 2016; van Dijk 2010). With the current rate, the Netherlands has reclaimed its traditional place among the least punitive countries in the Western world, in the company of the Scandinavian countries and Switzerland. Crime prevention has certainly become less pivotal, but whether this forms part of a fundamental punitive turn in the country remains a moot point. In an international perspective, it seems far-fetched to speak of a punitive turn in a country detaining less than half the numbers of prisoners per capita as the United Kingdom, and less than a tenth of the numbers in the United States.

The second possible interpretation that comes to mind is that heavy top-down structures for crime prevention at the level of central government went against the general political trend toward decentralization of government function as a means to bring policymaking closer to the people. From the outset, both police- and criminal justice–based support structures for crime prevention were resisted by the Ministry of the Interior, which feared for the autonomy of municipal authorities in maintaining public order and controlling local crime. This source of opposition gained political ground and, in fact, prevailed

---

* In 2007, the new coalition government consisting of Christian democrats and Labor issued a new program called Safety Begins with Prevention (Ministries of Justice and the Interior 2007). In an introductory statement, the new Minister of Justice Ernst Hirsch Ballin wrote that crime control could no longer be regarded as the sole responsibility of police and justice and that many other government agencies at all levels have important roles to play. Although this policy plan suggests a rebirth of the crime prevention philosophy of the 1980s, it has not led to a restrengthening of support structures within the ministry or elsewhere and seems to have had little lasting influence.

when decentralization became an official political priority of the government around 1995, propelled by politicians of the left Liberal Party D'66 and the Labor Party. With the integration of security policies in programs of urban renewal, or specifically empowerment of the most vulnerable neighborhoods in the country, support structures promoting specific social policies top-down, such as the Directorate of Crime Prevention, went blatantly against the political tide. Similar political dynamics had led in 1988 in France to the integration of the National Council on Crime Prevention (Le Conseil National de Prévention de la Délinquance) into an Interministerial Committee on Cities (La Delegation Interministerielle à la Ville) and the integration of Crime Prevention Contracts into comprehensive Urban Problem Contracts. In the United Kingdom, as mentioned, the Safer Cities Programme was relaunched in 1994 as Single Regeneration Programme. Its focus on situational measures was diluted and results in terms of crime reduction were disappointing (Knox et al. 2000).

In theory, crime prevention policies can be left to the local level (mayors or other local authorities), as propagated by the Paris-based European Forum on Urban Security. However, misgivings that such fully decentralized crime prevention policies will be unsustainable, without technical and financial support from a dedicated unit in central government, have been confirmed in both France and the Netherlands. In both countries, the integration of crime prevention structures into structures addressing urban problems (or social cohesiveness) has soon resulted in a complete loss of any focus on crime problems (Crawford 1998). In France, the crime prevention grants were renamed into security grants in 1992. In 1997, the national program of security-related grants for municipalities was refocused on crime control measures, such as neighborhood policing and houses of security (Dieu 2009). From 2002 onward, under the leadership of the conservative politician Nicolas Sarkozy, the pendulum has swung back 180° to a criminal policy of undiluted punitiveness (Wyvekens 2009). In the United Kingdom, the Safer Cities Programme, migrated to the Ministry of the Environment in 1994, was discontinued in 1998 without any form of succession. In the Netherlands, municipal crime prevention has, as explained, virtually ceased to exist soon after its transfer to the Ministry of the Interior and concurrent "decentralization."

Both the punitive shift and decentralization of government have undoubtedly played a part in the decline of crime prevention. Yet, these factors cannot fully explain it. In our view, the single most important, and probably decisive, factor was that, around 2000, crime had ceased to be a threat to the well-being of citizens and profitability of businesses. As a consequence, the need of supplementing conventional criminal justice with other means lost its urgency.

When reflecting on the trajectory of crime prevention since the early 1990s, its close synchrony with the movements in volume crime is hard to miss. Political support for crime prevention has matched overall trends in crime since 1980, booming from 1985 onward, peaking around 2000, and falling steeply thereafter. In hindsight, crime prevention in the Netherlands as a new policy concept seems to have been spawned by the emergency situation created by the prolonged crime boom of the 1970s and 1980s. Faced with chronic, and seemingly unsolvable, overburdening of its institutions by ever-increasing numbers of cases and arrested offenders, the law enforcement and criminal justice establishment felt obliged to invest in alliances with governmental and nongovernmental organizations that could address criminogenic situations in their respective operational domains. For this pragmatic reason, the Ministry of Justice initiated a police-based crime prevention organization, promoting target hardening by citizens in 1973, and, lifting its ambitions to a higher level in response to a deepening crisis, reached out to other ministries and local governments and the business community as partners in crime prevention in the mid-1980s. Principled opposition to the alignment of education, youth work, health care, and the leisure industry to the fight against crime was overruled by a shared feeling that crime and related fear of crime had to be brought under control with all possible means. Of symbolic importance in this respect is the leadership role of the Prime Minister whose Secretary-General chaired for some years the interministerial committee on crime prevention.* The readiness of large corporations to take part in the National Platform and to co-fund some of its projects has been portrayed as a manifestation of the Dutch tradition of pulling forces in times of a (nautical) crisis—known as Polderen† (van Dijk and de Waard 2009). This interpretation, however neat, only confirms that the participation of the corporate world was first and foremost driven by the conviction that the crime crisis harmed their business interests and that this could not be remedied with conventional criminal justice means alone. As was to be expected, the readiness of the governmental and nongovernmental partners in crime prevention decreased as soon as volume crime—and the costs incurred from it—looked more manageable. From the perspective of the Ministry of Justice, support structures to forge coalitions with other governmental and nongovernmental organizations in the fight against volume crime appeared luxuries as soon as caseloads of prosecutors and courts went down and prisoner rates started tumbling, as has been the case in the Netherlands now for many years.

---

* Similarly, in France, the National Council of Crime Prevention, established in 1983, was up to 1988 chaired by the Prime Minister and supported by a secretariat at the Ministry of Justice.
† A polder is a low-lying tract of land enclosed by embankments known as dikes, usually drained and reclaimed marshland, and a common feature of the Netherlands. Not coincidentally, a large proportion of all Dutch families are called van Dijk (or Winterdijk). Ever since the Middle Ages, competing elites in the same polder were forced to set aside their differences to maintain the polders, lest they all be flooded. The common fight against the sea is seen as the root cause of Polderen, meaning the Dutch tradition of pragmatic and consensual policies (Romein and Romein-Verschoor 1943). Whether or not these instances of collaboration are indeed rooted in the cultural heritage of the polder, coalition building across religious denominations and political parties has undeniably been a characteristic of Dutch society for a long time (Lijphart 1975).

The demise of crime prevention as well as the punitive turn around in 2000, should be interpreted against the background of stabilizing or decreasing crime rates at the time. Around this time, volume crime had dropped so much in most Western countries that governments could afford replacing evidence-based policies by ideologically inspired tough-on-crime policies. Actually, reducing crime had ceased to be an urgent and broadly shared political priority. It is fully in line with this interpretation that, at the present juncture, interest in crime prevention seems strongest among governments of developing and middle-income countries faced with extremely serious problems of crime (Shaw 2014; Waller 2014).

Conclusion: The Future of Crime Prevention

Crime prevention was presented by many of its propagators as an ideologically inspired reform movement. In hindsight, its institutional success in a country such as the Netherlands seems to have been short lived because it was predicated on a perceived law and order crisis lasting two decades. The case of evidence-based crime prevention as a cost-effective and humane alternative to criminal justice may be strong, but not necessarily strong enough to ensure the maintenance of dedicated support structures in the long run. In an optimistic scenario, preventive measures will somehow remain at least an element of rational and humane counter crime policies. In a pessimistic scenario, crime prevention will soon be remembered as one of the ideological peculiarities of the generation of criminologists 1968.

However, our own realistic perspective on crime prevention as an emergency response to a crime epidemic suggests a third scenario. If, as argued by some criminologists, the international drops in crime have been largely caused by spontaneous or government-sponsored primary, situational crime prevention, such as large-scale car and household security (Crawford 2009; van Dijk et al. 2012a), then crime prevention has become a victim of its own success. By effectively driving down levels of crime, crime prevention has made its own support structures superfluous.* This conclusion brings us to a final reflection on the potential for a new generation of crime prevention

---

* Well-researched examples of falls in types of crime caused by improved security are those of car theft and household burglary. In the case of the Netherlands, rates of car theft were driven down by the EU Directive on immobilizers of 1999 and by the complementary activities of the foundation Tackling Vehicle theft, co-funded by the Ministry of Justice and the car industry. The promotion of better secured houses has been a constant of Dutch crime prevention policies. In 1999, security requirements became mandatory for all newly built houses through an amendment of the National Building Code. Results of the ICVS show that, in 2010, Dutch houses were the best secured in Europe, with security locks present in 85% of all houses (van Dijk 2014).

programs in the future. According to the theoretical school explaining international crime drops as resulting from improved crime prevention, crime is a cyclical phenomenon (van Dijk et al. 2012a). When crime rates fall, so will risk perceptions, and the willingness to invest in self-protection. After some time, potential offenders will be tempted by expanded opportunities of crime, caused by reduced investments in security and by the arrival of new, unsecured technologies, for example, in cyberspace. In due time, crime rates will again increase. As soon as private and corporate victims will have noticed that their losses of crime have become unreasonably large, they will, once again, be ready to become partners in crime prevention. At the same time, Ministries of Justice and police forces will again be hard-pressed to look out for such partners. In this view, crime prevention, though in decline now, will be in demand again as soon as the next, near unavoidable crime boom has announced itself.

To be prepared, governments are advised to keep knowledge bases on evidence-based crime prevention measures up to date and to maintain the institutional capacity to monitor where such measures need to be implemented and which coalitions to this end need to be set up. If this advice is heeded, governments may not just be better placed to address a new crime boom but even be able to nip it in the bud.

Glossary of Key Terms

Administrative crime prevention: "the total of all private initiatives and state policies, other than the enforcement of criminal law, aimed at the reduction of damage caused by acts defined as criminal by the state" (van Dijk and de Waard 1991).

European Crime Prevention Network: One of the EUCPN's main tasks is to arrange an annual conference for sharing and disseminating experience and knowledge of best practices in preventing crime and increasing safety and security in the EU. The European Crime Prevention Award is a contest that aims to reward the best European crime prevention project. The nominated projects are presented each year during the Best Practice Conference (www.eucpn.org).

Neighborhood Watch 2.0: A new generation of citizen initiatives to improve safety in the neighborhood establishing WhatsApp groups with participation of local police officers, for example, in the Dutch city of Tilburg.

Security houses: A security house is a locality from where different governmental agencies, including police, prosecutors, and municipal service providers, operate together to monitor and support persons responsible for public disorder, domestic violence, or crime in the city. A key feature of the houses is the exchange of information on the target group from all participating organizations and the coordination of interventions.

Situational crime prevention: Strategies that are aimed at reducing the criminal opportunities that arise from the routines of everyday life. Such strategies include "hardening" of potential targets, improving surveillance of areas that might attract crime (e.g., closed-circuit television surveillance), and deflecting potential offenders from settings in which crimes might occur (e.g., by limiting access of such persons to shopping malls and other locales).

Tackling the top 800 project: A project designed to incapacitate and resocialize young repeat offenders who are in need of a highly structured, closely supervised program with the involvement of many other agencies besides the police and the prison and probation services. In Amsterdam, for example, the project focuses on the 800 most active young offenders in the city.

Target hardening: Target hardening means "making targets more resistant to attack or more difficult to remove or damage." A target is anything that an offender would want to steal or damage. It could be an object, property, person, or, in some cases, an animal. Examples of target hardening are fitting better doors, windows, or shutters; window or door locks; alarms; screens in banks; fencing systems; repairing damaged and derelict property; and fitting a wheel lock to a vehicle.

Discussion Questions

1. Is crime prevention rightly presented in the United Nations Guidelines on Preventing Crime of 2002 as a cost-effective and more humane alternative to conventional means of crime control?
2. What is the state of crime prevention in your own country? Which structures are in place to promote crime prevention, and have these structures been strengthened or weakened since 2000?
3. Which institutions are or have been leading in promoting crime prevention in your country (police, cities, national/federal ministries, public–private partnerships)?
4. Which types of crime prevention are currently the most popular in your country? What is neglected or poorly implemented?
5. Is the central and local government in your country prepared to address current or coming crime booms?

Suggested Reading

Crawford, A. (ed.). (2009). *Crime Prevention Policies in Comparative Perspective.* Cullompton, UK: Willan Publishing. A collection of essays on the different trajectories of crime prevention in a broad selection of European countries over the last three decades.

van Dijk, J. (2008). *The World of Crime: Breaking the Silence on Problems of Security, Justice and Development across the World.* CA: SAGE, 2008. An introduction into comparative international criminology, highlighting differences in levels of crime, crime prevention, criminal justice, and victim assistance across the world and their impact on sustainable development.

Waller, I. (2014). *Smarter Crime Control: A Guide to a Safer Future for Citizens, Communities and Politicians.* Maryland: Rowman & Littlefield. An update on innovative programs to tackle endemic crime problems such as domestic violence and gun violence from an international perspective.

Recommended Web Links

www.crimesolutions.gov
www.popcenter.org
www.crime-prevention-intl.org
www.hetccv.nl/
http://whatworks.college.police.uk/toolkit/Pages/Toolkit.aspx

References

Aebi, M. et al. (2016). *Council of Europe Annual Penal Statistics, Prison Stock on 01 January 2014 and 2015.* Strasbourg: Council of Europe. Retrieved from http://wp.unil.ch/space.

Aos, S. et al. (2001). *The Comparative Costs and Benefits of Programs to Reduce Crime.* Olympia (WA): Washington State Institute for Public Policy.

Aos, S. et al. (2004). *Benefits and Costs of Prevention and Early Intervention Programs for Youth: Technical Appendix.* Olympia, WA: Washington State Institute for Public Policy.

Berghuis, B. (2015). Hoe komt het dat al die cellen leegstaan? *Sancties* 12: 65–77.

Cairney, P. (2013). *Policy Concepts in 1000 Words: The Policy Cycle and Its Stages.* Wordpress.com. Retrieved from https://wordpress.com/2013/11/11/policy-concepts-in-1000-words-the-policy-cycle-and-its-stages/.

Clarke, R.V., and Eck, J.E. (2005). *Crime Analysis for Problem Solvers in 60 Small Steps.* London: Jill Dando Institute of Crime Science. Retrieved from http://www.cops.usdoj.gov/pdf/crimeanalysis60steps.pdf.

Crawford, A. (1998). *Crime Prevention and Community Safety: Politics, Policies and Practices,* London and New York: Longman.

Crawford, A. (2008). *Crimprev info n°16bis—Comparative Models of Crime Prevention and Delivery: Their Genesis, Influence and Development*. Retrieved from http://www.crimprev.eu.

Crawford, A. (ed.). (2009). *Crime Prevention Policies in Comparative Perspective*. Cullompton, UK: Willan Publishing.

Dieu, F. (March 30, 2009). *L'évolution des politiques publiques de prevention et de sécurité*, Martiques.

Ekblom, P., Law, H., and Sutton, M. (1996). *Safer Cities and Domestic Burglary*, Home Office Research Study, 164. London: Home Office.

Farrell, G., and Pease, K. (1993). *Once Bitten, Twice Bitten: Repeat Victimization and Its Implications for Crime Prevention*. London: Home Office, Police Research Group.

Farrington, D.P., and Welsh, B.C. (2003). Family-based prevention of offending: A meta-analysis. *Australian and New Zealand Journal of Criminology* 36(2): 127–151.

Garland, D. (2001). *The Culture of Control: Crime and Social Control in Contemporary Society*. Oxford, UK: Oxford University Press.

Greenwood, P.W. et al. (1996). *Diverting Children from a Life of Crime: Measuring Costs and Benefits*. Santa Monica: RAND. Retrieved from http://www.rand.org/pubs/monograph_reports/MR699-1.html.

Guerette, R. (2009). The pull, push, and expansion of situational crime prevention evaluation: An appraisal of thirty-seven years of research. In *Evaluating Crime Reduction Initiatives*, eds. J. Knutsson and N. Tilley, 29–58. Monsey, NY: Criminal Justice Press.

Hesseling, R. (1995). Functional surveillance in the Netherlands: Exemplary projects. *Security Journal* 6(1): 21–25.

Huisman, W., and Nelen, H. (2007). Gotham unbound Dutch style: The administrative approach to organized crime in Amsterdam. *Crime Law and Social Change*, 48: 87–103. Retrieved from http://link.springer.com/article/10.1007%2Fs10611-007-9083-3#/page-1.

Jongejan, A., and Woldendorp, T. (2013). A successful CPTED approach: The Dutch "Police Label Secure Housing." *Built Environment*, 39: 31–48. Accessed February 04, 2016. Retrieved from http://www.veilig-ontwerp-beheer.nl/publicaties/a-successful-cpted-approach-the-dutch-2018police-label-secure-housing2019/view.

Knox, J., Pemberton, A., and Wiles, P. (2000). *Partnerships in Community Safety: An Evaluation of Phase 2 of the Safer Cities Programme*. London: Department of the Environment, Transport and the regions Great Britain.

Laycock, G., and Heal, K. (1989). Crime prevention: The British experience. In *The Geography of Crime*, eds. D.J. Evans and D.T. Herbert. London: Routledge.

Lijphart, A. (1975). *The Politics of Accommodation: Pluralism and Democracy in the Netherlands*. Berkeley, CA: University of California Press.

Lub, V. (2016). *De burger op wacht; het fenomeen buurtpreventie onderzocht*. Rotterdam: Erasmus Universiteit.

Mayhew, P. et al. (1976). *Crime as Opportunity*. London: Her Majesty's Stationery Office. Retrieved from http://library.college.police.uk/docs/hors/hors34.pdf.

Ministries of Justice and the Interior. (2007). *Safety Begins with Prevention: Continuing Building a Safer Society*. The Hague: Ministries of Justice and Interior.

Ministry of Interior. (1994). *Integral Safety Report for* 1994. The Hague: Ministry of the Interior.

Romein, J., and Romein-Verschoor, A. (1943). *De Lage Landen bij de Zee; Een Geïllustreerde Geschiedenis van het Nederlandse Volk.* Utrecht: de Haan.

Shaw, M. (2014). Transnational organized crime: An overview from six continents. In *Transnational organized crime in Africa,* eds. J. Albanese and P. Reichel, 93–115. Sage, Los Angeles.

Sherman, L. et al. (1997). *Preventing Crime: What Works, What Doesn't, What's Promising.* Washington, DC: National Institute of Justice. Retrieved from https://www.ncjrs.gov/pdffiles/171676.PDF.

Smit, P., and van Dijk, J.J.M. (2014). History of the Dutch Crime Survey(s). In *Encyclopedia of Criminology and Criminal Justice,* eds. G. Bruinsma and D. Weisburd, 2286–2296. New York: Springer Press.

Society and Crime: A Policy Plan for the Netherlands. (1985). The Hague: Ministry of Justice.

T.M.C. Asser Instituut. (2000). *Prevention of Organised Crime: The Registration of Legal Persons and Their Directors and the International Exchange of Information.* The Hague: T.M.C. Asser Instituut. Retrieved from http://www.asser.nl/upload/eurlaw-webroot/documents/cms_eurlaw_id49_1_rapport.pdf.

United Nations. (2002). *UN Guidelines for the Prevention of Crime: Action to Promote Effective Crime Prevention.* Vienna: United Nations. ECOSOC Resolution 2002/13. Retrieved from https://www.unodc.org/documents/justice-and-prison-reform/crimeprevention/resolution_2002-13.pdf.

van Burik, A., van Dijk, E., and Molck, J. (1999). *Evaluatie Beleid Jeugd en Veiligheid Amsterdam 1995 tot en met 1998.* Amsterdam: DSP Groep.

van Dijk, J.J.M. (2010). Trends in Dutch prisoners rates: Regression to the mean or enduring exception? In *Punitivity,* eds. H. Kury and E. Sjae. Bochum: Brockmeyer. Retrieved from https://pure.uvt.nl/portal/files/1277657/Dijk_Trends_in_Dutch_prisoners_rates_101110_postprint_immediately.pdf.

van Dijk, J.J.M. (2014). Understanding the international falls in crime: Or why burglary rates dropped less steeply in Germany than in the Netherlands. In *International Perspectives of Crime Prevention,* eds. M. Coester and E. Marks, 23–47. Mönchengladbach: Forum Verlag Godesberg.

van Dijk, J.J.M., and de Waard, J. (1991). A two-dimensional typology of crime prevention projects: With a bibliography. *Criminal Justice Abstracts* 23: 483–503. Retrieved from https://pure.uvt.nl/portal/files/987925/TWO-DIME.PDF.

van Dijk, J.J.M., and de Waard, J. (2009). Forty years of crime prevention in the Dutch Polder. In *Crime Prevention Policies in Comparative Perspective,* ed. A. Crawford, 131–154. Cullomptom, UK: Willan Publishing.

van Dijk, J.J.M., and Junger-Tas, J. (1988). Trends in crime prevention in The Netherlands. In *Communities and Crime Reduction,* eds. T. Hope and M. Shaw, 260–277. London: Home Office, Research and Planning Unit.

van Dijk, J.J.M., and Steinmetz, C.H.D. (1979). *The Research and Documentation Centre Victimisation Surveys, 1974–1977: Results of a Study into the Volume and Trends in Petty Crime.* The Hague: Ministry of Justice, Research and Documentation Centre.

van Dijk, J.J.M., Tseloni, A., and Farrell, G. (eds.). (2012a). *The International Crime Drop: New Directions in Research*. Houndmills, Bastingstoke, Hampshire: Palgrave Macmillan.

van Dijk, J.J.M., van Dijk, B., van Soomeren, P., and Vollaard, B. (2012b). Politiële Preventie: Oude Uitdaging in Nieuw Jasje. In *Voer voor Kwartiermakers: Wetenschappelijke Kennis Voor de Inrichting van de Nationale Politie*, eds. F. Vlek and P. Van Reenen, 207–226. Apeldoorn: Reed Business. Retrieved from http://www.politieenwetenschap.nl/cache/files/56b89a37ced48kwarti ermakers.pdf.

van Dijk, J.J.M., Van Kesteren, J., and Smit, P. (2008). *Criminal Victimisation in International Perspective: Key Findings from the 2004-2005 ICVS and EU ICS*. Den Haag: Boom Legal Publishers. Retrieved from http://unicri.it/services/library _documentation/publications/icvs/publications/ICVS2004_05report.pdf.

Van Gemert, F., Petersen, D., and Lien, I.L. (eds.). (2008). *Street Gangs, Migration and Ethnicity*. Cullompton, UK: Willan Publishing.

Van Hees, A. (1998). De Ontwikkeling Van Halt in Cijfers. *Kwartaalbericht Rechtsbescherming en Veiligheid* 11: 48–50.

Van Nieuwaal, F.M., and Beunders, H.J.G. (2010). *Voorkomen Verdient Beter: Een Verkenning van de Rol van Preventie Binnen de Politie, Verleden, Heden en Toekomst*. Rotterdam: Erasmus Universiteit.

Van Ours, J.C., and Vollaard, B. (2015). The engine immobilizer: A non-starter for car thieves. *The Economic Journal*, Article first published online: April 6, 2015 doi: 10.1111/ecoj.12196. Retrieved from http://onlinelibrary.wiley.com/doi /10.1111/ecoj.12196/epdf.

van Soomeren, P., and Beerepoot, A. (2005). *Tegenhouden Als Nieuw Paradigma Voor de Politie?* Amsterdam: DSP-Groep. Retrieved from http://www.dsp-groep.nl /getFile.cfm?dir=rapport&file=11abTegenhouden_als_nieuw_paradigma_voor _de_politie.pdf.

Vollaard, B. (2013). Preventing crime through selective incapacitation. *The Economic Journal* 123: 262–284. Retrieved from http://onlinelibrary.wiley.com /doi/10.1111/j.1468-0297.2012.02522.x/epdf.

Vollaard, B., and Moolenaar, D. (2009). Beperkte Invloed Rechter op Gebruik Celstraf. *Nederlands Juristenblad* 85: 1208–1213.

Vollaard, B., and Van Ours, J.C. (2011). Does regulation of built-in security reduce crime? Evidence from a natural experiment. *The Economic Journal* 121: 485–504. Retrieved from http://onlinelibrary.wiley.com/doi/10.1111/j.1468-0297 .2011.02429.x/epdf.

Waller, I. (2006). *Less Law, More Order: The Truth about Reducing Crime*. Westport, CT: Praeger Publishers.

Waller, I. (2014). *Smarter Crime Control: A Guide to a Safer Future for Citizens, Communities and Politicians*. Lanham, MD: Rowman & Littlefield.

Willemse, H.M. (1996). Overlooking crime prevention: Ten years of crime prevention in the Netherlands. *Security Journal* 7: 177–184.

Wyvekens, A. (2009). The evolving story of crime prevention in France. In *Crime Prevention Policies in Comparative Perspective*, ed. A. Crawford, 110–130. Cullompton, UK: Willan Publishing.

The Value of Crime Prevention

19

Avoiding the Direct, Indirect, and Societal Costs of Crime

ANNE MILLER

Contents

Learning Outcomes

After reading this chapter, you should be able to

- Understand the concept of "cost of crime" and why it is pursued
- Learn about methods for measuring the tangible and intangible aspects of the cost of crime
- Consider the value of crime prevention in relation to the cost of crime
- Consider the implications of measuring the cost of crime for policy decision making around investing in crime prevention

Introduction

> Therefore, the correct question is not about the value of any single crime, but
> the value of crime reduction.
>
> **J. Czabanski**
> *2008*

Policymakers around the world continually face tough decisions about the
allocation of public funds. Should funds go to education, health, social services, justice, or any number of other important and essential services? In
making these resource allocation decisions, understanding the costs of different issues and intervention options can be extremely important in ensuring that society's needs are met while avoiding inefficient and costly public
investments. A frequently debated area of public investment is justice (Cohen
2005; Czabanski 2008). How do we, as a society, allocate public resources in
an efficient way to ensure the safety and security of citizens? How can public
funds be used to reduce victimization, recidivism, and fear of crime? Often,
when these questions arise, the "**cost of crime**" is cited as a demonstration
of the size of the issue or as justification for different policy options that seek
to reduce crime or garner some form of retribution from those who commit
crimes.

Crime prevention is one policy approach when investing in society's
safety and security. When deciding whether to invest in crime prevention
initiatives, the cost of crime is often weighed against the cost of crime prevention interventions in order to decide whether the investment is "worth
it" (Cohen 2005; Czabanski 2008). If the investment in crime prevention
garners results that create more benefit and value (e.g., reduced recidivism
[Fox and Albertson 2011] or reduction in fear of crime [Semmens 2007]) for
society than the cost of crime, justifying the investment and finding support
for the crime prevention initiative may be easier for policymakers. On the
other hand, if crime prevention is so costly that it will require more government resources than the cost of crime itself, policymakers may have a much
harder time finding support for the initiative (Roman and Farrell 2002). For
example, intensive early intervention crime prevention strategies like the
proven Functional Family Therapy model can be quite costly, possibly costing more than the potential crimes a youth may commit later in life, such
as theft or other minor misconduct (see, e.g., National Crime Prevention
Centre 2008).

While the cost of crime is often discussed and used to justify policy decisions, it can be very difficult to measure and can mean different things in
different contexts (Cohen 2005). Further, while many jurisdictions make
estimations of the cost of crime, they may be basing those estimations on

different things. For example, in the United States, it is estimated that the government spends upward of US$179 billion on police protection, judicial and legal activities, and corrections annually on top of US$15 billion in annual economic losses borne by victims of crime (McCollister et al. 2010). Meanwhile, in Canada, it is estimated that provincial and federal governments spend $20.3 billion CAD (Office of the Parliamentary Budget Officer 2013) on policing, courts (judges, prosecutors, legal aid, and youth justice) and corrections (including parole) while the cost of crime to society has been estimated at $31.4 billion CAD annually (Zhang 2008). In Italy, the total social cost of crime is estimated to be more than €38 billion annually, amounting to 2.6% of Italy's annual GDP (Detotto and Vannini 2010), while in Hungary, the social cost of crime is estimated at only €1.6 billion annually (Kerezsi et al. 2011). In Chile, the cost of crime has been estimated at US$1.35 billion or 2.06% of Chile's GDP (Olavarria-Gambi 2007).

The ambiguity present in the measurement of the cost of crime makes choices about public investment in justice even more difficult to make. This chapter will explore the methods for understanding the cost of crime in order to present a case for the value of crime prevention in relation to the cost of crime. The policy implications of understanding the value of crime prevention will be discussed.

Why Study the Cost of Crime?

Although crime and deviance are arguably purely social constructs (Schneider 1985), crime is often used as a "social barometer" for determining the overall well-being of a society (Sims and Johnston 2004). Therefore, before we investigate the intricacies of measuring the cost of crime, we first need to ask ourselves why crime should be measured in financial terms at all. One of the most cited reasons for valuing any social issue in monetary terms is the benefit of translating complexities of the social world into a single, measurable, unit— money—that is widely used and explicitly understood in our society (Abrams 2013). But then, why is it important to understand the complex issue of crime in a single, measurable, unit? According to Manning et al. (2013) who advocate for the use of costing methodologies to understand crime:

A structured method is essential because limitations to human cognitive capacity restrict our ability to capture all the salient information particularly if one wishes to incorporate multiple domains and the results of a meta-analysis of past experience into the decision-making framework.

M. Manning et al.
2003, p. 322

In other words, translating the complexities of crime into financial terms allows decision makers to grasp a broad range of information about crime, in a succinct and concrete way, facilitating their ability to choose between different policy options and ensure accountability to taxpayers. Abrams (2013, p. 908) points out that "this allows the policy maker to concretely identify the expected impact of any policy change and consider how different policies might yield superior net benefits." In a world of limited resources, where actual money will be spent on addressing the issue of crime in society, translating the effects of crime into monetary terms becomes essential in ensuring that these limited resources are allocated well (Marsh et al. 2008). Understanding the cost of crime can help show the relative importance of the issue of crime in society and reveal the seriousness of a particular type of crime based on the cost of the impacts of that crime. It helps put into perspective public spending that occurs to address crime in society and allows for cost–benefit calculations that reveal whether certain actions and investments are worth the cost (Czabanski 2008). For example, incarceration is often costlier than community justice initiatives (Greenwood et al. 1994) and understanding these costs can provide additional decision-making information for policymakers with constrained budgets.

In summary, by understanding the issue of crime in monetary terms as the "cost of crime," we are able to understand the magnitude of the issue, make different policy and resource allocation decisions, and measure the impact of those decisions in a concrete way. However, the costs to society of addressing the cost of crime should not be ignored. For example, while it may be beneficial to limit the hours of operation of convenience stores in terms of the cost of crimes like robberies, the impact on society may be costlier in terms of wages lost and limits on consumer purchasing options (Hunter 1999).

What Is the Cost of Crime?

When the cost of crime is discussed, it may be assumed that everyone understands the concept in the same way. In reality, estimations of the cost of crime often vary widely in reflection of what is being included in the estimates. The concept of measuring the financial costs of crime and the value of crime prevention or crime reduction has been around for many years. One of the first modern-day estimates began in 1931 under Herbert Hoover's National Commission on Law Observance and Enforcement (unofficially known as the **Wickersham Commission**). The Commission was charged with uncovering the causes of crime in America and making recommendations appropriate for public policy. Volume 12 of the Commission provided a report specifically on the cost of crime (Gray 1979).

Unfortunately, since 1931, no one standard method for estimating the cost of crime has emerged. Today, there are a number of different approaches to understanding what might constitute the cost of crime. Cohen (2005) and Czabanski (2008) provide two of the most comprehensive resources that explore the concept of cost of crime and how to measure it. The types of cost categories identified by these authors include the following:

1. Costs directly caused by criminal behavior
2. Costs society incurs in response to crime and in order to deter future incidents or extract retribution
3. Costs in anticipation of crime and in order to prevent future incidents
4. Costs incurred by the offender, such as the opportunity cost of the offender's time while either engaging in the criminal activity or being punished

These cost categories contribute to a "bottom-up" approach to understanding the cost of crime, whereby discrete costs, expenses, and losses are aggregated to understand the total cost of crime. On the other hand, a "top-down" approach to understanding the cost of crime looks at the entire societal cost of crime without looking at the cost of any one individual component of the cost of crime. Top-down calculations of the cost of crime use either macroeconomic indices and budget data to calculate the societal cost of crime or population-wide surveys to understand society's "price" of crime. This chapter will only explore the components of bottom-up methods of measuring the cost of crime as top-down methods are less common and are considered a less concrete way of understanding the cost of crime to society (Kerezsi et al. 2011).

Types of Costs

Any of the four cost categories presented by Cohen (2005) and Czabanski (2008) can be further broken down into a number of different types of costs, like victimization costs, cost of police, cost of lost property, cost of imprisonment, costs of changes in individual behavior, and so on. To better understand these different costs, we can consider them in terms of *tangible* and *intangible* costs (see, e.g., McCollister et al. 2010).

Tangible **costs** of crime are those costs that are already understood in monetary terms or that involve monetary payments. These can include things like the cost of property that is stolen or damaged, medical costs, the cost of incarceration, wages lost owing to the impacts of crime, spending on precautionary measures like alarm systems, police expenditures, and so on. While tangible costs are easy to understand conceptually and seem as though they would be easy to capture in cost of crime calculations as they are already articulated in monetary terms, the reality of capturing tangible costs of crime can be much more complicated. Aside from measures of direct expenditures by government on the criminal justice system, there is no universal accounting system for tallying up the out-of-pocket losses of crime victims. While some jurisdictions have victimization surveys (e.g., the International Crime Victimization Survey) that ask the population about information on recent criminal victimization, often these surveys underestimate the tangible costs of crime experienced, as these costs can be difficult for victims to estimate or remember. Further, while governments can provide information on budgets for the criminal justice system, the proportion of costs attributed to crime in other departments, for example, in government-supported health care systems, can be difficult to estimate (Cohen 2005, pp. 32–33).

Intangible **costs** of crime are costs not normally expressed in monetary terms. In other words, they are things not typically exchanged in private or public markets. Intangible costs of crime can include things like pain and suffering, loss of quality of life, and fear of victimization. These costs are even more difficult to estimate than tangible costs of crime as they first require conceptual definitions of the intangible (e.g., "fear," "quality of life," etc.) and then require techniques to assign a monetary value to something that does not normally get traded on a market using monetary value. For example, Semmens (2007) points out the difficulty of assigning monetary value to the fear of crime, where "fear" and "crime" must first be defined and operationalized as concepts before they can be rigorously operationalized for measurement and valuation. Similarly, the cost of pain and suffering or lost quality of life need conceptual differentiation as well as innovative methods for determining the monetary cost or value of the concepts.

> Pain and suffering is a monetized value of the physical and mental pain and anguish endured by the victim owing to the injury. Quality-of-life costs involve the monetization of enjoyable activities the victim is no longer able to undertake as a result of the injury.... Although we can conceptualize these differences it is virtually impossible to separate them out empirically.
>
> **M. A. Cohen**
> *2005, p. 37*

Tangible and *intangible* costs of crime can also be understood in terms of ***direct and indirect costs***. Any cost of crime, whether tangible or intangible, may be *directly* caused by a crime where it can be enumerated and attributed to an offender or offenders (*direct cost* of crime) or it may be *indirectly* caused by a crime or multiple crimes to which it cannot be directly attributed (*indirect cost* of crime) (Cohen 2005). For example, direct costs

BOX 19.1   UNDERSTANDING THE VALUE
OF CRIME PREVENTION THROUGH SOCIAL
RETURN ON INVESTMENT ANALYSIS

Social Return on Investment (SROI) is an emerging, internationally standardized, methodology that seeks to understand the value of interventions in a holistic way that includes economic, environmental, and social value. The methodology was first established in the United States in the 1990s by a man named Jed Emerson. He was working as a fundraiser for a nonprofit and wanted to develop a methodology for understanding the value of social investment in order to move nonprofit fundraising away from a relationship-based model to an evidence-based model. The SROI methodology has continued development and advancement in the United Kingdom since the early 2000s with the emergence of the SROI Network and the development of international standards of practice spearheaded by the SROI Network.

In SROI, investment costs are compared to the total value of social outcomes to create a ratio of costs to benefits. A positive SROI ratio indicates that for every dollar invested, a return of social value is created. For example, an SROI ratio of 1:3 would indicate that for every dollar invested, $3 is created in social value.

SROI also seeks to understand value from different stakeholders' perspectives, creating a clear distinction between value to government, value to program participants, value to victims, and value to other stakeholders. The monetary values that are included in an SROI analysis include both tangible and intangible values to different stakeholders (Nicholls 2009).

The SROI methodology has started to be used to estimate the value of community-level crime prevention initiatives. The method allows decision makers to quickly understand whether an investment in crime prevention has resulted in the creation of significant social value, and whether this value accrues to government, participants, potential victims, society, or other stakeholders. For example, in the Province of Alberta in Canada, the government invested approximately $60 million (CAD) in 88 community-based crime prevention initiatives across the province. They required every investee to complete an SROI analysis to demonstrate the social value created by their program. While not all programs had the capacity to complete rigorous analyses, those that were able to collect data and apply research could then demonstrate the value of the investment. SROI also enabled programs to highlight value to different stakeholders including participants, potential victims, and different government departments like health and education (Government of Alberta, Safe Communities Innovation Fund 2015).

Nevertheless, the SROI methodology does have drawbacks. Rigorous standards of practice have yet to emerge and many assumptions must be made in the process of mapping and valuing outcomes, leading to some skepticism of results (see, e.g., Fujiwara 2015). Regardless of these challenges, an increasing number of crime prevention initiatives are using SROI to express social value in a new way.

of crime may include the value of property that is stolen or damaged or the cost of pain and suffering experienced directly by a victim whereas the indirect costs of crime may involve changes in behavior of those who are not direct victims of crime, like individuals who buy security alarms because of fear of crime or those who feel their quality of life has been affected by crime in their community.

Finally, ***opportunity costs*** relate to the value of lost opportunity caused directly or indirectly by crime. For example, if a victim must spend time with police investigators as a result of a crime, that victim suffers a lost opportunity to enjoy leisure activities or pursue paid activities (employment). Even if no actual wages are lost, the *opportunity* for a victim to earn money has been lost and can be valued (see Box 19.1).

Techniques for Valuing Tangible and Intangible Costs of Crime

Economists and researchers have spent significant time and effort exploring methods for measuring the tangible and intangible, direct and indirect, costs of crime (Cohen 2005). The tangible costs of crime generally use primary and secondary data sources, such as government expenditures, to enumerate the value of specific aspects of crime. Information on the tangible costs of crime may come from sources such as the following:

- Public budgets (e.g., government department budgets, service budgets, etc.)
- Medical records
- Insurance records
- Demographic data (e.g., wage rates for different individuals in society)
- Household surveys of victimization

Studies typically combine all the different tangible cost dimensions that can be estimated from available data to measure the total tangible cost of crime (Soares 2015).

Uncovering the monetary value of intangible costs of crime involves techniques that go beyond secondary data sources on actual costs incurred. They seek to determine how financial terms can be applied to nonfinancial goods and services that are not traded in a market place. Valuation techniques include the following (see, e.g., Cohen 2005; Czabanski 2008; Fujiwara 2013; Soares 2015):

- Willingness to pay
- Willingness to accept
- Hedonic pricing
- Jury awards
- Contingent valuation
- Well-being valuation and QALYs

Willingness to Pay is a technique of determining the value of intangible outcomes by looking at what individuals pay for market-traded items that result in the same intangible outcomes. For example, we might look at what people spend on home security systems to determine the cost of the fear of crime in our society. According to some, the willingness-to-pay technique is ideal as it is "based on real preferences, assumes the possibility of compensation and measures all consequences of crime as feared by people" (Czabanski 2008, p. 110). Thus, economists often prefer the willingness-to-pay technique of intangible valuation as it is based on *actual* market behaviors (Soares 2015). The **Willingness to Accept** method of valuation also looks at real marketplace transactions related to intangible outcomes; however, this method considers how much, in monetary terms, individuals are willing to accept to have a risk of negative outcomes (Cohen 2005). For example, economists may look at the wage rate differentials for risky jobs and make assumptions about the value of quality of life based on how much more workers are willing to accept for a decreased quality of life or risk of decreased quality of life (e.g., police officers are paid for the risk that their life may be shortened or quality of life decreased as a result of injuries in the line of duty) (Cohen 2005). *Willingness to Pay* and *Willingness to Accept* methods of valuing intangibles are also called *revealed preference* techniques as analysts use market values to reveal the value of intangibles (Hoffman and Spitzer 1993).

Hedonic Pricing models are another approach that uses real market transactions to estimate the monetary value of intangible outcomes. This method uses statistical techniques to estimate the proportion of the marginal difference in home prices that is attributed to different neighborhood attributes, such as crime rate. Here, analysts infer consumers' willingness to pay for an intangible, like a feeling of safety in their neighborhood, by looking at the difference in property values in safer neighborhoods and statistically estimating the amount of value difference that is attributed to neighborhood safety (see, e.g., Ihlanfeldt and Mayock 2010). While this method relies on actual market transactions in relation to small differences in crime rates, it is limited in isolating specific values like the cost of any individual crime type (Soares 2015).

Using *jury awards* to estimate the cost of intangibles related to crime is a relatively new technique for translating things like pain and suffering into monetary value that can be included in estimations of the cost of crime (Cohen 2005, p. 35). Here, analysts examine the amount awarded by juries in tort cases with injuries from crimes (e.g., assault, sexual assault, etc.) to understand the monetary value of intangible outcomes, like fear, or pain and suffering. While this method directly assigns monetary value to the intangible consequences of different crimes, it is not currently a popular method among economists as many see the results of jury decisions as unpredictable and possibly unreasonably high in terms of the amounts received by victims (Cohen 2005, p. 35).

Gaining prominence in the 1980s, **contingent valuation** determines the monetary value of intangibles by asking a large sample of people what they feel they would pay to achieve or avoid an outcome. Soares (2015, p. 125) indicates that "the logic underlying the contingent valuation method is simple. In order to attribute value to a good that is not traded in the market, one should simply ask people how much they would be willing to pay for it." This technique requires a very large sample size in order to achieve reliable cost estimates since individuals may not have accurate opinions or knowledge about how to cost intangibles. In relation to the cost of crime, individuals could be asked things like "what would you pay to avoid an assault?" or "what would you pay to feel safe in your community?" Some economists are skeptical of the method as it does not look at actual market behavior of individuals, but rather asks people to speculate about what their behavior *would* be if certain intangibles were available on the market (see, e.g., Hanley 1989). **Contingent valuation** is also called **stated preference** as individuals are asked to state their subjective value for intangibles.

Finally, **well-being valuation** is an alternative method for valuing goods that do not rely on people's revealed or stated preferences (Berg and Ferrer-I-Carbonell 2007). This valuation technique looks at data on subjective well-being (life satisfaction) in comparison to data on income levels to compare marginal changes in well-being with equivalent changes in income (Fujiwara 2013, p. 1). For example, if a survey shows that living in a safe area increases life satisfaction by one point, we can determine what increase in income also leads to an increase of life satisfaction by one point and make an assumption that the value of living in a safe neighborhood is equivalent to the monetary value of that change in income. This example simplifies the method somewhat; a detailed account of recent developments in well-being valuation techniques is presented by Fujiwara (2013). The *well-being valuation* method is an important innovation as there is mounting evidence from behavioral economics that indicates that preferences, whether stated or revealed, may not be totally consistent, well-informed, or reliable (see, e.g., Lichtenstein and Slovic 2006). By using secondary data to infer intangible values, the subjective bias of individuals' stated preference or marketplace fluctuations is decreased.

Another technique of understanding the intangible value of well-being and quality of life are Quality Adjusted Life Years (QALYs). Researchers in health economics often consider the value of new medical treatments in terms of QALYs by considering the value of one QALY to be the value of one year in perfect health. If an individual's health is less than perfect, QALYs are added at a rate of less than one per year, with zero QALYs associated with death, and in some extreme cases negative QALYs reflecting a health status deemed "worse than death." Dolan et al. (2005) suggest that the impact of violence crimes such as rape, assault, murder, and so on can be valued in terms of the number of QALYs victims of different crimes lose. In other words, the cost of the crimes is the number of QALYs lost because of the crime. Using this method, Dolan et al. (2005) suggest the costliest crimes in terms of lost QALYs include rape, wounding, common assault, murder, robbery, and sexual assault.

Beyond the quality of life individuals may lose owing to crime, it is possible that actual lives are lost. Valuing the loss of life can be a difficult endeavor. *Value of life* estimations are a contentious area of valuation within economic and costing literature. In the realm of justice policy and law, life is generally considered priceless, with crimes that take away life (e.g., murder, assault, etc.) almost universally severely punished. When estimating the value of life as part of the cost of crime, economists are not arguing for a "price on life" or that the "value" of lives should be compared against one another. Rather, economic methods for estimating the *value of life* seek to statistically determine the impact of loss of life in monetary terms in order to better understand interventions in areas such as health, justice, and environment. Estimates of the *value of life* may be based on wage differences that account for risk, or estimations of lost productivity, or on contingent valuation. In different analyses, the *value of life* may be different, making some skeptical of the decision to include this intangible cost in calculations of the cost of crime (Mrozek and Taylor 2002). For further reading on the benefits and limitations of estimating the *value of life*, see Ashenfelter (2006).

While the techniques for valuing the intangible costs of crime seek to assign monetary value to things that would not normally be traded in a marketplace, Czabanski (2008) highlights that

> Estimates of costs of homicides, rapes, serious injuries, burglaries and so on are not meant to be like a price on the market. They do not represent any particular

license to commit a crime and when someone is prone to commit many crimes he does not get rebates, like on the market, but rather a life sentence quite quickly.

J. Czabanski
2008, p. 111

In other words, although estimating the monetary value of intangibles related to crime can contribute to a holistic understanding of the real cost of crime, it does not mean that these intangibles should be treated as market goods and decision makers should understand the distinction between real

---

BOX 19.2   FUNDING CRIME PREVENTION THROUGH SOCIAL IMPACT BONDS

Social Impact Bonds (SIBs), otherwise known as Pay for Success Bonds or Social Benefit Bonds, are an emerging financing model for the delivery of social outcomes (Fox and Albertson 2011). In a SIB model, private investors invest in the creation of social outcomes (e.g., reduced recidivism) that also benefit society and potentially reduce government costs (e.g., policing costs). If set outcome targets are achieved (e.g., 20% reduction in recidivism), then investors receive a rate of return from the government, with the assumption that the government is saving money owing to the outcomes achieved. If set outcomes are not achieved, investors do not receive a return on their investment. Proponents of SIBs suggest that the model allows for decreased investment risk for governments and increased innovation in achieving social outcomes (Liebman 2011). Detractors question the reliability of data used to measure the impact of programs funded using SIBs and suggest that innovation and government savings are not easily achieved through this financing model (Fox and Albertson 2011).

Justice investments, including investments in crime prevention, have been highlighted as a suitable area for SIBs to be used. The first SIB in the world was launched in 2010 at Peterborough Prison in the United Kingdom, sponsored by the Ministry of Justice and the Big Lottery Fund. The SIB funded a program called One Service, seeking to decrease recidivism rates of offenders joining the program voluntarily when they are released from the prison. Preliminary results of the pilot have been positive, but final results and investor payout have not yet occurred (Disley and Rubin 2014). Since the initial SIB pilot in 2010, jurisdictions in the United States, the United Kingdom, and Australia have been piloting SIB financing models to address crime.

cost savings and estimations of intangible value (Cohen 2005). For example, while Zhang (2008) estimated the intangible cost of pain and suffering attributed to assault in Canada to be $9547 CAD, this is not a direct monetary loss to victims or governments. Rather, it is a financial estimation of the value of something that does not have monetary value.

When crimes are prevented, the total value of avoiding a crime can be calculated in terms of both *tangible* and *intangible* costs. While intangible costs do not result in costs saved directly by converting intangible experiences into monetary value, valuation of intangibles presents a greater opportunity to fully understand the value of crime prevention (see Box 19.2).

The Value of Crime Prevention Compared to the Cost of Crime

Preventing crime, particularly from a social development perspective, involves investing in communities, families, and individuals by providing support programs and interventions for those most at risk of committing crime *before* they commit a crime, thereby *preventing* the crime from happening. Crime prevention interventions and support programs include social, educational, economic, and recreational activities as well as rehabilitation activities for individuals who are already involved in the criminal justice system (Fournier-Ruggles 2011). There is a growing body of evidence that crime prevention programs and initiatives lead to real and sustained reductions in crime in the long term (see, e.g., Jamieson and Hart 2003).

If a crime is not committed, then it follows that there will be no cost from the crime. This logic appears to support crime prevention as the best option for reducing the cost of crime over time. However, we must also consider the *cost* of crime prevention. According to McIntosh and Li (2012): "crime prevention programs are expensive to design and implement, so concerns about effectiveness must be balanced with concerns about fiscal reality" (p. 3). As decision makers then consider different justice policy options, including investing in crime prevention initiatives, it is thus imperative to consider not only the effectiveness of programs and the potential cost of crimes not committed, but also the value of crime prevention in comparison to the cost of investing in crime prevention. This provides additional information to decision makers around whether crime prevention is economically efficient and an effective use of public resources (McIntosh and Li 2012). Aos et al. (2001, p. 6) point out that "in this regard, crime prevention and intervention is like any business: in order to have a positive economic bottom line, not only does a product need to work and be successful, it also needs to be produced in a cost-efficient manner."

For example, if a crime prevention initiative is intended to reduce burglary in an area, the effectiveness can be measured by how many fewer burglaries are committed compared to the average before the initiative. The value of burglaries prevented can be calculated in terms of the value of goods not stolen or victimization that has not occurred. However, if the cost of the crime prevention initiative is so high that it costs even more than the goods that would have been stolen or the victimization that may have occurred, then the initiative is not cost-effective and may be seen as impractical or a poor use of public funds (Bowers 2010).

Understanding the economy and efficiency of crime prevention interventions needs to go beyond "cost-per" measures like the cost per program participant or cost per offender to consider the broader costs of crime, including intangible costs, as outlined in this chapter (Nicholls 2009). By going beyond standard measures of program effectiveness and program cost to understand the cost of crime prevention interventions in relation to the personal and societal tangible and intangible costs avoided, different decisions about effectiveness can be made. For example, in a review of 106 evaluations of crime prevention initiatives, Marsh et al. (2008) indicate that policy decisions related to more than 25% of interventions reviewed would have been different if a robust cost–benefit analysis, including tangible and intangible costs, was added to the evaluation of the program. Two things are essential, then, when considering whether crime prevention is cost-effective: rigorous program evaluation and research on the full cost–benefit of the intervention.

Understanding the full costs of crime against the investment in crime prevention can be particularly illuminating when small and targeted, yet impactful, programs are investigated. Although a program may only achieve a relatively small reduction in crime or may only affect a relatively small number of individuals, sometimes the *value* of that impact is well beyond the modest investment in the program (Aos et al. 2001).

For example, the Region of Waterloo in Ontario, Canada, wanted to prevent homelessness and criminal activity in their area, so they invested public funds in intensive housing-first homelessness prevention programs. Programs receive around $50,000 CAD per year to operate, and usually only work with a small number of individuals each year (10–15). This may seem like a costly initiative since the cost per client is, on average, more than $3000 to $5000. When compared to the cost of homelessness (including criminal activities associated with homelessness), however, the modest investment creates nearly 9.5 times its value in crimes not committed and health/other social services not used. In this context, even though only a few individuals engage in the programs each year, the value of preventing them from becoming homeless is nearly $29,000 to $47,000 per client (Robertson and Miller 2013).

Further, Cohen et al. (2010) indicate that targeted interventions for offenders on particular trajectories (e.g., high-frequency chronic young offenders) can lead to more significant cost savings than nontargeted interventions that treat all offenders equally. Thus, crime prevention initiatives designed to intervene in particular offender trajectories may be more desirable investments as a result of the cost savings garnered through program success.

Despite evidence of the cost-effectiveness of crime prevention, one of the biggest difficulties for decision makers with limited resources and multiple priorities is that crime prevention interventions need long-term investments with reductions in crime and victimization that are not seen immediately (Fournier-Ruggles 2011). This means that even while there may be compelling evidence as to the effectiveness and economic efficiency of crime prevention, governments may be tempted to invest in justice policies with immediately visible impacts, even if they are costlier in the long run than crime prevention initiatives.

For example, in 1994, in California, people voted overwhelmingly in favor of a "tough on crime" approach to justice within the State. The "three strikes" law, giving individuals three chances for encounters with the criminal justice system before long-term imprisonment (25 years to life in prison), was a politically popular policy with very costly results. The sweeping nature of the law meant that many nonviolent criminals were put into prison on long-term sentences, with an estimated cost of $18,000 to $50,000 per prisoner per year (Galloway 2011). While researchers pointed out that the initiative may save some police, court, and victimization costs with offenders taken out of the community, once they are incarcerated, greater prison costs overwhelm such savings (Greenwood et al. 1994). In the end, although the tough-on-crime approach was politically popular, investment in crime prevention could have resulted in significant cost savings for the State.

Further, effective measurement of long-term results from crime prevention initiatives may be difficult, leading to decisions to focus on interventions with measurable immediate or short-term impact. Developing common methods and metrics for measuring and valuing crime prevention could decrease the burden of data collection and increase the robustness of results, changing the public narrative on crime prevention and creating new public demands for investment in long-term solutions.

Summary and Conclusion

The primary objective of this chapter was to explore the concept of the cost of crime in relation to the value of crime prevention. We have described different methods for valuing the tangible and intangible aspects of the cost of crime in order to develop a deeper understanding of the value of crime prevention. While researchers have begun to refine the practice of financially valuing crime prevention, there remain difficulties around capturing all value in financial terms. For a full understanding of the value of crime prevention to be developed and integrated into decision making by governments, several things must occur:

1. Measurement of outcomes. The first step in understanding the value of crime prevention is understanding the effectiveness of crime prevention initiatives in terms of outcomes achieved. If crime prevention programs are rigorously evaluated, we are enabled to go a step further and consider the value of outcomes that have been achieved—or the cost of consequences that have been avoided.
2. Valuation of outcomes (including avoided consequences) and investment. Once we have an understanding of the effectiveness of crime prevention initiatives, we can begin to consider the value of outcomes like reduced crime as well as the value of avoiding consequences that contribute to the cost of crime as explored in this chapter. This can be compared to the cost of investing in crime prevention to understand the economic efficiency and cost–benefit of crime prevention initiatives.
3. Development of common methods and metrics. Finally, as more research and valuation is pursued, common evaluation and costing methods can be developed to ensure comparisons between crime prevention options are analogous. Common metrics for measuring and valuing outcomes can further standardize processes for understanding the social and economic impact of crime prevention.

Overall, then, the value of crime prevention in relation to the cost of crime is not as straightforward as "no crime, no cost." In order to fully understand the value of crime prevention, we must rigorously evaluate crime prevention effectiveness, fully value the outcomes of crime prevention, and make a comparison between this value and the cost of investing in crime prevention.

Glossary of Key Terms

Contingent valuation: determines the monetary value of intangibles by asking a large sample of people what they feel they would pay to achieve or avoid an outcome. This technique requires a very large sample size in order to achieve reliable cost estimates.

Cost of crime: is the total financial value of crimes committed within a society. The cost of crime can include tangible, intangible, direct and indirect costs. There is no one standard method for determining the cost of crime.

Direct costs of crime: are those costs *directly* caused by a crime where it can be enumerated and attributed to an offender or offenders. Direct costs of crime can include things like the value of property that is stolen or damaged or the cost of pain and suffering experienced directly by a victim.

Hedonic pricing: uses statistical techniques to estimate the proportion of the marginal difference in home prices that is due to different neighborhood attributes, like crime rate. Analysts infer consumers' willingness to pay for an intangible, like a feeling of safety in their neighborhood, by looking at the difference in property values in safer neighborhoods and statistically estimating the amount of value difference that is due to neighborhood safety.

Indirect costs of crime: are those costs *indirectly* caused by a crime or multiple crimes to which it cannot be directly attributed to an offender or offenders. Indirect costs of crime can involve changes in behavior of those who are not direct victims of crime, like individuals who buy security alarms because of fear of crime or those who feel their quality of life has been affected by crime in their community.

Intangible costs of crime: are costs not normally expressed in monetary terms or not typically exchanged in private or public markets. Intangible costs of crime can include things like pain and suffering, loss of quality of life, and fear of victimization.

Opportunity costs of crime: are the value of lost opportunity caused directly or indirectly by crime. For example, if a victim must spend time with police investigators as a result of a crime, that victim suffers a lost opportunity to enjoy leisure activities or pursue paid activities (employment). Even if no actual wages are lost, the *opportunity* for a victim to earn money has been lost and can be valued as the ***opportunity cost***.

Tangible costs of crime: are those costs that are already understood in monetary terms or that involve monetary payments. These can include things like the cost of property that is stolen or damaged, medical costs, the cost of incarceration, wages lost owing to the impacts of crime, spending on precautionary measures like alarm systems, police expenditures, and so on.

Willingness to accept: is a method of valuation that looks at real marketplace transactions related to intangible outcomes; this method considers how much, in monetary terms, individuals are willing to accept to have a risk of negative outcomes.

Willingness to pay: is a technique of determining the value of intangibles. It assumes that the value of an intangible can be determined by examining the value of things traded on a market that would result in similar intangibles. For example, we might look at what people spend on home security systems to determine the cost of the fear of crime in our society.

Well-being valuation: is a valuation technique that uses secondary data on subjective well-being (life satisfaction) in comparison to secondary data on income levels to compare marginal changes in well-being with equivalent changes in income. For example, if a survey shows that living in a safe area increases life satisfaction by one point, we can look to see what increase in income also leads to an increase of life satisfaction by one point and make an assumption that the value of living in a safe neighborhood is equivalent to the monetary value of that change in income.

Discussion Questions

1. What are the reasons why researchers try to estimate the cost of crime?
2. Why is it important to try to measure the intangible costs of crime and what methods may be most effective in estimating these intangible costs?
3. What impact does the method chosen to measure the cost of crime have on the total cost calculated?
4. How does the value of crime prevention relate to the cost of crime?
5. How does estimating the cost of crime influence policy and public investment decisions about crime prevention?
6. How might the method of estimating the cost of crime influence decisions about investing in crime prevention?

Suggested Reading

Abrams, D.S. (2013). The imprisoner's dilemma: A cost benefit approach to incarceration. *SSRN Electronic Journal SSRN Journal.*

Cohen, M.A. (2005). *The Costs of Crime and Justice.* London: Routledge.

Czabanski, J. (2008). *Estimates of Cost of Crime History, Methodologies, and Implications.* Berlin: Springer.

Dolan, P., Loomes, G., Peasgood, T., and Tsuchiya, A. (2005). Estimating the intangible victim costs of crime. *The British Journal of Criminology* 45: 958–976.

Moore, S., and Shepherd, J.P. (2006). The cost of fear: Shadow pricing the intangible costs of crime. *Applied Economics* 38: 293–300.

Recommended Web Links

Frontline two-part documentary *Locked Up in America* (April 22 and 29, 2014) http://www.pbs.org/wgbh/pages/frontline/locked-up-in-america/.

RAND Corporation Cost of Crime Calculator (USA) http://www.rand.org/jie/centers/quality-policing/cost-of-crime.html.

International Centre for the Prevention of Crime http://www.crime-prevention-intl.org/.

References

Abrams, D.S. (2013). The imprisoner's dilemma: A cost benefit approach to incarceration. *SSRN Electronic Journal.*

Aos, S., Phipps, P., Barnoski, R., and Lieb, R. (2001). *The Comparative Costs and Benefits of Programs to Reduce Crime.* Olympic, WA: Washington State Institute for Public Policy.

Ashenfelter, O. (2006). Measuring the Value of a Statistical Life: Problems and Prospects. Working Paper 11916, *National Bureau of Economic Research.* http://www.nber.org/papers/w11916.pdf (accessed September 25, 2015).

Berg, B., and Ferrer-I-Carbonell, A. (2007). Monetary valuation of informal care: The well-being valuation method. *Health Economics* 16: 1227–1244.

Bowers, K. (2010). Burglary, Prevention of. In *Encyclopedia of Victimology and Crime Prevention*, eds. B. Fisher and S. Lab, Vol. 1, 45–49. Thousand Oaks, CA: SAGE Publications.

Cohen, M.A. (2005). *The Costs of Crime and Justice.* London: Routledge.

Cohen, M.A., Piquero, A.R., and Jennings, W.G. (2010). Studying the costs of crime across offender trajectories. *Criminology and Public Policy* 9(2): 279–305.

Czabanski, J. (2008). *Estimates of Cost of Crime History, Methodologies, and Implications.* Berlin: Springer.

Detotto, C., and Vannini, M. (2010). Counting the cost of crime in Italy. *Global Crime* 421–435.

Disley, E., and Rubin, J. (2014). *Phase 2 Report from the payment by results Social Impact Bond pilot at HMP Peterborough.* Santa Monica, CA: RAND Corporation. Retrieved from http://www.rand.org/pubs/research_reports/RR473.

Dolan, P., Loomes, G., Peasgood, T., and Tsuchiya, A. (2005). Estimating the intangible victim costs of violent crime. *British Journal of Criminology* 45: 958–976.

Fournier-Ruggles, L. (2011). The cost of getting tough on crime: Isn't prevention the policy answer? *Journal of Public Policy, Administration and Law* 2: 19–28.

Fox, C., and Albertson, K. (2011). Payment by results and social impact bonds in the criminal justice sector: New challenges for the concept of evidence-based policy? *Criminology and Criminal Justice* 11(5): 395–413.

Fujiwara, D. (2013). A General Method for Valuing Non-Market Goods Using Wellbeing Data: Three-Stage Wellbeing Valuation. Discussion Paper 1233, London School of Economic Centre for Economic Performance, Retrieved from http://cep.lse.ac.uk/pubs/download/dp1233.pdf.

Fujiwara, D. (2015). The Seven Principle Problems of SROI. SIMETRICA. Retrieved form http://www.simetrica.co.uk/#!The-Seven-Principle-Problems-of-SROI/c1jf1/3 (accessed September 25, 2015).

Galloway, G. Canada Warned Not to Follow U.S. Tough-on-crime 'mistakes.' *The Globe and Mail*, March 3, 2011. Accessed December 16, 2015. http://www.theglobeandmail.com/news/politics/canada-warned-not-to-follow-us-tough-on-crime-mistakes/article569195/.

Government of Alberta, Safe Communities Innovation Fund (SCIF). (2015). Retrieved from https://justice.alberta.ca/programs_services/safe/Pages/scif.aspx.

Gray, C.M. (1979). *The Costs of Crime.* Beverly Hills, CA: Sage Publications.

Greenwood, P.W., Rydell, P., Abrahamse, A., Caulkins, P.P., James, C., Model, K., and Klein, S.P. (1994). *Three Strikes and You're Out: Estimated Benefits and Costs of California's New Mandatory-Sentencing Law.* Santa Monica, CA: RAND Corporation. http://www.rand.org/pubs/monograph_reports/MR509.html. Also available in print form.

Hanley, N.D. (1989). Valuing non-market goods using contingent valuation. *Journal of Economic Surveys* 3(2): 235–252.

Hoffman, E., and Spitzer, M.I. (1993). Willingness to pay vs. willingness to accept: Legal and economic implications. *Washington University Law Review* 71 (1).

Hunter, R. (1999). Convenience store robbery revisited: A review of prevention results. *Journal of Security Administration* 22(1): 1–13.

Ihlanfeldt, K., and Mayock, T. (2010). Panel data estimates of the effects of different types of crime on housing prices. *Regional Science and Urban Economics* 40: 161–172.

Jamieson, W., and Hart, L. (2003). *Compendium of Promising Crime Prevention Practices in Canada.* Ottawa: Caledon Institute of Social Policy. Retrieved from http://www.caledoninst.org/Publications/PDF/42ENG.pdf.

Kerezsi, K., Kó, J., and Antal, S. (2011). The social costs of crime and crime control. *Beijing Law Review* 2: 74–87.

Lichtenstein, S., and Slovic, P. (eds.). (2006). *The Construction of Preference.* Cambridge, UK: Cambridge University Press.

Liebman, J. (February 9, 2011). Social Impact Bonds. Report for Center for American Progress, Retrieved from https://www.americanprogress.org/issues/general/report/2011/02/09/9050/social-impact-bonds/.

Manning, M., Smith, C., and Homel, R. (2013). Valuing developmental crime prevention. *Criminology and Public Policy* 12(2): 305–332.

Marsh, K., Chalfin, A., and Roman, J.K. (2008). What does cost–benefit analysis add to decision making? Evidence from the criminal justice literature. *Journal of Experimental Criminology* 4: 117–135.

McCollister, K.E., French, M.T., and Fang, H. (2010). The cost of crime to society: New crime-specific estimates for policy and program evaluation. *Drug and Alcohol Dependence* 108: 98–109.

McIntosh, C., and Li, J. (2012). An Introduction to Economic Analysis in Crime Prevention the Why, How and so What. Research Report: 2012-5. Ottawa: National Crime Prevention Centre, Public Safety Canada.

Mrozek, J.R., and Taylor, L.O. (2002). What determines the value of life? A meta-analysis. *Journal of Policy Analysis and Management* 21(2): 253–270.

National Crime Prevention Centre (NCPC). (2008). Promising and Model Crime Prevention Programs. Public Safety Canada. Retrieved from http://www.publicsafety.gc.ca/cnt/rsrcs/pblctns/prmsng-mdl-vlm1/prmsng-mdl-vlm1-eng.pdf.

Nicholls, J. (2009). *A Guide to Social Return on Investment.* London: Cabinet Office, Office of the Third Sector.

Office of the Parliamentary Budget Officer. (2013). *Expenditure Analysis of Criminal Justice in Canada.* Ottawa. Retrieved from http://www.pbo-dpb.gc.ca/files/files/Crime_Cost_EN.pdf.

Olavarria-Gambi, M. (2007). The economic cost of crime in Chile. *Global Crime* 8(4): 287–310.

Robertson, S., and Miller, A. (2013). Region of Waterloo STEP Home SROI Roll-Up Report: The Story Behind the Number: Uncovering Hidden Value in STEP Home's Intensive Support Programs. Waterloo, ON: Regional Municipality of Waterloo.

Roman, J., and Farrell, G. (2002). Cost–benefit analysis for crime prevention: Opportunity costs, routine savings, and crime externalities. In *Evaluation for Crime Prevention: Crime Prevention Studies*, ed. N. Tilley, Vol. 14, 53–92. Monsey, NY: Criminal Justice Press/Willow Tree Press.

Schneider, J.W. (1985). Social problems theory: The constructionist view. *Annual Review of Sociology* 11: 209–229.

Semmens, N. (2007). Towards an understanding of 'FEAR' as an intangible cost of crime. *International Review of Victimology* 14: 219–235.

Sims, B., and Johnston, E. (2004). Examining public opinion about crime and justice: A statewide study. *Criminal Justice Policy Review* 15(3): 270–293.

Soares, R.R. (2015). Welfare costs of crime and common violence. *Journal of Economic Studies* 42(1): 117–137.

Zhang, T. (2008). *The Costs of Crime in Canada*. Ottawa: Department of Justice. Retrieved from http://www.justice.gc.ca/eng/rp-pr/csj-sjc/crime/rr10_5/rr10_5.pdf.

Index

Page numbers followed by f, t, and b indicate figures, tables, and boxes, respectively.

For Product Safety Concerns and Information please contact our EU
representative GPSR@taylorandfrancis.com Taylor & Francis Verlag GmbH,
Kaufingerstraße 24, 80331 München, Germany

Printed and bound by CPI Group (UK) Ltd, Croydon, CR0 4YY
01/05/2025
01858338-0001